The Transnationalization of Anti-Corruption Law

The last twenty years have witnessed an astonishing transformation: the fight against corruption has grown from a handful of local undertakings into a truly global effort. Law occupies a central role in that effort and this timely book assesses the challenges faced in using law as it too morphs from a handful of local rules into a global regime.

The book presents the perspectives of a global array of scholars, of policy makers, and of practitioners. Topics range from critical theoretical understandings of the global regime as a whole, to regional and local experiences in implementing and influencing the regime, including specific legal techniques such as deferred prosecution agreements, addressing corruption issues in dispute resolution, whistleblower protection, civil and administrative prosecutions, as well as blocking statutes. The book also includes discussions of the future shape of the global regime, the emergence of transnational compliance standards, and discussions by leaders of international organizations that take a leading role in the transnationalization of anti-corruption law.

The Transnationalization of Anti-Corruption Law deals with the most salient aspects of the global anti-corruption regime. It is written by people who contribute to the structure of the regime, who practice within the regime, and who study the regime. It is written for anyone interested in corruption or corruption control in general, anyone with a general interest in jurisprudence or in international law, and especially anyone who is interested in critical thinking and analysis of how law can control corruption in a global context.

Régis Bismuth is Professor of Law at Sciences Po Law School, France.

Jan Dunin-Wasowicz is an anti-corruption and arbitration associate, Hughes Hubbard & Reed LLP, Paris, France.

Philip M. Nichols is the Joseph Kolodny Professor of Social Responsibility in Business and Professor of Legal Studies and Business Ethics at the Wharton School, University of Pennsylvania, USA.

Transnational Law and Governance

Series Editor: Paolo Davide Farah, West Virginia University, USA and gLAWcal – Global Law Initiatives for Sustainable Development, UK

In recent years the concepts of 'transnational law' and 'governance' have been explored by both scholars and practitioners with the terms taking on new meaning and significance, particularly in light of the ongoing economic crisis and a corresponding critical reappraisal of global institutional structures and governance. This multidisciplinary series aims to provide a home for research exploring these issues.

Transnational law covers a broad theoretical definition which includes studies emerging from disciplines such as international law, comparative law, international economic law, and administrative law undertaken by legal scholars but also features extensive research undertaken by scholars from other disciplines, including but not limited to, political science, international relations, public administration, sociology, history, philosophy, and geography. Governance in particular is now seen as important when we refer to the general stability of the markets, to good faith, and other key principles which are fundamental to the notion of a fair market which is responsive to the needs of governments and citizens as well as businesses.

This series features cutting-edge works which critically analyze the relationship between governance, institutions, and law from a variety of disciplinary perspectives.

Titles in this series include:

A Radically Democratic Response to Global Governance
Dystopian Utopias
Margaret Stout and Jeannine M. Love

Sustainability and Peaceful Coexistence for the Anthropocene
Pasi Heikkurinen

Administrative Appeals in EU Law
Giacomo Gattinara and Alessandro Di Mario

Technocracy and the Law
Accountability, Governance and Expertise
Edited by Alessandra Arcuri and Florin Coman-Kund

The Transnationalization of Anti-Corruption Law
Edited by Régis Bismuth, Jan Dunin-Wasowicz and Philip M. Nichols

The Transnationalization of Anti-Corruption Law

Edited by Régis Bismuth,
Jan Dunin-Wasowicz, and
Philip M. Nichols

Routledge
Taylor & Francis Group
LONDON AND NEW YORK

First published 2021
by Routledge
2 Park Square, Milton Park, Abingdon, Oxon OX14 4RN

and by Routledge
605 Third Avenue, New York, NY 10158

Routledge is an imprint of the Taylor & Francis Group, an informa business

British Library Cataloguing-in-Publication Data
A catalogue record for this book is available from the British Library

Library of Congress Cataloging-in-Publication Data
A catalog record has been requested for this book

ISBN: 978-0-367-85301-3 (hbk)
ISBN: 978-1-032-00544-7 (pbk)
ISBN: 978-1-003-17463-9 (ebk)

Typeset in Galliard
by Deanta Global Publishing Services, Chennai, India

Contents

Figures

Tables

About the editors

Régis Bismuth is Professor of Law at Sciences Po Law School (Paris), specializing in public international law, international economic law, and international adjudication. His research interests include *inter alia* sovereign immunity, economic sanctions, anti-corruption, sovereign debt, state capitalism, financial regulation, and independent regulatory agencies. He is Co-Editor-in-Chief of *The Law and Practice of International Courts and Tribunals* and Director of Studies of the French Branch of the International Law Association. He has also advised public institutions and private entities on matters of international law.

Jan Dunin-Wasowicz is a member of the Anti-Corruption & Internal Investigations and Arbitration practice groups of Hughes Hubbard & Reed LLP. He is a member of the New York, District of Columbia, and Paris bars. Jan Dunin-Wasowicz has served as Vice-Chair and Chair of the American Society of International Law's Anti-Corruption Law Interest Group. He is an adjunct lecturer at Sciences Po Law School and the University of Paris I - Panthéon-Sorbonne.

Philip M. Nichols is the Joseph Kolodny Professor of Social Responsibility in Business and a Professor of Legal Studies and Business Ethics at The Wharton School of the University of Pennsylvania. Professor Nichols has served as the President of the Academy of Legal Studies in Business, and as Co-Chair of the American Society of International Law's Anti-Corruption Law Interest Group and its International Economic Law Group.

Contributors

Leah Ambler is a legal analyst at the Anti-Corruption Division of the OECD where she also manages the OECD Latin America and Caribbean Anti-Corruption Initiative. She is also Co-chair of the International Bar Association's Anti-Corruption Committee. Prior to joining the OECD, she worked for Australia's Department of Foreign Affairs and Trade and for an international law firm in Tokyo, Japan. She has a combined Law and Asian Studies degree from the Australian National University and is admitted as both a barrister and a solicitor.

Jessica Ansart is a corporate lawyer practicing with an international law firm in Paris. Prior to practicing law, she worked with several international anti-corruption and rule of law organizations, including the Interdisciplinary Corruption Research Network. Ansart received both a Juris Doctor from Georgetown University Law Center and an LLM in Droit Économique from Sciences Po in 2019.

Jeffrey R. Boles is Associate Professor and Chair of the Legal Studies Department at Temple University's Fox School of Business, where he holds a Dorothy S Washburn Research Fellowship and is a Fox Honors Faculty Fellow. He holds a PhD from the University of California, Berkeley, and a JD from the University of California, Berkeley School of Law.

Stéphane Bonifassi has practiced complex financial crime litigation for nearly 30 years. He counsels individuals, companies and states affected by illicit schemes and other financial crimes. In these endeavours, he is assisted by members of the Paris-based boutique law firm he leads, Bonifassi Avocats. He co-founded The International Academy of Financial Crime Litigators with the Basel Institute on Governance.

Jonathan Bourguignon is an Associate Expert in anti-corruption at the United Nations Office on Drugs and Crime (UNODC). He is also a PhD candidate at the Institut des Hautes Études Internationales (IHEI), Université Paris-II Panthéon-Assas, and has published several articles focusing on the interplay between international law and criminal law.

Rachel Brewster is the Jeffrey and Bettysue Hughes Professor of Law at Duke Law School as well as the co-director of Duke's Center for International and

Comparative Law. Her scholarly research focuses on the areas of international economic law, particularly international trade law, anticorruption law, and international relations theory.

Qingxiu Bu is an Associate Professor in Law and Senator at the University of Sussex. He was a Li Kashing Professor at Faculty of Law, McGill University, and docent at Institute of Global Law and Policy (IGLP). He was in charge of a core module of Transnational Business Law at the Center of Transnational Legal Studies, Georgetown University.

Vera Cherepanova has more than ten years' experience as a compliance officer. She is the founder of Studio Etica, a boutique consultancy that provides advice on corporate ethics and compliance programs to companies around the world. She speaks English, French, Italian, and Russian.

Robert Clark is the Manager of Legal Research at TRACE, the globally recognized anti-bribery business association founded in 2001 to provide multinational companies and their commercial intermediaries with anti-bribery compliance support.

Nuria Gonzalez currently serves in the ethics function of a multilateral organization headquartered in the US. Her professional experience encompasses the public, international, and private sectors. Gonzalez has always combined her work with academia, teaching and conducting research in Argentina. She graduated cum laude from Austral University School of Law (Buenos Aires). She also holds a Master's in International Law at University of Rome Tor Vergata and an LLM from the University of Illinois.

Caroline Goussé is an attorney licensed in New York and Paris, with a practice focused on criminal defense. She has experience working on complex financial crime cases involving top management officers and companies in diverse industries, advising on white-collar crime investigations, and more generally in criminal defense in both the United States and France.

Sean J. Griffith is the T J Maloney Chair in Business Law at Fordham Law School in New York City. Professor Griffith received his law degree magna cum laude from the Harvard Law School, where he was an editor of the Harvard Law Review and a John M Olin Fellow in Law and Economics. Prior to entering academia, Professor Griffith was an associate at the law firm of Wachtell, Lipton, Rosen & Katz in New York.

Tamar Hostovsky Brandes is a Senior Lecturer at Ono Academic College's Faculty of Law. She earned her JSD and LLM (cum laude) from Columbia Law School, where she was a Finkelstein Fellow, and her LLB (magna cum laude) from Tel Aviv University. She teaches and researches in the areas of international and constitutional law, focusing on the intersection between international law and domestic law.

Eduard Ivanov is Professor at the National Research University Higher School of Economics, and frequent visiting lecturer at the International Anti-Corruption

Academy. Professor Ivanov is an expert in international law, anti-corruption, compliance, combating money laundering, terrorism, and financing of terrorism. He has solid practical experience in the Russian FIU, and in the Eurasian Group on Combating Money Laundering and Financing of Terrorism.

Elitza Katzarova holds a PhD in international relations from the University of Trento, Italy. She has carried out anti-corruption research at the OECD and the UN. Her book *The Social Construction of Global Corruption: From Utopia to Neoliberalism* was published in 2019. She has worked and given invited lectures at universities in Germany, Austria, Italy, Bulgaria, and Portugal.

Thomas Kruessmann is a German-qualified lawyer with many years of experience working as attorney-at-law and consultant in Vienna and Moscow. Currently, he is the Academic Director of the Master's program 'International Corporate Compliance and Business Ethics' at the Higher School of Economics (Moscow). In addition, he is a Senior Expert Counsel with Lansky, Ganzger + partner, Vienna.

Thomas H. Lee is the Leitner Family Professor of International Law and Director of Graduate and International Studies at Fordham University School of Law in New York, and Of Counsel at Hughes, Hubbard & Reed. He has also been a Visiting Professor at Columbia Law School, Harvard Law School, and the University of Virginia School of Law. He has published many articles and book chapters on international law, international arbitration, US constitutional law, and the US federal courts. He is a member of the ICSID Panel of Conciliators and of the American Law Institute.

Claire Leger is a legal analyst at the Financial Action Task Force (FATF). She previously worked at the OECD's Anti-Corruption Division where she assisted the Working Group on Bribery in its country monitoring activity and carried out anti-corruption technical assistance programs. She also worked in a business and criminal law firm in Paris and as a Law and Economics researcher at the School of Law of the University Erasmus of Rotterdam, as a postdoc researcher at the University Paris Nanterre, and as an Amnesty International Delegate. Leger holds a PhD in Law and Economics (University Erasmus of Rotterdam), a Master's in Business Law and a Master's in Public Economics (University Paris 1 Panthéon Sorbonne).

Lucinda Low is a partner with Steptoe & Johnson, LLP, where she is a member of the Firm's Executive Committee and head of the FCPA/Anti-Corruption Practice. She works with clients on prevention, investigation, risk management, and remediation, and represents companies and individuals before US enforcement agencies and international financial institutions.

Alexandra Manea is Legal Counsel in the World Bank's Office of Suspension and Debarment, which is the first adjudicative tier of the Bank's anti-corruption sanctions system. Manea contributes to the Bank's anti-corruption policy and assists the Chief Suspension and Debarment Officer with reviewing accusations of fraud, corruption, and collusion against respondent firms and individuals brought by the Bank's investigative unit, and with determining whether (and how) to sanction a respondent. She is a published author in the international anti-corruption field.

Andres Ortiz is a compliance specialist at one of the world's largest financial institutions, focusing in financial regulation and compliance matters. Ortiz holds an LLM from the Duke School of Law and an LLB from the Pontificia Universidad Catolica del Ecuador.

Anna Lorem Ramos is Counsel at the World Bank Group Sanctions Board Secretariat, and was Dispute Settlement Lawyer at the WTO Appellate Body Secretariat. In the Philippines, she practiced litigation and thereafter clerked at the Supreme Court. She earned her Juris Doctor and Economics degree from the University of the Philippines, and LLM in Public International Law from Queen Mary, University of London.

Jimena Reyes is a Paris Bar human rights attorney. As FIDH's director for the Americas since June 2003, she has conducted investigations on human rights in Northern and Latin American countries, particularly on the rule of law, corruption, business and human rights and impunity of international crimes. She has also litigated before the Inter-American system of human rights and intervenes frequently as an expert before international organizations (European Union, UN).

Denis Saint-Martin is a full professor at the political science department, Université de Montréal. He specializes in comparative public administration and governance, including anti-corruption policies. He was a Fulbright Fellow at the Kennedy School of Government and Public Policy Advisor to the Office of the Prime Minister of Canada. He completed his doctoral and post-doctoral studies at Carleton and Harvard University.

Vishal Sharma is working as Assistant Professor of Law in the UPES School of Law, Dehradun, Uttarakhand, India. Prior to his current position, he worked as an assistant professor in various reputed law schools in Delhi National Capital Region in India (2015–2020), including the University of Delhi. His profile can be accessed at https://www.upes.ac.in/schools-faculty/law/vishal-sharma.

Jamieson Smith is the Chief Suspension and Debarment Officer for the World Bank, heading the Office of Suspension and Debarment, the first tier of the Bank's two-tiered adjudicative sanctions system. Smith reviews accusations of fraud and corruption against firms and individuals brought by the Bank's Integrity Vice Presidency. He has spoken at various anti-corruption conferences around the world.

Simon St-Georges is a lawyer and a political science PhD candidate at Université de Montréal. His practice in public markets at an international law firm led him to complete a master's thesis on Canadian deferred prosecutions under the supervision of Professor Saint-Martin. He is thankful for the financial support of the Vanier scholarship.

Camila Florencia Tort is a consultant at the Department of Legal Cooperation of the Organization of American States, which, among other functions, provides advisory and technical secretariat services to the Follow-Up Mechanism of the Inter-American Convention against Corruption (MESICIC). Her areas of expertise include public international law, anti-corruption, money laundering, transparency and open government.

Charlene Valdez Warner is an Associate in Linklaters' US Dispute Resolution Practice. She has experience in complex commercial litigation and international arbitration. She formerly worked at various arbitration institutions in Asia and the US, and with the international arbitration group of another magic circle firm in Paris. She obtained legal degrees in the Philippines, the UK, and the US.

Yueming Yan is a PhD candidate at McGill University Faculty of Law under the supervision of Professor Andrea Bjorklund. Yueming researches in areas of public international law, international investment and commercial arbitration, and corporate social responsibility. Her doctoral thesis concerns anti-corruption in international investment law from the perspectives of state responsibility, investor obligations, investor-state dispute settlement reform, and sustainable development.

Foreword

Corruption is a multiscale problem, affecting communities and permeating decision-making at all levels of governance. As globalization has opened transboundary markets over the past decades and continues to fuel international trade, corruption too has crossed borders, calling for coordinated action at the global level. In this context, the OECD countries and a few others adopted the Convention on Combating Bribery of Foreign Public Officials in International Business Transactions in 1997, setting in motion the fight against bribery worldwide. Some twenty years later, the Working Group on Bribery, which monitors the implementation of the Convention by its members, is reviewing its anti-bribery instruments to address new challenges and adjust to new trends.

Indeed, in the last twenty years, global trade has changed profoundly. New players emerged and supply chains have become increasingly integrated. High-risk industries, such as pharmaceutical, construction, and mineral extraction have continued to expand, to name just a few factors. In the meantime, corruption has conquered new ground, taken new shapes, and become more sophisticated.

To stay ahead of the curve, more countries have developed and implemented anti-corruption standards. In recent years, several state parties to the OECD Anti-Bribery Convention have enforced their anti-bribery legislation for the first time, and multijurisdictional enforcement actions have increased at a fast pace, as demonstrated by major bribery cases such as Odebrecht and Airbus. In other words, anti-corruption is pursuing its transnationalization.

While this phenomenon reflects a firm determination by some countries to fight bribery and maintain a level playing field in world markets, it raises multiple questions. For instance, what should be the parameters of multilateral enforcement actions? How to account for cultural differences in shaping new standards and practices? What role should be given to international organizations and multilateral development banks? How does the transnationalization of anti-corruption affect trade dynamics?

The insightful chapters that compose this publication shed light on these questions. Bringing together authors from academia, international organizations, the private sector, as well as civil society organizations, they canvass a wide range of perspectives, providing an invaluable contribution to the discussion. In particular, the contributions take stock of the current anticorruption landscape, examining how global standards, regional features, trade considerations, and other factors shape domestic anti-corruption efforts. The publication also explores some of the most compelling topics that emerged with the internationalization of anti-corruption law and practices: compliance, whistleblower protection, and the interaction of anticorruption law with key areas of the global legal landscape, notably arbitration, human rights, and international law.

This publication builds on a two-day conference organised in Paris in December 2018 by the Anti-Corruption Law Interest Group of the American Society of International Law, Sciences Po Law School, and the Zicklin Center for Business Ethics Research of the Wharton School of the University of Pennsylvania, with the support of the OECD Anti-Corruption Division. The authors of the chapters were invited to present their research in thought-provoking panel discussions, making for a remarkable event by both its quality and the diversity of topics covered. It is a privilege to congratulate Régis Bismuth, Jan Dunin-Wasowicz, and Phil Nichols for curating this research and bringing it together on paper in this rich publication. Their commendable engagement and genuine dedication were the driving force of this important project, in which the OECD was glad to actively participate.

As global trade pushes new frontiers and welcomes new players, the transnationalization of anti-corruption law is bound to continue its acceleration. Beyond shifting trade dynamics, unprecedented events such as the health crisis brought about by the COVID-19 pandemic, and environmental challenges, will inevitably lay a fertile ground for corruption and shape the development of global governance. A continued dialogue on the transnationalization of law, convening experts from all horizons, is critical to understand and therefore effectively combat bribery. In this context, policymakers need research, data, and insightful feedback from all stakeholders to move in the right direction. By exploring all these topics, this publication promises to significantly contribute to the fight against corruption.

Patrick Moulette* and Elisabeth Danon**

**Head of the OECD Anti-Corruption Division*
***Legal Analyst at the OECD Anti-Corruption Division*

Preface

The word corruption derives from Latin *con* (with) and *rumpere* (break) and emphasizes how a break of integrity is what matters the most. All forms of corruption, especially bribery, are related to this break of integrity. Since the beginning of time, the corruptive phenomenon has and continues to exist.[1]

In fact, corruption is an ongoing phenomenon that originated centuries ago, where officials in a given state used their positions to demand monetary or other benefits. Historically, no government has escaped from this phenomenon and until relatively recently, only little efforts have been employed at the international or regional levels to eliminate corruption.

In religious books, corruption stories served as warnings for the believers of the final harsh fate awaiting corrupted people and emphasized the importance of conducting economic activities in an honest manner. The stories about entire kingdoms and states failing in the past and revolutions erupting because of corrupted officials and authorities can be found in every history book, as some of these historical events have shaped and developed our current modern world. Examples include the 1789 French revolution where the corruption of the state, its alliance with the Church, and the lavish lifestyle of Louis XVI and his wife, Marie Antoinette, led to the eruption of one of the greatest revolutions of all times prompting the king's wife, when asked about how the poor could afford to buy bread, to make her famous statement 'Let them eat cake.'

Recent studies assert that without drastic improvement in the provision of education and other societal values, the reduction of these practices will not be possible.[2] However, the belief that the phenomenon is intrinsic with the functioning of all political systems is a widespread misperception which slowed down anti-corruption policies at a transnational level.

In fact, this universal phenomenon persists until today, despite all the state-level efforts to eradicate it and the technological developments that have occurred

1 Ramsay MacMullen, *Corruption and the Decline of Rome* (Yale University Press 1988).

2 Eric M Uslaner, *The Historical Roots of Corruption: Mass Education, Economic Inequality, and State Capacity* (Cambridge University Press 2017) 162 <http://ebooks.cambridge.org/ref/id/CBO9781108241281> accessed 8 July 2020.

in the last century, where numerous high-level corrupted employees and past corruption methods were busted by the police using extremely sophisticated technics. As a result, numerous stories and movies such as *The Wolf of Wall Street* and *Inside Job* were based off these great accomplishments and highlight the depth to which corruption is deeply ingrained within the economic system. Additionally, the 2008 economic crisis highlighted the depth to which a state would go to bail out large banks and corporations despite their questionable activities resulting in the crisis. More recently, the COVID-19 pandemic has again highlighted this phenomenon as large corporations such as airline companies and even big basketball teams like the Los Angeles Lakers are being bailed out by the state at the expense of small business owners and citizens that constitute the main tax payers and who are in desperate need of money.

While monetary forms such as bribery and embezzlement are prohibited almost everywhere today, other forms of corruption such as clientelism, cronyism, and favoritism are, in varying degrees, accepted by both governments and citizens. Ethics is shaped by culture; therefore, the acceptance of what could be perceived by others as a corruptive practice greatly varies across the globe.

With the advent of globalization, interstate cooperation, trade, and economic interdependence in the last century, corruption has developed greatly to suit the changes that occurred especially given the possibility of international cooperation over a network of highly corrupted groups. Such groups have emerged and created extremely sophisticated networks that go beyond the states' and international organizations' ability to track and address cross-border corruption. These networks have utilized technological advancements[3] to conduct all sorts of corrupted activities that fly under the radar and have benefitted from existing safe havens in several states that profit from such activities, mainly developing and least developing countries.

Before the 'new globalization,'[4] corruption was perceived as a political internal issue rather than a global one.[5] The increase of interlinkages amongst developed and developing nations as well as the rise of civil society as a key non-state actor coupled with the advancement of multilateralism resulted in a depoliticization of corruption.[6] Good governance is now accepted to break

3 Paolo Davide Farah and Marek Prityi, 'Public Administration in the Age of Globalization and Emerging Technologies: From Theories to Practice', (2019) 88, 2 UMKC Law Review 397, 397–417.

4 Richard E Baldwin, *The Great Convergence: Information Technology and the New Globalization* (The Belknap Press of Harvard University Press 2016) 142–175.

5 Susan Rose-Ackerman, 'What Does "Governance" Mean?' (2017) 30 Governance 23, 31, citing her personal experience 'Staff in private conversations instructed me that "weak governance" and related terms were often used in Bank documents as code words for corruption. A project suffering from admitted failures would be described as plagued with governance problems.'

6 Jon ST Quah, 'Governance and Corruption: Exploring the Connection' (2009) 16 American Journal of Chinese Studies 119, 121.

corruption. However, anti-corruption alone could not solve the devastating effects that this practice has on society.[7] Corruption breaches the trust amongst citizens and governors, further distancing both from the participation to the *res publica*. The increase in both abstentionism and populist movements (whether left or right) are typical responses of a corrupted environment in representative democracies.[8] By contrary, autocratic ones could leverage corruption to fortify implementation of national policies by officials, further reducing the already limited space of citizen participation.[9] Evidently, transnationalization of anti-corruption policies, regardless of government forms, fills this trust gap. On another note, anti-corruption could also be seen as a depoliticized and neutral governance tool balancing the excess of globalization.[10] In fact, if anti-corruption manages to become an acknowledged transnational law and governance field, national states could benefit in turn. Punishment of corrupted politicians could be therefore recognized as a task of the international community that not only has the financial means and capacity to hunt down the corruption network, but also the legitimacy in light of the mobility of capital. If a corrupted politician moves resources to a tax haven, the national judiciary has limited capacity to counteract this behaviour. In addition, against this background, an approach to corruption encompassing not only bribery, but also other forms of undue influences over local concerns, could be beneficial to align globalization with social values.[11]

This is why the establishment of global regulatory frameworks targeting cross-border corruption has been evolving in the last decades where numerous international agreements and non-binding instruments have been adopted to that end. These legal mechanisms were the result of events that occurred over decades, prompting states and the international community to push towards their adoption given the need for such instruments. The establishment of such mechanisms should be seen in the general framework of constant development and progress of international law and its fragmentation. In that sense, the increasing common challenges that have been recognized since the 1950s and 1960s, the emergence of new challenges, and the need for a global response have put pressure on international law to develop and progress to tackle all these matters. Therefore, the binding and nonbinding applicable rules to anti-corruption are just one of the numerous international instruments

7 Ibid 135.

8 Yves Mény and Yves Surel, 'The Constitutive Ambiguity of Populism' in Yves Mény and Yves Surel (eds), *Democracies and the Populist Challenge* (Palgrave Macmillan UK 2002) 1–21.

9 James R Hollyer and Leonard Wantchekon, 'Corruption and Ideology in Autocracies' (2015) 31 The Journal of Law, Economics, and Organization 499, 22 ('governments may systematically manipulate corruption as a means to address the moral hazard problem inherent in motivating lower-level officials.')

10 Paolo Davide Farah, 'Trade and Progress: The Case of China' (2016) 30 Columbia Journal of Asian Law 51, 111.

11 Ibid 112.

established to address fields such as international trade, human rights, natural resources management, and so on.[12] These rules are developed, because of the increasing technicalities in each of these fields and require specific knowledge and expertise as well as an interdisciplinary approach to each topic including anti-corruption.

A focus on strengthening governance rather than the provision of socio-economic and cultural rights has been followed by international and regional organizations. As an example, *The OECD Risk Awareness Tool for Multinational Enterprises in Weak Governance Zones* frames corruption as a result of bad governance and government failures when 'public sector actors are unable or unwilling to assume their roles and responsibilities in protecting rights (including property rights), providing basic public services (e.g. social programmes, infrastructure development, law enforcement and prudential surveillance) and ensuring that public sector management is efficient and effective.'[13]

It is in this context that this book has been written where the focus is mainly on examining the great developments that occurred in the anti-corruption field within the last few decades. Indeed, the fight against corruption has shifted from the local and national level to the global stage. The role of laws and regulations in such a shift is extremely important, especially for the establishment of a global regime. The contributors of this book are addressing the abovementioned shift from the local to the global scale, the reasons and challenges facing such shift, and the new rules adopted to tackle corruption globally while examining specific national rules that are considered as a model example in the fight against corruption. The contributors examine the future shape that the global regime will take, the role of international organizations in this regard, and the interplay between all of these elements from a global governance perspective. In that sense, this book is embracing a new approach to the topic of transnationalization of anti-corruption law, basing the analysis of the different contributors on the last few decades when great developments have occurred from a legal perspective. Such developments emerged not only in the anti-corruption field, but also in other areas of international law given the great progress made in the last decades.

When reading the book, it can be noticed that the contributors analyzed the international sources of anti-corruption law at the global level and the influence of different international conventions, such as the Organisation for Economic Co-operation and Development (OECD) convention and the human rights conventions. The impact of corruption on the implementation of international

12 Angelica Bonfanti, Business and Human Rights in Europe: International Law Challenges (Routledge 2018).

13 Organization for Economic Co-operation and Development (OECD), 'OECD Risk Awareness Tool for Multinational Enterprises in Weak Governance Zones' (8 June 2006) <https://www.oecd.org/daf/inv/mne/weakgovernancezones-riskawarenesstoolformultinationalenterprises-oecd.htm> accessed 8 July 2020.

rules has also been examined in detail. In fact, the contributors have also explored the ways through which the current anti-corruption laws can be further enhanced by examining the failures of anti-corruption laws and the different methods that can be used to tackle these failures, such as the introduction of standardized procedures and the development of a global peace-promoting anti-corruption regime. More suggestions and analysis are included in the book by the different contributors, where a debate over anti-corruption compliance standards and guidance, anti-corruption initiatives, standards, and guidelines, transnationalization of anti-corruption training, and fighting corruption through contract law took place. Still, many challenges need to be tackled despite the authors' suggestions. This is why the book also provides a detailed analysis of many of these challenges such as the impact of blocking statutes on enforcement of anti-corruption laws and foreign anti-bribery enforcement. This is a non-exhaustive list of the issues that are covered in the book, where topics such as the role of international dispute settlement resolution, the regional dimension of anti-corruption, the national experiences of selected states, and the role of international organizations have all been examined through detailed sections and individual chapters. Political co-optation, for instance, is a common feature of several East Asian countries and in the People's Republic of China (PRC) enabled preservation of power of the leading party.[14] Another example of how ethical considerations play a key role in corruption is the little divide between lobbyism and corruption. Lobbyism is, in fact, entirely accepted in some countries while opposed in others.

Influence over decision-making should be reduced if the lobbyist promotes the violation of human rights, the exploitation of workers and the environment, or favors with its actions other negative externalities. By contrast, lobbying should be promoted and supported, if the actor brings on positive changes for the society.[15] Political and economic inequalities shape representation of interests in policy making.[16] Civil society organizations have been frontrunners in the promotion of anti-corruption policies. They have been often more vocal and influential than the states to make 'bad' corporations accountable for their illegal or corrupting activities.[17] They have also supported policies for limiting the lobbying power of corporations merely promoting economic interests without due considerations of their impact on Non-Trade Concerns (NTCs).

Corruption practices have tremendous negative effects on the relation between citizens and government. This relationship should be accompanied by the increased focus on governance, which attempts to bridge the gaps between

14 Minxin Pei, 'Is CCP Rule Fragile or Resilient?' (2012) 23 Journal of Democracy 27, 32.

15 The concept of good lobby is an interesting example on this regard, see Alberto Alemanno, *Lobbying for Change: Find Your Voice to Create a Better Society* (Icon Books 2017)

16 Leslie Holmes, *Corruption: A Very Short Introduction* (Oxford University Press 2015) 28.

17 Régis Bismuth, Jan Dunin-Wasowicz, and Philip M Nichols 'The Transnationalization of Anti-Corruption Law: An Introduction and Overview' (Chapter 1 to this Volume).

developed and developing countries to counteract the societal crises that we are facing.[18] Good governance is closely linked with anticorruption and 'implies that the techniques used to produce policies further political legitimacy; the goal is not only policies that are scientifically advanced and technically sound but also policies that respond to public concerns.'[19] Measuring and assessing governments based on democracy indicators, such as the ones used by the *Democracy Index*,[20] appears to be no longer fashionable. The rise of actors placing greater emphasis on the quality of governance rather than on democracy has had the role of creating a fertile ground for anti-corruption policies. Weak governance and corruption undermine profitability of corporations and legitimacy even in autocratic regimes.

These issues have become particularly important in the context of globalization and fit perfectly into the broader discussions related to the necessary changes and improvements of the international legal norms and systems of governance towards the protection of Non-Trade Concerns (NTCs).[21] These topics are constitutive and pivotal of the gLAWcal book series on 'Transnational Law and Governance' published by Routledge Publishing (New York/London). In fact, through research, policy analysis, and advocacy, gLAWcal attempts to shed new light on NTCs issues such as good and global governance, human rights, right to water, rights to food, social, economic and cultural rights, labor rights, access to knowledge, public health, social welfare, consumer interests and animal welfare, climate change, energy, environmental protection and sustainable development, product safety, food safety and security. All these values are directly affected by the global expansion of world trade and should be upheld to balance the excesses of globalization

This book is an important addition to the gLAWcal book series on 'Transnational Law and Governance' regarding the broader meaning of good and global governance.[22]

18 Margaret Stout and Jeannine M Love, *Integrative Governance: Generating Sustainable Responses to Global Crises* (Routledge 2018).

19 Rose-Ackerman (n 5) at 31.

20 The EIU Democracy Index uses the following categories scores to assess the current state of: electoral process and pluralism; functioning of government; political participation; political culture; civil liberties. The Economist Intelligence Unit, 'EIU Democracy Index 2019 – World Democracy Report' (2019) <https://www.eiu.com/topic/democracy-index> accessed 9 July 2020.

21 Paolo Davide Farah, 'Trade and Progress: The Case of China' (2016) 30 Columbia Journal of Asian Law 51-112; Paolo Davide Farah and Elena Cima (eds), *China's Influence on Non-Trade Concerns in International Economic Law* (Routledge 2016). See also, Margaret Stout and Jeannine M Love, *A Radically Democratic Response to Global Governance: Dystopian Utopias* (Routledge 2016).

22 For other relevant contributions in the field included in the gLAWcal book series, *see* Angelica Bonfanti (n 12) and Jernej Letnar Černič, *Corporate Accountability under Socio-Economic Rights* (Routledge 2018).

The work accomplished by the editors is commendable. Régis Bismuth, Jan Dunin-Wasowicz, and Philip M Nichols have organized a conference with the best scholars and experts around the world on these topics and during which the various chapters of this volume were discussed. This international conference was organized in partnership with the American Society of International Law (ASIL) Anti-Corruption Law Interest Group (Washington DC, USA), Science Po Law School (Paris, France), and the Zicklin Center for Business Ethics Research of the Wharton School of University of Pennsylvania and it was held at Science Po Law School in Paris, France on December 6–7, 2018.

The editors have reached the goal of compiling a manuscript capable of becoming a point of reference for both scholars and practitioners in the field. This book contributes to the current literature on this topic in two main aspects. On one hand, it analyzes the already occurred transnationalization of the anti-corruption regime by placing particular emphasis on the institutional, legal, and economic underpinnings of the phenomenon. Multilevel and multiscalar interactions of the national anti-corruption regime bring fresh perspectives in particular to the study of transnational governance.[23] On the other hand, the book emphasizes howa transnational regime has been established. Interestingly, non-state actors and civil society organizations have been the catalyzer of this bottom-up integration of widely diverging interests and views on the corruptive phenomenon. The editors did an excellent job of including inter and multidisciplinary perspectives on anti-corruption and opened a discussion that will shape the current understanding of the regime. Scholars, civil society, the business community, and international organizations will greatly benefit from this book.

Hence, this edited volume by Régis Bismuth, Jan Dunin-Wasowicz, and Philip M Nichols provides a holistic and comprehensive analysis of the development of anti-corruption laws at the global level, benefiting from the experiences of different contributors across various legal professions and countries which provide an extremely added value to the debate occurring in the context of each chapter. This is relevant given the role corruption plays in the modern world and across borders and the many challenges posed by it, in particular the distortion of the decision-making process affecting governmental policies, but most importantly the lives of populations everywhere. It is in this context that this book is emerging at an extremely important moment, especially as numerous revolutions and civil movements are taking place globally as a direct result of the corruption of governments in places like Lebanon, Chile, and so on. The chapters of this

23 For an example of the importance of a multiscalar and multilevel approach in energy policy see: Paolo Davide Farah and Piercarlo Rossi, 'National Energy Policies and Energy Security in the Context of Climate Change and Global Environmental Risks: A Theoretical Framework for Reconciling Domestic and International Law through a Multiscalar and Multilevel Approach' (2011) 20 European Energy and Environmental Law Review 232.

edited collection provide an antidote that could help tackle corruption at the global scale as well as corrupted governments' practices that are affecting citizens directly and indirectly.

Professor Paolo Davide Farah
Editor-in-Chief for the gLAWcal book series 'Transnational Law and Governance' published by Routledge (New York/London).
West Virginia University, USA and gLAWcal – Global Law Initiatives for Sustainable Development, UK

Acknowledgements

Over three years have passed since the idea of launching a research project on the transnationalization of anti-corruption law sprang up over coffee in Paris. A central element of this project was the organization of a two-day conference that took place on December 6–7, 2018 in Paris at Sciences Po Law School during which the chapters of this book were presented and discussed. The conference and the following collective book would not have been possible without the assistance of several individuals and institutions.

The research project was initiated and led by the Anti-Corruption Law Interest Group of the American Society of International Law, Sciences Po Law School, and the Carol and Lawrence Zicklin Center for Business Ethics Research at the Wharton School, University of Pennsylvania.

Significantly, this project was also organized in close cooperation with the Organization for Economic Co-operation and Development. We are grateful to Nicola Bonucci (then OECD Director for Legal Affairs), Patrick Moulette (Head of the OECD Anti-Corruption Division), and Elisabeth Danon (Legal Analyst at the OECD Anti-Corruption Division) for their fruitful support and contribution.

In connection with the preparation of the conference, we would like to thank the team of Sciences Po Law School students who kindly volunteered, beginning with Clément Drouhard, Alexandre Dedo, Léna Dufeutrelle, Marc Steiert, Giovanni Volpe, Laura-May Weil, as well as the Sciences Po Law School staff, and Bérangère Gavaudo in particular. We are also grateful to Eloïse Glucksmann for her useful assistance.

Concerning the preparation of this book, we thank Paolo Davide Farah, Editor of the Transnational Law and Governance book series as well as our publisher Routledge, for the opportunity to publish this work. We are very grateful to Matilda Gillis, Stanislas Julien-Steffens, Claire Ren, and Gideon Gross for their useful editorial assistance.

Last but not least, we would like to thank all the participants of the Paris conference for their meaningful contribution to the discussions and, of course, we would like to thank all the contributors to this book.

The Editors,
Régis Bismuth, Jan Dunin-Wasowicz &
Philip M. Nichols

Abbreviations

ACHR	American Convention on Human Rights
ADB	Asian Development Bank
AfDB	African Development Bank
APEC	Asia-Pacific Economic Cooperation
APG	Asia/Pacific Group on Money Laundering
AU	African Union
AUCPCC	African Union Convention on Preventing and Combating Corruption
CFATF	Caribbean Financial Action Task Force
CLCC	Council of Europe Criminal Law Convention on Corruption
CoE	Council of Europe
CPTPP	Comprehensive and Progressive Agreement for Trans-Pacific Partnership
DOJ	US Department of Justice
EAG	Eurasian Group on Combating Money Laundering and Financing of Terrorism
EBRD	European Bank for Reconstruction and Development
ESAAMLG	Eastern and Southern Africa Anti-Money Laundering Group
EU	European Union
FATF	Financial Action Task Force
FCPA	US Foreign Corrupt Practices Act
FIU	Financial Intelligence Unit
FSRBs	FATF-style regional bodies
GABAC	Task Force on Money Laundering in Central Africa
GAFILAT	Financial Action Task Force of Latin America
GDPR	EU General Data Protection Regulation
GIABA	Inter-Governmental Action Group against Money Laundering in West Africa
GIACC	Global Infrastructure Anti-Corruption Centre
GRECO	The Group of States against Corruption of the Council of Europe

IACAC	The Inter-American Convention against Corruption
IBA	International Bar Association
IBRD	International Bank for Reconstruction and Development
ICC	International Chamber of Commerce
ICC Rules	ICC Rules on Combating Corruption
ICCPR	International Covenant on Civil and Political Rights
ICESCR	International Covenant on Economic, Social and Cultural Rights
ICSID	International Centre for the Settlement of Investment Disputes
ICSID Convention	Convention on the Settlement of Investment Disputes Between States and Nationals of Other States
IDA	International Development Association
IIA	International Investment Agreement
IMF	International Monetary Fund
INT	The World Bank Group Integrity Vice Presidency
ISO	International Organization for Standardization
MDB	Multilateral Development Bank
MENAFATF	Middle East and North Africa Financial Action Task Force
MNC	Multi-National Corporation
MONEYVAL	Council of Europe Committee of Experts on the Evaluation of Anti-Money Laundering Measures and the Financing of Terrorism
OAS	Organization of American States
OECD	Organisation for Economic Co-operation and Development
OECD Convention	The Convention on Combating Bribery of Foreign Public Officials in International Business Transactions
OECD WGB	OECD Working Group on Bribery
OSCE	Organization for Security and Co-operation in Europe
SADC	South African Development Community Protocol on Corruption
SEC	US Securities and Exchange Commission
SFO	UK Serious Fraud Office
SMEs	Small and Medium-Sized Enterprises
TI	Transparency International
UKBA	UK Bribery Act 2010
UN	United Nations
UNCAC	United Nations Convention against Corruption
UNCITRAL	United Nations Commission on International Trade Law
UNCTAD	United Nations Conference on Trade and Development

UNCTOC	United Nations Convention against Transnational Organized Crime
UNGA	United Nations General Assembly
UNODC	United Nations Office on Drug and Crime
UNSC	United Nations Security Council
WBG	World Bank Group

1 The transnationalization of anti-corruption law

An introduction and overview

Régis Bismuth, Jan Dunin-Wasowicz, and Philip M. Nichols

Before October of 1996, international organizations and actors rarely discussed corruption. Within the World Bank Group, the topic was considered dangerously political and thus outside the range of appropriate issues for the Group. In 1996, however, then-President James Wolfensohn delivered an opening speech to the Group's annual meeting in which he acknowledged that corruption significantly interfered with the objectives of the Group, and in which he described corruption as a 'cancer' that inflicted numerous harms on the people of the world.[1]

Wolfensohn's speech highlighted a turning point in the study of and concern about corruption. Just a year before Wolfensohn's speech, the nongovernmental organization Transparency International, founded in part by persons who had left the World Bank Group in frustration with the way that corruption impeded their work, released the first Corruption Perceptions Index, which gave the world its first standard quantitative measure of corruption. Just a few months before Wolfensohn's speech, the Organization of American States concluded negotiation of and opened for signature the Inter-American Convention Against Corruption, the first international instrument specifically focused on corruption.

Since 1995, the study of corruption and practice of anti-corruption have changed in ways that can only be described using superlatives. The study of corruption has grown exponentially. Where once only a small handful of scholarly articles might address corruption in any given year, there are now entire journals dedicated to the subject and its study is commonplace. Practice has exceeded scholarly study; entire industries are built around providing advice and training, around risk assessment and avoidance, and around prosecution and defense. Once barely discussed, corruption is now at the forefront of conversations.

This book examines one aspect of the changes that have occurred in those decades. Legal systems have always attempted to control corruption, but have largely done so from a domestic perspective. In the last few decades, that changed. Corruption is recognized as a transnational phenomenon, and its control has

1 James Wolfensohn, 'Address to the Board of Governors at the Annual Meetings of the World Bank and the International Monetary Fund' in *Voice for the World's Poor* (World Bank 2005) 50.

been transnationalized. The contributions to this book explore discrete aspects of that transnationalization (4). Before discussing those contributions, however, it is useful to review what is meant by 'corruption' (1), 'transnational' (2), and the 'global anti-corruption regime' (3).

1 Corruption

This is not a book about corruption, but instead about laws and rules created to control corruption. Nonetheless, it is important to understand the object of these rules. As a phenomenon, corruption defies easy definition. Its effects, however, are much easier to describe.

1.1 Defining corruption

The authors in this book, and the anti-corruption community in general, use the word 'corruption' to mean several phenomena. Each of these has relevance to efforts to control corruption and to the subject matter of this book.

The definition of corruption as a social phenomenon has engendered substantial debate among political scientists and sociologists. Arnold Heidenheimer and Michael Johnston suggest that the myriad attempts to define corruption can be parsed into three broad categories: market-based, public interest-centered, and public office-centered types of definitions.[2] Market-based definitions tend to discuss corruption as a product of markets for influence or as a consequence of market failures. As Mark Philp notes, however, these sorts of analyses 'are certainly one way of understanding corruption, they may also provide a fruitful model for the explanation of the incidence of corruption, but they are not a way of defining it.'[3] Public interest-based definitions, on the other hand, view corruption through the lens of its deleterious effects on the public interest and good governance. This type of analysis similarly illuminated effect but provides little in terms of definition.[4]

Ulrich von Alemann warns that 'perhaps it is wrong to search for one true and correct universal definition. Maybe such a definition is like the Holy Grail, i.e. something unattainable that can only be a kind of guiding star.'[5] Von Alemann suggests that rather than seeking a crisp definition of corruption, scholars should

2 Arnold J Heidenheimer, *Political Corruption: Readings in Comparative Analysis* (Holt, Rinehart & Winston 1970) 4.

3 Mark Philp, 'Conceptualizing Political Corruption' in Arnold J Heidenheimer and Michael Johnston (eds), *Political Corruption: Concepts and Contexts* (3rd edn, Transaction 2002) 50.

4 For an example of the use of a public interest-based definition, see Maryvonne Gnaux, 'Social Sciences and the Evolving Concept of Corruption' (2004) 42 Crime, Law and Social Change 13, 18–22.

5 Ulrich von Alemann, 'The Unknown Depths of Political Theory: The Case for a Multidimensional Concept of Corruption' (2004) 42 Crime, Law and Social Change 25, 26.

instead attempt to understand it.[6] This approach, however, risks becoming tautological: according to this definition the phenomenon that a researcher attempts to understand is by definition whatever the scholar understands. This approach also renders comparisons and the sharing of knowledge difficult.

Practitioners and scholars therefore require a definition, and seem to have settled on the third of Heidenheimer and Johnston's definitions, a public office-based definition. Joseph Senturia used an early version of this definition in an encyclopedia entry on corruption,[7] but Joseph Nye brought it into broader discourse.[8] No single iteration of this definition exists, but in its broad form, capable of encompassing private sector as well as public sector corruption, a credible articulation would define corruption as:

> The abuse or misuse of trust or authority for self-serving reasons rather than the reasons for which trust or authority was conferred.

The International Chamber of Commerce, the International Monetary Fund, the Organisation for Economic Cooperation and Development, Transparency International, and the World Bank Group each use variations of this definition.[9] Most of the authors in this book explicitly or implicitly use the same definition of corruption, as does almost all of the research on which they rely.

The United Nations, on the other hand, not only does not use this definition but also eschews any attempts to define corruption. Like von Alemann, the parties that negotiated issues of corruption within the United Nations worried that attempting to define corruption was less important than acting on corruption, and avoided definition 'so as to allow greater flexibility for future implementations and interpretations.'[10] Scholars and practitioners require a definition, but von Alemann and the United Nations offer an important reminder: when considering

6 Ibid. Von Alemann, like Heidenheimer and Johnston, parses theories of corruption into categories, although von Alemann suggests seven categories rather than three: at 26–27.

7 Joseph J Senturia, 'Corruption, Political' (1931) IV Encyclopaedia of the Social Sciences 448.

8 Joseph S Nye, 'Corruption and Political Development: A Cost-Benefit Analysis' (1967) 61 American Political Science Review 417, 419.

9 International Chamber of Commerce, *Memorandum to the OECD Working Group on Bribery in International Business Transactions: Recommendations by the International Chamber of Commerce (ICC) on Further Provisions to be Adopted to Prevent and Prohibit Private-to-Private Corruption* (ICC 2006) 2; International Monetary Fund, 'The Role of the Fund in Governance Issues—Review of the Guidance Note—Preliminary Considerations—Background Notes' (2017) IMF Policy Papers, 9; 'What is Corruption?' (Transparency International) <www.transparency.org/en/what-is-corruption#> accessed 1 June 2020; 'Glossary of Statistical Terms' (OECD 2013) <stats.oecd.org/glossary/detail.asp?ID=4773> accessed 1 June 2020; World Bank, *Helping Countries Combat Corruption: The Role of the World Bank* (World Bank Group 1997) 8.

10 Antonio Argandoña, 'The United Nations Convention against Corruption and Its Impact on International Companies' (2007) 74 J Bus Ethics 481, 488.

the social phenomenon, pedantic insistence on strict enforcement of a definition is unlikely to result in insights into the nature of that phenomenon.

That reminder stands in stark contrast to the second way in which the authors of this book use the word 'corruption.' The objects of study in this book are laws, rules, and regulations. Definitions used to define social phenomena encompass the nature of a phenomenon rather than drawing sharp lines. Legal definitions, on the other hand, must draw clear lines. Basic fairness requires that people subject to that law know which behaviors fall within prohibitions and which do not. Fair processes require that the state prove that a person charged with violating a rule did violate that rule.

The criminal law of the Falkland Islands amply illustrates a precise definition:

> (1) A person ('P') commits an offence in either of the following cases.
> (2) Case 1 is where —
>   (a) P offers, promises or gives a financial or other advantage to another person; and
>   (b) P intends the advantage —
>   (i) to induce a person to perform improperly a relevant function or activity; or
>   (ii) to reward a person for the improper performance of such a function or activity.
> (3) Case 2 is where —
>   (a) P offers, promises or gives a financial or other advantage to another person; and
>   (b) P knows or believes that the acceptance of the advantage would itself constitute the improper performance of a relevant function or activity.
> (4) In Case 1 it does not matter whether the person to whom the advantage is offered, promised or given is the same person as the person who is to perform, or has performed, the function or activity concerned.
> (5) In Cases 1 and 2 it is irrelevant whether the advantage is offered, promised or given by P directly or through a third party.[11]

The criminal law repeats this exercise for the offense of accepting a bribe, and for bribing foreign officials.[12]

Because this is a book about the control of corruption through law and other rules, the authors in this book therefore use the word 'corruption' in two different ways. The word denotes a general social phenomenon without sharp boundaries. The word also is used as a blanket phrase encompassing several very sharply defined actions.

11 Crimes Ordinance 2014, §490. This legislation is to a large extent modeled on the UK Bribery Act.

12 Crimes Ordinance 2014, §491, §495.

The word 'corruption' is also used in a third way that sometimes causes confusion. As a phenomenon, corruption can take many forms, such as nepotism, embezzlement, cronyism, or extortion. Most often, however, the word 'corruption' actually refers only to one particular form: bribery. Susan Rose-Ackerman, a pioneer in the study of corruption, is unabashed: 'I shall always keep bribery in the analytical foreground.'[13] Michael Johnston, on the other hand, laments the confusion and imprecision engendered by the conflation of 'corruption' and 'bribery.'[14] Whether one sides with Rose-Ackerman or with Johnston, one cannot fight common usage. The word corruption now means only bribery. The anti-corruption regime discussed in this book, therefore, although sounding expansive, is actually designed almost entirely to control bribery and not other forms of corruption.

1.2 The effects of corruption

Corruption inflicts innumerable harms. In a foreword to the United Nations Convention Against Corruption, then-Secretary General Kofi Annan observed that:

> Corruption is an insidious plague that has a wide range of corrosive effects on societies. It undermines democracy and the rule of law, leads to violations of human rights, distorts markets, erodes the quality of life and allows organized crime, terrorism and other threats to human security to flourish.[15]

Annan's condemnation of corruption echoes that of Wolfensohn a decade earlier.[16]

Corruption inflicts profound damage on people and the planet they inhabit.[17] The World Economic Forum estimates that the costs of corruption equals five percent of the world's gross domestic product.[18] The International Monetary Fund estimates that endemic corruption costs countries four percent of national

13 Susan Rose-Ackerman, *Corruption: A Study in Political Economy* (Academic Press 1978) 4.

14 Michael Johnston, *Syndromes of Corruption: Wealth, Power, and Democracy* (CUP 2005) 20–21.

15 Kofi Annan, *Foreword to United Nations Convention against Corruption* (UN Sales No V.04-56160, UN Office on Drugs & Crime 2004).

16 Wolfensohn states that 'corruption diverts resources from the poor to the rich, increases the cost of running businesses, distorts public expenditures, and deters foreign investors … it erodes the constituency for aid programs and humanitarian relief … it is a major barrier to sound and equitable development.' See Wolfensohn (n 1) 50.

17 See generally Susan Rose-Ackerman and Bonnie J Palika, *Corruption and Government: Causes, Consequences and Reform* (2nd edn, CUP 2016).

18 Security Council, press release, UN doc no SC/13493 (10 September 2018) <www.un.org/press/en/2018/sc13493.doc.htm> accessed 1 June 2020.

gross domestic product in tax revenues.[19] It also estimates that the most corrupt emerging economies waste twice as much money as do the least corrupt.[20] A study of 105 countries found that bribery costs the private sectors in developing countries 3.7 times the amount that those countries receive in development aid.[21]

Corruption also inflicts profound human costs. Corruption contributes to shorter lifespans, higher rates of infant mortality, lower levels of health, and lower levels of literacy and education.[22] Corruption causes the misallocation of resources and results in substandard or unwanted infrastructure.[23] Corruption degrades the physical environment and undermines efforts to protect it.[24] Corruption diminishes quality of life.

Corruption disrupts the relationship between people and governance. In a corrupt system, officials act in their own interest rather than in the interests of their constituencies.[25] Corrupt bureaucracies tend to be of lower quality than clean bureaucracies,[26] and corrupt bureaucrats conceal information and create

19 Vitor Gaspar, Paolo Mauro, and Paulo Medas, 'Tackling Corruption in Government' (*IMFBlog*, 4 April 2019) <http://blogs.imf.org/2019/04/04/tackling-corruption-in-government/> accessed 1 June 2020.

20 Ibid.

21 Sadika Hameed and Jeremiah Magpile, *The Costs of Corruption: Strategies for Ending a Tax on Private-Sector-Led Growth* (Rowman & Littlefield 2014) 3.

22 See Sanjeev Gupta, Hamid Davoodi, and Erwin Tiongson, 'Corruption and the Provision of Health Care and Education Services' (2000) International Monetary Fund Working Paper 116; Maureen Lewis, 'Governance and Corruption in Public Health Care Systems' (2006) Center for Global Development Working Paper 78.

23 See Jonathan Lehne, Jacob N Shapiro, and Oliver Vanden Eynde, 'Building Connections: Political Corruption and Road Construction in India' (2018) 131 J Dev Econ 62; Shuhong Wang, Danqing Zhao, and Hanxue Chen, 'Government Corruption, Resource Misallocation, and Ecological Efficiency' (2020) 85 Energy Econ 104573; Bingyong Zheng and Junji Xiao, 'Corruption and Investment: Theory and Evidence from China' (2020) 175 J Econ Behav & Org 40; Elisa Gamberoni, Christine Gartner, Claire Giordano, and Paloma Lopez-Garcia, 'Is Corruption Efficiency-Enhancing? A Case Study of Nine Central and Eastern European Countries' (2016) ECB Working Paper 1950.

24 See Chun-Ping Chang and Yu Hao, 'Environmental Performance, Corruption and Economic Growth: Global Evidence Using a New Data Set' (2017) 49 Applied Econ 498; Lorenzo Pellegrini and Reyer Gerlagh, 'Corruption, Democracy, and Environmental Policy: An Empirical Contribution to the Debate' (2006) 15 J Env & Dev 332.

25 Robert Klitgaard, *Controlling Corruption* (UCLA Press 1988) 1–12.

26 Bola Dauda, 'Corruption, Nepotism, and Anti-Bureaucratic Behaviors' in Nimi Wariboko and Toyin Falola (eds), *The Palgrave Handbook of African Social Ethics* (Palgrave Macmillan 2020) 317; Thomas Herzfeld and Christoph Weiss, 'Corruption and Legal (In)Effectiveness: An Empirical Investigation' (2003) 19 Eur J Pol Econ 621, 629.

obstacles to service.[27] Corruption engenders substantial mistrust of and disengagement from institutions of governance.[28]

Corruption negatively affects markets and the conduct of business. Corruption perverts the operation of markets: rather than production and consumption decisions being made on the basis of cost, quality, and need, those decisions are based on the quality of bribes. Indeed, much of the impetus for passage of the United States' Foreign Corrupt Practices Act was the legislature's desire to safeguard the integrity of the global market.[29] Several chapters in this book choose to focus on the effect of the global corruption regime on producers, but readers should not interpret that as suggesting that only producers are affected. Distortions to markets affect consumers as much as producers.

Corruption, particularly bribery, does impose costs on individual business firms. Business firms that pay bribes spend more time and incur greater costs when dealing with government than business firms that do not pay bribes.[30] Business firms that pay bribes incur higher costs when raising capital.[31] Firms that pay bribes are less productive, and experience slower rates of growth.[32] They

27 See Robert Wade, 'The Market for Public Office: Why the Indian State is Not Better at Development' (1985) 13 World Dev 467, 474–80; Robert Wade, 'The System of Administrative and Political Corruption: Canal Irrigation in South India' (1982) 18 J Dev Stud 287, 314–315.

28 See Eric M Uslaner, 'Trust and Corruption' in Johann Graf Lambsdorff, Markus Taube, and Matthias Schramm (eds), *The New Institutional Economics of Corruption* (Routledge 2005) 76, 82–87.

29 The United States Congress emphasized their intention to preserve market integrity through passage of the Act. At the opening of committee hearings, a Chair warned that '[t]he practice of bribing foreign officials has corrupted ... the free market system, under which the most efficient producers with the best products are supposed to prevail.' Foreign and Corporate Bribes: Hearings on S 3133 Before the S Comm on Banking, Hous & Urban Affairs, 94th Cong (1976) 1 (statement of Sen William Proxmire, Chair). The Senate Report that accompanied the Senate version of the Act described bribery as 'fundamentally destructive of th[e] basic tenet' of business and warned that bribery threatened 'the very stability of overseas business.' S Rep No 95-114 (1977). 4. The House Report stated that bribery 'short circuits the marketplace ... by directing business to those companies too inefficient to compete in terms of price, quality or service, or too lazy to engage in honest salesmanship, or too intent upon unloading marginal products.' HR Rep No 95-640 (1976) 4.

30 See Francisco Ciocchini, Erik Durbin, and David TC Ng, 'Does Corruption Increase Emerging Market Bond Spreads?' (2003) 55 J Econ & Bus 503, 512–513; Charles MC Lee and David Ng, 'Corruption and International Valuation: Does Virtue Pay?' (2005) 18 J Investing 23, 31–33.

31 See Alejandro Gaviria, 'Assessing the Effects of Corruption and Crime on Firm Performance: Evidence from Latin America' (2002) 3 Emerging Mts Rev 245, 267; Daniel Kaufman and Shang-Jin Wei, 'Does 'Grease Money' Speed Up the Wheels of Commerce?' (1999) World Bank Policy Research Working Paper No. 2254.

32 Raymond Fisman and Jakob Svensson, 'Are Corruption and Taxation Really Harmful to Growth? Firm-Level Evidence' (2007) 83 J Dev Econ 63, 64; Johann Graf Lambsdorff, 'How Corruption Affects Productivity' (2003) 56 Kyklos: Intl Rev for Soc Sci 457, 468.

also encounter more difficulties when trying to form partnerships and other relationships.[33]

All of these harms can be measured and discussed in a clinical way. As Tamar Hostovsky Brandes reminds the reader, however, there are other less quantifiable aspects to corruption that merit attention.[34] Corruption inflicts indignities both small and large. In the last few years, millions of people around the world have protested against corruption. Protesters have endured bitter Eastern European winters and suffocating Middle Eastern summers. They have braved snipers, beatings by security forces, and imprisonment. People have even self-immolated to protest corruption. People despise corruption, and the anger it engenders cannot be ignored.

2 Transnationalization of law

The phrase 'transnational law' has the same imprecise boundaries as the word 'corruption.'[35] As with the phenomenon of corruption, the concept may be more important than a precise definition. Conceptually, transnational law fills a lacuna in doctrinal theories of law. The term 'domestic law' addresses laws generated unilaterally by sovereign states and generally applicable to parties and actions over which they have jurisdiction. The term 'international law' addresses laws generated jointly (bilaterally, plurilaterally, or multilaterally) by sovereign states or the international organizations they have created. There should be, however, a jurisprudential lexicon or theories for activities that transcend political borders and cannot be understood, captured, or effectively regulated solely within the confines of traditional legal categories.

Business scholars, in particular, have observed the gap in traditional legal thinking, perhaps because business activities increasingly occur without reference to political borders. Stephen Kobrin notes, for example, that whereas multinational business firms operate as a unitary whole and 'emphasize control exercised by the center over the enterprise as a whole,' legal thinking continues to conceive of 'a transnational firm as "stringing together corporations created by the laws of different states."'[36] Kobrin explains how the reality of business does not conform to a world in which relationships exist only within the confines of a polity or between nations:

33 See Philip M Nichols, 'The Business Case for Complying With Bribery Laws' (2012) 49 Am Bus LJ 325, 334–352.

34 Tamar Hostovsky Brandes, 'The Relevance of Moral Arguments against Foreign Bribery: Israel as a Case Study', ch 5.

35 The phrase 'transnational law' was used as early as 1956, in Philip C Jessup, *Transnational Law* (Yale UP 1956).

36 Stephen J Kobrin, 'Private Political Authority and Public Responsibility: Transnational Politics, Transnational Firms, and Human Rights' (2009) 19 Bus Ethics Q 349, 356.

> Borders are 'transcended' rather than crossed, relations become increasingly 'supraterritorial' as distance, borders and geographic space itself lose economic and political significance. Markets no longer need to be defined in terms of geographic proximity and, in some instances, the location of transactions and organizations has become indeterminate.[37]

Kobrin and other business scholars do not suggest that domestic or international law has become obsolete, nor do they argue for the replacement of domestic or international law by some other paradigm.[38] Instead, they lament the failure of legal theory to accurately describe the world that they occupy. The concept of transnational law aims to remedy that failure.

In an ever-globalizing world, many sectors have come to recognize the usefulness of the transnational paradigm. Capital is both extremely liquid and relatively impervious to political borders; many who study financial regulation now embrace the concept of transnational rules.[39] Environmental protection, human rights, the internet, labour, migration, narcotics control, terrorism, and more all lend themselves to transnational regulation.[40] As David Zaring points out, many human activities now seem to fall within the ambit of the transnational.[41]

As a concept, transnational law is no more fully theorized than other jurisprudential theories,[42] and deliberately the choice has been made not to circumscribe our project to a single theory of transnational law. It should be

37 Stephen J Kobrin, 'Globalization, Transnational Corporations and the Future of Global Governance' in Andreas Georg Scherer and Guido Palazzo (eds), *Handbook of Research on Global Corporate Citizenship* (Edward Elgar 2008) 250.

38 See Kobrin, 'Private Political Authority' (n 36) 361 (acknowledging the power and relevance of sovereign states).

39 E.g., Abraham Newman and Elliot Posner, 'Transnational Feedback, Soft Law, and Preferences in Global Financial Regulation' (2016) 23 Rev Intl Pol Econ 123; David Zaring, 'Finding Legal Principle in Global Financial Regulation' (2011) 52 Va J Intl L 683.

40 See Tilmann Altwicker, 'Explaining the Emergence of Transnational Counter-Terrorism Legislation in International Law-Making' (2018) 24 Finnish YB Intl L 3; Tilmann Altwicker, 'Transnationalizing Rights: International Human Rights Law in Cross-Border Contexts' (2018) 29 EJIL 581 (2018); Adelle Blackett and Laurence R Helfer, 'Introduction to the Symposium on Transnational Futures of International Labor Law' (2019) 113 AJIL Unbound 385; Laura Mai, '(Transnational) Law for the Anthropocene: Revisiting Jessup's Move From "What?" to "How?"' (2020) 11 Transnatl Legal Theory 105; Neha Mishra, 'Building Bridges: International Trade Law, Internet Governance, and the Regulation of Data Flows' (2019) 52 Vand J Transnatl L 463; Bruce Zagaris and Alex Psilakis, 'International Narcotics Control and Transnational Organized Crime' (2019) 35 Intl Enforcement L Rep 41.

41 David Zaring, 'Rulemaking and Adjudication in International Law' (2008) 46 Colum J Transnatl L 563, 565–566.

42 See Craig M Scott, 'Transnational Law as Proto-concept: Three Conceptions' (2009) 10 German LJ 859, 868–875 (parsing theories of legal realism into three categories—traditionalism, decisionism, and pluralism—but arguing that pluralism has the strongest explanatory power).

noted, nonetheless, that most theorists agree that transnationalization consists of something different than an expansion of domestic jurisdiction:

> [T]he term transnational does not merely signify the extension of … normativity across borders … Instead, the term transnational identifies an intricate connection of spatial and conceptual dimensions: in addressing … the demarcation of emerging and evolving spaces and … the construction of these spaces as artifacts for human activity, communication and rationality.[43]

Gregory Schaffer offers a cohesive model of the creation of transnational networks of rules.[44] He suggests a plurality of sources from which rules emerge, including 'bureaucratic networks of public officials, hybrid public-private networks, and networks of purely private parties.'[45] These sources interact in dynamic and recursive ways.[46] In this dynamic process, 'the transnational and local are held in tension, the actors engaged in transnational legal processes seek to influence local lawmaking and practice, and the national legal norms, adaptations, and resistance provide models for and feed back into transnational law.'[47] The product of this dynamic process changes constantly, and manifests itself differently across the breadth of its application.

Describing this process reveals many open questions. What roles and how much influence do the many actors play and have? Does the absence of democratic ratification render transnational law undemocratic? Do hegemons have undue influence over the process, or does it decentralized nature give voice to less powerful actors? It is those sorts of questions that chapters of this book address.

3 The global anti-corruption regime

As with so many other terms used in this book, the phrase 'global anti-corruption regime' lacks precise boundaries. The term exists for the convenience of those who study or practice in the realm of corruption control, who use it to designate an uncoordinated network of rules, laws, processes, and norms that operate to control corruption. That network clearly constitutes transnational law and is a natural object of study.

43 Peer Zumbansen, 'Comparative, Global and Transnational Constitutionalism: The Emergence of a Transnational Legal-Pluralist Order' (2012) 1 Global Constitutionalism 16, 22.

44 Gregory Shaffer, 'Transnational Legal Process and State Change' (2012) 37 L & Soc Inquiry 229.

45 Ibid 236.

46 Ibid 238. See Terence Halliday and Bruce Carruthers, 'The Recursivity of Law: Global Norm-Making and National Lawmaking in the Globalization of Corporate Insolvency Regimes' (2007) 112 Am J Sociol 1135 (describing dynamism and recursivity in the creation of transnational rules).

47 Shaffer (n 44) 238.

Many strands work together to create the network that constitutes the global anti-corruption regime. The regime constantly changes and grows,[48] but its basic components can be described.

3.1 Domestic activities

The domestic law of every country in the world criminalizes the bribery of its own officials, and most criminalize other forms of corruption as well. The law of the Falkland Islands, the southernmost polity in the world, has already been mentioned.[49] Greenland, the northernmost polity, also criminalizes corruption.[50] Russia, the easternmost country in the world, has enacted a plethora of laws and rules to control corruption, as has the westernmost, the United States.[51] Every country or state-equivalent in between those four corners prohibits the corruption of its own officials.

A growing body of domestic legal systems also prohibits the bribery of foreign officials. Once, only the laws of the United States and Sweden prohibited transnational bribery.[52] Now, the laws of virtually all of the major trading or investing countries have similar provisions.[53] These laws vary in scope and jurisdictional reach; the most common iteration criminalizes the payment of bribes to foreign government officials for purposes that have to do with business.

Laws, however, are not the only domestic contribution to the global anti-corruption regime. Many polities also contribute processes, administrative regulations, and training and norm creation. One of the most controversial processes, the conclusion of criminal investigations by deferred prosecution agreements or non-prosecution agreements, is the subject of a chapter in this book.[54] Administrative rules, on the other hand, tend to generate less debate. Both the federal government of the United States and the central government of China, for example, debar actors who act corruptly from further business with those

48 Gwendolyn Gordon observes that legal scholars tend to mistake culture as static when in reality it constantly changes. Gwendolyn Gordon, 'Culture in Corporate Law' (2016) 39 Seattle UL Rev 353, 363.

49 Text to note 11.

50 Criminal Code 1954, § 17.

51 See V Shorokhov, 'Anti-Corruption Policy in the Russian Federation' (2017) 3 Eur J Natural History 22; Mark S Gaioni, 'Federal Anticorruption Law in the State and Local Context: Defining the Scope of 18 USC Sec. 666' (2012) 46 Colum JL & Soc Probs 207.

52 15 USC § 78dd-1 (1978); Brottsbalken, SFS § 103 (1997).

53 See Nichols (n 33) 362–363 (reviewing laws of major trading and investing countries).

54 See Simon St-Georges and Denis Saint-Martin, 'The Global Diffusion of DPAs: The Not So Functional Remaking of the Rules against Business Corruption', ch 20. See also Mike Koehler, 'Measuring the Impact of Non-Prosecution and Deferred Prosecution Agreements on Foreign Corrupt Practices Act Enforcement' (2015) 49 UC Davis L Rev 497 (describing and discussing the controversial use of these agreements).

governments.[55] These are not small contributions to the global anti-corruption regime. In 2018, the United States government alone debarred 1,334 entities from procurement activities.[56]

States also robustly educate and generate norms. Hong Kong's Independent Commission Against Corruption stands out as a leader.[57] The Independent Commission is empowered to investigate and prosecute allegations of corruption, but that is only one of the three prongs in its anti-corruption portfolio. The Commission also assists with regular audits of every agency in the Hong Kong government, as required by Hong Kong law, to not only account for spending and other decisions but also find weaknesses in the decision-making and reporting processes that might lend themselves to corruption.[58] The third prong of the Commission's charge is education. The Commission conducts educational seminars in secondary schools, and has produced an extensive catalogue of educational videos and publications that are available for public consumption.[59]

3.2 Private dispute settlement

Arbitral bodies have developed a set of rules distinct from local laws and regulations. These rules may have more influence on transnational business than domestic law.[60] Arbitration usually operates less expensively and more quickly than judicial bodies. In polities with unstable, weak, or inexperienced institutions, arbitration offers a more reliable and trustworthy alternative to judicial bodies.[61]

Business firms that engage in corruption cut off their access to arbitration. The seminal case, ICC 1110, decided in 1963, involved an agent's request for payment of commissions on oil contracts in Argentina. The agent clearly had been involved in corrupt activities. Judge Gunnar Lagergren observed that:

55 Federal Acquisitions Regulations System—Causes for Debarment, 48 CFR § 9.406-2; Tong Xin-chao, 'Chinese Procurement Law: Current Legal Frameworks and a Transition to the World Trade Organization's Government Procurement Agreement' (2003) 17 Temple Intl & Comp LJ 139, 163–164.

56 *Annual Report of the Interagency Suspension and Debarment Committee to Congress* (30 October 2019) 7.

57 See Jon ST Quah, 'Anti-Corruption Agencies in Four Asian Countries: A Comparative Analysis' in Bidya Bowornwathana and Clay Wescott (eds), *Comparative Governance Reform in Asia: Democracy, Corruption, and Government Trust* (Emerald 2008) 85 (describing and comparing anti-corruption agencies).

58 ICAC, 'Internal Audit Functions' <www.icac.nsw.gov.au/prevention/foundations-for-corruption-prevention/internal-audit-functions> accessed 1 June 2020.

59 ICAC, 'Anti-Corruption Resources' <www.icac.org.hk/en/resource/publications-and-videos/ps/index.html> accessed 1 June 2020.

60 See Christopher R Drahozal and Richard W Naimark, *Towards a Science of International Arbitration: Collected Empirical Research* (Kluwer 2005) 59 (noting that 95% of transnational business contracts include an arbitration clause).

61 See Ilias Bantekas, *Introduction to International Arbitration* (CUP 2015) 16–20.

> Whether one is taking the point of view of good governance or that of commercial ethics it is impossible to close one's eyes to the probable destination of amounts of this magnitude, and to the destructive effect thereof on the business pattern with consequent impairment of industrial progress. Such corruption is an international evil; it is contrary to good morals and to international public policy common to the community of nations. [Firms engaged in corruption] have forfeited any right to ask for assistance of the machinery of justice.[62]

In the context of transnationalization, Judge Lagergren's ruling exhibits both rulemaking and the expression of norms that transcend locality.

More recently, relying on the principle that agreements to arbitrate are separable from otherwise unenforceable contracts,[63] arbitral bodies have granted limited access to arbitration even when bribery is alleged, but will not enforce contracts tainted by corruption.

> [B]ribery is contrary to the international public policy of most, if not all, States or, to use another formula, to transnational public policy. Thus, claims based on contracts of corruption or on contracts obtained by corruption cannot be upheld by this Arbitral Tribunal.[64]

In other words, arbitral panels will hear a case that involves corruption, but will not enforce the underlying contract.[65]

Arbitral bodies actively contribute to the global anti-corruption regime in other ways. Tribunals may, for example, investigate the possibility of corruption on their own initiative; if they fail to investigate and the occurrence of bribery is found in later proceedings, a tribunal's decision may legally be set aside by a national court.[66]

3.3 *International instruments*

Although transnational law encompasses sources other than those that govern relations between states, the instruments that govern those relationships have contributed substantially to the global anti-corruption regime. Most of those

62 ICC Case No 1110, Award (1963) [20], reprinted in (1994) 10 Arbitration Intl 282, 294.

63 Bantekas (n 61) 27–29.

64 *World Duty Free Company Ltd v. Republic of Kenya*, ICSID (World Bank) Case No ARB/00/7, Award (4 October 2006) [157].

65 See Matt Reeder, 'Estop That! Defeating a Corrupt State's Corruption Defense to ICSID BIT Arbitration' (2016) 27 Am Rev Intl Arb 311, 313–314.

66 Bernardo Cremades and David Cairns, 'Transnational Public Policy in International Arbitral Decision-Making: The Cases of Bribery, Money Laundering, and Fraud' in Kristine Karsten and Andrew Berkeley (eds), *Arbitration, Money Laundering, Corruption and Fraud* (Kluwer 2003) 67.

instruments require signatories to criminalize bribery, particularly the bribery of foreign officials.

The Organization of American States, led by Venezuela, promulgated the first of these conventions. Venezuela was then at a flection point in its democratic and economic progressions, both of which had been set back by bank failures caused by corruption.[67] The Inter-American Convention on Corruption requires all members of the organization to criminalize transnational bribery, and also requires members to cooperate with one another in the investigation, apprehension, and prosecution of persons and entities that pay bribes.[68]

The Organisation for Economic Cooperation and Development, universally known as the OECD, soon followed. Members of the OECD presented even more ripe conditions for an international instrument than did the Americas. Several Western European members were beset by wrenching corruption scandals, perhaps most painfully in Germany, where the corruption scandal engulfed the respected architect of German reunification.[69] The political and commercial reintegration of Central and Eastern Europe with Western Europe following the end of the Cold War also focused Western European attention on corruption. As Mark Pieth notes, 'Suddenly corruption abroad no longer happened on a remote continent, far away from home.'[70] In East Asia, Japan endured a series of corruption scandals so severe that Japan amended its constitution and changed the structure of its government.[71] A positivist international law account of these instruments might give scant attention to these background conditions; the plurality of sources considered in transnational law accounts makes them relevant. The OECD Convention on Combating Bribery of Foreign Public Officials in International Business Transactions was adopted one year after the Inter-American Convention; it too requires members to criminalize transnational bribery and to cooperate with one another in investigation and enforcement.[72]

Other international organizations followed with similar instruments. The African Union, the Council of Europe, and the European Union have each

67 See Bruce Zagaris and Shaila Lakhani Ohri, 'The Emergence of an International Enforcement Regime on Transnational Corruption in the Americas' (1999) 30 L & Poly Intl Bus 53, 65 (describing Venezuela's leadership).

68 Inter-American Convention against Corruption, 29 March 1996, 35 ILM 724. See 'Developments in the Law—International Criminal Law' (2001) 114 Harv L Rev 1943, 2032 (describing requirements).

69 See Kyle James, 'The Scandal that Rocked the Government of Helmut Kohl' (*DeutchesWelt* 2010) <www.dw.com/en/the-scandal-that-rocked-the-government-of-helmut-kohl/a-5137950>.

70 Mark Pieth, 'International Efforts to Combat Corruption' in *The Foreign Corrupt Practices Act: How to Comply Under the New Amendments and the OECD Convention* (Am Bar Assn 1999) E-1.

71 See Fakutsa Masumi, 'Political Reform's Path of No Return' (1994) 41 Japan Q 254, 255 (describing the scandals and their aftermath).

72 (Adopted 17 December 1997, entered into force 15 February 1999) 37 ILM 1.

agreed to similar requirements.[73] More recently, the United Nations General Assembly adopted a Convention Against Corruption, which requires signatories to criminalize transnational bribery.[74] Just to give a glimpse of its universal acceptance, it must be noted that the UN Convention Against Corruption has to date 187 State Parties, even more than the UN Convention against Torture and Other Cruel, Inhuman or Degrading Treatment or Punishment (170), the UN Convention on the Elimination of All Forms of Racial Discrimination (182), the Convention on the Prevention and Punishment of the Crime of Genocide (152).

The contributions of international organizations go well beyond the promulgation of conventions. The OECD is particularly active in anti-corruption activities. The OECD Working Group on Bribery, for example, monitors each member's compliance with the Convention and publishes lengthy, very detailed reports.[75] The OECD publishes myriad working papers, maintains a publicly accessible knowledge portal, and funds numerous anti-corruption programs in non-member countries, many of which attempt to create or strengthen local laws and legal systems.[76] The United Nations has also engaged in activities beyond the promulgation of its Convention. The Sustainable Development Goals established by the United Nations include Goal 16: 'Promote peaceful and inclusive societies for sustainable development, provide access to justice for all and build effective, accountable and inclusive institutions at all levels.' Target 16.5 within this goal is to 'substantially reduce corruption and bribery in all their forms' as measured by indicator 16.5.1, the 'proportion of persons who had at least one contact with a public official and who paid a bribe to a public official, or were asked for a bribe by those public officials, during the previous 12 months,' and indicator 16.5.2, the 'proportion of businesses that had at least one contact with a public official and that paid a bribe to a public official, or were asked for a bribe by those public officials during the previous 12 months.'[77] The interplay between these quantified measures, the requirements of its international instruments, and the norms expressed by the United Nations exemplifies the plurality of sources embraced by transnational law theory.

73 African Union, Convention on Preventing and Combating Corruption (adopted 11 July 2003) 43 ILM 5; Council of Europe, Criminal Law Convention on Corruption, ETS No 173, 27 January 1999, 38 ILM 505.

74 United Nations Convention against Corruption (opened for signature 9 December 2003, entered into force 14 December 2005) 2349 UNTS 41, arts 15–20.

75 OECD, 'Country Monitoring of the OECD Anti-Bribery Convention' <www.oecd.org/corruption/countrymonitoringoftheoecdanti-briberyconvention.htm> accessed 1 June 2020.

76 See OECD, 'Anti-Corruption and Integrity Hub' <www.oecd.org/corruption-integrity/> accessed 1 June 2020.

77 United Nations, Department of Economic and Social Affairs, 'SDG Indicators' <http://unstats.un.org/sdgs/metadata/?Text=&Goal=16&Target=16.5> accessed 1 June 2020.

3.4 Civil society and international financial institutions

Members of civil society make significant contributions to the global anti-corruption regime. A few months before the OECD promulgated its convention, for example, the International Chamber of Commerce adopted a rule forbidding the payment or acceptance of bribes or kickbacks by members, requiring members to control payments by their agents, and requiring members to adopt accounting procedures that would preclude the hiding of illicit payments.[78] The Chamber maintains a Commission on Anti-Corruption, which regularly publishes model codes of corporate conduct and other guidelines for business behavior.[79]

Transparency International plays an even more prominent role than the International Chamber of Commerce. In addition to publishing its very influential Corruption Perceptions Index, Transparency International conducts and publishes 'National Integrity Assessments,' which include evaluations of political structures, laws, and legal enforcement.[80] Transparency International makes recommendations on changes to these systems, and also publishes hundreds of documents that include model codes and laws, as well as suggested transnational standards. Transparency International also articulates norms and indicators that transcend political borders.[81]

The International Chamber of Commerce and Transparency International are only two of hundreds, perhaps thousands, of civil organizations that contribute to the global anti-corruption regime. To describe all of them, or even just to list them, would overwhelm this chapter. The activities of the World Bank Group, however, must be noted.

The World Bank Group has promulgated rules that forbid corruption in any project involving the Group. These are not toothless rules; the World Bank Group enforces them through hearings and debarment. The Integrity Vice Presidency division of the World Bank actively investigates and holds hearings on such claims.[82] If bribery is found to have occurred, then the responsible person or firm is placed on an embargo list and may not become involved in any project involving the World Bank Group.[83] The International Monetary Fund and each of the Regional Development Banks have similar processes, and maintain similar

78 Rules of Conduct to Combat Extortion and Bribery, arts 1, 2 & 4.

79 See, e.g., Commission on Anti-Corruption, *Combating Extortion and Bribery: ICC Rules of Conduct and Recommendations* (ICC 2005).

80 Transparency International, 'National Integrity Systems Assessment' <www.transparency.org/en/national-integrity-system-assessments> accessed 1 June 2020.

81 See, e.g., Transparency International, 'Ethics and Integrity' <www.transparency.org/en/the-organisation/ethics-integrity> accessed 1 June 2020.

82 Pascale Hélène Dubois, 'Domestic and International Administrative Tools to Combat Fraud & Corruption: A Comparison of US Suspension and Debarment with the World Bank's Sanctions System' (2012) U Chi Legal F 195, 218–226.

83 Sope Williams, 'The Debarment of Corrupt Contractors from World Bank-Financed Contracts' (2007) 36 Pub Contract LJ 277, 278.

lists; reciprocal agreements among these institutions result in cross-debarment.[84] As of June 2020, more than twelve hundred entities were debarred.

The World Bank Group contributes far more than its own administrative rules and processes. The World Bank Group actively promotes good governance programs, and frequently works with countries to change their laws, their legal institutions, and their enforcement processes. The World Bank constitutes a microcosm of transnational law creation. It is fitting that this chapter begins with an iconic speech by a former President, and that this section ends with reference to the significant contributions of the Group.

4 This book

This book does not use the global anti-corruption regime as a tool to create another jurisprudential theory of transnational law. Instead, the chapters in this book address discrete questions or issues raised by the transnationalization of anti-corruption law. The book is divided into five parts, each of which asks questions about both the content of the global anti-corruption regime and the transnational nature of that regime.

4.1 Part I: International, regional, and domestic sources of anti-corruption law – eclecticism or convergence?

The first part of this book addresses fundamental questions about transnational legal regimes, regarding the sources of and influences on the rules that make up the regime. Some models of transnational law suggest, for example, that rules are transplanted from one jurisdiction to another while other models suggest a diffusion of rules across networks.[85] Some models suggest that hegemons influence the content and structure of transnational regimes, while others suggest that the nature of transnational regimes gives greater voice to a plurality of sources.[86]

This part begins with a chapter by Elitza Katzarova and Jessica Ansart, which investigates the extent to which the United States' Foreign Corruption Practices Act influenced international instruments and the role played by the United States as a political actor.[87] The chapter finds that the Foreign Corrupt Practices Act served as a model for the instruments promulgated by the Organisation of American States and the Organisation for Economic Cooperation and Development, which, in turn, influenced other instruments. The chapter also

84 Dubois (n 82) 232.

85 See David Marsh and JC Sherman, 'Policy Diffusion and Policy Transfer' (2009) 30 Poly Study 269, 270–274 (discussing differences in the models).

86 See, e.g., Boaventura de Sousa Santos and César A Rodríguez-Garavito (eds), *Law and Globalization from Below: Towards a Cosmopolitan Legality* (CUP 2005) (edited volume that addresses questions of hegemony and plurality in transnational regimes).

87 Elitza Katzarova and Jessica Ansart, 'The Americanization of International Anti-corruption: The Influence of the FCPA on the OAS and OECD Conventions', ch 2.

argues that not only did the United States as a political actor strongly influence international instruments, but also that its activities with respect to corruption are part of a broader effort to influence transnational criminal regimes and enforcement. The chapter concludes that US influence is so extensive that US enforcement techniques must be understood in order to understand enforcement of the global anticorruption regime.

The second chapter in the part, by Sean Griffith and Thomas Lee, expands on that argument by asking why countries succumbed to the United States' influence by enacting laws to prohibit transnational bribery.[88] They suggest that following the promulgation of international instruments, the United States expanded the jurisdictional reach of its own laws so as to encompass foreign firms that conducted business in the United States. These firms were subject to restrictions that did not apply to compatriot firms that did not conduct business in the United States. In order to even the competitive field, therefore, these firms applied pressure to their home governments to enact domestic rules similar to those of the United States. Griffith and Lee's contribution constitutes a carefully argued analysis of the creation of one strand of the global anti-corruption regime.

The third chapter in this part examines the role of another powerful actor, the Organisation for Economic Cooperation and Development.[89] Rachel Brewster and Andres Ortiz scrutinize recent corruption scandals in South America and subsequent reactions, through the lenses of a theory of government decision-making and theories of reform. Brewster and Ortiz particularly observe the role of the OECD as a political entrepreneur. They find that South American countries with membership in the OECD reacted differently and instituted different reforms than nonmember countries. Theories of transnational law creation emphasize the role that knowledge plays as well as the influence of politics;[90] this chapter provides a close examination of both in the ongoing creation of the global anti-corruption regime.

The fourth chapter, by Tamar Hostovsky Brandes, also contemplates sources that contribute to the global anti-corruption regime.[91] Brandes examines the adoption and implementation of anti-corruption laws in Israel, and finds that although the economic aspects of these laws were recognized, the moral aspects played a powerful role in their adoption and in their subsequent implementation. Brandes's analysis somewhat rebukes those who argue that the creation of

88 Sean J Griffith and Thomas H Lee, 'Toward an Interest Group Theory of Foreign Anti-Corruption Laws', ch 3.

89 Rachel Brewster and Andres Ortiz, 'Never Waste A Crisis: Anticorruption Reforms in South America', ch 4.

90 E.g., Peter M Haas, 'Introduction: Epistemic Communities and International Policy Coordination' (1992) 46 Intl Org 1 (emphasizing the importance of knowledge as technical uncertainty grows, and suggesting that 'epistemic communities'—groups of technical experts—have substantial political influence in the political aspects of regime creation).

91 Tamar Hostovsky Brandes, 'The Relevance of Moral Arguments against Foreign Bribery: Israel as a Case Study', ch 5.

the global anti-corruption regime only became possible when advocates abandoned moral arguments and transformed the discussion into one of economics and business rationality.[92] Brandes's analysis of the critical influence that moral notions have on Israel's enforcement of anti-corruption rules, and her argument for explicitly addressing moral questions when implementing laws, amply demonstrate the plurality of not only sources but also drivers that contribute to the global anti-corruption regime.

The fifth chapter takes the reader from Israel to France. Jonathan Bourguignon examines a recently enacted anti-corruption law, particularly the extraterritorial reach of that law.[93] The reach of Loi Sapin II of 2016[94] might exceed that of the United States' Foreign Corrupt Practices Act and the United Kingdom's Bribery Act. In this case, Bourguignon finds that France acts as the social entrepreneur. By enacting a law with such extensive reach, Bourguignon argues, France applies pressure on other states to avoid jurisdictional conflicts by coordinating and distributing prosecution. Bourguignon provides insights into Loi Sapin II, but by showing how the choices that France makes in crafting its domestic law influence the practices of other countries, also demonstrates the dynamism of the creation of the global anti-corruption regime.

The final chapter in this part takes the reader to yet another part of the world and involves yet another set of influential actors. Qingxiu Bu examines the relationships among China and several countries in Africa.[95] Bu warns that the Chinese practice of guanxi, highly institutionalized networks of social relationships and obligations, might interact with embedded corruption in parts of Africa in a way that increases corruption.[96] Bu emphasizes, however, that guanxi differs little from the social and professional networks nurtured by Western business firms. Bu suggests that the lack of sophisticated understandings of the real nature of guanxi in Western courts, and a lack of understanding of African systems by Chinese enforcement bodies, will result in uneven application of anti-corruption laws that disadvantage business firms from each side. Interestingly, Bu argues that the resolution of these conflicts lies not in the West nor in China but instead within Africa. Bu therefore not only demonstrates the dynamism of the global

92 See Beverley Earle, 'The United States' Foreign Corrupt Practices Act and the OECD Anti-Bribery Recommendation: When Moral Suasion Won't Work, Try the Money Argument' (1996) 14 Dick J Intl L 207, 209 (discussing this argument).

93 Jonathan Bourguignon, 'France's New Approach Towards Extraterritoriality in Anti-Corruption Law: Paving The Way for a Protective Principle in Economic Matters?', ch 6.

94 Loi no 2016–1691 du 9 décembre 2016 relative à la transparence, à la lutte contre la corruption et à la modernisation de la vie économique, Journal Officiel de la République Française No 0287 of 10 December 2016, Text No 2.

95 Qingxiu Bu, 'Chinese Multinational Corporations' Obligations in the Global Anti-Corruption: Levelling the Playing Field in Africa', ch 7.

96 In general, the relationship between guanxi and corruption generates substantial interest. See Jack Barbalet, 'Guanxi as Social Exchange: Emotions, Power and Corruption' (2018) 52 Sociology 934; Danielle E Warren, Thomas W Dunfee, and Naihe Li, 'Social Exchange in China: The Double-Edged Sword of Guanxi' (2004) 55 J Bus Ethics 353.

anti-corruption regime, but also makes a convincing argument for a wide plurality of sources for that regime.

4.2 Part II: Traditional methods reconsidered

Transnational law is dynamic and recursive, interacting with and reexamining itself in a process of constant change. This part of the book engages in that process. Each of the five chapters examines a given process, discusses its weaknesses, and suggests changes to the global anti-corruption regime.

The first chapter in this part, by Thomas Kruessmann, observes that despite frequent reference to the role that they could play, civil actions account for very little of the global anti-corruption regime.[97] Kruessmann argues that the paucity of civil law actions stems from a lack of imagination on the part of those who contribute to the creation of the regime. The traditional means of imposing liability – through breach of contract or infliction of a tort – are too uncertain and expensive when used to litigate issues of corruption. Kruessmann suggests looking elsewhere, and offers collective redress, as in consumer liability actions, and personal accountability, as imposed on corporate executives by supervisory boards, as examples of reimagined and more effective civil actions.

The second chapter in this part examines the effectiveness of voluntary standards and guidelines.[98] These privately developed tools are often called 'soft law' and constitute an important component of transnational regimes.[99] Vera Cherepanova begins by describing the emergence of myriad standards, and then usefully creates a four-part typology of existing standards.[100] Cherepanova examines the effectiveness of standards in controlling corruption and concludes that in the absence of accountability they have little effect. Cherepanova does not, however, argue that standards should be discarded; instead, she suggests that scholars and practitioners continue to study them so as to improve their effectiveness.

The third chapter in this part also examines standards and guidelines.[101] Eduard Ivanov reports on an empirical study he conducted, comparing the 'ocean' of standards and guidelines within the global anti-corruption regime to the relatively straightforward guidelines promulgated to curtail international money laundering and the financing of terrorists. Ivanov suggests that the

97 Thomas Kruessmann, 'The Failure of Transnational Anti-Corruption Law: Civil Law Strategies Reconsidered', ch 8.

98 Vera Cherepanova, 'The Proliferation of International Anti-Corruption Initiatives, Standards, and Guidelines: Classification, Benefits and Shortcomings, Future Prospects', ch 9.

99 See Christine M Chinkin, 'The Challenge of Soft Law: Development and Change in International Law' (1989) 38 ICLQ 850, 852.

100 See ibid 850–851 (criticizing the failure of scholars to realize the many forms taken by standards).

101 Eduard Ivanov, 'In the Ocean of Anti-Corruption Compliance Standards and Guidelines: Time for Codification?', ch 10.

multiplicity of resources, models, and guidance may work to the detriment of the goals of the anti-corruption regime, by leaving individual organizations confused and uncertain. He suggests standardization and codification of standards and guidelines.

Jimena Reyes, in the fourth chapter in this part, suggests a reconceptualization of the international anti-corruption instruments in Latin America.[102] Reyes notes that corruption has severely undermined the democratic revolutions throughout Latin America. She finds notions of grand corruption and theories of state capture to be too limited, in that they do not reflect the means through which corruption has undermined these states, and suggests new definitions. She also expresses frustration at the lack of connectivity between human rights regimes and anti-corruption regimes.[103] Reyes suggests that explicitly linking corruption to human rights would allow victims of corruption and of state capture to hold states and corrupt actors accountable in ways that are not available within the current global anti-corruption regime.

The final chapter in this part applies a similar analysis to international criminal law.[104] Vishal Sharma notes the many harms inflicted on society by large-scale corruption. In light of these harms, Sharma criticizes the failure of international criminal law to consider large-scale corruption as an international crime. He also notes that corruption undermines the prosecution of other crimes. Sharma suggests that corruption be considered an international crime prosecutable under the Statute of Rome, and proposes changes to the Statute of Rome to inoculate it against corruption. Sharma's chapter, along with the chapter contributed by Reyes, suggests a relatively unexplored process in the creation of transnational law. Sharma and Reyes suggest dynamic interaction not just within the context of a single transnational regime, but also between regimes. Their proposals demonstrate that this kind of interaction could enhance each of the interacting regimes.

102 Jimena Reyes, 'State Capture Through Corruption: How Can Human Rights Help?', ch 11.

103 Although only tangential to Reyes's arguments, the debate over whether corruption itself is a human rights violation or only contributes to and enables human rights violations may be of interest to some readers. Anne Peters provides a thorough introduction to this debate in 'Corruption and Human Rights' (2015) Basel Institute on Governance Working Paper No 20. The United Nations Office of the High Commissioner on Human Rights, on the other hand, provides an example of sidestepping the debate, opining that 'corruption itself is best seen as a structural obstacle to the enjoyment of human rights' but at the same time 'promot[ing] a human rights-based approach to anti-corruption.' Office of the United Nations High Commissioner for Human, 'Corruption and Human Rights' <www.ohchr.org/EN/Issues/CorruptionAndHR/Pages/CorruptionAndHRIndex.aspx> accessed 1 June 2020.

104 Vishal Sharma, 'Impact of Corruption on the Implementation of International Law: An International Criminal Law Perspective', ch 12.

4.3 Part III: The new frontiers of compliance

As discussed in this chapter, practitioners not only use transnational anti-corruption rules but also substantially contribute to the creation and content of those rules. Practitioners are naturally less interested in jurisprudential theory than in actual effectiveness. In this part of the book, contributors address practical problems with compliance, and propose meaningful solutions to those problems.

The first chapter in this part addresses the difficult issue of whistleblowers.[105] Corruption usually occurs out of sight; inside information may be the only means of discovering corrupt behavior. Leah Ambler and Claire Leger point out, however, that even though more countries actively investigate and prosecute corruption, only two percent of all investigations are initiated by information from a whistleblower. Several factors contribute to this surprisingly low percentage, but Ambler and Leger determine that fear and a failure to offer meaningful protection affect behavior the most. They attribute the failure in protection to a lack of requirements in international instruments, and to a subsequent lack of clarity in guidance provided to business firms. Business firms do not provide well-structured or consistent protection to potential whistleblowers, and potential whistleblowers do not receive a consistent or reassuring message regarding the consequences of whistleblowing. Ambler and Leger suggest that the global anti-corruption regime as a whole adopt techniques modeled on the OECD and the Group of 20.

In the second chapter,[106] Jeffrey Boles describes a business reality similar to that observed by Stephen Kobrin in his criticism of the narrow perspective of doctrinal law.[107] In this world of networks and value chains, created with little reference to political borders, any given business firm is associated with a number of other firms. The global anti-corruption regime often imposes liability for corrupt conduct engaged in by those firms. Boles argues that private contracts offer the most security for a business firm that seeks to shield itself from that risk. Boles draws from the experiences of business firms and their advisors to suggest the most effective way to harness the protection of private contracts.

The third chapter also focuses on empirical issues.[108] Knowledge generation and distribution is an important aspect of the creation and dynamism of transnational regimes. Indeed, in the third chapter of this book Rachel Brewster and Andres Ortiz demonstrate the importance of the role of the Organisation for Economic Cooperation and Development as a knowledge creator and

105 Leah Ambler and Claire Leger, 'Whistleblower Protection: The Next Frontier in the Transnationalization of Anti-Corruption Law', ch 13.

106 Jeffrey R Boles, 'The Contract as Anti-Corruption Platform for the Global Corporate Sector', ch 14.

107 Kobrin, 'Globalization, Transnational Corporations' (n 37) 250.

108 Robert E Clark, 'Linear and Non-Linear Modeling Techniques in Transnational Corruption Risk Assessment', ch 15.

disseminator.[109] Transparency International has also become one of the most widely known and used creators and distributors of knowledge. In this chapter, Robert Clark evaluates the validity and usefulness of Transparency International's influential Corruption Perceptions Index, as well as the World Bank's 'Control of Corruption' measures in its World Governance Indicators. Clark argues that the fact that these indexes treat a country as a whole rather than mapping the extent and nature of corruption within its borders greatly reduces the utility of the indexes. More granular information would assist business firms in assessing risk and designing appropriate anti-corruption programs, and would aid anti-corruption efforts. Clark suggests techniques that could improve the granularity of these types of measures.

In the final chapter in this section, Nuria González examines anti-corruption training.[110] González explicitly embraces the goal of creating an *acquis* on corruption control, and considers training to have a role in creating that corpus of hard and soft law. Her arguments strongly resonate with earlier explorations of norm generation in transnational law, which emphasized the powerful roles of nonstate actors and education.[111] Using comparative methods and analyzing programs used in numerous countries, González finds commonalities that suggest a nascent *acquis*, which she predicts will continue to become stronger and clearer.

4.4 Part IV: Anti-corruption considerations in international dispute resolution

Private dispute settlement plays a prominent role in the global anti-corruption regime. Gunnar Lagergren's decision took an early, and very firm, position against corruption, and has influenced countless subsequent disputes. This part of the book examines current issues in private dispute settlement related to corruption.

In the first chapter in this part, Lucinda Low addresses the role of 'red flags' in arbitral proceedings.[112] 'Red flags' are incidents or facts that put observers on notice that corruption might exist. The United States Department of Justice publishes a list of red flags, and warns that it will not excuse parties that ignore those warning signs.[113] The United Kingdom's Serious Fraud Office also emphasizes the necessity to heed red flags.[114] Low wrestles with the evidentiary value of red flags. She concludes that red flags indicate risk and thus merit investigation, but

109 Rachel Brewster and Andres Ortiz, 'Never Waste A Crisis: Anticorruption Reforms in South America', ch 4.

110 Nuria González, 'Transnationalization of Anti-Corruption Trainings', ch 16.

111 See, e.g., Martha Finnemore and Kathryn Sikkink, 'International Norm Dynamics and Political Change' (1998) 52 Intl Org 887.

112 Lucinda A Low, 'Methodologies for Proving Corruption in Arbitration: Uses and Limitations of Red Flags', ch 17.

113 *A Resource Guide to the Foreign Corrupt Practices Act* (2012) 22.

114 *Guidance About Procedures Which Relevant Commercial Organisations Can Put Into Place to Prevent Persons Associated With Them From Bribing* (2011) 38–39.

that indicators of risk do not sufficiently prove that a party in fact engaged in corrupt activities. Low acknowledges that in some cases, the sheer volume of red flags suggests corruption, but stands firm that 'connecting the dots' does not rise even to the level of circumstantial evidence.

The second chapter in this part examines the role of another prominent set of private actors: the Sanctions Board of the World Bank Group, and ICSID, the International Center for the Settlement of Investment Disputes.[115] Both bodies have long experience in hearing and resolving disputes over transactions that involved corruption, and have accumulated extensive jurisprudential corpuses. Anna Lorem Ramos and Charlene Valdez Warner thoroughly explicate those bodies of rulings with respect to three issues: burden of proof, standard of proof and evidence, and red flags. They find a reassuring level of rigor and fairness in the workings of these tribunals. The sophistication of the rules developed by these supranational bodies markedly demonstrates that private dispute settlement must be considered an integral part of the global anti-corruption regime.

The final chapter in this part addresses issues that echo broader questions about the sources of transnational rules and the dynamic interactions among different sources.[116] In this chapter, Yueming Yan investigates the effect that anti-corruption provisions in international investment agreements and in international treaties and conventions have on arbitral proceedings and decisions. Yan finds that few existing international investment agreements actually contain anti-corruption provisions, although such provisions are included in some more recently concluded agreements. Yan also finds that arbitral bodies rarely make specific references to anti-corruption conventions. Yan acknowledges that arbitral bodies strongly embrace anti-corruption norms, and thus the lack of interaction between these possible sources of transnational law might not be significant. Yan argues, however, that interaction between these sources of law would provide greater clarity for business firms operating under the rules of each.

4.5 *Part V: Challenges in the transnational enforcement of anti-corruption laws*

The final part of this book explores issues in the enforcement of the global anti-corruption regime. Three of the four chapters scrutinize domestic courts. Domestic courts are, in fact, the *loci* of much of the enforcement of transnational rules, and thus, argue scholars such as Hannah Buxbaum, 'participate in implementing effective regulatory strategies for global markets.'[117] After an exhaustive study

115 Anna Lorem Ramos and Charlene Valdez Warner, 'The World Bank Group in International Dispute Resolution of Fraud and Corruption: Examining the Practice and Jurisprudence of the Sanctions Board and ICSID Arbitral Tribunals', ch 18.

116 Yueming Yan, 'References to International Anti-Corruption Conventions in International Investment Arbitration and International Investment Agreements', ch 23.

117 Hannah L Buxbaum, 'Transnational Regulatory Litigation' (2006) 46 Va J Intl L 251, 316.

of the roles played by domestic courts, Christopher Whytock finds that their participation goes beyond implementation: 'for better or worse, domestic courts are pervasively involved in the regulation of transnational activity,' involvement that includes norm dissemination and rule creation.[118]

The first chapter in this part supports Buxbaum and Whytock's conclusions.[119] Simon St-Georges and Denis Saint-Martin study the diffusion of deferred prosecution agreements and non-prosecution agreements throughout OECD jurisdictions. They find functionalist explanations for this diffusion unconvincing; the agreements offer little utility and thus are unlikely to have been adopted to accomplish goals. St-Georges and Saint-Martin then apply theoretical explanations from political science and from sociology, and find that each have some explanatory power. They conclude that it is too early to discount any theory for the diffusion of these agreements, but also observe that the diffusion of the use of deferred prosecution agreements and non-prosecution agreements presents a fruitful opportunity to test theories of the creation of transnational regimes.

In the second chapter in this part, Stéphane Bonifassi and Caroline Goussé analyze domestic attempts to prevent domestic courts from participating in the creation and enforcement of transnational law.[120] Blocking statutes forbid local entities from responding to subpoenas or other inquiries, from participating in judicial proceedings, and from sanctioning other local entities with respect to the enforcement of laws in another jurisdiction. Blocking statutes are often aimed at the extraterritorial application of domestic law, including the United States' Foreign Corrupt Practices Act. Bonifassi and Goussé examine the effects on the global anti-corruption regime of blocking statutes in China, France, and Switzerland. They find that these laws have little effect, in part because business firms are bound by and subject to so many different strands of the regime that the blocking of one strand is inconsequential, and in part because the business firms benefit from participation in the transnational regime. Bonifassi and Goussé also note that the use of blocking statutes by these countries is somewhat disingenuous; the United States would not need to prosecute foreign business firms for corrupt activities if those firms' home countries were more effective in enforcement of their own laws.

The penultimate chapter in this part and in this book seriously examines what may seem a utopian dream: the creation of an international body to coordinate anti-corruption laws, rules, and policies.[121] Although this may seem an idle dream, it is worth noting that only a few years before its creation, few people thought

118 Christopher A Whytock, 'Domestic Courts and Global Governance' (2009) 84 Tul L Rev 67, 69.

119 Simon St-Georges and Denis Saint-Martin, 'The Global Diffusion of DPAs: The Not So Functional Remaking of the Rules Against Business Corruption', ch 20.

120 Stéphane Bonifassi and Caroline Goussé, 'The Impact of Blocking Statutes on Enforcement of Anti-Corruption Laws', ch 21.

121 Camila Florencia Tort, 'The Search for Synergies: The Utopian Ideal of Cooperation between International Anti-Corruption Mechanisms', ch 22.

that the creation of the World Trade Organization was even remotely possible.[122] Camila Florencia Tort acknowledges the argument that the creation of an international corruption body would substantially reduce transaction costs for all actors, particularly member countries, by coordinating policies and especially by coordinating prosecution and enforcement. Nonetheless, after working through the structural obstacles to the creation of such a body, Tort concludes that it is unlikely and might not work as effectively as proponents suggest. The creation of such a body will remain, at least for the foreseeable future, a dream.

The final chapter in this book departs from domestic courts but continues to explore enforcement. In this chapter, Alexandra Malina Manea and Jamieson Smith undertake an ambitious review of sanctions imposed by multilateral development banks upon finding that an entity has engaged in corruption in a project that involves that bank, with a focus on the use of financial sanctions.[123] They find a lack of consensus and divergent approaches to the use of financial sanctions. They then survey various domestic laws to find appropriate measures to use as models for the coordination of sanctions. They suggest that multilateral development banks take advantage of contractual remedies that include aspects of common law liquidated damages and the civil law *clause pénale*. Their suggestion vividly demonstrates the dynamism of transnational anti-corruption law; in this case, nonstate actors would borrow norms and procedures from domestic courts to improve the adjudication of transgressions in nonstate forums. Manea and Smith observe that multilateral development banks are involved in transactions worth billions of euros, and have developed very sophisticated mechanisms to protect the integrity of these transactions, but are confident that these mechanisms will continue to improve.

5 Conclusion

This book does not attempt to create yet another meta theory of transnational law. Instead, this book closely examines a legal regime already recognized as transnational. By doing so, the chapters in this book provide insights into the transnationalization of law in general. Chapters in this book explore the sources of transnational law, the dynamic interactions of those sources, the application of transnational rules in various forums, and recursive evolution of a transnational regime. The global anti-corruption regime is a fruitful object of study.

122 See Philip M Nichols, 'Corruption in the World Trade Organization: Discerning the Limits of the World Trade Organization's Authority' (1996) 28 NYU J Intl L & Pol 711, 711–712 (discussing the creation of the World Trade Organization).

123 Alexandra Manea and Jamieson Smith, 'In Search of a Tailored Approach to Anti-Corruption Sanctions in the International Development Context: Financial Remedies by the Multilateral Development Banks', ch 23.

This book also considers the control of corruption. Corruption diminishes human wellbeing and degrades the planet. Controlling corruption should be among the highest priorities. A deeper understanding of the regime that attempts to control corruption should help to make that regime more effective. A more effective regime, in turn, could help to improve the lives of people around the world. That, alone, merits giving attention to the global anti-corruption regime.

Part I

International, regional, and domestic sources of anti-corruption law: eclecticism or convergence?

2 The Americanization of international anti-corruption

The influence of the FCPA on the OAS and OECD conventions

Elitza Katzarova and Jessica Ansart

This chapter traces the political and legal influence of the US Foreign Corrupt Practices Act (FCPA) on international anti-corruption law. It argues that the FCPA has influenced global definitions of corruption and enforcement of anti-corruption legislation, and has shaped international anti-corruption debates since the mid-1970s. Part I traces the historical influence of the FCPA on international anti-corruption debates since the 1970s. The analysis shows that prior to the adoption of the FCPA (and early drafts in the US Congress), debates at international organizations, such as the United Nations (UN) and the Organization for Economic Cooperation and Development (OECD), offered different content, different regulatory measures, and a different scope for the definition of the offense. First, in terms of content, international debates were much broader and concerned with corporate (rather than governmental) abuse of power, mostly in the form of corporate political influence. Second, international debates prior to the FCPA were based on disclosure and not criminalization. They also promoted a much broader framework for international binding regulation of multinational corporations. Third, the scope of the offense expanded beyond bribery to include political influence of multinational corporations, encompassing the interaction of states and corporations in a global economy.

After the adoption of the FCPA, the US executive received a very specific mandate for the ongoing intergovernmental talks: to internationalize the FCPA. The unilateral move by the United States was not well-received by OECD partners, while related demands of developing countries also complicated the talks. When the US delegation placed the issue back on the OECD agenda in 1989, a different strategy was required. The UN was to be avoided, but the agreement of developing countries would be required to show other OECD member states that global consensus on corrupt practices was possible. The United States used the agreement reached at the Organization of American States (OAS) to shape talks at the OECD. At the same time, European partners used agreements reached at the Council of Europe (CoE) and the European Union (EU) to influence debates at the OECD. Altogether, as was part of US strategy in the 1990s, the countries of the G7 were decisive in the internationalization of anti-corruption measures. After showing the role of the OAS Convention, Part I concludes with the adoption of the OECD Convention. Part II shows that after the adoption of the two conventions, the '*Americanization*' of global anti-corruption law progressed in several ways.

To explain the FCPA's continued dominance on international efforts to combat corruption and its Americanizing effect, Part II argues that the OAS and OECD conventions were not ends, but means to achieve this effect. In other words, the conventions served as vehicles for the FCPA's Americanizing of anti-bribery laws. This legal analysis is two-fold, focusing on (i) a comparison of the legal texts, and (ii) an examination of implementation and enforcement of the texts. First, textual analysis shows how the OAS and OECD conventions deviated from the existing FCPA. They provided grounds for expanding the FCPA, particularly in terms of expanding its jurisdictional basis, and gave other states flexibility for implementation, while emphasizing cooperation among signatories in enforcement. Second, a look at implementation, especially expansion of the FCPA's jurisdictional basis, demonstrates how a surge in US foreign investigations and prosecutions pressured other states to implement the conventions and do so in a more 'American' style. In particular, the processes around newly implemented national legislation in the United Kingdom and France show how these laws emerged in response to the FCPA and as a means to compete rather than to comply with international conventions.

1 Negotiating global anti-corruption standards

In the early 1970s, a series of corporate scandals started when the involvement of the International Telegraph and Telephone (ITT) corporation in Chilean elections and politics came to public attention in the United States and the rest of the world.[1] In response to the revelations, at the third UN Conference on Trade and Development (UNCTAD III) in April 1972 in Santiago, the Chilean President, Salvador Allende, defined corruption as a problem caused by the involvement of business in politics and the rising influence of corporate power over the democratic process. Specifically, President Allende referenced corporations' 'powerful corruptive influence on public institutions in rich and poor countries alike.'[2] The framing of the ITT affair as corruptive corporate influence on politics and democracy cast a long shadow on anti-corruption debates at the UN and

1 On March 21, 1972, syndicated journalist, Jack Anderson, published an article in the *Washington Post* on the inappropriate involvement of the ITT company in the political life of Chile. Based on leaked internal memos, the ITT corporation had been allegedly trying to prevent Allende's election in 1970 due to fears that his policies would impact negatively ITT's investments in the country. See Jack Anderson, 'Memos Bare ITT Try for Chile Coup' *The Washington Post* (21 March 1972).

2 UNCTAD, 'Address Delivered by Mr. Allende, President of Chile at the Inaugural Ceremony on 13 April 1972', vol 1, annex VIII (Proceedings of UNCTAD Third Session) 353.

made anti-corruption consensus at the organization impossible for more than two decades.[3]

1.1 Chronicle of a death foretold: US failure to internationalize the FCPA in the 1970s

In the United States, a string of corporate scandals was heading in a different direction with the outbreak of the Watergate affair. The Watergate Special Prosecutor Force, investigating the 1972 campaign of President Richard Nixon, discovered that the slush funds used at home for illegal party contributions, were also used to bribe foreign officials abroad.[4] Judge Stanley Sporkin, employed by the Securities and Exchange Commission (SEC) at the time (1961–1981), and who later became Director of the Division of Enforcement (1974–1981), explained in an interview for the SEC that the investigative team 'had developed a horrendous situation' where they found out that 'those slush funds that were being used to give money to political parties … were also being used for other various activities, such as bribing officials in foreign countries to get business.'[5]

The disclosure program, consequently instituted by the SEC, had hundreds of companies participating on a voluntary basis, and in 1975 revealed a world-wide bribery web, a global scheme that Kissinger referred to as 'the Watergate of private industry.'[6] Given the particular post-Watergate environment, publicity surrounding these disclosures created strong support for a unilateral measure that would forbid US companies from employing these illicit practices abroad, leading eventually to the FCPA. What is not well known, is that in 1975, prior to the adoption of the FCPA, the US executive approached the OECD and the UN about the foreign corporate bribery problem, which emerged from the SEC disclosure program.[7] In September 1975, US Secretary of the Treasury

3 Elitza Katzarova, *The Social Construction of Global Corruption: From Utopia to Neoliberalism* (Palgrave Macmillan 2018).

4 Irving Pollack, Interview with Stanley Sporkin (Securities and Exchange Commission Historical Society, 23 September 2003).

5 Ibid 16.

6 Martin T Biegelman and Daniel R Biegelman, *Foreign Corrupt Practices Act Compliance Guidebook: Protecting Your Organization from Bribery and Corruption* (John Wiley & Sons 2010) 17.

7 The United States submitted a proposal to the OECD for the inclusion of 'illicit payments' in the Guidelines for Multinational Enterprises. The formal claim was made on September 17, 1975, just before the opening of the regular session of the UN General Assembly in the third week of September where a similar claim was reiterated. At the UN, the US claims on illicit/corrupt payments were incorporated in discussions about the repercussions of the activities of transnational corporations within the framework of the UN Commission on Transnational Corporations, which held its first annual session in 1975. Three countries submitted draft resolutions concerning the treatment of international corrupt practices to the General Assembly—the United States, Iran, and the Libyan Arab Republic. See IME(75)18, *Draft Guidelines on Political Involvement of Multinational Enterprises* (Note by the United States Delegation, 17 September 1975).

William Simon carried out informal talks with a number of finance ministers from developed nations at the IMF and the World Bank.[8] Until President Carter signed the FCPA into law in December 1977, the US approach to international organizations followed a disclosure approach promoted by the Ford administration.[9] This approach drastically changed with the adoption of the FCPA. Criminalizing corrupt payments and getting the United States out of the competitive disadvantage it had maneuvered itself into became the priority. The US delegation to the UN managed to influence the Draft Agreement on Illicit Payments in 1979, making it so that these early UN drafts were largely based on the FCPA.[10] Nonetheless, there were some divisive issues, unappealing to the US delegation and other developed nations, that made their way into the draft agreement.[11,12]

The failure of the UN agreement on illicit payments can be pinned down to South–North tensions. In the 1970s, the UN became the major venue for talks on illicit/corrupt payments. OECD discussions became entangled with the UN pre-negotiation talks. Furthermore, at the UN, the agreement on illicit payments was made conditional on the adoption of the Code of Conduct on Transnational Corporations. These developments can be seen as a coherent strategy by the Global South to influence the US-sponsored issue of illicit payments. For the

8 Protecting the ability of the United States to trade abroad: hearing before the Subcommittee on International Trade of the Committee on Finance, United States Senate, Ninety-fourth Congress, first session on S. Res. 265, a resolution to protect the ability of the United States to trade abroad, 6 October 1975.

9 Gerald Ford, 'Statement on the Task Force on Questionable Corporate Payments Abroad' 31 March 1976.

10 Mark Pieth, 'International Cooperation to Combat Corruption' in Kimberly Ann Elliott (ed), *Corruption and the Global Economy* (Peterson Institute 1997) 119.

11 The most divisive issue embedded in the draft agreement was the inclusion of payments to the apartheid regime in South Africa and Namibia. The claims on payments to the Apartheid regime were also supported by the G-77. The position of the Global South was that the Code of Conduct on Transnational Corporations was more important in trying to solve the problem of corporate influence than was the US limited preoccupation with corporate bribery. This is why conditioning the adoption of the agreement on illicit payments on the adoption of the Code of Conduct was consistent with the developing nations' demands to bound corporate behavior in a legal framework of collectively agreed-upon rules.

12 A couple of months prior to President Carter signing the FCPA into law, the UN report on the final session of the Working Group on the Problem of Corrupt Practices presented the US position on payments to South Africa as counter-productive, 'The underlying basic political problem is that the US which (partly for reasons of domestic—i.e. presidential/ congressional—policy) is pushing hard for a treaty on bribery and illicit payments, is not, at present at least willing to pay the price asked for it by the African countries, i.e., a corresponding criminalization of the payments of royalties and taxes to the illegal minority regimes in southern Africa. Moreover, many developed countries other than the US are indifferent to the idea of setting up elaborate standards for reporting and disclosure of illicit payments.' See UNCTC, *Inter-office Memorandum Final Session of the Working Group on the Problem of Corrupt Practices* (Series 0897, Box 7, File 4, UN Archives, New York Headquarters, 7 July 1977) 1.

Stage	Time frame	Characteristics
I.	1972-1976	*debates prior to the FCPA and early drafts in US Congress*
II.	1977-1980	*first attempts to internationalize the FCPA*
III.	1981-1988	*no efforts but rather weak FCPA enforcement*
IV.	1989-1993	*second attempt to internationalize without much success*
V.	1994-1997	*anti-corruption boom*

Figure 2.1 Stages in the early internationalization of anti-corruption law.

developing nations in the G-77, UNCTAD, and the Commission on Transnational Corporations (and its secretariat, the UNCTC), the US-sponsored issue of bribery was part and parcel of a larger agenda to curb corporate abuse of power in the legacy of the Allende UNCTAD and General Assembly talks in 1972.[13] This can be seen as the major difference in anti-corruption talks between the 1970s and 1990s. While corruption as government abuse of power dominated debates in international organizations in the 1990s, the 1970s were dominated by the topic of corporate abuse of power. The agenda of drafting a binding code of conduct on transnational corporations was in the spirit of these 1970s debates on corporate corruption, which came as a consequence of the Allende initiative and the complaint by the Chilean delegation to UNCTAD regarding the behavior of ITT prior to the 1973 military coup.[14]

In the 1970s, the US approach to transnational bribery was challenged by countries both in the Global North and the Global South.[15] After the FCPA's adoption (and even as early as when initial drafts of the FCPA, sponsored by Senator Proxmire, promoting a criminalization approach, started being discussed in the US Congress), the strategy of the US executive at international organizations also had to pivot towards international criminalization. Prior to the FCPA, there was already an international debate on corruption springing from a string of corporate scandals in the early to mid-1970s. This fact can partially explain the hostility with which other states met the unilateral approach taken by the United States in the form of the FCPA. The FCPA unilaterally defined the problem of corruption as one of criminalized bribery, while different understandings of corruption were being discussed at global venues.

13 Salvador Allende, 'Speech delivered by Dr. Salvador Allende, President of the Republic of Chile, before the General Assembly of the United Nations' (Embassy of Chile, Washington DC, 4 December 1972).

14 Amos Yoder, *The Evolution of the United Nations System* (Taylor & Francis 1993).

15 Katzarova (n 3).

1.2 Fighting the good fight in the 1990s

The US re-launched formal claims to address corruption or bribery as a global problem at the OECD during a Special Session of the Executive Committee, held on 28 February and 1 March 1989. The United States proposed a feasibility study, or an 'inventory of relevant legislation' on illicit payments to be completed through a questionnaire distributed to member states.[16] The US proposal provided a succinct background report on the FCPA and the consequences of the 1988 Omnibus Trade and Competitiveness Act. The OECD members were meant to put forward a common position at the UN. However, the significance of the question of transnational bribery did not have unequivocal support within the group. Nevertheless, in 1979, a decision was reached to sign an OECD agreement in case the UN talks faltered. Although US-sponsored consultations in Paris in spring 1978 did not show much promise for a common OECD position at the UN, the G7 Venice Summit in 1980 produced a Communiqué in which 'governments committed themselves to the ongoing UN effort and pledged, in the event that initiatives faltered, to conclude an agreement among themselves with the same objective.'[17,18]

This political commitment, however, proved to be unstable. The United States appeared to be the only state actor with a strong interest in addressing the question of illicit payments. The choice to tackle the problem unilaterally with the adoption of the FCPA, and without consulting other negotiating partners, further complicated the matter and alienated hesitant partners in the developed world. The adoption of the FCPA was viewed unfavorably by other OECD members, despite the fact that it put their multinational corporations at a competitive advantage over American multinationals. With the FCPA, the US government showed that it was unilaterally making decisions about addressing the corrupt payments problem, decisions that it intended to later impose on other countries. US partners were suspicious of a hegemonic trade agenda,[19] so, confronted with the impasse at the UN, OECD members did not pursue

16 C(89)49, *United States Proposal on the Issue of Illicit Payments* (Note to the Secretary General, 22 March 1989) 1.

17 C(90)87, *Illicit Payments in International Commercial Transactions* (Note to the Secretary General, 12 June 1990) 37.

18 The G7 Summit took place from June 22–23, 1980 in Venice, Italy and the final communiqué made the political commitment that the G7 members would pursue the question further, 'As a further step in strengthening the international trading system, we commit our governments to work in the United Nations toward an agreement to prohibit illicit payments to foreign government officials in international business transactions. If that effort falters, we will seek to conclude an agreement among our countries, but open to all, with the same objective.' Venice G7 Summit, 'Communiqué' (22–23 June 1980) <http://www.g8.utoronto.ca/summit/1980venice/communique/trade.html> accessed 1 June 2020.

19 Mark Pieth, 'International Efforts to Combat Corruption' (International Anti-Corruption Conference (IACC), Durban, October 1999).

the issue further.[20] The talks in the 1990s were thus re-opened in the shadow of the impasse from the 1970s, but also as an outstanding issue to be resolved by OECD members.

The catalyst for progress within the OECD was the change of leadership in Washington in 1993. President Clinton gave new impetus to the US initiative by making the anti-bribery agenda a foreign policy priority.[21] Furthermore, Warren Christopher, who became Secretary of State under Clinton, had been personally involved in drafting and discussing the FCPA in 1977 under Carter.[22] Together with the Assistant Secretary of State for Economic and Business Affairs, Daniel Tarullo, who was also a lawyer with good knowledge of the FCPA, Warren Christopher turned the OECD anti-bribery agenda into a major US priority.[23]

1.2.1 The OAS convention

With increased political dedication and resources, the United States was very influential in the drafting of the Recommendation on Bribery in International Business Transactions (RBIBT) in 1994. Having made some progress with European partners at the OECD with the RBIBT, the US government approached the member states of OAS. The US Office of Government Ethics and the US Information Agency launched the First International Conference on Ethics in Government in Washington DC in November 1994.[24] The following month, the Summit of the Americas in Miami made addressing corruption a priority for the organization. Richard Feinberg, former special assistant to President Clinton for National Security Affairs and senior director of the National Security Council's (NSC) Office of Inter-American Affairs, who was personally involved in the negotiations, traced how the US government engaged other state actors prior to the topic being raised for the first time in OAS.[25] An Interagency Working Group (IWG) was created in 1993 to deal with corruption in the framework of Inter-American relations and was later renamed the Democracy IWG. Michael Skol, who became Head of the IWG, had excellent knowledge of Venezuelan domestic politics through his work as US Ambassador to Caracas and expected that the US bid would be well-received by the new Venezuelan government, since the country's

20 C(90)87.Annex 2, *Description of the Work Done on the Issue of Illicit payments in International Transactions at an International Level* (12 June 1990) 37.
21 Alan Larson, 'US Policy on Corruption' in Kimberly Ann Elliott (ed), *Corruption and the Global* (Peterson Institute 1997) 237; Patrick Glynn, Stephen Kobrin, and Moises Naim, 'The Globalization of Corruption' in Kimberly Ann Elliott (ed), *Corruption and the Global* (Peterson Institute 1997) 7.
22 Mark Pieth, 'Introduction' in Mark Pieth, Lucinda A Low, and Nicola Bonucci (eds), *The OECD Convention on Bribery: A Commentary* (2nd edn, CUP 2013).
23 Glynn (n 21); Kenneth W Abbott and Duncan Snidal, 'Values and Interests: International Legalization in the Fight against Corruption' (2002) 31 The Journal of Legal Studies 141.
24 Richard E Feinberg, *Summitry in the Americas: A Progress Report* (Peterson Institute 1997).
25 Ibid.

recent corruption-related scandals had resulted in the president's impeachment.[26] Feinberg singled out winning Venezuela as an ally and receiving its support for the internationalization of the FCPA (in exchange for the inclusion of measures on extradition) as one of the major factors for the successful anti-corruption campaign in OAS. As part of the US consensus-building strategy, a series of meetings were organized in Washington through the embassies of a small core of member states (Venezuela, Chile, Honduras, and Ecuador) that carried out a considerable amount of work prior to the official announcement of corrupt practices as an agenda item at the Miami Summit.[27] The OAS Working Group on Probity and Ethics worked in close cooperation with the Washington Working Group. The drafts produced by the two groups paralleled each other and the US government managed to imprint its influence on the final draft of the Convention.[28]

Even though the anti-bribery agenda constituted a top priority for the United States at the Summit, President Clinton avoided explicitly naming the practices 'corrupt.'[29] As much as the word 'corruption' had a negative connotation, the trouble was that calling the practices 'corrupt' was also a direct reference to the Foreign 'Corrupt' Practices Act that the US executive was trying to internationalize. It was the Vice President of Ecuador, Alberto Dahik, who chaired the Advisory body of Transparency International (TI), who promoted the explicit use of 'corruption' as an agenda item.[30] The anti-corruption project was introduced into the general theme of probity and civic ethics raised by Chile in the post-Pinochet era.[31,32] During the Summit of the Americas in Miami, the United States persuaded its partners to establish cooperation with the Working Group on Bribery at the OECD.[33] As a consequence of this liaison, the OAS Group adopted a definition of the offense that reproduced almost verbatim the

26 Ibid.
27 Ibid.
28 Ibid 119.
29 Kimberly Ann Elliott, 'Corruption as an International Policy Problem: Overview and Recommendations' in Kimberly Ann Elliott (ed), *Corruption and the Global* (Peterson Institute 1997) 175.
30 Fredrik Galtung and Jeremy Pope, 'The Global Coalition against Corruption: Evaluating Transparency International' in Andreas Schedler, Marc Plattner, and Larry Jay Diamond (eds), *The Self-Restraining State: Power and Accountability in New Democracies* (Lynne Rienner Publishers 1999).
31 Carlos A Manfroni and Richard S Werksman, *The Inter-American Convention Against Corruption: Annotated with Commentary* (Lexington Books 2003).
32 The Chilean Ambassador to OAS, Edmundo Carreño presided over the Working Group on Probity and Ethics: see ibid. The Working Group, comprised of national experts mandated by almost all member governments, met at the Washington headquarters of OAS a number of times in order to amend and prepare the draft text of the Convention. Edmundo Vargas Carreño, 'The Inter-American Convention Against Corruption' (Conference for Transparency and Development in Latin America and the Caribbean, Lima, February 2000).
33 Elliott (n 29).

OECD preliminary definition.[34] The OAS Convention was successfully adopted on 29 March 1996 and Article VIII internationalized, in practice, the FCPA for the first time.[35]

The leadership of the US executive through a technique of issue-specific coalition building was instrumental in the successful adoption of the Convention.[36] Feinberg credited careful US preparatory work with diffusing the North–South tension on the global anti-bribery initiative. Furthermore, the liaison between the OAS and the OECD working groups proposed by the United States showed that the inter-American consensus would have positive repercussions for furthering the work of the OECD. The OAS Convention was indicative of an agreement between developing and developed nations on a common anti-bribery approach. The primarily US interest remained in the OECD, as internationalizing the FCPA among the members of OAS would not have been as consequential as convincing the major European investors to impose restrictions on their companies. The OAS progress, therefore, provided a bargaining chip for the United States at the OECD. Developing countries were finally on board with the US-sponsored anti-bribery campaign.

The OAS agreement was also a testament that the US issue-specific coalition-building approach was effective. An essential aspect of the coalition building was that intergovernmental cooperation was enriched by meetings between the Democracy IWG and several NGOs such as the US branches of the International Chamber of Commerce (ICC) and TI. Feinberg, who was a special assistant to President Clinton and senior director of Inter-American Affairs at the National Security Council, sought out TI's support in early 1994.[37] Vogl, co-founder of TI, agreed to leverage TI's connections in Latin America to convince another government to officially raise the question of corruption on the OAS agenda because, as Vogl put it, 'the United States could not diplomatically raise the issue itself as this would be resented.'[38,39] The US success building this broader coalition with non-governmental actors even before the topic was raised in OAS was fundamental for the quick negotiation and successful adoption of the OAS Convention.

34 DAFFE/IME/PI(93)1, *Elements of Recommendation – General Considerations* (Ad Hoc Group on Illicit Payments, Notes by the Netherlands Delegation, 23 August 1993).

35 Elliott (n 29).

36 Feinberg (n 24).

37 Frank Vogl, *Waging War on Corruption: Inside the Movement Fighting the Abuse of Power* (Rowman & Littlefield 2012).

38 Ibid 185.

39 This is how the support of the President of Costa Rica, Oscar Arias, and the Vice President of Ecuador, Alberto Dahik, was secured: ibid.

1.2.2 The OECD Convention

If we were to look at the anti-corruption eruption of the mid-90s with the fresh eyes of a person unaware of the confidential intergovernmental talks that had been going on for decades, a clear picture would emerge. An explosion of corruption scandals in the mid-90s was clearly driving the anti-corruption campaign. That was particularly valid for European OECD member states. Italy, France, Germany, Spain, and the United Kingdom all experienced a series of corruption-related political scandals and instability.[40] However, the corruption-related political scandals of the 1970s were no less turbulent.[41] They were severe in the United States, but also concerned other Western democracies. The corruption scandals of the 1970s did not generate enough support for the US international ban on bribery. What was different in the 1990s? It was the US strategy to connect these national, highly reported occurrences of corruption to the issue of transnational bribery through the 'calculated use of public diplomacy' that made the difference in the 1990s.[42]

The corruption accusations within OECD member states, such as France,[43] the United Kingdom, and Spain, influenced the climate of the OECD negotiation process in the mid-90s,[44] but were in no way sufficient in and of themselves to steer an international approach to corruption, and in particular to transnational bribery. The 'sensitization' of the European public to the subject of corruption was successfully employed by US officials, who 'observed the high level of European public interest in all aspects of corruption, including the OECD discussions.'[45] Political scandals culminating in the mid-90s made the European public highly attentive to issues of corruption, and State Department officials managed to link the preoccupation with domestic corruption to the question of transnational bribery.[46] It is likely that these national corruption scandals made some US partners more susceptible to supporting an OECD-sponsored anti-corruption instrument. This is why the success of the 'vague' RBIBT has been attributed to the US attempt to bring 'domestic political pressure, motivated by value considerations' to the negotiation table.[47] At the same time, there was no indication that these national troubles with corruption would become a global issue with a formidable global governance architecture.

After the RBIBT, the battle was not to agree on the existence of a problem, which the United States managed to narrow down to bribery, but to push for

40 Donatella Della Porta and Yves Mény (eds), *Democracy and Corruption in Europe* (Pinter 1997).

41 Vogl (n 37).

42 Glynn (n 21) 20.

43 Christophe Fay, 'Political Sleaze in France: Forms and Issues' (1995) 48 Parliamentary Affairs 663.

44 Della Porta (n 40).

45 Abbott and Snidal (n 23) 164.

46 Ibid.

47 Ibid.

criminal measures. European partners, in particular Germany and France (at first joined by the United Kingdom), were resisting the US attempt to promote criminalization by internationalizing the FCPA.[48,49] The US State Department wanted a binding treaty, but as this appeared unfeasible, was content with the recommendation on tax deductibility and the revision of the RBIBT in the direction of criminalization.[50] Germany and France, however, proposed a binding treaty, with the former choosing the UN as the venue for negotiation and the latter preferring the WTO.[51] This seemingly counter-intuitive joint move by the German and French delegations was done in order to deflect talks for a binding instrument to organizations that were chosen because of the likelihood of stalemate. The pre-negotiation talks at the UN were still referred to as the 'disaster of 1976'[52] and the US executive had historically avoided raising the issue of illicit payments at GATT (and the WTO).[53,54]

The deputy-director of DAFFE at the time, Rainer Geiger, called the European 'bluff' and proposed a convention at the OECD.[55] While prior to the RBIBT in 1994, the US delegation was pushing for a treaty, Pieth managed to convince them to explore the recommendation option, based on the positive experience with FATF.[56] The return to the convention route at the OECD, therefore, came as an unexpected turn of events at this stage. The threat by the reluctant European partners to move the talks to the UN or the WTO exemplifies the instrumental use of venues during the pre-negotiation talks.

The OECD partners were also bringing agreements reached in other organizations to the negotiation table. Work underway in regional organizations, such as OAS, the EU, and the CoE became part of the persuasion strategies of

48 DAFFE/IME/BR/RD(95)1, *Criminalization of Bribery of Foreign Public Officials* (Working Group on Bribery in International Business Transactions, 11 October 1995).

49 The 're-discovery' of the 1906 Prevention of Corruption Act and the repercussions of the 'cash for questions' controversy had a definitive impact on the UK position and the new government (formed in May 1997) wanted to take a strong stance against corruption. Peter Alldridge, 'The UK Bribery Act: "The Caffeinated Younger Sibling of the FCPA"' (2012) 73 Ohio State Law Journal 1181.

50 Abbott (n 45).

51 Pieth 'Introduction' (n 22).

52 Jack Blum, 'Testimony on the Problem of Curbing Grand Scale Global Corruption before the Committee on Financial Services, US House of Representatives' (111th Congress, 1st session, 19 May 2009) 2.

53 Senate Resolution 265 of 1975 specified GATT as the institutional forum for negotiations, but representatives of the US executive did not concur with this strategy, as they judged it would have been highly unlikely to reach consensus at GATT.

54 The United States did raise the issue of transparency in procurement at the WTO, but after the adoption of the OECD Convention. International Trade Commission, *Operation of the Trade Agreements Program, The Year in Trade, 49th Report* (Diane Publishing 1997).

55 Mark Pieth, 'Bribing Foreign Officials. The OECD Anticorruption Instruments' in Fritz Heimann and Mark Pieth (ed), *Confronting Corruption: Past Concerns, Present Challenges, and Future Strategies* (OUP 2018) 82.

56 Ibid.

both camps. The United States was using the OAS Convention to invalidate the argument that criminalizing the supply side of bribes constituted interference in the domestic affairs of another state (or the sovereignty of the so-called 'host' countries). In fact, after the adoption of the OAS convention, Tarullo argued that the member states of OAS 'suggest that governments of developed countries ... by failing to act against foreign bribery by their own multinationals, [are] complicit in the bribery.'[57] While the US delegation used the agreement at OAS as a bargaining tool, the European partners used the agreements reached at the CoE and the EU to set the tone of the OECD agreement. France and Germany presented a draft convention based on the texts negotiated at the EU and the CoE.[58] The EU Convention against Corruption Involving Public Officials (May 26, 1997) was adopted prior to the negotiations for a binding treaty at the OECD, which commenced in October 1997, and it criminalized bribery of holders of public office in other EU member states, but not in third counties.[59] If this approach were to be applied to the OECD Convention, as Germany and France wanted, it would have entailed criminalization only among members of the OECD (or the countries that signed the convention). This would mean that Germany, for example, would have made it illegal for a German company to bribe an official in Canada, but not in Bangladesh or Venezuela. This, albeit significant, concession would not have been satisfactory for the US delegation, because it would not have provided global coverage and would have only partially internationalized the FCPA. The United States rebuffed the European *inter partes* approach, arguing that only global coverage would be legitimate.[60] The US delegation's goal was to reach an agreement for the criminalization of bribery in countries outside the OECD area.

Targeting the OECD as the primary forum to address the corrupt payments issue in 1989 was a strategic move to internationalize the FCPA among the main US investment competitors at the time. While OECD member states were the target audience for US efforts to internationalize the FCPA, the US strategy from the start was to concentrate on the G7.[61] A series of meetings were organized prior to the 23rd G7 Summit in Denver. The meeting of the G7 Ministers and Central Bank Governors on April 27, 1997 in Washington produced a Statement of Support for the Anti-corruption Work of the International Financial Institutions

57 Quoted in Daniel Patrick Ashe, 'The Lengthening Anti-Bribery Lasso of the United States: The Recent Extraterritorial Application of the US Foreign Corrupt Practices Act' 73 (2005) Fordham Law Review 2897, 2912.

58 Pieth 'Introduction' (n 22).

59 Convention Drawn Up on the Basis of Article K.3(2)(C) of the Treaty on European Union on the Fight Against Corruption Involving Officials of the European Communities or Officials of Member States of the European Union (26 May 1997) ILM 37, 12.

60 Abbott (n 45).

61 Pieth 'Bribing Foreign Officials' (n 55).

and the OECD.[62] Following the Communiqué of G7 Finance Ministers was a series of preparatory meetings between Washington, DC and Airlie Center, VA on May 22–24, 1997 that proved to be decisive for reaching a compromise between OECD member states.[63]

The US executive was prepared to move forward without France and Germany and requested the support of the United Kingdom, but Tarullo, who was Clinton's personal representative to the Summit, attempted to secure the Franco-German agreement.[64] Lobbying US partners was another essential element. Between spring and autumn 1997, intensive lobbying took place through US embassies in key capitals.[65] Reaching the 'compromise of May 1997' ensured that in case the negotiations of a binding instrument failed by April 1, 1998, members would nonetheless enact criminalization measures in accordance with the Revised Recommendation.[66] The fate of the OECD Convention was also decided when the G7 members agreed to proceed with ratification.[67] The exact way in which the compromise of May 1997, which essentially secured the criminalization of bribery, was reached remains unspecified, but the change of venues, the instrumental use of publicity, and the 'embarrassment factor' remained an effective part of the persuasion arsenal of the US President's personal representative. 'Tarullo carried with him (or told people he did) a list of the 10 largest bribe-paying companies in the world' and he would threaten to make the list public with a tap on his pocket.[68] Through public diplomacy and the threat of publicity, the US executive would essentially re-create the consequences of the public revulsion that took over Europe and the United States in the 1970s, but the public distaste for corrupt practices in Europe was not mobilized in the 1970s, the way it was in the 1990s.[69]

The key to signing the convention on December 17, 1997 can be seen to lie in the compromise enshrined in section 3 of the Revised Recommendation. Section 3 ensured that criminalization measures would be enacted by April 1998, even if the negotiation of a binding instrument failed. This development reveals

62 'Statement of G7 Finance Ministers and Central Bank Governors' (Washington DC, 27 April 1997) <http://www.g8.utoronto.ca/finance/fm970427.htm> accessed 1 June 2020.

63 The White House, 'Summit of the Eight: The Sherpas' <https://clintonwhitehouse4.archives.gov/textonly/WH/new/Eight/sherpa.html> accessed 1 June 2020.

64 As the following telegram from the OECD Archives reveals: 'He [US Representative to OECD, Alan Larson] thought that the Germans might be prepared to move towards accepting the US conditions. Since the ECSS, the US had lobbied them at high level (letters from Attorney General Reno and Commerce Secretary Daley to their counterparts). In circulating the revised draft G7 statement, they had made clear US readiness to take this to the Summit. Tarullo would be pressing hard at Airlie House. Kohl would not wish to be embarrassed at Denver.' 'Washington Embassy Telegram to Foreign and Commonwealth Office' (United Kingdom) (RefN 1160, 21 May 1997).

65 Pieth 'Bribing Foreign Officials' (n 55) 83.

66 Pieth 'Introduction' (n 22) 19.

67 Ibid.

68 Abbott (n 45) 164.

69 Ibid.

how the neglected period of pre-negotiations is much more important than usually assumed. This is not to say that the negotiation of the binding treaty was not a difficult process. The negotiation of the OECD treaty was an abrasive process, that the participants were not particularly fond of.[70] The main reason for that, however, lied in the last minute introduction by the United States of the divisive issue of criminalization of payments to foreign political parties.[71] The particular issue did not make it into the final text, but criminalization as the 'strongest form of condemnation'[72] testified to the formal seriousness that OECD member states now attributed to the problem of corrupt payments.

2 Americanizing global anti-corruption after the conventions

From a legal perspective, the FCPA was a global innovation when enacted in 1977. As already mentioned in Part I, the US legislation, buttressed by strong political will, went farther than any other country's political and legal culture would permit anti-corruption law to go. The FCPA criminalized foreign bribery and provided significant means for enforcement against US businesses. Just as other states lacked the political will to adopt an FCPA-type legislation, they also lacked the legal culture needed to mobilize such a law. Thus, when international support for combating transnational bribery finally coalesced as a concerted effort in the mid-90s in the form of the OAS and OECD conventions, the conventions purposefully created flexible guidelines. This flexibility would permit the United States to strengthen the FCPA on the basis of certain provisions in the conventions, in line with its political ambitions, while simultaneously allowing other signatory states room to implement laws more aligned with their own political and legal cultures.

Despite the flexibility offered by the conventions, newly enacted national-level anti-bribery laws showcased strong elements of the FCPA. To explain the FCPA's *Americanizing* effect on other states' anti-bribery laws, we assert that the OAS and OECD conventions were vehicles for achieving this outcome. Our legal analysis is two-fold, focusing on (i) a comparison of legal texts, and (ii) an examination of implementation and enforcement of the texts. First, we argue that a textual analysis shows how the OAS and OECD conventions provided grounds for expanding the FCPA, particularly in terms of its jurisdictional basis. Second, we assert that this expansion of the FCPA's jurisdictional basis led to a surge in US enforcement actions that ultimately pressured foreign jurisdictions to implement the conventions, and to do so in a more American style.

70 David D Metcalfe, 'The OECD Agreement to Criminalize Bribery: A Negotiation Analytic Perspective' (2000) 5 International Negotiation 129, 150.

71 Ibid.

72 Abbott (n 45) 167.

2.1 *Comparing the texts: conventions expanding upon and reforming the FCPA*

The 1977 adoption of the FCPA represented a moral victory for those who felt US companies should not be in the business of exporting bribery.[73] The moral high ground sustaining this principled view, however, eroded over two decades when no other country adopted similar legislation. In fact, other countries, including Germany, whose businesses often competed with US business overseas, provided tax regimes permitting foreign bribes paid by their companies to be tax deductible.[74] Between 1994 and 1996, US companies lost an estimated $11 billion in foreign contracts because of bribes paid by foreign competitors to foreign officials.[75] Thus, by the mid-90s, there was a strong feeling that, as Acting Assistant Attorney General Ann M Harkins wrote in a letter to then-Speaker of the House Newt Gingrich, 'the application of the FCPA to US businesses only and the lack of any similar legislation anywhere else in the world ha[d] taken their toll on US business interests.'[76]

The OAS and OECD conventions provided the US with a means to solving this problem. The texts provided guidelines for effective national-level anti-bribery legislation. These guidelines became the basis for amending the FCPA's jurisdiction in two important ways. First, to whom the FCPA applies was broadened to include all foreign persons committing an act in furtherance of a foreign bribe while in US territory.[77] Second, nationality jurisdiction was incorporated making it so that US businesses and nationals acting wholly outside the US could be liable.[78] These jurisdictional expansions broadened the FCPA's applicability to both US and foreign offenders.[79]

While the conventions had almost instantaneous influence on US law, they did not have the same immediate effect in other states. This was, however, likely by design. Both conventions left room for signatory states to adopt anti-bribery

73 Mark Romaneski, 'The Foreign Corrupt Practices Act of 1977: An Analysis of Its Impact and Uncertain Future' (1982) 5 Boston College International and Comparative Law Review 405, 409.

74 'Germany, Where Bribery Is Tax Deductible' *Bloomberg* (7 August 1995) <https://www.bloomberg.com/news/articles/1995-08-06/germany-where-bribery-is-tax-deductible-intl-edition> accessed 1 June 2020.

75 Franklyn P Salimbene, 'The OAS and the OECD Move against Transnational Bribery: Implications for US Businesses and the Foreign Corrupt Practices Act' (1999) 104 Business and Society Review 91, 94.

76 Letter from Acting Assistant Attorney General Ann M Harkins to Speaker of the US House of Representatives, the Honorable Newt Gingrich (4 May 1998) <https://www.justice.gov/sites/default/files/criminal-fraud/legacy/2012/11/14/transltrs.pdf> accessed 1 June 2020 ('Ann Harkins Letter').

77 Ibid.

78 Ibid.

79 The 1998 reform also clarified what types of payments were liable, which, among other things, also broadened the FCPA's application, although to a lesser extent than the jurisdictional expansions discussed herein.

laws aligned with their respective domestic political and legal systems. They also called for increased international cooperation in cross-border efforts to combat transnational bribery. The conventions reflected a political compromise between signatories as demonstrated in Part I, which, although driven by the US desire to spawn FCPA clone legislations worldwide, ultimately left room, though limited, for other national approaches to emerge.

2.1.1 The OAS and OECD conventions as means of expanding the FCPA's jurisdictional reach

The initial FCPA's application was limited to 'domestic concerns' and followed the territoriality principle for jurisdiction (see Table 2.1, column 1).[80] 'Domestic concerns,' as defined under 15 USC § 78dd-2(h)(1) (1988), referred to any individual who was 'a citizen, national, or resident of the United States' or any business entity with its principal place of business in the United States or organized under US laws. Meanwhile, the territoriality principle held that a state could only adopt criminal laws that govern the conduct of individuals while on its sovereign territory.[81] According to these limitations, the US Department of Justice ('DOJ') could only police US individuals or corporations whose conduct within the United States amounted to an act in furtherance of foreign bribery.[82] The 1998 amendments to the FCPA broadened its jurisdiction, however, to reflect provisions included in the OAS and OECD conventions.

The OAS and OECD conventions contained provisions regarding jurisdiction that deviated from the FCPA and would spark its reform. First, the conventions advocated that states prohibit their nationals from committing acts of bribery outside of the state's territory, according to the nationality principle. Unlike the territoriality principle, a sovereign is considered to have jurisdiction over all its nationals under the nationality principle regardless of whether they act within the sovereign's territory.[83] Article V(2) of the OAS Convention states that 'Each State Party may adopt such measures … necessary to establish its jurisdiction … when the offense is committed by one of its nationals.'[84] Accordingly, the key to establishing jurisdiction is *who* commits the act—a national—rather than where the act is committed. Similarly, the OECD Convention in Article 4(2) states that 'Each party which has jurisdiction to prosecute its nationals for offences committed

80 The FCPA was first amended in 1988; however, changes made at that time had no bearing on provisions related to the jurisdictional aspects of the original 1977.

81 Cedric Ryngaert, 'The Concept of Jurisdiction in International Law' in Alexander Orakhelashvili (ed), *Research Handbook on Jurisdiction and Immunities in International Law* (2015) 50.

82 See Table 1, column 1; 15 US Code s 78dd-2(a).

83 Ryngaert (n 81) 2; Salimbene (n 75) 96.

84 Inter-American Convention Against Corruption (entered into force March 6, 1997) (1996) 35 ILM 724, art V(2) (OAS Convention), stipulates that jurisdiction may also be found over someone who habitually resides in the sovereign's territory.

abroad shall take such measures as may be necessary to establish its jurisdiction to do so.'[85] Accordingly, signatory states who already govern jurisdiction by the nationality principle, should take measures to establish jurisdiction over foreign bribery committed by their nationals while abroad.

Although the United States did not previously apply the nationality principle, and despite the fact that neither convention created an obligation for states to start applying the principle upon signing, the United States amended the FCPA to include jurisdiction based on the nationality principle. The US government's immediate willingness to adopt a great extra-territorial reach indicated that it may have envisioned the conventions as an excuse for reforming the FCPA in this regard. In fact, there is also significant evidence from political negotiations leading up to adopting the conventions indicating that extraterritoriality jurisdiction was among the issues pushed by the United States, much to the dislike of other parties.[86] Section 78dd-1(g)(1) of the 1998 amendment provides for alternative jurisdiction based on the nationality principle. It states, 'It shall also be unlawful for any issuer organized under the laws of the United States ... or for any United States person ... to corruptly do any act outside the United States.'[87] Thus, US businesses acting entirely outside US territory to further a bribery scheme would be liable. This amendment, therefore, greatly strengthened the DOJ's jurisdictional reach over US businesses, which would facilitate enforcement.

In addition to the nationality principle, the OECD Convention also authorized states to apply the territorial principle. This was particularly important because, when taken together with the convention's expanded definition for who may be liable ('any person'), a state can assert jurisdiction over foreign nationals acting within its sovereign territory. Article 1(1) states, 'Each Party shall take such measures as may be necessary to establish that it is a criminal offence under its law for any person intentionally to offer, promise or give any undue pecuniary or other advantage.'[88] Therefore, *who* may be liable for bribery is not limited by nationality, unlike under the initial FCPA. A state only has jurisdiction over the person, however, 'when the offence is committed in whole or in part in its territory,' per Article 4(1).[89] Thus, under the OECD Convention, a state has jurisdiction over its nationals or foreign nationals whenever the offence occurs in whole or in part on its sovereign territory.

The FCPA was subsequently expanded to cover foreign persons committing an offense in whole or in part on US territory. Until 1998, the FCPA only covered issuers with securities registered under the 1934 Securities Exchange Act

85 Convention on Combating Bribery of Foreign Public Officials in International Business Transactions, adopted by the Negotiating Conference, November 21,1997, art 4(2) (OECD Convention).

86 C(90)87, Illicit Payments in International Commercial Transactions (Note to the Secretary General, 12 June 1990).

87 15 US Code 15 s 78dd-1(g)(1).

88 OECD Convention, art 1(1).

89 Ibid art 4(2).

and 'domestic concerns.'[90] To comply with the OECD's call on state parties to cover 'any person,' the text was amended in 1998 to cover 'all foreign persons who commit an act in furtherance of a foreign bribe while in the United States.'[91] The DOJ, thenceforth, wielded a tool to enforce the FCPA against foreign businesses committing acts of foreign bribery in whole or in part on US territory. US businesses would no longer be the only ones accountable under the FCPA.

These jurisdictional expansions significantly bolstered the FCPA's capacity to enforce against foreign and domestic businesses, thereby leveling the playing field for business competition abroad. Additionally, the OAS and OECD conventions were aimed at spurring signatory states to adopt national criminal laws against foreign bribery, which could give them a legal basis for policing their own businesses. The conventions, however, created some uncertainty as to what form these developments would take.

2.1.2 The OAS and OECD conventions as applied to other states: leaving room for creativity, cooperation … and uncertainty

The OAS and OECD conventions left room both for states to customize their anti-bribery laws and for international cooperation.[92] The OAS Convention achieved this by being less binding on signatories and promoting a principle of cooperation between parties. The text of the OECD Convention does obligate signatories to adopt specific measures, but simultaneously provides flexibility for them to do so in line with their legal cultures. The OECD Convention also encourages, although it does not always explicitly require, its members to cooperate on their efforts to combat foreign bribery. While this flexibility likely helped garner widespread support for the conventions, it also created uncertainty concerning what types of national legislation would be implemented and how they would be enforced.

The dual mission of the OAS Convention was to provide (i) guidelines on national legislation criminalizing acts of corruption; and (ii) a legal framework for cooperation among state parties.[93] On the first point, the convention was considered the first such international effort to commit signatories to combat transnational bribery.[94] Its transnational bribery provisions were, however, non-self-executing to let signatories define the crime according to their constitutions

90 Ann Harkins letter (n 76); see Table column 1.

91 Ibid. See Table column 4.

92 Salimbene (n 75) 98.

93 Luis F Jiménez, 'The Inter-American Convention Against Corruption' (1998) 92 Proceedings of the Annual Meeting, American Society of International Law 157, 158; OAS Convention, art 2.

94 Jorge Garcia-Gonzales, 'The Organisation of American States and the Fight against Corruption' in OECD (ed), *Public Sector Transparency and Accountability: Making it Happen* (2002) 175, 177.

and fundamental legal principles.[95] Furthermore, the convention authorizes, although does not obligate ('may adopt measures'), states to exercise nationality jurisdiction in addition to territoriality jurisdiction.[96] As to the second point, the OAS Convention has been considered 'a roadmap for collective action' due to its express call for states to extend broad technical assistance to each other.[97] But to capitalize on opportunities for cooperation, national legislations and enforcement structures would have to be adequately strengthened.[98] Thus, the extent to which the convention could spur cooperation would hinge on states' efforts to adapt their legal systems to the goals of the convention.

The OECD Convention also left space for state parties to develop their approaches to combatting bribery according to their national political and legal cultures. This is particularly evident in its lenient definition of corporate criminal liability.[99] Article 2 provides a broad, flexible standard for the responsibility of legal persons, stating: 'Each Party shall take such measures as may be necessary, in accordance with its legal principles, to establish the liability of legal persons for the bribery of a foreign public official.'[100] Annex I (B) also recommends that states consider the role played by high-level corporate agents, particularly senior management, in the bribery scheme.[101] This overall guidance provided flexibility to states with less developed corporate criminal liability standards than that of, for example, the United States, which recognized the principle of *respondeat superior*. Under a theory of *respondeat superior*, corporations could be held liable for acts taken by their officers, directors, agents, or stockholders acting on behalf of the corporation.[102] Therefore, US prosecutors could easily impute actions by a corporation's agents to the corporation itself, making findings of corporate criminal liability extremely likely. This was, however, highly unique to the US legal system at the time, and the OECD Convention was regarded as striking an appropriate balance with its flexible standard.[103]

Regarding coordination between signatories, the OECD Convention encouraged and provided guidance on coordination without explicitly mandating it in all circumstances. Article 4 states, 'When more than one Party has jurisdiction

95 Jiménez (n 93) 160.

96 Use of this permissive language, as opposed to that used in the OECD Convention, which expressly requires ('shall adopt measures') states to exercise nationality jurisdiction, is also why the US did not feel it needed to reform the FCPA to comply with the OAS Convention, but only to later comply with the OECD convention. See Ann Harkins Letter.

97 Garcia-Gonzales (n 94) 177.

98 Giorleny D Altamirano, 'The Impact of the Inter-American Convention Against Corruption' (2007) 38 University of Miami Inter-American Law Review 487, 503.

99 Salimbene (n 75) 97.

100 OECD Convention, art 2.

101 Fritz F Heimann, Mark Pieth, *Confronting Corruption: Past Concerns, Present Challenges, and Future Strategies* (OUP 2018) 204.

102 R Christopher Cook and Stephanie Connor, *The Foreign Corrupt Practices Act: An Overview* (Jones Day 2010) 4.

103 Heimann (n 101) 204.

over an alleged offence described in this Convention, the Parties involved shall, at the request of one of them, consult with a view to determining the most appropriate jurisdiction for prosecution.'[104] While the use of the word '*shall*' made this clause mandatory, there remained an ambiguity as to when this consultation process would occur.[105] Professor Matthew Stephenson recently noted that the '*shall*' likely only refers to making consultations when one of the involved parties with jurisdiction requests it.[106] Furthermore, just because multiple parties may find jurisdiction and there may be a determination made about one jurisdiction being the most appropriate, Article 4 does not seem to limit other jurisdictions from proceeding with parallel prosecutions. Given that the OECD Convention broadly advocated for cooperation, the intention behind this provision was to lead to a handing off of investigations to the most appropriate jurisdiction. The text does not, however, expressly mandate full cooperation to that effect, thus leaving open questions as to when cooperation would occur.

The textual comparison between the conventions and the FCPA demonstrates that the conventions were far from mirror images of the 1988 FCPA. In fact, the conventions prompted significant amendments to the FCPA in terms of jurisdictional reach and expansion of who was covered by the legislation. Furthermore, the conventions' efforts to leave room for signatories to craft their national legislations in line with national political and legal cultures left gaps between the FCPA and whatever national laws would arise in other states. Although both conventions were aimed to promote cooperation between states, ambiguity concerning what types of legislation would be implemented and how they would be enforced also created uncertainty around what shape any international cooperation would take. In the context of this uncertainty, the strengthened 1998 FCPA would play a significant role in shaping other nation's implementation and enforcement stories.

2.2 Implementation and enforcement: the FCPA and its laggards

2.2.1 FCPA enforcement actions surge post-1998 strengthened by DOJ guidance

Given the US desire to put its businesses back in contention for foreign contracts, it is unsurprising that the DOJ wasted little time making use of its expanded jurisdiction under the amended FCPA. There was a dramatic uptake in actions against both domestic and foreign firms following 1998 (see Figure 2.2). The US capitalized on its new extraterritorial reach and was willing, in part due to

104 OECD Convention, art 4.

105 Matthew Stephenson, Comment to 'Guest Post: The Result in US v. Hoskins is Required by the OECD Anti-Bribery Convention' (*Global Anticorruption Blog*, 27 September 2018) <https://globalanticorruptionblog.com/2018/09/27/guest-post-the-result-in-us-v-hoskins-is-required-by-the-oecd-anti-bribery-convention/> accessed 1 June 2020.

106 Ibid.

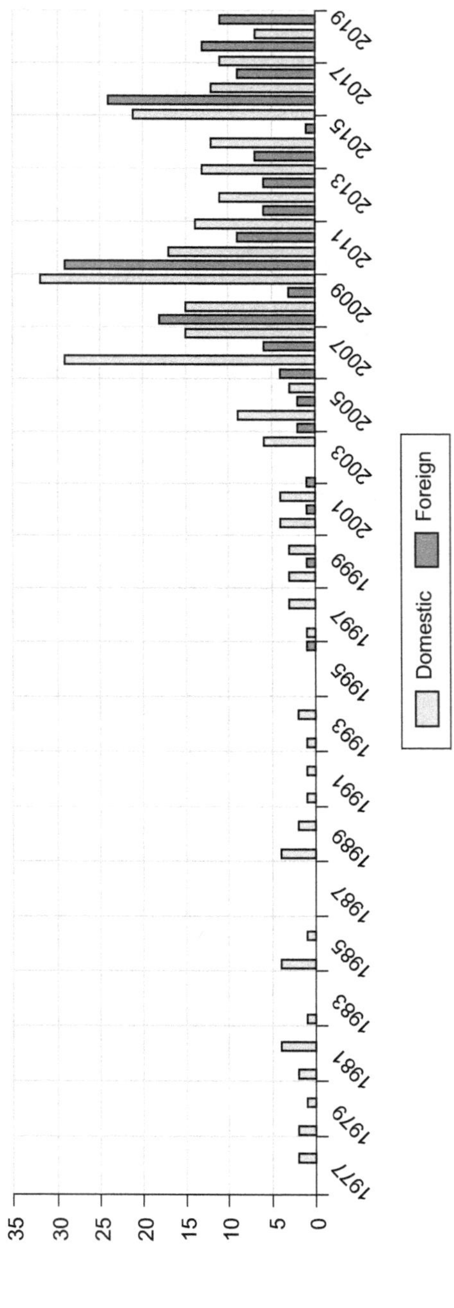

Figure 2.2 Foreign and domestic entities charged per year. 'DOJ and SEC Enforcement Actions per Year' (*Stanford Law School: Foreign Corrupt Practices Act Clearinghouse*, 2018) <http://fcpa.stanford.edu/statistics-analytics.html?tab=1> accessed 26 September 2019.

domestic developments, to expand guidelines and tools to facilitate its enforcement. Three legal developments beyond the scope of the conventions helped the DOJ to employ the FCPA more zealously. First, the DOJ applied ***respondeat superior*** to sanction foreign firms for the acts of their agents on US territory.[107] Second, it determined that the test for finding a nexus between the act and US territory could be easily fulfilled. Finally, the DOJ pioneered the use of deferred prosecution agreements (DPAs) or non-prosecution agreements (NPAs) to more efficiently enforce actions against corporations.[108] These developments were important first, because they spurred much US enforcement activity post-1998, but also because they have since emerged in foreign legal practice, despite not being part of either the conventions or these states' legal cultures.

Whereas the OAS and OECD conventions did not impose on signatories a high standard for corporate criminal liability because the practice was not well-developed in most countries, the US did not refrain from imposing its own standard of ***respondeat superior*** on foreign actors. Guidelines issued by the DOJ note that the US government would leverage the doctrine of ***respondeat superior*** to impose liability on an employer for the conduct of its employees or agents that is 'undertaken within the scope of their employment and intended, at least in part, to benefit the company.'[109] Since the 1998 FCPA amendment expanding jurisdiction, the DOJ has regarded the anti-bribery provisions to 'appl[y] to foreign persons and foreign non-issuer entities that, either directly or through an agent engage in ***any*** act in furtherance of a corrupt payment … while in the territory of the United States.'[110] Since, the DOJ has brought numerous actions against foreign firms including two of the largest ever brought, against French power and transportation company, Alstom SA, and against Brazilian state-owned energy company, Petróleo Brasileiro SA ('Petrobras'), applying ***respondeat superior*** to find corporate criminal liability and impose heavy fines.[111]

The US further expanded its extraterritorial reach by selecting a low threshold for what may qualify as a prohibited act while in US territory. DOJ Guidelines indicated that the threshold may be met by as little as an email sent from, to, or

107 Salimbene (n 75) 98.

108 Julie R O'Sullivan, 'How Prosecutors Apply the 'Federal Prosecutions of Corporations' Charging Policy in the Era of Deferred Prosecutions, and What That Means for the Purposes of the Federal Criminal Sanction' (2014) 51 American Criminal Law Review 29.

109 Aaron Murphey and Matthew L Kutcher, 'What the SEC and DOJ Resource Guide to the FCPA Means for Multi-National Companies' (*Business Law Today*, July 2013) <https://www.americanbar.org/groups/business_law/publications/blt/2013/07/02_murphy/> accessed 1 June 2020.

110 US Department of Justice and US Securities and Exchange Commission, *FCPA: A Resource Guide to the US Foreign Corrupt Practices Act* (2015) 11.

111 'United States of America v. Alstom SA Plea Agreement' (US District Court of Connecticut 2014) Ex. 2, B-1 ('Alstom Plea Agreement'); 'Petroleo Brasileiro SA—Petrobras Non-Prosecution Agreement' (United States Department of Justice, 26 September 2018) A-12 [52].

through the United States or a wire transfer sent through the United States.[112] Indeed, in *SEC v. Straub*, the SEC successfully proved jurisdiction over foreign national defendants where emails in furtherance of the bribery scheme were sent from locations outside the United States, but were routed through and/or stored on networks located within US territory.[113] Foreign firms aware of this low threshold have even structured bribery schemes specifically to evade a US territorial nexus. French company Alstom SA notoriously 'maintained an unwritten policy to discourage, where possible, consultancy arrangements that would subject [it] to the jurisdiction of the United States.'[114] Alstom 'used consultants who were not based in the United States, and intentionally paid consultants in bank accounts outside of the United States and in currencies other than US dollars.'[115] Thus, the DOJ's low threshold for finding a nexus to US territory has impacted its enforcement actions against foreign actors.

Finally, the innovative prosecutorial practice of using DPAs/NPAs as enforcement tools greatly bolstered US efforts starting in the early 2000s. The DOJ began using these agreements with corporate actors following the Enron scandal in 2001 that brought the giant accounting firm, Arthur Andersen, to its knees with widespread societal consequences.[116] These negotiated agreements allow the DOJ to delay or avoid prosecution and most of its negative side-effects, while still guaranteeing that the target corporation admits to the facts of the case, pays fines, and implements compliance policies, among other things.[117] DPAs/NPAs also greatly reduce the costs of carrying out extensive investigations and evidence collection required to take behemoth multinational corporations to trial and win.[118] Since beginning to use DPAs/NPAs, the DOJ has accelerated its enforcement activities. Between December 2004, when the DOJ first issued such an agreement and 2014, 70 out of 80—or approximately 85%—of the DOJ's FCPA enforcement actions against business organizations were resolved by a DPA or NPA.[119] Despite this success, the DOJ's embrace of DPAs/NPAs has not been without criticism as some argue that such prosecutor-led negotiated agreements lack judicial scrutiny, permitting the DOJ to 'occup[y] the role of

112 US Department of Justice and US Securities and Exchange Commission (n 110) 11.

113 *SEC v. Straub*, Case No. 11 civ 9645 (S.D.N.Y.); Mike Koehler, 'Into The FCPA's Jurisdiction Thicket' (*FCPA Professor*, 28 April 2015) <http://fcpaprofessor.com/into-the-fcpas-jurisdictional-thicket/> accessed 1 June 2020.

114 Alstom Plea Agreement (n 111) Ex. 2, B-1.

115 Ibid.

116 O'Sullivan (n 108) 35.

117 Mike Koehler, 'Measuring the Impact of Non-Prosecution and Deferred Prosecution Agreements on Foreign Corrupt Practices Act Enforcement' (2015) 49 UC Davis Law Review 497, 505.

118 Rick Messick, 'Analyzing Settlements in Corruption Cases: A Primer' (*Global Anticorruption Blog* 6 December 2017) <https://globalanticorruptionblog.com/2017/12/06/analyzing-settlements-in-corruption-cases-a-primer/> accessed 1 June 2020.

119 Koehler, 'Measuring the Impact of Non-Prosecution and Deferred Prosecution Agreements on Foreign Corrupt Practices Act Enforcement' (n 117) 521.

prosecutor, judge, and jury all at the same time.'[120] Nevertheless, these more amicable arrangements have facilitated a surge in FCPA enforcement and have propelled the US to the top of the anti-bribery enforcement leader-board.

2.2.2 US enforcement efforts lead the way for the OAS and OECD enforcement lag

Other signatory countries continued to straggle behind the US in terms of implementation and enforcement of the conventions well into the 2000s. Meanwhile, the US with its broadened FCPA statute and new enforcement tools, began to fill this global enforcement gap. As a result, states previously slow to fulfill their obligations under the conventions, began to fall in line. These states followed the American blueprint closely, adhering to practices pioneered by the DOJ rather than those strictly inspired by the international conventions.

The US has become the undisputed leader in anti-bribery enforcement globally in the two decades since the signing of the international conventions. OECD statistics for the period 1999–2016 show that US sanctions against legal persons (entities as opposed to individuals) accounted for nearly 70% of all actions brought by the 41 signatory states.[121] In raw figures, the US brought 109 actions, with 67 of those ending in a DPA or NPA.[122] In comparison, countries like Brazil and France sanctioned zero legal persons during this same period.[123] The OECD also praised US efforts to implement and enforce the anti-bribery convention including its use of 'innovative methods like … Deferred Prosecution Agreements (DPAs) [and] Non-Prosecution Agreements (NPAs).'[124] The OECD added only a brief cautionary note regarding these practices to encourage the US to enhance 'transparency and public awareness of these measures.'[125] Overall, the US remained the standard-bearer in terms of national-level implementation and enforcement of an effective anti-bribery regime.

Regarding the international convention's second aim of increasing cooperation in cross-border enforcement, OECD monitoring also shows the US at the center of these efforts. The 2016 report finds that for that year, US authorities were involved in all six multi-jurisdictional cases in which prosecutions for a single foreign bribery scheme were brought in multiple countries.[126] Figure 2.3 further shows that up until 2016, there were effectively no sanctions imposed

120 Ibid.

121 OECD Working Group on Bribery, *2016 Data on Enforcement of the Anti-Bribery Convention* (November 2017) 6.

122 Ibid.

123 Ibid 5.

124 OECD Working Group on Bribery, *Phase 3 Report on Implementing the OECD Anti-Bribery Convention in the United States* (October 2010) 5.

125 Ibid.

126 OECD Working Group on Bribery, *2016 Data on Enforcement of the Anti-Bribery Convention* (n 121) 9.

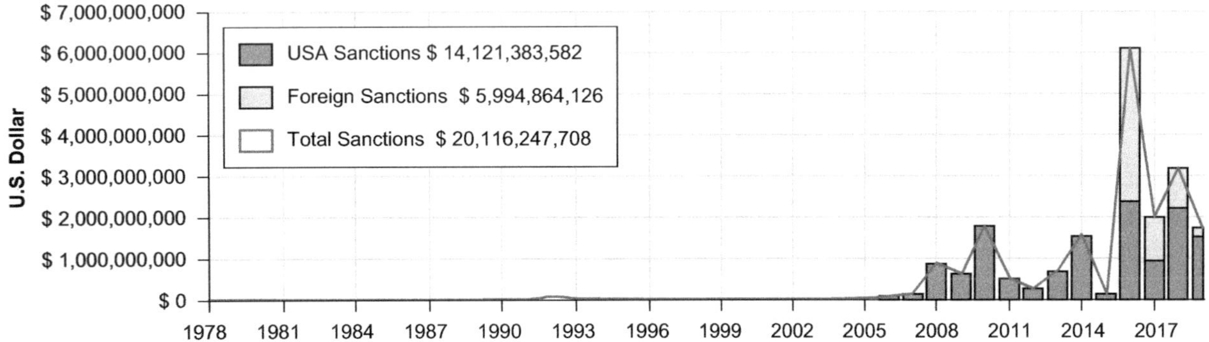

Figure 2.3 Total and average sanctions imposed on entity groups per year. 'Total and Average Sanctions Imposed on Entity Groups per Year' (*Stanford Law School: Foreign Corrupt Practices Act Clearinghouse*, 2018) <http://fcpa.stanford.edu/statistics-analytics.html?tab=2> accessed 26 September 2019.

by foreign states on cases brought by US authorities, even though foreign states presumably had jurisdiction over the cases thanks to the conventions. Thus, for nearly 20 years after the conventions came into force, other states have lagged behind the US in terms of enforcement and sanctioning efforts, while the United States has spearheaded action globally.

2.2.3 Resentment of US extraterritorial enforcement spurs implementation of FCPA-like criminal laws

The great irony of this story is that as the US increased its enforcement efforts, other states began to resent US extraterritorial action despite that action stemming from provisions introduced in the OAS and especially the OECD treaty. This resentment grew perhaps strongest in Europe. A 2018 report by the Institut Jacques Delors, a European think tank, criticized the overreach of US law. In addition to lamenting that the US applies the norms and sanctions it alone has decided to foreign entities and persons, the article asserts that US extraterritorial enforcement threatens European state sovereignty.[127] The report calls upon Europe to impose similar extraterritorial laws to preserve sovereignty and '*au nom de la nécessité de rééquilibrer un rapport de forces avec les États-Unis*' (for the sake of the necessity to rebalance a ratio of power with the United States).[128] These critics of US action against foreign entities have seemingly forgotten that inspiration for extraterritoriality came from international conventions and not US practice. It is, however, zealous extraterritorial action by US authorities that inspires other states to copy US law and practice in order to compete.

The development of the UK Bribery Act and French law Sapin II exemplifies this trend. The UK Bribery Act, introduced in April 2010, was largely 'seen as an indirect response to [the] BAE case.'[129] BAE Systems, a British defense contractor, participated in a global bribery scheme starting in the early 2000s.[130] Although BAE was ultimately penalized by both the DOJ and the UK's Serious

127 'Par extraterritorialité, on entend généralement l'utilisation unilatérale par un État des instruments pris en vertu de ses compétences souveraines pour faire appliquer sa propre loi, dans un territoire autre que le sien, pour des actions commises hors de son territoire, par des entités ou personnes relevant d'autres pays. *C'est bien le cas lorsque les États-Unis appliquent à des entités et personnes non-américaines des normes et des sanctions décidées par eux seuls.*' Institut Jacques Delors, *L'Europe Face Aux Sanctions Américaines, Quelle Souveraineté?* (October 2018).

128 Ibid 3.

129 Afua Hirsch, 'New Bribery Law Puts Overseas Payments under Scrutiny' *The Guardian* (London, 11 April 2010) <https://www.theguardian.com/uk/2010/apr/11/law-bribery-bae-overseas> accessed 1 June 2020.

130 US Department of Justice, 'BAE Systems PLC Pleads Guilty and Ordered to Pay $400 Million Criminal Fine' (1 March 2010) <https://www.justice.gov/opa/pr/bae-systems-plc-pleads-guilty-and-ordered-pay-400-million-criminal-fine> accessed 1 June 2020.

Fraud Office, the United States was seen as going further with its sanctions.[131] At the time, the $400 million fine against BAE placed it in the top three all-time FCPA fines.[132] The UK felt that its international reputation was damaged due to its inability to adequately handle the scandal, and passed the Bribery Act in response.[133] The Act, coming over a decade after the UK signed the OECD Convention, went beyond guidelines provided in that treaty by taking on some of the most effective aspects of the FCPA. For example, the UK set a low threshold for what could constitute a foreign business's acts on UK territory, triggering jurisdiction even when the bribery occurs abroad.[134] Although the UK, at first, hesitated to include negotiated agreements into its enforcement regime, it ultimately conceded that incorporating DPAs based on the US model would assist its efforts.[135] Today the UK Bribery Act is highly regarded as one of the most robust anti-bribery regimes in the world.

The more recent 2016 implementation of the French anti-corruption law Sapin II further demonstrated that states once critical of US practices were now willing to implement American methods to regain sovereignty and a competitive edge. The French have long criticized the FCPA's extraterritorial reach that has ensnared numerous French multinationals in international bribery scandals, including the already mentioned Alstom scandal that brought in the second largest FCPA fine on record in 2014.[136] Indeed, the lead story in the January 2017 edition of *Le Monde Diplomatique* titled, '*Au nom de la loi … Americaine*,' expounded French disdain for the FCPA as a tool of American economic imperialism and explained how Sapin II could be France's counterattack.[137] Despite that criticism, the French law adopts a broad extraterritoriality standard

131 Richard L. Cassin, 'BAE Pleads Guilty' (*The FCPA Blog*, 1 March 2010) <http://www.fcpablog.com/blog/2010/3/1/bae-pleads-guilty.html> accessed 1 June 2020; ibid.

132 Richard L. Cassin, 'Petrobras Smashes the Top Ten List (And We Explain Why)' (*The FCPA Blog*, 28 September 2018) <http://www.fcpablog.com/blog/2018/9/28/petrobras-smashes-the-top-ten-list-and-we-explain-why.html> accessed 1 June 2020.

133 Hirsch (n 129).

134 A foreign company that carries on any part of its business in the UK could be prosecuted for failure to prevent bribery even where the bribery takes place wholly outside the UK and the benefit or advantage to the company is intended to accrue outside the UK. See Peter Wilkinson, *The 2010 UK Bribery Act Adequate Procedures* (Transparency International UK, July 2010) 9.

135 Koehler, 'Measuring the Impact of Non-Prosecution and Deferred Prosecution Agreements on Foreign Corrupt Practices Act Enforcement' (n 117) 561.

136 Assemblée Nationale Française, Rapport d'information sur l'extraterritorialité de la législation américaine (No. 4082, 5 October 2016); Richard L Cassin, 'New French Anti-Corruption Law Allows DPAs' (*The FCPA Blog*, 10 November 2016) <http://www.fcpablog.com/blog/2016/11/10/new-french-anti-corruption-law-allows-dpas.html> accessed 1 June 2020.

137 Jean-Michel Quatrepoint, 'Au nom de la loi … américaine' *Le Monde Diplomatique* (Paris, January 2017) 1, 22–23.

that could sweep up foreign firms who usually reside in French territory.[138] The DOJ's prosecutorial discretion in negotiating agreements with corporations had also long bemused the French. Yet the French also acquiesced to incorporating a type of DPA option, called the *Convention judiciaire d'intérêt public* (CJIP).[139] Although some French commentators and criminal lawyers continue to scrutinize what they deem an 'Americanization' of French law with these reforms, the government has been undeterred in implementing what Minister Sapin saw as necessary for 'France [not to] remain one step behind or under the authority of foreign justice, in particular that of the United States.'[140]

While these two cases raise the question of whether recent national-level anti-bribery law developments will lead to increased cooperation or competition between states on enforcement matters, a May 2018 DOJ policy shift, followed closely by international resolutions of the Société Générale and Petrobras scandals, signaled that the US, at least, is now trying to lead on international cooperation.

In May 2018, US Deputy Attorney General Rod Rosenstein announced that the DOJ would pursue a new policy with regard to enforcing the FCPA. The policy would better reflect the reality that most cases span jurisdictions and involve multiple regulatory and enforcement actors. As such, the policy would 'encourag[e] Department attorneys, when possible, to coordinate with other federal, state, local, and foreign enforcement authorities seeking to resolve a case with a company for the same misconduct.'[141] In doing so, the DOJ could avert what Rosenstein referred to as the 'piling on' of penalties against multinational corporate defendants that can otherwise occur when authorities do not coordinate.[142] To better implement this policy, the DOJ would also detail a senior US prosecutor to work with the UK's Serious Fraud Office in London in order to strengthen cooperative enforcement efforts between the two authorities.[143] Thus, just on the heels of countries like the UK and France beefing up their enforcement capacities, the US decided to transition from being a lone

138 Ludovic Malgrain, Jean-Lou Salha, 'Update on Sapin II Law' (*White & Case Alert*, 10 January 2017) <https://www.whitecase.com/publications/alert/update-sapin-ii-law> accessed 1 June 2020.

139 Justin P Campbell, 'Michel Sapin: Sapin II retakes French Sovereignty' (*The FCPA Blog*, 20 June 2018) <http://www.fcpablog.com/blog/2018/6/20/michel-sapin-sapin-ii-retakes-french-sovereignty.html> accessed 1 June 2020.

140 BT, 'Rolls-Royce relève la tête après deux ans de restructuration' *Les Echos* (7 August 2017) <https://www.lesechos.fr/07/08/2017/LesEchos/22502-061-ECH_rolls-royce-releve-la-tete-apres-deux-ans-de-restructuration.htm> accessed 1 June 2020; 'Première séance du lundi 06 juin 2016' (Assemblée Nationale Française, 6 June 2016) 5 (remarks of M. Michel Sapin), 20 (remarks of M. Olivier Marleix).

141 US Department of Justice, 'Deputy Attorney General Rod Rosenstein Delivers Remarks to the New York City Bar White Collar Crime Institute' (9 May 2018) <https://www.justice.gov/opa/speech/deputy-attorney-general-rod-rosenstein-delivers-remarks-new-york-city-bar-white-collar> accessed 1 June 2020.

142 Ibid.

143 US Department of Justice, *Fraud Section Year in Review* (2018) 21.

wolf enforcer to coordinating joint efforts with foreign authorities. Furthermore, Rosenstein's words were quickly followed by action against non-compliant companies, demonstrating just how seriously the DOJ was taking this new policy.

The June 2018 enforcement action against Société Générale, concluded jointly by US and French authorities, showcased both the impact of France's new *Americanized* enforcement tools as well as a US policy shift towards cooperation. The newly implemented DPA *a la française*—the CJIP—substantially emboldened French prosecutorial authorities, facilitating enforcement actions in seven cases between its creation at the end of 2016 and September 2019.[144] This enforcement rate over two and a half years marks a substantial increase from that achieved by French authorities during the 17 years beginning in 1999, when the OECD Convention took effect. Until Loi Sapin II came into force in December 2016, the French authorities had penalized only one legal entity.[145] Furthermore, the enforcement action against Société Générale represented the first coordinated resolution in a foreign bribery case between French and American authorities.[146] Prior to this joint effort, the French had achieved only one enforcement action in a foreign bribery case while American authorities had successfully brought large actions against French corporations such as Alstom.[147] Thus, the coordinated effort against Société Générale along with the six other CJIPs represent major steps in French enforcement, spurred in part by the recent US policy shift.

Following the Société Générale resolution, the DOJ also collaborated closely with Brazilian authorities in investigating and bringing action against the Brazilian state-owned and controlled energy company, Petrobras, in September 2018.[148] Petrobras eventually entered into the largest FCPA settlement in history yet, totaling $1.78 billion of which $853.2 million was a criminal penalty payable to the DOJ.[149] On the other hand, 80% of the criminal penalty was to be paid directly to the Ministerio Publico Federal in Brazil, greatly reducing the total amount paid to the DOJ for the resolution.[150] The DOJ demonstrated what

144 Agence Française Anticorruption, 'La convention judiciaire d'intérêt public' (2019) <https://www.agence-francaise-anticorruption.gouv.fr/fr/convention-judiciaire-dinteret-public> accessed 1 June 2020.

145 OECD Working Group on Bribery, *2017 Data on Enforcement of the Anti-Bribery Convention* (November 2018) 5.

146 'Fraud Section Year in Review' (n 143) 6; US Department of Justice, 'Société Générale SA Agrees to Pay $860 Million in Criminal Penalties for Bribing Gaddafi-Era Libyan Officials and Manipulating LIBOR Rate' (4 June 2018) <https://www.justice.gov/opa/pr/soci-t-g-n-rale-sa-agrees-pay-860-million-criminal-penalties-bribing-gaddafi-era-libyan> accessed 1 June 2020.

147 Ibid.

148 US Department of Justice, 'Petróleo Brasileiro SA—Petrobras Agrees to Pay More Than $850 Million for FCPA Violations' (27 September 2018) <https://www.justice.gov/opa/pr/petr-leo-brasileiro-sa-petrobras-agrees-pay-more-850-million-fcpa-violations> accessed 1 June 2020.

149 Cassin, 'Petrobras smashes the top ten list (and we explain why)' (n 132).

150 Ibid.

some have called 'exceptional leniency' in this case as a result of its policy move to discourage the 'piling on' of penalties and encourage coordination with foreign enforcement agencies who share jurisdiction.[151] Thus, the US joint operations with French and Brazilian authorities demonstrated how the US is poised to have even more of an Americanizing effect on international anti-bribery enforcement, this time by spurring collaborative enforcement efforts.

This section has demonstrated that there has been an Americanizing effect on global anti-bribery laws. This effect has largely materialized as US enforcement efforts filled a gap between the conventions taking effect and other state signatories implementing and enforcing their own laws. US actions against large British and French companies sparked a need to protect their own sovereignty for those countries and a desire to fight back against US authorities. As a result, even those most critical of US extraterritorial action are adopting legal regimes enabling them to act similarly to US authorities. The concern resulting from this trend, however, is whether these laws and attitudes behind them will breed international competition rather than the cooperation envisioned by the international conventions. A recent policy change by the US DOJ followed by cooperative international efforts led by American prosecutors may indicate that the US intends again to lead international anti-bribery efforts, but this time towards a cooperative model.

3 Conclusion

In this chapter, we have argued that the United States heavily influenced the definition and content of international anti-corruption law with the FCPA forming the backbone of its approach to internationalizing corruption control. The chapter traced the history of the OECD and the OAS conventions and their role in US strategy since the 1970s. It also put forward the argument that after the adoption of the two conventions, the Americanization of international anti-corruption practice continued through implementation and enforcement efforts.

Given the immense influence that the United States has had over the internationalization of anti-corruption law, the US experience in defining and fighting corruption must also be relevant to a broader understanding of corruption as a global phenomenon. The FCPA was a regulatory measure that emerged out of a particular constellation of domestic factors peculiar to the United States. Regulation of 'corrupt practices' also has a long pedigree in US (and English) law. Judging from its name, the 'Foreign Corrupt Practices Act' appears as the international counterpart to the Federal Corrupt Practices Act, which remained active until Nixon signed a new campaign financing law in 1971. The state and federal Corrupt Practices Acts emerged out of a deep concern with corporate

151 Ibid. US Department of Justice, 'Deputy Attorney General Rod Rosenstein Delivers Remarks to the New York City Bar White Collar Crime Institute' (n 141).

influence on elections and politics.[152] The regulation of 'corrupt practices' in the United States has developed in a progressive tradition and is often concerned with limiting corporate (rather than government) abuse of political power. It therefore resonated strongly with developing nations who, in the 1970s, were concerned by corporate political influence. Not much of this progressive anti-corruption politics is reflected in the way corruption became institutionalized as a global problem in the 1990s. An understanding of the richness of the US debate on corruption might, therefore, be relevant to a global understanding of corruption as corporate as well as government abuse of power.

To acknowledge US influence on criminalizing transnational bribery means also to understand the US anti-corruption initiative in a broader context of transnational crime control. As a global leader, the United States has done much to define global 'goods and evils' in the framework of global crime governance[153] From this perspective, the criminalization of transnational bribery is but one example of US leadership in international crime control.[154] The case of corruption can thus be understood as an example of a much broader Americanization of global crime governance.

152 Jeff Wiltse, 'The Origins of Montana's Corrupt Practices Act: A More Complete History' (2012) 73 Montana Law Review 299.

153 Anja Jakobi, *Common Goods and Evils? The Formation of Global Crimes Governance* (OUP 2013).

154 Peter Andreas and Ethan Nadelmann, *Policing the Globe: Criminalization and Crime Control in International Relations* (OUP 2006).

Annex: Table 2.1

Table 2.1 Provisions governing jurisdiction in major anti-corruption instruments.

	FCPA (1977/1988)[a]	*OAS Convention*	*OECD Convention*	*FCPA (1998)*
Relevant provisions governing jurisdiction	15 USC §78dd-2(a) states: (a) Prohibition. It shall be unlawful for any **domestic concern**, other than an issuer which is subject to section 78dd–1 of this title, or for any officer, director, employee, or agent of such domestic concern or any stockholder thereof acting on behalf of such domestic concern, to make use of the mails or any means or instrumentality of interstate commerce corruptly in furtherance of an offer, payment, promise to pay, or authorization of the payment of any money, or offer, gift, promise to give, or authorization of the giving of anything of value to …	Article V (2) states: Each State Party **may** adopt such measures as may be necessary to establish its jurisdiction over the offenses it has established in accordance with this Convention ***when the offense is committed by one of its nationals*** or ***by a person who habitually resides in its territory.*** Article VIII on Transnational Bribery states, in part:	Article 1(1) states: Each Party **shall** take such measures as may be necessary to establish that it is a criminal offence under its law for **any person** intentionally to offer, promise or give any undue pecuniary or other advantage, whether directly or through intermediaries, to a foreign public official, for that official or for a third party, in order that the official act or refrain from acting in relation to the performance of official duties, in order to obtain or retain business or other improper advantage in the conduct of international business.	15 USC §78dd-1(a) states: (a) Prohibition. It shall be unlawful for any **issuer** which has a class of securities registered pursuant to section 78l of this title or which is required to file reports under section 78o(d) of this title, or for any officer, director, employee, or agent of such issuer or any stockholder thereof acting on behalf of such issuer, to make use of the mails or any means or instrumentality of interstate commerce corruptly in furtherance of an offer, payment, promise to pay, or authorization of the payment of any money, or offer, gift, promise to give, or authorization of the giving of anything of value to … The **1998** amendment also adds § 78dd-1(g), which provides for **alternative jurisdiction**, stating that:

Where 'domestic concern' is defined under § 78dd-2(h)(1) as: (A) any individual who is a citizen, national, or resident of the United States; and (B) any corporation, partnership, association, joint-stock company, business trust, unincorporated organization, or sole proprietorship which has its principal place of business in the United States, or which is organized under the laws of a State of the United States or a territory, possession, or commonwealth of the United States.	Subject to its Constitution and the fundamental principles of its legal system, each State Party shall prohibit and punish the offering or granting, directly or indirectly, by its nationals, persons having their habitual residence in its territory, and businesses domiciled there, to a government official of another State, of any article of monetary value, or other benefit, such as a gift, favor, promise or advantage, in connection with any economic or commercial transaction in exchange for any act or omission in the performance of that official's public functions.	Article 4 provides: (1) Each Party **shall** take such measures as may be necessary to establish its jurisdiction over the bribery of a foreign public official *when the offence is committed in whole or in part in its territory.* (2) Each Party which has jurisdiction to prosecute its nationals for offences committed abroad shall take such measures as may be necessary to establish its jurisdiction to do so in respect of the bribery of a foreign public official, according to the same principles.	(1) It shall also be unlawful for **any issuer** organized under the laws of the United States, or a State, territory, possession, or commonwealth of the United States or a political subdivision thereof and which has a class of securities registered pursuant to section 78l of this title or which is required to file reports under section 780(d) of this title, **or for any United States person** that is an officer, director, employee, or agent of such issuer or a stockholder thereof acting on behalf of such issuer, **to corruptly do any act outside the United States** in furtherance of an offer, payment, promise to pay, or authorization of the payment of any money, or offer, gift, promise to give, or authorization of the giving of anything of value to any of the persons or entities set forth in paragraphs (1), (2), and (3) of subsection (a) of this section for the purposes set forth therein, **irrespective** of whether such issuer or such officer, director, employee, agent, or stockholder makes use of the mails or any means or instrumentality of interstate commerce in furtherance of such offer, gift, payment, promise, or authorization. (2) As used in this subsection, the term 'United Statesperson' means a national of the United States (as defined in section 1101 of title 8) or any corporation, partnership, association, joint-stock company, business trust, unincorporated organization, or sole proprietorship organized under the laws of the United States or any State, territory, possession, or commonwealth of the United States, or any political subdivision thereof.

Note: All italics and bold has been added by the author for emphasis.

[a] The FCPA was first amended in 1988; however, the changes to the law made at this time, unlike those later made in 1998, did not affect the jurisdictional elements of the original 1977 legislation. Michael V Seitzinger, 'Foreign Corrupt Practices Act (FCPA): Congressional Interest and Executive Enforcement, In Brief' (*Congressional Research Service*, 15 March 2016) 3–5 <https://fas.org/sgp/crs/misc/R41466.pdf> accessed 26 September 2019.

3 Toward an interest group theory of foreign anti-corruption laws

Sean J. Griffith and Thomas H. Lee[1]

Foreign anti-corruption laws—laws that prohibit businesses from paying bribes abroad—have proliferated around the globe. The United States took the lead in 1977 with the passage of the Foreign Corrupt Practices Act (FCPA), which criminalized what many then considered an ordinary cost of doing business abroad.[2] Multilateral international treaties came two decades later, with the Organization for Economic Cooperation and Development (OECD) Anti-Bribery Convention in 1998,[3] followed by the United Nations Convention Against Corruption in 2003.[4] Individual states' domestic laws against foreign corruption came next, in large part because the treaties obligated ratifying countries to enact domestic laws penalizing the payment of bribes to foreign officials.[5] But enforcement, as we shall see, trailed enactment.

Foreign anti-corruption laws present a puzzle. Why would the government of one country care to prevent corruption in another? Laws against *domestic* corruption are longstanding and easy to justify. Corruption—the abuse of public power for private gain—distorts political decision-making and leads to the misallocation

1 An earlier version of this chapter was first published as an article in the University of Illinois Law Review.

2 Foreign Corrupt Practices Act of 1977, Pub. L. No. 95–213, 91 Stat. 1494 (1977), *amended by* the Omnibus Trade and Competitiveness Act of 1988, Pub. L. No. 100–418, tit. V, §§ 5001–03, 102 Stat. 1415 (1988), and the International Anti Bribery and Fair Competition Act of 1998, Pub. L. No. 105–366 (1998) (codified as amended at 15 US Code ss 78m, 78dd-1, 78dd-2, 78dd-3, 78ff (2018)).

3 Convention on Combating Bribery of Foreign Public Officials in International Business Transactions, adopted by the Negotiating Conference, 21 November 1997 37 ILM 1 (OECD Convention).

4 United Nations Convention against Corruption (opened for signature 9 December 2003, entered into force 14 December 2005) 2349 UNTS 41 (UNCAC).

5 Article 2 of the OECD Convention provided that 'Each Party shall take such measures as may be necessary, in accordance with its legal principles, to establish the liability of legal persons for the bribery of a foreign public official.' Article 16 of the UNCAC mandated that ratifying states 'adopt such legislative and other measures as may be necessary to establish as a criminal offence, when committed intentionally … the promise, offering or giving to a foreign public official … directly or indirectly, of an undue advantage' to 'act or refrain from acting in the exercise of his or her official duties' related to international business.

of government revenues, the degradation of civil services, and the disenfranchisement of the poor. Governments designed for the benefit of their people thus have a plain interest in preventing corruption at home. The reasons for promulgating laws to curtail *foreign* corruption, however, are much less apparent, especially considering that the principal means a government has at its disposal is to regulate the extraterritorial conduct of the domestic businesses paying the bribes to foreign officials. But without the ability to pay bribes abroad, domestic businesses may be at a competitive disadvantage vis-à-vis unregulated foreign businesses that will continue to supply bribes in bidding for the same international business contracts. The foreign competitor pays the bribe and wins the business while the domestic company suffers. Imposing pain on domestic business interests, given their lobbying power, is a dangerous political strategy for any government. So why would a government enact and then enforce foreign anti-corruption laws when the principal beneficiaries are the citizens of other countries? And, given the limited impact on the global supply of corruption of any unilateral state action, why even bother? Yet foreign anti-corruption laws exist and are increasingly being enforced across the globe.

This chapter seeks to solve the puzzle by offering an interest-group account for the spread of foreign anti-corruption laws across the globe. It is important to distinguish at the start between enactment and enforcement of foreign anti-bribery laws, because the two trends do not go together. The FCPA, for example, was sparsely enforced for more than two decades after being enacted.[6] The bevy of foreign anti-corruption laws passed by countries around the world in the wake of the OECD Anti-Bribery Convention and the UN Convention Against Corruption have also been rarely enforced until very recently in a select few signatory countries.[7] As of 2017, 23 of the 43 states that ratified the OECD Convention had not conducted a single foreign-bribery prosecution.[8] Moreover, despite the fanfare for the OECD and the UN conventions, and the ratification of regional anti-corruption conventions in Africa, the Americas, and Europe, direct treaty-based enforcement has generally failed to materialize.

The pace of enforcement of foreign anti-corruption laws has accelerated dramatically in the 21st century. Most significantly, FCPA enforcement in the US has ramped up not only against US-based companies but also against multinational companies, mostly from capital-exporting economies.[9] More recently, many of the countries whose companies have been the targets of FCPA enforcement—notably, the United Kingdom, Germany, France, and Brazil—have now not only enacted foreign anti-bribery laws, but have also begun to enforce them.[10] Many

6 See text at n 96ff.

7 See text at n 148ff.

8 See OECD, *Fighting the Crime of Foreign Bribery: The Anti-Bribery Convention and the OECD Working Group on Bribery* (2018).

9 See text at n 96ff.

10 See text at n 148ff.

other countries, meanwhile, continue *not* to enforce foreign anti-corruption laws, though most capital-exporting countries have enacted such laws.[11]

The explanation for trends in enactment and enforcement of foreign anti-corruption laws outlined in this chapter breaks from the existing literature. Much of the prior academic work focused exclusively on the FCPA and explains it either as a tool for the altruistic advancement of human rights[12] or, alternatively, as a tool for prosecutorial rent extraction.[13] Our account eschews both normatively tinged framings and looks instead to the political interest groups affected by the passage of foreign anti-bribery laws in various capital-exporting countries—not just the United States—to explain evolving trends. Our explanation also differs from institutionalist accounts that emphasize international organizations and domestic governance organs as the primary causal mechanisms for the spread of anti-corruption norms.[14] Our analysis, by contrast, is bottom-up and focused on private interest groups, rather than top-down and focused on state institutions.

Our interest-group based theory posits that observed patterns of enactment and enforcement can be explained by looking to the incentives of each country's domestic business lobby. Consider first the United States. Immediately after the FCPA was passed in 1977, US business interests favored lax enforcement, if not outright repeal.[15] That was the status quo for over two decades. At the same time, a second-best preference of US multinational corporations was to obtain a 'level playing field' vis-à-vis foreign competitors not subject to the FCPA.[16] This goal was eventually attained in the form of the 1998 OECD Convention and, just as critically, in resultant amendments to the FCPA empowering the US Department of Justice (DOJ) to enforce the statute vigorously against foreign companies with some connection to the US.[17] Achieving robust enforcement against foreign

11 Ibid.

12 See, e.g., Andrew Brady Spalding, 'Corruption, Corporations, and the New Human Right' (2014) 91 Washington University Law Review 1365. See also Matthew Murray and Andrew Spalding, *Freedom from Official Corruption as a Human Right* (Brookings Institute 2015) 2.

13 See, e.g., Mike Koehler, 'Measuring the Impact of Non-Prosecution and Deferred Prosecution Agreements on Foreign Corrupt Practices Act Enforcement' (2015) 49 UC Davis Law Review 497, 522 (arguing that 'the use of NPAs and DPAs also allows the DOJ to feed its lucrative FCPA enforcement program'). See also Mike Koehler, 'The Uncomfortable Truths and Double Standards of Bribery Enforcement' (2015) 84 Fordham Law Review 525, 541–544 (pointing to inconsistencies between the aspirational goals of ending bribery and enforcement patterns of the FCPA).

14 See, e.g., Rachel Brewster, 'Enforcing the FCPA: International Resonance and Domestic Strategy' (2017) 103 Virginia Law Review 1611, 1619 (arguing that the FCPA required 'international resonance' through the OECD before it could be meaningfully enforced). See also Rachel Brewster and Samuel W Buell, 'The Market for Global Anticorruption Enforcement' (2017) 80 Law and Contemporary Problems 193, 198–200 (explaining FCPA enforcement patterns by reference to the institutional incentives of enforcers).

15 See text at n 57ff.

16 See text at n 57ff.

17 See text at n 82ff.

competitors was a key component of getting US business interests on board.[18] But our story does not end there.

Now consider the incentives facing a foreign multinational corporation in the wake of the OECD Convention. The best case would be for its home jurisdiction not to enact any foreign anti-bribery law, but that option is foreclosed by the explicit provisions of the Convention.[19] The second-best option is lax home-state enforcement after enactment, which was the outcome multi-national corporations in OECD countries with foreign-corruption laws did achieve for over a decade.

The incentives of foreign multi-nationals changed, however, after the US Congress amended the FCPA in 1998 to permit enforcement against foreign companies based on minimum contacts with the United States—for example, by currency passed through a US depository institution—and the DOJ and Securities and Exchange Commission (SEC) demonstrated willingness to carry out aggressive enforcement against them. Those that bore US enforcement risk now had a substantial incentive to stop paying bribes anywhere and to implement strong FCPA compliance programs. Such compliance measures put these foreign companies at a competitive disadvantage with respect to regional and domestic competitors who operated without significant US enforcement risk and who therefore continued to pay bribes to win international business contracts. Consequently, foreign multinationals subject to FCPA enforcement developed a level playing field interest parallel to that of US multinationals prior to enactment of the OECD. But for foreign companies, a level playing field entailed enactment and enforcement of foreign anti-bribery laws in home jurisdictions as against their domestic and regional competitors. This is the world the multinationals eventually got, starting in the United Kingdom and Germany.[20]

This chapter argues that this private business interest-group account explains observed global patterns of enactment and enforcement of foreign anti-corruption laws better than existing explanations grounded in altruism, governmental interests, or international institutional analysis. This account also enables us to make better predictions about future trends in foreign anti-corruption laws than the alternative theories. Specifically, our interest-group explanation allows us to make two concrete predictions regarding enactment and enforcement patterns going forward.

Countries are more likely to adopt and enforce foreign anti-corruption laws on businesses operating within their borders once multinational businesses based in those jurisdictions face significant risks of enforcement in other jurisdictions, such

18 See Brewster (n 14) 1615 (arguing that 'the FCPA could not be robustly enforced until federal prosecutors could adopt … an enforcement strategy that allowed them to charge both American corporations and their foreign rivals, thus creating a level playing field in international commerce').

19 See (n 5) and accompanying text.

20 See text at n 148ff.

as the United States or the United Kingdom. This leads to a critical implication for the fight against global corruption: the best way to get countries to enact and enforce foreign anti-corruption laws is to enforce your own anti-corruption laws against their companies. In other words, the best way to get France to enforce its Law on Transparency, Combating Corruption and Modernization of Economic Life, commonly referred to as 'Sapin II,'[21] is to enforce the FCPA or the UK Bribery Act against French multinationals.

Countries with few or no multinational corporations and therefore no realistic extra-territorial enforcement risk will be relatively immune to pressure from foreign anti-corruption laws. Even if such a jurisdiction were to enact such laws, insofar as businesses operating within it are not subject to an appreciable threat of extra-jurisdictional enforcement, there will be no real incentive for that country to enforce its own foreign anti-corruption laws. Foreign anti-bribery laws, in other words, are the supply-side solution to a first-world problem: multinational companies paying big bribes abroad. They may fail to solve the problem of bribes paid by companies beyond the reach of first-world enforcement.

But the lens of an international relations theory shows a way that the global anti-corruption norm might yet prevail. 'Hegemonic stability theory' examines the conditions under which a global hegemon might provide a public good that benefits all nations, like free trade or a corruption-free international economic order.[22] A variant on the theory posits that a critical mass of leading countries that are enforcing foreign corruption laws, known as a 'k-group,' might also jointly provide a public good under certain conditions.[23] It may be the case that we are witnessing the formation of a hegemonic k-group of states forming around a global anti-corruption regime—the United States, Brazil, and Western European nations.

The presence of a foreign anti-corruption k-group of capital-*exporting* countries may change the incentives in capital-*importing* states in the following way. Imagine a government official in a capital-importing country who is considering taking a bribe in awarding the contract for a large infrastructure project. Companies from the k-group will not pay bribes, fearing enforcement of foreign anti-corruption laws; companies from non-k-group countries will pay bribes. But if the official accepts a bribe and awards a contract to a non-k-group company, he or she will have to explain why the bids from k-group companies were rejected. Insofar as k-group companies may be viewed as offering higher-quality work than non-k-group companies, this may be a difficult decision for the official to rationalize. In other words, if the traditional competitors of American companies—British, German, and French companies with good reputations—are no longer willing to offer bribes, the official will have a harder time explaining why he or she awarded the contract to a less established company from a country that still does not

21 See text at n 148ff.
22 See text at n 121ff.
23 See text at n 121ff.

enforce foreign anti-corruption laws. This realignment of demand-side incentives on the part of potential bribe recipients will only increase as the k-group spreads due to supply-side incentives.

China is a wild card in both stories. Because many of its international businesses are state-owned or state-influenced, China may be immune to the business-interest incentive story we are telling. In other words, because our model depends upon the incentives of *private* business interests—interests that are not as pronounced in China given the role of the Chinese state in enterprise—it does not allow us to venture a strong prediction regarding China. And to the extent that China commands a large share of international business contracts, the willingness of its state-owned or state-influenced companies to bribe may suffice to counteract the anti-corruption norm of the k-group. It is possible that we are headed toward a world of dueling hegemons.

This chapter proceeds as follows. Part 1 highlights important conceptual distinctions between foreign versus domestic corruption and why eliminating foreign corruption became a global policy priority. Part 2 develops our interest-group causal story, tracing the path of enactment and enforcement of the FCPA—the first and most prominent national foreign anti-corruption law—through the lens of domestic business interests. The US business community's successful lobbying for multilateral treaties to 'level the playing field,' which culminated in the OECD Convention, is a key part of this story. Part 3 surveys existing literature and explanations for the rise of foreign anti-corruption laws. It then introduces our contending explanation, which brings in international relations theory by applying hegemonic stability theory and its offshoot k-group theory to explain evolving patterns in the enactment and enforcement of foreign anti-corruption laws. Part 3 also offers predictions on the future trajectory of laws in this area as well as a framework that can be applied to other international legal contexts. Part 4 then tests our explanation against observed patterns in the enactment and enforcement of foreign anti-corruption laws in other countries in the wake of the OECD Convention. A brief conclusion follows.

1 Why do we care about foreign corruption?

Political scientist Joseph Nye defined corruption as 'behavior which deviates from the formal duties of a public role because of private-regarding (personal, close family, private clique) pecuniary or status gains.'[24] Corruption has long been perceived as detrimental to good domestic governance, especially in liberal democratic countries like the United States.[25] Government receipts and revenues are diverted from uses of greatest benefit to the public in favor of sub-optimal uses

24 J S Nye, 'Corruption and Political Development: A Cost-Benefit Analysis' (1967) 61 American Political Science Review 417, 419.

25 See generally Zephyr Teachout, *Corruption in America: From Benjamin Franklin's Snuffbox to Citizens United* (Harvard University Press 2016).

sought by bribe-payers.[26] For instance, a public official who takes a bribe may award a government contract to an inexperienced builder or let a criminal go free to commit more crimes. Those who do not bribe, whether because of integrity or a lack of resources, may lose meritorious bids, receive second-class treatment, or suffer generally from degraded public services. Additionally, bribes often entail falsified accounting records by both the taker and the giver of a bribe. Such subterfuge contributes to a lack of transparency that imposes transaction costs to monitor and police, and it may distort public policy decisions if widespread. Hence, most countries have longstanding domestic anti-bribery laws, and domestic political orders have routinely—if episodically—prosecuted egregious cases of domestic corruption.[27]

In the post-World War II, post-colonial era, however, opinions among economists and political scientists regarding the relative benefits of corruption in the international—as opposed to domestic—order became divided.[28] The animating concern was that it seemed unrealistic to expect impeccable public-regarding conduct from officials in post-war or post-colonial developing nations with weakened or fledgling governance institutions. In this context, it seemed moralistic and even counter-productive to condemn governments as 'corrupt'—a charge leveled against newly installed ruling regimes not only by rueful former colonial powers but also by indigenous contenders for power. From the perspective of macroeconomic theory, corruption might have a net positive effect on growth in a developing country if the size of the public pie in the country grew despite greater marginal growth for those in power taking bribes. At the level of petty officials in such countries, graft supplied an essential supplement to the meager public salaries developing countries could provide.[29] Furthermore, some economists viewed bribes as necessary grease to get things done in countries with copious laws and regulations on paper that might be invoked to block beneficial investments or economic activity.[30]

26 See, e.g., Norimitsu Onishi and Selam Gebrekidan, 'Hit Men and Power: South Africa's Leaders Are Killing One Another' *NY Times* (30 September 2018) <https://www.nytimes.com/2018/09/30/world/africa/south-africa-anc-killings.html> accessed 1 June 2020 (detailing rampant corruption involving government contracts in South Africa that has sparked assassinations against whistleblowers). The article details one particularly egregious instance of corruption involving the refurbishment of a historic building in a South African province. See ibid ('after five years and more than $2 million in public money, the project was a sinkhole of dubious spending, with little to show for it').

27 See Susan Rose-Ackerman, *Corruption and Government: Causes, Consequences, and Reform* (CUP 1999).

28 See John Brademas and Fritz Heimann, 'Tackling International Corruption: No Longer Taboo' (1998) 77 Foreign Affairs 17, 21.

29 See Nye (n 24) 427.

30 See Brademas and Heimann (n 28) 17.

In the past couple of decades, however, consensus has formed that corruption in the developing world has net negative effects that are worth eradicating.[31] Indeed, some contemporary voices go so far as to condemn corruption as 'an unrecognized threat to international security.'[32] The notion that there should be different standards for domestic corruption as between developed and developing countries was always problematic.[33] The same economic arguments about inequity, inefficient allocation of public resources, and lack of transparency and transaction costs are valid in all domestic political orders, regardless of the relevant order's state of economic development. What changed, then? As the imperatives of the Cold War ended and the colonial era faded into history, the paternalistic instinct to condone anti-corruption measures in the developing world also faded. At the same time, the demise of superpower rivalry opened the possibility of fully global cooperation toward public goods, like free trade or the eradication of corruption.

Consequently, a global norm against corruption was promulgated on the international plane. Multilateral treaties like the OECD Convention of 1998 and the UN Convention against Corruption of 2005 are the formal international law manifestations of the norm. These treaties, among other things, require signatory nations to pass domestic laws creating civil and criminal liability for the payment of foreign bribes. At the same time, international financial institutions like the World Bank and the regional development banks made anti-corruption initiatives a priority and a condition for sponsored development projects.[34] In this way, soft law complemented hard law on the international level.

The germinal insight behind the global anti-corruption movement is that a corruption-free world order is a public good, analogous to a free-trade world without tariffs.[35] Public goods, however, are not so easy to achieve despite the common benefit of all, as witnessed by the centuries it took to establish a global near-free-trade regime and the threats to it even at present. This is in part because no one country can be assured of capturing enough of the benefit to make the first move to attain it. Moreover, the countries bearing the most costs for providing the public good have an incentive to defect out of resentment against others' free-riding. With specific respect to global anti-corruption, a government, despite

31 See ibid 18; James Wolfensohn, 'Address to the Board of Governors at the Annual Meetings of the World Bank and the International Monetary Fund' (1 October 1996).

32 Carnegie Endowment for International Peace Working Group on Corruption and Security, *Corruption: The Unrecognized Threat to International Security* (2014).

33 Ibid 3–4.

34 See Wolfensohn (n 31).

35 A public good is non-rivalrous (more than one person can consume the good at the same time) and non-excludable (i.e., non-payors for the good cannot be denied access to it). See generally Tyler Cowen, 'Introduction' in Tyler Cowen (ed), *Public Goods & Market Failures: A Critical Examination* (Transaction Publishers 1999) 1, 3–4. Paradigmatic examples of public goods are lighthouses and national defense. See R H Coase, 'The Lighthouse in Economics' (1974) 17 Journal of Law and Economics 357, 358.

its interest in combating corruption at home, has an incentive to defect from laws barring bribes in foreign countries paid by its own companies to secure lucrative international business contracts and resultant foreign revenues. Without the bribes, companies from other countries would obtain the contracts. The predictable outcome of this collective action problem is that any effort to build a global anti-corruption regime is doomed to failure. Yet this regime appears to be forming, presenting an interesting puzzle to be explained.

To summarize, Part 2 makes two important conceptual points about foreign anti-corruption laws. First, the oddity of laws outlawing *foreign* corruption as opposed to the obvious justification and ubiquity of *domestic* anti-corruption laws is often overlooked. The latter is intuitive; the former is not. Understanding the differing incentives between the two is essential to perceiving the puzzle and grasping our solution. Second, many people forget that for most of the post-World War II period, economists and policymakers viewed foreign corruption in developing and rebuilding states as something to be tolerated or even as a good thing. It is only with the end of the Cold War in the 1990s that a consensus has formed that corruption anywhere is bad, and that a corruption-free world is an achievable and desirable public good.

2 A history of the enactment and enforcement of foreign anti-corruption laws

2.1 Foreign policy and the genesis of the FCPA

The genesis of foreign anti-bribery law was the Watergate scandal in the United States. The notorious break-in to Democratic Party headquarters by operatives working for President Richard Nixon's reelection campaign was discovered to have been financed by secret slush funds. Further investigation into the Watergate scandal revealed that such funds were not limited to domestic political uses.[36] Specifically, investigations led to the discovery of US corporate slush funds used to finance bribes and contributions to officials and politicians in foreign countries for favorable business treatment.[37] These disclosures spurred a worldwide backlash against American corporations and the evils of US-led market capitalism that damaged US allies and empowered its adversaries during the Cold War. The FCPA emerged as an instrument of American foreign policy in response to this backlash.

In 1973, the US Senate's Watergate hearings revealed that American corporations had made illegal payments into the President's reelection campaign, leading the SEC Director of Enforcement to launch an inquiry into how companies recorded these payments. The inquiry found that companies had intentionally

36 See Stanley Sporkin, 'The Worldwide Banning of Schmiergold: A Look at the Foreign Corrupt Practices Act on its Twentieth Birthday' (1998) 18 Northwestern Journal of International Law and Business 269, 272.

37 See ibid 271–272.

concealed the payments by falsifying their financial statements.[38] An expanded SEC investigation then found that not only were the mislabeled accounts used for making illegal political contributions, but they were also being used to make other illegal payments, including bribes to foreign officials.[39] In addition to the SEC's investigation, Congress itself convened a series of public hearings on the matter, most notably the Senate Foreign Relations Subcommittee on Multinational Corporations, chaired by Senator Frank Church.[40] The Church Committee ultimately discovered that 'over 400 US companies admitted making questionable or illegal payments in excess of $300 million to foreign government officials, politicians and political parties.'[41]

These revelations embarrassed prominent US companies and soured sensitive US relationships and negotiations with foreign nations. Lockheed Corporation, for example, was embroiled in scandal following revelations that it had bribed numerous foreign politicians and members of government, including officials in Italy and Japan, to win procurement contracts.[42] The Lockheed revelations brought down the government of Prime Minister Tanaka in Japan.[43] 'Both Chilean President Allende and Venezuelan President Perez broke off talks with US officials on compensation for nationalized property when they learned of corporate payments [by US companies].'[44] Congress and the American public were concerned that the disclosures not only revealed the excesses of US capitalism but

38 Ibid 271 ('The political contributions were disguised on the contributing corporations' books and records. At no time did the books and records disclose that an illegal political contribution had been made. This was not an oversight; it was the product of careful planning by top corporate officials.').

39 Securities and Exchange Commission, *Report of the Securities and Exchange Commission on Questionable and Illegal Corporate Payments and Practices* (1976) 3. ('The staff discovered falsifications of corporate financial records, designed to disguise or conceal the source and application of corporate funds misused for illegal purposes, as well as the existence of secret 'slush funds' disbursed outside the normal financial accountability system.').

40 'Political Contribution to Foreign Governments: Hearings Before the Subcomm. on Multinational Corp. of the S. Comm. On For. Rels.', 94th Congress 2 (1975) (statement of Sen. Frank Church, Chairman, Subcomm. On Multinational Corp) ('Church Committee').

41 H.R. Rep. No. 95–640, 4 (1977) (Conf. Rep.) (further noting that those acknowledging illegal or questionable payments included 117 companies in the Fortune 500).

42 The disclosures were particularly newsworthy because Lockheed was the beneficiary of a $200 million bail-out by the US government in 1971 to avoid bankruptcy. See Anthony Sampson, 'Lockheed's Foreign Policy: Who, in the End, Corrupted Whom?' *NY Magazine* (15 March 1976) 53, 56, 58. Additional allegations involved payments to ruling-party politicians in West Germany, and to members of the Saudi and Dutch royal families.

43 See 'Foreign Payments Disclosure: Hearing on H.R. 15481 and H.R. 13870 Before the Subcomm. on Consumer Prot. and Fin. of the H. Comm. on Interstate and Foreign Com.', 94th Congress 2 (1976) (statement of Rep. John M Murphy, Chairman, Subcomm. On Consumer Prot. and Fin.).

44 'Unlawful Corporate Payments Act of 1977: Hearing on H.R. 3815 Before the Subcomm. on Consumer Prot. and Fin. of the H. Comm. On Interstate and Foreign Com.', 95th Congress 169 (1977) (statement of Rep. Michael Harrington).

also risked undermining foreign allies facing Communist opposition.[45] Congress enacted the FCPA to address and neutralize the adverse foreign policy consequences of US companies' payments of foreign bribes.

The FCPA targets both bribery and bad accounting. It prohibits bribes—the giving of anything of value with a corrupt intent—paid to foreign officials as well as the failure to keep books and records that accurately reflect the disposition of company assets.[46] The FCPA is unprecedented: it is the first law to criminalize the payment of bribes to officials in a *foreign* country. It is remarkable that the US chose to act unilaterally to prohibit what was widely known to be a common practice worldwide; indeed, foreign bribes were treated as tax-deductible business expenses in many countries. It was, accordingly, a problem that the US could not solve alone.[47] Even more remarkable is the willingness of the US government to act despite the fact that doing so threatened to put American businesses at a disadvantage in competing for lucrative international business contracts.[48] Why would elected representatives disregard domestic business interests in a quixotic effort to prevent bribery in foreign countries?

45 See Church Committee (n 40).

46 15 US Code ss 78m, 78dd-1, 78dd-2, 78dd-3, 78ff (2018). An important difference between the two parts of the statute is that the bribery aspect requires intent, but the books and records part is strict liability. Because the two often go together in practice, however, the books and records aspect of the statute eventually became a tool of prosecutors, excusing them of the difficulty of proving intent.

47 See, e.g., 'Protecting the Ability of the United States to Trade Abroad: Hearing on S. Res. 265 Before the Subcomm. on Int'l Trade of the S. Comm. on Fin.', 94th Congress (1975) (statement of Sen. Abraham Ribicoff, Chairman, Subcomm. On Int'l Trade) ('[A]nybody who knows what is going on worldwide knows this is a worldwide phenomenon; that business houses and business corporations in every nation of the world are paying under the table and are guilty of bribes but none of them paint them this way.'); 'Lockheed Bribery: Hearing Before the S. Comm. on Banking, Hous., and Urban Affairs', 94th Congress 27–28 (1975) (statement of D J Haughton, Chairman of the Board, Lockheed Aircraft Corp.) (acknowledging payments to foreign officials but emphasizing that 'so did everyone else who was at all knowledgeable about foreign sales' because 'it appeared to be necessary to make such payments in order to compete successfully in many parts of the world.').

48 See, e.g., 'Abuses of Corporate Power: Hearing Before the Subcomm. on Priorities and Econ. in Gov't of the Joint Econ. Comm.', 94th Congress 153–154 (1976) (statement of Robert S Ingersoll, Deputy Secretary of State) ('There is widespread recognition in the Congress that such unilateral action [on corporate payment of foreign bribes] would put US companies at a serious disadvantage in the export trade.'); 'Unlawful Corporate Payment Acts of 1977: Hearing on H.R. 3815 and H.R. 1602 Before the Subcomm. on Consumer Prot. and Fin. of the H. Comm. on Interstate and Foreign Commerce', 95th Congress 164 (1977) (statement of Rep. John E. Moss, Member, H. Comm. on Interstate and Foreign Commerce) (emphasizing that 'to think that no loss of business would occur in every instance would be unrealistic. Can we allow this to occur? Yes, if that is the small price we must pay to return morality to corporate practice.'); ibid 187–188 (statement of W Michael Blumenthal, US Secretary of the Treasury) ('[A]ll right, we will be at a slight competitive disadvantage and we will all sleep better for it.').

The initial enactment of the FCPA reflected the temporary subordination of business interests to foreign diplomacy and balance-of-power calculations during the fraught times of the Cold War. Senator Church made the point crystal clear in the opening statement of his subcommittee's investigation: 'This subcommittee is concerned with the foreign policy consequences of these payments by US-based multinational corporations.'[49] Underscoring the point, the Senator read an extended quotation into the record from a book emphasizing the Communist dogma that 'capitalism breeds corruption' and emphasizing that 'the elimination of corruption has been advanced as the main justification for military takeovers.'[50] Over the course of many hearings in both Houses of Congress focusing on foreign bribes paid by US corporations, speakers repeatedly emphasized that foreign bribery weakened US allies and strengthened US enemies.[51] Bribery was linked to Communist Party gains in Italy,[52] the fall of pro-US governments in Honduras and Libya,[53] and political difficulties facing allied governments in

49 Church Committee (n 40). See also Mike Koehler, 'The Story of the Foreign Corrupt Practices Act,' 73 Ohio State Law Journal 929, 932–943 (2012) (describing how foreign policy concerns motivated the passage of the FCPA).

50 Church Committee (n 40) 2–3 (quoting Gunnar Myrdal, Asian Drama: An Inquiry into the Poverty of Nations (1968)).

51 See, e.g., 'Abuses of Corporate Power: Hearing Before the Subcomm. on Priorities and Econ. in Gov't of the Joint Econ. Comm.', 94th Congress 154 (1976) (statement of Robert S Ingersoll, Deputy Secretary of State) ('Preliminary results have included serious political crises in friendly countries ... Many foreign commentators and opinion makers have expressed concern about the effects of US processes in their countries and suggested that the United States has a responsibility to take into account the interests of its allies when it is cleaning up its own house.'); 'The Activities of American Multinational Corporations Abroad: Hearing Before the Subcomm. on Int'l Econ. Policy of the H. Comm. on Int'l Relations', 94th Congress 22–23 (1975) (statement of Mark B Feldman, Deputy Legal Advisor, Department of State) ('The head of a friendly government has been removed from office and other friendly leaders have come under political attack [because of bribery revelations].').

52 'The Activities of American Multinational Corporations Abroad: Hearing Before the Subcomm. on Int'l Econ. Policy of the H. Comm. on Int'l Relations', 94th Congress 1–2 (1975) (statement of Rep. Robert N C Nix, Chairman, Subcomm. on Int'l Econ. Policy) (noting among other things that 'the Communist party is using the fact of multinational bribery in Italy against the political friends of the United States.').

53 Ibid 4 (statement of Rep. Stephen J Solarz, Member, Subcomm. on Int'l Econ. Policy) ('One government has already been toppled and political parties in several other countries have been seriously compromised.'). In the words of Senator Church: 'There is also little doubt that widespread corruption serves to undermine those moderate democratic and pro-free-enterprise governments which the United States has traditionally sought to foster and support. Several oil companies testified before the subcommittee that they had made huge political contributions in Italy and Korea, for example. They claimed to be supporting the democratic forces who are friendly to foreign capital in those countries, but in fact, they were subverting the basic democratic processes of those two countries by making illegal contributions and were, at the same time, providing the radical left with its strongest election issue. The large and steady gains made by the Italian Communist Party in recent elections are due in no small part to the fact that it is believed to be the only non-corrupt political force in the

Japan, the Netherlands, and elsewhere around the world.[54] An anti-corruption backlash leading to the downfall of friendly governments is an omnipresent trope in the legislative history. Senator Church summed it up nicely: 'The Communist bloc chortles with glee at the sight of corrupt capitalism.'[55]

Given these broad geostrategic aims, the statute Congress and President Carter passed was not the narrow corrective to corporate accounting and book-keeping favored by the more business-conscious SEC.[56] In outlawing the payment of foreign bribes, Congress went further, guided more by the Church Committee's Cold War strategic vision than the SEC's original investigation and its narrower corporate responsibility and sound business ethics aims. By criminalizing the payment of foreign bribes, Congress sought to make a strong statement against American instigation of corruption abroad. The ultimate aim was to buttress friendly governments and to deny succor and rhetorical force to Communist movements around the world that had zeroed in on US corporate payments to fuel anti-capitalist, anti-American sentiment. The FCPA, in other words, was a political weapon of the Cold War, wielded in the interests of national security.

2.2 Business interests intervene

US businesses with foreign operations and their lobbyists could not stop the FCPA from being adopted given the perceived national security interests behind the statute's enactment. Indeed, they hardly tried. The American Chamber of

---

country, while the other parties are seen as the handmaidens of foreign and domestic financial interests. … [Such practices] only serve to discredit them and the United States. Ultimately, they create the conditions which bring to power political forces that are no friends of ours, whether a Quaddafi in Libya, or the Communists in Italy.''Protecting the Ability of the United States to Trade Abroad: Hearing on S. 265 Before the Subcomm. on Int'l Trade of the S. Comm. on Fin.', 94th Congress 9 (1975) (statement of Sen. Frank Church, Chairman, Subcomm. on Multinational Corp.).

54 'Foreign Payments Disclosure: Hearing on H.R. 15481 and H.R. 13870 Before the Subcomm. on Consumer Prot. and Fin. of the H. Comm. on Interstate and Foreign Commerce', 94th Congress 2 (1976) (statement of Rep. John M Murphy, Chairman, Subcomm. on Consumer Prot. and Fin.) ('The foreign policy implications for the United States are staggering and in some cases, perhaps irreversible. Payments by Lockheed alone may well have advanced the Communist cause in Italy. In Japan, a mainstay of our foreign policy in the Far East, the government is reeling as a consequence of such payments. On August 16, former Prime Minister Tanaka was indicted on charges of accepting $1.7 million from Lockheed. And most recently, the monarchy in the Netherlands has been rocked by the Lockheed scandal. All of this lends substantial credence to the suspicions by extremists that US businesses operating in their country have a corrupting influence on their political systems.').

55 122 Cong. Rec. 12, 604–605 (1976) (statement of Sen. Church).

56 'The Activities of American Multinational Corporations Abroad: Hearing Before the Subcomm. on Int'l Econ. Policy of the H. Comm. on Int'l Relations', 94th Congress 189 (1975) (statement of Philip A Loomis, Jr., Commissioner, SEC) ('[O]ur obligation … is to obtain disclosure of information which is material to investors in the buying and selling of securities in the company. We are not here to police the morality of American industry as such, but the responsibilities of disclosures to investors.').

Commerce and a special committee of the New York City Bar did testify that while bribery of foreign officials was abhorrent, new legislation was not necessary because existing law was sufficient to deal with the problem.[57] Although some members of Congress were sympathetic to this view,[58] and others were concerned that unilateral action would put US businesses at a competitive disadvantage,[59] these arguments could not overcome the momentum in favor of the statute. Given that its preferred outcome of preventing the FCPA from being enacted was politically impossible, the business community took action toward a second-best outcome: pursuing the twin goals of a level playing field internationally and lax enforcement domestically.

The US Government's efforts to export the new foreign anti-corruption norm coincided with the conception of the FCPA. As early as 1975, the Senate passed a unanimous resolution urging the Executive Branch to raise anti-corruption initiatives in negotiations with trading partners.[60] The US did try to include anti-corruption measures in the Tokyo round of General Agreement on Tariff and Trade (GATT) negotiations (1973–1979), but the other GATT nations balked at treating corruption as a trade issue.[61] The Senate Report on the FCPA also urged the Executive Branch to coordinate anti-bribery efforts with other capital-exporting nations through targeted multilateral or bilateral international agreements, although it did not make FCPA enactment contingent upon simultaneous

57 See 'Foreign Corrupt Practices and Domestic and Foreign Investment Disclosure: Hearing on S. 305 Before S. Comm. on Banking, Hous., and Urban Affairs', 95th Congress 185–186 (1977) (statement of J Jefferson Staats, Staff Associate, Chamber of Commerce of the United States) ('The Chamber condemns the payment ... of bribes ... [But] US securities law already requires public disclosure of material payments ... It is important to note, as well, that misrepresentations to the Internal Revenue Service of certain payments may constitute violations of the Internal Revenue Code. The Chamber, therefore, is not convinced that new legislation is needed to confront the problems caused by questionable overseas business payments.'); 'Foreign Payments Disclosure: Hearing on H.R. 15481 and H.R. 13870 Before the Subcomm. on Consumer Prot. and Fin. of the H. Comm. on Interstate and Foreign Commerce', 94th Congress 178 (1976) (statement of William F Kennedy, Co-Chairman, Special Comm. on Foreign Payments, Ass'n of the Bar of the City of New York) ('There was never a lack of law applicable to the situation. What there was, was a lack of law enforcement.').

58 'Foreign Payments Disclosure: Hearing on H.R. 15481 and H.R. 13870 Before the Subcomm. on Consumer Prot. and Fin. of the H. Comm. on Interstate and Foreign Commerce', 94th Congress 147 (1976) (statement of Rep. Michael Harrington) ('I feel very strongly that the existing legislation is adequate.').

59 'Protecting the Ability of the United States to Trade Abroad: Hearing on S. 265 Before the Subcomm. on International Trade of the Securities Commission on Finance', 94th Congress 1 (1975) (statement of Sen. Abraham Ribicoff, Chairman, Subcomm. on Int'l Trade) (noting that once American companies were barred from making payoffs, 'the business that they should be getting would be going to foreign competitors who were undertaking the same practices').

60 S. Res. 265, 94th Congress (1975).

61 See Peter W Schroth, 'The United States and the International Bribery Convention' (2002) 50 American Journal of Comparative Law 593, 596–597.

international or foreign legal initiatives.[62] The Executive Branch focused its ensuing global mobilization efforts in the 1970s on the OECD and the UN's Economic and Social Council (ECOSOC).[63] Neither initiative bore much fruit. The OECD did agree to include a general anti-bribery statement in the 1976 Declaration on International Investment and Multinational Enterprises.[64] But the other OECD countries would go no further because they did not share the United States' unique perception of foreign bribery as a national security threat. Rather, they continued to view it as an ordinary cost of doing business in the developing world. The UN initiatives did not even get as far as a statement of general principles due to Cold War divisions and disagreements about how to deal with apartheid in South Africa.

Unsure of the prospects for leveling the playing field by diplomacy or public international law, the US business community also pursued private initiatives to spread the foreign anti-corruption norm within the global business community. As the US moved to adopt the FCPA, the Paris-based International Chamber of Commerce (ICC), a business association promoting international trade and investment, promulgated a set of anti-bribery commitments that could be incorporated into cross-border contracts at the urging of US business interests.[65] Because the contractual language was not mandatory, however, the best the ICC could do was encourage its members to opt in to anti-bribery commitments. Non-US businesses, aware of their advantages vis-à-vis their US competitors, routinely chose not to make the commitment.

By 1981, the failure to mobilize a multilateral anti-bribery coalition that would relieve perceived disadvantages for US businesses abroad caused the General Accounting Office (GAO) to issue a report entitled *The Impact of the FCPA on US Business*.[66] The report was based on a survey of 250 of the largest US companies and offered strong critiques of both the FCPA's accounting and substantive provisions.[67] The central criticism of the substantive anti-bribery

62 S. Rep. No. 94–1031, 6 (1976).

63 See Schroth (n 61) 597–598.

64 OECD, *Declaration on International Investment and Multilateral Enterprises* (25 May 2011) <http://www.oecd.org/daf/inv/investment-policy/oecddeclarationoninternationalinvestmentandmultinationalenterprises.htm> accessed 1 June 2020.

65 International Chamber Commerce on Corporate Responsibility and Anti-Corruption, *ICC Rules on Combating Corruption* (2011). The mechanism for contractual incorporation was the ICC's form Anti-Corruption Clause. See International Chamber Commerce on Corporate Responsibility and Anti-Corruption, *ICC Anti-Corruption Clause* (2012).

66 US Government Accounting Office, B-198581, Impact of Foreign Corrupt Practices Act on US Business (1981) <http://archive.gao.gov/d46t13/114503.pdf> accessed 1 June 2020.

67 The basic criticism of the accounting provisions was that they were vague and generated excessive and inefficient compliance costs. About 55% of the respondents reported that their efforts to comply with the Act have resulted in costs that were greater than the benefits received. About half of these respondents believed the cost burden increased their accounting and auditing costs by 11–35%. Another 20% estimated these costs increased by more than 35%. See ibid 6.

provision was that it left American business at a competitive disadvantage to foreign competitors:

> More than 30 percent of the questionnaire respondents engaged in foreign business reported they had lost overseas business as a result of the act. In addition, while more than 70 percent of the questionnaire respondents believed the act has been effective in reducing questionable foreign payments by American companies, over 60 percent of the respondents perceived that, assuming all other conditions were similar, American companies could not successfully compete against companies abroad that are not subject to the same prohibitions.[68]

The ultimate recommendation of the report was to push for 'an effective international ban against bribery,' emphasizing that most respondents 'believed an international agreement would strengthen America's competitive position abroad.'[69] Noting that efforts at the United Nations had failed for four years in a row, the report closed by urging the President to make 'a strong international anti-bribery agreement' a priority as well as recommending that Congress demand an annual report of progress made toward that end.[70] Nevertheless, foreign governments—lacking a coherent domestic interest group in favor of banning foreign bribery and, in many cases, harboring a clutch of companies that happily paid foreign bribes to win business—continued to resist.[71]

Despite the lack of success on leveling the playing field, American businesses did manage to achieve the second part of their second-best outcome: minimal *enforcement* of the FCPA within the US itself. In the early years of the statute, neither the SEC nor the DOJ aggressively pursued cases involving foreign bribes.[72] Although the SEC did pursue enforcement actions under the FCPA's accounting provisions, the agency brought only one action under the substantive anti-bribery

68 'The Impact of the Foreign Corrupt Practices Act on US Business: Hearing Before the Subcomm. on Int'l Fin. and Monetary Policy and Subcomm. on Sec. of the S. Com. on Banking, Hous., and Urban Affairs', 97th Congress 4 (1981) (statement of Donald L Scantlebury, Div. Dir. and Chief Accountant of GAO Accounting and Fin. Mgmt. Div.).

69 Ibid 45.

70 Ibid 48.

71 The American companies pointed out that some US trading partners have explicitly encouraged such bribes by permitting businesses to claim them as tax-deductible business expenses. S. Rep. No. 105–277 (1998) 2. The Commerce Department has stated that it has learned of significant allegations of bribery by foreign firms in approximately 180 international commercial contracts since mid-1994, contracts that were valued at nearly $80 billion. See ibid.

72 See Department of Justice, 'Related Enforcement Actions' <http://www.justice.gov/criminal-fraud/related-enforcement-actions> accessed 1 June 2020. Securities Exchange Commission, 'SEC Enforcement Actions: FCPA Cases' <http://www.sec.gov/spotlight/fcpa/fcpa-cases.shtml> accessed 1 June 2020.

provisions in the statute's first ten years.[73] Likewise, the DOJ reported few bribery investigations, bringing only those cases that involved glaring violations of the law—substantial cash payments to senior foreign officials.[74] By the late 1980s, enforcement was effectively as moribund as any serious effort to forge an international agreement against bribery.[75]

Indeed, the domestic enforcement situation had reached such a nadir that business interests grew hopeful in 1988 for a repeal of the FCPA.[76] Although Congress did not have the stomach to repeal the decade-old foreign anti-corruption statute, it did lighten the Act's burden by permitting specified foreign payments and providing an affirmative defense for 'reasonable and bona fide expenditures.'[77] At the same time, Congress doubled down on efforts to build a coalition of governments opposed to foreign bribery, expressly charging the President to 'pursue the negotiation of an international agreement, among the members of the Organization of [sic] Economic Cooperation and Development, to govern persons from those countries concerning acts prohibited' under the FCPA.[78] Towards this end, Congress required the President to report back annually on his efforts, as the GAO report had recommended in 1981.[79]

Consequently, the US approached the OECD in early 1989 to propose the creation of an *ad hoc* group to work towards creating a 'binding obligation by members to enact … penalties to punish their nationals and corporations who commit bribery in connection with [international commercial] transactions.'[80] These efforts ultimately bore fruit in the OECD's Convention on Combating

73 See Securities Exchange Commission (n 72). The SEC was somewhat more active in enforcing the accounting provisions. Over the same ten-year period, the SEC pursued 109 injunctive actions and 24 administrative proceedings under the accounting provisions.

74 See Adam Fremantle and Sherman Katz, 'The Foreign Corrupt Practices Act Amendments of 1988' (1989) 23 International Law 755, 759.

75 See Elizabeth K Spahn, 'Implementing Global Anti-Bribery Norms: From the Foreign Corrupt Practices Act to the OECD Anti-Bribery Convention to the UN Convention Against Corruption' (2013) 23 Indiana International and Comparative Law Review 1, 1–6 (describing the United States' push for international anti-bribery efforts); Department of Justice, 'Related Enforcement Actions' (n 72).

76 Brewster (n 14) 1656–1657.

77 Foreign Corrupt Practices Act Amendments of 1988 s 5003(c), Pub. L. No. 100–418, 102 Stat. 1107, 1415 (codified as amended at 15 US Code s 78dd-1 (2018)). See also Fremantle and Katz (n 74) 767 ('Domestic concerns engaged in foreign business appear to have obtained in the 1988 amendments a modicum of relief from the more onerous of the anti-bribery provisions of the FCPA.').

78 Foreign Corrupt Practices Act Amendments of 1988 s 5003(d).

79 Ibid.

80 See OECD, 'United States Proposal on the Issue of Illicit Payments' (OECD Doc. C(89)49, 22 March 1989) 2 (noting goal of creating 'comparable national legal standards governing bribery in conducting international commercial transactions').

Bribery of Foreign Public Officials in International Business Transactions (the 'OECD Convention') discussed in greater detail below.[81]

2.3 Multilateral treaties and ensuing domestic enactments

In 1994, the OECD Council adopted the 'Recommendation on Bribery in International Business Transactions,' a US-backed proposal urging member countries to take 'effective measures to deter, prevent and combat the bribery of foreign public officials in connection with international business transactions' and to coordinate on bringing their domestic laws into conformity with respect to the bribery of foreign public officials.[82] The Recommendation led to the establishment of the Working Group on Bribery in International Business Transactions. The Working Group, in turn, published a 'Revised Recommendation on Combating Bribery in International Business Transactions' in 1997.[83] In this stronger initiative, the OECD Council moved to outlaw foreign bribery in an 'effective and co-ordinated manner' by opening negotiations on 'an international convention to criminalize bribery.'[84]

Pursuant to the Revised Recommendation, the OECD Convention was adopted and opened for signature by the end of 1997.[85] The OECD Convention calls on all parties to make it a crime:

> for any person intentionally to offer, promise or give any undue pecuniary or other advantage, whether directly or through intermediaries, to a foreign public official, for that official or for a third party, in order that the official act or refrain from acting in relation to the performance of official duties, in order to obtain or retain business or other improper advantage in the conduct of international business.[86]

It further calls on all adopting parties to assert *territorial* jurisdiction broadly to enforce the criminal prohibition, to the extent allowed by national legal and

81 OECD, *OECD Convention and Related Documents* <https://www.oecd.org/daf/anti-bribery/ConvCombatBribery_ENG.pdf> accessed 1 June 2020.

82 OECD, 'Recommendation of the Council on Bribery in International Business Transactions' (OECD Doc. C(94)75/FINAL, 11 July 1994) 2–3.

83 OECD, 'Revised Recommendation of the Council on Combating Bribery in International Business Transactions' (OECD Doc. C(97)123/FINAL, 23 May 1997).

84 Ibid 2–3. The agreed common elements of criminal legislation and related actions were outlined in the Annex to the Recommendation. See ibid 7–9.

85 OECD Convention. To date, the Convention has been adopted by 43 parties, including 34 OECD member countries and nine non-member countries including Argentina, Brazil, Bulgaria, Colombia, Latvia, Russia, and South Africa. For the status of the convention, see OECD, 'OECD Convention on Combating Bribery of Foreign Public Officials in International Business Transactions: Ratification Status as of May 2018' <http://www.oecd.org/daf/anti-bribery/WGBRatificationStatus.pdf> accessed 1 June 2020.

86 OECD, *OECD Convention and Related Documents* (n 81) 7.

constitutional principles.[87] It also directs extension of extraterritorial jurisdiction with respect to nationals consistent with applicable national laws.[88] The US ratified the OECD Convention and promptly enacted domestic legislation to implement the treaty.[89]

This required the US Congress to amend the FCPA to extend its jurisdictional hook—an event with significant consequences for subsequent trends in the statute's enforcement. First, the amendments provided for jurisdiction over the acts of US businesses and nationals in furtherance of unlawful payments that take place wholly outside the US.[90] Second, the amendments clarified that territorial jurisdiction could be asserted over foreign actors as long as the chain of transactions touched and concerned the territory of the US.[91] Third, the amendments eliminated a pre-existing disparity in penalties between US nationals and foreign nationals employed by or acting as agents of US companies.[92] The latter had formerly been subject only to civil penalties.[93] The Act abolished this restriction and subjected all employees or agents of US businesses to both civil and criminal penalties, regardless of their nationality.[94]

87 Ibid 16.

88 Ibid 16–17.

89 International Anti Bribery and Fair Competition Act 1998, Pub. L. No. 105–366, 112 Stat. 3302.

90 OECD, *United States: Review of Implementation of the Convention and 1997 Recommendation* (1999) 13. ('Prior to its amendment in 1998, the FCPA asserted only territorial jurisdiction. In light of the requirements of the Convention, the FCPA has added a jurisdiction basis for acts committed abroad by US nationals and businesses (nationality jurisdiction).') Even before its amendment, it was not necessary, however, that the payment, gift, offer, or authorization itself have taken place in the United States, only that an act in furtherance have taken place. Thus, if two officials of a corporation, at least one of whom was in the United States, corresponded (by mail, fax, or email) or spoke with each other over the telephone concerning a planned unlawful payment, that would be sufficient for the United States to assert jurisdiction, even if the payment itself, the official to be bribed, the person actually paying the bribe, and the money to be used to pay the bribe are all outside the territory of the United States. See ibid 13–15. This exercise of extraterritorial jurisdiction over US businesses and nationals for unlawful conduct abroad was believed to be consistent with US legal and constitutional principles. Specifically, Congress's power was justified under the constitutional grants of power to Congress to 'regulate Commerce with foreign Nations' and to 'define and punish ... Offenses against the Law of Nations.' US Constitution art 1, s 8, cl. 3, 10.

91 The United States interprets 'territory' broadly. It includes the actual territorial boundaries of the 50 States, as well as territories, possessions, and commonwealths. In addition, it includes areas within its territorial waters, aboard ships and airplanes flying under its flag, and aboard aircraft en route to the United States. The 1998 amendments expanded the FCPA to cover 'any person.' For non-US nationals and non-US companies, the amended FCPA requires that the person to be prosecuted actually have committed an act in furtherance of a bribe within the US. See OECD, *United States: Review of Implementation of the Convention and 1997 Recommendation* (n 90) 13–14.

92 International Anti Bribery and Fair Competition Act 1998, s 3.

93 See 15 US Code s 78ff(c)(2)(A) (1994) (current version at 15 US Code s 78ff(c)(2) (2018)).

94 15 US Code s 78ff(c)(2) (2018).

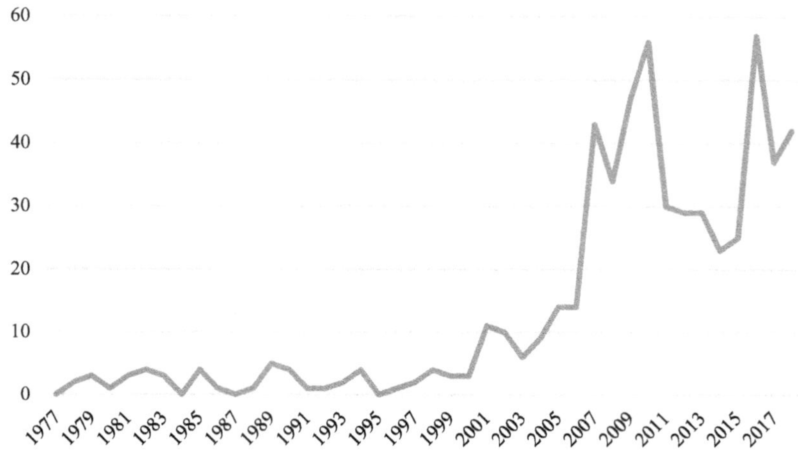

Figure 3.1 FCPA enforcement actions by year.

The ratification of the OECD Convention led to a spurt of national enactments not just in the United States but also in all signatory states. These national statutes, however, remained largely dormant for several more years outside of the United States.[95] The lack of enforcement was due to the same concern that US companies had expressed when the FCPA was enacted: business interests in the relevant states perceived that strictly enforcing the prohibition on bribes would disadvantage their efforts to obtain lucrative international business contracts. Governments were receptive to these concerns until very recently. As with enactment, the United States took the lead in the new trend toward enforcement of foreign anti-corruption laws, as section 2.4 explains.

2.4 A new era of FCPA enforcement

As described above, although the US adopted the FCPA in 1977, enforcement was minimal for its first several decades. According to a database of FCPA enforcement actions maintained by Stanford University, from 1977 through 2001, there was a total of 52 FCPA enforcement actions.[96] Between 2001 and 2018, however, there were 516.[97] Figure 3.1 below demonstrates this graphically. Not only have the numbers of enforcement actions increased, so too has the size of settlements to those actions.

95 See text at n 148.

96 Arthur and Toni Rembe Rock Center for Corporate Governance, 'DOJ and SEC Enforcement Actions per Year' *FCPA Clearinghouse* (2015) <http://fcpa.stanford.edu/statistics-analytics.html> accessed 1 June 2020.

97 Ibid.

In other words, in the 18-year period since 2001, there have roughly been ten times as many enforcement actions as there were in the 24-year period prior to 2001. Not only has the frequency of FCPA enforcement actions increased, so too has the size of settlements to those actions. As Professor Mike Kohler has observed:

> The $1.8 billion in combined corporate fines, penalties and disgorgement in 2010 is most striking when compared to 2000 FCPA enforcement. In 2000, there was one FCPA enforcement action (by the SEC) with a total fine amount of $300,000. The past decade has thus witnessed a remarkable transformation—not as to the FCPA itself (the statute has not changed since 1998), but as to FCPA enforcement and theories of prosecution.[98]

Additionally, the pattern of US enforcement actions in the past several years has centered on *foreign* companies subject to FCPA jurisdiction under the post-OECD amendments by virtue of their operations or contacts with the United States. Stephen Choi and Kevin Davis reported that from 2004 through 2011, one-third of all resolved enforcement actions involved non-US companies.[99] They also found that the 'SEC and DOJ impose greater sanctions, all else equal, on foreign companies.'[100] Consistent with their analysis, a tally of the ten largest FCPA enforcement actions, as of September 2017, includes only three US companies versus two French companies, and one each from Sweden, Germany, Israel, the UK, and the Netherlands.[101] More recent data are in line with this trend: in 2016, one US company (Och-Ziff), one Israeli company (Teva Pharmaceuticals), and one Brazilian company (Odebrecht/Braskem) paid FCPA settlements on the scale of the payments made by the top ten settlements that Choi and Davis reported.[102] And on September 27, 2018, Petrobras, the Brazilian state-owned energy company, reached the largest bribe-paying settlement in history—$1.78 billion to be paid to US and Brazilian authorities, dwarfing the previous high of $800 million paid by the German company Siemens in 2008.[103] We will discuss

98 Mike Koehler, 'Big, Bold, And Bizarre: The Foreign Corrupt Practices Act Enters A New Era' (2011) 43 University of Toledo Law Review 99, 104.

99 Stephen J Choi and Kevin E Davis, 'Foreign Affairs and Enforcement of the Foreign Corrupt Practices Act' (2014) 11 Journal of Empirical Legal Studies 409, 412.

100 Ibid 440.

101 Richard L Cassin, 'Telia Tops Our New Top Ten List (After We Do Some Math)' (*FCPA Blog*, 22 September 2017) <http://www.fcpablog.com/blog/2017/9/22/telia-tops-our-new-top-ten-list-after-we-do-some-math.html> accessed 1 June 2020.

102 Richard L Cassin, 'Reconsidered: Odebrecht and Braskem Are on Our FCPA Top Ten List' (*FCPA Blog*, 29 December 2016) <http://www.fcpablog.com/blog/2016/12/29/reconsidered-odebrecht-and-braskem-are-on-our-fcpa-top-ten-l.html> accessed 1 June 2020.

103 Richard L Cassin, 'Petrobras Reaches $1.78 Billion FCPA Resolution' (*FCPA Blog*, 27 September 2018) <http://www.fcpablog.com/blog/2018/9/27/petrobras-reaches-178-billion-fcpa-resolution.html> 1 June 2020.

in greater detail in Part 3 the reasons for, and the ramifications of, this relatively recent trend in FCPA enforcement against foreign companies.

We believe that two factors explain the dramatic escalation in FCPA enforcement in 2001 and then in 2007. First, from a regulatory perspective, the passage of the OECD Convention and the amendments to the FCPA in its wake enhanced the legal instruments available for US authorities to prosecute foreign corruption and raised the issue's profile. In particular, the significant rise in FCPA prosecutions after 2007 was anchored in the expansive jurisdictional reach of the statute owing to the 1998 amendments that allowed US enforcement authorities to target the conduct of foreign companies, thereby sparing their superiors and themselves the political backlash that might come from markedly increased enforcement against US businesses. At the same time, the multilateral treaty obligated the other capital-exporting countries that signed it to enact their own foreign corruption laws, raising the possibility of a level playing field for US businesses at risk of FCPA prosecution. And if enactments by other countries did not necessarily mean enforcement, the DOJ and SEC no longer had to fear active interference by foreign governments and could even invoke treaty-based cooperation from them. Furthermore, having achieved the level playing field (at least on the books) that US business interests had lobbied for so strenuously, US enforcement authorities were emboldened to craft a more aggressive enforcement strategy. This shift in US enforcement culture was enhanced by the enactment of the Sarbanes-Oxley Act and the accompanying onset of greater demands for corporate compliance and regulatory oversight.[104]

Second, from a geopolitical perspective, just as Watergate almost three decades earlier triggered the enactment of the FCPA because of the discovery of the role illicit corporate money played in the scandal, increasing awareness of the centrality of illegal money in laundering the proceeds of drug and other criminal enterprises and in terrorist financing focused attention on the FCPA as a powerful instrument for disrupting illegal cash flows.[105] This was particularly true after the September 11th terrorist attacks, when US and other anti-terrorism authorities focused on the flow of money to terrorist networks.[106] Whether related to terrorism, drugs, or other crimes, illicit capital flows went through banks and were uncovered through an increased focus on anti-money laundering rules.[107] Money laundering is a first cousin of bribery and corruption—the funds used for bribery are frequently laundered through shell businesses or sham transactions akin to

104 Brewster (n 14) 1673–1676.

105 US Department of Justice and US Securities and Exchange Commission, *FCPA Resource Guide to the US Foreign Corrupt Practices Act* (2012).

106 Juan C Zuarate, *Treasury's War: The Unleashing of a New Era of Financial Warfare* (Public Affairs 2013) 7. ('After 11 September 2001, the United States unleashed a counter-terrorist financing campaign that reshaped the very nature of financial warfare. The Treasury Department waged an all-out offensive, using every tool in its toolbox to disrupt, dismantle, and deter the flows of illicit financing around the world.')

107 Ibid 8–12.

the circulatory system for money laundering. Investigators naturally uncovered evidence of bribery once they started looking harder at money laundering and capital flows to terrorists, drug cartels, and rogue states. Having examined in detail the history of the enactment and enforcement of the FCPA, we turn, in the next part, to theoretical explanations for the rise of foreign anti-corruption laws.

3 Contending theories of foreign anti-corruption laws

Prior work on the development of foreign anti-bribery laws can be divided into three general approaches. The first takes human rights norms as the prime source of foreign anti-corruption laws.[108] On this view, such laws are enacted to signify commitment to anti-corruption as a human or civil right. And, as with anti-discrimination law, enforcement of the anti-corruption norm occurs when the political and moral orders align to permit it.[109] Second, the 'realist' orientation focuses on the motivations of the states enacting and enforcing the legislation. The basic intuition is that a state will enact or enforce foreign anti-corruption laws when to do so is perceived to be in the state's national interest. Third, the 'institutionalist' approach shares with the human rights view the basic idea that anti-corruption is a public good that needs to be advanced. Institutionalists, however, focus explanatory leverage on the design and workings of institutions: (1) on the international level, multilateral treaties (like the OECD Convention) and financial organizations (like the World Bank) for achieving the public good; and (2) on the domestic level, national laws (like the US FCPA) and government agencies (like the SEC) and actors (like prosecutors).

All three explanations have much to contribute to understanding the history of the enactment and enforcement of foreign anti-corruption laws. Each explanation, however, fits only part of the story. Human rights-based theories may explain why some capital-exporting states might wish to regulate foreign corruption in poor, developing countries, but they cannot explain how this interest overcomes the public goods problem. Such theories also fail to explain prevailing patterns of enforcement. Why, for instance, has the enforcement of foreign anti-corruption laws accelerated so greatly since 2010, despite a worldwide retrenchment in international human rights activism and a countervailing trend toward political authoritarianism and inward-looking nativism among developed countries? Similarly, theories emphasizing rent-seeking may explain some aspects

108 See Spalding (n 12) 1385–1402.

109 To illustrate the analogy to anti-discrimination law, consider that the US civil rights revolution only happened after *Brown v. Board of Education*, 347 US 483 (1954), and the passage of the Civil Rights Act of 1964, despite that the relevant formal law—the Civil War Amendments to the US Constitution—were ratified in 1868. Notwithstanding an initial attempt at meaningful enforcement during Reconstruction, the United States was not ready to enforce the law on the books until a century later. Similarly, the enactment of the FCPA in 1977 did not result in meaningful widespread enforcement until 2000, after the end of the Cold War.

of enforcement such as the recent trend toward large FCPA settlements against foreign companies. But they fail to account for the timing of enactments and worldwide patterns of enforcement beyond the United States. Both human rights and rent-seeking accounts also fail to explain the FCPA's dormancy from 1977 to 2000. Finally, institutionalist theories help us to understand the process and formal mechanisms by which enactment and enforcement happen, but they do not tell us how the key institutions form their preferences. For that, we believe, a deeper understanding of the interests, incentives, and causal influence of interest groups is necessary.

3.1 Rights-based accounts

One leading theory of foreign anti-corruption laws hypothesizes human rights norms as the prime cause.[110] On this view, states are principally motivated by moral or altruistic aims. Rich nation-states know that corruption is corrosive not only to their own domestic political orders but also to those of other states, particularly poorer ones, and seek to eradicate corruption everywhere. This human rights orientation is shared and advanced by the World Bank and other global NGOs.[111] All other things being equal, a human rights theory would seem especially strong as an explanation for the *enactment* of domestic anti-corruption laws like the FCPA and multilateral anti-corruption treaties. Both are outcomes with high symbolic value and the potential to serve as focal points in reform efforts. In human rights accounts, business interests are characterized as profit-maximizing actors that the state needs to regulate, not the primary engines of anti-corruption norm enforcement, as we argue. Professor Spalding asserts, for instance, that tweaking the FCPA to ensure that its enforcement better aligns with human rights justice (e.g., paying fines forward to victims in developing countries) is a better path to 'holding corporations liable for overseas rights abuses' than the Alien Tort Statute.[112] He writes:

> What the world needs now is a federal statute that holds both US and foreign companies liable for overseas human rights abuses; a statute that contains an express congressional statement of extraterritorial application and rests on well-established principles of corporate liability ... That statue already exists. It is the US Foreign Corrupt Practices Act.[113]

110 See Murray and Spalding (n 12); Spalding (n 12) 1385–1402; Andrew Brady Spalding, 'The Irony of International Business Law: US Progressivism and China's New Laissez-Faire' (2011) 59 UCLA Law Review 354, 370–388.

111 See Brewster (n 14); Wolfensohn (n 30) 6.

112 Spalding (n 12) 1366–67.

113 Ibid 1367.

Professor Spalding is surely right that multinational corporations paying bribes is a part of the problem of global corruption. But our account frames corporations not as bad actors that need to be regulated. Rather, it focuses on how the transnational environment can align their interests to solve the public good problem. No company wants to pay bribes; they pay them because they fear that others will pay them instead and take their business.

3.2 Realist accounts

A second theory for the spread of foreign anti-corruption regulation focuses more squarely on patterns in *enforcement* of domestic laws, not just their enactment or the ratification of treaties. On this view, what is driving greater enforcement is not an altruistic commitment to furthering human rights abroad but rather rent-seeking by governments who prosecute and sanction bribe-paying firms.[114] The United States, in particular, has imposed very large sanctions on companies for alleged FCPA violations in the 21st century.[115] It and other countries that have recently become more aggressive about enforcement typically do not return moneys collected to the state in which bribes occurred, instead depositing them into their own treasuries.[116] This result suggests that the motive for prosecutions is not to advance the good of the country in which corruption took place but rather to levy a 'bad act' tax on companies in the enforcing state.

In terms of US FCPA enforcement, the targets of sanctions have increasingly been non-US companies based in capital-exporting countries engaged in activities related to the United States. This suggests an additional, nationalistic dimension to rent-seeking by US government agencies and prosecutors. This impression seems reinforced by the fact that often the connection of such activities to the United States has been exceedingly minimal.[117]

The trend to bigger fines against foreign companies—funds that are kept in the capital-exporting enforcement jurisdiction—appears to confirm the suspicion that growing foreign anti-bribery enforcement is not motivated by an altruistic desire to ameliorate the human rights conditions in capital-importing states. Professor Koehler suggests that the enforcement patterns indicate rent-seeking, pure and simple.[118] And Professors Choi and Davis frame a model explaining enforcement trends by primary reference to the national interests of the enforcing states.[119] Country *A* will enforce foreign bribery laws against Country *B*'s corporations if to do so is in Country *A*'s national interest. The state and its institutions are the focal point of both explanations. But the predictions of those who posit

114 See Choi and Davis (n 99) 414.
115 See ibid.
116 See ibid.
117 See, e.g., Cassin, 'Petrobras Reaches $1.78 Billion FCPA Resolution' (n 102).
118 Koehler (n 98) 129–131.
119 See Choi and Davis (n 99) 410, 419–428.

national interest or rent-seeking as the principal explanation for enforcement patterns do not line up with facts on the ground, as we shall see in part 4. Why, for instance, have the principal targets of the US government's largest FCPA investigations and settlements hailed from closely allied countries like the United Kingdom, Israel, and Germany? Why, by contrast, have Chinese companies not been subject to any FCPA sanctions until December 2018, and then only for a relatively small amount?

3.3 *Institutional accounts*

A third group of commentators emphasizes institutions over altruism, national interests, or rent-seeking to explain the spread of global anti-corruption measures. The key actors and variables are the US President, Congress, the SEC, the DOJ (particularly prosecutors), their foreign counterparts, domestic laws like the FCPA, and international treaties like the OECD Convention. Professor Rachel Brewster, for example, emphasizes 'international resonance' in describing how enactment of the FCPA inspired the OECD Convention, which in turn triggered an amendment to the FCPA enabling US prosecutors to pursue an '"international-competition neutral" enforcement strategy, investigating domestic corporations and their foreign rivals alike.'[120] Institutionalist explanations like Professor Brewster's focus on state actors and how collective action at the international level feeds back to the domestic level. Our account, by contrast, starts with private actors and their ability to influence law-making at the state level.

3.4 *Our interest-group model*

In this section, we invoke international relations theory to build our interest-group model to explain patterns in enactment and enforcement of foreign anti-corruption laws. The primary causal actors in our model are business interest groups—not states, international organizations of states, or non-governmental organizations. In our view, states are not the prime cause but rather the fora in which interest groups interact to achieve their preferences. With respect to a global anti-corruption norm, we focus on how it might be achieved not from the top-down by states and state actors, but from the bottom-up by the linked acts and preferences of business groups. We do not claim that state actors have no role. Rather, our central claim is that state action is motivated principally by private actors in each state—namely, the business lobby. But how do private interests motivate state actors? And how, once motivated by private actors, do states coordinate with each other? For answers to these questions, we turn to international relations theory—in particular, hegemonic stability theory and the concept of two-level games.

120 Brewster (n 14) 1612.

3.4.1 Hegemony to k-group theory

As noted above, freedom from official corruption in cross-border transactions has the character of a public good.[121] All participants in the international system—sovereign states and firms engaged in cross-border trade—would prefer to have the public good, but no state or firm has sufficient incentive to bring it about due to collective action and free-rider problems. If one state prevents its private companies from paying bribes to get lucrative international business contracts, the contracts (and any profits from them) will go to companies based in other states that permit bribe giving. Without the ability to coordinate and punish defectors, each individual participant has an incentive to continue to bribe, especially if doing so is perceived as a source of competitive advantage.

Nevertheless, despite the structural roadblocks posed by the collective-action and free-rider dynamics, public goods are in fact supplied in the international economic system. For example, the world order has realized advances in free trade, stable mediums of financial exchange, effective property rights enforceable across borders, and a host of other preconditions for stability and aggregate growth in the international economic realm. How is this so?

International relations theorists developed 'hegemonic stability theory' to explain the provision of public goods in the global economy.[122] Hegemonic stability theory focuses on the distribution of power.[123] The earliest versions of the theory argued that a single hegemonic state is necessary to ensure provision of a public good in the international economy, such as economic stability or free trade.[124] When a single superpower extracts sufficient benefit from international stability, it will expend effort to coordinate other states and tolerate occasional defections, thereby creating a stable international economic order.[125] Under the original articulation of hegemonic stability theory, the provisions of public goods sufficient to support international economic cooperation could be expected only under conditions of true hegemony, i.e., the presence of a single hegemonic state.[126]

121 See Coase (n 35) and accompanying text.

122 See Robert Gilpin, *The Political Economy of International Relations* (Princeton University Press 1987) 72–92 (articulating the core elements of hegemonic stability theory and responding to critics).

123 See ibid.

124 Charles P Kindleberger, *The World in Depression: 1929–1939* (University of California Press 1986) 298 (drawing parallels between the *Pax Britanica* and the *Pax Americana* to argue that a hegemonic power is necessary to overcome collective action problems among states).

125 See Gilpin (n 122) 74.

126 This raises the vexed question of how to measure and define hegemony. Theorists have offered definitions in absolute and relative terms focusing on whether one nation's GNP, volume of international trade, and volume of international borrowing and lending dominate all others or whether such measures predominate over others on a relative basis. For the purposes of this chapter, we take Transparency International's lead in presuming that a country's share of global exports is a serviceable benchmark for gauging its power in the global economy.

Later versions of hegemonic stability theory focused on the role of other non-hegemons in creating or supporting international economic stability.[127] These revisions to the theory drew upon Mancur Olson's insight that a small group of actors, numbering *k* where *k* > 1, may be able to overcome collective action and free-rider problems under two conditions.[128] First, each member of the 'k-group' must extract sufficient benefit from the public good to justify its investment in bringing the good about.[129] Second, each member of the k-group must know that its defection from the collective order would result in the failure of the good being produced.[130] Applying these insights to international relations, theorists argued that a small k-group of states could provide the necessary conditions for international economic cooperation just as well as a single hegemon could.[131]

For a time after the end of the Cold War, it was believed that the United States and the European Union had sufficient leverage in the world economy to constitute a k-group. In 2007, political scientist Daniel Drezner asserted that:

> [The United States and the European Union] are the only two entities that combine relatively large markets with relatively low vulnerability. As measured by aggregate size, the United States and the European Union both have economies over $10 trillion at the end of 2003. The American and European shares of global merchandise trade are more than twice that of any other 'candidate' great power. Using market exchange rates, both the United States and European Union are twice as large as Japan, the next biggest economy. When their market size is combined, the United States and the European Union are responsible for roughly 40 percent of global output, 41 percent of world imports, 59 percent of inward foreign direct investment, 78 percent of outward foreign direct investment, and 99 percent of global mergers and acquisitions.[132]

Presuming the validity of k-group theory and sufficient unity of interest and information, the United States and the European Union could together supply public goods in the global economic order based on Drezner's assessment of the state of

127 See Robert Keohane, *After Hegemony: Cooperation and Discord in the World Political Economy* (Princeton University Press 1984) 39, 46 (discussing the prospect for international economic coordination to arise among small groups of state actors in the absence of hegemony); David A Lake, 'Leadership, Hegemony, and the International Economy: Naked Emperor or Tattered Monarch with Potential?' (1993) 37 International Studies Quarterly 459, 467 (critiquing and extending hegemonic stability theory).

128 Mancur Olson, *The Logic of Collective Action* (Harvard University Press 1965) 33.

129 Ibid.

130 Ibid.

131 Duncan Snidal, 'The Limits of Hegemonic Stability Theory' (1985) 39 International Organization 579, 599 (modeling the possibility of collective action in the absence of hegemonic leadership).

132 Daniel W Drezner, *All Politics is Global: Explaining International Regulatory Regimes* (Princeton University Press 2007) 36.

play in 2007.[133] Unity of interest and information, however, may be issue specific. If so, because each great power must calculate its national interest with regard to each separate issue before deciding whether to cooperate, international regimes organized by k-group coalitions may be more fragmented than those created by hegemons.[134] Of course, the rise of China as a great economic power and the decline of the European Union in the 21st century throws into doubt prevailing assumptions about the sufficiency of the United States and the European Union to constitute a k-group. But it does not contradict the theory of the k-group as a means of providing a public good like an international anti-corruption regime. The question is whether China will join the k-group or spoil its effectiveness.

3.4.2 Two-level games

Coordination among states on the international plane, whether through a tightly focused k-group or a more general and looser multilateral cooperation, depends to a large extent on the scope of possible agreement by any state, which may, in turn, be constrained by domestic politics. Accordingly, an analytical tool that international relations theorists have used to model the forces at play in international deal making is the two-level game.[135] A state seeking to negotiate international agreement faces pressures at both the international and domestic levels simultaneously—a two-level game between the state and its domestic interest groups and among other states.[136]

The logic of the two-level game was originally applied to treaty negotiation where the negotiator for a state must deal with international counterparties (Level I) but must also ratify the agreement with his or her domestic constituency (Level II).[137] This analytic construct enabled theorists to define 'win-sets'—that is, a range of outcomes that could be both agreed among the international

133 See generally James D Morrow, 'Modeling the Forms of International Cooperation: Distribution Versus Information' (1994) 48 International Organization 387 (emphasizing problems of information and distribution in the formation of coalitions).

134 Daniel W Drezner, 'The Contradictions of Post-Crisis Global Economic Governance' in Manuela Moschella and Catherine Weaver (eds), *Handbook of Global Economic Governance: Players, Powers and Paradigms* (Routledge 2014) 345, 353 (summarizing literature and noting that increasing the number of relevant actors increases both transaction and bargaining costs as well as the possibility of a wider dispersion of preferences).

135 Robert D Putnam, 'Diplomacy and Domestic Politics: The Logic of Two-Level Games' (1988) 42 International Organization 427, 434.

136 Two-level games emphasize the role of domestic constituents, even in explaining international outcomes. At the national level, domestic groups pursue their interests by pressuring the government to adopt favorable policies, and politicians seek power by constructing coalitions among those groups. At the international level, national governments seek to maximize their own ability to satisfy domestic pressures, while minimizing the adverse consequences of foreign developments. See ibid.

137 Ibid 436.

counterparties at Level I and ratified by the domestic constituency at Level II.[138] This construct leads to a number of insights, including that the Level I negotiating position is largely determined by what is feasible at Level II.[139] A negotiator may have more success against his or her international counterparts if he or she can demonstrate very little 'deal-space' vis-à-vis the domestic constituency. And developments in domestic politics may expand or restrict the deal space in Level I. By contrast, and perhaps counterintuitively, the greater the ability of a negotiator to win approval at home, the more likely the negotiator can be pushed around by his or her counterparts internationally at Level I.[140] Moreover, it is theoretically possible that a state (say, the United Kingdom) might be moved by cross-cutting alliances between domestic interest groups (like UK businesses with operations in the United States and, therefore, subject to FCPA compliance) and a foreign state (say, the United States) to acquiesce to an international outcome (say, enforcement of its own foreign anti-corruption laws). Finally, the best sanction for deterring defection might be different in design if aimed at the specific domestic constituency most likely to militate for defection at Level II.[141]

3.4.3 Putting it all together

Our account has five parts, with the last two parts incorporating insights borrowed from the international relations theory concerning k-groups and two-level games. First, as soon as the FCPA was enacted in response to the exogenous shock of Watergate, US companies, realizing that repeal was a political impossibility, urged the US government to push *international* anti-corruption regulation to level the playing field.[142] US companies would be at a competitive disadvantage if their foreign rivals could pay bribes to win lucrative procurement, arms, and infrastructure contracts while they could not. If foreign companies, however, could be brought into the anti-bribery fold, then the disadvantage to US companies from the FCPA would be neutralized. At the same time, these same business interests lobbied for lax enforcement of the FCPA domestically.

Second, these lobbying efforts bore fruit in the OECD Convention of 1997. The capital-exporting states that signed the Convention passed implementing legislation as per their treaty obligations. At the same time, they did not make serious efforts to enforce these statutes on the books.[143] In the United States, Congress passed important amendments to the FCPA to implement the Convention including a very broad jurisdictional provision that extended coverage to foreign companies with minimal connections to the United States.

138 Ibid 437.
139 Ibid 442–443, 448.
140 Ibid 440.
141 Ibid 460 (noting 'the importance of targeting international threats, offers, and side payments with an eye towards their domestic incidence at home and abroad').
142 See text at n 120ff.
143 See text at n 148ff.

Third, the US government, particularly the DOJ, stepped up FCPA enforcement, especially after 9/11, as part of a renewed focus on the financial aspects of transnational crimes and national security threats. Because of the broad jurisdictional scope of the amended FCPA, some foreign companies doing business in the United States were also swept up into the greater FCPA enforcement dragnet, including UK, German, French, Israeli, and Brazilian companies. So far, our causal account is principally descriptive and in general agreement with realist, institutionalist, and altruist explanations. The next two parts are where we deploy international relations theory and diverge from existing accounts.

Fourth, these foreign companies, after being brought within the jurisdictional reach of the FCPA, supported, or acquiesced in, enforcement by their home countries of the foreign anti-corruption laws that had been enacted pursuant to the OECD Convention but left dormant. In other words, a two-level game played out, with the interests of foreign companies subject to FCPA jurisdiction aligned with the United States in ensuring enforcement of foreign anti-corruption laws in their home jurisdictions. This would level the playing field against ***their*** domestic and regional competitors who might not be subject to US FCPA enforcement. At the same time, the implicated foreign governments could, in theory, use the laws to reciprocate against US companies. But generally, US companies were more compliant with foreign anti-bribery laws, having had to live with FCPA compliance for a much longer time.

Fifth and finally, once companies from a k-group of leading countries—for instance, the US, the UK, Germany, France, and Brazil—can plead an inability to give bribes due to a real risk of enforcement of foreign anti-corruption laws in their home jurisdictions when they bid for international contracts in the developing world, the officials in those countries will be left with a difficult choice. Should they award contracts to top US, UK, German, French, or Brazilian companies who cannot offer bribes, or to competitors who can because their home countries do not have foreign anti-bribery laws or only minimally enforce them? In other words, the successful proliferation of a truly global anti-corruption regime depends upon the formation of a k-group of enforcing countries and multinational corporations with sufficient leverage to curtail the giving of bribes on the supply side. It is conceivable that as the k-group grows (e.g., to include other European countries, Japan, or Korea), a tipping point will be reached where potential bribe takers cannot justify taking inferior bids from bribe-paying companies for fear of exposing their bribe taking.

The wild card in our model remains China, which is not currently enforcing foreign anti-corruption laws. Due to its explosive economic growth, China and its companies may command a sufficient share of global capital exports to prevent the formation of a k-group if they continue to pay bribes absent Chinese regulatory enforcement. But enforcing the FCPA against Chinese businesses subject to FCPA jurisdiction while also operating in capital-importing countries may not pressure the Chinese government to enforce its own foreign anti-bribery laws on Chinese companies (although it may enforce them against foreign companies operating in China), since the Chinese government is effectively the entity paying the bribe. Indeed, Chinese foreign policy may be to encourage—not to prohibit—foreign bribes given Xi Jinping's 'Belt and Road' Initiative (BRI), China's ambitious program of funding and building infrastructure projects in the developing world.[144] Chinese companies may thus continue to pay bribes to build political capital among developing-world elites. They might even do the work at lower rates thanks to state loans, subsidies, and programs designed to deploy slack capacity from the Chinese construction industry to infrastructure projects abroad.[145]

On the other hand, Chinese companies paying frequent bribes may find themselves blacklisted by the World Bank and other development banks.[146] Chinese companies might then begin to comply with international norms, and China might enforce its foreign anti-corruption laws to preserve Chinese companies' eligibility for development-bank sponsored projects. Additionally, some developing countries, Malaysia for example, are beginning to push back against BRI, wary of being too much under the influence of China.[147] And growing economic tensions with the United States may increase US government agencies' scrutiny of Chinese companies with US connections, including FCPA enforcement by the DOJ and the SEC. In any event, China is an important case that needs to be examined and analyzed carefully. Part 4 tests our model with actual case studies.

4 Case analysis of our interest group theory

The OECD Anti-Bribery Convention required ratifying nations to enact domestic foreign-corruption laws similar to the FCPA. Article 2 of the Convention provides that '[e]ach Party shall take such measures as may be necessary, in accordance with its legal principles, to establish the liability of legal persons for the bribery of a foreign public official.'[148] Most of the 44 OECD signatory countries have in fact passed foreign corruption legislation to comply with the treaty, but enforcement patterns have varied dramatically. According to the 2018 report of Transparency International (TI), a non-governmental organization dedicated to monitoring foreign corruption, only seven capital-exporting countries with an aggregate 27% share of global exports can be characterized as pursuing

144 Peter Thomson, 'Statement at the Plenary Session of the Belt and Road Forum for International Cooperation' (UN General Assembly, 14 May 2017).

145 See Spalding (n 12) 394–395.

146 See The World Bank, 'Combatting Corruption' <http://www.worldbank.org/en/topic/governance/brief/anti-corruption> accessed 1 June 2020. See, eg, The World Bank, 'World Bank Group Announces Debarment of Two Chinese Construction Companies Working on Energy Product' (19 July 2018) <https://www.worldbank.org/en/news/press-release/2018/07/19/world-bank-group-announces-debarment-of-two-chinese-construction-companies-working-on-energy-project> accessed 1 June 2020.

147 Hannah Beech, '"We Cannot Afford This": Malaysia Pushes Back Against China's Vision' *NY Times* (20 August 2018) <https://www.nytimes.com/2018/08/20/world/asia/china-malaysia.html> accessed 1 June 2020.

148 OECD Convention, art 2.

'active' enforcement: the US, Germany, the UK, Italy, Switzerland, Norway, and Israel.[149] TI's 2018 report counts four countries (Australia, Sweden, Brazil, and Portugal) with aggregate global exports of 3.8% as 'moderate' enforcers, and 11 countries (including France, the Netherlands, and Canada) with aggregate exports of 12.3% as 'limited' foreign-corruption law enforcement countries.[150] TI reports that 22 countries—nearly half of the OECD Convention's signatories (including Japan, South Korea, India, Mexico, and Russia) pursue 'little or no' enforcement of foreign corruption laws.[151]

What explains the varying levels of enforcement of foreign corruption laws and how can we predict the future of enforcement patterns? Even among the 'active' and 'moderate' signatories, enforcement has been a relatively recent trend in the last few years except for the United States, which, as described above, dramatically increased FCPA enforcement early in the new millennium.

As set forth in part 3, our explanatory model focuses on the interests of the US and foreign companies. The basic insight is that as businesses face enforcement of foreign anti-corruption laws in other countries (e.g., the FCPA in the United States), they will push for or acquiesce in enforcement in their own capital-exporting countries to 'level the playing field' vis-à-vis competitors who do not face the same enforcement risk. For instance, a German company that is subject to US FCPA enforcement will seek or acquiesce in Germany's enforcement of its own foreign anti-corruption laws. Over time, this will result in more and more capital-exporting countries enforcing their formerly moribund foreign anti-bribery laws that were enacted upon ratification of the OECD Convention. At some point, a k-group on the supply side may trigger a rejection of the bribes that are still being offered on the buy side. This is on the presumption that the bribe-free services or goods provided by the k-group are so objectively superior to what bribers can provide that the potential bribe-taker will have no other option than to take a bid from a k-group provider.

It may help to give concrete examples to understand the model. Recall the extent to which the OECD Convention itself resulted from US businesses lobbying for an international level playing field. Consider, then, the cases of the UK and Germany—two of the earliest active enforcement jurisdictions.[152] In fact, the UK Bribery Act, which came into force in 2011, is more far-reaching than the FCPA, most prominently in its applicability to foreign commercial bribes paid to private actors, not just foreign officials.[153] The UK Act came into law the year after

149 See Gillian Dell and Andrew McDevitt, *Exporting Corruption—Progress Report 2018: Assessing Enforcement of the OECD Anti-Bribery Convention* (Transparency International, 2018) 4.

150 Ibid.

151 Ibid.

152 Ibid 49–51, 88–91.

153 See Ministry of Justice *Guidance About Procedures Which Relevant Commercial Organisations Can Put Into Place to Prevent Persons Associated With Them From Bribing (section 9 of the Bribery Act 2010)* (2011).

BAE Systems, a British aerospace and defense company, settled a long-running FCPA investigation that resulted in a $400 million settlement—the third-largest ever at the time.[154] Germany has become perhaps the second leading jurisdiction for enforcement of foreign corruption laws in the past few years. From 2007 to 2017, German authorities initiated 40 investigations, commenced 13 actions, and disposed of 49 cases with sanctions—a level of enforcement commensurate to US enforcement of the FCPA prior to 2007 in terms of volume, although the targets of investigations were individuals not corporations, and the amounts of sanctions were considerably smaller.[155] The German technology giant Siemens paid $800 million in 2008 to settle an FCPA enforcement action.[156] That settlement was the largest in the history of foreign-corruption law enforcement until the September 2018 Petrobras settlement.

A pattern emerges, reinforced by the interesting fact that nearly all the 'active' or 'moderate' enforcement jurisdictions in 2018 are home states of foreign companies subject to FCPA actions by US enforcement authorities that result in very public and large settlements and non-prosecution agreements. For instance, Transparency International's 2018 Report counts Israel as an active enforcer of foreign corruption laws, with 13 investigations opened between 2014 and 2017 and the country's first ever foreign corruption case reaching settlement in 2016.[157] Earlier in 2016, Teva Pharmaceuticals Industries—a generic drug maker—paid $519 million to settle US FCPA charges that it had paid bribes in Russia, Ukraine, and Mexico.[158]

The causal mechanism is straightforward. When prominent foreign companies like BAE (UK), Siemens (Germany), and Teva (Israel) paid fines and made non-prosecution agreements to settle US FCPA prosecutions, they stopped resisting enforcement of analogous laws in their home jurisdictions. Because the expansive jurisdictional reach of the post-OECD Convention FCPA meant that these giant multinational companies could not escape foreign anti-corruption regulation in the United States—a large market they could not forego, their interest in lobbying their home governments for lax enforcement faded. These companies would have needed to implement effective FCPA compliance regimes in any event as part of their respective non-prosecution agreements with US authorities. Consequently, companies like BAE, Siemens, and Teva confronted their own level playing field problem vis-à-vis domestic and non-US competitors who were not subject to potential FCPA enforcement because of *de minimis* operations

154 Richard L Cassin, 'BAE Pleads Guilty' (*FCPA Blog*, 1 March 2010) <http://www.fcpablog.com/blog/2010/3/1/bae-pleads-guilty.html> accessed 1 June 2020.

155 Dell and McDevitt (n 149) 49.

156 Richard L Cassin, 'Siemens to Plead Guilty' (*FCPA Blog*, 12 December 2008) <http://www.fcpablog.com/blog/2008/12/12/siemens-to-plead-guilty.html> accessed 1 June 2020.

157 Dell and McDevitt (n 149) 56.

158 SEC, 'Teva Pharmaceutical Paying $519 Million to Settle FCPA Charges' (22 December 2016) <https://www.sec.gov/news/pressrelease/2016-277.html> accessed 1 June 2020.

or contacts within the US. And so they acquiesced and even lobbied for more aggressive enforcement in their home countries like the UK, Germany, and Israel as their level-playing-field antidote. At the same time, the US FCPA prosecutions often required cooperation with home-jurisdiction enforcement authorities which built up capacity and expertise to enforce their own anti-corruption laws. It is telling, for instance, that one recent target of German prosecutors was a subsidiary of ThyssenKrupp Marine Systems—an erstwhile rival (and sometimes ally) of Siemens.[159] The case was settled by the subsidiary's agreement in 2017 to disgorge 49 million euros—the largest German domestic settlement to date and the first notable one involving a corporate defendant.[160]

The only OECD signatory that was a home jurisdiction for companies subject to high-profile FCPA actions that Transparency International did *not* characterize in its 2018 report as an 'active' or 'moderate' enforcer is France.[161] Three French companies were investigated for FCPA violations and agreed to sizable disgorgement settlements: Technip for $338 million in 2010; Total for $398 million in 2013; and Alstom for $772 million in 2014.[162] And yet TI concluded that France was a 'limited' enforcement jurisdiction.[163] This finding would appear to contradict our model.

But more recent events on the ground indicate that the model is accurate in its predictions even as to France, but on a longer time horizon. France, despite having ratified the OECD Convention, did not have the legal tools (e.g., an enforcement agency or non-prosecution agreements) to ensure meaningful enforcement of foreign anti-corruption laws. That changed, in large part because of the French government's experience and cooperation with US authorities regarding the three high-profile FCPA actions against French companies mentioned above. In December 2016, France passed the Law on Transparency, Combating Corruption and Modernization of Economic Life, commonly referred to as 'Sapin II.'[164] The law created a new national Anti-Corruption Agency, charged with anti-corruption oversight of big companies including mandated compliance regimes.[165] The law also instituted much-needed whistleblower protections and excised preexisting rules that the victim or alleged offender be a French citizen and that the conduct at issue must be an offense in both France and the

159 Dell and McDevitt (n 149) 49.

160 Ibid. The relevant German laws were changed in 2015 to allow prosecution of juridical persons like corporations.

161 Ibid 46.

162 Richard L Cassin, 'With Alstom, Three French Companies Are Now in the FCPA Top Ten' (*FCPA Blog*, 23 December 2014) <http://www.fcpablog.com/blog/2014/12/23/with-alstom-three-french-companies-are-now-in-the-fcpa-top-t.html#sthash.fFBa7gKy.dpuf> accessed 1 June 2020.

163 Dell and McDevitt (n 149) 2.

164 Ibid 47.

165 Ibid.

territory in which it took place.[166] Perhaps most importantly, Sapin II introduced a new tool analogous to the US deferred prosecution agreement—the *convention judiciaire d'intérêt public* (CJIP).[167] The first CJIP was made with Hong Kong Shanghai Banking Corporation (HSBC) Private Bank Suisse (a Swiss subsidiary of the storied Hong Kong banking institution), involving secret bank accounts of French taxpayers.[168] In November 2017, the Paris High Court approved the CJIP to settle the matter without admitting guilt subject to a 300 million euro settlement including disgorgement and fines.[169]

As with France, it is possible to make a prediction on the future course of the enforcement of foreign anti-corruption laws in Brazil based on our model. In light of the historic Petrobras settlement—the first to pass the $1 billion mark in terms of total value[170]—one would expect Brazil to ramp up enforcement of its own foreign anti-corruption laws, particularly against foreign companies. Because Petrobras was a state entity, the Brazilian authorities cooperated very closely with the United States SEC and DOJ in the matter, and a significant portion of the recovery will go to Brazil.[171] Like their French counterparts, the Brazilian enforcement agencies likely learned a great deal from their cooperation with the US authorities. At present, TI reports that Brazil is a 'moderate' enforcer.[172] If we are right, that characterization will change in the future, although Brazil, like France, may need some time to develop the necessary legal architecture, including the development of a specialized enforcement agency, enhanced whistleblower protections, and the implementation of non-prosecution agreements.

According to TI, the three largest economies with 'little or no' enforcement of foreign corruption laws between 2014 and 2017 are China (10.8% of global exports), Japan (3.8%), and South Korea (3.0%).[173] China is not a signatory of the OECD Convention (although it has ratified the UNCAC), and, as noted above and discussed below, is a special case given the role of the state in the economy. Consequently, our model, which is premised on the influence of business interests as independent actors, cannot explain China well. Japan and South Korea are different: they are signatories to the OECD convention, and big business groups have been dominant players in both of these capital-exporting Asian economies. What explains the recent lack of enforcement in those countries?

166 Ibid.
167 Ibid.
168 Ibid.
169 Ibid.
170 Department of Justice, 'Petroleo Brasileiro S.A.-Petrobras' (26 September 2018) <https://www.justice.gov/opa/press-release/file/1096706/download> accessed 1 June 2020; Petróleo S.A.-Petrobras, Securities Act Release No. 10561, Exchange Act Release No. 84295, 2018 WL 4628173 (27 September 2018).
171 Cassin, 'Petrobras Reaches $1.78 Billion FCPA Resolution' (n 102).
172 Dell and McDevitt (n 149) 4.
173 Ibid 10.

Japan is a particularly interesting case because there have, in fact, been several FCPA settlements involving Japanese companies. In April 2018, Panasonic Corporation agreed to pay $143 million in disgorgement of profits and prejudgment interest to settle FCPA claims related to bidding for in-flight entertainment and communications systems.[174] Its US subsidiary, Panasonic Avionics Corporation, agreed to a criminal fine of more than $137 million as part of a deferred non-prosecution agreement in conjunction with the same crime.[175] In 2011, JGC Corporation, a Japanese energy, procurement, and construction (EPC) company paid $219 million to settle FCPA charges for conspiring with the US company KBR/Halliburton to pay bribes to Nigerian officials on the Bonny Island Liquid Natural Gas project.[176] KBR/Halliburton, the principal conspirator, itself paid a $579 million settlement in 2009, the largest FCPA settlement paid by an American corporation.[177] The Japanese trading company Marubeni paid $54.6 million in connection with the Bonny Island project in 2012.[178] Marubeni also pleaded guilty in 2014 to FCPA violations for payments made relating to the Tarahan power project in Indonesia and paid $88 million.[179] Olympus of America, a wholly owned subsidiary of Olympus Corporation of Japan, also paid a $22.8 million in FCPA fines as part of a deferred prosecution agreement in 2016 with respect to bribes paid for medical equipment contracts in Latin America.[180] Hitachi reached a settlement with the SEC in 2015 to pay $19 million to settle bribery charges with respect to power station orders in South Africa.[181]

174 SEC, 'Panasonic Charged With FCPA and Accounting Fraud Violations' (20 April 2018), <https://www.sec.gov/news/press-release/2018-73> accessed 1 June 2020.

175 Ibid.

176 Richard L Cassin, 'JGC Resolves Criminal Charges' *FCPA Blog* (6 April 2011) <http://www.fcpablog.com/blog/2011/4/6/jgc-resolves-criminal-charges.html> accessed 1 June 2020.

177 Ibid.

178 Department of Justice, 'Marubeni Corporation Resolves Foreign Corrupt Practices Act Investigation and Agrees to Pay a $54.6 Million Criminal Penalty' (17 January 2012) <https://www.justice.gov/opa/pr/marubeni-corporation-resolves-foreign-corrupt-practices-act-investigation-and-agrees-pay-546> accessed 1 June 2020.

179 Department of Justice, 'Marubeni Corporation Agrees to Plead Guilty to Foreign Bribery Charges and to Pay an $88 Million Fine' (19 March 2014) <https://www.justice.gov/opa/pr/marubeni-corporation-agrees-plead-guilty-foreign-bribery-charges-and-pay-88-million-fine> accessed 1 June 2020.

180 Deferred Prosecution Agreement, *United States v. Olympus Latin America, Inc.*, No. 16-CR-3525 (D.N.J. March 1, 2016) 7.

181 Arthur and Toni Rembe Rock Center for Corporate Governance, 'Case Information: Securities and Exchange Commission v. Hitachi, Ltd.' *FCPA Clearinghouse* (2015) <http://fcpa.stanford.edu/enforcement-action.html?id=576> accessed 1 June 2020. The Japanese company Bridgestone also agreed to pay a fine of $28 million to settlement charges of Sherman Antitrust Act and FCPA violations concerning marine-hose orders. The maximum amount chargeable for the FCPA violation, however, was $500,000, so the overwhelming part of the settlement was for the antitrust violations. Department of Justice, 'Bridgestone Corporation Agrees to Plead Guilty to Participating in Conspiracies to Rig Bids and Bribe

Why have Japanese business interests not mobilized to encourage the Japanese government to 'level the playing field' and ramp up enforcement of its own foreign anti-corruption laws given this track record of FCPA enforcement against Japanese multinational companies? Several factors may be at work. First, it may be that the scale of the penalties, while large, has not reached headlines level, i.e., $500 million or $1 billion. And the optics and demonstration effect of the largest settlement—the $219 million paid by JGC in 2011—was watered down by the fact that Japanese companies were junior partners in the Bonny Island project syndicate. The leader was a US company, KBR/Halliburton, which had paid $579 million two years earlier.[182] Second, Japan may lack the legal infrastructure to enforce foreign anti-bribery laws effectively against corporations. Like France before it enacted Sapin II, Japan did not have a mechanism to allow deferred prosecution agreements until an amendment to their criminal procedural code came into effect on June 1, 2018.[183] Moreover, Japanese law does not afford strong protection for whistleblowers, a critical catalyst to foreign anti-bribery prosecutions. Finally, implementation of the OECD Anti-Bribery Convention in Japan largely falls under the remit of the Ministry of Economy, Trade, and Industry, which is also responsible for the promotion of Japanese businesses abroad, a dual mandate which creates obvious tensions.[184]

By contrast to Japanese companies, no South Korean company has entered into a deferred prosecution agreement with US authorities and paid sizable fines regarding FCPA violations. That may change in the future, but it seems that a high-profile, big-number FCPA settlement may be a necessary catalyst to the change. Additionally, South Korea lacks some of the same safeguards and cultural norms regarding whistleblowers as Japan. But we believe that our model will eventually apply to Japan and South Korea, given the strength of business interests in both countries and their liberal democratic political orders. As such, we predict that:

(1) there will be a large-scale US FCPA (or other k-group) investigation and settlement involving flagship multinational companies in the two countries (in the hundreds of millions of dollars range);
(2) the respective national enforcement authorities will be involved;
(3) Japan and South Korea will subsequently enforce their national foreign anti-bribery laws, with the acquiescence or encouragement of the multinational companies already subject to enforcement in k-group jurisdictions; and

---

Foreign Government Officials' (15 September 2011) <https://www.justice.gov/opa/pr/bridgestone-corporation-agrees-plead-guilty-participating-conspiracies-rig-bids-and-bribe> accessed 1 June 2020.

182 Cassin, 'JGC Resolves Criminal Charges' (n 176).

183 Dell and McDevitt (n 149) 60.

184 Ibid.

(4) eventually, Japan and South Korea will join the k-group, increasing the momentum toward a truly global anti-corruption regime.

China is the country with the largest share of global exports—10.8%, by comparison to the US share of 9.9%.[185] Although it is not a signatory of the OECD Convention, it acceded to the UN Convention Against Corruption (UNCAC) in 2006.[186] In 2011, China amended its criminal code to criminalize the bribery of foreign officials:

> Whoever gives any property to a staff member of a company, an enterprise or any other entity for any improper benefit shall be sentenced to imprisonment of not more than 3 years or criminal detention if the amount of property is relatively large; or be sentenced to imprisonment of not less than 3 years but not more than 10 years and a fine if the amount of property is huge. Whoever gives any property to a functionary of a foreign country or an official of an international public organization for any improper commercial benefit shall be punished according to the provision of the preceding paragraph. Where an entity commits a crime as provided for in the preceding two paragraphs, a fine shall be imposed on it, and its directly responsible person and other directly liable persons shall be punished according to the provision of paragraph 1 of this chapter. A briber who voluntarily confesses to his bribery before a criminal investigation on him is opened may be given a mitigated penalty or be exempted from penalty.[187]

Although this amendment—known as the Foreign Bribery Provision—satisfied UNCAC's requirement to enact domestic foreign anti-bribery laws, UNCAC does not require enforcement.[188] UNCAC does allow and encourage signatories to engage in peer or expert review of their respective anti-corruption initiatives and programs, and China has 'firmly opposed review mechanisms that go beyond self-assessment.'[189] Commentators and observers have generally concluded that the enactment of the new Chinese foreign-bribery law was a symbolic gesture,

185 Ibid 10.

186 UNODC, 'Signature and Ratification Status' <https://www.unodc.org/unodc/en/corruption/ratification-status.html> accessed 1 June 2020.

187 Eight Amendment (中文版) [Criminal Law] (promulgated by the Standing Comm. Nat'l People's Cong., 25 February 2011, effective 1 May 2011), art 164, 2011.

188 Jeffrey Young, 'Corruption Concerns Taint Burgeoning China-Africa Trade' *VOA News* (1 September 2014) <https://www.voanews.com/a/corruption-concerns-tain-buregeoning-china-africa-trade/2432469.html> accessed 1 June 2020. See also Samuel R Gintel, 'Fighting Transnational Bribery: China's Gradual Approach' (2013) 31 Wisconsin International Law Journal 1, 26.

189 Gintel (n 188) 26.

with little or no possibility for enforcement.[190] Indeed, the OECD has criticized the enacted law as:

> being deliberately designed to avoid strict enforcement. The absence of any meaningful sanctions against Chinese companies for offences abroad to date corroborates this criticism. Overall, China's approach has been one of attentively observing and selectively transposing transnational anti-bribery standards without showing any signs of enforcement.[191]

Additionally, one US commentator has asserted that the Chinese law relating to bribery of foreign officials requires intent that appears to be facially more limited than the requisite intent for domestic bribery: 'It therefore appears that giving a bribe to a foreign public official to secure non-commercial benefits, which would be prohibited in the domestic context, may be permissible in a foreign context.'[192] To date, China has not brought any reported charges against Chinese nationals or corporations for paying foreign bribes.

There is some reason for hope. Since taking power, President Xi Jinping has made the fight against *domestic* corruption a high priority.[193] Thus, he created a powerful new anti-corruption agency, the National Supervision Council, with the mission of overseeing 'all public servants exercising public power.'[194] As with Watergate in the United States, illegal funds used domestically may lead to the discovery of such funds used abroad. And the payment of bribes by Chinese companies has led to many of them being blacklisted from participating in infrastructure projects sponsored by the World Bank and regional development banks like the Asia Development Bank.[195] There were reports in October 2015, for instance, that Chinese officials were investigating individuals possibly connected with corruption related to Sinopec's oil exploration in Angola.[196] At the same time, the Chinese government has done nothing to address western news reports

190 Ibid 9.

191 Bertram Lang, 'Engaging China in the Fight Against Transnational Bribery: "Operation Skynet" as a New Opportunity for OECD' (OECD Global Anti-Corruption & Integrity Forum, 2017) 8.

192 Gintel (n 188) 19.

193 The Economist 'China is Conducting Fewer Local Policy Experiments Under Xi Jinping' (18 August 2018) <https://www.economist.com/leaders/2018/08/18/china-is-conducting-fewer-local-policy-experiments-under-xi-jinping> accessed 1 June 2020.

194 Pratik Jakhar, 'China's Anti-Corruption Campaign Expands With New Agency', *BBC* (20 March 2018) <https://www.bbc.com/news/world-asia-china-43453769> accessed 1 June 2020.

195 Asian Development Bank, 'Anticorruption and Integrity: Sanctions' <https://www.adb.org/site/integrity/sanctions> accessed 1 June 2020.

196 Sun Hong, *Bribery and Corruption Offences, Enforcement and Penalties: China* (Thomson Reuters Practical Law, updated January 2019).

of rampant payment of bribes on behalf of Chinese business in Africa, for example, by Hong Kong businessman Chi Ping Patrick Ho.[197]

At the end of the day, it is not clear that Chinese multinational companies subject to FCPA or other anti-corruption law enforcement abroad can mobilize the Chinese government to enforce its own foreign anti-bribery laws against all Chinese companies to level the playing field. Most daunting is the fact that the present Chinese government perceives an affirmative strategic interest in *paying* bribes to secure infrastructure contracts in the developing world and developing economic and political bonds. That is the point of the so-called 'Belt and Road' initiative. And given the large share of world exports originated by Chinese companies, China's intransigence may be enough to stymie the k-group.

In December 2018, the DOJ and the SEC announced an FCPA settlement with Polycom, a US telecommunications technology company, based on bribes paid to Chinese officials by its Chinese subsidiary. Polycom agreed to pay the SEC $16.3 million ($10.7 million to disgorge illicit profits, $1.8 million for prejudgment interest, and $3.8 million fine)[198] and an additional $20.3 million to the US Treasury and Postal Service Consumer Fraud Fund pursuant to a DOJ non-prosecution letter agreement.[199] A $36.6 million dollar settlement is not large by the standards of recent FCPA settlements, and the company in question was a US corporation that had recently acquired the Chinese company which had paid the bribes to Chinese officials before its acquisition. But it may signal a start to more robust FCPA enforcement against Chinese companies, particularly in the context of the current trade war between the United States and China. And if so, it may be an early sign that the model we have set forth may yet have explanatory purchase to Chinese business interests.

5 Conclusion

In this chapter, we have sought to make four contributions to the literature. First, this chapter is the first to examine *global* enactment and enforcement patterns of foreign corruption laws in a theoretically informed way. Prior accounts have focused primarily on explaining the enactment of the FCPA and its enforcement trends and have devoted much less effort to explaining other states' foreign corruption laws. Others have told a story about the US government's interests or rent-seeking by prosecutors to explain the international spread of such laws. By contrast, this chapter has focused on the organic growth of such laws, spurred by the interests of each state's domestic business lobby. Under the right

197 Jenni Marsh, 'How a Hong Kong Millionaire's Bribery Case Exposes China's Corruption Problem in Africa', *CNN* (10 February 2018) <https://edition.cnn.com/2018/02/09/world/patrick-ho-corruption-china-africa/index.html> accessed 1 June 2020.

198 Polycom, Inc., Exchange Act Release No. 84978, 2018 WL 6804090 (26 December 2018).

199 Letter from US Department of Justice to Caz Hasemi about Polycom, Inc (20 December 2018).

circumstances, we have shown that these incentives could create a domino effect in the enforcement of national foreign anti-corruption laws that would explain the actual patterns we observe in the world.

Second, our account has illuminated a critical distinction between foreign anti-corruption laws and anti-corruption laws more generally. This analytical isolation has emphasized just how unusual outbound foreign anti-corruption laws are as well as how they differ in form and function from strictly domestic anti-corruption laws.

Third, our account generates predictions and a normative vision for the future. On the assumption that eradicating corruption is a public good, our story shows that it does not necessarily follow that achieving the goal requires top-down norm enforcement along the lines of the traditional international governance model. It is possible, rather, that the same result might be achieved among decentralized sovereign states by the independent actions of leading states brought about by business interests seeking to maximize their own profits. Such a market-based model may have applications in other international contexts where the conventional wisdom emphasizes international laws and institutions as the principal causal mechanism.

Finally, from a methodological perspective, the chapter highlights the value of interdisciplinary approaches that combine legal analysis with international relations theory. In particular, hegemonic stability theory, which had its heyday in international relations scholarship pertaining to international political economy and free trade in the 1980s and 1990s, has never been applied to anti-corruption scholarship despite its obvious fit and explanatory leverage to the issue. We do not claim that our theory of the transmission of foreign anti-bribery laws explains every case. In some cases, there may indeed be rent-seeking prosecutors or altruistic policymakers. Still, we think it is an important contribution with real explanatory traction and predictive power. We hope that it will inform the debate of how best to spread anti-corruption norms worldwide.

4 Never waste a crisis

Anti-corruption reforms in South America

Rachel Brewster and Andres Ortiz[1]

In the last five years, corruption scandals have rocked South America, leading to the indictment and conviction of top elected officials as well as civil and criminal charges against some of the region's largest and most powerful corporations. The largest corruption investigation, the Operação Lava Jato (Operation Carwash) scandal in Brazil,[2] has ensnared the former president Lula da Silva,[3] led to the arrest of industrial magnates,[4] and uncovered similar bribery schemes in 12 other countries, including Peru, Argentina, Panama, and Venezuela.[5] In Peru, all of the three living former presidents have been implicated in the corruption investigation.[6] A fourth former Peruvian president, Alan Garcia, took his own life as police

1 An earlier version of this chapter was first published as an article in the Virginia Journal of International Law. The authors would like to thank Katy Garcia for excellent research assistance.

2 Natalia Mori, 'Operation Car Wash and Its Impact on Peru' (2018) NYU Journal of Legislation & Public Policy Quorum (describing Lava Jato as 'the largest bribery case in the history of Brazil and Latin America').

3 Samantha Pearson and Luciana Magalhaes, 'Former Brazilian President Is Convicted of Corruption' *The Wall Street Journal* (12 July 2017) (describing Lula's conviction as 'highest-profile sentence yet in the Car Wash case').

4 Andrew Jacobs and Paula Moura, 'At the Birthplace of a Graft Scandal, Brazil's Crisis Is on Full Display' *The New York Times* (10 June 2016) (reporting that the Lava Jato 'has led to the arrest of more than 150 business tycoons and elected officials').

5 Stephanie Nolan, 'Corruption beyond Brazil: Where the 'Car Wash' Scandal Has Splashed across Latin America' *The Globe & Mail* (12 November 2017) (observing that the Lava Jato scandal has spread outside of Brazil and has led to the investigation of prominent politicians in half a dozen Latin American countries).

6 Andrea Zarate and Nicholas Casey, 'Alan Garcia, Ex-President of Peru, Is Dead After Shooting Himself During Arrest' *The New York Times* (17 April 2019) (discussing how Peruvian officials are investigating all of the country's living former presidents, including Pedro Pablo Kuczynski—predecessor to the current president, Martin Vizcarra, Alejandro Toledo, and Ollanta Humula). Former President Alejandro Toledo is currently living in the United States, and was recently arrested by American authorities based on an extradition request by the Peruvian government. Nicholas Casey and Andrea Zarate, 'Former Peru President Arrested in US as Part of Vast Bribery Scandal' *The New York Times* (16 July 2019) (discussing how Toleda was arrested by American authorities after he repeatedly refused requests from Peruvian courts to return).

raided his home as part of the corruption investigation.[7] In response to this and other scandals, protestors have taken to the streets to demand changes to how government and businesses operate.[8]

The crisis brought on by corruption scandals—including Operação Lava Jato, but also others—has created the political conditions necessary for major legal reforms in the region.[9] Governments, responding to popular pressure, are motivated to prosecute high-ranking government officials and corporations, and to adopt new legislation.[10] However, this has not led to harmonization across South America.[11] While there are certain themes present in many legal reforms—*ex ante* controls, the possibility of deferred prosecution agreements, leniency agreements, and independent prosecutors—there remains significant variance among the anticorruption regimes in South American countries.[12]

For all of the economic and political upheaval that the corruption scandals have created, there has been surprisingly little academic analysis of how these crises have changed the policy landscape in South America.[13] This chapter provides a holistic evaluation of how governments in South America have responded and why they have adopted specific reforms. Importantly, we find that one of the major explanations for the change in national policy is international law. Specifically, we argue that membership in the Organization for Economic Cooperation and

7 Ryan Dube and Juan Forero, 'Former Peruvian President Dies After Shooting Himself During Police Raid' *The Wall Street Journal* (17 April 2019) (describing how Garcia committed suicide as police came to arrest him due to corruption investigations tied to the Odebrecht scandal).

8 Simon Romaro, 'In Nationwide Protests, Angry Brazilians Call for Ouster of President' *The New York Times* (15 March 2015) (reporting that hundreds of thousands of Brazilians took to the streets to protest and demand reforms); David Segal, 'Petrobras Oil Scandal Leaves Brazilians Lamenting a Lost Dream' *The New York Times* (7 August 2015) (putting the number of protesters at one million).

9 See Americas Society, *Latin America's Battle Against Corruption: A Path Forward* (Americas Quarterly, 10 April 2018) (discussing how corruption scandals have changed the political and legal environment in Latin America).

10 Ibid (discussing region wide reform efforts). For specific country developments, see, e.g., Ligia Maura Costa, 'The Dynamics of Corruption in Brazil: From Trivial Bribes to a Corruption Scandal' in Omar E Hawthorne and Stephen Magu (eds), *Corruption Scandals and their Global Impacts* (Routledge 2018) 189, 196–201 (analyzing legal reforms in Brazil after Lava Jato); Luis Vieira, 'Argentina to Expand Use of Plea Bargaining, Inspired by Brazil' *Americas Quarterly* (24 March 2016) (discussing legal reforms in Argentina resulting from the Lava Jato scandal); Mori (n 1) (analyzing legal reforms in Peru).

11 See text at n 108ff.

12 Ibid.

13 There are excellent academic articles examining individual country's responses. See, e.g., Costa (n 10) 196–201 (describing the corruption scandal and its impact on Brazilian politics); Guillermo Jorge, 'The Impact of Corporate Liability for Corruption in Latin America' (2019) 113 AJIL Unbound 320 (discussing the impact of corruption scandals in Brazilian politics).

Development (OECD) Convention[14] has a significant effect on the government's policy reforms for member states. This chapter provides the foundations for demonstrating how treaty membership can change national government policy, particularly in moments of political crisis.

This chapter examines how the anti-corruption reform process has unfolded in South America by providing case studies of several OECD Convention members and a non-member. We examine how governments' responses to corruption have been driven by their own national politics, their experiences and interactions with other nations' anti-corruption laws, and the influence of international treaties (most notably the OECD Convention) and international organizations. Specifically, we explore how South American countries' laws have developed along similar lines, adopting several foreign legal concepts—both over the last two decades and the last five years—but have retained important differences. A process of transnational legal exchange is clearly taking place, but each exchange occurs in a unique national system and thus has its own local qualities.

The chapter also presents a theoretical framework for understanding legal change in South America. As we discuss in the chapter, South American states that have joined the OECD Convention respond to corruption crises in systematically different ways than non-OECD Convention members. We argue that this is because there is an existing set of policy recommendations, along with transnational pressure to adopt these policies, that are particularly relevant for policymakers in OECD Convention member states. We discuss how treaty membership not only influences countries' responses to corruption but also provides a legal structure to make sure that the responses to the crisis produce meaningful policy change. Restated, it improves the likelihood that countries will make substantive anti-corruption reforms in response to a crisis and not simply adopt weak measures that satisfy political demands for change.

This chapter proceeds in four parts. In section 1, we discuss the corruption scandals that have shaken South America's political establishment. In particular, we discuss the Operação Lavo Jato case, which is the largest corruption scandal in the history of South America, if not the world.[15] We also analyze how the discovery of Brazilian construction giant Odebrecht's corrupt practices led to the scandal spreading across South America.[16] The political scandals and popular

14 Convention on Combating Bribery of Foreign Public Officials in International Business Transactions (adopted 17 December 1997, entered into force 15 February 1999) 37 ILM 1 (OECD Convention).

15 Jonathan Watts, 'Operation Car Wash: Is this the Biggest Corruption Scandal in History?' *The Guardian* (1 June 2017) (discussing the web of corruption between Brazilian construction companies, Petrobras, and Brazilian government officials and how it may be the largest corruption scandal ever uncovered). See also Costa (n 10) 196–201 (discussing how the Lava Jato scandal is likely the world's largest corruption scandal in terms of dollars involved).

16 Anthony Faiola, 'The Corruption Scandal Started in Brazil. Now It's Wreaking Havoc in Peru' *The Washington Post* (23 January 2013) (reporting how the Lava Jato corruption scandal has spread to fourteen countries due to Odebrecht's practice of bribery). See also n 35.

outrage that followed provided the requisite conditions for corruption reform proposals to be viable.

In section 2, we present a theory of how governments act in a political crisis and apply it to South America's current crises. Drawing on Professor John Coffee's concept of the 'regulatory sine curve,' we examine the political dynamics of government decision-making during and after a crisis.[17] The popular demands for policy action during a crisis create the political space for corruption reforms that are not possible during times of 'normal' politics.[18] However, these policies are vulnerable to backsliding when the crisis passes and politics returns to normal.[19] We discuss how membership in the OECD Convention influences government leaders responding to popular demands by placing certain reforms on policymakers' radar screens. We argue that this is a positive effect because it prevents policymakers from opportunistically choosing reforms that are unlikely to be effective going forward. In addition, monitoring by international organizations may prevent backsliding in the post-crisis period.

In section 3, we describe how various South American countries have responded to corruption crises, highlighting the variance between OECD Convention member countries, but also showing how this group, on the whole, responds differently than non-OECD Convention countries. These case studies demonstrate how unique each country's political situation is. The details of the crisis, the national government's particular goals, and the existing legal framework all influence the administration's reform proposals. Yet for all of the contextual nature of national politics, the influence of the OECD Convention and its recommendations are identifiable in each member country. The case studies illustrate how the theory set out in section 2 works in practice in the middle of complicated and chaotic domestic politics.

In section 4, we conclude by summarizing how corruption crises have brought legal reforms to many South American countries in the last decade. We further examine the changing global prosecution picture, specifically, the challenges of having multiple nations' prosecutors pursuing the same corporations. We discuss how the future will likely require even greater cooperation between national governments on anti-corruption prosecutions and some of the hurdles that this deeper cooperation will face.

17 John C Coffee, 'The Political Economy of Dodd-Frank: Why Financial Reform Tends to Be Frustrated and Systemic Risk Perpetuated' (2012) 97 Cornell Law Review 1019, 1020–1042.

18 Ibid 1020–1031.

19 Ibid 1030.

1 The corruption scandals

The Operação Lava Jato (Operation Car Wash) investigation in Brazil is the largest corruption scandal in the nation's history,[20] leading to the conviction of top government officials[21] and industry leaders,[22] and aiding the fall of the government.[23]

20 For a discussion of the Lava Jato scandal, see Claire Felter and Rocio Cara, 'Brazil's Corruption Fallout' (*Council on Foreign Relations*, 7 November 2018) <https://www.cfr.org/backgrounder/brazils-corruption-fallout> accessed 1 June 2020 (describing the corruption scandal and noting that the probe 'reached the highest levels of Brazilian government and corporate elite, implicating President Michel Temer, former presidents, and dozens of cabinet officials and senators'); Watts (n 15) (discussing the web of corruption between Brazilian construction companies, Petrobras, and Brazilian government officials); Mori (n 2) (describing Lava Jato as 'the largest bribery case in the history of Brazil and Latin America' and explaining the links between Odebrecht, Petrobras, and Brazilian public officials); Nicholas Zimmerman, 'How Brazil Went From Neoliberal Success Story to Total Political Chaos in 10 Years' *New York Magazine* (19 December 2017) (tracing origins of the scandal from 2005 to 2017); Costa (n 10) 196–201 (describing the corruption scandal and its impact on Brazilian and Latin American politics). For the role of Petrobras in the Lava Jato investigation, see generally, Segal (n 8). The Lava Jato scandal has become so notorious that Netflix is creating a series, 'The Mechanism,' based on it. See Larry Rohter, 'Brazil's Jaw-Dropping Corruption Scandal Comes to Netflix' *The New York Times* (16 March 2018).

21 The most notable conviction was that of 'Lula,' Brazilian former President, Luiz Inácio Lula da Silva, who was found guilty of accepting bribes for Petrobras's contracts. See Pearson and Magalhaes (n 3) (describing Lula's conviction as the 'highest-profile sentence yet in the Car Wash case' and 'the first verdict to emerge from five graft-related charges against Mr. da Silva'). Other convicted government leaders include Brazilian House Speaker Eduardo Cunha, who brought the impeachment charges against President Dilma Rousseff. Paul Kiernan, 'Brazil's Former House Speaker Eduardo Cunha Sentenced to Prison for Corruption, *The Wall Street Journal* (30 March 2017) (reporting that House Speaker Cunha was sentenced to 15 years in prison for corruption charges coming out of the Operation Car Wash probe).

22 Over 120 others have been convicted in the Lava Jato investigation, including the CEO of Odebrecht, Marcelo Odebrecht, and other Odebrecht executives. See Manuela Andreoni et al, 'Ex-President 'Lula' of Brazil Surrenders to Serve a 12-year Jail Term' *The New York Times* (7 April 2018) (noting that Lava Jato 'has so far resulted in the conviction of 120 people and billions of dollars in restitution'); Jacobs and Moura (n 4) (reporting that the Lava Jato 'has led to the arrest of more than 150 business tycoons and elected officials'); Luciana Magalhaes, 'Odebrecht to Cooperate with Prosecutors in Corruption Probe' *The Wall Street Journal* (22 March 2016) (reporting that the CEO of Odebrecht was sentenced to 19 years in prison for bribery); Luciana Magalhaes and Reed Johnson, 'Marcelo Odebrecht Agrees to Plea Deal in Brazilian Corruption Probe' *The Wall Street Journal* (1 December 2016) (reporting that Marcelo Odebrecht and many other former and current Odebrecht executives were signing plea deals with prosecutors regarding bribery schemes).

23 The Lava Jato scandal is widely attributed as one of the primary causes of President Dilma Rousseff's impeachment, which ended her hold on power. See Jacobs and Moura (n 4) (noting that '[a]lthough her alleged crimes are not directly tied to Lava Jato, her downfall has been fueled by public anger over the scandal's revelations of epic and systematic corruption.'); Mica Rosenberg and Nate Raymond, 'Brazilian Firms to Pay Record $3.5 Billion Penalty in Corruption Case' *Reuters* (21 December 2016) (observing that the Lava Jato scandal 'contributed to the downfall of Brazil's former president, Dilma Rousseff').

The scandal is wide-ranging and complicated, involving a host of industries and national government leaders.[24] The scandal gets its name from a police wiretap of a gas station involved in a money laundering investigation.[25] From that original investigation, Brazilian authorities began to collect evidence that private corporations, largely construction firms, were offering bribes to Petrobras, the Brazilian state-owned oil company, to secure contracts from Petrobras.[26] The result was billions and billions of dollars in bribes and stolen state assets.[27] The bribes were then funneled to Petrobras executives and the Brazilian government officials who supported the oil company for their own enrichment and to finance their political campaigns.[28]

The scandal was a political earthquake in Brazil.[29] Even though Brazil has had a history of corruption, the scale of the corruption and the involvement of Petrobras were shocking.[30] Petrobras, whose revenues represented 10% of Brazilian gross domestic product, was viewed as a symbol of Brazil's economic success and development.[31] It also tarnished the ruling government, which had governed during Brazil's economic boom.[32] Former President Luiz Inacio da Silva was drawn into the scandal and subsequently convicted of corruption.[33] The

24 See Segal (n 8) (discussing how the initial money laundering investigation expanded to include grand corruption involving the state-owned oil company, a host of industrial giants, and the most powerful politicians in Brazil).

25 Will Connors and Paulo Tervisani, 'Brazil "Carwash" Shrugs Off Notoriety Tied to Petrobras Scandal' *The Wall Street Journal* (21 2015). Several commentators have noted that the term 'carwash' is a misnomer given that the gas station, Posto da Torre (Tower Gas Station) had a laundromat, not a carwash. Segal (n 8); Jacobs and Moura (n 4).

26 See Joe Leahy, 'What is the Petrobras Scandal that is Engulfing Brazil' *Financial Times* (31 March 2016) (noting that the bribes were distributed to Petrobras executives and directors as well as to politicians and political parties). See also Watts (n 15) (discussing the wide ranging investigation); Segal (n 8) (examining in detail how the investigation expanded from the wiretaps to uncover widespread corruption at the highest levels of Brazilian industry and government). See also n 20.

27 The exact amounts involved in the Lava Jato scandal are uncertain but range between $3 billion and $5 billion. See Watts (n 15) (describing the sums involved as $5 billion); Segal (n 8) (pegging the number at $3 billion).

28 See Felter and Cara (n 20) (discussing the corrupt schemes uncovered by the Lava Jato investigation); Watts (n 15); Segal (n 8).

29 Costa (n 10) 196 (describing the scandal as one that has 'shaken Brazil's foundations'); Segal (n 8) (describing the sense of national anger this way: 'Brazilians are in the midst of an identity crisis. Much of Brazil's recently acquired cachet looks as if it was the product of fraud, and for an added touch of humiliation, a fraud cooked up at a company long regarded as an emblem of Brazil's success and aspirations.')

30 See Segal (n 8) (describing the scandal that 'convulsed the country with fury and a stinging sense of betrayal'); Watts (n 15).

31 See Segal (n 8) (discussing the importance of Petrobras to the nation's aspirations and the Brazilian economy); Watts (n 15) (describing Petrobras as the 'flagship' for Brazil's emerging economy and noting that it accounted for 1/8 of all investment in Brazil).

32 See Segal (n 8); Watts (n 15).

33 Andreoni et al. (n 22) (describing Lula's imprisonment as 'perhaps the biggest triumph' of the Lava Jato investigation while noting that the bribes that Lula accepted 'were a small

scandal further contributed to the fall of the government of da Silva's successor, President Dilma Rousseff.[34]

The discovery of the extensive corruption further hurt the Brazilian economy, which was already beginning to slide by the time the scandal made headlines. Petrobras's market capitalization plunged, in part due to the decline in oil prices but also due to the bribery revelations.[35] Petrobras subsequently paid $2.95 billion to settle a class-action investor suit based on its corrupt practices[36] and another $853 million to American and Brazilian authorities to settle corruption charges.[37]

The Lava Jato scandal did not end in Brazil. The investigations of alleged bribery by Odebrecht, the Brazilian construction giant, which was one of the primary sources of bribes for Petrobras, spread to at least 12 other countries, including

---

chapter in the annals of Lava Jato'). The fall of President Luiz Inacio da Silva, known as 'Lula,' was dramatic, as he had been one of the most popular presidents in Brazil's history and was considering a re-election bid. For more discussion of the impact of Lula's conviction, see Editorial Board, "Lula' Is in Prison, and Brazil's Democracy is in Peril' *The New York Times* (12 April 2018) (describing Lula's conviction as 'only one outcome, albeit the most dramatic' of the Operation Car Wash bribery investigation). However, a recent Brazilian Supreme Court decision may open the door to having Lula's and others' corruption sentences overturned. See Brad Brooks, 'Brazil Supreme Court Decision Seen as "Blow" to Car Wash Probe' *Reuters* (14 March 2019) (analyzing the Brazilian Supreme Court opinion finding that corruption cases against politicians should have been heard by electoral courts, not federal criminal courts).

34 The Lava Jato scandal, along with the failing Brazilian economy, is generally viewed as one of the primary causes of President Dilma Rousseff's impeachment, which ousted her from power. See Jacobs and Moura (n 4) (noting that '[a]lthough her alleged crimes are not directly tied to Lava Jato, her downfall has been fueled by public anger over the scandal's revelations of epic and systematic corruption'); Paulo Trevisani and Reed Johnson, 'Dilma Rousseff Ousted in Historic Brazil Impeachment Vote' *The Wall Street Journal* (31 August, 2016) (observing that Rousseff's ouster 'was widely expected, though only partly because of the legal evidence marshaled against her. Well before the trial's final phase opened last week, Ms. Rousseff's administration had come under pressure over the brutal recession and a massive corruption scandal at the state oil company that splintered her political base and devastated her popular support.'); Zimmerman (n 20) (noting that '*Lava Jato* hit Rousseff hard. After all, she had chaired the Petrobras board from 2003–2010. Although the investigation has not implicated her personally, her professed ignorance of the scheme, despite her proximity to its most influential players, has struck few as credible … As Rousseff's popularity ratings dropped to single digits, the pace of the recession quickened, and as *Lava Jato* progressed, talk of her impeachment grew.'); Rosenberg and Raymond (n 23) (observing that the Lava Jato scandal 'contributed to the downfall of Brazil's former president, Dilma Rousseff').

35 See Segal (n 8) (noting that Petrobras lost half of its market value after the bribery revelations, which was worse than other oil companies who were also suffering due to lower oil prices); Watts (n 15) (noting that Petrobras was ordered by courts to suspend business after the bribery scandal was public, hurting its bottom line).

36 Paul Kiernan, 'Petrobras to Pay $2.95 Billion to Settle US Suit Over Corruption' *The Wall Street Journal* (3 January 2018).

37 Aruna Viswanatha, Jeffrey T Lewis, and Samuel Rubenfeld, 'Petrobras to Pay $853.2 Million to Settle Corruption Probes in US, Brazil' *The Wall Street Journal* (27 September 2018).

Peru, Panama, Colombia, Argentina, and Venezuela.[38] Odebrecht used its business model of bribing governments for large construction contracts almost everywhere in South America.[39] In fact, Odebrecht's business model of corruption was so institutionalized that the company centralized bribes into its 'Division of Structured Operations,' which prosecutors have dubbed its 'division of bribery.'[40] Odebrecht's Chief Executive Officer, Marcelo Odebrecht, and other Odebrecht executives ended up cooperating with the Lava Jato investigation and signed plea deals.[41] Marcelo Odebrecht was sentenced to 19 years in prison for bribery.[42]

38 Nicholas Casey and Andrea Zarate, 'Corruption Scandals With Brazilian Roots Cascade Across Latin America' *The New York Times* (13 February 2017) (discussing how 14 Latin American countries are investigating whether the Brazilian construction giant, Odebrecht, which is at the center of the Lava Jato scandal, bribed their government officials); Faiola (n 16) (stating the corruption scandal has spread to 14 countries); 'Odebrecht Case: Politicians Worldwide Suspected in Bribery Scandal' *BBC* (15 December, 2017) (listing the total bribes paid by Odebrecht in Brazil ($349 million), Venezuela ($96 million), Dominican Republic ($92 million), Panama ($59 million), Angola ($50 million), Argentina ($35 million), Ecuador ($33.5 million), Peru ($29 million), Guatemala ($18 million), Colombia ($11 million, and an alleged additional $16 million), Mexico ($10 million), Mozambique ($1 million), Antiqua (alleged $10.5 million), El Salvador (alleged amount uncertain), and further investigations into Chile and Portugal); Nolan (n 5) (observing that the Lava Jato scandal has spread outside of Brazil and has led to the investigation of prominent politicians in half a dozen Latin American countries); Mori (n 2) (observing that Odebrecht has acknowledged paying '$778 million in bribes in twelve different countries in Latin America and Africa'); Alexandra Stevenson and Vinod Sreeharsha, 'Secret Unit Helped Brazilian Company Bribe Government Officials' *The New York Times* (21 December 2016) (reporting that Odebrecht's bribery scheme 'lasted more than two decades and involved bribes to government officials in a dozen countries across three continents').

39 Casey and Zarate (n 38) (reporting on Odebrecht's corrupt business practices throughout South America and other parts of the world).

40 See Matthew M Taylor, 'The Odebrecht Settlement and the Costs of Corruption' (*Council on Foreign Relations*, 27 December 2016) <https://www.cfr.org/blog/odebrecht-settlement-and-costs-corruption> accessed 1 June 2020 (noting that Odebrecht's 'business model was rooted in a remarkable amount of subterfuge, including a shadow budget administered by a 'Division of Structured Operations' using two shadow computer systems (one of which was destroyed to hide evidence)'); *BBC*, 'Odebrecht case' (n 38) (reporting that Odebrecht used its Division of Structured Operations 'essentially as a bribery department' to bribe 'government officials and political parties at home and abroad'); Stevenson and Sreeharsha (n 38) (quoting Department of Justice officials as saying 'Odebrecht and Brasken used a hidden but fully functioning Odebrecht business unit—a 'Department of Bribery,' so to speak—that systematically paid hundreds of millions of dollars to corrupt government officials in countries on three continents'); Magalhaes and Johnson (n 22) (reporting that prosecutors argue that Odebrecht 'maintained a clandestine 'department of bribes' along with a detailed accounting of payment to potentially hundreds of political figures').

41 Magalhaes and Johnson (n 22) (reporting that Marcelo Odebrecht and many other former and current Odebrecht executives were signing plea deals with prosecutors regarding bribery schemes).

42 Magalhaes (n 22).

The corruption probe into Odebrecht has resulted in the investigation or indictment of top government officials in Peru,[43] Colombia,[44] and Ecuador.[45] The allegations of bribery in those countries have also been dramatic.[46] This is particularly true in Peru, where all of its former presidents, most well regarded, are now under investigation for accepting bribes from the construction company.[47] Odebrecht's actions have also had serious economic repercussions in South America: 25 major infrastructure projects totaling $7 billion have been suspended as part of lenders' investigations into Odebrecht's practices.[48]

The wave of corruption investigations in South America is unprecedented, leading to public protests and a new push to pass anti-corruption legislation.[49]

43 Four former Peruvian presidents have been accused of receiving bribes from Odebrecht. See Faiola (n 16) (noting that Presidents Kuczynski, Humala, Garćia, and Toledo have either been arrested or are under investigation for receiving bribes from Odebrecht for construction projects); BBC, 'Odebrecht Case' (n 38) (reporting that two ex-presidents from Peru are under investigation and that a third, Ollanta Humala, and his wife, Nadine Heredia, are in pre-trial detention for alleged receipt of bribes from Odebrecht); Nolan, (n 5) (noting that the then current Peruvian president and two former presidents are under investigation resulting from the Lava Jato scandal); Mori, (n 2) (noting that the then Peruvian President Pablo Kuczynski was implicated in the Lava Jato scandal and ultimately was forced to resign).

44 Then Colombian president Juan Manual Santos, who won the Nobel Peace Prize in 2016, was investigated for receiving bribes from Odebrecht. See Nolan (n 5) (noting that Santos was under investigation from bribery allegations stemming from Lava Jato); Casey and Zarate (n 38) (discussing allegations that Santos received $1 million for his campaign from Odebrecht); BBC, 'Odebrecht Case' (n 38) (reporting that Colombia had charged a former vice-minister for transport and a former senator with bribery related to Odebrecht contracts). President Santos has subsequently acknowledged that his 2010 campaign received $400,000 in illegal contributions from Odebrecht but maintains that he was unaware of the payment. See Helen Murphy, 'Colombia's Santos Apologizes for Illegal Funds Paid into Campaign' *Reuters* (14 March 2017) (reporting on President Santos's statement that he did not have knowledge of the illegal payments).

45 Ecuador's Vice-President Jorge Glas was convicted of receiving bribes from Odebrecht and sentenced to a six-year prison term. See BBC, 'Odebrecht Case' (n 38) (reporting that Glas was convicted of receiving $13.5 million in bribes from Odebrecht); Nicholas Casey, 'Ecuador's Vice President Is Jailed in Bribery Investigation' *The New York Times* (3 October 2017) (reporting on Glas's arrest for allegedly receiving bribes from Odebrecht).

46 Casey and Zarate (n 38) (reporting that 'Latin America's biggest corruption scandal is shaking the continent's political establishment.It can all be traced back to Odebrecht, the Brazilian construction company, which has built major projects throughout the region.').

47 See Faiola (n 16).

48 Nolan (n 38) (reporting that Brazilian development bank loans 'for 25 projects in nine countries worth $7 billion (US) are now frozen' due to investigations into Odebrecht resulting from Lava Jato); Luciana Magalhaes, 'Brazil's BNDES Working to Unlock Close to $5 Billion in Loan Disbursements' *The Wall Street Journal* (22 February 2017) (noting that the Brazilian development bank had suspended close to $5 billion in payment on 25 projects valued at $7 billion because 'they were linked to companies involved in the sweeping Operation Car Wash corruption probe').

49 In addition to being the largest corruption scandal ever in dollar terms, the Lava Jato probe has led to changes in legislation and prosecutorial practices in many South American countries. See Vieira (n 10) (noting that the Lava Jato investigation 'is changing the legal and

These protests upended each nation's normal politics.[50] In each state, protestors took to the streets demanding that the government 'do something' to address corruption.[51] This chapter examines governments' responses to these demands and how international law was instrumental (or not) in putting proposals on the governments' agendas.[52]

In the background to this discussion is the concept of transnational legal exchange.[53] The idea is that countries are influenced by each other's laws, unilateral legal actions, and multilateral legal endeavors. Scholars discuss how legal ideas are transplanted,[54] translated,[55] diffused,[56] and acculturated.[57] Studies of transnational legal exchange study the process by which national and international legal concepts move between states and international organizations. This chapter fits within that tradition.

In the area of anti-corruption law, scholars have noted that countries' influences on each other can be complementary or antagonistic (and possibly both at once).[58] In the case of transnational anti-corruption prosecutions, transnational

---

political landscape not just in Brazil, but also around Latin America'); Report by the Americas Society (n 9) (noting that Latin America is experiencing a 'truly regional anti-corruption movement, even if results have varied widely among countries,' and also crediting the Lava Jato prosecutors with demonstrating the effectiveness of plea bargains in corruption investigations.)

50 See n 38 (discussing the political fallout region-wide of these corruption scandals).

51 Ibid.

52 See section 3.

53 The transnational flow of ideas and legal concepts is a core part of modern law and legal processes. See Gregory Shaffer and Daniel Bodansky. 'Transnationalism, Unilateralism and International Law' (2012) 1 Transnational Environmental Law 31 (noting that '[w]e have long lived in an age of transnationalism but transnational processes have intensified with economic and cultural globalization following the fall of the Berlin Wall.')

54 Ugo Mattei, 'Efficiency in Legal Transplants: An Essay in Comparative Law and Economics' (1994) 14 Int'l Rev. L & Econ. 3, 3–4 (noting that '[i]n most cases changes in a legal system are due to legal transplants.')

55 Maximo Langer, 'From Legal Transplants to Legal Translations: The Globalization of Plea Bargaining and the Americanization Thesis in Criminal Procedure' (2004) 45 Harvard International Law Journal 1 (highlighting how the same rules act differently in various national legal traditions and broader legal system and, thus, translation is a better metaphor than transplantation.)

56 Katerina Linos, *The Democratic Foundations of Policy Diffusion: How Health, Family and Employment Laws Spread across Countries* (OUP 2013) (noting that legal ideas often flow through observation and diffusion).

57 Ryan Goodman and Derek Jinks, 'How to Influence States: Socialization and International Human Rights Law' (2004) 54 Duke Law Journal 621 (emphasizing the importance of acculturation in countries adoption of human rights law).

58 Kevin E Davis, Guillermo Jorge, and Maíra R Machado, 'Transnational Anticorruption Law in Action: Cases from Argentina and Brazil' (2015) 40 Law & Social Inquiry 664, 666–671. See also Kevin E Davis, 'Does the Globalization of Anti-Corruption Law Help Developing Countries?' in Julio Faundez and Celine Tan (eds), *International Law, Economic Globalization and Development* (Edward Elgar 2010) 9; Susan Rose-Ackerman, 'Introduction: The Role of International Actors in Fighting Corruption' in Susan Rose-Ackerman and Paul

legal processes can increase the country's legal capacity to address corruption by bringing additional resources or providing superior legal expertise in how to prosecute cases.[59] Yet the same positive processes can concurrently contain negative undercurrents. Foreign actors may have political blind spots or their own political agendas that do not align well with the interests of the local population.[60] There are also accountability concerns as the local population has little voice in the policy processes that lead to the opening and settlement of cases.[61] In addition, the intervention of foreign officials may lead local actors to introduce legal reforms without a proper analysis or without prioritizing the systemic causes of corruption.

This chapter focuses more on the process by which national and international legal ideas are translated into domestic law. Our definition adheres closely to the definition adopted by Professors Davis, Jorge, and Machado that '[transnational law] can be imagined as a rather disorderly series of interactions between local, foreign, and supranational legal institutions, prompted by specific actions or events, with each set of interactions both being shaped by and shaping the institutions involved.'[62] This is a less direct transnational intervention than foreign prosecutions (although we argue that the possibility of foreign prosecutions is an important factor in understanding the flow of legal concepts across borders).

In the next section, we present a political framework that provides specific mechanisms to understand when countries will be open to foreign and international legal exchange. We emphasize the importance of crisis in anti-corruption policy adoption, and the important roles of foreign law and supranational recommendations in providing policy models to respond to domestic crises. Section 4 then applies this framework to the process of corruption reform in South America.

2 Politics and legal reform during crisis

Politics are different in a crisis. This section presents a theory for understanding government decision-making in periods of crisis. As this section highlights, a crisis creates the political opportunity for new coalitions to form and generate policies that would not be possible in ordinary politics. It also highlights the structural threat to these policies as the moment of crisis passes. The first part draws out this political dynamic by examining the work of Professor John Coffee in

---

Carrington (eds), *Anti-corruption Policy: Can International Actors Play a Constructive Role?* (Carolina Academic Press 2013) 3.

59 See Davis and others (n 58) 668–668. See also Juan O Perla, 'A Game Theoretic Analysis of the Inter-American Convention against Corruption' (2017) 16 Rich J Global L & Bus 61 (discussing how Latin American countries have used foreign prosecutions to fight corruption).

60 See Davis and others (n 58) 670.

61 Ibid.

62 Ibid 667.

American financial regulation. Like in anti-corruption policy, financial policy change often results from moments of crisis and involves complex regulatory measures. This part highlights Coffee's idea of a 'regulatory sine curve,' where political entrepreneurs have a limited time to enact policies before normal politics returns. At that point, the predominant interest groups regain their control of issue governance and attempt to roll back reforms.

The second part applies this analysis to the area of anti-corruption law. It discusses how anti-corruption law also comes out of periods of scandal and national crisis. The demand that the government do something to address corruption can lead to a multitude of policy proposals, some of which are likely to be more effective than others. We argue that in this moment, countries that are members of the OECD Convention will act systematically differently than countries that are not members. The OECD Convention and its organizational staff act similarly to political entrepreneurs. In moments of crisis, the treaty body has policy recommendations for member countries that enter domestic legislative discussion. The OECD Convention can be a beneficial force in this situation by having a set of policies that have had some vetting in other nations. In addition, in the post-crisis return to normal politics, the OECD Working Group and other OECD Convention countries can monitor and support continued enforcement of the policies. At the margins, this can reduce the rollback of anti-corruption reforms or their lax enforcement.

2.1 *The regulatory sine curve in financial regulation*

It is a mantra in politics that politicians 'should never let a good crisis go to waste.'[63] Crises create the space for *unusual* political alignments, permitting a range of constituencies to unite and demand political reforms in a manner that would not be possible outside of the crisis. In his work on the Dodd-Frank financial reforms that followed the 2008 financial crisis in the United States, Professor John Coffee discusses how corporate regulation—an area normally dominated by a small group of well-financed insiders—was open to broad new federal rules in a manner that would not have been possible without strong popular demands that the government take action.[64] Yet this window for legislative change is short. The

63 The quote has been attributed to many political figures including Winston Churchill (although the Churchill source may be a misattribution). Its most famous use in the last decade is attributed to Rahm Emanuel discussing the 2008 financial crisis and the opportunity crisis created to pass financial regulatory laws. See Fred Shapiro, 'Quotes Uncovered: Who Said No Crisis Should Go to Waste?' (*Freakonomics*, 13 August 2009) <http://freakonomics.com/2009/08/13/quotes-uncovered-who-said-no-crisis-should-go-to-waste/> accessed 1 June 2020.

64 See Coffee (n 17). See also Christopher H Schroeder, 'Rational Choice Versus Republican Moment-Explanations for Environmental Laws, 1969–73' (1998) 9 Duke Environmental Law & Policy Forum 29, 33–38 (applying and critiquing Olson's framework in explaining the development of American environmental law).

popular demands for change lessen as the crisis passes and politics return to their normal course. As the predominant interest groups regain their control on the policymaking process, reforms will be rolled back or only weakly implemented. Coffee refers to this as the 'regulatory sine curve,' and he argues that it explains both the passing of strong statutory reforms and their erosion.[65]

Drawing on the work of Mancur Olson,[66] Coffee discusses how financial regulation is controlled by the financial services industry, which is compact, knowledgeable, well-funded, and organized.[67] The major groups who could counterbalance the financial services industry are shareholders and other investors.[68] These groups are more numerous, but their members are dispersed, disorganized, and not necessarily knowledgeable about recent policy proposals or what the impact of these proposals would be.[69] The relative organizational advantages of the financial services industry over shareholders and investors (well-funded and targeted lobbying, a consistent message, group cohesion) allow the industry to dominate the often-competing interests of shareholders and investors in the legislative and regulatory process.[70]

This business-as-usual approach to lawmaking is upset by the onset of a crisis.[71] Crises change politics in several ways. First, crises shine a spotlight on a particular policy area. Instead of being one of many issues on a national agenda, scandals or crises focus national attention on a specific set of policies and how the current governance structure has failed to prevent the current crisis.[72] The public has a heightened awareness of the importance of the policy area and will demand change. Yet the demands by the public for the government to take some action can remain diffuse.

Into this political gap come policy entrepreneurs.[73] Policy entrepreneurs attempt to focus the public's discontent into a concerted push for a set of policy reforms, a new institution, or a combination of both.[74] Policy entrepreneurs are able to put proposals on legislators' agendas.[75] The ability to propose governance

65 Coffee (n 17) 1020–1031.

66 Mancur Olson, *The Logic of Collective Action* (2d ed. Harvard University Press 1971).

67 Coffee (n 17) 1021–1042.

68 Ibid.

69 Ibid.

70 Ibid. See also Dan Awrey, 'Complexity, Innovation, and the Regulation of Modern Financial Markets' (2012) 2 Harvard Business Law Review 235, 262–265 (discussing the regulatory dominance of financial firms and their ability to innovate around regulation).

71 Coffee (n 17) 1021–1022.

72 Ibid.

73 Ibid.

74 Ibid.

75 Michael Mintrom, 'Policy Entrepreneurs and the Diffusion of Innovation' (1997) 41 American Journal of Political Science 738; for an application to international organizations, see Peter M Haas, 'Introduction: Epistemic Communities and International Policy Coordination' (1992) 46 International Organization 1.

changes in response to a crisis is a powerful role.[76] They can harness the public's general demands, build coalitions, shape the policy debate, and fill in regulatory details for policy areas that are often opaque and complex.[77]

For instance, in the wake of the US 2008 financial crisis caused by the subprime mortgage market, Professor Elizabeth Warren acted as a policy entrepreneur in the passage of the Dodd-Frank Act.[78] Professor Warren previously argued that American consumer financial protection regulations were insufficient to protect American consumers from the profit-focused strategies of the American financial industry.[79] In normal politics, Professor Warren's proposals made little headway as the financial industry successfully beat back attempts to regulate mortgage lending or banking.[80] But in the midst of the financial crisis, the American public's focus on the governance failures in the mortgage industry was at its height, and new alignments became possible.[81] Professor Warren was able to successfully lobby the Obama administration and top Democratic lawmakers to propose a consumer protection agency as part of the Dodd-Frank Act that would have significant autonomy from Congress (fearing that the agency's powers would be trimmed back once the moment of crisis had passed).[82]

The opportunity that a crisis presents will often be short lived. Politics are such that public attention turns quickly to new issues or other scandals.[83] The return of normal politics means that the window for passing any reforms is narrow and that there is a constant threat of weak implementation post-crisis.[84] As Coffee describes, '[t]he standard cyclical progression along the Regulatory Sine

76 Coffee (n 17) 1021–1022.

77 See Mintrom (n 75) 738–70.

78 See Todd Zywicki, 'The Consumer Financial Protection Bureau: Savior or Menace' (2013) 81 George Washington Law Review 856, 857–864 (referring to Warren as both the 'founding mother' and the 'intellectual godmother' of the institution); John C Coffee Jr., 'The Retreat from Systemic Risk Regulation: What Explains It? (And Why It Was Predictable)' (2018) 2018/4 *Annales des Mines—Réalités industrielles* 80 (stating that '[t]he CFPB was clearly the brainchild of Senator Elizabeth Warren'). See also Susan Block-Lieb, 'Accountability and the Bureau of Consumer Financial Protection' (2012) 7 Brook. J. Corp. Fin. & Com. L. 25, 27–28 (discussing how the financial service industry's normal lock on interest group politics was broken for a time and the interests of diffuse consumer groups won).

79 The specific article that discussed a consumer financial protection agency was Oren Bar-Gill & Elizabeth Warren, 'Making Credit Safer' (2008) 157 University of Pennsylvania Law Review 1.

80 See Zywicki (n 78) 860–864 (discussing the founding of the institution as part of the subprime mortgage crisis); Block-Lieb (n 77) 27–28.

81 See n 78.

82 See Zywicki (n 78) 860–864 (critically analyzing the institution but acknowledging that it was the product of entrepreneur lobbying). See also Leonard J Kennedy, Patricia A McCoy, and Ethan Bernstein, 'The Consumer Financial Protection Bureau: Financial Regulation for the Twenty-First Century' (2012) 97 Cornell Law Rev 1141, 1144–1150 (discussing the institution's autonomy).

83 Coffee (n 17) 1030.

84 Ibid.

Curve from intense to lax enforcement is driven by a basic asymmetry between the power, resources, and organization of the [diffuse] group (i.e. investors) and the interest groups affected by the specific legislation. Cohesion among investors begins to break down once "normalcy" returns.'[85]

Moreover, many critics argue that legislation passed in a crisis is poorly thought out.[86] Although these critics might have their own agendas or represent particular interests, popular policies are often characterized as blunt or insufficiently sophisticated approaches to addressing complex and dynamic relationships.[87] For instance, in a now famous article, Professor Roberta Romano referred to previous American financial legislation, the Sarbanes-Oxley Act, as 'quack' corporate governance.[88] The Dodd-Frank Act also has many critics who argue that it was adopted at the height of public fury over the financial crisis and will be counter-productive.[89]

All of this leaves policies that result from a crisis under siege.[90] Any significant changes have to be made quickly and are thus often open to the charge that they are substantively unsophisticated.[91] In addition, the policies are the result of a public demand that is unlikely to last as ordinary politics return. The lack of support from the predominant interest groups, whose preferences were put aside in the crisis, can lead to the erosion of the policy mandate and the lax enforcement of the reforms going forward.[92]

2.2 The regulatory sine curve in anti-corruption law

Anti-corruption laws are subject to a similar political dynamic as financial reform legislation. In times of normal politics, the dominant interest groups that control the regulatory environment are politicians themselves (who may or may not prefer strong anticorruption laws) and domestic corporations who understand the channels by which government contracts are granted and business is operated. In normal politics, neither of these groups may have much of an incentive to change the status quo. While certain politicians, specific firms, and citizen groups might adamantly demand anti-bribery reforms, the power of these groups is

85 Ibid.

86 See, e.g., Zywicki (n 78) 864–917 (criticizing the Bureau of Consumer Protection).

87 Ibid.

88 Roberta Romano, 'The Sarbanes-Oxley Act and the Making of Quack Corporate Governance' (2004) 114 Yale Law Journal 1521. See also Coffee (n 16) 1027–1039 (critiquing this position).

89 Stephen M Bainbridge, 'Dodd-Frank: Quack Federal Corporate Governance Round II' (2011) 95 Minn L Rev 1779 (stating that the act was a response to 'populist outrage' and adopted quickly without any serious analysis); Zywicki (n 78) 864–917 (discussing the Bureau of Consumer Financial Protection as having a poor agency design and counterproductive substantive policy).

90 Coffee (n 17) 1029–1037.

91 See n 89.

92 Coffee (n 17) 1029–1037.

generally too diffuse and unorganized to provide a sufficient counter-balance. The dominant groups generally will have little incentive to disrupt the existing order. Thus, any demands for major anti-corruption reforms can be pushed back or ignored without much political cost.

The existence of a corruption scandal changes this calculus. Major news reports of bribery focus the public's attention on the injustice of corruption: how government officials are becoming personally enriched, how corporations are stealing from the country, how the country's priorities are distorted by the existence of bribes, how elected officials fail to represent their constituents, and on and on. The public's demand for the government to take action against corrupt practices can overwhelm ordinary politics and provide the space for a new alignment of interests. In the moments of crisis, an opportunity for governance reform emerges.

In South America, the recent Lava Jato corruption scandal has been such a moment of crisis for many countries. Although civil society in much of South America had treated corruption with resignation for many decades, a number of changes in these countries have made the population less willing to accept the status quo.[93] A growing middle class, more representative democracy, as well as the possible influence of social media have all made South American populations less willing to accept corruption as the evitable byproduct of historical, structural, and systemic governance problems.[94] These factors, as well as others, have opened the door to possible reform. As Professor Eduardo Engle (University of Chile and Former Chair of the Presidential Advisory Council on corruption in the Bachelet administration) noted, '[t]here is a silver lining to these scandals: you have a window of opportunity to make major reforms in favor of accountability. In normal times, these reforms are almost impossible.'[95]

Political entrepreneurs can have an important function in crisis politics. The lasting regulatory changes from the crisis will depend on what proposals are put forward as the relevant demands for action. As section 3 discusses in detail, South American countries that have joined the OECD Convention have responded systematically differently than non-OECD Convention countries to the Lava Jato scandal (and other contemporaneous or more recent scandals).

In this situation, the OECD Convention and the organization's staff work similarly to political entrepreneurs. South American countries that have joined the OECD Convention not only have international legal obligations to adopt anti-bribery measures, they also face regular monitoring and peer-review that come with recommendations to adopt specific measures to limit corruption. In particular, the OECD Working Group provides regular monitoring and produces reports (Phases 1–4) on countries' compliance with the OECD Convention

93 Americas Society (n 9).

94 Ibid. See also Brian Winter, 'The Amazing Case That Proved Latin America's Crackdown on Corruption Is For Real' (2016) 10 Americas Quarterly 1.

95 Report by the Americas Society (n 9) 6.

commitments. These peer review reports hold significant legitimacy in the international community as they are viewed as objective and the result of iterative and multilateral legal processes. The reports also provide recommendations for policy changes or refinements that can be readily placed on national legislative agendas in a period of crisis.[96]

In addition, these measures are likely to be good policy. Compared to the financial sector, where accusations of 'quack policies' are regularly attached to new financial regulations, OECD Convention commitments (and the recommendations of the OECD Working Group) have been debated by scholars, policy analysts and government leaders, and have been generally adopted in multiple jurisdictions. While we certainly do not want to argue that there is one optimal anti-corruption policy for all countries, the OECD Convention policies are more tested and conceptually thought out than many quickly considered crisis policy proposals. Thus, OECD Convention commitments and the OECD Working Group recommendations are likely to lead to positive changes in the states and are, therefore, a good (if not necessarily the optimal) source of policy innovation.

For OECD Convention members, pressure from the international organization as well as from other member countries makes the OECD Convention commitments politically salient. As in the financial sector, the governments need to do something quickly that will appear legitimate and meaningful to the domestic audience. This leads governments to turn to ideas that are vetted and readily adoptable.[97] As Professor Bainbridge notes, '[in a crisis], the pressure of time tends to give advantages to interest groups and other policy entrepreneurs who have prepackaged purported solutions that can be readily adapted into legislative form.'[98]

Moving along the political cycle, the period of crisis is generally followed by a period of return to normalcy. In these periods, the major interest groups often regain their grip on legislative and regulatory control. This can also be followed in the general population with a sense of disillusionment with corruption reforms. The optimism that comes with broad demands for change can lead to disappointment with the lack of structural transformation.[99] In addition, the perception that

96 The OECD also launched the Latin America and Caribbean Anti-Corruption Initiative in 2007 to help implement the convention in Latin America and to provide a forum for law enforcement officials to share ideas, experiences, and best practices. See OECD, *Fighting Transnational Corruption in Latin America and the Caribbean* (2018).

97 For a view of the negative side of this process, see Romano (n 88) 1591 (noting that, '[t]he dismal saga of the SOX governance mandates demonstrates that congressional lawmaking in times of perceived emergency offers windows of opportunity to well positioned policy entrepreneurs to market their preferred, ready-made solutions when there is little time for reflective deliberation').

98 See Bainbridge (n 89) 1786.

99 Report by the Americas (n 9) 5 (noting that 'Regionwide [in South America], some countries have seen a perceptible decline in popular support for anti-corruption efforts. This may be partly due to natural fatigue as time passes. But many citizens see a pattern of selective justice, in which some parties or individuals are singled out for prosecution while others continue to operate with impunity.').

anticorruption measures are politically directed to favor some political parties over others can lead to cynicism.[100] In these moments, the major interest groups can either try to push back against the crisis' reforms or only selectively enforce the new provisions. Here, continuing pressure from the OECD Working Group and other OECD Convention member countries can work to prevent backsliding.

In this stage, the OECD Convention can serve an important function by monitoring and reporting on the country's implementation of its laws. The OECD Working Group's peer review process monitors a country's continued compliance with the OECD Convention as well as other aspects of the country's anticorruption law (such as the even application of the law, resources dedicated to enforcement, and transparency in the standards that the country is using in bringing and resolving cases).[101] This monitoring and reporting process helps prevent, but by no means precludes, the rolling back of anticorruption reforms after the period of crisis has passed.

Beyond the influence of the OECD Convention, the US Foreign Corrupt Practices Act (FCPA) likely has an influence on legal reforms in South American countries. The US is the most active prosecutor of foreign corruption and has a very broad set of jurisdictional bases, including listing on American exchanges.[102] South American companies are frequent targets of FCPA probes. Approximately one third of all FCPA cases arise out of allegations of corruption in Central and South America.[103] Moreover, some of the most significant FCPA settlements have involved activity in South America. The first 'blockbuster' FCPA settlement of $800 million with Siemens was the result of that corporation's activities in Argentina (as well as Venezuela and Bangladesh).[104] In addition, the global

100 Felter and Cara (n 20).

101 See, e.g., OECD Working Group on Bribery, *Phase 3 Report on Implementing the OECD Convention in Brazil*, (OECD, October 2014). For instance, that report made recommendations on clarifying the liability of corporations, corporations' responsibility for their employees' actions, and the sanctions that applied to them. See ibid 69. In addition, the report called for the consistent application of cooperation and leniency agreements as well as greater transparency for the reasons for cooperation and leniency agreements in specific cases. Ibid 71.

102 See Rachel Brewster, 'Enforcing the FCPA: International Resonance and Domestic Strategy' (2017) 103 Virginia Law Review 1611 (discussing the very broad basis for FCPA jurisdiction particularly based on accessing American capital markets even indirectly as a 'deposit receipt').

103 James G McGovern and Robert Toll, 'Anti-Corruption trends across Latin America' (*Ethical Boardroom*, Spring 2017) <https://ethicalboardroom.com/anti-corruption-trends-across-latin-america/> accessed 1 June 2020.

104 See US Department of Justice Press Release, Siemens AG and Three Subsidiaries Plead Guilty to Foreign Corrupt Practices Act Violations and Agree to Pay $450 Million in Combined Criminal Fines: Coordinated Enforcement Actions by DOJ, SEC and German Authorities Result in Penalties of $1.6 Billion (15 December 2008) (another $800 million was paid to German authorities).

settlement between the US, Switzerland, and Brazil regarding Odebrecht was the result of that corporation's activities in Brazil.[105]

The American FCPA model functions almost exclusively on settlements: the so-called deferred prosecution agreements (DPA) or non-prosecution agreements (NPA) that the US Department of Justice (DOJ) and the Securities and Exchange Commission (SEC) reach with corporations to resolve foreign corruption charges.[106] The American openness to plea agreements allows it to resolve cases quickly and without trial, although it is subject to critique from multiple angles. Importantly for South American countries, however, the ability to join forces with American law enforcement officials and become part of a global settlement requires domestic legal authority to establish a cooperation or leniency agreement with corporations. These types of agreements have not traditionally been available in South American countries for allegations of significant crimes.[107]

As Section 3 describes, a number of South American countries have altered their legal codes to provide for more leniency and cooperation agreements. Such legal changes provide the tools necessary to enter into multination global settlements regarding corrupt activity that falls within the country's jurisdiction. The desire to join these settlements, particularly American resolutions under the FCPA, can be a strong reason for South American countries to consider adopting these legal reforms. For instance, the Brazilian government was able to join the global settlement regarding Odebrecht with the US and Switzerland and receive 80% of the criminal fine assessed in that case.

In the next section, we apply this framework to policy reforms adopted in South America after the corruption crisis. We argue that South American countries that have joined the OECD Convention behave systematically differently during a crisis than countries that have not. Although there is variation among OECD Convention members as well, these countries are more likely to respond to a crisis by adopting (or expanding) the liability of legal persons (i.e., corporations), and developing (or increasing) the ability of law enforcement officials to form leniency or cooperation agreements.

105 See US Department of Justice Press Release, 'Odebrecht and Braskem Plead Guilty and Agree to Pay at Least $3.5 Billion in Global Penalties to Resolve Largest Foreign Bribery Case in History' (21 December 2016). The case was part of a global settlement between the US, Switzerland, and Brazil. The US and Switzerland each claimed 10% of the total fine with Brazil receiving the remaining 80%. See ibid. The US share was initially set at $260 million but, due to Odebrecht's inability to pay, the fine was reduced to $93 million.

106 Joseph W Yockey, 'FCPA Settlement, Internal Strife, and the Culture of Compliance' [2012] Wis L Rev 689, 696–705; Annalisa Leibold, 'Extraterritorial Application of the FCPA Under International Law' (2014) 51 Willamette L Rev 225, 239–240.

107 The legal hurdles can be significant. States may not have expansive liability for corporations (legal persons) and corporations may not be liable for all of the actions of their employees. In addition, the ability to resolve these cases without trial may be limited. See generally Daniel Pulecio Boek, 'The United States Foreign Corrupt Practices Act and Latin America: The Influence of Local Prosecutorial Efforts in Transnational White-Collar Litigation' (2014) 24 International Law: Revista Colombiana de Derecho Internacional 21.

3 South American countries' responses to corruption crises

This section describes how South American countries have responded to recent corruption scandals. It demonstrates how countries that have become members of the OECD Convention have adopted different laws than countries that have not joined the convention. It also notes the changing priority given by governments to fulfill their international commitment of implementing the OECD Convention, and what has guided the legislative discussion for the enactment of specific statutes and legal reforms. Moreover, it exposes the impact of regional corruption scandals, such as the Odebrecht case, that have not been common, but are likely to keep growing due to international cooperation in the investigation and prosecution of corruption.

The OECD Working Group reports can provide countries with valuable recommendations for the implementation of legislation. One of the main concerns of the OECD Working Group regarding the implementation of the convention in South America was the lack of enactment of legislation that would hold legal persons (corporations) responsible for foreign corruption. As examined in detail in the country studies below, this resulted in the Working Group repeatedly recommending that South American OECD Convention member countries adopt and strengthen laws related to the liability for corporations. This is a particularly meaningful reform because it focuses liability on the entity that gains from corrupt business practices and creates an incentive for corporate leaders to adopt measures to prevent bribery.[108] In addition, it prevents corporations from avoiding liability for the entity's actions by scapegoating individual employees.

Although it took several years for these countries to implement such recommendations, many began doing so after 2009, often in response to a corruption scandal. These laws were frequently accompanied by a provision that required or incentivized corporations to adopt anti-corruption compliance programs. The reforms also often included the possibility that corporations could settle corruption charges with prosecutors or regulatory agencies. Several South American countries that are not part of the OECD Convention have enacted anti-corruption statutes and reforms in recent years, but these countries have not incorporated all of these features into their legal frameworks.

This section provides case studies of several South American countries. We begin with legal reforms undertaken in Argentina and Peru, where the effects of the OECD Convention and the recommendations of the Working Group are clearest. We next discuss Brazil, Colombia, and Chile, where there is more variation but where similar themes unfold. We end by examining several non-OECD Convention countries and highlight how reform proposals differ significantly in those countries.

108 Philip M Nichols, 'The Business Case for Complying with Bribery Laws' (2012) 49 American Business Law Journal 325 (discussing the impact of corruption liability on corporations). See also Brewster (n 102) (examining the impact of strong anticorruption enforcement policies against corporations in the United States).

One issue that we do not address, as it is outside the scope of our already broad chapter, is why countries choose to join (or not) the OECD Convention. In our interviews, we heard local observers discuss that joining the OECD Convention was important (or perceived as important) for attracting foreign investment. If true, there is a possibility that these changes are more directly the result of pressure to draw in foreign capital, rather than a response to the transnational legal process. While we cannot disprove that hypothesis with our current data, we believe that our case studies show that the OECD Convention has at least had an intervening effect. That is, even if countries are primarily adopting these reforms to attract foreign investment (which we are skeptical of given the intensity of domestic pressures on these issues), the OECD Convention nonetheless has an important effect in identifying and elaborating what specific policies are desirable.

3.1 Argentina

Argentina was one of the first South American countries to join the OECD Convention. In spite of this early action in joining the treaty, Argentina failed to implement several key aspects of the convention.[109] It was not until the Odebrecht scandal rippled through Argentina that the legislature was willing to adopt laws establishing liability for legal persons. The Working Group, in its Phase 3 Report on 2014, expressed its concern regarding the state's commitment to fight foreign bribery, considering that the majority of key observations made since 2001 had not been implemented, such as holding legal persons liable for transnational corruption.[110] In 2015, Mauricio Macri became Argentina's President, ending 12 years of Kirchner presidency. Macri's campaign promised to make substantial changes to Argentina's economy and had announced his intention to analyze the possibility of becoming a full OECD member.[111] His campaign was also based on the promise to fight corruption, considering that there were several allegations of corruption against the former president Cristina Kirchner.[112] In March 2017, Argentina presented an Action Plan to the OECD with the aim of implementing

109 See OECD Press Release, 'Argentina must urgently enact Corporate Liability Bill to rectify serious non-compliance with Anti-Bribery Convention' (24 March 2017).

110 See OECD Working Group on Bribery, *Phase 3 Report on Implementing the OECD Anti-bribery Convention in Argentina* (OECD, December 2014) 5–6.

111 Argentina was interested joining the broader OECD organization, not just the Anti-Bribery Convention. See 'Macri's OECD Seduction to Continue at G20 Summit' *Buenos Aires Times* (11 November 2018) <https://www.batimes.com.ar/news/world/macris-oecd-seduction-to-continue-at-g20-summit.phtml> accessed 1 June 2020 (noting that among President Macri's 'key objectives is his desire for Argentina to become a full member of the Organisation for Economic Co-operation and Development').

112 Roberto P Bauza, 'Argentina's Fight against Corruption: New Reality, New Tools' (*International Bar Association,* 19 December 2017) <https://www.ibanet.org/Article/NewDetail.aspx?ArticleUid=08A16322-5602-4141-8A57-F8B1F55DF94C> accessed 1 June 2020.

OECD standards and best practices.[113] In the same month, the OECD Working Group issued its Phase 3bis report. That report noted that the current government was making a serious effort to implement changes, but Argentina was still not compliant with key recommendations such as incorporating legal person liability for corruption crimes.[114] Although the president had presented a bill to Congress in October 2016 to address the issue of liability for legal persons, it was not passed until December 2017.

The Odebrecht scandal was important to accelerate the legislative process considering that scholars, media, and even President Macri had commented on several occasions about the importance of this law's passage in order to move forward with Odebrecht investigations.[115] Law 27,401 implemented criminal liability for legal persons for the commission of: (i) local or international bribery and influence peddling; (ii) negotiations incompatible with public office; (iii) extortion by public officers; (iv) unjust enrichment by public officers and employees; and (v) falsification of balance sheets and reports. This law also introduced compliance programs into Argentina's legislation. It provided that adopting and implementing a compliance program could mitigate and even exempt legal persons from responsibility. However, it also provided that implementing a compliance program would be mandatory for those entities that engaged with the Federal Government.

The Lava Jato scandal also had an important impact on Argentinian anticorruption policy by leading to the adoption of cooperation agreements with defendants. The Argentinian government was heavily criticized for its slow investigation into Odebrecht and other cases, particularly compared to Brazil's ability to move quickly to form plea agreements. In response, Argentina adopted Law 27,401 providing that legal persons were able to enter into effective collaboration agreements, where they could seek reduction of penalties in exchange for accurate, useful, and verifiable information regarding facts, principals, and participants in the crime, or permitted the recovery of assets.[116] This type of settlement, designed to fight corruption, was new in Argentinian legislation. In October 2016, Law

113 See 'Argentina, A Mutually Beneficial Relationship' (OECD) <https://www.oecd.org/latin-america/countries/argentina/> accessed 1 June 2020.

114 Argentina had already implemented legal person liability for tax offences, insider trading and other securities offences, money laundering, and terrorism financing. For example, joint liability for companies and individuals has existed in Argentina since 1981.

115 See Stephanie Keith, 'Argentina Congress Passes Law to Fight Corporate Corruption' *Reuters* (8 November 2017) <https://www.reuters.com/article/us-argentina-corruption/argentina-congress-passes-law-to-fight-corporate-corruption-idUSKBN1D83AX> accessed 1 June 2020; Carlos Jasso, 'Argentina Bans Brazil's Odebrecht from New Projects for 12 Months' *Reuters* (3 July 2017) <https://www.reuters.com/article/us-argentina-odebrecht-idUSKBN19O2JV> accessed 1 June 2020; Natalia Violosin and Susan Rose-Ackerman, 'Argentina Must Reform to Tackle Government-Business Corruption' (*The Hill*, 20 June 2017) <https://thehill.com/blogs/pundits-blog/international/338612-argentina-needs-reform-to-tackle-government-and-business> accessed 1 June 2020.

116 The agreement is subject to the conditions established in Art. 18 of Law 27,401.

27,304 was enacted and provided that defendants that cooperate with accurate and verifiable information of crimes that they participated in, could receive a sentence reduction through a written agreement with prosecutors, subject to the judge's approval after a hearing.[117] These reforms aimed to address the OECD Working Group observations made in 2014, regarding the delays in the investigation and prosecution of economic crimes.[118] Although this law arguably does not provide the same broad prosecutorial powers to enter into plea agreements that Brazilian and American law enforcement officials have, it does provide prosecutors with greater flexibility in reaching multistate settlements.[119]

3.2 Peru

In 2014, the Peruvian Government launched an OECD Country Program, aiming to become a member of the Organization.[120] The Program, which was developed with the OECD, was built upon five key areas, including anti-corruption.[121] This Program consisted of 'policy reviews, implementation and capacity building projects, participation in OECD Committees and adherence to selected OECD legal instruments.'[122] Based on this commitment, during the first month of Kuczynski's presidency, Peru enacted Law 30424 in April 2016 to adhere to the OECD Convention requirements and to implement liability of legal persons. Due to this, the law only provided administrative liability for legal persons for transnational corruption. The law contemplated sentencing bonuses or even exemption of liability to those companies that adopted or had implemented compliance programs. Though there was no provision regarding settlements, it permitted companies to receive sentencing bonuses for cooperation, disclosure, and other factors.

As the Lava Jato scandal expanded into Peru, it set the conditions for Peru to expand the liability for legal persons engaged in corruption. At the end of 2016, with the DOJ's release of the bribes paid by Odebrecht in Latin America, Peru's

117 The information must incriminate another person of equal or greater responsibility for the crime. This figure already existed in Argentina legislation, but did not apply to bribery crimes.

118 See OECD Working Group on Bribery, *Phase 3 Report on Implementing the OECD Anti-bribery Convention in Argentina* (OECD, 2014). The Working Group observed that systemic deficiencies in Argentina's criminal justice system identified in Phase 2 still persist and that widespread delays in economic crime cases continue to plague the criminal justice system. Moreover, the few cases of foreign corruption opened to investigate foreign bribery had progressed very slowly.

119 See Benjamin N Gedan and Christopher Phalen, 'In Argentina, Why Is All Quiet on the Odebrecht Front?' *Americas Quarterly* (9 April 2018).

120 See 'Argentina, A Mutually Beneficial Relationship' (OECD) <https://www.oecd.org/latin-america/countries/argentina/> accessed 1 June 2020.

121 Ibid. The five areas were economic growth, public governance, anti-corruption and transparency, human capital and productivity, and environment.

122 Ibid.

government went through a severe political crisis. Pedro Kuczynski, who had promised in his presidential campaign to fight against corruption and who had obtained powers from Congress to do so, was under pressure.[123] On 5 January 2017, Odebrecht agreed with prosecutors to collaborate with the investigations and disgorged $8.5 million of profits in bribes. Two days later, Peru enacted Law Decree 1352. The decree's preamble stated that its objective was to fulfill several international commitments including the OECD Convention, as well as to remedy deficiencies highlighted by the Financial Action Task Force (FATF) regarding legal person liability for money laundering and terrorism financing. This Decree reformed Law 30,424 by expanding its scope, holding legal persons liable under administrative law for domestic and transnational bribery, money laundering, and terrorism financing.

Other legal reform, aimed at expanding plea bargaining, also appears to be a direct result of the Lava Jato scandal. Although plea bargaining already existed in Peru for individuals facing charges related to organized crimes beginning in 2000, President Kuczynski issued an important legal reform (enacted through Law Decree 1301) days after the DOJ's release of Odebrecht payments. This law aimed to strengthen the 'efficient cooperation' process in order to facilitate the investigation of crimes and prosecution of criminal organizations. Under this law, a defendant could make a request to the Prosecutor's Office to be considered a cooperator in a plea deal in exchange for obtaining an exoneration, reduction or suspension of penalty, by providing verifiable information that permitted the Prosecutor's Office to identify those criminally liable for certain crimes, including national and transnational bribery.[124] Though this law initially did not apply to legal persons, Law 30,737, enacted in March 2018, allowed entities to enter into 'efficient cooperation' agreements that would permit prosecutors to exempt, suspend, or reduce sanctions in exchange for timely, efficient, and corroborated information that would permit the identification of others involved in the crime. Law 30,737's main purpose was to guarantee the payment of civil fines imposed on legal persons in corruption cases. At that moment, the only case that would have been subject to such regulation was the agreement between Peru and Odebrecht.[125]

123 Pedro Kaczynski obtained through law 30,506, enacted in October 2010, a delegation from congress to legislate for a period of 90 days in a limited number of subjects, that included the necessary law to implement OECD instruments and measures to fight corruption. These laws are referred to as law decrees, rather than decrees.

124 See Peru Ministry of Justice and Human Rights News, 'Ministra: Decreto Legislativo N° 1301 facilitará investigación y sanción del crimen organizado' Ministerio de Justicia y Derechos Humanos del Perú (13 March 2017). The Minister of Justice of Peru discussed the specifics of this law with the special commission created by Peru's Congress to investigate the Lava Jato case. She argued that the reform gave prosecutors more power to negotiate, protects the identity of the cooperator, and allowed criminal organization leader to be subject to this process as long as they identify a higher leader of the organization.

125 IUS 360°, '¿Cómo pretende la Ley 30737 asegurar el pago inmediato de la reparación civil a favor del Estado en el caso Lava Jato?' (*IUS 360*, 20 March 2018) <https://ius360.com/

3.3 Brazil

Although Brazil ratified the OECD Convention in August 2000, it did not hold legal entities responsible for transnational corruption until 2013. The OECD Working Group expressed its concern regarding this issue in 2004, 2007, and 2010.[126] However, before the Working Group's 2010 follow up report was issued, the Comptroller General of Brazil in cooperation with the Ministry of Justice and the Federal Attorney General's Office, presented to Congress (Chamber of Deputies) Bill 6,826 that proposed to implement civil and administrative liability for legal entities for acts against national and foreign public administrations.[127] The Chamber of Deputies formed a special committee in October 2011 to review the bill and present its report. The committee did not issue a report until April 2013.

As the committee worked on this legislation, the Brazilian public was dissatisfied with the government's spending priorities and the growing number of corruption cases. In June 2013, Brazil had historic protests due the costs of the FIFA World Cup and the Olympic Games, both due to take place in the next three years. Brazilians insisted that the government should increase the public spending for health, education, and transportation and also demanded actions against corruption. This last demand was motivated by the Mensalão scandal, which was concurrently on trial in Brazil's Supreme Court.[128] This case caught the attention of the media and caused public debates that led to an anti-corruption campaign through social media, which contributed to Brazilians' growing intolerance of corruption.[129]

Public discontent and demands for corruption reform led to the passage of new legislation in record time. Bill 6,826, which had been in the Chamber of Deputies for over three years, flew through the rest of the legislative process and was enacted as Law 12,846 in August 2013. The law not only incorporated civil and administrative liability for legal persons that committed illicit acts against national and foreign public administrations, but it also established a regime

notas/como-pretende-la-ley-30737-asegurar-el-pago-inmediato-de-la-reparacion-civil-favor-del-estado-en-el-caso-lava-jato/> accessed 1 June 2020.

126 See OECD Working Group on Bribery, *Brazil: Phase 2 Follow-up Report on the Implementation of the Phase 2 Recommendations* (OECD, June 2010) 4.

127 See Willian Coelho and Leticia Barbabela, 'The New Brazilian Anticorruption Law: Federation Challenges and Institutional Roles' (2015) 6 World Bank Legal Review 365, 371–374 (arguing that this bill was inspired by the FCPA and the UK Bribery Act).

128 See ibid 372 (This scandal has been taking place since 2004, during Lula da Silva's government. Congressional representatives of the Workers Party were requiring monthly payments in exchange for political support inside the Congress. This scandal also involved high ranking political figures, financial institutions and public institutions. Ministerio Publico accused 40 people that included important politician of the Workers Party and official that worked closely with Lula da Silva.) This case was considered the biggest corruption scandal until the Lava Jato investigation.

129 Ibid 372.

through which legal persons could enter into leniency agreements. This would allow fines against a legal person to be reduced by up to two thirds. A legal person could also be exempt from certain sanctions, in exchange for cooperation with and disclosure in, the investigation. In addition, the law introduced compliance programs into Brazilian legislation by allowing corporations to reduce sanctions for the 'effective' implementation of programs.

The same political dynamics also led to the quick passage of a previously slow-moving reform bill regarding cooperation agreements. One day after the enactment of Law 12,846, Brazil enacted Law 12,850, which had been in the legislative process since 2009. It addressed cooperation agreements and judicial pardons, and reformed the definition of criminal organization. The law gave prosecutors an important new tool in the fight against corruption. It allowed individuals to enter into a settlement with prosecutors, approved by a judge, at any stage of any criminal prosecution, including after sentencing. The individual would receive judicial pardon, reduction of sentence by up to two thirds, or replacement of a custodial sentence with a sentence of restrictive rights in exchange for individual voluntary cooperation and aid in the investigation.[130]

Before the enactment of this law, Brazilian legislators had issued a number of different statutes since 1990 that would allow plea bargains only for the commission of certain crimes, but not for corruption.[131] As with many other states in the region, Brazilian legislation contemplated an abbreviated process for crimes punished by one-year imprisonment or less, where natural persons could enter into plea bargains.[132]

3.4 Colombia

Colombia's decision to join and implement the OECD Convention occurred during a domestic corruption scandal. In June 2010, a bribery scheme, known as 'Carrusel de la Contratacion,' at that time considered the biggest corruption

130 According to Article 4 of the law, such cooperation had to produce one or more of the following results: (I) identification of joint principals and accessories that integrate a criminal organization and of the criminal offenses committed by them; (II) the disclosure of the hierarchical structure and the division of tasks within a criminal organization; (III) prevention of criminal offenses arising from the activities performed by a criminal organization; (IV) full or partial recovery of the products or proceeds derived from criminal offenses committed by a criminal organization; (V) location of any victims of a criminal organization provided their physical integrity is preserved.

131 See Andrew B Spalding, 'Brazil's Olympic-Era Anti-Corruption Reforms' (2017) 32 Maryland Journal International Law 188, 216 ('Under the previous regime, judges could only reduce the penalty by one to two thirds, or grant a pardon post-conviction if the judge determined that the defendant's cooperation was useful to the conviction. A defendant could thus not be sure, at the time of confession, of the plea bargain's effects on his or her conviction and sentence.')

132 Ibid.

scandal in Colombian history, shook the nation.[133] This case brought Colombia's corruption problem into public debate, and put pressure on the government to take action. President Juan Manuel Santos took office in August 2010, soon after the scandal came to light. His National Plan had key priority issues such as gaining international relevance and improving good governance.[134] This plan also highlighted the importance and the benefits of becoming a full member of the OECD, and the necessity to strengthen the fight against corruption.[135] In the first months of Santos's presidency, the executive branch presented a bill that was passed in 2011, known as the Anti-corruption Statute.[136] This statute aimed to respond to public demands that resulted from the 'Carrusel de la Contratacion' scandal and to implement the OECD Convention.[137]

The law provided that legal entities are subject to administrative liability if they had sought benefits from the commission of crimes against public administration, or any criminal offence related to public property.[138] However, the OECD Working Group in its Phase 2 Report stated its concern regarding deficiencies of legal person liability in the Anti-Corruption Statute, such as lack of liability for certain legal entities, the impossibility of enforcing an action against a company without establishing the responsibility of a natural person, and the ineffectiveness of sanctions to produce their expected effects.[139] Based on these observations, a bill was presented to Congress expressing that its objective was to implement the OECD Convention accordingly. In February 2016, Law 1778 established an administrative procedure for the investigation and sanction of legal persons for bribery of foreign officials, independent and not subject to the criminal responsibility of an individual. The law introduced compliance programs by permitting entities to receive a sentencing bonus or to even be exempt from liability for adopting and implementing compliance programs. However, it also provides that the Superintendence of Legal Entities would establish, based on relevant

133 Diego Escallón Arango, 'Reacción del Estado colombiano frente al carrusel de la contratación en Bogotá: ¿eficacia o discurso?' (2014) 32 Revista de Derecho Público de la Universidad de los Andes 1, 6–11 (The Carrusel de la Contratacion scandal implicated the former mayor of Bogota, city council members, congressmen, and politicians. The scandal revealed a network where these officials would award projects to important private firms in exchange for commissions. Illicit payments were funneled through contracts awarded to fake companies and consultancies that where never provided.).

134 See generally Departamento Nacional de Planeacion, *Resumen Ejecutivo Plan nacional de desarrollo 2010–2014: prosperidad para todos* (2010).

135 Ibid.

136 Ley 1474 de 2011, Art. 34, 12 de julio de 2011. D.O. No. 48.128.

137 The OECD Working Group on Bribery in its Phase 1 Report in Implementing the OECD Convention recognized that the Anti-Corruption Statute aimed to bring Colombia's legislation into compliance with the Convention.

138 While the majority of state members of the Convention in the region did not established legal persons liability for bribery in their first reforms to implement the Convention requirements, Colombia did.

139 See OECD Working Group on Bribery, *Phase 2 Report on implementing the OECD Anti-bribery Convention in Colombia* (OECD, October 2015) 5.

factors, which entities should implement compliance programs. In addition, Law 1778 introduced a leniency process that could allow legal persons to receive even a full exemption of the sanction in exchange for disclosure and cooperation.[140]

3.5 *Chile*

Chile ratified the OECD Convention in 2001 and quickly enacted legislation to implement the convention, which entered into force in 2002.[141] The Working Group on Bribery, while analyzing Chile's implementation of the OECD Convention in its Phase 2 Report in October 2007, expressed its concern regarding Chile's noncompliance with key recommendations expressed in the Phase 1 Report issued in 2004.[142] One of those recommendations was to adopt legislation that held legal persons accountable and subject to sanctions.[143] Based on the seriousness of Chile's noncompliance with the Convention, the Working Group decided to do an additional review in 2008, which took place in 2009.[144] Chile took important steps in those two years in order to fulfill several of the key recommendations. In March 2009, the president of Chile presented to the Congress a bill to implement corporate criminal liability in Chile.[145] The vice president explained that Chile had been invited in May 2007 to be a full member of the OECD, but this was subject to the State implementing OECD regulations. After explaining the benefits of being an OECD full member, the vice president described the observations of the 2nd Report of the Working Group regarding legal person liability and the need to fulfill the Working Group's key recommendations.[146] Congress acted promptly and enacted Law 20,393, which entered into force in December 2009.

140 Under Colombian criminal procedure, which only applies to individuals, a defendant can only enter into a plea bargain for the commission of specific crimes. Private corruption is considered as one of those. However, under Colombian criminal law, private corruption takes place when an individual gives a bribe to the agents of a private entity in exchange for a benefit for him or a third party that is against the private entity's interest.

141 See Law No. 19,829, which reforms Chile's Criminal Code regarding bribery, promulgated on September 30, 2002.

142 OECD Working Group on Bribery, *Chile: Phase 2 report on the application of the Convention on Combating Bribery of Foreign Public Officials in International Business Transactions and the 1997 Revised Recommendation on Combating Bribery in International Business Transactions* (OECD, October 2007) 4.

143 Ibid.

144 See OECD Working Group on Bribery, *Chile: Phase 2 report Follow-up on the application of the Convention on Combating Bribery of Foreign Public Officials in International Business Transactions and the 1997 Revised Recommendation on Combating Bribery in International Business Transactions* (OECD, October 2009).

145 'Historia de la Ley 20,393' (*Biblioteca del Congreso Nacional de Chile*, 2 December 2009) 4–15 https://www.bcn.cl/historiadelaley/nc/historia-de-la-ley/4785/ accessed 1 June 2020.

146 Ibid 5.

This law only holds legal persons criminally liable for bribery of local or foreign officials, money laundering, and financing of terrorism. With this reform, anti-corruption compliance programs were also included in Chile's legislation. Article 3 of the Law provided that, for a legal entity to be held liable, the criminal offense must be the result of a breach of the entity's 'duty of direction and supervision.' The law deems such duties to be met if the legal person has adopted and implemented a 'sufficient' organization, administration, and supervision model before the commission of the offense.[147]

Law 20,393 also allowed entities to settle through a 'conditional suspension' similar to a deferred prosecution agreement, permitting the criminal process to be terminated without trial if the defendant observed the conditions of the suspension. This was completely different to what natural persons could do while facing prosecution for bribery.[148] Chile's general rule of criminal procedure for mandatory prosecution, which applies to bribery of local and foreign officials, did not allow prosecutors to close an investigation without presenting charges, unless there was no evidence of the commission of a crime. This law granted prosecutors more flexibility to enter into a conditional suspension in any bribery case where there was no sentence or other conditional suspension of the ongoing proceeding against a legal person.

Although the legislative process of Law 20,393 could appear to show that Chile did not require a period of scandal or national crisis for the enactment of anti-corruption laws, this would not be accurate. Since 2014, several corruption scandals focused the nation's attention on Chile's lobbying, campaign financing, and conflicts of interest regulations.[149] These cases resulted in a growing lack of confidence in democratic institutions in Chile and led Bachelet to create an advisory commission that would draft regulations in a 45-day window to address this problem.[150] In August 2016, an anti-corruption agenda was established with the

147 Law No. 20,393 Art 4.

148 See OECD Working Group on Bribery, *Chile: Phase 2 report on the application of the Convention on Combating Bribery of Foreign Public Officials in International Business Transactions and the 1997 Revised Recommendation on Combating Bribery in International Business Transactions* (OECD, October 2007) 25–27. See also OECD Working Group on Bribery, *Phase 3 report on implementing the OECD Anti-bribery Convention* (OECD, March 2014) 26–27 (noting that criminal proceedings involving individuals could also be suspended without trial only if the offense was punishable with prison time for three or less time). Chile, like many South American countries, has established a process that allows abbreviated procedures when a prosecutor seeks a sentence of five years or less and the accused agrees to it. See ibid.

149 See Simon Romero, 'Chile Joins Other Latin American Nations Shaken by Scandal' *The New York Times* (9 April 2017) <https://www.nytimes.com/2015/04/10/world/americas/chile-joins-other-latin-american-nations-shaken-by-scandal.html> accessed 1 June 2020; Pascale Bonnefoy, 'As Graft Cases in Chile Multiply, a "Gag Law" Angers Journalists' *The New York Times* (7 April 2016) <https://www.nytimes.com/2016/04/08/world/americas/chile-corruption-press-gag-law.html> accessed 1 June 2020.

150 Consejo Asesor Presidencial contra los Conflictos de Interés, el Tráfico de Influencias y la Corrupción, *Informe Final* (24 April 2015).

purpose of initiating the legislative process of such reforms that concluded in the enactment of several laws such as Law 20,880 and Law 20,900, which regulated conflict of interests and disclosure of assets and interest by public officials, and prohibited firms from financing campaigns.[151]

3.6 Non-OECD convention countries

South American non-member countries to the OECD Convention have not followed the recent patterns seen in member countries to OECD Convention. The only non-OECD Convention countries that have adopted legal person liability for bribery are Ecuador and Venezuela, but they have not required or incentivized legal persons to adopt and implement anti-corruption compliance programs. Neither has there been a trend to enhance or grant prosecutors new legal tools to investigate and prosecute corruption crimes in a faster and more efficient way.

In Ecuador, there had been no enactment of significant anti-corruption laws for over ten years until the Odebrecht scandal. With the release by the DOJ of the bribes paid by Odebrecht in Ecuador, the media and Ecuadorians demanded immediate action from the government and judicial institutions. The information provided by the United States and Brazil led the General Prosecutor to open investigations against the former vice president, several ministers, the State Comptroller General, and officials of the state-owned oil company Petro Ecuador for corruption-related charges. After the imprisonment of the vice president in December 2017, recently elected President Lenin Moreno called for a general referendum to fight corruption that was approved with 65% of votes in February 2018.

The referendum proposed several reforms, which included an amendment to the criminal code to implement criminal liability for corporate entities that commit national bribery and influence peddling.[152] The amendment did not require the government to give any sentencing bonus for companies that implemented a compliance program, nor did it allow legal persons to settle at any stage of the proceedings. Recently, several congressional representatives have presented anti-corruption bills as a response to the Odebrecht Scandal. The Justice Commission of the Ecuadorean Congress analyzed the bills and presented a consolidated project for congressional debate. Though several scholars emphasized the need for strengthening legal person liability by implementing compliance programs and

151 'Conoce la Agenda de Probidad y Transparencia, Agenda de Probidad y Transparencia' Gobierno de Chile <http://www.lasnuevasreglas.gob.cl/> accessed 1 June 2020.

152 Ecuador had already incorporated criminal liability for legal person but only for specific crimes that did not include bribery. The referendum also prohibited those found guilty of bribery or other corruption crimes from running for office, to obtain public employment, and to contract with public entities. The referendum also proposed different measures to strengthen the independence of Ecuadorean institutions, and prohibited re-election of public officials.

other measures, the Commission focused on asset recovery.[153] The President vetoed the bill in September 2017 and presented a new bill that would implement whistleblower provisions for public officials and enhance plea bargaining. However, this law has not been taken as a priority by Congress.

In Venezuela, there have been two significant anti-corruption reforms. The Law against Organized Crime and Terrorism Financing of 2012 incorporated legal person criminal liability in a broad manner, holding legal persons responsible for bribery payments. However, it did not require or incentivize legal persons to implement compliance programs, nor did it allow them to enter into settlement agreements with prosecutors. The law stated that its purpose was to investigate, prosecute, and regulate crimes related to organized crime and terrorism financing in accordance with the Constitution and international instruments. In November 2013, due to the severe economic crises in Venezuela, corruption allegations, and raising protests, Congress delegated to President Maduro, for one year, legislative power to enact laws to fight corruption and defend the economy.[154] In November 2014, through a Presidential Decree published in Official Gazette 6.155, President Maduro enacted the Anti-Corruption Law. The main reforms in this law were the creation of the Anti-Corruption National Body that would report directly to the President, asset recovery provisions, and disclosure of assets by public officials. It also criminalized transnational corruption in order to fulfill international commitments.

In 2010, Bolivia enacted the Marcelo Quiroga Santa Cruz Anti-Corruption Law in order to comply with the United Nations Convention Against Corruption (UNCAC) and the Inter-American Convention Against Corruption (IACAC) commitments[155] and with the electoral promise of Evo Morales of zero tolerance for corruption.[156] The law criminalizes active and passive corruption, and bribery of foreign officials. It also enhances whistleblower provisions, including preservations of labor protection. It does not hold legal persons liable for corruption or bribery. However, it provides that the legal representative of a legal person can be charged for illicit enrichment committed by an entity. Since then, there have not been any significant legal reforms in Bolivia.

153 This was due to a great number of public complaints regarding the lack of asset recovery in the Odebrecht investigations and the impunity of officials that have avoided trial by fleeing from the country.

154 See Nicolas Maduro Moros, Presidencia de la Republica Bolivariana de Venezuela, *Contra la corrupción y la guerra económica (Sesión especial con motivo de solicitud de Ley Habilitante Asamblea Nacional)* (2013) (Maduro alleged that elite groups have declared a war against Venezuela, requiring them to take special measures in order to face such challenges.).

155 See Ley 004, Art.1, 2, 31 de marzo de 2010.

156 See Evo Morales, *Discurso de posesión del Presidente Constitucional de la República* (2006). Evo Morales was the first indigenous president of Bolivia. His campaign offered radical changes in Bolivia politics. One of the main promises of his first presidential campaign was the fight against corruption, which had been constantly present throughout Bolivia's history.

Paraguay had not enacted any anti-corruption legislation in over ten years when a 2012 presidential decree created a National Anti-corruption Secretary that implemented anti-corruption policies and international commitments of the UNCAC and IACAC. Paraguay's fight against corruption has advanced at a slow pace.[157] However, in recent months, there has been an unprecedented number of student-led protests in Paraguay. These protests began after several congressional representatives were re-elected despite being charged with corruption. Protests have led to new investigations and prosecutions of high-ranking officials. Yet, no reforms have been adopted yet. Andrew Nickson, an expert on Paraguay at the University of Birmingham, stated that '[u]nless convictions and reforms happen quickly, the recent anti-corruption protests could run out of steam.'[158]

Uruguay's corruption index is significantly better than other countries in the region, and it has been referred to as the cleanest country in Latin America.[159] There have not been significant anti-corruption reforms since 1998.[160]

4 Conclusion and challenges ahead

The political maxim to never waste a crisis is only the starting point for understanding government decision-making in times of political upheaval. Crises create the necessary conditions for reform, but the process of getting meaningful and effective proposals before legislators is the critical next step.

Corruption crises present unique opportunities to pass meaningful anti-corruption reform. The question often is whether governments will use the crisis to do so. This chapter examines this question in the context of the recent wave of corruption scandals in South America and analyzes whether international law can help ensure that new legislation includes robust and effective measures. By comparing how South American countries that were members of the OECD Convention responded to these crises to countries that did not join the OECD Convention, we can test for the treaty's effect in national legislative reform efforts.

We find that the OECD Convention did have a significant impact on the content of anti-corruption reforms. The OECD Anti-Bribery Working Group in their reports and recommendations continually emphasized the need for corporate liability for acts of domestic and foreign bribery. Most South American countries did not have such liability, but rather only held individuals liable. In

157 Iñaki Albisu Ardigó 'Paraguay: Overview of Corruption and Anti-corruption' (*Transparency International*, 2016) 1–2 <https://knowledgehub.transparency.org/helpdesk/paraguay-overview-of-corruption-and-anti-corruption> accessed 1 June 2020.

158 Laurence Blair, 'Long Overdue, Can an Anti-Corruption Surge in Paraguay Last?' *World Politics Review* (14 November 2018) <https://www.worldpoliticsreview.com/articles/26747/long-overdue-can-an-anti-corruption-surge-in-paraguay-last> accessed 1 June 2020.

159 Ardigó (n 157) 1–2.

160 See Law N° 17.060 of December 23, 1998 (Rules of this legislation were enacted in 2003 Decree N° 30).

addition, most South American countries did not have procedures for settling such claims without a full trial.

In the aftermath of the crises, countries that had joined the OECD Convention overwhelmingly adopted or meaningfully strengthened their national laws regarding corporate liability for corruption. This is a significant and consequential reform because it centers liability on the entity that profits from corrupt conduct and incentivizes corporate leaders to prevent bribery in their business dealings. Countries that had joined the OECD Convention also generally provided mechanisms for corporations to limit this liability (or at least mitigating factors) by offering incentives for creating corporate compliance programs *ex ante* and introducing pre-trial settlements of these charges. By contrast, countries that did not join the OECD Anti-Bribery treaty did not focus their reforms on creating a system of corporate liability, corporate compliance programs, or prosecutorial mechanisms to have pre-trial resolution.

Notwithstanding the success of the reforms in many South American states, there are challenges on the horizon. The fight against corruption has caused some economic losses in the region. While the fight against corruption can be costly, it is important to acknowledge that the costs of corruption are even higher (by a large order of magnitude) and thus robust anticorruption reform is extremely important to a nation's economic success.[161] Corruption distorts political leaders' focus from public goods to private gain, redirects state resources away from socially optimal projects to projects where the opportunity for bribes is highest, and distorts market competition away from price to illicit payments.[162]

Nonetheless, fighting corruption can have economic impacts as well, particularly in the short term. This has been true for the recent South American corruption investigations and prosecutions. Two economic impacts stand out and are worth addressing here.

First, the corruption allegations throughout South America regarding Odebrecht's business practices (and the business practices of some other major firms revealed by the Lava Jato investigation) have led to the suspension of major infrastructure projects. The Brazilian development bank (Banco Nacional de Desenviolvimento Economico e Social (BNDES)), froze 25 infrastructure projects across South America, valued at $7 billion, due to concerns of corruption with the construction companies, including Odebrecht.[163] Not only does this hurt the companies and individuals who would be employed by the projects, it also imposes losses on those who would benefit from the projects' completion.[164]

161 Jakob Svensson, 'Eight Questions about Corruption' (2005) 19 Journal of Economic Perspectives 19.

162 Ibid 19–21. See also Nichols (n 108) 325–368 (discussing the direct and indirect costs of corruption to businesses).

163 Magalhaes (n 48).

164 Jorge (n 13).

Second, there is the risk of multiple governments 'piling on' the same allegations.[165] Because governments prohibit foreign as well as domestic corruption, several countries can have jurisdiction over the same activity. Between nations, there is not a 'double jeopardy' bar to adjudicating the same charges. The legal resolution of charges in one nation does not necessarily resolve those charges in other nations' legal system.[166] For instance, Odebrecht entered into a settlement of its transnational bribery scheme with the United States, Switzerland, and Brazil together.[167] The United States had jurisdiction under its Foreign Corrupt Practices Act because Odebrecht listed on an American stock exchange.[168] As a result, American prosecutors had jurisdiction over bribes by Odebrecht in Brazil just as Brazilian prosecutors did. However, Odebrecht still faces potential claims in other countries where it engaged in bribery.

The difficulty of resolving all of the possible claims can result in continued uncertainty for the corporation and make rehabilitation of the corporation difficult.[169] Indeed, Odebrecht filed for bankruptcy in the summer of 2019, which is set to be the largest bankruptcy in South American history.[170] This bankruptcy will additionally hurt Brazilian taxpayers by shifting losses to BNDES, which holds over $2 billion of Odebrecht's debt.[171] Although Odebrecht's bankruptcy was at least partly due to the downturn in the Brazilian economy, the company's continued problems due to its corrupt practices certainly contributed.[172]

165 'Piling On' is the term used by the US Justice Department and others to describe the challenge of uncoordinated prosecutions of the same activity by multiple governments. Henry Cutter, 'Morning Risk Report: DOJ Takes Aim at Enforcement "Piling On"' *The Wall Street Journal Blogs* (10 May 2018) <https://blogs.wsj.com/riskandcompliance/2018/05/10/the-morning-risk-report-doj-takes-aim-at-enforcement-piling-on/> accessed 1 June 2020.

166 Lindsay B Arrieta, 'How Multijurisdictional Bribery Enforcement Enhances Risks for Global Enterprises' (*American Bar Association*, 20 June 2016) <https://www.americanbar.org/groups/business_law/publications/blt/2016/06/08_arrieta/> accessed 1 June 2020. The idea of dual sovereignty gives each sovereign the right to adjudicate violations of its laws. Some nations may take into account foreign prosecutions and thus bar domestic prosecution, but this would be a matter of national legal doctrine; see Fredrick Davis, 'Does International Law Require an International Double Jeopardy Bar?' *Global Anticorruption Law Blog* (18 October 2016) <https://globalanticorruptionblog.com/2016/10/18/guest-post-does-international-law-require-an-international-double-jeopardy-bar/> accessed 1 June 2020 (discussing French law on this issue and in specific corruption investigations).

167 Samuel Rubenfeld, Paul Kiernan, and Luciana Magalhaes, 'Brazil's Odebrecht to Pay Up to $4.5 Billion to Settle Bribery Case' *The Wall Street Journal* (21 December 2016).

168 Brewster (n 102) (discussing in detail the basis for American extraterritorial jurisdiction over corporations listed on American exchanges).

169 Jorge (n 13).

170 Paulo Trevisani, Samantha Pearson, and Luciana Magalhaes, 'Odebrecht Bankruptcy to Hurt Brazilian State-Owned Bank' *The Wall Street Journal* (18 June 2019) (discussing Odebrecht's bankruptcy filing).

171 Ibid.

172 Ibid.

These challenges should not be dismissed lightly, but neither should they be barriers to continued progress in fighting corrupt practices. On the first point, the economic costs of fighting corruption are real and, more importantly to the politics of fighting corruption, the costs of fighting corruption are more visible than the direct and indirect costs of corruption. For instance, bribes are hidden so citizens do not directly see these economic costs but citizen are very aware when loans are suspended due to corruption concerns. But these are short term costs that are vastly outweighed by the benefits of deterring corrupt behavior. In addition, the public may be willing to accept these costs as part of the process of cleaning up the government and the market. In fact, many in Brazil celebrated the bankruptcy as a type of 'cleansing' of corporate behavior.[173]

The concern of piling on allegations is also a genuine challenge. The overlapping jurisdiction for anti-corruption cases is a source of concern for many corporations and national governments, which worry that their national corporations may be too harshly punished for past practices. However, the answer to this concern is deeper cooperation between nations on anti-corruption enforcement, not a retreat from enforcement. The US government has officially adopted a policy of trying to coordinate with other nations to resolve anti-corruption cases where multiple claims of jurisdiction exist. The goal of the policy is to achieve an 'equitable result' and avoid duplicative penalties.[174] To this end, countries have recently started to frequently engage in multinational settlements. In addition, countries that formally have jurisdiction over a corruption case often will not bring charges if they believe that another countries' courts have adequately resolved the matter.[175] Barriers still remain to this approach, particularly in countries where pre-trial settlements of corruption charges are not permitted.[176] Nonetheless, the clear trend is toward greater international cooperation as countries pool their resources to bring meaningful enforcement to anticorruption law worldwide.[177]

173 Ibid (reporting that '[m]any in Brazil viewed the bankruptcy—and the at least $2.6 billion anticorruption settlement it paid US, Brazilian, and Swiss authorities—as a sort of cleansing of corporate Brazil').

174 Henry Cutter, 'DOJ Targets "Duplicative Penalties" Through Increased Coordination' (*Wall Street Journal Blogs*, 9 May 2018) <https://blogs.wsj.com/riskandcompliance/2018/05/09/doj-targets-duplicative-penalties-through-increased-coordination/> accessed 1 June 2020.

175 Rachel Brewster and Christine Dryden, 'Building Multilateral Anticorruption Enforcement: Analogies between International Trade & Anti-Bribery Law' (2017) 57 Virginia Journal of International Law 221, 255–257.

176 The inability to settle charges makes a timely and internationally coordinated settlement more difficult.

177 Arrieta (n 166); Brewster and Dryden (n 175) 257–261.

5 The relevance of moral arguments against foreign bribery

Israel as a case study

Tamar Hostovsky Brandes

The OECD Convention on Combating Bribery of Foreign Public Officials in International Business Transactions (OECD Convention) establishes an elaborate and rigorous peer-review enforcement mechanism, which is based on close monitoring by a working group, established by the OECD Convention, of member states' compliance. Compared with the monitoring mechanisms of other international instruments, the OECD Convention's monitoring process is exceptionally meticulous: it involves the review of each member state's legislative framework and the compatibility of its laws with the requirements of the OECD Convention, the review of the capability of the domestic institutions and bodies responsible for enforcing the prohibition of foreign bribery to perform their role, and the review of the actual actions taken by each country. The review process is based not only on written material and information provided by state officials but also on country visits by examiners. Visits include meeting with official actors from the various branches of government, as well as with representatives of the private sector, representatives of the media, and members of civil society. The process is thus tailored to examine not only formal compliance but also 'softer' measures such as education and awareness-raising efforts and the results of such efforts. The in-depth, hands-on examination process is crucial to reveal possible gaps between the official steps a state has taken and the implementation of the OECD Convention in practice, and it recognizes the importance of collaborative efforts by various branches and industries in achieving compliance. Despite this recognition, it is often still difficult to assess to what extent has the OECD Convention achieved its goal with regard to a particular country—the reduction of the number foreign bribes by individuals and entities from a particular state.

This chapter argues, drawing on the example of Israel, that there is an indication that despite considerable efforts on various fronts: legislation, investigation, and awareness-raising, the attitude of at least some prominent actors towards foreign bribery has not significantly changed. That is, despite the fact that countries, in this particular case, Israel, have explicitly acknowledged the wrongfulness of foreign bribery, many of the revenant actors have yet to fully internalize such wrongfulness. The chapter argues that our knowledge of why people obey the law suggests that the normative stance towards a legal norm is likely to affect compliance with it. It argues that in the area of awareness-raising, the emphasis with respect to international bribery has been, at least in Israel, on spreading knowledge regarding the existence of the offence of foreign bribery and the enhancement of enforcement efforts, and on highlighting the negative economic and reputational consequences bribery may have on companies. While these are important arguments, there is indication that they do not suffice to change attitudes towards the offence by various industry actors.

Awareness raising efforts in Israel lack reference to the moral and ethical aspects of foreign bribery, to its negative influence on democracy world wide, and to the implications of corruption for human rights. This is in stark contrast to the heated public debate on domestic bribery that has taken place in Israel in recent years.

The lack of reference to ethical arguments is perhaps a reflection of the belief that such arguments are ineffective. I argue that our experience in other areas, including our knowledge of why people comply with the law, suggests that the effectiveness of moral and ethical considerations is, in this case, undermined. Moreover, the difficulty of transforming attitudes and opinions based on deterrence alone indicates that emphasizing economic and reputational ramifications is not enough.

The chapter proceeds as follows: section 1 introduces the OECD Convention and its implementation mechanism. Section 2 reviews theories of compliance with the law, and highlights the distinction between deterrence-based compliance and compliance based on normative commitment to the law. Section 3 examines Israel's compliance with the OECD Convention and its enforcement efforts as reviewed in the Phase 1, Phase 2, and Phase 3 reports. Section 4 discusses the lack of ethical and normative arguments in the compliance process and argues that in the case of Israel, such arguments could, eventually, support and enhance compliance. It further argues that such arguments have both domestic and international dimensions. Section 5 concludes.

1 The OECD Convention and its implementation mechanisms

The initiation of the OECD Convention is attributed to the United States. The Foreign Corrupt Practices Act of 1977, enacted in the US following the Watergate scandal, rendered it illegal for certain US individuals and entities to bribe public officials of other countries.[1] The FCPA itself was initiated by an SEC prosecutor, and in addition to the general claim that bribery was morally wrong, the negative impacts of bribery on the economy were brought as the main justifications for its

1 15 US Code ss 78dd-1.

enactment.[2] The economic harms caused by bribery also stood at the center of the emerging body of research of that era on the impacts of corruption.[3]

Following the enactment of the FCPA, US corporations began to push for a global ban on foreign briberies, in order to level the playing field and ensure that US companies are not disadvantaged is the global market. The US thus sought to ensure that prohibitions similar to those imposed on US companies by FCPA are imposed on European companies, and negotiations towards the adoption of an anti-bribery convention begun. These negotiations eventually resulted in the acceptance of the OECD Convention in 1998.[4]

While free market arguments dominated the public discourse regarding foreign bribery, Elizabeth K Spahn notes that during the 1980s, arguments related to the negative relationship between corruption and development began occupying a more central role in the public discourse on corruption. This change, she explains, was tied to the realization that the failure of several major investment plans of the World Bank was due to corruption, and the following demands of investors, which required governance reform as a condition for investment. Finally, in the past decade, the relationship between corruption and human rights has been highlighted, and a growing body of literature stressing the relationship between corruption, democracy, and human rights has emerged.

The research and public discourse on corruption has thus evolved in the past four decades, from emphasizing mostly the economic harms of corruption to discussing its negative implications for development, human rights, and democracy. However, the question that I seek to examine is whether, and to what extent, is this evolvement in the academic and international discourse reflected in the domestic realm of compliance, and whether it can or should be reflected in this realm.

The OECD Convention includes a rigorous peer-review monitoring process, which is compulsory for all parties to the OECD Convention.[5] It is based on four separate Phases: Phase 1 focuses on the evaluated country's legal framework and examines its compatibility with the requirements of the OECD Convention. Phase 2 examines the application of such framework in practice. Phase 3 focuses on enforcement, and examines whether the recommendations given in Phase 2 were implemented. Phase 4 strives to fine-tune the examination based on a country's

2 Elizabeth K Spahn, 'Implementing Global Anti-Bribery Norms: From the Foreign Corrupt Practices Act to the OECD Anti-Bribery Convention to the UN Convention against Corruption' (2013) 23 Indiana International and Comparative Law Review 1.

3 See, e.g., Susan Rose-Ackerman, *Corruption: A Study in Political Economy* (Elsevier 1978).

4 Elizabeth Acron, 'Twenty Years of the OECD Anti-Bribery Convention: National Implementation and Hybridization' (2018) 51 University of British Columbia Law Review 613. See also Kevin E Davis, 'Why Does the United States Regulate Foreign Bribery: Moralism, Self-Interest, or Altruism?' (2012) 67 Annual Survey of American Law 497.

5 OECD, 'Country Monitoring of the OECD Anti-Bribery Convention' <https://www.oecd.org/corruption/countrymonitoringoftheoecdanti-briberyconvention.htm> accessed 1 June 2020.

specific enforcement issues, and examines whether the recommendations given in Phase 3 were implemented.

The monitoring process involves on-site visits and face-to-face conversations not only with government officials, but also with non-government actors. The reports reflect the formal actions taken by a country in order to fight foreign bribery, as well as the position of government officials, and the perceptions, attitudes, and opinions of private individuals required to comply with such actions. The reports thus provide a rich source of information for examining various facets of compliance in particular countries, and assessing the strength and dominance of the different justifications for anti-bribery obligations in countries' internal discourses. Understanding local perceptions may, in turn, assist us in identifying possible impediments to compliance.

2 Why do people obey the law?

The question of compliance is, of course, one of the essential questions jurists are concerned with. While a comprehensive analysis of theories of compliance is beyond the scope of this chapter, a rough distinction can be drawn between instrumental theories of compliance and normative theories of compliance. Tom R Tyler explains that the instrumental perspective:

> underlies what is known as the deterrence literature: people are viewed as shaping their behaviour to respond to changes in the tangible, immediate incentives and penalties associated with following the law—to judgments about the personal gains and losses resulting from different kinds of behaviour.[6]

Empirical evidence is conflicted regarding the extent to which deterrence actually achieves compliance. What appears to be clear, however, is that to the extent the deterrence—in particular criminal deterrence—contributes to compliance, it cannot be relied on exclusively.

In contrast to deterrence-based theories of compliance, normative theories of compliance suggest that people obey the law not because of their fear of the consequences of disobedience, but because they perceive such obedience as right and just. Tyler explains that:

> If people view compliance with the law as appropriate because of their attitudes about how they should behave, they will voluntarily assume the obligation to follow legal rules. They will feel personally committed to obeying the law, irrespective of whether they risk punishment for breaking the law.[7]

6 Tom R Tyler, *Why Do People Obey the Law?* (Princeton University Press 1991) 3.
7 Ibid.

The normative theory of compliance is thus based on peoples' attitudes towards the law. There are various reasons for why people may feel that a law should be respected. One important distinction, in this regard, is the distinction between personal morality and legitimacy of the law itself. Under a normative commitment that is based upon morality, people obey the law because they perceive it as just. Under a normative commitment that is based on legitimacy, people obey the law because they perceive it as stemming from a legitimate authority. Both are non-instrumental in the sense that they are based on the nature of the law, rather than the consequences of infringing it. However, the first focuses on the content of the law, while the second focuses on its source.

Precisely because it is difficult to empirically assess the strength of each theory of compliance in particular cases and scenarios, it is advisable to build a multi-faceted compliance scheme, which does not build exclusively on deterrence but also on the two aspects of normative adherence.

Achieving moral normative commitment to the prohibition on foreign bribery may prove to be especially challenging. While many actors perceive domestic bribery as wrong, foreign bribery was historically justified as being part of the 'business culture' of the foreign country, part of its 'way of life' and generally 'the way things are'. This perception, whether genuine or convenient, allowed actors to draw and justify to themselves a distinction between domestic bribery and foreign bribery. Once such distinction is drawn, individuals that are not prone to offer bribes in the domestic setting may perceive it as legitimate to do in a foreign country.

Achieving normative compliance with the prohibition on foreign bribery based on the legitimacy of the prohibition itself may also prove to be challenging. It is generally perceived as legitimate for states to regulate behaviour within their territory. However, the offence of bribery of a foreign public official is an extra-territorial offence, where the state extends its authority to acts committed in another country. Since such extensions are the exception to the rule, extra-territorial legislation inherently suffers from weaker legitimacy, and must be justified.

3 Israel and the OECD

Israel joined the OECD in 2010 and ratified the OECD Convention in 2009. In preparation for its accession to the OECD Convention, Israel's Penal Code was amended on July 7, 2008, to include the offence of 'bribery of foreign official'.[8] Section 291A, titled 'Bribing a Foreign Public Official,' states as follows:

(a) A person who gives a bribe to a foreign public official for an act in relation with his functions, in order to obtain, to assure or to promote business

8 For background regarding the enactment of the law see: Amichai Cohen, Tal Filberg, and Yuval Shany 'The Effect of International Human Rights Law on the Legislation in Israel' (2017) 10 Hukim 69 (in Hebrew).

activity or other advantage in relation to business activity, shall be treated in the same manner as a person who commits an offence under Article 291.

(b) No indictment shall be issued in respect to an offence under this article unless given written consent from the Attorney General.

(c) For the purpose of this article: 'foreign country' includes, but not limited to, any governmental unit in the foreign country, including national, district or local unit. 'foreign public official' includes any of these: (1) An employee of a foreign country and any person holding a public office or exercising a public function on behalf of a foreign country; including in the legislative, executive or judiciary branch of the foreign country, whether by appointment, by election or by agreement; (2) A person holding a public office or exercising a public function on behalf of a public body constituted by an enactment of a foreign country, or of a body over which the foreign country exercises, directly or indirectly, control; (3) An employee of a public international organization, and any person holding a public office or exercising a public function for a public international organization; 'public international organization' means an organization formed by two or more countries, or by organizations formed by two or more countries.

The Israeli offence of 'bribery of a foreign public official' builds on and is closely linked to the domestic offence of bribery of a foreign official in s 291. No special exemptions have been made, for example, with respect to facilitation payments, and Israel has explained that the similarity between the two offences was intentional as it allowed, among other things, the authorities to apply the case law related to Article 291 to Article 291A.[9]

In accordance with the OECD Convention's four-phased monitoring scheme, Israel's Phase 1 report recommendations concentrated on the facial compatibility of Israeli law with the OECD Convention. While the conclusions indicated that it appears that Article 291A provides a foundation for compatibility with the OECD Convention, they did raise some concerns, in particular with respect to the low sanctions imposed by Israeli law for violation of Article 291 and, accordingly, also Article 291A.

The recommendations following the Phase 2 report suggested that Israel enhance its awareness-raising efforts in both the public and the private sectors. They specifically referred to the importance of raising awareness in the defence industry, and stressed the importance of raising awareness of the 'detrimental effects of foreign bribery.'[10] They also referred in detail to the need to enhance and improve various measures required for compliance, including whistle-blower

9 Ibid.

10 OECD, *Israel Phase 2: Report on the Application of the OECD Convention on Combating Bribery of Foreign Public Officials in International Business Transactions and the 1997 Recommendation on Combating Bribery in International Business Transactions* (11 December 2009) 69.

protection, statutory reporting obligations, implementation of anti-corruption measures in the instruments and working processes of export insurance companies and the licensing process of defence companies (at the time in which Phase 2 was performed, the licensing process of companies in the defense sector contained no anti-bribery clauses), the detection of foreign bribery through tax information (including the sharing of such information), and other issues. In particular, the working group expressed concern regarding the enforcement efforts in Israel, the lack of independent investigation efforts, and the fact that allegations regarding offences committed by Israeli companies, including a prominent state-owned company in the defense sector, were neither investigated nor prosecuted.[11]

Israel responded positively to the Phase 2 report—the majority of required changes were made, either through legislation, through implementation of anti-corruption measures in various stages in the export process, and through proactive education initiatives regarding foreign bribery. These efforts did not go unnoticed—in the response to the Phase 2 follow up report, Israel was praised for implementing the majority of the working group's recommendations. The examiners concluded that,

> With the progress of time, we have witnessed great positive developments in the understanding of the Israeli public and private sector of the need to curb foreign bribery, and we are confident that this would be apparent in future stages of the monitoring process.[12]

The positive tone of the Phase 2 follow up comments somewhat changed in Phase 3. While Israel has indeed taken a range of actions to bring its legal and institutional framework in line with the requirements of the OECD Convention, in 2015, when the Phase 3 report was concluded, no prosecutions had yet taken place. Here, again, an abundance of recommendations was made with regard to required additional changes and clarifications of Israel's internal framework. However, the picture depicted began to be one in which extensive changes are made, yet their practical implementation was still lacking.

Shortly after, in 2016, Israel prosecuted its first (and, to date, only) case of bribery of a foreign public official. Nip Global, an information technology company, was convicted by a Tel Aviv court pursuant to a plea bargain for bribery of a foreign official in Lesotho. A fine of 2.25 million NIS and confiscation in the sum of 2.25 million NIS were imposed on the company.[13] In accepting the plea bargain, the court referred to the OECD Convention and indicated that the bribery of a foreign public official was a serious offence. However, it determined that in light of the company's cooperation, and in light of the fact that the case was the first of its kind, the plea bargain was acceptable despite the fact that

11 Ibid pt 14.

12 Ibid 39.

13 *Tel-Aviv District (Fiscal and Financial) v. NIP Global Ltd* [2016] TP 57177-11-16.

the fine was low relative to the company's revenues from the project at stake (an estimated $30,000,000). Nip Global was acquired in 2018 by US company Pangea.[14]

4 The Israeli discourse regarding bribery of foreign public officials

As discussed above, the OECD Convention's enforcement scheme not only refers to legal enforcement but also stresses the importance of education and awareness-raising efforts. Indeed, the reports submitted by Israel highlights the efforts conducted in this regard in both the private and public sectors. These include education of public officials, conducting seminars and conferences in both the private and public sectors, and distributing information regarding the offence in both sectors.

However, a deeper look into the awareness-raising efforts in Israel reveals that the content of these efforts focuses almost exclusively on information regarding the existence of the offence in Israeli law and on the instrumental justifications for it. Thus, for example, Attorney General Guideline 4.1110 regarding the 'Prohibition on Payments of Bribes to a Foreign Public Official – Article 291A of the Penal Law, 1977' explains that the offence was introduced pursuant to Israel's obligations under the OECD Convention.[15]

Except for a single and vague sentence stating that the offence will make 'a contribution to the strengthening of domestic ethical standards' the Guideline contains no reference to the ethical or moral dimensions of the offence. It does, however, refer to its instrumental benefits, explaining that 'Maintaining these international standards will render it easier for Israeli companies to operate in international business transactions and will increase the competitiveness of the Israeli market.'[16] Similar themes were also highlighted in Israel's reports. Thus, for example, the Phase 2 report follow-up states that: 'Israeli authorities particularly strive to highlight the detrimental effects of foreign bribery on Israeli society, Israeli economy and the conduct of international business.'[17]

Despite the ongoing educational and awareness-raising efforts, it appears from the reports that the normative stance of at least some relevant actors is slow to change. For example, the examiners of Phase 2 indicate that during an onsite visit 'one Knesset Member stated that "we know that you sometimes have to hire local

14 Yasmin Yablonko, 'Pangea Buys Israeli co NIP Global for $30m' *Globes* (14 June 2014) <https://en.globes.co.il/en/article-pangea-buys-israeli-co-nip-global-for-30m-1001241392> accessed 1 June 2020.

15 Attorney General Guideline 4.1110, 'Prohibition on Payments of Bribes to a Foreign Public Official—Article 291A of the Penal Law, 1977' <https://www.justice.gov.il/Units/YoezMespati/HanchayotNew/Seven/41110.pdf> accessed 1 June 2020.

16 Ibid.

17 OECD, *Follow-Up Report on the Implementation of the Phase 2 Recommendation* (March 2012) 6.

agents when the arms industry trades abroad" but that "thousands of Israelis have jobs as a result of the deal."'[18] The examiners stated, in this regard, that 'some views expressed by panelists' were concerning, including the view that foreign bribery has been 'the only way for Israeli companies to compete abroad.'[19]

Despite the fact that the report noted the problematic attitudes of some of the interviewees, it focused on the instrumental justifications for the offence. Thus, for example, the working group noted that:

> There appeared to be only a low level of understanding that the bribery of foreign public officials can be damaging to the reputation of Israel's economic relations with other countries and to the reputation of its companies operating abroad. Israel promised to rectify this, ensuring that its awareness-raising campaign on foreign bribery aims to change this position by sending the message that foreign bribery has great negative impacts, including on the economic reputation of Israel and Israeli companies engaged in international business.

Similar issues regarding the attitudes of the relevant actors came up during phase 3: examiners noted that during an onsite visit to Israel 'a senior official from the Ministry of Finance stated that Israel "needs to balance fighting corruption with financial concerns".'[20] The evaluation team raised concerns that this statement might suggest that bribery is perceived as a necessary part of doing business abroad, and that 'a senior representative from the business community expressed the view that Israeli companies cannot compete without corruption.'[21]

Regarding the private sector, the Phase 3 examiners indicated that, while some panellists with whom they met acknowledged the importance of enforcement efforts by Israel, 'the outdated view that foreign bribery is a necessary part of doing business abroad appears to remain, at least in some sectors.' The examiners noted that 'During the on-site visit, a representative of a high-risk industry (with operations in high-risk countries) passionately asserted that Israeli companies must bribe foreign officials in order to compete abroad and ensure the sustainability of the industry which would otherwise rapidly decline (as occurred in another country with large operations in this sector). The panellist forcefully stated that Israel should not be prosecuting such conduct as this was the responsibility of the foreign state. A second panellist from the same organisation indicated agreement with these assertions.'[22]

18 Ibid pt 16.
19 Ibid pt 19.
20 OECD, *Phase 3 Report on Implementing the OECD Anti-Bribery Convention in Israel* (11 June 2015).
21 Ibid 9.
22 Ibid, pt 123.

Doubts regarding the legitimacy of Israel's enforcement efforts were also openly raised recently, for example, by Adv. Yaron Lipshes, who represented the defendant in the case of Nip Global. In an interview conducted in connection with news regarding two companies being probed for bribing foreign public officials, Lipshes, who is a white-collar crime attorney and a partner in a prominent Israeli law firm, challenged the desirability of enforcement efforts. 'The steps being carried out by law enforcement authorities in this context may be understandable', he argued, 'and there are those who would say it is admirable, but you need to remember that this involves the most significant industrial activity being carried out by Israel companies, which could disappear altogether.'[23]

'These investigations', argued Lipshes, 'are trying to undermine a practice of many years that is widespread in these countries, and in many cases it's impossible to do business there without it.' Lipshes demonstrated his claim by explaining that the problem derives from the fact that the definition of the crime of 'bribery of a foreign official' draws on the Israeli notion of bribery. He then moved in to explain that using an intermediary related to the government who receives a 'bonus' for bringing in business is perceived as bribery under Israeli law. Because the Israeli offense of bribery of foreign officials is based on the domestic offence of bribery, working with such an 'intermediary' in a foreign country will be considered as bribery, despite the fact, he claims, that this is a 'common practice' in some countries.[24]

While Israel has taken an official stance which recognizes the importance of the prohibition on foreign bribery, the attitudes expressed by panelists and by Lipshes are prevalent both among some public officials and certainly among private actors. Despite the fact that almost a decade has passed since Israel acceded to the OECD Convention, and despite the many implementation measures, including education and awareness raising efforts, such opinions are far from being eradicated.

Despite the fact that these positions were flagged by the working group as concerning, these concerns were not reflected in the recommendation, as the compliance approach of the working group is deterrence-focused. This, in turn, has dictated both the focus of Israel's efforts and the public discourse in Israel. For example, one of the main concerns of the phase 2 examiners with respect to Israel regarded the relatively low penalties imposed on violators, deemed too low to deter offenders.[25] Israel responded to this critique, amending the law with

23 Yasmin Gueta, 'If Israelis Won't Pay Bribes, Companies from Other Countries Will Push Them Out of Africa' *The Marker* (19 March 2018) <https://www.themarker.com/law/1.5913336> accessed 1 June 2020.

24 Ibid.

25 OECD, *Israel: Phase 1 Review of Implementation of the OECD Convention and 1997 Revised Recommendation* (19 March 2009).

regard to both domestic and international bribery, and introduced stricter punishments and higher fines.[26]

The gains and losses stemming from the prohibition on foreign bribery dominate the awareness raising efforts. As the reports indicate, Israel has invested considerable efforts in dispersing information both regarding the existence of the criminal offence of bribery of foreign officials and regarding the fact that enforcement efforts have been enhanced. In addition, efforts have been made to explain to the relevant actors that such bribery has negative economic implications. Among actors in the public sector, emphasis has been placed on the importance of membership in the OECD for Israel and on the negative implications that lack of proactivity in enforcement of the OECD Convention may have for Israel. Indeed, the need to comply with the requirements of the OECD is a recurring theme in the communications and explanations of the Ministry of Justice to public actors involved in the implementation of compliance measures.

This line of argument, however, carries some risks. While it is not difficult to explain that membership in the OECD carries benefits, the social legitimacy of international law in Israel is relatively weak, and appears to be in even further decline.[27] International law is often perceived as not paying due regard to Israel's national interests, and in other areas of law, public opinion generally appears to be that the requirements of international law should be accorded limited weight in policy making.

The fact that the prohibition on foreign bribery was imposed on Israel through an international obligation may thus weaken, rather than strengthen, its internal legitimacy. The comments made by several actors regarding the alleged negative impact enforcement of the prohibition will have on key industries in Israel reflects a common perception, according to which national interests should override international obligations.

In the private sector, the emphasis of awareness-raising efforts was on the negative reputational implications for companies suspected to be involved in bribery, and on the negative effects of foreign bribery on markets, which could harm all actors.

With respect to the private sector, awareness-raising efforts concentrated on the claim that involvement in bribing scandals may have negative reputational impacts for Israeli companies. However, this claim may prove to be more convincing in some areas, for example, in pharmaceuticals, than in industries such as the defense sector or infrastructure. The identity of other actors in the field and

26 In introducing the bill, representatives of the Ministry of Justice explained that the amendment was necessary both to combat corruption but also to comply with the OECD requirements. In light of the fact that only a single case has been prosecuted, to date, under Article 291A, the main influence actually appears to be on domestic bribery. See discussion in Gil Eshet, 'Economic Offences in Israel' in Ohad Gordon and others (eds), *Edmund Levy Book* (Nevo 2017).

27 Tamar Hostovsky Brandes, 'International Law in Domestic Courts in an Era of Populism' (2019) 17 International Journal of Constitutional Law 576.

the existing business culture is also relevant, in this regard. Lipshes argued, for example, that Israeli companies are competing against Chinese companies, which often don't abide by international rules, and that enforcement efforts may thus place Israel at a disadvantage.

To sum up, the working group's recommendations, the awareness-raising efforts, and the current public discourse in Israel on foreign bribery all focus on deterrence—on highlighting the criminal, political, and economic consequences of violation. Ethical and moral arguments are astoundingly lacking from the discussion, as are any arguments regarding the impact of foreign bribery on democracy and human rights.

Interestingly, in the case law concerning the tax deductibility of bribes paid to foreign officials that was adjudicated prior to Israel joining the OECD Convention, ethical and moral arguments were actually central to the Courts' decisions to ban such deductions. One example is the case of Income Tax Appeal 1015/03 *Company Ltd v. Netanya Assessing Officer*,[28] which concerned the deductibility of bribes paid in a foreign country during the tax year of 1999–2003 (prior to Israel joining the UNCAC). The appellants argued that paying bribes was 'a necessity of doing business' in the foreign country, and that bribes in a foreign country should not be examined under the same moral values prevalent in Israel.

The Court dismissed these claims. Despite the fact that there was no explicit prohibition, at the time, on bribery of foreign officials, the Court stated that 'the values of the states do not stop at its borders.'[29] Recognizing bribe payments as deductible expenses, the Court explained, would turn Israeli citizens into accomplices. The Court further argued that even if the acts were not prohibited in the foreign country, this would be incompatible with the values of Israel and contrary to public policy in Israel.

It should be noted, in this regard, that despite the fact that the acts preceded Israel's accession to the OECD and the UNCAC, the Court reviewed extensively the practice of other states in the area of bribery of foreign officials as an indication of the standards Israel aspires to and as examples of the types of states Israel strives to resemble. The comparative examination did not serve to establish an international obligation, nor did it serve, on its own, as proof of the moral wrongness of such bribes. It did serve, however, as reinforcement of the Court's claim that the acts were morally wrong and that the perception that moral values were not bounded within borders was not improbable. Since Israel was not a party to relevant international instruments prohibiting such acts, it was not bound by them. However, both international and comparative law served to demonstrate the existence of shared values, which Israel should adopt.

The Supreme Court decision of *Hydrola*, delivered shortly after, similarly regarded the deductibility of payments made to public officials by a company

28 Income Tax Appeal 1015/03 *Company Ltd v. Netanya Assessing Officer* [2008].
29 Ibid [20].

that operated in the former USSR. Justice Rubinstein discussed in length the development of the international ban on foreign bribery, again despite the fact that it was not binding upon the appellants at the time, and indicated that it was important for Israel, in the foreign affairs sphere, to act in line with the global standard. However, Rubinstein emphasized the moral wrong embedded in foreign bribery, explaining that bribery was an act that was both universally and domestically wrong. Determining that bribery payments were not deductible, Rubinstein rejected the claim that 'public policy' in Israel was different than 'public policy' in Russia, and stated that 'some matters of public policy are universal, in terms of values, even if not in reality, and bribery, a biblical offence which is also part of the cultural heritage of the Russian people, is one of them.'[30] Rubinstein devotes long paragraphs to reviewing the severity of the offence of bribery in Jewish religious sources, anchoring its wrongfulness not only in international sources, but also in domestic culture and tradition.

Oddly, arguments pertaining to the nature of bribery are absent from the domestic discourse and awareness-raising efforts that followed Israel's accession to the OECD, which focused, as indicated above, on stressing the instrumental justifications for complying with the OECD Convention. They are also absent from the single case in which an entity was convicted of bribery of a foreign public official, the case of Nip Global, discussed above.

5 Conclusion

While some may be skeptical regarding the power of ethical and moral arguments, theories of compliance suggest that normative commitment is central to adherence to the law. While Israel has conformed to the majority of the working group's recommendation, there appears to be a gap between the appearance of compliance, and compliance in practice. It is difficult to assess the full extent of this gap, but the fact that many relevant actors still perceive foreign bribery to be an essential business practice, together with the small numbers of investigations and prosecutions in a country with relatively many actors operating in high-risk industries and high-risk countries, raises suspicion that foreign bribery is still a prevalent practice.

Israel is a small country, with a close-knit business community. Some high-risk industries, in particular, the defense industry, are closely linked to the security services and to the government. The intertwined interests of business entities and government, in particular in the defense industry, may create negative enforcement incentives against actors in these industries, as may the perception that the success of Israeli companies abroad is a matter of national interest. In this context, deterrence-based compliance may be particularly weak.

In Israel, there is a solid foundation for normative commitment towards the prohibition on bribery. In the past years, a number of high-profile public officials

30 CA 6726/05 *Hydrola v. Assessing Officer Tel Aviv* [2008].

have been indicted on corruption allegations. These include former prime minister Ehud Olmert, who served prison time for accepting a bribe, and current prime minister Benjamin Netanyahu, who was indicted on January 28, 2020, for bribery, fraud, and breach of trust. The prohibition on bribery is, accordingly, prominent in the public debate in Israel.

What is striking, in this regard, is the gap between the attitudes regarding foreign bribery, as expressed in the reports, and the attitudes towards domestic bribery. It is doubtable whether the same individuals that portray foreign bribes as a necessity would openly endorse bribes as a legitimate practice within Israel. Despite the similar wording, in Israel, of the domestic offense of bribery of a public official and the offense of bribery of a foreign public official, the normative commitment towards each of the two offenses is very different.

Interestingly, it appears that accession to the OECD Convention placed the emphasis of the public discourse on foreign bribery in Israel on deterrence-related compliance, pushing aside moral arguments against foreign corruption, despite the fact that a foundation for such arguments had begun to develop in the Israeli case law. This is regrettable: such arguments could support normative commitment towards the prohibition on foreign bribery that would supplement and strengthen the impact of deterrence.

Without normative commitment, and as long as the prohibition on foreign bribery is perceived as an externally-imposed prohibition, compliance will be based on deterrence only, and is likely to be an ongoing cat-and-mouse game. Three arguments against the prohibition on foreign bribery currently exist in the public discourse in Israel. The first is that Israeli companies will be in an inferior position if they are constricted by anti-bribery laws, and that the Israeli legislation actually harms Israeli companies, while it should be protecting them. The second is that the prohibition of foreign bribery is based on a misunderstanding of the 'local culture' of foreign countries and that it thus is a mistake to apply the same standards to business practices in Israel and abroad. The third, related argument is that enforcement of the prohibition on foreign bribery unjustly portrays those involved as criminals, and that they are essentially harassed by such investigations. The latter two arguments demonstrate that the normative weight accorded to the prohibition on foreign bribery is very different from that accorded to domestic bribery. Deterrence alone cannot address these arguments. They can only be responded to by addressing the moral wrongfulness of foreign bribery, and anchoring the justification of the international and domestic commitment to fight such bribery in this wrongfulness.

6 France's new approach towards extraterritoriality in anti-corruption law

Paving the way for a protective principle in economic matters?

Jonathan Bourguignon[1]

On January 31, 2020, the multinational Airbus reached a judicial agreement with the Parquet National Financier regarding an important corruption case in which French prosecutors took 'the driving seat.'[2] The company was accused of participation in the setting-up of a multiyear bribery scheme for trade in civil and military aircrafts in various countries, including Indonesia, Malaysia, Nepal, Russia, China, and Colombia. To resolve the charges, the company accepted to pay a fine of 2.1 billion euros to French authorities, in parallel with deferred prosecution agreements (DPAs) with US and British authorities.[3] While such agreements have become a common tool in the United States, their use is much more recent in France. The case was also the first coordinated resolution of a foreign bribery case between the three countries.

The adoption on December 9, 2016 of a landmark piece of legislation against corruption, namely '*Loi Sapin II*,'[4] was a key factor to this success. This legislative development was an obvious response to the constant criticism faced by French authorities in the last decade for the poor results achieved in the fight against transnational corruption. Until its coming into force, the gradual protection of the probity and integrity of public officials through criminal law (which started long ago with Napoléon's *Code pénal* of 1810) had proven rather ineffective in ensuring the punishment of offenders in complex transnational cases. Law enforcement agencies had long been unable to restrain the setting-up by French companies or their subsidiaries of bribery schemes abroad involving foreign

1 The views and opinions expressed in this article are those of the author and do not necessarily reflect those of the United Nations or its member states.

2 Kate Beioley, 'Airbus Case Shows France's New-Found Anti-Corruption Drive' *Financial Times* (17 February 2020).

3 Parquet national financier, 'Press Release of 31 January 2020' <https://www.tribunal-de-paris.justice.fr/75/publications> accessed 1 June 2020.

4 Loi n° 2016–1691 relative à la transparence, à la lutte contre la corruption et à la modernisation de la vie économique, adopted on 9 December 2016.

public officials. The Organization for Economic Cooperation and Development (OECD) expressed its concern on many occasions, highlighting that during the period of 2000–2012, only 33 investigations were launched, a number that was 'low in relation to the size of the French economy and the exposure of French companies to the risk of transnational bribery.' The OECD also deplored the fact that French courts had ruled on a 'very low number of convictions for bribery of foreign public officials', namely five since the criminalization of such conduct.[5] Needless to say, all other intergovernmental bodies fighting corruption unanimously shared these concerns, be it the Conference of the States Parties to the United Nations Convention against Corruption (UNCAC), the Council of Europe's Group of States against Corruption (GRECO), or the EU's European Commission.[6]

In parallel, US authorities have demonstrated their strong willingness and capacity to prosecute foreign companies—including major French companies. Indeed French companies have consistently found themselves with the unpalatable honor of featuring in the rankings of the top ten Foreign Corrupt Practices Act (FCPA)[7] enforcement actions of all time (based on penalties and disgorgement assessed in the US enforcement documents). Every ranking of the past decade has included at least two French companies: namely Technip and Alcatel-Lucent in 2012, and currently even three—Airbus, a Dutch-French company ($2.3 billion), Alstom (8th, $772 million), and Société Générale (9th, $585 million) in the last assessment available as of early 2020;[8] the latter company indeed replaced another French multinational, Total ($398 million), in the list.[9] The extensive reach of the FCPA, combined with the significant powers of the US Department of Justice (DOJ), have demonstrated their impressive efficacy against the malpractices of France's banking, energy, and services giants. In comparison, the United Kingdom's Bribery Act 2010 (UKBA)[10] has demonstrated an equally strong capacity to punish foreign companies but has not affected French multinationals to the same extent so far. Still, French multinational companies must monitor very carefully the activities of their UK subsidiaries to avoid severe penalties. It was not until 2016 that French national institutions fully realized—and assessed—the impact of these frameworks on the national economy.

5 OECD Working Group on Bribery, *Phase 3 Report On Implementing the OECD Anti-Bribery Convention in France* (2012) 11 [15].

6 The EU Commission summarised most of these observations in its 2014 anti-corruption report; see EU Commission (DG Home Affairs), *EU Anti-Corruption Report* (3 February 2014) annex no 10.

7 US Foreign Corrupt Practices Act (FCPA) 1977. See especially 15 US Code ss 78dd-1ff.

8 See Leslie Wayne, 'Foreign Firms Most Affected by a US Law Barring Bribes' *The New York Times* (3 September 2012); Harry Cassin, 'Airbus Pays $4 Billion to Settle Global Bribery and Trade Offenses' *The FCPA Blog* (31 January 2020).

9 Regarding the *Total* case, see US Department of Justice, 'French Oil and Gas Company, Total, S.A., Charged in the United States and France in Connection with an International Bribery Scheme' (29 May 2013).

10 Bribery Act 2010 (UK).

Shortly before the adoption of Loi Sapin II, the Assemblée Nationale adopted a high-profile report on *The extraterritoriality of US legislation*. Its conclusions rebuked US authorities over the reach of US law and stressed that its implementation 'might be perceived as a form of legal *imperium*.'[11] Yet, the failure of French authorities to fight transnational corruption effectively was described in even harsher words:

> The best way to counter foreign extraterritorial mechanisms against corruption is to demonstrate the efficacy of our justice in this field. We thus need results. Yet, such results are, to date, cruelly lacking: twenty-years on, not even one final conviction has been handed down against French legal persons on charges of corruption. This odd situation ... is weakening [France's position] internationally.[12]

The final convictions pronounced since then against Total and Vitol in the '*Oil for Food*' case, by a judgment of the *Cour de cassation*,[13] has left untouched the overall picture. Among other explanatory factors, critics blamed certain features of the criminal justice system (procedural impediments applying to transnational offences, absence of a DPA mechanism), together with the shortcomings of the then anti-corruption body.

Against this backdrop, the French Government decided in the spring of 2016 to introduce a bill in Parliament to strengthen France's legal and institutional framework against corruption. The bill was presented by Michel Sapin, Minister for the Economy and Finance, who already played a leading role in the 1990s in the adoption of a previous piece of legislation on the same topic (Loi Sapin)[14]. The law, which was adopted under a fast-track legislative process, addresses the main aspects of the long-standing criticism expressed by international organizations and NGOs. Its goal is clear: to bring France up to the level of protection afforded by key partner countries against transnational corruption, namely the FCPA and the UKBA.

The contribution of Loi Sapin II to the fight against corruption is threefold: first, it sets up a new anti-corruption compliance framework, which applies to several categories of legal and natural persons. In many aspects, its requirements

11 See Karine Berger and Pierre Lellouche, *Rapport d'information sur l'extraterritorialité de la législation américaine*, n°4082 (5 October 2016).

12 Karine Berger, 'Commission des lois de l'Assemblée nationale, meeting of 25 May 2016', quoted in Sébastien Denaja, *Rapport au nom de la Commission des lois* (n° 3785 and 3786, 26 May 2016).

13 Cour de cassation (criminal division) (n° 16-82.117, 14 March 2018). The two oil companies were sentenced for the bribery of Iraqi public officials in the context of the UN 'Oil for Food' programme (1996–2003), which allowed Saddam Hussein's Iraq to sell crude in exchange for humanitarian goods.

14 Loi n° 93–122 du 29 janvier 1993 relative à la prévention de la corruption et à la transparence de la vie économique et des procédures publiques.

appear even more stringent than the US or UK programs. To monitor the implementation of this framework, the law creates a new anti-corruption body, the *Agence Française Anticorruption*. Its resources and powers have been substantially strengthened compared to those of its predecessor. Besides, French prosecutors are permitted to conclude deferred prosecution agreements (*Convention Judiciaire d'Intérêt Public* (CJIP)) with legal persons charged with corruption and influence peddling. This sensitive feature of the law, which breaks with France's longstanding opposition to negotiated justice, was much debated among anti-corruption stakeholders, including NGOs.[15] Eventually, Loi Sapin II eases substantially the exercise of extraterritorial jurisdiction against corruption, i.e., the legal power of French authorities to try and punish persons for corruption conducts that took place abroad.

Article 21 of the Loi waives the traditional procedural conditions applying to the prosecution of extraterritorial offenses, including dual criminality and the requirement of a formal complaint filed by the victim or the foreign authority; more importantly, it introduces two new provisions in the French *Code pénal* (arts 435-6-2 and 435-11-2) which extend France's extraterritorial jurisdiction against corruption. Both provide that French law applies to certain corruption and influence-peddling offenses committed abroad 'by a French national, or by a person having habitual residency in France *or carrying out her economic activity, either in whole or in part, on French territory*, in any circumstances.'[16] Surprisingly, this puzzling phrase has failed to attract intense scrutiny of commentators, with the exception of certain anti-corruption practitioners. While this feature of the legislation has not yet been implemented,[17] its potential impact on foreign multinational companies and natural persons is significant. From a legal perspective, it challenges existing categories of criminal jurisdiction in international law and reopens the debate on the core principles applying to extraterritorial jurisdiction.

This study aims to demonstrate that France's Loi Sapin II enshrines a distinctive and very broad conception of the protective principle that goes partly beyond the already extensive approaches of the FCPA and the UKBA (1). On these premises, it examines the validity of such a jurisdiction claim in international law, with mixed results (2), before turning to desirable solutions in a multijurisdictional context (3).

15 Code de procédure pénale, as amended by art 22 of the Loi 'Sapin II,' art 41-1-2. For diverging opinions, see reports published in 2016 by Transparency International (in favor), Sherpa and Anticor (against), in the context of the discussion of the *Loi Sapin II* bill.

16 See Code pénal, created by art 21 of the Loi 'Sapin II,' arts 435-6-2, 435-11-2. The translation and emphasis are ours.

17 This information was confirmed by Mr Jean-Luc Blachon, Vice-Head of the Parquet National Financier (National Financial Prosecutor's Office), during an interview conducted on November 8, 2018.

1 Article 21 of the Loi Sapin II: a distinctive conception of the protective principle

1.1 Applying the protective principle to economic matters at large

As noted above, Article 21 of Loi Sapin II provides that French criminal law applies to listed offenses committed 'by a French national, or by a person having habitual residency in France *or carrying out her economic activity, either in whole or in part, on French territory*, in any circumstances.' The first element ('by a French national'), obviously refers to active personal jurisdiction, which is one of the main jurisdictional tools used by French authorities against offenses committed abroad.[18] The second element ('by a person having habitual residency in France') is based on a rather common variation of territorial jurisdiction. Both can be said to rely on well-accepted heads of jurisdiction in international law: active personal jurisdiction is one of the most commonly used heads of jurisdiction, the existence of which is also required or permitted by several multilateral instruments against corruption, including the Council of Europe's and United Nations Conventions.[19] Territorial jurisdiction based on a status of habitual or permanent residence, which has regrettably avoided academic scrutiny, finds strong support in state practice.[20] However, 'carrying out economic activities' in a country seems to challenge existing categories of criminal jurisdiction in international law: the 'territorial' aspects to which the phrase refers do not concern the alleged commission of corruption offenses, but the location of the professional activity of the economic operator involved. It does not point either to 'personal' connections such as nationality or other forms of legal status in domestic law. Thus, it must be considered as an autonomous connecting factor, the nature of which is scarcely identifiable *prima facie*. This situation is, in itself, problematic in international law; states are expected to rely on recognizable criteria when asserting extraterritorial jurisdiction in order to protect the interests of other states and ensure legal certainty to the subjects of domestic law. Anti-corruption stakeholders such as the NGO Transparency International even went as far as qualifying the provision as 'quasi-universal' jurisdiction, and recommended a clarification of its meaning.[21]

18 See Code pénal, art 113-6.

19 Council of Europe Criminal Law Convention on Corruption, ETS No. 173, 27 January 1999, art 17 [1](b) ('Council of Europe Criminal Law Convention on Corruption') lists active personal jurisdiction under the compulsory heads of jurisdiction, but para. 2 leaves open the possibility for States parties to make reservations to this provision; United Nations Convention against Corruption (opened for signature 9 December 2003, entered into force 14 December 2005) 2349 UNTS 41, art 42 [2](b), makes it a permissible head of jurisdiction.

20 See James Crawford, *Brownlie's Principles of Public International Law* (8th edn, OUP 2012) 459–460. The authors list this criterion under the variations of the nationality principle, which is debatable, but the general remark remains relevant.

21 Transparency international, *Dispositif anticorruption de la loi Sapin II—Guide pratique* (2017) 14.

This being said, Article 21 of the Loi may find its support through reference to the protective principle, understood as the 'principle of international criminal jurisdiction permitting a state to grant extraterritorial effect to legislation criminalizing conduct damaging to national security or other central State interests.'[22] The most straightforward argument is of pure common sense: in the absence of other identifiable jurisdictional basis, the assertion enshrined in Article 21 of the Loi must necessarily be based on the (bold) presumption that the behaviour of a person which carries out an 'economic activity' on the territory of a State has the potential to affect this state's essential economic interests—even when the said conduct is adopted by a foreign person abroad. More precisely, the corruption of foreign public officials, even by a private person acting abroad, may bear consequences for the authority and international relations of the states involved. This interpretation is supported by the position of the relevant criminal provisions within the *Code pénal*,[23] that is the division on 'Serious crimes against the Nation, the State and Public Peace' (Book IV), subdivision on offenses undermining the state's authority (title III). A careful analysis of the *travaux préparatoires* confirms that the provision was adopted 'to defend France's economic interests' at large.[24] This is also in line with the historical link binding the protective principle to France, as the principle emerged in the aftermath of the French Revolution.[25]

Although Article 21 of Loi Sapin II does not affect general rules of jurisdiction, its potential impact should not be underestimated. The new jurisdictional rule applies to a wide range of corruption and influence-peddling conducts having a manifest transnational or international character. The first set of offenses to which these criteria apply are passive corruption by a foreign or international public official (art 435-1 of the *Code pénal*),[26] passive influence peddling by any person, in relation to a foreign public official (art 435-2), active corruption, by any person, of a foreign public official (art 435-3), and active influence peddling by any person, in relation to a foreign public official (art 435-4).[27] The same jurisdictional criteria apply to offenses of passive corruption by a person taking part to

22 The term is 'compétence de protection' or 'compétence réelle' in French, 'Staatsschutzprinzip' in German. Iain Cameron, 'International Criminal Jurisdiction, Protective Principle' *in Max Planck Encyclopedia of Public International Law* (OUP 2015). See also Iain Cameron, *The Protective Principle of International Criminal Jurisdiction* (Dartmouth 1994) 2–3.

23 Criminal Code of France, arts 435-6-2, 435-11-2.

24 In this respect, a prominent participant to the *travaux*, Pierre Lellouche, goes as far as saying that the vagueness of the provision is 'intentional' (*à dessein*). See Berger (n 12).

25 Criminal Procedure Code of 1808, ss 5–6. See Monika Krizek, 'The Protective Principle of Extraterritorial Jurisdiction: A Brief History and an Application of the Principle to Espionage as an Illustration of Current United States Practice' (1988) 6 Boston University International Law Journal 337.

26 By 'foreign public official' and 'international public official,' one means a person holding public office or discharging a public service mission, or an electoral mandate, respectively in a foreign state or within a public international organization.

27 Loi, art 20 also extends the criminalization of influence peddling by adding the words 'in a foreign State' in the relevant criminal provisions (*Code pénal* arts 435-2, 435-4).

the activities of an international court (judge, clerk, expert, among others positions) or of a foreign arbitral body (art 435-7 of the *Code pénal*), passive influence peddling in relation to a person in such position, by any person (art 435-8), active corruption, by any person, of a person taking part to the activities of an international court or of a foreign arbitral body (art 435-9), and active and passive influence peddling, in relation to a person taking part to the activities of an international court (art 435-10). Moreover, it must be recalled that Loi Sapin II waives several requirements that apply in principle to the exercise of extraterritorial jurisdiction; thus, neither dual criminality with the state where the offense was committed nor a formal complaint by the victim or the foreign state are required to implement this distinctive conception of the protective principle.

As a consequence, French authorities are now able, on the basis of a narrow connecting factor, to try and punish foreign natural and legal persons for various acts of corruption committed abroad involving foreign public officials. Arguably, this goes beyond the reach of the already extensive approaches of the FCPA and UKBA.

1.2 The questionable claim of horizontal alignment with the FCPA and UKBA

Legislative alignment with partner states was among the main arguments put forward by proponents of the extension of France's criminal jurisdiction against corruption. In substance, the issue was as much about fighting corruption as ensuring economic competitiveness: according to some drafters, the reach of the FCPA and UKBA could harm the strategic interests of French multinationals in countries where they compete with other foreign companies, thus requiring the adoption of 'extraterritorial tools comparable to those used by [France's] main competitors.'[28] Yet, the degree of alignment of Loi Sapin II with the FCPA and UKBA on the issue of jurisdiction needs to be ascertained. Needless to say, it is almost impossible to undertake a rigorous comparison of specific aspects of domestic law against corruption in different countries. The scope of each piece of legislation is inevitably unique, be it regarding the definition of 'foreign public officials,' the forms of corruption criminalized (and the existence of an intention requirement), as well as more general features of domestic law such as the accepted forms of liability.

Still, the comparison of several features of Loi Sapin II, the FCPA, and the UKBA challenges the idea that the new French legislation merely comes up to the level of its US and UK counterparts—at least in terms of assertion of jurisdiction. Contrary to common belief, the FCPA does not have an unlimited extraterritorial reach.[29] The FCPA's anti-corruption provisions apply broadly to three categories

28 Denaja (n 12).

29 In this respect, see (in French and English speaking literature), *inter alia*, Régis Bismuth, 'Pour une appréhension nuancée de l'extraterritorialité du droit américain—Quelques réflex-

of persons and entities: (1) *issuers* and their officers, directors, employees, agents, and shareholders; (2) *domestic concerns* and their officers, directors, employees, agents, and shareholders; and (3) *other persons and entities*, acting while in the territory of the United States.[30] The first category refers to companies with a class of securities listed on a national securities exchange in the United States, or any company with a class of securities quoted in the over-the-counter market in the United States. It may well rely on the protective principle, although some classify it under territorial jurisdiction.[31] The 'domestic concerns' category combines personal and territorial elements, by encompassing any individual who is a US citizen or a resident of the United States, or any legal person organized under US law or who has its principal place of business in the United States.[32] The third category, 'other persons and entities' is obviously based on territorial jurisdiction, although the phrase 'acting while in the territory' has been interpreted quite widely to include tenuous connection with the US (routing payment through US bank accounts; sending an email to a US company).

Leaving aside the issue of territorial jurisdiction, the FCPA seems to be based on a slightly narrower approach of economic interests (US securities; *principal* place of business) than Loi Sapin II. Also, recent developments in the *United States v. Hoskins* case confirm that judges will not easily allow US law enforcement to apply the FCPA to foreign nationals acting exclusively outside the US territory, unless they strictly qualify as 'domestic concerns.'[33] It should be stressed that the Act applies only to active forms of corruption, while French law applies to both active and passive forms of corruption and influence peddling. Ironically, France's alleged 'retaliation' against US extraterritoriality might further the latter's objectives. It may be argued that the US leadership in the fight against transnational corruption was not mainly designed as an economic weapon, aiming to subject foreign multinationals competing with US majors; rather, it supported publicly the adoption of similar probity rules in the countries where the biggest

ions autour des procédures et sanctions visant Alstom et BNP Paribas' (2015) AFDI 785; Emmanuel Breen, *FCPA—La France face au droit américain de la lutte anti-corruption* (Joly éditions 2017); Mateo J de la Torre, 'The Foreign Corrupt Practices Act: Imposing an American Definition of Corruption on Global Markets' (2016) 49 Cornell International Law Journal 469; Lauren A Ross, 'Using Foreign Relations Law to Limit Extraterritorial Application of the FCPA' (2012) 6 Duke Law Journal 445.

30 See respectively 15 US Code s 78dd-1 ('issuers'); 15 US Code s 78dd-2 ('domestic concerns'); US Code s 78dd-3 ('territorial jurisdiction').

31 Cedric Ryngaert, *Jurisdiction in International Law* (2nd edn, OUP 2015) 84.

32 US Department of Justice, *FCPA—A Resource Guide to the U.S. Foreign Corrupt Practices Act* (2012) 10–11.

33 In this case, which relates to the DOJ's investigation into Alstom SA, the US Court of Appeals for the Second Circuit ruled that a non-resident foreign national could not be held criminally liable for aiding or abetting or conspiring to violate the FCPA, unless the government could show that he acted as an agent of a 'domestic concern' or while physically present in the US. See US Court of Appeal (2d Cir.), *United States v Hoskins*, 24 August 2018, n° 16-1010-cr.

companies engaged in global competition are based. This is illustrated by the US's leading role in the adoption of multilateral treaties, especially the OECD instrument on the matter, and the sudden rise of enforcement actions following its adoption.[34]

The UK Bribery Act provides for another suitable point of comparison with Loi Sapin II. Members of the Assemblée Nationale who suggested the introduction of the broad 'economic activities' nexus explicitly mentioned the UKBA to argue that such criteria were an admissible and advisable addition to French law. Interestingly, the British piece of legislation was already heralded as a response to the extraterritorial reach of the FCPA, thus confirming the 'ripple effect' created by the US initiative. Looking closely at the UKBA, the identification of a jurisdictional link similar to Loi Sapin II's 'economic activities' nexus is not self-evident. The main provision defining the jurisdiction reach of the UKBA (s 12, 'territorial application'), provides that the courts have jurisdiction over the s 1, 2,[35] or 6 offenses committed at least partly in the UK, as well as over offenses committed abroad by persons having a 'close connection' with the UK (esp. British nationals, ordinarily residents in the UK, and bodies incorporated in the UK). This 'close connection' is based on well-defined territorial and personal nexus with the offense, which makes it much narrower than Loi Sapin II's 'economic activities' criterion.

The 'close connection' condition is only waived for the application of one specific provision, that is, s 7 ('Failure of commercial organisations to prevent bribery').[36] Section 7(3) provides that relevant commercial organisations can be liable for conduct amounting to a s 1 (general bribery offense) or a s 6 offense (bribery of a foreign public official) on the part of a person who is neither a UK national or resident in the UK, nor a body incorporated or formed in the UK. Here, 'relevant commercial organisations' are defined as a body or partnership incorporated or formed in the UK irrespective of where it carries on a business, or an incorporated body or partnership *which carries on a business or part of a business in the UK* irrespective of the place of incorporation or formation.[37] The key concept here is that of an organisation which 'carries on a business.' This phrase was undoubtedly used as the model for Loi Sapin II's 'economic activities' criteria. Yet, the two jurisdictional rules must be distinguished on several grounds. First and foremost, the UKBA's nexus, based on 'business in the UK,' only applies to a very specific offense of corruption prevention ('failure to prevent bribery') while Loi Sapin II's jurisdictional reach applies to various forms of active and passive

34 See Rachel Brewster, 'Enforcing the FCPA: International Resonance and Domestic Strategy' (2017) 103 Virginia Law Review 1611.

35 This particular offense is not relevant for the purposes of s 7.

36 See Bribery Act 2010 (UK) ss 12(5), 7.

37 See ibid s 7(5)(b), (d); our emphasis. The first successful prosecution under s 7 only took place in March 2018, in the case of *R v Skansen Interiors Ltd*, and involved a small-scale UK based refurbishment company. See Crown Prosecution Service, 'Company Directors Jailed for Bribery' (23 April 2018).

corruption offenses. Besides, a common understanding of 'economic activities' (*activités économiques*) encompasses, but is not limited to, business activities (*activité commerciale*). In this respect, the UK Ministry of Justice published a *Bribery Act Guidance*[38] that narrows down substantially the meaning of 'carrying on a business in the UK.' For instance, the fact that a foreign company has a UK subsidiary is deemed to be insufficient for the parent company to qualify as 'carrying on business in the UK.'[39] No guidelines of this sort have been published so far regarding Loi Sapin II, hence leaving wide open the interpretation of the 'economic activities' criterion by French authorities.

This brief comparative analysis indicates that, to some extent, Loi Sapin II's extraterritoriality may well surpass the jurisdictional rules of both the FCPA and UKBA. This conclusion leaves unaddressed the question of how far states can go in extending the reach of criminal law on the ground of economic interests. This question, for which the answer is to be found in international law, is of paramount importance in the context of the fight against transnational corruption.

2 Criminal jurisdiction based on 'economic' or 'business' activities in the territory: A valid basis in international law?

2.1 A dubious basis in customary law

Any assessment of a jurisdiction claim in international law necessarily mentions a famous *obiter dictum* of the Permanent Court of International Justice (PCIJ) in its *Lotus* case:

> Far from laying down a general prohibition to the effect that States may not extend the application of their laws and the jurisdiction of their courts to persons, property, and acts outside their territory, it leaves them in this respect a wide measure of discretion which is only limited in certain cases by prohibitive rules; as regards other cases, every State remains free to adopt the principles which it regards as best and most suitable.[40]

38 UK Ministry of Justice, *The Bribery Act 2010—Guidance* (2011).

39 Whilst recalling that 'courts will be the final arbiter as to whether an organisation "carries on a business" in the UK,' the *Guidance* applied a common-sense approach to stress that 'organisations that do not have a demonstrable business presence in the United Kingdom would not be caught. The Government would not expect, for example, the mere fact that a company's securities have been admitted to the UK Listing Authority's Official List and therefore admitted to trading on the London Stock Exchange, in itself, to qualify that company as carrying on a business or part of a business in the UK … Likewise, having a UK subsidiary will not, in itself, mean that a parent company is carrying on a business in the UK, since a subsidiary may act independently of its parent or other group companies': see UK Ministry of Justice (n 38) 15–16 [36]. See also, in the same publication, at 9 [15]–[16].

40 *The Case of the SS 'Lotus' (France v. Turkey)* PCIJ Rep Series A No 10, 18–19.

Although the judgment dates from almost a century ago (1927), neither the International Court of Justice (ICJ) nor any other international judicial body has had—or taken?—the opportunity to re-examine the regime of criminal jurisdiction in international law. For this reason, state practice and international law literature still commonly refer to the *Lotus dictum* as a point of reference, which somehow renews its validity.[41] However, given that few prohibitive rules applying to assertion of jurisdiction have been identified and relied upon, another approach seems to be favored in practice. It consists in placing the *onus probandi* on the state asserting jurisdiction, whose claim must be based on a recognized connecting factor.[42]

If one applies this general conception to our subject, the US, the UK, and France must, thus, be able to demonstrate that the reach of their anticorruption legislation is based on territoriality, personality, or any other recognized criteria. The protective principle, which seems to be loosely relied upon in Loi Sapin II, enjoys a particular status in this respect. On the one hand, it is unanimously held that the principle is based on a recognized connecting factor, the essential interests of the State. On the other hand, the list of interests which may qualify as 'essential' is quite controversial.[43] This distinguishes the principle from other factors that are overall internationally defined, such as 'territory,' 'nationality,' or 'legal registration'. As a consequence, it is a very difficult task to assess the validity in international law of claims based on it. As Iain Cameron stressed in the only monograph on the subject, the scope of the principle is 'flexible' and 'unpredictable,' which explains why it is used 'to legitimize the extraterritorial application of all manner of unpalatable offences, [such as] vague offences against the economic interests of the State.'[44] Regardless of this obstacle, one should strive to determine whether state practice includes 'economic interests' among admissible 'essential interests,' and as the case may be, *which* economic interests are encompassed.

Leaving aside the (rather few) states that do not rely at all on the protective principle, practice resulting from domestic legislation and case law may be classified into two broad categories: First, states that point to specific protected interests, either through a general jurisdictional rule or in specific criminal provisions. Of course, defense and national security are among the most common

41 See cf Ryngaert (n 31) 30–37.

42 See, for instance, Malcolm D Evans, *International Law* (4th edn, OUP 2014) 314–15; Malcolm N Shaw, *International Law* (8th edn, CUP 2017) 487.

43 This is illustrated by the approach chosen by many books to define the principle, that is, via a non-exhaustive list of examples rather than in abstract terms. See, e.g., Bernard H Oxman, 'Jurisdiction of States' in *The Max Planck Encyclopedia of International Law*, vol IV (OUP 2012) 550–551.

44 See Cameron, *The Protective Principle of International Criminal Jurisdiction* (n 22) 49; Cameron, 'International Criminal Jurisdiction, Protective Principle' (n 22).

essential interests mentioned.[45] Specific interests relating to a State's economic and financial power are also often encompassed, especially protecting the national currency (counterfeiting of currency)[46] and to a lesser extent, securities and other financial instruments issued by the state.[47] Only the US seems to base the *use* of its national currency in an illegal transaction as a valid nexus. Such practice does not seem to extend the protection to economic interests at large, hence calling into question the possibility for states to rely on the mere existence of an 'economic' or 'business' activity to extend jurisdiction to extraterritorial offenses. Reference to unspecified 'economic interests,' such as in Bolivia's and Costa Rica's *Código penal*,[48] are indeed very rare. Even the *Restatement of the Law (Fourth), Foreign Relations Law of the US* (2018), which approach to jurisdiction cannot be blamed for its rigidity, confines the protective principle to 'security of the state' and a 'limited class of other fundamental state interests.' The only economic interest mentioned here is again the state's currency.[49] Yet, the practice of a larger group of states may blur the picture that was just starting to emerge. A significant number of states do not define 'interests' and assert criminal jurisdiction over any conduct 'affecting' or 'against' the state or its interests at large. It is the case of quite a few states around the world, including the People's Republic of China, Russia, Sweden, or Italy.[50] Other states are well aware of such claims, but never

45 Including Criminal Procedure Code of Algeria s 588; Criminal Code of Cambodia s 22(1); Criminal Code of Cape Verde s 4(1)(a); Criminal Code of Denmark s 8(1); Criminal Code of France s 113–10; Criminal Code of Ethiopia s 13; Criminal Procedure Code of Gabon s 516; Criminal Code of Iraq [8(1)]; Criminal Code of Japan s 2 (ii)–(v), (viii); Criminal Code of Jordan s 9; Criminal Code of Lebanon s 19(1); Criminal Code of the Netherlands s 4(a); Criminal Procedure Code of Niger s 647; Criminal Code of Oman s 8; *Criminal Code* of Tchad s 7(b); Criminal Code of Uruguay s 10(1); Criminal Code of Thailand s 7(1); American Law Institute's *Restatement of the Law (Fourth), Foreign Relations Law of the US* (2018) [216] (Fourth Restatement). This is without mentioning specific fields, such as counterterrorism law.

46 Including Criminal Code of Albania s 8(7); Criminal Code of Cambodia s 22(3); Criminal Code of Cape Verde s 4(1)(a); Criminal Code of Ethiopia s 13; Criminal Code of France s 113–10; Criminal Procedure Code of Gabon 516; Criminal Code of Iraq [8(1)]; Criminal Code of Japan s 2 (ii)–(v), (viii); Criminal Code of Jordan s 9; Criminal Code of Lebanon s 19(1); Criminal Code of the Netherlands s 4(c), (d); Criminal Procedure Code of Niger s 647; Criminal Code of Oman s 8; Criminal Code of South Korea art 5(4); Criminal Code of Chad s 7(b); Criminal Code of Thailand s 7(2); Criminal Code of Uruguay s 10(3); US Fourth Restatement [216].

47 Including Criminal Code of Japan ss 2 (ii)–(v), (viii); Criminal Code of the Netherlands s. 4(d); Criminal Code of Rwanda s 12; Criminal Code of South Korea s 5 (5); Criminal Code of Uruguay s 10(3). See also Cedric Ryngaert, 'Jurisdiction in International Law: US and European Perspectives' (PhD thesis, University of Leuven, Netherlands, 2007) 372ff.

48 Criminal Code of Bolivia s 1(4) of the refers to offenses 'against the national economy' (*delitos contra la economía nacional*); Criminal Code of Costa Rica, s 5(1), mentions offenses committed abroad 'which harm [its] economy' (*hechos contra su economía*).

49 §216 of the American Law Institute's *Restatement of the Law (Fourth), Foreign Relations Law of the US.*

50 Among many others: Criminal Code of Armenia s 15 [3(2)]; Criminal Code of Azerbaijan s 12 [2]; Criminal Code of Belarus s 6(2); Civil and Criminal Procedure Code of Bhutan s

formally denied their validity. Therefore, one must admit that no clear definition of the 'essential interests' protected can be identified in State practice. Such a conclusion is rather disturbing, as it provides us with no clear answer as to the validity of the Loi Sapin II jurisdictional rule and similar provisions in customary international law. However, these extensive assertions may find strong support in treaty law.

2.2 *The solid basis provided by multilateral instruments against corruption*

Since the late 1990s, a significant number of multilateral instruments have been adopted to strengthen the fight against corruption, either at the regional level by the Organization of American States (OAS) (1996), the OECD (1997), the Council of Europe (1999) and the African Union (AU) (2003), or universally (UNCAC).[51] Their respective scope differs in various aspects (e.g., focus on prevention or corruption, forms of corruption addressed), but they all share as a common spirit that only multilateralism and cooperation can ensure an effective fight against transnational corruption. As the Preamble of the UNCAC stresses (para 3), 'corruption is no longer a local matter but a transnational phenomenon that affects all societies and economies.' Against this background, anticorruption treaties provide for several legal tools that are commonly found in criminal law treaties, including provisions on criminal jurisdiction. Interestingly, these provisions often refer to the protective principle as one of the principles on the basis of which a State Party 'may establish its jurisdiction.' In particular, the UNCAC provides that a State Party may establish its jurisdiction when '[t]he offence is committed *against* the State Party.'[52] Arguably, such a provision allows states to assert jurisdiction on the basis of the protective principle in its broadest form, since the protected interests are never defined elsewhere.[53] The Convention of the African Union on Preventing and Combating Corruption goes even further by providing that each State Party has jurisdiction over acts of corruption 'when

20(d); Criminal Code of Bulgaria s 5; Criminal Code of the People's Republic of China s 8; Criminal Code of Italy s 10; Criminal Code of Kazakhstan s 8(4); Criminal Code of Latvia s 4(3); Criminal Code of Russia s 12(3); Criminal Code of Sweden s 3(4)(ch 2); Criminal Code of Turkmenistan s 8(2).

51 Respectively Inter-American Convention Against Corruption (entered into force 6 March 1997) (1996) 35 ILM 724 (the OAS Convention); Convention on Combating Bribery of Foreign Public Officials in International Business Transactions (adopted 17 December 1997, entered into force 15 February 1999) 37 ILM 1 (OECD Convention); Council of Europe Criminal Law Convention on Corruption; United Nations Convention against Corruption (opened for signature 9 December 2003, entered into force 14 December 2005) 2349 UNTS 41 (UNCAC).

52 UNCAC, art 42(2)(d); such authorization is subject to art 4, which protects state sovereignty.

53 UNODC, *Legislative guide for the implementation of the United Nations Convention against Corruption* (New York, 2012) 134 [495].

the offence, although committed outside its jurisdiction, affects, in the view of the State concerned, its vital interests or the deleterious effects or harmful consequences or effects of such offences impact on the State Party.'[54] Of course, the relative effect of treaties entails that these jurisdictional provisions only apply *inter pares*, and with regard to the specific offenses they criminalize; but this caveat is of little relevance regarding the UN instrument, which is binding on the vast majority of states.

Besides, other treaty provisions explicitly encourage the expansion of the jurisdiction reach of state parties. The OECD Convention—which is binding on the US, the UK, and France—adopts a rather radical stance on the issue by providing that each State Party shall 'review whether its current basis for jurisdiction is effective in the fight against the bribery of foreign public officials and, if it is not, shall take remedial steps.'[55] In addition to this rather exceptional legal obligation, other treaties address this issue in their related materials. The *Legislative Guide* to the UN Convention emphasizes the adverse effects of existing 'jurisdictional gaps,'[56] while the explanatory report to the Council of Europe's instrument refers explicitly to the protective principle: 'In the field of corruption, [territorial and national] principles may … not always suffice to exercise jurisdiction, for example over cases occurring outside the territory of a Party, not involving its nationals, but still affecting its interests.'[57] Logically, the same liberal approach is followed by the monitoring bodies of anticorruption treaties, such as the Group of States against Corruption (GRECO) or the OECD Working Group. Through these legal obligations and criminal policy-setting, multilateral instruments against corruption give ground to the extensive claims enshrined in Loi Sapin II's Article 21 and other pieces of legislation.

This encourages the overlap of jurisdictional claims over transnational corruption, the result of which is well-known. As was recalled recently by the Agence Française Anticorruption, 'in this context, a company may face simultaneous controls or prosecutions by several States and be required to provide important information about its contracts and business partners, including on the territory of other States.'[58] The Agency referred specifically to the FCPA, the UKBA, and Loi Sapin II examined above. Despite some coordination efforts, the situation is

54 African Union Convention on Preventing and Combating Corruption (adopted 11 July 2003) (2004) 43 ILM 5, art 13(1)(d). Although the US, the UK and France are obviously not parties to this instrument, this illustrates the (very) liberal approach sometimes adopted towards the protective principle.

55 OECD Convention, art 4(4). For a commentary, see Mark Pieth, 'Article 4—Jurisdiction' in Mark Pieth, Lucinda A Low, and Nicola Bonucci (eds), *The OECD Convention on Bribery—A Commentary* (2nd edn, CUP 2014) 322.

56 'Jurisdictional Gaps that Enable Fugitives to Find Safe Havens Need to be Reduced or Eliminated': see UNODC (n 53) [492].

57 *Explanatory Report on the Council of Europe Criminal Law Convention on Corruption* (1999) 17 [83].

58 Agence française anticorruption (AFA), *Rapport annuel d'activité 2017* (22 May 2018) 6.

for now rather chaotic for multinational companies and other persons involved in international business, and very far from the ideal of a 'normative global village.'[59] Thus, the crafting of policy and legal solutions is urgently needed.

3 Addressing jurisdictional overlaps: policy and legal solutions in the fight against transnational corruption

3.1 Unilateral initiatives: a plea for jurisdictional self-restraint

Legal and natural persons involved in international business should be able to know with enough clarity which anti-corruption law they must comply with, so as to adapt their behaviour and avoid criminal punishment. This 'predictability' issue is key to the protection of both crucial legal principles and economic interests—that is legal certainty and investment security, among others. Jurisdictional self-restraint could play an interesting role in this respect, especially when applied to the selection of connecting factors by states. The liberal approach towards jurisdiction in international law should not encourage states to pick nebulous factors, in the name of the fight against transnational corruption. Ideally, a connecting factor should characterize a close or genuine contact with the State.[60] Thus, a general standard of reasonableness should be applied to assertions of jurisdiction to prevent unnecessary conflicts of (exercise of) criminal jurisdiction. In this regard, Professor Mann stressed in his famous Hague Lecture on jurisdiction that 'a merely political, economic, commercial or social interest does not in itself constitute a sufficient connection.'[61] In the context of Loi Sapin II, several stakeholders of the legislative debate criticized the 'economic activities' criteria as being based on a 'dubious link' with France's interests. Rapporteur Pillet (Senate), pointing to the risk of encompassing a very large number of legal persons carrying out most part of their activity abroad, advocated for a careful consideration of the issue, 'in order to determine whether French justice is best fit to punish conduct that concern France only very indirectly.'[62] In this spirit, it would be advisable as a minimum to amend the relevant provision, by replacing

59 For a discussion of the concept in the context of anticorruption law, see Steven Salbu, 'Extraterritorial Restriction of Bribery: A Premature Evocation of the Normative Global Village' (1999) 24 Yale Journal of International Law 22.

60 Ryngaert (n 31) 156–57. In our study, the concept is only used as a *guideline*, without prejudice to the existence of a potential customary obligation formulated in the same spirit.

61 Frederick A Mann, 'The Doctrine of Jurisdiction in International Law' vol 111 (RCADI, 1964-I) 49. Again, our study does not go as far as adopting the uncompromising approach of jurisdiction followed by Frederick Mann, according to whom 'a State has jurisdiction, if its contact with a given set of facts is so close, so substantial, so weighty, that legislation in respect of them is in harmony with international law and its various aspects (including the practice of states, the principles of non-interference and reciprocity and the demands of inter-dependence):' ibid.

62 French Senate, 'Verbatim Reports of Parliamentary Proceedings' (Session of 23 November 2016).

'economic' by 'business' interests and by adding the word 'substantial' to characterise the '(business) activity in the country.'[63] In this way, French courts would be led to interpret the factor much more narrowly than the 'economic interests' phrase allows. For instance, this would prevent the 'jurisdictional hook' of Loi Sapin II to reach a company on the sole basis that it has registered securities with France's competent authorities. As in the case of the UKBA, judicial authorities will be the final arbiters of the scope of the jurisdictional rule.

It should be stressed that these propositions would not go against the objectives set by the anti-corruption instruments and their monitoring bodies. In spite of the 'liberal approach' identified above, the recommendations of the treaty bodies focus mainly on the removal of procedural impediments to the exercise of (uncontroversial) extraterritorial jurisdiction, rather than the assertion of unlimited jurisdiction based on vague connecting factors. For instance, the OECD Working Group underlined in 2004 that the scope of France's criminal law was 'extensive,' thanks notably to its broad conception of territoriality. The OECD body required mainly from French authorities to consider waiving the 'procedural requirements which can make [the use of personal jurisdiction] particularly difficult when prosecuting the offence of bribery of foreign public officials.'[64] This is what France undertook through certain provisions of Loi Sapin II, and it is less than certain that it needed to do more: Suffice to say that while the new criterion of 'economic activity' has not been implemented to a single case so far, the numbers of investigations opened in France on cases of corruption of foreign public officials has in parallel significantly increased.[65] In fact, an economy-orientated protective principle seems not to be needed by prosecutors to address the most common hypothesis faced, namely corruption schemes used by French companies or their subsidiaries of foreign or international public officials. Two main situations arise in practice: (a) the company, the company staff, and the public official involved are foreign citizens, but a legal element of the conduct occurs—or is legally considered as having occurred—in France. Here, French territorial jurisdiction will apply. These situations are very numerous as many elements are deemed relevant (e.g., payment of a sum of money in France, payment order issued in France, etc.); (b) the conduct occurs wholly abroad, the public official involved is a foreign citizen, but the company itself or the staff involved are 'French' persons according to French law: French active personal jurisdiction will apply in most cases. Ambitious pieces of legislation adopted recently, such as Ireland's recent Criminal Justice (Corruption Offences) Act of 5 June 2018,

63 In French, 'activité commerciale substantielle.'

64 OECD Working Group on Bribery, *Phase 2 Report on Implementing the OECD Anti-Bribery Convention in France* (2004) 1 [116]–[122].

65 Information up to date as of November 8, 2018, date of the aforementioned interview conducted with the Parquet National Financier.

confirm that it is possible to fight transnational corruption without leaving familiar patterns.[66]

These developments confirm that judicial restraint is both advisable and achievable without harming the objectives at stake. The key answer to ineffective mechanisms against transnational corruption lies in procedure and practices rather than in filling alleged 'jurisdictional gaps.' This is not to say that situations of concurrent jurisdiction can and should be totally avoided. Rather, multilateral solutions need to be developed to articulate responsibilities between the states involved in the fight against corruption.

3.2 Multilateral solutions: articulating States' responsibilities

The regime of jurisdiction set out in anti-corruption treaties apparently leads to an odd situation: Instruments adopted at a multilateral level to protect common interests facilitate unilateral and self-centred responses by States. Fortunately, the liberal approach applied to assertion of extraterritorial jurisdiction is partly mitigated by several mechanisms applying at the stage of its exercise. In particular, the OECD Convention provides that when more than one party has jurisdiction over a corruption offense, 'the Parties involved shall, at the request of one of them, consult with a view to determining the most appropriate jurisdiction for prosecution.'[67] This is especially important since no general obligation exists in international law that prohibits a State from prosecuting or punishing a person who has already been punished in another forum—i.e., a 'transnational form of the *non bis in idem*' standard. Thus, persons whose conduct falls within the scope of the anticorruption law of several states might face double jeopardy and be left without legal remedy. Now that France has joined the US and UK in the 'long arm' jurisdiction club, these states—and arguably several others—have for a fact the capacity to punish even those corruption offenses committed by a foreign person abroad regarding foreign public officials. This makes cooperation and coordination an increasingly important issue. Unfortunately, treaty obligations requiring cooperation and coordination have a very limited content,[68] and cannot by themselves articulate State responsibilities in a systematic and coherent fashion. In particular, they do not address the tricky issue of determining which venue is best fit for prosecution. When dealing with multijurisdictional situations, it matters little whether a State can rely on 'protective,' 'personal,' or 'territorial' nexus with the conduct, since much depends on the location of the suspects, the witnesses, the evidence, and of course the human and logistical resources available in each potential forum.

66 See Criminal Justice (Corruption Offences) Act 2018 (Ireland) ('Corruption occurring outside the State'), s 12(2), which lists only various forms of territorial and personal jurisdiction criteria.

67 OECD Convention, art 4(3).

68 See Pieth (n 55).

The issue can be better understood through the lens of prosecutorial policy. The development of 'negotiated justice' mechanisms (in the US, the UK, France, and beyond) has given more flexibility to prosecutors at the domestic level, but also in the relations with their foreign counterparts. This is well illustrated by the landmark *Société Générale* case. On May 25, 2018, the French multinational Société Générale reached a judicial agreement with French prosecutors regarding an important bribery case. The company was accused of participation in the setting-up of a multiyear bribery scheme regarding Libyan public officials under the rule of Muammar Gaddafi. To resolve the charges, the company accepted to pay a fine of 250 million euros to French authorities, in parallel with a deferred prosecution agreement with the US Department of Justice.[69] An agreement was adopted between the DOJ and the Parquet National Financier in the first coordinated resolution between the two countries.[70] More recently, the *Airbus* case brought coordination a step further, with a trilateral arrangement between France, the UK, and the US. The coordination scheme was also more ambitious: investigations were conducted as part of a joint investigation team set up between the French PNF and the British Serious Fraud Office (SFO), with parallel investigations in the United States by the DOJ and the Attorney General for the District of Columbia.[71] The PNF, SFO, and US authorities then coordinated in order to reach simultaneously with Airbus a 'CJIP' in France and deferred prosecution agreements in the US and the UK.

In order to anchor these practices, authorities of partner countries should set up best practices and memoranda of understanding to articulate parallel exercises of jurisdiction. This seemingly technical issue is also a political and financial one: in high-profile cases against multinational companies, fines can involve enormous amounts, which can destabilise even strong businesses. This does not escape the attention of French authorities, given the high number of French multinationals in the global economy. More ambitious solutions may also be considered at the regional level, especially within the European Union. The EU has recently made a historical step in the construction of a European criminal justice, by setting up the European Public Prosecutor's Office (EPPO), a financial prosecutor having competence in 22 Member States. For now, its material competence includes not only corruption offenses 'affecting the *Union*'s financial interests,' but also offenses 'inextricably linked' to such offenses; it may well be extended further in the future.[72]

69 Parquet National Financier (PNF), 'Convention judiciaire d'intérêt public conclue entre le Procureur de la République financier et la Société Générale SA' (doc. PNF-15 254 000 424, 24 May 2018).

70 US Department of Justice, 'Société Générale S.A. Agrees to Pay $860 Million in Criminal Penalties for Bribing Gaddafi-Era Libyan Officials and Manipulating LIBOR Rate' (4 June 2018).

71 Parquet national financier (n 3).

72 Emphasis added. See Council Regulation (EU) 2017/1939 of 12 October 2017 implementing enhanced cooperation on the establishment of the European Public Prosecutor's Office (EPPO) ss 22ff.

7 Chinese multinational corporations' obligations in the global anti-corruption arena

Levelling the playing field in Africa

Qingxiu Bu

Both China and Africa confront a similar problem of corruption, which erodes the rule of law, and stifles economic development.[1] Combatting bribery is a global challenge, which contributes primarily to social instability. The global community has taken a more streamlined and unified approach toward bribery, that is, objections to bribery are commonly shared. China has also made a crusade against corruption an important rhetorical part of its globalization policy. This trend leads multinational corporations (MNCs) to reassess their anti-bribery programs to ensure adequate compliance. Many questions arise as to whether Western MNCs would be disadvantaged in competing with their Chinese counterparts for the lucrative African markets, and whether China's approaches in Africa would facilitate the anti-corruption sustainably. The chapter focuses on the role that China could play in helping African countries curb corruption. It proceeds in seven sections below.

Section 1 posits that China has become one of Africa's main trading partners and Chinese investment and aid in Africa outstrip those of all other countries. Section 2 moves to a theoretical discussion of demand-side anti-corruption and supply-side anti-bribery. Section 3 examines the relationship between the Chinese custom of gift giving and an African practice of prevalent corruption which may provide a toxic mix. It analyzes the Chinese cultural practice of *guanxi* which may clash superficially with Western notions of corrupt practices. It is argued that Western networking serves the same role as that of *guanxi*-building in substance. Such a hypothesis may complicate anti-bribery in Africa both in theory and in practice. Section 4 discusses an uneven playing field in combating corruption between China and the West in Africa. Hypothetically, the uneven enforcement places Western MNCs in Africa at a competitively disadvantaged position, which argument is to be challenged dialectically. Section 5 explores the extraterritorial effect of China's anti-bribery law abroad, with particular regard to its potential spill over effect in Africa. It discusses the amendments made to Article 164 of

1 Jennifer Whitman, 'Fighting the Natural Resource Curse in Sub-Saharan Africa with Supply-Side Anti-Bribery Laws: The Role of China' (2014) 11 Manchester Journal of International Economic Law 121, 145.

the People's Republic of China (PRC) Criminal Law, which criminalises bribery beyond China's borders, as well as the Ninth Amendment with a primary focus on the bribe suppliers. Section 6 further examines a role China could play in helping African countries curb corruption. This part challenges a hypothesis that the combination of these two factors, i.e., China's anti-corruption campaign and its substantial economic engagement with Africa, will give a boost to anti-corruption efforts in Africa. It also presents a case study of China's activities in Africa, illustrating how irregular enforcement of anti-corruption regulations combined with foreign engagement lacking sensitivity to the fragility of the rule of law, particularly in poorly-governed African states, can exacerbate corruption and its associated ills. Section 7 explores and proposes some feasible strategies to catalyse realistic changes. To mitigate the exposure to litigation risks requires a relentless focus on compliance. It is observed that a more sustainable shift to less corrupt governance is dependant primarily on the transformation of inner causes, instead of those external ones. A conclusion is given in summary of the above core arguments. Given that Africa's corruption has become a scourge to sustainable development, China can advance anti-corruption initiatives on the continent, but incrementally. More comprehensive endeavours need to be undertaken in the longer run.

1 China's presence in Africa and rent-seeking

Africa has established its strategic geopolitical position, not only because it is a global natural resource supplier, but also because it is a potentially lucrative export market. The economic growth in Africa is driven by a high demand for natural resources primarily from China. The country has become Africa's biggest trading partner through forming a close economic relationship with various African countries.[2] Many of the activities of Chinese MNCs relate to the mineral resources industry, which investment in Africa's infrastructure fills a critical need on the continent. It also allows for better quality infrastructure at lower cost. However, this is only one side of the narrative.

1.1 China's unconditional policy compromises Africa's efforts in combating corruption

The current theory holds that there is one key difference between Chinese and Western conceptions of responsibility for Africa's development, namely, Western states apply strict supply-side anti-corruption measures against its MNCs operating abroad. China's foreign policy has always focused on building economic relationships and securing investments. One of the tests is to ascertain

2 Ian Bremmer, 'The Future Belongs to the Flexible' *Wall Street Journal* (27 April 2012); 'China Surpassed the United States as Africa's Largest Trade Partner in 2009 and in 2010 China's Trade with Africa Grew by Over 43 Percent.'

whether, and if so, the extent to which their practices reinforce or undermine local legal and political institutions.[3] China has consistently taken a hard line against interference in other countries' internal affairs. The country's involvement in Africa is with no strings attached.[4] China does not require recipient countries to implement rigorous anti-corruption measures upon which the West normally insists. It emphasises its no-strings policy, and contrasts it with the supposedly imperialist approach of the West.

The Chinese government does not desire to eradicate public corruption in Africa. Though China may sometimes opportunistically deviate from that non-interference policy, in general, non-intervention is so fundamental to Chinese foreign policy that the government is unlikely to significantly impose pressure on Africa with regard to corruption. As such, Chinese MNCs involve foreign investment in the continent where no conditions are mandated, such as democracy, rule of law, and anti-corruption. It has always refrained from getting entangled in the social and political affairs of other nations, including anti-corruption in Africa. This attitude affects China's willingness to overlook the anti-corruption records of its trade partners. Inadequate measures attached with cash inflow negatively impact on the building of a healthy anti-corruption ecology in the recipient countries.

While the Western approach to overcoming state corruption in managing natural resource revenues is based on encouraging transparency, the Chinese model of state capitalism has tended to rely on direct provision of public infrastructure. Many African governments favor the unconditional approaches.[5] The non-attachment policies erode African states' incentives to combat corruption.[6] They also contribute to unaccountable leaders' rent seeking. The lack of enforcing anti-corruption measures negatively impacts on the rule of law and sustainable development of the recipient regimes. China's policy incentivizes officials in power to misappropriate a country's natural resources unsustainably. This is prone to compromise the anti-corruption efforts. In consequence, China does not impose sanctions on its enterprises working in Africa when they pay bribes or engage in other acts of corruption on the continent. In this regard, China's policy of engagement in Africa, to some extent, facilitates official corruption. China should change its non-conditional policy and enforce international-level standards of

3 James Odia, 'Foreign Direct Investments, Corporate Social Responsibility, and Economic Development: Exploring the Relationship and Mitigating the Expectation Gaps' in Marianne Ojo (ed), *Analysing the Relationship between Corporate Social Responsibility and Foreign Direct Investment* (IGI Global 2016) 228.

4 Richard Aidoo and Steve Hess, 'Non-Interference 2.0: China's Evolving Foreign Policy towards a Changing Africa' (2015) 44 (1) Journal of Current Chinese Affairs 107, 139.

5 Patrick J Keenan, 'Curse or Cure? China, Africa, and the Effects of Unconditioned Wealth' (2009) 27 Berkeley Journal of International Law 84, 105–106.

6 Reagan R Demas, 'Moment of Truth: Development in Sub-Saharan Africa and Critical Alterations Needed in Application of the Foreign Corrupt Practices Act and Other Anti-Corruption Initiatives' (2011) 26 American University International Law Review 315, 369.

anti-corruption.[7] One example of how China's policy of non-interference with regard to corruption provides such incentives is Chinese investment in Angola.

Oil constitutes over 95% of all Angolan exports and corruption in Angola's oil and gas-related ministries is rampant.[8] Years of conflict have left the country dependent on the International Monetary Fund (IMF) for emergency assistance during periods of hardship. In 2007, the IMF helped but conditioned assistance on democratic elections and other important governance reforms. Concurrently, China's Eximbank loaned $2 billion to Angola to rebuild infrastructure crippled by Angola's civil war. This aid had no conditions of transparency and accountability.[9] Angola ultimately rejected the IMF's assistance, which caused the country to lose an opportunity to reduce corruption and enhance the rule of law. It is noteworthy to look into who has benefited more from China's investment in Angola's oil and gas industry: government officials or the Angolan people in general. To finance an unaccountable government may be unlikely to enable the whole society to benefit in the long run. China may need to reshape its pure capitalism engagement by enforcing good governance and anti-corruption standards. Doing so will, to some extent, catalyze the super power's global governance obligations.

1.2 Rent-seeking

Corruption is the largest hindrance to Africa's economic growth, due largely to the lack of rule of law. The risk of China's policy in Africa is that the offer of wealth to unaccountable regimes, unconditioned on good governance, fosters increased corruption and ultimately impedes development sustainably.[10] Rent-seeking officials take advantage of the lack of transparency in resource deals with China to personally profit from the transactions. Some African officials with control over natural resources seek to illicitly profit from the 'rents' obtained by leasing access to natural resources, typically to Chinese state-owned enterprises (SOEs). Notably, flows of money from natural resources can be more easily diverted through corruption than those earned through diversified commerce.[11] There is big room for rent-seeking when Chinese MNCs seek to secure permits to operate. It is noted that Illicit Financial Flows (IFFs) out of Africa might surpass

7 Ibid.

8 Alex Vines, 'Thirst for African Oil: Asian National Oil Companies in Nigeria and Angola' *Chatham House Report* (1 August 2009).

9 John Reed, 'Angolan Oil Likely to Raise Transparency Issues' *Financial Times* (11 October 2005).

10 Keenan (n 5) 105–106.

11 Maya Forstater, Simon Zadek, and others, 'Corporate Responsibility in African Development: Insights from an Emerging Dialogue' (2010) Working Paper No. 60 (Corporate Social Responsibility Initiative, Harvard Kennedy School) 10.

the amount received as foreign assistance.[12] As the level of Chinese investment increasingly flows into infrastructure and development projects, it is questionable whether this relationship will boost Africa's anti-corruption efforts. It remains unclear whether the Chinese involvement in Africa does catalyze the local ability-building to reduce poverty on the continent, given that the Chinese government shows no interest in reshaping the ecology of anti-bribery. An overview of China's presence in Africa is instructive before addressing whether uneven enforcement of supply-side anti-bribery laws can impact Africa.

1.3 Theoretical interaction between demand-side anti-corruption and supply-side anti-bribery

Many factors influence corruption but inner causes are the main ones. The internal causes in the context of Africa are the absence of strong institutions and the absence of rule of law culture. The success of anti-corruption depends on an even global enforcement of supply-side anti-bribery standards on the one hand, and on an affirmative commitment of demand-side anti-corruption effort on the other. The actions of foreign MNCs operating in Africa can help solve corruption by incentivising change and reducing corruption from both the supply- and demand-sides, but lasting reforms in the rule of law must take place internally. As Picci argued, whereas developing countries appear very frequently at the receiving end of the corrupt relation, it happens relatively less often that their firms bribe foreign officials abroad.[13] This does not apply differently to Africa's anti-bribery. The demander of a bribe is an official who has the power to offer a government contract, to issue a license, or to allocate some scarce resource, and the supplier is an MNC which is keen to secure these favors.[14] Normally, external causes become operative through internal causes. However, they contain the potential for the two causes to transform into each other under certain circumstances. Bribery is not always related to corrupt deals between governments. Private firms often play a significant role in the development of bribery. In this regard, it is essential to look into interaction among three parties, that is, Chinese and Western MNCs and interested persons in Africa. Both Western and Chinese actors catalyze changes of the African anti-corruption metrics, which practice in Africa is supposed to incentivize change and reduce corruption, at least, from a supply side. It remains uncertain which approach would lead to a more sustainable

12 United Nations Economic Commission for Africa, *Illicit Financial Flows: Report of the High-Level Panel on Illicit Financial Flows from Africa* (2015). Addis Ababa, Ethiopia; Dev Kar and Devon Cartwright-Smith, *Illicit Financial Flows from Africa: Hidden Resource for Development* (Global Financial Integrity 2010).

13 Laarni Escresa and Lucio Picci, 'A New Cross-National Measure of Corruption' (2017) 31 The World Bank Economic Review 196, 219.

14 Avinash Dixit, 'Corruption: Supply-side and Demand-side Solutions' in S Mahendra Dev and P G Babu (eds), *Development in India: Micro and Macro Perspectives* (Springer 2016) 57.

result. One well-known measure of the supply-side of corruption, Transparency International (TI)'s Bribe Payers Index (BPI), together with the TI's Corruption Perception Index (CPI), inform a narrative that China's MNCs are more likely to pay bribes in securing business opportunities in Africa. Within the interaction between the foreign MNCs and African actors, one of the inherent variables that cannot be ignored is culture, which always plays a paramount role in anti-corruption scenarios.

2 The main-theme of culture: *guanxi* vis-à-vis network

Perceptions of bribery do not vary much by culture. Confucianism, deeply embedded in Chinese society, condemns bribery as other civilisations commonly do.[15] The Confucian ideology not only discourages corruption by advocating integrity and morality, but also stresses the importance of human relationships.[16] The principles of reciprocity and trust espoused in Confucianism are manifest in *guanxi*, which implies a continuous exchange of favors.[17] These notions determine how a person should act within a community.[18] As Chinese society slides into mercantilism, gift giving has long been a component of business operations.[19] Ethical concerns arise due to an improper application of *guanxi*, which often leads to bribery. In this vein, *guanxi* helps to ascertain the prevalence of the corruption epidemic, which is intrinsically bound within the cultural norms of Chinese society. It remains unclear whether there are substantive differences between Western facilitation payments and the prevalent gift-giving practice in China *guanxi*. The latter is readily seen as a catalyst of bribery in China, while the former is lawful under the US Foreign Corrupt Practices Act (FCPA),[20] though unlawful under the Bribery Act (UKBA).[21] *Guanxi* is widely perceived by the West as a sordid form of favoritism and nepotism.[22] According to the *Guide/Guidelines* to the two major anti-bribery laws, certain business expenditures, like reasonable hospitality,

15 Philip Nichols, 'Regulating Transnational Bribery in Times of Globalization and Fragmentation' (1999) 24 Yale Journal of International Law 257, 278.

16 Clyde Stolenberg, 'Globalization, Asian Values, and Economic Reform: The Impact of Tradition and Change on Ethical Values in Chinese Business' (2000) 33 Cornell International Law Journal 711, 722.

17 Jone Pearce and Katherine Xin, 'Guanxi: Connections as Substitute for Formal Institutional Support' (1996) 39 Academy of Management Journal 1641, 1658.

18 Stolenberg (n 16).

19 Paul Steidlmeier, 'Gift Giving, Bribery and Corruption: Ethical Management of Business Relationships in China' (1999) 20 Journal of Business Ethics 121, 132.

20 15 US Code s 78dd-2(B): The FCPA 'shall not apply to any facilitating or expediting payment to a foreign official, political party, or party official the purpose of which is to expedite or secure the performance of a routine governmental action.'

21 'Bribery Act 2010: Joint Prosecution Guidance of The Director of the Serious Fraud Office (SFO) and The Director of Public Prosecutions (DPP)' s 6(1).

22 IY Yeung and Rosalie Tung, 'Achieving Business Success in Confucian Societies: The Importance of *Guanxi* (Connections)' (1996) 25 Organisational Dynamics 54, 65.

are not considered bribery.[23] To understand the rationale behind the delicate distinction may help MNCs to be alert to potential pitfalls across jurisdictions, particularly in Africa. It is essential to ascertain the extent to which the divergent statutory approaches respectively by the three jurisdictions impose on the intersection of culture and anti-bribery endeavor.

2.1 Guanxi *with unique Chinese characteristics*

China is experiencing a period of transition to a market economy, shifting from a *guanxi* predominance to an orientation characterized by the rule of law.[24] Nevertheless, *guanxi* still explicitly exemplifies a continued predominance of act utilitarianism over weakness of rule utilitarianism in China.[25] In the business world, the art of *guanxi* is arguably seen as a negative phenomenon; the corruption of officialdom in contemporary Chinese society.[26] Across the globe, attitudes towards what bribery exactly comprises vary. Given the inherent conflict between the socially embedded nature of some common practice and legal definitions of bribery, it makes sense to distinguish culturally appropriate gift giving from outright bribery.

2.1.1 Is guanxi*-oriented culture inherently wrong?*

Guanxi per se is not an 'original sin.' It is a deeply embedded system of interpersonal relationships. As Hamilton observed: 'Chinese society consists of networks of people whose actions are oriented by normative social relationships.'[27] A pragmatic theory holds that *guanxi* is used to build privileged networks to secure potential advantages; the recipient of a gift obligates itself to return the favor in the form of an undefined reciprocal service in the future.[28] *Guanxi* falls in line with Confucian benevolence, which expects the recipient to repay favors. It is this reciprocating dimension that ensures respect of the *guanxi* obligations among the network. *Guanxi*, in this dimension of the Chinese culture, acts as a means to advance personal interests. Gift giving can serve as a facilitating scheme in a *guanxi*-related context. Apart from the pragmatic perspective, *guanxi* functions

23 'Bribery Act 2010: Joint Prosecution Guidance' (n 21) s 6(2); Securities Exchange Commission and Department of Justice, *A Resource Guide to the US Foreign Corrupt Practices Act*' (14 November 2012) 17.

24 Philip Nichols, 'A Legal Theory of Emerging Economies' (1999) 39 Virginia Journal of International Law 229, 302.

25 Chad Hansen, *A Daoist Theory of Chinese Thought: A Philosophical Interpretation* (OUP 1992) 115–121.

26 Mayfair Mei-hui Yang, *Gifts, Favours, and Banquets: The Art of Social Relationships in China* (Cornell University Press 1994) 56–62.

27 Gary Hamilton, *Commerce and Capitalism in Chinese Societies* (Routledge 2006) 45.

28 John Rice and Fang Huang, 'Firm Networking and Bribery in China: Assessing Some Potential Negative Consequences of Firm Openness' (2012) 107 Journal of Business Ethics 533, 545.

as an efficient coordination mechanism, which ostensibly lowers transaction costs in a transitional period characterized by high intuitional uncertainty.[29] It makes up for the defectiveness of an incomplete market economy.[30] Theoretically, bribery is inversely proportional to its costs. As the costs associated with corrupt transactions increase, *guanxi* gradually reduces in importance, and incidences of bribery should decline. However, this has not been the case during China's transition to a market economy. With central-administrative mechanisms diminishing, new market-oriented substitutes are emerging placed to effectively govern the transition.[31] The growing liberalization of the Chinese economy demands a well-established anti-bribery regime, which can provide legal certainty, and thus steadily eliminate reliance on *guanxi* to safeguard transactions. The mere institutionalization of sophisticated laws does not displace the reliance on *guanxi* in the short term. There should be common consensus among businesses that regulatory regimes perform more effectively than *guanxi*, before they could be viewed as preferable in regulating their transactions.[32]

2.1.2 Pluralistic attitudes towards bribery—the cultural tolerance of bribery in China

Guanxi-based bribery has been increasingly common in contemporary Chinese society. As a form of significant social capital, *guanxi* is cultivated over time based on trust and reciprocity, which may facilitate binding bribery.[33] The cultural tolerance of corruption may partly account for the complexity of anti-bribery efforts in China. Firstly, sentiments of moral repugnance and censure towards corruption are not so prevalent in China as in Western countries.[34] Chinese culture indicates that people's social status rests overwhelmingly with their wealth, which incentivizes people to pursue even illicit gains at any expense. Bribery *per se* serves as a symptom of both opportunity and lack of restraint. The restraints on such activities have weakened as China's guiding ideology has shifted from one of social purification to one of overwhelming materialism.[35] Such a perception affects the

29 Matthias Schramm and Markus Taube, 'The Institutional Economics of Legal Institutions, *Guanxi*, and Corruption in the PR China' in John Kidd and Frank-Jürgen Richter (eds), *Fighting Corruption in Asia: Causes, Effects, and Remedies* (World Scientific 2003) 271.

30 Vivian Zhan, 'Filling the Gap of Formal Institutions: The Effects of *Guanxi* Network on Corruption in Reform-Era China' (2012) 58 Crime, Law and Social Change 93, 109.

31 Richard Posner 'A Theory of Primitive Society, with Special Reference to Law' (1980) 23 Journal of Law and Economics 1, 53.

32 David Richardson and Alesya Tepikina, 'Anti-corruption Campaign in China—Causes of Corruption, and Hope?' *Global Investigations Review* (25 August 2014).

33 Carolyn Hsu, 'Capitalism without Contracts versus Capitalists without Capitalism: Comparing the Influence of Chinese *guanxi* and Russian blat on Marketization' (2005) 38 Communist and Post-Communist Studies 309, 327.

34 Ling Li, 'Performing Bribery in China: *guanxi* Practice, Corruption with a Human Face' (2011) 20 Journal of Contemporary China 1, 20.

35 Stolenberg (n 16).

public's attitude towards corruption. Secondly, sensitivity to culture in China leads to tolerance of certain actions that may be labelled bribery under the UKBA and FCPA.[36] Gift giving is fundamental to the entrenched practice of developing *guanxi* and plays a delicate role in securing a potential business.[37] Gifts foster a sense of indebtedness.[38] A common form of *quid pro quo* relational expectations is evinced via tacit understanding. As a result, bribery is plausibly accepted as a valid means in conducting business, running rampant throughout China. *Guanxi* is often abused to advance the interests of firms at the price of distorting the commercial culture.[39] It was indicated that 94.2% of participants prosecuted for bribe giving said that they would warm up relations with *guanxi* before paying bribes.[40] For this reason, culturally competent MNCs should become aware of its ethical and legal ramifications. Furthermore, cultural differences render it difficult to distinguish between actionable and acceptable behaviour,[41] blurring the line between regular transactions and bribery in the current hybrid system. The issue arises as to where the line should be drawn.[42] Noonan suggests that:

> a gift is given in a context created by personal relations to convey a personal feeling and concluding that a gift-giver does not give by way of compensation or by way of purchase.[43]

It depends largely on whether a reasonable person would regard a gift as unduly extravagant in particular circumstances.[44] Within Chinese culture, there are moral parameters in distinguishing regular gift giving from bribery, based on 'intentions, purpose, means, and the result.'[45] These ideological differences in value and Western ethnocentric prejudice often lead to the assumption that China does not

36 Susan Rose-Ackerman, 'Corruption: Greed, Culture and the State' (2010) 120 Yale Law Journal Online 125, 140.

37 Alan Smart and Carolyn Hsu, 'Corruption or Social Capital? Tact and the Performance of *Guanxi* in Market Socialist China' in Monique Juijten and Gerhard Anders (eds), *Corruption and the Secret of Law: A Legal Anthropological Perspective* (Ashgate 2007) 167.

38 Jean-Sébastien Marcoux. 'Escaping the Gift Economy' (Journal of Consumer Research, 20 May 2009).

39 Jessica Silver-Greenberg and Ben Protess, 'JP Morgan Hiring Put China's Elite on an Easy Track' *The New York Times* (29 August 2013).

40 Li (n 34) 20.

41 Steven Salbu, 'Extraterritorial Restriction of Bribery: A Premature Evocation of the Normative Global Village' (1999) 24 (1) Yale Journal of International Law 223, 240–241.

42 Ibid 250.

43 John Noonan, Jr., *Bribes: The Intellectual History of a Moral Idea* (Diane Publishing Company 1984) 695.

44 Securities Exchange Commission and Department of Justice (n 23) 15–18.

45 Richard Andrulis, Huang Quanyu, and Chen Tong, *A Guide to Successful Business Relations with the Chinese: Opening the Great Wall's Gate* (Routledge 1994) 218.

regard the act of bribery as shameful in the way Westerners regard it.[46] Guthrie raised a counterargument refuting this presumption that:

> powerful economic actors often pay increasing attention to the laws, rules and regulations that are part of the emerging rational-legal system which is being constructed by the Chinese state.[47]

Chinese culture has steadily taken on a new lens, aligned with a more Western view on bribery. Never before in China has the practice of gift giving come under such stringent scrutiny. Foreign MNCs' policy against bribery must apply the same in China, despite different presuppositions. Regardless of the plausible 'mother of all path dependence,' culture does not play a decisive role in building China's anti-bribery laws following the track of FCPA and UKBA, nor will culture be considered as a mitigating element in the cross-border corporate criminal liability.

2.2 *A classical preposition: the Chinese* guanxi *vis-à-vis the western network*

Gift giving manifests, to some degree, favors that are not uniquely a Chinese phenomenon. Pervasive corruption reinforces a negative perception of *guanxi*. Corruption being endemic in China, gift giving is not to blame since it represents only part of the wider landscape of *guanxi*. There is little difference between *guanxi* and Western networking practices. Favors can be regarded as the ultimate carrier of *guanxi*, and are typically of a more personal nature than those performed in Western networking.[48] As a means of expressing respect and honor, gift giving shows that a relationship is valued. It expresses good will and gratitude, which is considered a dynamic form of social contracting.[49] The concept of *guanxi* overlaps, to a large degree, with the Western concept of networking. For this reason, it is not justified to differentiate these two social phenomena extensively. As stated in the *Guide* to the FCPA, giving a small gift is an appropriate way for business people to display respect for each other.[50] The FCPA does not prohibit gift giving, but only illegitimate bribes disguised as a gift.[51] By means of reduction to absurdity, one of the Transparency International comments indirectly proves the negligible difference between the two, proposing that: 'small companies are

46 Nii Lante Wallace-Bruce, 'Corruption and Competitiveness in Global Business—The Dawn of a New Era' (2000) 24 Melbourne University Law Review 349, 354.

47 Douglas Guthrie, 'The Declining Significance of *Guanxi* in China's Economic Transition' (1998) 154 The China Quarterly 254, 255.

48 Snejina Michailova and Verner Worm, 'Personal Networking in Russia and China: Blat and *Guanxi*' (2003) 21 European Management Journal 509, 510.

49 OECD Anti-Corruption Unit, 'Commentaries on the Convention on Combating Bribery of Officials in International Business Transactions' (1998) 37 ILM 8.

50 Securities Exchange Commission and Department of Justice (n 23) 15.

51 Ibid 16.

far more vulnerable to corruption since they often do not have the connections to bypass individual officials.'[52] In practice, such circumstances are usually blurred, where it is nearly impossible to ascertain what kind of payment could constitute bribery, and what could be acceptable as regular gifts or hospitality. The softened interpretations by the *Guide* to the FCPA complicate the African anti-bribery efforts, despite the golden rule of 'prevention is better than cure.'

Typically, an individual offers a gift in their *guanxi* network for an indefinite return, whilst their Western counterparts expect a prompt return following the facilitation payment. The latter is, in substance, not a *guanxi*-related giving, but targets particularly the recipient's routine performance. The use of facilitation payments is one of the methods to build a pragmatic and instant *guanxi*. Some commentators have echoed such a discourse, stating that: 'the US society has a tradition which pursues specificity and decisiveness.'[53] Both *guanxi* and Western networking share similar underlying cultural implications of a moral and ethical indebtedness. Some differences manifest themselves in more psychological rather than substantive perspectives. From a legal perspective, the only plausible difference appears that the gift giving in the West has been sophisticatedly institutionalised. *Guanxi* stands as an informal antagonistic relationship to the formal Western system of legal rights.[54] In the West, some pre-existing institutions produce relatively clear jurisdictional lines. As such, a prerequisite to establish criminal liability rests with a sufficient causal link between the advantage/bribe and the intention to influence,[55] whereas within a *guanxi* network, the influence could take shape long after the gift giving. Chinese institutions, to some extent, do not reside in jurisdictions, but within relationships. Although gift giving is explicitly regulated even in China's codified law, it has never been robustly enforced. This contradiction promotes the perception that gift giving constitutes a part of the Chinese culture uniquely, or at least, it differs substantively from that in the West.

2.3 *The dialectical analysis of* guanxi *in comparison: the institutional void*

Corruption is pervasive with tentacles reaching into every arena of Chinese society.[56] Because of the culture of gift giving, Chinese MNCs have been accused

52 'When a Bribe is Merely Facilitating Business' *The Economist* (1 June 2011).

53 Xiaohua Lin and Shavin Malhotra, 'To Adapt or Not Adapt: The Moderating Effect of Perceived Similarity in Cross-Cultural Business Partnerships' (2012) 36 (1) International Journal of Intercultural Relations 118, 121.

54 Gary Hamilton, 'Civilizations and the Organization of Economics' in Neil J Smelser and Richard Swedberg (eds), *The Handbook of Economic Sociology* (Princeton University Press 1994) 183.

55 UK Ministry of Justice, *The Bribery Act 2010 Guidance* (2010) 13.

56 William Wan, 'China's New Leaders Focus on Culture of Corruption' *Washington Post* (29 December 2012).

of being promiscuously corrupt in their business practices.[57] However, it is an institutional void that contributes primarily to prevalent bribery in China. Many variables contribute to the prevalent corruption, among other things, such as weak rule of law, poor enforcement of anti-bribery, and low governance standards. Similarly, legal frameworks and institutional frameworks are fundamental for the development of Africa's anti-corruption scheme. Strong institutions and accountability entail necessary deterrence, which also helps to foster a compliance culture under a governance framework. As such, African countries with a strong rule of law will be better positioned to manage their natural resources.

2.3.1 Empirical evidence

The cause of bribery is not the culture of a society, but rather the result of institutional void, which contributes mainly to China's ranking as 77th out of the 180 countries on the Corruption Perceptions Index (CPI).[58] In addition, Transparency International rated China next to last in its 2011 Bribe Payers Index (BPI) for its measured propensity to pay bribes. It was ranked the 27th of 28 world's largest economies in the BPI, which indicates that Chinese companies are the most likely to offer bribes when doing business abroad.[59] Nevertheless, the Chinese diaspora does not exhibit similar degrees of corruption in the diverse range of countries in which they reside. In the CPI 2017, Hong Kong was ranked 13th and Singapore's rank was even higher at 6th out of 180 countries.[60] According to the Ease of Doing Business Index 2019, Singapore was ranked the second, Hong Kong the fourth and China the 46th out of 190 countries.[61] These results are consistent with corresponding CPI rankings. It also shows that Singapore and Hong Kong are among the least corrupt cohorts, while China (77th) is among the more corrupt in the world. A myriad of factors has driven the intensification of bribery in China, of which it is the institutional weakness that constitutes an inherently fundamental element. The gap can be attributed to the fact that corruption is firmly rooted in China's institutional foundations,[62] although it could be argued that Singapore and Hong Kong may have become less corrupt because of their colonial histories.

57 Steidlmeier (n 19) 132.

58 Transparency International, 'Corruption Perceptions Index 2017' <https://www.transparency.org/news/feature/corruption_perceptions_index_2017> accessed 1 June 2020.

59 Transparency International, 'Bribe Payers Index Report 2011' <http://www.transparency.org/bpi2011/results> accessed 1 June 2020.

60 Transparency International, 'Corruption Perceptions Index 2017' (n 58).

61 World Bank, *Doing Business 2019* (World Bank Group 2019).

62 Steven Salbu, 'A Delicate Balance: Legislation, Institutional Change, and Transnational Bribery' (2000) 33 Cornell International Law Journal 657, 678.

2.3.2 Enhance the institutional building

Even the most prudent anti-bribery provisions may not reduce corruption where bribery represents routine ways of doing business. However, law equipped with rigorous institutions can transform culturally constructed practices.[63] The three jurisdictions share similar cultural values, but there are dramatic differences between the institutions. In addition, these differences suggest that culture plays a less significant role in contributing to the CPI rankings. *Guanxi* is perceived as a negative activity linked inextricably with bribery practices. However, they are not necessarily directly linked. *Guanxi* only transitions into bribery when the exchange taking place involves corrupt intent. Whilst culture could represent an obstacle for fighting bribery, cultural pluralism is not an excuse to undermine efforts in tackling bribery extraterritorially. The Chinese economy is more robust than before, its culture has growing significant global implications and corresponding cultural values exert influence in Africa. Such repercussions will be limited when both foreign MNCs and their Chinese counterparts operate on a level playing field, which can be ensured through rule-based institutional restraint. If the anti-bribery institutional change is path dependent, China needs to build more effective institutions, as these have a significant influence on culture.[64] At stake is the potential to ensure that the behavior and attitudes of those in power are subject to stringent law and genuine threat of punishment when involved in bribery. Although cultural transformation takes time, this institutional building may act as a catalyst for changes in cultural norms. It is worth undertaking extrinsic analysis of the process of cultural change and its implications for anti-bribery regimes in the three major jurisdictions.

3 A pseudo-proposition: the argument of an unlevelled playing field

The UK Bribery Act 2010 (UKBA) and FCPA may make Western MNCs less competitive in Africa due to the uneven enforcement of law. Despite a growing number of FCPA prosecutions against foreign MNCs, it is argued that the Chinese MNCs are not subject to similar stringent anti-bribery laws. Chinese firms may not have to bear the costs of additional due diligence and scrutiny under the FCPA or UKBA. With increasing convergence of the global anti-bribery regimes, uneven law enforcement will undercut the aim of the OECD Convention on Combating Bribery of Foreign Public Officials in International Business Transactions (OECD Convention) to harmonise international anti-bribery standards. This may plausibly harm those in high-enforcement nations. Paradoxically, the uneven playing field may create a systematic risk that could

63 Salbu, 'Extraterritorial Restriction of Bribery' (n 41) 226.

64 Matthias Schramm and Markus Taube, 'The Institutional Economics of Legal Institutions, *Guanxi*, and Corruption in the PR China' in John Kidd and Frank-Jürgen Richter (eds), *Fighting Corruption in Asia: Causes, Effects and Remedies* (World Scientific Press 2003) 271.

prevent those Western MNCs from securing businesses while competing with their Chinese counterparts in Africa. It is, however, noteworthy that both the US and UK authorities have increased their prosecution of foreign entities. A long-standing debate centers on whether the UKBA and FCPA really place British and American businesses at a disadvantage. Some specific provisions under FCPA and UKBA provide delicate leverage in response to the hypothesis. Meanwhile, the international community has endeavored to create a level playing field to combat bribery beyond its own territories.

Hypothetically, the Western MNCs incur a competitive disadvantage against their counterparts in Africa, where anti-bribery laws are not enforced as rigorously as in the US and the UK.[65] Would the FCPA and UKBA enforcement counterproductively chill business by discouraging corporate entry into the African market? Firstly, both the US and UK's anti-bribery regimes are characterized by their extraterritoriality. If enforced properly, the Western anti-bribery measures can better align the incentives of companies operating in Africa and reduce the incidence of bribery.[66] On the other hand, Western MNCs may be beaten at securing a contract because they did not pay a bribe, which may, in substance, chill investment appetite as a result. Arguably, fearful of prosecution under the tough anti-bribery laws, Western MNCs have been retreating. The resultant asymmetrical market opportunities limit the ability of Western MNCs to compete in Africa. As such, the loss of Western MNCs' competitiveness is attributed to a paradoxical theory of availability heuristic,[67] that is, the Western heightened anti-bribery enforcement results in an uneven playing field in Africa. Secondly, the West pushes democracy and capitalism while the Chinese state capitalism is politically appealing in Africa. The West always requires African governments to alter their social and political agendas so as to meet their investment preconditions. As such, widespread corruption in Africa could put Western MNCs between the proverbial rock and a hard place.[68] Generally, the Western MNCs are reluctant to involve themselves in deals with African states of poor legal structure. Paradoxically, given that corruption poses significant risks for investors, substantial compliance costs could pressure the West to undermine its commitment in combatting bribery in Africa. The uneven enforcement limits the ability of the West to achieve its ultimate objective, that is, reducing corruption in Africa. It is argued that its Chinese rivals are not subject to similar investigations and even prosecutions. As such, Chinese MNCs are filling the gap and further expanding their presence in Africa, seeking out its natural resources. Nevertheless, some statistics provide empirical evidence to the contrary.

65 Eric Pedersen, 'The Foreign Corrupt Practices Act and Its Application to US Business Operations in China' (2008) 7 (1) Journal of International Business and Law 13, 47.

66 Demas (n 6) 369.

67 Amos Tversky and Daniel Kahneman, 'Availability: A Heuristic for Judging Frequency and Probability' (1973) 5 Cognitive Psychology 207, 232.

68 Patrick Norton, 'The Foreign Corrupt Practices Act Dilemma' *China Business Review* (November/December 2006) 22.

3.1 Empirical evidence

MNCs' home state laws cannot completely reach transnational bribery, and the host state's legal framework is therefore required for effective control.[69] In 2011, 72% of the financial penalties in FCPA cases were assessed by US authorities against non-US companies, even though these companies comprised only 41% of those investigated.[70] From 2009 to 2011, 16 of the 36 FCPA enforcement cases have involved non-US parent companies.[71] Nine of the ten largest penalties until 2011 imposed by US authorities for alleged FCPA violations were levied against foreign companies.[72] Several of the most high profile FCPA enforcement actions of all time have also been against foreign companies. Further research puts forward 90% of small-and-medium enterprises (SMEs) have had no problems with the provisions of the UK Bribery Act 2010 and 89% of SMEs felt that UKBA had no impact on their ability to export.[73] In reality, China-based MNCs are faced with a rapidly evolving anti-bribery compliance environment. They are not exempt from the FCPA and UKBA's reach either. Taking advantage of the lucrative African markets, the Chinese MNCs have been running into the challenges of complying with the FCPA and UKBA as well. As some commentators revealed: 'nearly one-half of all China-related corporate prosecutions under the FCPA since 2002 involved the provision of gifts.'[74]

3.2 An invalidated pseudo-proposition

The empirical analysis invalidates the above-mentioned argument that US and UK corporations are being disadvantaged. Firstly, China has accelerated criminalization of paying bribes to foreign officials, mirroring the exterritorial restrictions provided under both the UKBA and the FCPA. Those internationally accepted norms are reflected in China's amended Article 164. Chinese MNCs operating abroad are, thus, treated the same as their counterparts, at least, under the law in paper. Secondly, neither the Chinese nor the Western MNCs are penalized out of either protectionism, nationalism, or selective enforcement. Without solid evidence that UK and US multinationals are being disadvantaged, such a perception is only to be viewed as a pseudo-proposition. Lastly, the

69 Nichols (n 15); Philip Nichols, 'Are Extraterritorial Restrictions on Bribery a Viable and Desirable International Policy Goal Under the Global Conditions of the Late Twentieth Century?: Increasing Global Security By Controlling Transnational Bribery'(1999) 20 Michigan Journal of International Law 451, 476

70 US Department of Justice, Related Enforcement Actions, Chronological List 2011. <http://www.justice.gov/criminal/fraud/fcpa/cases/2011.html> accessed 1 June 2020.

71 Ibid.

72 Ibid.

73 HM Government, *Insight into Awareness and Impact of the Bribery Act 2010 Among Small and Medium Sized Enterprises (SMEs)* (2015) 37, 38.

74 F Joseph Warin, Michael S Diamant, and Jill M Pfenning, 'FCPA Compliance in China and the Gifts and Hospitality Challenge' (201) 5 Virginia Law & Business Review 33, 59.

empirical data mentioned above proves to be counterintuitive. The anti-bribery efforts have been taking place in both international as well as domestic fora,[75] although the effectiveness of extraterritorial restrictions on bribery remains to be seen. The global challenge from corruption requires an international solution. In order to create a level playing field, global anti-bribery initiatives have been emerging toward the development of an avenue to deter transnational bribery. Under the UN and OECD Conventions, the signatory countries are committed to outlawing extraterritorial bribes throughout the world.

4 The extraterritorial effect of China's anti-bribery law

There is increasingly a global trend towards the strengthening of existing anti-bribery regimes. Cultural change being incremental, institutional globalisation in anti-bribery laws can minimize the negative and accentuate the positive.[76] Albeit restrained by the traditions of culture, Chinese institutional development has shown growth in its sophisticated anti-bribery laws, which are not confined to domestic bribery. China has begun to catch up with its Western counterparts in criminalizing bribery to foreign officials. In 2011, China took a key step, enacting legislation that criminalizes paying bribes to foreign government officials for the purpose of seeking illegitimate commercial benefit.[77] The intention of the Amendments is to create legislation similar to the FCPA and the UK Bribery Act. Being geopolitically constructive, Article 164 has become a source of systemic risk for multinational corporations.[78] The law's extraterritorial effect pressures MNCs to take more proactive steps to prevent foreign bribery in Africa.

4.1 The Eighth Amendment to Article 164 of the Chinese Criminal Law (CCL 2011)

China has adopted domestic legislation criminalizing corrupt foreign business practices in line with those key multilateral treaties setting global anti-bribery standards. The Amendments in Article 164 create a legal avenue to ensure full compliance with the OECD Convention. With the update to the provisions, China's anti-bribery law complies with comparable texts issued by signatory

75 Stuart Deming, '1998 International Legal Developments in Review: Foreign Corrupt Practices' (1999) 33 International Lawyer 507, 514.

76 Kevin Davis, 'Does the Globalization of Anti-Corruption Law Help Developing Countries?' in Julio Faundez and Celine Tan (eds), *International Law, Economic Globalisation and Development* (Edward Elgar 2010) 283.

77 The Eighth Amendment to the Criminal Law was adopted by the Standing Committee of China's National People's Congress (NPC) on February 25, 2011, which came into force on May 1, 2011 (CCL 2011).

78 Alice Gartland, 'Bribery and Corruption: Caught between Three Regimes' *Practical Law* (24 October 2014).

members of the OECD.[79] It also represents an integral part of China's effort to conform to the United Nations Convention against Corruption (UN Convention), to which China is a signatory.[80] Broadening the efforts beyond its own borders, the Amendment criminalizes the providing of 'money or property to any foreign party performing official duties or an official of international public organisations' for the purpose of 'seeking illegitimate business benefits.'[81] Prior to this Amendment, the CCL did not have extraterritorial effect. The Amendment marks the first time in which the law addresses bribery of African officials. Chinese MNCs are thus obliged to abide by strict domestic laws and those in Africa. The enforcement is not so robust compared to those under the FCPA and the UKBA, explaining the shortfall in why there have been no prosecutions so far under the Amended Article 164. After all, deterrence is only achievable through credible threat. The absence of a genuine threat of criminal liability may give Chinese MNCs an advantage over their counterparts in the African marketplace.

Generally, Chinese anti-bribery laws tend to lack specificity as to the elements that constitute a violation,[82] which leaves much room for the exercise of discretion in enforcement. It does not specify any exceptions, such as facilitation payments under FCPA and the 'adequate procedures defence' under UKBA. Justifiable as it is under FCPA, making a facilitation payment in China would still be actionable. The vagueness may allow for inconsistent and at times politically motivated enforcement.[83] In fact, Chinese MNCs are already subject to the UKBA and FCPA, due to their activities in the UK and the US given the increased cross-border transactions; there could be a scenario where the same set of facts that causes a violation of Article 164 can also constitute a violation of the FCPA and UKBA, and *vice versa*. The transnational interaction has resulted in a number of exposures initiated by FCPA investigations in the first instance. Previously, China has generally not taken action even after investigations initiated by other countries with respect to bribery have been disclosed. It is argued that the Eighth Amendment is rather more of symbolic importance, since the new provision does not include some integral components which have been specially designed to trigger criminal liability under UNCAC Article 16. It is, however, a significant step in its gradual approach to fighting transnational bribery. The Amendment empowers the Chinese authorities to exercise greater vigilance in monitoring

79 Convention on Combating Bribery of Foreign Public Officials in International Business Transactions (adopted 17 December 1997, entered into force 15 February 1999) 37 ILM 1 (OECD Convention).

80 China signed the UN Convention on December 10, 2003 and ratified it on January 13, 2006. See: <https://www.unodc.org/unodc/en/treaties/CAC/signatories.html> accessed 1 June 2020.

81 CCL 2011, art 164 (2). The Eighth Amendment took effect on 1 May 2011.

82 Kyle Wombolt and Matthew Galvin, 'Why Multinational Must be Wary of China's Anticorruption Authorities' *International Financial Law Review* (30 January 2012).

83 'Strong Arm of the Law: China's Commercial Corruption Laws Are Undermined by Politically Driven Enforcement' *China Economic Review* (13 July 2012).

its MNCs' activities in Africa. It is still an early stage, but reflective of China's intention to apply the Amendment against foreign bribery. Furthermore, the provision's expanded scope is significant in light of the increasingly aggressive application of extraterritorial jurisdiction over bribery under the FCPA and UKBA. In consequence, compliance with the two anti-bribery laws does not necessarily ensure compliance with the provision under CCL 2011. This complicates MNCs' efforts to structure their compliance. The multinationals must take this uncertainty into account when determining the level of litigation risk posed by the Amendment. As such, the Eighth Amendment should, in principle, improve Chinese MNCs' ethical standard and help to level the playing field in the African markets.

4.2 The Ninth Amendment to the Chinese criminal law (CCL 2015)

The Chinese government is increasingly determined to change the long-standing culture of graft and backhanders. The Ninth Amendment to the PRC Criminal Law came into effect on November 1, 2015.[84] Previous legal regimes generally targeted only officials who accept bribes.[85] The Ninth Amendment revised several anti-bribery provisions, mainly to impose harsher punishment on offenders who provide bribes. This approach reinforces the compliance in broader scope with the UN Convention against Corruption.[86] In particular, the Ninth Amendment echoes Article 21 of the UN Convention, which covers both active and passive bribery. It imposes additional grounds of liability as well as harsher penalties for bribery offences, which represents China's escalating effort in fighting bribery. The Amendment differs from the FCPA in that the latter aspires to 'concentrate on the supply side by targeting the MNCs that offer bribes to government officials.'[87]

It adds a new provision to Article 390, targeting those giving bribes to a person who may exert influence on a current or former government official.[88] The Chinese Criminal Procedure Law defines 'close relatives' as 'husband, wife, father, mother, son, daughter, and siblings,'[89] there is no guidance in the Amendment as to who will qualify as a person 'closely related' to the state

84 The National People's Congress of China promulgated the Ninth Amendment to the Criminal Law on 29 August 2015 (CCL 2015).

85 The FCPA does not provide a mechanism to prosecute foreign officials for receiving bribes, presumably for reasons of international comity. Unlike the FCPA, the Bribery Act criminalizes the receipt of bribes, in addition to the payment of bribes.

86 UN Convention covers 'Bribery of national public officials (art 1)'; Bribery of foreign public officials and officials of public international organisations (art 16); and Bribery in the private sector (art 21).

87 Warin and others (n 74) 41.

88 The Ninth Amendment adds a crime (as art 390(a)) of offering bribes to 'state functionaries' close relatives or other persons closely related to them, or former state functionaries, their close relatives, or other persons closely related to them.'

89 Criminal Procedure Law (China), art 106.

functionary. A lack of definition may give the authorities broader discretion and flexibility in prosecuting a bribe-giver.[90] Such 'influential persons' include anyone who is closely associated with a current or former government official.[91] This Amendment mirrors an approach in the *US v. Liebo*, where it was illegal to corruptly influence a foreign official via influencing his connected persons.[92] It represents a further effort to prevent government officials from receiving bribes through their inner circle during their government service or *ex post*.[93] Corporate compliance due diligence should broaden payee background checks to 'red flag' not only current and former government officials, but also any of their close associates to prevent such a delicate violation. The provision tries to resolve an inherent problem in the practice where bribers were penalised far less harshly than were the bribees. This disparity was based on an assumption that the former is often a reluctant participant in bribery. However, bribers and bribees are often interdependent on each other.

4.3 The impact on MNCs' global compliance strategies

China's anti-corruption landscape has become more stringent than ever with the above Amendments. The approaches bring China's statutory enforcement authority standards to levels among the world's toughest anti-bribery laws, which stand aloof from the traditional Chinese culture of gift giving. The updating of the Chinese Criminal Law represents a positive step, given China's growing role in the African market. The global anti-bribery regimes have thus been reinforced with China moving forward on the recent Amendments. Enforcement of China's new law would send a strong message that China is assuming a position of global leadership consistent with both its commitment to rule of law and its stature as the second largest economy in the world. Given the general lack of affirmative defenses or exceptions, the Amendments seek to impose harsher penalties than those under the FCPA and UKBA, which target mainly on the supply side of the bribery. As such, MNCs should proactively review and ensure that their due diligence and stringent compliance programmes rise to this new challenge. They need to reassess their existing internal control procedures to ensure even their African subsidiaries are properly protected adequately. MNCs subject to investigations by UK or US regulators should operate conforming to global resolutions, including those created by Chinese anti-bribery authorities. Plausibly, it still remains unclear whether the stringent Amendments could meaningfully change the scenario between the anti-bribery institutions and the long-standing culture

90 K Lesli Ligorner, 'Expanding the Dragnet of the Law in China's Fight against Corruption' *Insight* (November 2015).

91 CCL 2015, art 46.

92 *United States v. Liebo*, 923 F.2d 1308, 1311 (8th Cir. 1991); Securities Exchange Commission and Department of Justice (n 23) 16.

93 The Ninth Amendment of the CCL 2015, art 390.

with particular regard to gift giving. The Eighth Amendment provides a macro framework outlawing bribery of African officials, while the Ninth one is more micro entailing constructive constraints over the briber givers, likely, in the name of gift-giving. More specifically, it is argued that gift giving and *guanxi*-building are not unique in China, while the institution matters via the anti-bribery law in terms of the universal social phenomena in essence.

5 Would China's anti-corruption campaign have positive spill over effects in Africa?

Bribery deals are more expectant between China and Africa in comparison to other international deals. Corruption is something entrenched in the culture. Whereas China is characterised by its *guanxi* and gift-giving culture, African deals are known to involve bribes often wrapped as 'good service gifts'. A toxic mix when it comes to the determent of global bribery. The duty to combat corruption appears to be predominantly a political duty. Corruption has been a decades-long problem with little indication of political change in the near future; the prospect of looking to China for a glimmer of hope could be enticing. It is doubtful that China's anti-corruption campaign will substantially decrease corruption in Africa.[94] It remains to be seen whether it is possible for a country with a poor record of anti-corruption to export an efficient model to Africa. Chinese MNCs' proactive actions could help incentivise behavioural change and thus reduce corruption in Africa. However, this must be based on certain circumstances. It is worth examining the Chinese approaches' spill over effect on African anti-corruption.

5.1 Beijing model's ideological inspiration

Ideologically, China's anti-corruption campaign may serve as a model, inspiring some of Africa's more authoritarian leaders. The Beijing Model could convince those governments that undertaking a serious anti-corruption campaign does not necessarily mean opening the door to full democracy. Even so, the credibility of China's campaign may inspire African leaders to address the largest hindrance to economic development while keeping their power. China's anti-corruption campaign has been removing key players who facilitated corruption in Africa. There is the case, for instance, of Sam Pa, the 'controversial businessman credited with spearheading China's spectacular drive into Africa over the last two decades.'[95]. While functioning as dealmaker for the Queensway Group, a shadowy organisation responsible for many multibillion-dollar transactions between African countries and Chinese businesses, Pa allegedly bribed countless

94 Katie King, 'What Does China's Anticorruption Campaign Mean for Africa?' *The Global Anticorruption Blog* (25 January 2016).

95 Ibid.

African officials, in addition to providing support to some of the continent's unaccountable governments. Pa was then swept up in a Chinese anti-corruption investigation. The removal of corrupt and corruption-inducing figures like Pa could decrease corruption, as well as signal that the Chinese government is moving away from allowing purely profit-driven capitalism, and toward a more formalized, less corrupt form of engagement.[96]

5.2 Anti-corruption in China's national interests

Getting increasingly international in its anti-corruption campaign, China joins in the fight against bribery by passing similar standards on its MNCs operating in Africa. In accordance with its non-intervention policy, China is unlikely to prioritize corruption in Africa. Chinese MNCs could feel even more pressure to offer bribes, so as to ensure they win contracts. Despite the Amendments of the Chinese Criminal Law, China seems far less interested in prosecuting its MNCs who committed bribery in Africa. To deter corruption, China might pressure its African partners to keep bribery out of China–Africa deals.[97] If the need to pay bribes decreased profit margins for Chinese firms, China could decide that it is in its own best interest to pressure African countries to prevent their own nationals from requesting them, in particular, if the Chinese government believed its own MNCs could out-compete others in a fair market. In this regard, China's judiciary does not function independently unless its national interest and the processes of judiciary integrity align. Chinese MNCs are thus not likely to be concerned about prosecution by the Chinese authorities for bribery committed in Africa. Arguably, Africa's sustainable economic development depends on a reduction in corruption and triggers essential changes to the current battle against corruption in order to ensure that it is enforced effectively.[98] In this sense, China's anti-corruption drive is not reliable in terms of eradicating Africa's corruption. More problematically, Africans still need to be vigilant against China-connected corruption, and that the most effective solutions are likely to come from within.[99] With China's profit-driven and competitive attitude, it is argued that it is open to adjusting to bribery culture in Africa. The United Nation Office on Drugs and Crime (UNODC) once reported that an ethically compromised judiciary is 'a serious impediment to the success of any anti-corruption strategy.'[100] China lacks applicability of the recent amendments of its criminal law and does not enforce anti-corruption standards on the operations of its own companies in Africa. It is no wonder that there has been no prosecution so far against China's MNCs operating in Africa.

96 Ibid.
97 Ibid.
98 Demas (n 6) 369.
99 King (n 94).
100 UNODC's Action against Corruption and Economic Crime, UNODC (2013) <www.unodc.org/unodc/en/corruption/index.html> 1 June 2020.

6 Sustainable strategies: catalyze the change through compliance

Chinese culture influences the way people think, act, and hence the extent to which they should be held responsible for their behavior. As a double-edged sword, the culture *per se* can contribute to illegal behaviour like bribery, while it can also be a vehicle for promoting good ethical conduct.[101] As transactions cross borders, simultaneously satisfying each of the overlapping anti-bribery laws of multiple jurisdictions can be challenging. It is never enough to stress the need for a culture of compliance. This section explores how to tackle bribery through taking preventive measures and fostering a culture of integrity.

6.1 Make gift-giving policies jurisdiction specific

MNCs' compliance regimes tend to reflect their parent companies' corporate culture and strategic imperatives. One of the primary risks that the African culture posed to MNCs is that they could run afoul of the FCPA or the UKBA. Foreign MNCs may attempt to defend their bribery in reference to the local prevalent corrupt culture. The claim that bribery exists intrinsically in local culture remains a plausible pseudo proposition, which misleads the MNCs' African anti-bribery efforts. Extraterritoriality arguably disregards the values of other cultures, given that gift policies vary considerably from jurisdiction to jurisdiction.[102] What might well constitute a reasonable gift in one country may violate anti-bribery laws in other jurisdictions. The UKBA provides that: 'any local custom or practice is to be disregarded unless it is permitted or required by the written law applicable to the country or territory concerned.'[103] Law transforms a culture that tolerates corruption, while simultaneously the culture triggers a response of enacting more anti-bribery laws. In this regard, the law is not merely a reflection or by-product of culture, but can also serve a legitimate constitutive role in forming culture.[104] With more anti-bribery laws with extraterritorial effect, the room for customary gift-giving practices is shrinking, even though they do not truly constitute bribery.[105] None of Article 164, FCPA, or Bribery Act 2010 grants a culture

101 Thomas Donaldson, 'Values in Tension: Ethics Away from Home' *Harvard Business Review* (September–October 1996).

102 Duane Windsor and Kathleen Getz, 'Multilateral Cooperation to Combat Corruption: Normative Regimes Despite Mixed Motives and Diverse Values' (2000) 33 (3) Cornell International Law Journal 731, 772.

103 Bribery Act 2010 s 5.

104 Menachem Mautner, 'Three Approaches to Law and Culture' (2011) 96 Cornell Law Review 839, 867; Philip Nichols, 'The Viability of Transplanted Law: Kazakhstani Reception of a Transplanted Foreign Investment Code' (1997) 18 University of Pennsylvania Journal of International Economic Law' 1235, 1271.

105 Timothy Fort and James Noone, 'Gifts, Bribes, and Exchange: Relationships in Non-Market Economies and Lessons for Pax E-Commercia' (2000) 33 Cornell International Law Journal 515, 546.

defense, so it is a challenge for MNCs to ensure that they are upholding the law.[106] MNCs should display subcultures and countercultures in their various African operations, instead of behaving in a 'when in Rome do as the Romans do' way.

The concept of *guanxi* is central to Chinese society and thus heavily influences corporate behaviour. It is a misconception that a corporate culture of corruption exists in which bribery is an integral part of doing business. MNCs are thus expected to focus increasingly on strengthening their anti-bribery compliance programs, simply because they are forbidden to pay bribes across jurisdictions. Both Chinese and Western MNCs must prohibit bribery despite local custom.[107] The environment of pervasive corruption does not justify that MNCs should follow the local way to secure business opportunities. Bribery is normally disguised in the African customary practices and facilitated by MNCs' local subsidiaries. A cultural sensitivity card is sometimes played by foreign MNCs, although it is often driven by profit motives.[108] However, invoking culture as a justification for making bribes can, by no means, be considered as a defense if prosecuted. The MNCs should in all circumstances respect the value of free market, but not use the local culture as an excuse for committing bribery.[109] There is substantial convergence on values about bribery across various cultures. As discussed in previous sections, bribery is never justified as a paradoxical reflection of cultural norms. Otherwise, such plausible sophistry will compromise efforts to produce justice and integrity.[110] The mitigation considerations enshrined in both the Bribery Act *Guidelines* and the FCPA *Guide* remain the same, in substance, as rationales behind China's *guanxi*-oriented cultures.

6.2 *The shifting landscape of localized compliance risks*

Culture is arguably resistant to institutional changes. It can hardly be affected simply by changes in new laws. Anti-bribery results depend upon the extent to which the company's incentives are tied to its performance. There is need for a broader and multijurisdictional compliance scenario. Otherwise, foreign MNCs would be misled and further suffer without an adequate corresponding global anti-bribery governance regime. Fostering a culture of compliance enables multinationals to

106 Matt Vega, 'The Sarbanes-Oxley Act and the Culture of Bribery: Expanding the Scope of Private Whistleblower Suits to Overseas Employees' (2009) 46 Harvard Journal on Legislation 425, 454.

107 Drury Stevenson and Nicholas Wagoner, 'FCPA Sanctions: Too Big to Debar?' (2011) 80 (2) Fordham Law Review 775, 820 at 788.

108 Daniel Patrick Ashe, 'The Cultural Sensitivity Card is Often Played by Foreign MNCs Which Pay Bribes in Achieving Their Profit-Maximising Goals' (2005) 73 Fordham Law Review 2897, 2945.

109 Rose-Ackerman (n 36) 140.

110 UK Ministry of Justice, *The Bribery Act 2010 Guidance* (n 55).

localize their global governance compatibly into Africa's socio-legal and cultural settings and transform the anti-bribery system. Through fostering the culture that fuses high integrity, MNCs will be likely able to complete the process of such a transformation. Otherwise, there will be massive repercussions across significant international business.

6.2.1 The feasibility to foster a compliance culture against bribery

The enforcement agencies give meaningful credit to companies which implement in good faith a comprehensive and risk-based compliance programme. Assessment of risk is fundamental to developing a strong compliance programme,[111] which needs to be updated to ensure it accounts for anti-bribery risks on a global basis. Mere global compliance programs superimposed upon Africa's regulatory environment are inadequate. MNCs must assess the bribery risk of each jurisdiction where they operate. Failure to take these steps will result in exposure to massive bribery liability on a global scale. It is imperative for an MNC to enhance the due diligence process in dealing with the presence of any red flags.[112] Although adequate compliance subjects a company to the least amount of exposure to criminal liability, the short-term commercial incentive renders it unattractive for the entity to adhere to such strategies. It is unlikely to inhibit every employee from acting outside of the parameters of a company's compliance policy.[113]

It is highly feasible to design a set of anti-bribery compliance rules, which has far-reaching implications for MNCs with global presence. The cultural dimension is important to the implementation of a compliance program, given that cultures exert a powerful influence on the corporate behavior. The impact encompasses changes in both formal institutions and laws and MNCs' legal behaviour. The strong tradition of gift giving creates a high-risk corrupt business environment. Globalising anti-bribery compliance efforts will mitigate the risks. However, delivering the anti-bribery culture is a challenging area and also difficult to quantify. It could contribute to bribery, while the cultural elements, to some extent, rationalize such behaviour. MNCs must understand the cultural uniqueness that shapes business transactions in Africa. Seeking to transform social norms, MNCs' willingness to nurture a corporate culture of zero-tolerance for bribery is in fact contrary to the African local customs and is thus doomed from the start. Differences in cultural values may increase likelihood of violations of anti-bribery law, but do not necessarily create practical problems in extraterritorial

111 Securities Exchange Commission and Department of Justice (n 23) 58.

112 *SFO v. Standard Bank plc* (Case No U20150854, 2015).

113 Peter Henning, 'Be Careful What You Wish for: Thoughts on a Compliance Defence under the Foreign Corrupt Practices Act' (2012) 73 (5) Ohio State Law Journal 883, 928.

enforcement.[114] Overestimation of the cultural variable would not only compromise the institutional globalization of anti-bribery law, but also compromise the localization of MNCs' global compliance efforts in Africa.

Convergence on a single set of cultural norms seems to be highly implausible.[115] To achieve purportedly objective righteous conduct, hard law to criminalize bribing foreign officials can ultimately not only transcend the cultural distinctions, but also restrain certain cultural declination for unlawful behaviour.[116] It is critical to make integrity and ethics a part of the overall evaluation scheme, which provides positive incentives for compliance. Foreign MNCs' success will require more than simply developing greater cultural sensitivity.[117] A policy of zero tolerance for bribery is the most effective way to comply on a global scale. Such a policy renders MNCs' compliance exceedingly challenging. A high level of commitment is required to prevent persons acting on the firms' behalf from engaging in bribery, and to foster a corporate culture in which bribery is never tolerated.[118] MNCs' African subsidiaries and branches must show evidence of their commitment to a culture of compliance.

6.2.2 Make the global compliance regimes compatible

With global presence, it will never be enough to highlight the compatible integration of the MNCs' global compliance designed into the local anti-bribery framework in Africa. Various developments in the African legal enforcement landscape suggest that compatible anti-bribery compliance needs to be warranted. Bribery *per se* may not be a cultural issue; it is imperative to integrate the specifics of a given culture into an anti-bribery compliance program and, specifically, its implementation. The challenge is to adapt compliance programs to specific environments while respecting the same standards and principles of integrity. Bribery presents legal and regulatory challenges, but these challenges cannot be addressed by the law in isolation. It is imperative to integrate MNCs' compliance programs by efficiently tailoring their efforts into the local legal and enforcement settings. An integrity system integrates a set of mechanisms that both reinforce desired behaviour *via* value-orientated cultural path and deter bribery via rule-based law

114 Michael Runnels and Adam Burton, 'The Foreign Corrupt Practices Act & New Governance: Incentivizing Ethical Foreign Direct Investment in China and Other Emerging Economics' (2012) 34 Cardozo Law Review 295, 327.

115 Nichols, 'The Viability of Transplanted Law' (n 105) 1271.

116 Lan Cao, *Culture in Law and Development: Nurturing Positive Change* (Oxford, OUP 2016) 145.

117 Coimbatore Krishnarao Prahalad and Kenneth Lieberthal, 'The End of Corporate Imperialism' (2003) 81 Harvard Business Review 109, 117.

118 SFO, *Serious Economic Crime: A Boardroom Guide to Prevention and Compliance* (White Page Ltd., 16 November 2011) 89.

enforcement.[119] The compatible integration needs to be carefully adapted for the African market and designed for effective implementation. Inevitably, implementation of an adequate anti-bribery compliance program may be resisted, in particular, when a foreign MNC ensures that bribery is not countenanced so as to reduce the incidence of passive and active bribery.[120] There is no one-size-fits-all compliance approach. It takes time for the current global anti-bribery regime to converge on a set of conceptual standards for theoretically defining corruption, given the universal disapproval of bribery.[121] Most foreign MNCs may have to adjust their focus on compliance, which used to be driven primarily by external influences, such as under UKBA and FCPA, rather than Chinese legislation.

7 Conclusion

China's unprecedented engagement in Africa has triggered a long-standing debate in terms of its role in combating corruption. The Western involvement complicates the anti-bribery landscape in the continent. This study presents a cultural analysis of bribery as an essential tool for shaping an effective legal apparatus. There has been a convergence of global anti-bribery norms toward outlawing the bribery of foreign officials. The pace of consolidating domestic institutions is escalating as globalization continues. MNCs trying to embed ethical values into compliance regimes will need to consider the particular cultural characteristics and Confucian influences on employees' behaviour. However, China's culture represents only one of the variables that are likely to contribute to bribery. A paradoxical defense by attributing to an exclusive cultural influence is not well justified. The cultural effect should not be read too widely with the amendment to Article 164 integrated into the global anti-bribery regime. While cultural sensitivity to China's anti-bribery laws is imperative, MNCs must cover the overlap across jurisdictions. A presumption takes shape that Chinese MNCs are not subject to FCPA-like laws, which has put Western companies in a disadvantaged position. It is argued that UKBA and FCPA do not necessarily weaken the Western MNCs' competitiveness in Africa. It is further held that whether to pay bribes is largely based on rational and economic calculation of benefit and costs. Anti-bribery is a section within a wide range of inroads that travel to the heart of the institutional cultures of MNCs, of which ethical culture should be clearly articulated. MNCs should have rigorous and well-established compliance programs. An adequate compliance culture can protect against violations and help mitigate liability in case bribery should arise, while the most reliable approach is to enhance institutional building in compliance programs. This approach is neither dichotomous nor between a rock and a hard place. Anti-bribery efforts are still in their infancy

119 Lynn Paine, 'Managing for Organisational Integrity' (March–April 1994) Harvard Business Review 85, 113.

120 UK Ministry of Justice, *The Bribery Act 2010 Guidance* (n 55) 8.

121 Salbu, 'Extraterritorial Restriction of Bribery' (n 41) 241.

in Africa, but are likely to grow as the world trends towards a greater emphasis on ethically responsible global business practices. It holds particularly true with the African governments' initiative to prioritize their campaign against the prevalent corruption. MNCs should ensure that their due diligence and compliance programs rise to this new challenge. The increasingly aggressive enforcement of the global anti-bribery law unquestionably poses further challenges for MNCs operating in Africa. This highlights a renewed focus on the importance of MNCs' effective compliance strategies for their long-term success globally.

Part II

Traditional methods reconsidered

8 The failure of transnational anti-corruption law

Civil law strategies reconsidered

Thomas Kruessmann

The transnationalization of anti-corruption law received its impetus from the United States which, after adopting the FCPA in 1977, began to use its international weight to expand anti-corruption rules abroad. The goal was to level the playing field for US businesses with foreign competitors who were not under such stringent anti-corruption legislation as the FCPA. As a result of political pressure, in a variety of regional fora (Europe, Latin America, Africa) multilateral conventions were adopted and finally consolidated into a UN convention.[1] In this way an international legal standard emerged ('the anti-corruption norm')[2] which subsequently served as a normative framework for national lawmakers to adopt the relevant legislation.

Looking at corruption from a transactional business-bribery point of view and seeing it primarily as deviant or unethical behavior,[3] the US essentially adopted a 'bad apples' approach which underestimated the cultural significance of what is considered corruption in many societies. Not surprisingly, this strategy brought mixed results at best. And although the debate on 'what works and what doesn't' is an ongoing one, it is fairly clear that civil law is among the weakest performing elements of the overall strategy. So far, there is little research on the reasons for such failure.[4] Furthermore, there is no meaningful discussion on how civil law strategies could be revived and whether some specific country experience could serve as an example. Young argues that across the world there has been a rise in civil litigation related to corruption. He presents the following classifications:

1) Regime change lawsuits;
2) Breach of trust lawsuits;

1 For a more detailed background, see Gerry Ferguson, *Global Corruption: Law, Theory and Practice* (University of Victoria 2018).

2 Ellen Gutterman and Mathis Lohaus, 'What is the "Anti-Corruption" Norm in Global Politics?' in Ina Kubbe and Annika Engelbert (eds), *Corruption and Norms* 241, 247.

3 Ibid.

4 The Group of States Against Corruption (GRECO) has so far gone through four rounds of evaluating the implementation of the Council of Europe Criminal Law Convention, but has not touched upon the Civil Law Convention yet.

3) Overpayment and recovery lawsuits;
4) Unfair competition lawsuits;
5) *Qui tam* lawsuits.[5]

This classification is a useful, yet overly broad one. Cases of grand corruption and asset recovery are often of a different magnitude. The goal of this chapter is instead to look at the weakness of civil law in everyday cases and examine some examples of innovative practices that could be used as a bottom-up contribution to the debate. By presenting two case studies this chapter argues that it is time to move beyond the realm of codified transnational law and look for laboratories and good practice examples in individual countries.

1 The international anti-corruption standard

Today's undisputed 'gold standard' in anti-corruption, the UN Convention against Corruption (UNCAC), codifies *inter alia* a rule that had been expressed in regional anti-corruption conventions earlier:

> Each State Party shall take such measures as may be necessary, in accordance with principles of its domestic law, to ensure that entities or persons who have suffered damage as a result of an act of corruption have the right to initiate legal proceedings against those responsible for that damage in order to obtain compensation.[6]

Comparing the language of this article to other UNCAC prescriptions, it is relatively vague. While the obligation appears to be unconditional ('shall'), it is qualified by necessity and made dependent on principles of domestic law. Substance-wise, it mixes a procedural requirement ('the right to initiate proceedings') with a substantive one ('the right to obtain compensation for damage suffered as a result of an act of corruption'). From a strictly legal point of view, this may be an odd approach, but it should not be forgotten that the drafters of UNCAC were not lawyers, but diplomats. It also does not address a number of critical issues, such as damage to *which* legal interests are liable for compensation, how causality ('as a result of') should be defined, and what standard of culpability should be used.

It is true, though, that older regional conventions do not express a clearer standard. Article 1 of the Council of Europe Civil Law Convention on Corruption appears to be more strongly worded than UNCAC in that it provides fewer loopholes for national law-makers. But the scope of the obligation is actually wider

5 Simon Young, 'Why Civil Action Against Corruption?' (2009) 16 Journal of Financial Crime 144, 145.

6 United Nations Convention against Corruption (opened for signature 9 December 2003, entered into force 14 December 2005) 2349 UNTS 41, art 35 (UNCAC).

because the right to claim compensation for damages is treated as only one example of the possibility to defend one's rights and interests:

> Each Party shall provide in its internal law for effective remedies for persons who have suffered damage as a result of acts of corruption, to enable them to defend their rights and interests, including the possibility of obtaining compensation for damage.

One's rights and interests can typically also be defended by a court order to abstain from a certain practice. This is important when it comes to a company director's unwillingness to investigate allegations of corruption and to establish compliance systems to preventively monitor his or her company's business. Perhaps the most critical word in this article is 'effective.' It goes back to the Council of Europe Twenty Guiding Principles for the Fight against Corruption,[7] which required member states:

> to ensure that civil law takes into account the need to fight corruption and in particular provides for effective remedies for those whose rights and interests are affected by corruption.[8]

Arguably, by insisting on effective remedies the Civil Law Convention on Corruption is less concerned with technicalities of the national legal orders, but addresses its attention to the results to be achieved. It is therefore more straightforward than the comparable UNCAC norm. Other regional conventions do not offer any further clues. The Inter-American Convention against Corruption as well as the African Union Convention on Preventing and Combating Corruption are silent on the issue of civil law remedies. As for the OECD, only the 2009 Recommendations for Further Combating Bribery of Foreign Public Officials in International Business Transactions address the issue, but only in the most careful manner:

> The Council … recommends that each member country take concrete and meaningful steps in conformity with its jurisdictional and other basic legal principles to examine or further examine the following areas: … civil, commercial and administrative laws and regulations, to combat foreign bribery.

The list of declarations and reservations to UNCAC[9] does not contain any specific mentioning of Article 35. This is most likely a result of the vagueness of

7 Council of Europe Committee of Ministers Resolution 97 (24) of 6 November 1997.

8 Ibid [17].

9 For the list of Declarations and Reservations to the UNCAC see: UNODC, 'Declarations and Reservations' <http://www.unodc.org/documents/treaties/UNCAC/ReservationsDeclarations/DeclarationsAndReservations14Aug2008.pdf> accessed 1 June 2020.

the article which makes it uncontroversial. Moving from the universal to the European standard, the Council of Europe Civil Law Convention on Corruption with its relatively more stringent prescription has so far (by April 2019) attracted 35 ratifications (with seven additional countries having signed but not yet ratified). Compared to the 48 ratifications that the Council of Europe Criminal Law Convention has achieved so far, this is a small, but still marked difference in success. It speaks of the fact that a number of European countries which had no hesitation in embracing the Criminal Law Convention do, obviously, have second thoughts on its Civil Law cousin.

2 Practical limits to making civil law work

2.1 Background

In the Explanatory Report to the Civil Law Convention on Corruption the Council of Europe claims that 'the possibility to tackle corruption phenomena through civil law measures is an outstanding feature of the Council of Europe approach to the fight against corruption.'[10] History has obviously proved the authors of the Explanatory Report wrong, but the question is why this civil law approach has nevertheless been adopted into UNCAC and elevated to the status of a universal norm of international law. While there is no conclusive answer, there is at least an argument to be made that the insistence on civil law measures is part of the US agenda to promote a universal 'anti-corruption norm' derived from US law.

The private enforcement of public law is a specific feature of a political system[11] that has always maintained a critical distance to federal and/or state authority and trusted the wisdom of citizens more than that of public officials.[12] European continental legal systems, by contrast, are more state-centered and place higher trust in their public officials. There is also a certain difference in the approach to legal standing and thus access to justice in a wider sense. European continental courts usually tie admissibility of the action to the breach of the plaintiff's own right (*Klagebefugnis*). Unless he or she can show authority to act on behalf of a collective or a legal person, a single plaintiff should have no legal standing to claim

10 Council of Europe, *Explanatory Report to the Civil Law Convention on Corruption* (1999). Emphatic also Wolfgang Rau, 'The Council of Europe's Civil Law Convention on Corruption' in Olaf Meyer (ed), *The Civil Law Consequences of Corruption* (Nomos 2009) 21, 23. Rau refers, in particular, to a feasibility study commissioned by the Council of Europe's Multidisciplinary Group on Corruption which attested that an international initiative in the area of civil law was 'both possible and necessary'. The study itself does not seem to be published though.

11 By comparison, Young does not view the US as a leader in anti-corruption litigation: 'The USA is no stranger to corruption litigation, yet even there, cases seem to be on the rise.' See Young (n 5) 145.

12 Paul Carrington, 'Law and Transnational Corruption' (2007) 70 Law and Contemporary Problems 109, 111.

that he or she is acting as a trustee of the common good. E.g., in the German legal order there are only very limited instances, like in Bavarian constitutional law, in which a 'popular action' (*Popularklage*) is admissible.

In US law, there are no comparable limitations. Instead, private enforcement of the 'anti-corruption norm' is realized in some rather peculiar ways. The FCPA as the most important federal law is enforced by the Securities and Exchange Commission in its public law dimension and by the Department of Justice in its criminal law dimension, with no private enforcement of the FCPA itself. Instead, in tender situations in which a bidder secures victory by paying a bribe, the aggrieved competitor is entitled to resort to legal action under the (federal) Racketeer Influenced and Corrupt Organization Act (RICO)[13] or claim damages under state tort law, if the bribe caused foreseeable harm.[14]

The idea of private enforcement of public law is perhaps most strongly expressed in various types of *qui tam* litigation under common law, mostly in cases in which a government has been defrauded by contractors. *Qui tam* stands short for '*qui tam pro domino rege quam pro se ipso in hac parte sequitur*,' translated as 'he who pursues this action on our Lord the King's behalf as well as his own.' It allows for any third person (called the relator, quite often a whistleblower from inside the company) to bring a private action in the name of the government against any person or company claiming that he or she defrauded the government. Under current US federal law, the relator, if successful, may earn a minimum of 25% of the treble damages that will be recovered from the fraudulent contractor, plus reimbursement of costs including attorney's fees. While not necessarily corruption-related, *qui tam* actions have a number of advantages that make them suitable also for private enforcement in corruption cases. Under the US False Claims Act which currently embodies this type of litigation, proceedings are not criminal, so they do not require proof beyond reasonable doubt, but only a preponderance of the evidence. Full use may be made of the civil procedural right to compel disclosure of possible evidence and to compel non-party witnesses to supply their evidence as well. Under the US Freedom of Information Act, large parts of the Government's files must be disclosed to private investigations. The Department of Justice is entitled to intervene and take control of the proceeding, but even if it does, the case continues as a civil action and the relator remains a party. And if the Department of Justice does not intervene, the relator is entitled to maintain the action in the name of the United States.

In short, there is in the United States a powerful legacy of bringing private enforcement into the fight against corruption. But there are also highly specific preconditions which make this system difficult to work in a European continental context. In order to assess these difficulties in a practical manner, let us look into a number of case scenarios to ask how effective civil law strategies might be.

13 Racketeer Influenced and Corrupt Organization (RICO) Act, 18 US Code s 1961 (1994).
14 *Korea Supply Co. v. Lockheed Martin Corp.*, 29 Cal.4th 1134, 131 Cal. Rptr. 2d 29 (2003).

2.2 Tender competition

This is the classical constellation that lies at the heart of most US examples on the use of civil law strategies. Companies A and B compete in a tender. A's tender offer is objectively stronger, but B bribes the tender officer to win. A suffers harm in that it cannot realize the profit that it was certain to make based on its stronger offer.

It is important to note that apart from the primary contract between B and the tender officer to rig the tender, there are no contractual relationships between A and B and also between the 'loser' A and the tendering authority. In accepting the crooked tender offer of B, a so-called secondary contract is concluded between B and the tendering authority.

As explained earlier, under US law, B's bribe may violate RICO and state laws. Courts therefore acknowledge the possibility of a private tort action to be brought by A for the loss of expected pecuniary gain. In continental European countries, a similar tort action is possible only when an absolute right is concerned, e.g., in the current case if the property of B suffered harm. The concepts of property and absolute right thus go hand in hand, referring primarily to physical items that form the core of the property (e.g., buildings, machinery). An expected profit or pecuniary advantage may be part of the financial credit (*Vermögen*) of A when it is certain to be realized, but it is not an absolute right. In German case law, there is an acknowledged extension of the concept of absolute right, namely the so-called right to an established and executed business (*Recht am eingerichteten und ausgeübten Gewerbebetrieb*). In certain limited cases, aggressive behavior against an established and executed business is accepted as a violation of an absolute right, thus opening the possibility of tort action. So far, however, the courts have not accepted that offering a bribe in a tender situation, thereby depriving the competing company of its certain chance of winning, constitutes a violation of the right to an established and executed business by the dishonest competitor.

One major difference between US and continental European jurisdictions is, therefore, the extent to which tort action is admissible, depending on the legal interest to be protected. By requiring the violation of an absolute right, tort action in the continental European context is available only in a smaller number of cases. To overcome this reliance on tort law, *Makinwa* proposes to include into the class of public procurement contracts a sleeping third-party clause. Based on a certain threshold of evidence of a bribe having rigged the tender process, an identifiable group of third-party beneficiaries should automatically become a party to the contract and obtain standing to sue on the basis of the contract.[15]

15 Abiola Makinwa, Empowering the Victims of Corruption: The Potential of Sleeping Third-Party Beneficiary Clauses (Open Society Foundations 2016).

2.3 School

Parents A send their child to a state school. Due to corruption in the local school administration, the funds to improve the schooling situation got syphoned off. The level of education at the school is below the national average. After a year of attending this school, the level of achievement of students, including A's child, is significantly lower than in other schools where the funding is at normal levels.

Assuming that attending school is based on a contract, there may be a way of suing the school for breach of contract if the level of educational services is below the agreed one. But it will be difficult to show causality, i.e., that the corruption of school administrators and the resulting lower levels of available funding caused the lower level of achievements of A's child. It is easy to argue that due to learning deficits etc., A's child would not have been able to reach the normal level of achievement, even if the funding had been appropriate.

If the school were a state school, attendance would most likely be governed by public law. In this case, common law may provide for a *qui tam* action: even without having sent their child to this particular school, A can adopt the position of a whistleblower and sue the relevant school administrator on behalf of the government. Under ordinary *qui tam* principles, this would be a powerful weapon because the relator is entitled to demand treble damages. Looking at this situation in more detail, it will have to be ascertained, however, whether the fraudulent school administrator is in a position comparable to a government contractor and whether the same conditions are to be found in this case.

In continental European systems, assuming that the schooling is public and attendance not based on a contract, neither parent nor child will be able to argue that they have been violated in an absolute right. In a similar constellation, there may be the possibility of bringing a human rights action based on a violation of the right to education. The first case of human rights litigation based on corruption claims occurred before the ECOWAS Court of Justice.[16] In 2007, a Nigerian civil society group argued that systematic high levels of corruption and theft amounted to a violation of the right to education of every Nigerian child. The ECOWAS Court of Justice agreed that the right to education is judiciable, but required that 'there must be a clear linkage between the act of corruption and a denial of the rights to education.'[17]

2.4 Hospital

Under national law, patient A is entitled to a three-bed room which is also acknowledged in the contract concluded with the hospital. The contract contains

16 Adetokunbo Mumuni, *Litigating Corruption in International Human Rights Tribunals: SERAP before the ECOWAS Court* (Open Society Foundations 2016).

17 Ibid 7.

a clause that allows the hospital administration to place more beds into one room in case of emergency or a temporary over-crowding. Patient B knows that there is the possibility of obtaining a one-bed room when a payment under the counter is made to the head doctor. As a result of B's payment, two beds are moved into the room of A, explaining this as the result of temporary overcrowding. Due to the higher stress level in the five-bed room, A's recuperation takes significantly longer.

Looking at this case from a contractual perspective, A could sue the hospital for damages because the hospital triggered the emergency clause despite the fact that there was no overcrowding. The damage would most likely be that A had to put up with being accommodated in a five-bed room while under his contract in line with national legislation he was entitled to a three-bed room. There would be no need to show negative effects on his health, although it would be difficult to assess the lack in quality accommodation in monetary terms. From a tort law perspective, even under continental European systems, A's health is an absolute right (compared to the right to education in the school example) so that its violation may give rise to tort action. However, like in the school case, it will be difficult to show that the higher stress levels in the five-bed room were the sole (or at least the main) cause for A's slower recuperation.

2.5 Road

Local resident A uses a state road to commute to work. As the road was in bad shape, road works were planned by the state. In the tender, company B failed to win the bid despite its better offer because company C paid a bribe to the tender officer. Subsequently, C recouped the money paid on the bribe by executing the road work in a manner that violated certain standards and saved money. As a result, after only one winter the road was in worse shape than before. A is able to show that due to the poor quality of the road maintenance his car was suffering higher wear and tear than under normal conditions.

In the given scenario, there is the primary contract between C and the tender officer on rigging the tender and the subsequent secondary contract between C and the tendering authority on the road works. In the absence of a third-party clause, A is not a party to the contract between C and the tendering authority, although as a local resident he would clearly be a beneficiary compared to others who may be using the road only accidentally. Under US law, the bribe paid by C may give rise to a violation of RICO and state laws. Consequently, competitor B may bring a tort action. A, by comparison, may bring *qui tam* litigation if he had been the first to obtain knowledge of C's manipulations.

Under continental law, the increased wear and tear of A's car is a violation of the absolute right to property. A could therefore bring tort action in his own name. However, there is an issue of causality. It may be impossible even for an expert to ascertain with certainty that the damage to A's car is caused primarily by using the given road.

2.6 Conclusion

Trying to systematize the outcomes from the foregoing discussion, the following observations can be made:

1) Constructing remedies under *contract law* is often not possible. Private parties may be users or beneficiaries of services provided, but with no legal recourse against the company that offers the services. This is evident in the road case where the road is maintained by a state authority or a delegated company, but no contract is concluded for using the road (except for toll roads). Using hospital or school services may be based on a contract, depending on the circumstances. In the most classical case of the crooked tender, there are typically no third-party beneficiary clauses included.
2) Under tort law, it is essential that the plaintiff shows that he or she has been *violated in his or her own right.* The *qui tam* action is an exception. Most continental legal systems abhor this approach as a *Popularklage* and would always insist on showing that the plaintiff has suffered the violation of his or her own right.
3) There is a difference between what US and continental legal systems consider to be the *protected legal interest* when it comes to tort action. US legal systems acknowledge any type of harm or damage, particularly if a pecuniary advantage cannot be realized. In continental legal systems, tort action is only possible based on the violation of an absolute right, e.g., life or limb, property, etc.
4) There may be problems with *causality* in that it is difficult or even impossible to show that paying a bribe started the chain of events that ultimately led to the damage. Other factors may intervene. The Council of Europe, in its Explanatory Report to the Civil Law Convention on Corruption, adopts a reasonable middle ground by claiming that the causal link should be adequate (thus, not giving all elements in the causal chain the same weight) and that damage should be an ordinary and not an extraordinary consequence of corruption.[18]

Levels of *culpability* did not appear to be problematic in all the aforementioned cases. However, this was due to the fact that offering or paying a bribe, defrauding, or embezzling funds is by necessity done with intent and cannot be the result of negligence. There are other cases, however, where negligence might play a role. When the question is whether a company director can be sued because he omitted to adopt in his or her company reasonable compliance management systems, a determination needs to be made whether his or her negligence contributed to the fact that middle management was engaging in bribery.

18 Explanatory Report (n 8) [45].

The observations lead us to conclude that when it comes to tort action, there is probably little one can do in terms of harmonizing the criteria for liability. Having juxtaposed here only a roughly sketched US legal position with a continental European one, it becomes clear that the approaches are deeply engrained in the respective legal traditions and cannot easily be changed without far-reaching consequences.

It is true though that a contractual perspective will often offer more leverage than a tort action. When it comes to contracts, we observe that civil law, as a rule, is disinterested in the reasons for the poor performance. There can be a third-party bribe affecting the level of performance by one party to the contract to the detriment of the other (e.g., in the hospital case where we observe a zero-sum game). And there can be cases in which corruption is not transactional, embodied in the offering and accepting of a bribe, but rests on the behavior of a single contract partner alone who embezzles, defrauds, or misappropriates the entrusted funds. In both cases this is advantageous for the potential plaintiff because he or she does not even need to know why the partner to the contract is performing the contract poorly or not at all.

In the literature there is one more factor discussed that was not captured in the cases above: the issue of access to justice in terms of the cost of bringing an action. There is the claim[19] that US law facilitates the bringing of civil action because attorneys can be more entrepreneurial, agreeing on a success fee with their clients and taking the risk of losing the case upon themselves. Also, under the American Rule each party is responsible for paying its own fees. This is in contrast to the English rule (widely accepted also in continental Europe) that the losing party pays the prevailing party's attorneys' fees. As an argument, this may be convincing but in general it omits the impact of legal expenses insurance.

The more relevant argument to be made in terms of access to justice is whether national law allows for the bundling of claims or even for class action to mitigate risk. In the corruption cases described above, this would be an advantage in most, but not all cases. In bribery cases, e.g., the classical tender or the hospital situation, the negative effects are felt only by one party. In non-transactional corruption cases, e.g., the school situation, the effects are felt widely, e.g., for all students of a particular school or the entire school district. In these cases, being able to bundle claims minimizes risks and makes legal action more likely. The road situation is a mix of both because there is a bribe paid, but subsequently the crooked tenderer performs his public work in a substandard manner, thus harming a large number of road users who may not even notice the damage.

19 Carrington (n 12) 114, 121.

3 Possible avenues for activating civil law strategies

3.1 Strengthening collective action

3.1.1 Background and EU initiatives

Civil law strategies are often conflated with civil society strategies.[20] Looking at the origin of UNCAC, this is understandable because strengthening civil society has been a hallmark of the Convention. Article 13 (1) UNCAC calls upon State Parties to:

> take appropriate measures, within its means and in accordance with fundamental principles of its domestic law, to promote the active participation of individuals and groups outside the public sector, such as civil society, non-governmental organizations and community-based organizations, in the prevention of and the fight against corruption and to raise public awareness regarding the existence, causes and gravity of and the threat posed by corruption.

UNCAC does not specifically require that anti-corruption NGOs employ civil law strategies. Such decisions are for the relevant NGOs to take in light of national legislation and in the concrete situation. But UNCAC clearly opens a perspective on public interest litigation in which NGOs and other civil society organizations step in to defend the common good. Likewise, citizens, united in collective action, are called upon to join their individual grievances and seek collective redress. Moving away from classical NGOs and strengthening collective action is perhaps the single most powerful trend in current anti-corruption politics. And in this spirit, it may be worthwhile to explore the role of intermediaries that can facilitate the bringing of legal action.

The case examples discussed above operated along the distinction of user (road,[21] school attendance without contract) and contract partner (school attendance with contract, hospital). There was thus either a single person affected or a large group of more or less identifiable persons. Clearly, what can be seen is a lack of intermediary organizations that could help to unite individual claimants and catalyze collective action.

The EU has for several years been pursuing the goal of creating a coherent approach to collective redress. Based on a European Parliament Resolution of 2 December 2012,[22] the Commission adopted a Recommendation on June 11,

20 Mohamed Abdelsalam, 'Applying Civil Law to Curb Corruption: A tool for Civil Society and Individuals' (Global Anti-Corruption & Integrity Forum, OECD, Paris, 31 March 2017).

21 A toll may indicate that a contract is concluded between the user and the entity in charge of maintaining the road. Most often, however, the toll is some kind of public fee attached to using the road without creating contractual obligations.

22 See 'Towards a Coherent European Approach to Collective Redress', European Parliament resolution of 2 February 2012 (2013/C 239 E/05).

2013 entitled 'On common principles for injunctive and compensatory collective redress mechanisms in the Member States concerning violations of rights granted under Union Law.'[23] Whereas the European Parliament expressed concern about cases of scattered and dispersed damages, the European Commission highlighted the need to address cases of mass harm. In both scenarios it was held that the cost risks associated with litigation might deter consumers from bringing action, unless there would be ways to bundle their claims and allow for collective action.

In the Commission document, strengthening collective redress is defined in a twofold way: either as injunctive collective redress, aimed at ensuring the possibility to claim cessation of illegal behavior collectively, or compensatory collective redress, aimed at ensuring the possibility to claim compensation collectively. 'Collectivity' can be achieved by simply bundling the claims of two or more natural or legal persons. But it can also mean the idea of 'representative action,' defined as an action which is brought by a representative entity, an *ad hoc* certified entity or a public authority on behalf and in the name of two or more natural or legal persons.[24] The Commission Recommendations suggest that member states should designate representative entities to bring representative action on the basis of clearly defined conditions of eligibility. These conditions should include at least the following:

- the entity should have a non-profit making character;
- there should be a direct relationship between the main objectives of the entity and the rights granted under Union law that are claimed to have been violated in respect of which the action is brought;
- the entity should have sufficient capacity in terms of financial resources, human resources, and legal expertise, to represent multiple claimants acting in their best interest.

In general, when allowing for representative action, the task is to achieve a balance between building a reliable system that works also in light of increased cross-border commerce, and avoiding frivolous litigation by self-proclaimed protectors of rights. In the preamble to its Recommendations, the Commission explained that:

> amongst those areas where the supplementary private enforcement of rights granted under Union law in the form of collective redress is of value, are consumer protection, competition, environment protection, protection of personal data, financial services legislation and investor protection.

It is striking to see that in all the areas listed by the Commission, corruption may be an important *modus operandi*. But it is not explicitly mentioned even once.

23 OJ L 201/60 of 26 July 2013.
24 Ibid [3](d).

Obviously, there is no effort to mainstream an anti-corruption perspective into the ways we analyze situations that are harmful to EU citizens and businesses.

When looking at EU citizens, the idea of consumer protection is perhaps still the one that opens up the best angle to consider cases of corruption. In an approach that is partly overlapping with the idea of strengthening collective redress in general, the EU Commission on April 11, 2018 proposed to repeal Directive 2009/22/EC on injunctive relief that stands at the center of EU consumer protection law, and replace it by a Directive on representative action for the protection of the collective interests of consumers.[25] Interestingly, in this proposal the Commission defined a consumer as 'any natural person who is acting for purposes which are outside their trade, business, craft or profession.' This definition is remarkable because it goes beyond viewing the consumer as somebody who purchases a product. In our cases above, it opens up the possibility of including also hospital patients and students at school in the category of consumers.

The main idea of the proposal is to enable qualified entities to bring representative action seeking an injunction order to establish that a so-called trader's practice constitutes an infringement of law, and if necessary, stopping the practice or, if the practice has not yet been carried out but is imminent, prohibiting it.[26] This main purpose of injunctive relief is coupled with the idea of redress, by enabling representative action also to seek a redress order which obligates the trader to provide for, *inter alia*, compensation, repair, replacement, price reduction, contract termination, or reimbursement of the price paid, as appropriate.[27] So, from an anti-corruption point of view, this will be another example to see how EU member states in the future will go about the task of structuring representative action. But it will most likely not be a strong example for allowing civil action because redress is clearly subordinate to injunctive relief. Still, we are seeing innovation in the way consumer protection is structured. And this may open up new perspectives also for collective action in anti-corruption.

3.1.2 The Musterfeststellungsklage in German law

Unrelated to the Directive discussed above, but very much in line with its thinking, the German Parliament recently adopted an innovation, adding a new type of action to its Code of Civil Procedure. It is called *Musterfeststellungsklage*, which roughly translates as 'action aimed at a sample determination.' The background for this innovation is the diesel scandal that rocked the German automobile industry. The Act is phrased in more general consumer protection terms, but

25 European Commission, 'Proposal for a Directive of the European Parliament and of the Council on representative actions for the protection of the collective interests of consumers, and repealing Directive 2009/22/EC' (2018/0089, 11 April 2018).

26 Ibid art 5(2).

27 Ibid art 6(1).

the idea was to have it enter into force before the end of the year 2018 when the claims for damages against German car manufacturers will expire. And so, the German Bundestag hurried to make the necessary amendments enter into force by November 1, 2018, just in time to give consumer protection associations the chance to take the German car manufacturers to court.

In the debate on new perspectives on collective action in anti-corruption, this new type of action is an interesting one. Compared to the earlier EU initiatives which were aimed at collective redress in general or injunctive relief coupled with redress, the *Musterfeststellungsklage* merely takes an intermediary step, i.e., allowing a consumer protection association to apply to the court to give a binding determination whether the factual and/or legal preconditions for a claim are given or not. By its nature, the action's goal is a court determination, so it is neither injunctive relief nor the award of damages. This solution has been criticized because of its supposed 'half-bakedness,' still requiring a plaintiff to bring an individual action once the court has determined that the conditions for the claim are met. And furthermore, it is no class action in the US understanding because a court decision will only be binding on those plaintiffs who joined the action and not for others who abstained, but are in factually the same situation. On the other hand, there are advantages which seem particularly relevant in the field of anti-corruption: when the foundation of the individual claim is weak and issues of causality are worrisome, joining forces to ask a consumer protection association to obtain a court's clarification first significantly lowers the risk of bringing action and encourages victims of corruption to come forward.

The technical details of the law are rather complex because, again, it has to strike a balance between catalyzing individual plaintiffs who are fragmented and fear the cost of bringing action, and preventing frivolous litigation in the name of self-proclaimed consumer protection agencies. It sets a minimum requirement of ten individual plaintiffs who claim that the results of the determination are materially relevant for their claim, and requires in addition that in the course of two months a minimum of 50 consumers register to join the action.

Compared to *qui tam* litigation, an important aspect is here that eligible consumer protection associations must not act on a for-profit motive. Also, in their total funding the share of corporate donations must not exceed 5% to make sure that no conflicts of interest occur. The *Musterfeststellungsklage* is explicitly understood to be an instrument of consumer protection, but, as shown above, a number of corruption situations can actually be seen as involving consumers as victims.

3.2 Strengthening corporate compliance

A second avenue for activating civil law strategies to counteract corruption is in the area of corporate compliance. Corporate compliance systems are not *per se* concerned with corruption. The risk of having bribes affect the business is rather one of many risks that a company may face.

Having a corporate compliance system installed and up to date is not only a sign of an enlightened management practice, but also a defensive strategy for any manager to avoid liability. Under the business judgement rule, managers should be encouraged to take entrepreneurial risk, even if it means that negative consequences may fall back on the shareholders. The shareholders, by contrast, will accept the consequences of failed risk-taking, i.e. corporate losses and diminished dividends, if the management observed reasonable care and acted on the basis of the best information available. Only if this invisible line is crossed and management acted frivolously or without due care may shareholders sue for compensation. Thus, fear of personal liability is arguably the strongest motivational factor behind successful corporate compliance.

Encouraging shareholders to bring legal action against corporate directors is not a new idea, and its realization depends on a number of factors in the respective legal systems. Often, corporate law requires a certain quorum of shareholders to support the action, and there may be other obstacles in the law to balance the process. Most often, this model is also discussed irrespective of the fact whether in the company law there is a unitary or a two-tier board system. But when it comes to two-tier board systems, the situation may be more complicated in some countries.

In Western corporate practice, e.g., in Germany, the supervisory board tends to be not an active corporate player, but rather a dignified place for former executive managers to continue to offer their advice. There is often talk of a 'cozy' relationship between executive managers and the supervisory board. So, while management is naturally wary of shareholders, it can count on the supervisory board for support in most situations. Keeping this distinction in mind, there is an interesting development in the corporate world taking place that merits a closer look: supervisory boards suing former executive directors for damages. Again, there can be relevant examples drawn from Germany:

> In the wake of the Siemens corruption scandal in January 2008, the Siemens supervisory board claimed compensation from its former executive managers and simultaneously offered the possibility of reaching settlements. This route was taken by two former chief executive officers and seven other ex-managers. Among them, the former chief executive officer Heinrich von Pierer agreed to pay 5 Mio. Euros in settlements. A settlement of 4 Mio. Euros was also offered to the former chief financial officer, Heinz-Joachim Neubürger. However, Neubürger refused, claiming that he did not violate any relevant duties. Siemens then sued Neubürger for 15 Mio. Euros damages and won this claim in full. As a result, Neubürger committed suicide.[28]

28 Daniel Schäfer, 'Legal Action by German Boards to Rise' *Financial Times* (2 December 2009). For more background see Holger Fleischer, 'Aktienrechtliche Compliance-Pflichten im Praxistest' (2014) 17:9 Neue Zeitschrift für Gesellschaftsrecht, 321; Christoph E. Hauschka, 'Fünf Jahre Siemens-Entscheidung des LG München I' (2018) 9:4 Corporate Compliance Zeitsdhrift 159.

> In the ongoing Volkwagen diesel scandal, the Volkswagen supervisory board was reported to be examining civil action against the former chief executive officer Martin Winterkorn in the amount of up to 1 Bio. Euros.[29] In May 2018, Winterkorn renounced the right to invoke the statute of limitations by another year until May 2019 to enable a court clarification of the situation to go forward.[30]

The two aforementioned cases have a rather complex legal background. Based on para 111 of the Joint Stock Companies Act, the German Federal High Court of Justice (*Bundesgerichtshof*) in 1997 adopted the famous *ARAG / Garmenbeck* ruling.[31] In it, the Court clarified the duty of the supervisory board, as part of its *ex post* monitoring, to assess possible claims against (former) executive directors who violated their duties, and decide on bringing action against them. The Court stated that this assessment and decision, understood as two distinct stages, needs to be made in light of the company's well-being. For the second stage, there should be, as a rule, an obligation to proceed with civil claims, unless, in an overall assessment of the arguments, there are 'weighty reasons' (*gewichtige Gründe*) mitigating against it. Later changes in the law, relating to the standards for shareholders to bring action, introduced the criterion of a preponderance of reasons mitigating against bringing action (*bei überwiegenden Gegengründen*). In the ensuing debate, there is now a group of scholars who argue that the same standard should be applied to the supervisory board bringing action, thus making it even harder to tilt the argument in favor of *not* bringing action.

In the light of the aforementioned legal changes, the debate has moved to a related question: when making the overall assessment and weighing the reasons for and against bringing civil action, does the supervisory board have discretion so that the core of its decision is not subject to judicial review, or are the courts able to review the decision in every detail? Advocates of a 'cozy' relationship argue that even if the tightening of standards in counter-indications needs to be accepted, the supervisory board remains free to make its assessment as a matter of discretion, without being subject to a full review by the courts. This position is useful, e.g., when judging the risk of reputational damage by bringing court

29 'VW prüft Milliardenklage gegen Winterkorn' *Spiegel Online* (5 May 2018) <https://www.spiegel.de/wirtschaft/unternehmen/volkswagen-will-martin-winterkorn-haftbar-machen-a-1206403.html> accessed 1 June 2020. Von Georg Mec, Rainer Hank and Thomas Gutschker, 'Martin Winterkorn droht der Ruin' *Frankfurter Allgemeine Zeitung* (5 May 2018) <https://www.faz.net/aktuell/wirtschaft/auto-verkehr/ex-volkswagen-chef-martin-winterkorn-droht-der-ruin-15575610.html> accessed 1 June 2020.

30 'Schadenersatz gegen Ex-VW-Chef? Winterkorn verzichtet vorerst auf Verjährung' *NTV* (21 May 2018) <https://www.n-tv.de/wirtschaft/Winterkorn-verzichtet-vorerst-auf-Verjaehrung-article20443827.html> accessed 1 June 2020.

31 BGHZ 135, 244.

action. The counter-position holds that there is no discretion involved and the assessment is fully under the review of the courts.[32]

The interesting feature in this legal background is not how legal arguments are used to bolster the traditionally 'cozy' relationship between executive and supervisory board. It is rather that the issue of violation of duties that lies at the heart of the executive directors' wrongdoing is 'color blind,' i.e., it does not look at the type of violation and possible consequences that might be attached to it. If, for instance, the omission of the executive board is due to corruption, it may be quite possible to argue that in this case the Civil Law Convention against Corruption would oblige Germany to strengthen the duty to bring action against executive directors even more. Alas, Germany is among the countries which have not yet ratified the Convention. So, the argument is a hypothetical one. But it shows the potential of strengthening the use of civil law in the fight against corruption.

The cases of seeking damages from former executive directors may usher in a new era of corporate responsibility. Compliance management systems critically hinge on the 'tone from the top,' i.e., a coherent message from the chief executive officers repeatedly sent to all employees that emphasizes the ethical/value orientation of the company and declares corruption and other types of violations as unacceptable. Practically, when middle- or lower level management engages in corruptive acts there is usually a pre-determined set of consequences, ranging from reprimand to a promotion freeze to firing. In fact, firing the culprits is often used also to make a statement that a company is adamant about its anti-corruption values. But rarely is the relevant manager sued for compensation, most simply because his or her financial situation will not be in the range that significant damages for the company can be expected. This is, of course, different with top management. The latest developments thus do not merely represent a more aggressive use of civil litigation to recoup some of the damage by corruptive practices. It is also a powerful tool to reinforce the 'tone from the top' that a company is serious about protecting its integrity. And very often, it is sufficient to announce the willingness to take the culprits to court. As in the Siemens case, settlements leaked to the media can be a sensible strategy to create financial compensation while passing on the message that the company is serious in its anti-corruption stance. Actual litigation, by contrast, may still have an uncertain outcome and carries the risk of negative publicity.

4 Conclusion

The goal of this chapter was to argue that it is time to move beyond the realm of codified transnational law and to look for laboratories and good practice examples in individual countries. As the cases have shown, there is at first sight

32 For detailed references see Uwe Hüffer and Jens Koch, *Aktiengesetz* (14th edn, CH Beck 2020) s 111, n 7ff.

a similar approach in seeking damages either under contract or under tort law in the major jurisdictions of the world. So, the drafters of transnational anti-corruption conventions may be forgiven for believing that civil law action could become an important vector in counteracting corruption both nationally and transnationally. When looking deeper, it emerges that the specificities of national law are still overwhelmingly strong and cannot be harmonized on the basis of a rather superficial clause in an international convention

The two examples brought here from German law show that creative use of civil law has hardly made it onto the agenda and should be considered much more strongly. The US approach in preferring individual over public enforcement is a potentially powerful one, but it tends to underestimate the unwillingness of individuals due to risk and cost aversion. If collective action is the hallmark of the current era of anti-corruption efforts, then access to justice should be eased and individual claimants be offered tools to unite their cause and bring representative action. If the EU were serious about addressing mass harm scenarios and opening up collective redress, it should start to consider the mass harm caused by corruption.

9 The proliferation of international anti-corruption initiatives, standards, and guidelines

Classification, benefits and shortcomings, future prospects

Vera Cherepanova

Corruption, which is broadly defined as 'the abuse of entrusted power for private gain,'[1] is a permanent feature of political systems and is hardly new.[2] According to the evidence from law court speeches and comic drama sources, corruption was widespread in the political and judicial systems of Ancient Greece. Claire Taylor notes that 'every level of Athenian politics was riddled with corruption, from the most important orators to the smallest deme election.'[3] In Rome, the corruption was institutionalized and the sums required were so enormous that it even contributed to the civil war: massive borrowing needed for bribes led to financial and political instability among the aristocracy in the sixties and fifties BC.[4] In his historical analysis of the railroad industry in 19th century America, Charles Perrow argues that the spread of corruption was so wide that it should have been added to the usual factors of production, e.g., land, labor, capital, technology, and organizational form.[5] At the same time, throughout the centuries, past societies and polities designed specific mechanisms to pursue anti-corruption agenda: anti-corruption laws have been enacted, violators have been prosecuted and even executed.

However, the re-emergence of corruption as a genuinely global issue occurred in the context of the continuing processes of globalization.[6] Economic

1 Transparency International, 'What is Corruption?' <https://www.transparency.org/what-is-corruption> accessed 1 June 2020.

2 James W Williams and Margaret E Beare, 'The Business of Bribery: Globalization, Economic Liberalization, and the 'Problem' of Corruption' (1999) 32 Crime, Law and Social Change 115.

3 Claire Taylor, 'Bribery in Athenian Politics—Part I: Accusations, Allegations and Slander' (2001) 48 Greece & Rome 53.

4 Andrew Lintott, 'Electoral Bribery in the Roman Republic' (1990) 80 The Journal of Roman Studies 1.

5 Charles Perrow, *Organizing America: Wealth, Power and the Origins of Corporate Capitalism* (1st edn, Princeton University Press 2002).

6 Patrick Glynn, Stephen J Kobrin, and Moises Naim, 'The Globalization of Corruption' in Ann E Kimberley (ed), *Corruption and The Global Economy* (1st edn, Institute for International Economics 1997).

liberalization, the increase in foreign investment and international transactions facilitated the uprise of multi-national corporations (MNCs), which were now enabled to shift their operations out of 'home' countries.[7] Inevitably, numerous ethical, cultural and legal differences among nations have been brought up to the surface as never before due to this new business practice. It has become apparent that bribery is perceived differently in different cultural contexts, and, therefore, is treated differently by the regulators.

Due to the diversity of national legal systems, the harmonization of anti-corruption legislation is a complex multi-dimensional process that requires considerable effort and resources together with a certain extent of political interest to push through this agenda. Needless to say, this is a project with a long-term outlook. In the meantime, the post-Westphalian world order explicitly called for global governance instruments—the ones that would align, at least to some extent, the omnipresent heterogeneity of national legal regimes in the global playfield. [8]

Over the recent decades, the world has witnessed a proliferation of a myriad of initiatives, guidelines, and standards intended to guide the conduct of MNCs in terms of corporate responsibility and business ethics, anti-corruption and bribery, social and environmental practices. From an anti-corruption perspective, some of the prominent examples include the UN Global Compact, ISO 37001:2016 'Anti-bribery Management Systems,' WEF's Partnering Against Corruption Initiative, and TI's Business Principles for Countering Bribery, to name a few.

These voluntary rules attempt to hold MNCs accountable for their decisions and actions.[9] Recent corporate scandals connected with non-compliance of MNCs with ethical expectations of society underscored the importance of these regulations. Gilbert, Rasche, and Waddock propose to label these initiatives as 'international accountability standards' (IASs) and define them as 'voluntary predefined rules, procedures and methods to systemically assess, measure, audit and/or communicate the social and environmental behavior and/or performance of the firms.'[10]

The IASs fall under the category of soft law regulations and are not directly enforceable. In the context of international law, these are the rules that set

7 Manuel Velasquez, 'Globalization and the Failure of Ethics' (2000) 10 Business Ethics Quarterly 343.

8 Andreas G Scherer and Guido Palazzo, 'The New Political Role of Business in a Globalized World: A Review of a New Perspective on CSR and Its Implications for the Firm, Governance, and Democracy' (2011) 48 Journal of Management Studies 899.

9 Dirk U Gilbert and Andreas Rasche, 'Opportunities and Problems of Standardized Ethics Initiatives: A Stakeholder Theory Perspective' (2008) 82 Journal of Business Ethics 755; Andreas Rasche, '"A Necessary Supplement": What the United Nations Global Compact Is and Is Not' (2009) 48 Business and Society 511.

10 Dirk U Gilbert, Andreas Rasche, and Sandra Waddock, 'Accountability in a Global Economy: The Emergence of International Accountability Standards' (2011) 21 Business Ethics Quarterly 23.

standards of conduct. Brunsson and Jacobsson (2000) define a standard as a form of regulation that outlines how the one who accepted it should (and should not) behave.[11] In contrast to the traditional or 'hard' law, soft law provisions are usually formulated with less precision and are not legally binding. However, it would be incorrect to call IASs completely voluntary at least for two reasons. First, over time certain soft law regulations become the basis for binding laws. This is what happened with the EU Directive 2014/95/EU on non-financial reporting. The Directive requires large public-interest companies with more than 500 employees to include non-financial statements in their annual reports from 2018 onwards. Companies which are subject to this requirement have to disclose their efforts in relation to environmental protection and social responsibility, treatment of employees and diversity on company boards, anti-corruption and bribery policies.[12] The Directive provides for certain flexibility in how to disclose this information and encourages companies to use EU, national or international guidelines/reporting frameworks including the UN Global Compact, ISO 26000 'Social Responsibility' standard or the OECD Guidelines for multinational enterprises. Clear enough, soft law guidelines are referred to by a legally binding EU government regulation.[13]

Second, it is possible for compliance with anti-corruption standards to become a legal or contractual requirement for certain industries or organizations including public procurement and supply chains. The adoption of an anti-corruption standard may then be considered a prerequisite to start or continue business with an organization. The additional assurance provided by the certification/implementation of a standard can bring operational efficiencies to compliance function. It streamlines the due diligence process, allowing companies to choose third parties who have been certified/have implemented certain IASs.

At the same time, because of their non-binding nature, IASs have their limits. As long as there are no mechanisms to neither directly enforce compliance with their provisions nor impose meaningful sanctions for non-compliance, the actual impact of anti-corruption guidelines, standards, and initiatives is regularly questioned. In the absence of a clear regulatory framework, they appear to lack accountability *per se*. However, in a situation of fragmented and sometimes inconsistent application of extraterritorial anti-corruption provisions, the IASs might be the only viable solution to the issue of countering corruption on a global scale.

This chapter takes a closer look at the proliferation of anti-corruption IASs. Despite their swift expansion in recent decades and a steady demand from business,

11 Nils Brunsson and Bengt Jacobsson, 'The Contemporary Expansion of Standardization' in Nils Brunsson and Bengt Jacobsson (eds), *A World of Standards* (1st edn OUP 2000).

12 Directive 2014/95/EU of the European Parliament and of the Council of 22 October 2014 amending Directive 2013/34/EU as regards disclosure of non-financial and diversity information by certain large undertakings and groups [2014] OJ L330/1 (Non-Financial Reporting Directive).

13 Non-Financial Reporting Directive, rec. 9.

this type of regulation has not received due attention in academic literature. So far, the scholars were mainly studying IASs from a broader perspective of social and environmental accountability, with anti-corruption agenda included as one of the components. However, lately, there have been so many developments specifically in the domain of bribery and corruption that it is about the time to consider them on their own. A more profound examination of anti-corruption IASs is required, and this chapter seeks to fill in this research gap.

The chapter is organized as follows. In the next section, I assess the proliferation of international anti-corruption initiatives, standards, and guidelines through the lens of IASs classification introduced by Gilbert, Rasche, and Waddock.[14] Using several examples in each category, the IASs are analyzed along a set of criteria to arrive at a comprehensive overview in terms of their underlying characteristics including target audience, applicability, expectations from adopters and presence of assurance/sanctions mechanisms. Next, I discuss the benefits and shortcomings of current IASs focussing on the positive and negative aspects of their inherent features. I conclude with a number of suggestions of what needs to be addressed by future research.

It is important to note that the resource guides issued by national anti-corruption authorities including 'A Resource Guide to the FCPA,' 'Guidance on adequate procedures' under the UK Bribery Act, or 'AFA Guidelines' under the Sapin II law were not considered for the purposes of this analysis. Although not legally binding from a formal perspective, these guidelines are intended to help organizations understand better what the statutory requirements are and how to meet them. Based on their main objective, these guidelines cannot be referred to as voluntary accountability standards and are, therefore, excluded from the scope of this chapter.

1 Classification of anti-corruption standards

Corporate accountability implies the timely provision of comprehensive information to organizational stakeholders on the consequences of a firm's operations and decisions. With this information, stakeholders are better equipped to judge a firm's actions and are able to hold it duly accountable.[15] IASs have emerged and proliferated to streamline and structure corporate accountability for (un)ethical decisions. They constitute a large institutional infrastructure designed to address the transparency expectations of society towards the business.

Anti-corruption IASs are diverse in their nature. They provide various mechanisms to facilitate corporate accountability, ranging from a public commitment to anti-corruption principles to vigorous auditing and certification procedures. In other words, the standards differ because of the differences in their underlying accountability mechanisms. But not only—their content, scope,

14 Gilbert, Rasche, and Waddock (n 10) 26.

15 Andrew Crane and Dirk Matten, *Business Ethics* (2nd edn, OUP 2007).

and target audience can vary from one to another as well. To help managers cut through this complexity of diverse yet oftentimes overlapping initiatives, and choose which standards to implement, there is a clear need for classification. Categorizing anti-corruption IASs is no easy task—some of them compete with each other, others complement, and again others overlap. However, the classification introduced by Gilbert, Rasche, and Waddock for corporate responsibility standards[16] appears complementary to the purposes of this analysis and fits very well into the anti-corruption context. This classification allows us to cluster anti-corruption IASs along four different categories:

- principle-based standards;
- certification standards;
- reporting standards;
- process standards.

Next, using several examples of anti-corruption initiatives from each of the four categories, the IASs are examined in detail by applying the following analysis criteria:

- background information;
- current number of participants;
- target audience;
- implementation guidelines: flexibility and scalability of application;
- actions required to adopt the IASs;
- expectations from participants;
- presence of external assurance/sanctions mechanisms;
- participation renewal procedures.

2 Principle-based standards

The first category of anti-corruption IASs is referred to as principle-based standards (WEF Partnering Against Corruption Initiative, TI Business Principles for Combating Bribery, OECD Good Practice Guidance on Internal Controls, Ethics, and Compliance). These are the standards that outline broadly defined principles, rather aspirational than directive. They do not embody sharp clarity in terms of expectations from their members and may be used as a guideline or as a starting point for anti-corruption program implementation. The underlying accountability mechanism of this category is reduced to asking organizations to make statements of commitment with regards to fundamental ethical norms of transparency and zero-tolerance to corrupt practices.

'Soft-commitment' collective action initiatives are an illustrative example of the principles-based IASs. The WBI guide defines collective action as 'a

16 Gilbert, Rasche, and Waddock (n 10) 26.

collaborative and sustained process of cooperation among stakeholders ... [that] brings vulnerable individual players into an alliance of like-minded organizations and levels the playing field between competitors.'[17] In other words, collective action projects require multiple parties to enter into some sort of agreement to refrain from unethical business practices, with the selected third parties (often civil society organizations) acting as facilitators. The level of participants' commitment may vary significantly from one initiative to another: high-level commitment initiatives involve contractual agreements subject to third-party audits and sanctions, while the low-level projects are limited to the expression of public aspirational commitments and do not provide for enforcement mechanisms. Low-level commitment initiatives can be short-term or long-term.[18] The former require a public commitment from the participants for the duration of a project/transaction. The latter have a longer duration and are sector or country specific. One example of the aforesaid initiative is the PACI Principles for Countering Corruption.

The PACI Principles for Countering Corruption (previously known as 'The PACI Principles for Countering Bribery') were first formulated in 2004 by a group of mining companies executives from the WEF's Industry Partnership programme. Today it is one of the major Forum's cross-industry collaborative efforts with close to 90 signatories from multiple industry sectors and global locations.[19] PACI membership is restricted to the members of the WEF. To become a member of PACI, a company is required to submit a membership application together with the PACI Principles signed by the CEO or equivalent company officer. The Principles are formulated in an aspirational way and request the signatory *to strive* to foster transparency, set the 'tone from the top' and build an internal commitment to a culture of zero-tolerance.[20] To maintain active membership, PACI signatories are required to (a) recommit to the PACI Principles and complete an anti-corruption survey every two years, and (b) participate in at least one biannual PACI community of signatories meeting every two years.[21] The only sanctions that PACI has at its disposal is to delist the company from the list of signatories, not allow it to use the PACI logo or attend PACI events.

Other notable examples of principles-based anti-corruption IASs include ICC Rules on Combating Corruption first published by International Chamber of Commerce as early as 1977 and later updated multiple times up to the present

17 World Bank Institute, *Fighting Corruption through Collective Action: A Guide for Business* (2008).

18 United Nations Global Contact, *A Practical Guide for Collective Action against Corruption* (2015).

19 World Economic Forum, 'Partnering against Corruption Initiative (PACI) Signatories' (March 2020) <http://www3.weforum.org/docs/WEF_PACI_Members.pdf> accessed 1 June 2020.

20 World Economic Forum, *Partnering Against Corruption Initiative: Global Principles for Countering Bribery. Application & General Terms of Partnership* (2016).

21 Ibid 7.

2011 version, Business Principles for Countering Bribery, originally developed by Transparency International in 2002 and revised in 2013, and the Good Practice Guidance on Internal Controls, Ethics, and Compliance issued by the Organization for Economic Cooperation and Development (OECD) in 2010. These initiatives constitute what is considered a 'good practice' and are intended as a method of self-regulation. Companies may accept them voluntarily and use them as a reference for the development of anti-corruption compliance programs; however, there is no follow-up monitoring or control of the effect of their implementation provided for in the guidelines.

3 Certification standards

In contrast to principles-based IASs, certification standards (e.g., ISO 37001:2016 Anti-Bribery Management Systems, and TRACE certification) involve external assurance. Certification standards measure companies' performance against the predefined criteria. The external validity is claimed to be ensured through the process of independent audit. In other words, these standards are designed to ensure that the company's activities comply with the provisions of the adopted standard through an independent assessment, which may be considered an undisputable advantage of this category. However, the quality of external verification is regularly questioned because of the lack of quality control over the corresponding auditing standards.[22]

ISO 37001:2016 'Anti-Bribery Management System – Requirements with Guidance for Use' was published in late 2016. It is a new international anti-corruption standard that specifies requirements for designing, implementing and optimizing anti-corruption management system. Over 80 experts, from 37 participating countries, 22 observer countries and eight liaison organizations were involved in developing the standard, which used the UK national standard BS 10500 Anti-Bribery Management as a baseline.[23] The standard builds upon existing guidelines ('A Resource Guide to the FCPA,' 'Guidance on adequate procedures' under the UK Bribery Act, and OECD Good Practice Guidance on Internal Controls, Ethics, and Compliance) and is a 'homogenization' of anti-bribery best practices. It requires organizations to implement a series of measures and controls to help prevent, detect, and deal with bribery including anti-bribery policy, risk assessment procedures, due diligence, and management commitment.[24] The requirements are formulated in a very broad way—measures and controls are expected to be 'reasonable and proportionate,'[25] however, the

22 Gilbert, Rasche, and Waddock (n 10) 30.

23 Neill Stansbury, *The Purposes and Benefits of ISO 37001* (Ethic Intelligence 2018).

24 ISO, 'ISO 37001: Anti-Bribery Management System Standard' <https://www.iso.org/files/live/sites/isoorg/files/standards/popular_standards/iso_37001_anti-bribery_management/iso.37001.slides.nov_15.pptx >accessed 1 June 2020.

25 Ibid slide 8.

standard does not specifically define what it means in practice. This broadness is claimed to allow the standard to be implemented by a wide range of organizations, irrespective of size, sector, structure, geography, or jurisdiction.

ISO 37001 is a requirements standard that allows organizations implementing it to go through an independent certification. However, the certification is not mandatory—a company may decide to use the standard as guidance material to design, benchmark or improve an anti-corruption program. Certification is done by a certification body, not by ISO. Organizations are free to select a certification body at their own discretion: its accreditation at a national accreditation body is recommended, but not compulsory.[26] After passing a two-stage onsite audit, the organization gets three-year certification with a re-certification audit at the end of the third year. In between certification years, there are annual surveillance audits to ensure continuous conformity and improvement. In case an audit reveals non-conformity with some aspect of the ISO 37001, sanctions can range from suspension (for major non-conformities) to corrective action requests (minor non-conformities). As of 2017, a total of 40 companies and organizations have been ISO 37001 certified.[27]

TRACE certification is another notable example of anti-corruption certification standard. US-based provider of third-party risk management solutions, TRACE International has developed a certification for individuals and SMEs interested in obtaining their own verified due diligence information. To be certified, an entity has to complete an online anti-bribery questionnaire, adopt an anti-bribery Code of Conduct and participate in TRACE's online anti-bribery training. After two to three weeks of due diligence process administered by TRACE analysts, the entity will get a comprehensive report containing information on its business structure, government/military ties of key owners and their family members, the results of the list, media, and internet-based searches. The report can then be shared with all business partners as a proof of completion of 'internationally accepted due diligence procedures.'[28] Businesses and individuals who successfully passed the certification process are included into TRACE Intermediary Directory, a public database of 'vetted' SMEs. The certification has to be renewed annually.

4 Reporting standards

Reporting standards provide a framework for disclosure on corporate economic, social, and environmental activities and their impact. The idea is to institutionalize sustainability reporting in a similar way to financial reporting

26 ISO, 'FAQ on ISO 37001: 2016' (December 2017) <https://committee.iso.org/sites/tc309/home/projects/published/ongoing-2/faqs-on-iso-37001.html> accessed 1 June 2020.

27 Pierre Simon, 'ISO 37001 Update November 2017' (LinkedIn Pulse, 20 November 2017) <https://www.linkedin.com/pulse/iso-37001-update-november-2017-pierre-simon-ccep-i/> accessed 1 June 2020.

28 TRACE, 'TRACE Certification Brochure—Portable Due Diligence for SMEs' (2017) <https://www.traceinternational.org/get-certified> accessed 1 June 2020.

standards. Organizations publish standardized reports on their impacts on the economy, environment, and society. The reporting framework defines indicators and guidelines the organizations may use to communicate their non-financial information to interested stakeholders.[29] The use of a common set of indicators and principles enables benchmarking and data comparison between companies, industries, and geographical regions. The reporting standards claim to enhance the global comparability and quality of information on these impacts, fostering transparency and accountability of organizations. Although there are no reporting frameworks designed for anti-corruption alone, the major sustainability reporting standards (GRI Sustainability Reporting Standards, The United Nations Global Compact and its Communication on Progress (COP) requirement) contain an anti-corruption component with corresponding disclosure requirements/ reporting elements.

The Global Reporting Initiative (GRI), an Amsterdam-based non-profit organization, was initiated by the Coalition for Environmentally Responsible Economies (CERES) and Tellus Institute in 1997. Since that time, the reporting framework went through several revisions to arrive at the 'first global sustainability reporting – The GRI Standards' effective from July 1, 2018.[30] GRI Standards can be used by an organization of any size, type, sector, or geographic location. Currently, more than 12,000 organizations across the globe use GRI standards for their sustainability reporting purposes, which makes them the most widely used sustainability standard in the world.[31]

GRI 205: Anti-corruption is a topic-specific standard in the series of GRI standards on economic topics. An organization *may* choose to use GRI 205, *or parts of its content*, with or without preparing a non-financial report in accordance with the GRI Standards. In any case, the reported information will include a 'GRI-referenced' claim and the organization will be listed as a participant on the GRI website.[32] Offering this level of flexibility raises questions on consistency and comparability of information reported under the GRI standards. Furthermore, GRI does not monitor or sanction an organization's performance, only to the extent to which it adheres to the reporting framework. GRI 205 sets out the reporting requirements on three anti-corruption topics: operations assessed for risks related to corruption and information on material corruption risks identified; communication and training about anti-corruption policies and procedures delivered to governance body members, employees, and business partners; confirmed incidents of corruption involving employees and business partners

29 Andreas Rasche, 'Collaborative Governance 2.0' (2010) 10 Corporate Governance: The International Journal of Business in Society 500.

30 GRI, 'GRI's History' (GRI, 2016) <https://www.globalreporting.org/information/about-gri/gri-history/Pages/GRI's%20history.aspx> accessed 1 June 2020.

31 GRI, 'Sustainability Disclosure Database' <http://database.globalreporting.org/> accessed 1 June 2020.

32 GRI, *GRI 205: Anti-Corruption 2016* (2016).

and actions taken.[33] Although the disclosures are detailed and unambiguous, they cover only certain parts of an anti-corruption compliance program. Other key elements including leadership role and 'tone-from-the-top,' whistleblowing mechanisms, as well as continuous monitoring and improvement of the program, are not reflected in the disclosure requirements.

The UN Global Compact was launched in 2000, and today it is the world's largest voluntary corporate responsibility initiative with more than 9,000 business and 3,000 non-business signatories.[34] It initially consisted of nine principles in the areas of human rights, labor, and environment, and was subsequently expanded to include the tenth principle on anti-corruption. The principle is formulated in an aspirational way and states that 'businesses should work against corruption in all its forms, including extortion and bribery.'[35] The tenth principle supports the sustainable development goal on peace and justice strong institutions.[36] The initiative seeks to align business operations and strategies with ten universally accepted principles. To join the initiative, a business organization has to complete the application form and prepare a letter of commitment signed by a CEO expressing commitment to UNGC ten principles and annual submission of a Communication on Progress (COP) report.[37] Originally quite flexible in terms of COP submission contents and deadlines, there has been a policy shift to enforce this reporting mechanism more swiftly.

In this way, starting from 2013[38] all participants are required to report in their COP against basic reporting elements set out in the reporting guidance developed by UNGC together with Transparency International. Seven elements cover three aspects of anti-corruption management including policy and commitment to comply with applicable laws, implementation (leadership support, communication and training for employees, internal controls), and monitoring and improvement.[39] Similar to the GRI 205 standard, the mandatory reporting requirement covers only some of the aspects of an anti-corruption program. The reporting indicators which cover the missing aspects are described as 'desired

33 Ibid 7–9.

34 United Nations Global Compact, 'See Who's Involved' <https://www.unglobalcompact.org/what-is-gc/participants/search?utf8=%E2%9C%93&search%5Bkeywords%5D=&search%5Bper_page%5D=10&search%5Bsort_field%5D=&search%5Bsort_direction%5D=asc> accessed 1 June 2020.

35 United Nations Global Compact, 'The Ten Principles of the UN Global Compact' <https://www.unglobalcompact.org/what-is-gc/mission/principles> accessed 1 June 2020.

36 United Nations Global Compact, '17 Goals to Transform our World' <https://www.unglobalcompact.org/sdgs/17-global-goals#sdg16> accessed 1 June 2020.

37 United Nations Global Compact, 'Application Process' <https://www.unglobalcompact.org/participation/join/application> accessed 1 June 2020.

38 United Nations Global Compact, 'UN Global Compact Policy on Communicating Progress' (2013) <https://www.unglobalcompact.org/docs/communication_on_progress/COP_Policy.pdf> accessed 1 June 2020.

39 United Nations Global Compact and Transparency International, *Reporting Guidance on the 10th Principle against corruption* (2009).

reporting elements,'[40] i.e., participants may choose to report on them but it's not required.

Besides a mandatory disclosure framework, UNGC does not provide for other accountability mechanisms. It doesn't assess the information provided in COP, nor does it make judgments on participants' performance. The only sanction that UNGC has at its disposal is a de-listing on UNGC site. Failing to submit COP on an annual basis results in a downgrading of participant status from active to non-communicating. Participants who do not communicate progress for two years in a row are expelled with their name published.[41]

5 Process standards

The categories analyzed above focus on the question of *what* organizations need to do to meet the expectations of stakeholders in terms of integrity and responsible business practices. Process standards (ISO 19600:2014 Compliance Management Systems, OCEG GRC Capability Book) on the contrary seek to define *how* corporate accountability can be achieved.[42] These are high-level management guidelines on how to incorporate an anti-corruption agenda into organizational culture, daily processes, and operations. Process standards define components, methods, and practices necessary to develop an organization-wide accountability framework. Therefore, they equally apply to general compliance management as well as risk-specific areas including anti-bribery, anti-corruption, antitrust, fraud, misconduct, and others.

ISO 19600:2014 Compliance Management Systems provides guidance on how organizations can design, implement, maintain, evaluate, and optimize compliance management systems. Based on the principles of good governance, proportionality, transparency, and sustainability, it seeks to aid in building a comprehensive compliance framework based on a risk-oriented approach. The basic guidance it provides covers key topics including compliance obligations, their scope, and context, defining compliance objectives, understanding the crucial role of leadership and the best ways to monitor the effectiveness of a compliance program.[43] Consistent with other management systems, ISO 19600 is based on a four-step method used for the control and continuous improvement of processes (plan-do-check-act).[44] The standard is applicable to all types of organizations, with the extent of application depending on the organization's size, structure, and complexity. ISO 19600 has been developed as a 'high-level structure' standard that doesn't provide for a certification. Therefore, there are

40 Ibid 12.

41 United Nations Global Compact, 'About the UN Global Compact' <https://www.unglobalcompact.org/about/faq> accessed 1 June 2020.

42 Deborah Leipziger, *The Corporate Responsibility Code Book* (2nd edn, Greenleaf 2010).

43 ISO, 'ISO 19600:2014 Compliance Management Systems' <https://committee.iso.org/sites/tc309/home/projects/published/ongoing-1.html> accessed 1 June 2020.

44 Ernst and Young, *ISO 19600 International Standard for Compliance Management* (2015).

no enforcement mechanisms associated with its use. However, the standard is currently under revision and is planned for release in 2020 as a requirement standard allowing a certification.[45]

The OCEG GRC Capability Model or Red Book 3.0 is another notable example of a process standard. The Open Compliance and Ethics Group (OCEG), a US-based non-profit organization, was founded in 2002 with a broad mission to improve corporate compliance and ethics. Together with an expert community, the organization claims to have 'invented' the GRC (Governance, Risk, and Compliance) in 2003,[46] followed by a publication of a rigorous study of GRC best practices called a 'GRC Capability Model.' Having undergone several revisions, the current version 3.0 provides a blueprint for the integration and strategic alignment of governance, risk management, and compliance. The GRC Capability Model, the central piece of the OCEG framework, rests on four components including L-learning about context, culture and stakeholders, A-aligning performance, strategies, and objectives with the learnings; P-performing by addressing requirements and risks through actions and controls, and R-reviewing and improving effectiveness and continued alignment of actions and controls.[47] To help organizations evaluate and audit GRC Capabilities, the OCEG has also developed GRC Assessment Tools (referred to as 'Burgundy Book'). This standard may be used for self-assessment as well as external assurance by third-party auditors.[48] Both 'books' are applicable to individual risk-specific programs (i.e., anti-corruption, anti-fraud, etc.), business units, and entire organizations. The standards are intended as a self-regulation tool and do not provide any seal of approval or performance assessment. Currently, there are 85,000 members in the OCEG community.[49]

The four categories proposed by Gilbert, Rasche, and Waddock[50] provide an overview of the differences between anti-corruption standards. At the same time, it is clear that the standards share important similarities. Some of them compete with each other, others complement, and again others overlap. Moreover, some of the standards exhibit characteristics of several categories, e.g., UNGC is primarily a principles-based standard yet with reporting requirements. In other words, the current situation with IASs is not streamlined, which fosters uncertainty and confusion for those who develop the standards and for the end-users. The

45 ISO, 'ISO 37301 Compliance Management Systems—Requirements with Guidance for Use' (ISO) <https://committee.iso.org/sites/tc309/home/projects/ongoing/ongoing-3.html> accessed 1 June 2020.

46 OCEG, 'What is OCEG' <https://www.oceg.org/about/what-is-oceg/> accessed 1 June 2020.

47 OCEG, 'GRC Capability Model Version 3.0' <https://go.oceg.org/grc-capability-model-red-book> accessed 1 June 2020.

48 OCEG, 'GRC Assessment Tools. Version 3.0' <https://go.oceg.org/grc-assessment-tools-burgundy-book> accessed 1 June 2020.

49 OCEG (n 46).

50 Gilbert, Rasche, and Waddock (n 10) 26.

developers of the standards do not explore in a sufficient manner the existing complementarities between IASs, remaining too focused on their own projects. The convergence between the standards should be encouraged. In the following section, I continue the analysis by discussing the benefits and shortcomings of current anti-corruption IASs.

6 Discussion: benefits and shortcomings of anti-corruption standards

The vast institutional infrastructure of anti-corruption IASs that has emerged to address the society's growing concern over business accountability and actual impact of corporate decisions provides many opportunities to demonstrate commitment to integrity and ethical practices. However, the strand of academic research suggests that the proliferation of IASs brings not only opportunities[51] but also a comparable number of problems.[52] This section extends these discussions by analyzing inherent features of anti-corruption standards in a two-fold way, with each feature having both positive and negative aspects.

6.1 Variety

As we have seen in the previous section, the variety of anti-corruption initiatives is compelling. Currently there is a great number of IASs which differ from one another in terms of scope, content, activities involved, target audience, and method of application. This diversity provides an opportunity for companies to select and apply the standard mostly suited to reflect their economic reality and activities relevant to their anti-corruption efforts.

However, it may create uncertainty which standard should be used and in what circumstances. Overlapping requirements cause confusion for those who develop the standards as well as for the end-users. In the absence of a dominant standard, organizations regularly choose to adopt several initiatives at the same time. That leads to management overload, increased associated compliance costs,

51 John G Ruggie, 'Reconstituting the Global Public Domain: Issues, Actors and Practices' (2004) 10 European Journal of International Relations 499; Steven Bernstein and Benjamin Cashore, 'Can Non-State Global Governance be Legitimate? An Analytical Framework' (2007) 1 Regulation and Governance 347; Julia Black, Constructing and Contesting Legitimacy and Accountability in Polycentric Regulatory Regimes' (2008) 2 Governance and Regulation 137.

52 Dara O'Rourke, 'Outsourcing Regulation: Analyzing Nongovernmental Systems of Labor Standards and Monitoring' (2003) 31 Policy Studies Journal 1; Petra Christmann and Glen Taylor, 'Firm Self-Regulation through International Certifiable Standards: Determinants of Symbolic Versus Substantive Implementation' (2006) 37 Journal of International Business Studies 863; Gilbert and Rasche (n 9) 761; Michael Behnam and Tammy L McLean, 'Where is Accountability in International Accountability Standards? A Decoupling Perspective' (2011) 21 Business Ethics Quarterly 45; Gilbert, Rasche, and Waddock (n 10) 37–42.

as well as the reduced impact of each of the applied standards.[53] Several standards competing for dominance can also adversely affect the perception of the IASs' legitimacy in general.[54] Organizations may not clearly determine the standards which will remain on the market, and maybe it will be the government that would eventually 'intervene to impose a different mandatory regime.'[55] In these circumstances, general support in terms of the number of signatories/participants for a stand-alone initiative is difficult to attain.

6.2 Multi-stakeholder approach

In most of the cases, the development of anti-corruption IASs involves a multi-stakeholder process bringing together non-government organizations, business associations, government entities, businesses, and academia. For example, over 80 experts, from 37 participating countries, 22 observer countries and eight liaison organizations were involved in developing ISO 37001.[56] A multi-stakeholder approach has been recognized to be beneficial for problem-solving in terms of increased effectiveness[57] and enhanced legitimacy of the decision-making.[58] The collaboration between public and private actors fosters inclusiveness of diverse perspectives and more informed decisions.

At the same time, inclusiveness requires a balanced input from all of the participating stakeholders, which is no easy task to arrange. Some of the stakeholders may have more financial and other resources to influence the standard-setting process and its content. This would not lead to a well-balanced discourse. Moreover, the more stakeholders are involved in the standard-setting, the broader the standard's contents may get. Trying to embrace the inputs from a large number of participants from a wide range of countries, cultures and legal systems bears a serious risk of arriving at a very basic compromise document with a limited practical capacity.

53 Michael Behnam and Tammy L McLean, 'Where is Accountability in International Accountability Standards? A Decoupling Perspective' (2011) 21 Business Ethics Quarterly 45.

54 Gilbert, Rasche and Waddock (n 10) 40.

55 John J Kirton and Michael J Trebilcock, *Hard Choices, Soft Law. Voluntary Standards in Global Trade, Environment and Social Governance* (1st edn, Ashgate Publishing 2004) 6.

56 Stansbury (n 23).

57 Tanja A Börzel and Thomas Risse, 'Public-Private Partnerships: Effective and Legitimate Tools of Transnational Governance' in Edgar Grande and Louis W Pauly (eds), *Complex Sovereignty: Reconstituting Political Authority in the Twenty-First Century* (1st edn, University of Toronto Press 2005).

58 Scherer and Palazzo (n 8) 933.

6.3 Global impact

The process of globalization as the main driver of the IASs' emergence and proliferation explicitly calls for a global policymaking. This is the issue that IASs are primarily designed to tackle. With the regulatory authority getting more fragmented, there is a clear need to fill in the voids in the global legal environment.[59]

However, the work of international organizations is regularly criticized because of the remoteness of the global policymaking from the local realities.[60] Moreover, given the developed countries currently dominate in the standard-setting process,[61] it is not surprising that some experts go to extremes in their opinions and explicitly call it a 'colonization' of local cultures.[62] The fact that the standards are 'imported' and not 'home-grown' explains criticism and lack of trust. For example, Doraev refers to the continuing transnationalization of anti-corruption norms as 'a threat to the national sovereignty.'[63]

6.4 Perceived value vs. hard law

On the other hand, the perceived legitimacy of an international anti-corruption standard may sometimes be higher than the one associated with the extraterritorial legislative norms. It is no easy task to explain to the employees of a Saudi Arabian, Russian, or Brazilian subsidiary of an MNC why they should comply with the requirements of the US/UK extraterritorial legislation (FCPA or UK Bribery Act), whereas the requirement to comply with an international standard appears more coherent.

That said, the anti-corruption IASs are in any case based on the legislative norms. For example, ISO 37001 and TRACE due diligence standard build upon existing legal acts and accompanying guidelines ('A Resource Guide to the FCPA', etc).[64] The fact that IASs do not bring anything new to the table is a widespread criticism. It is more than likely that companies familiar with the requirements of anti-corruption regulations won't find anything new in the standards. Then what is their benefit?

Moreover, the continuous evolution of legislation can create differences between the requirements of the standards and what is required by law. ISO 37001 was published in late 2016. In November 2017, the US Department

59 Scherer and Palazzo (n 8) 900–905.

60 Robert A Dahl, 'Can International Organizations Be Democratic? A Skeptic's View' in Ian Shapiro and Casiano Hacker-Cordon (eds.), *Democracy's Edges* (1st edn, CUP 1999).

61 Bobby S Banerjee, 'Who Sustains Whose Development? Sustainable Development and the Reinvention of Nature' (2003) 24 Organization Studies 143.

62 Glen Lehman, 'A Critical Perspective on the Harmonization of Accounting in a Globalizing World' (2005) 16 Critical Perspectives on Accounting 975, 982.

63 Mikhail G Doraev, 'Globalization of Anti-corruption Legislation: A Long Arm of the Foreign Law or a Threat to the Russian Sovereignty?' (2015) Legislation 61.

64 Stansbury (n 23); ISO (n 24).

of Justice updated its FCPA Policy.[65] As a result, the requirements for ISO 37001 certification need to continually change and evolve as well. Otherwise the standard may become outdated and lend itself to obsolescence. Ultimately, this could lead to companies having to seek recertification which would increase associated costs and management effort.

6.5 Flexibility

Elaborating further on the broad nature of IASs, it brings an important benefit of flexibility to the standards. Most of them are applicable to organizations of any size, type, sector, or geographic location. They are designed to be scalable to apply to individual risk-specific programs, subsidiaries, business units, or entire organizations, with the extent of application depending on the size, structure, and complexity of operations. The standards are formulated in a generic way which leaves room for interpretation possibilities. This leads to a variety of implementation strategies with every organization being able to adopt a standard in the way to meet its particular needs. For example, organizations are free to choose which GRI standards, or parts of their content, they use for sustainability reporting purposes.[66]

This flexibility inherent to IASs can also turn into a problem. The requirements may get so general that they are literally meaningless.[67] Ambiguous language provides less structure and guidance in terms of implementation, which can lead to a 'symbolic' adoption with the standard adopted, but not implemented. In these circumstances, organizations are more likely to decouple formal standards from daily operations.[68] Although the disclosure requirements under the GRI standards are formulated unambiguously, the flexibility of application allows companies to produce 'piecemeal sustainability reports' that contain incomplete or inconsistent data exhibiting the most appealing sides of their business operations.[69] This calls into question the usefulness of such reporting: as Reynolds and Yuthas note, 'for reports to be useful ... they must have qualities of comparability and consistency.'[70]

65 *FCPA Corporate Enforcement Policy 9-47.120* (November 2017).

66 GRI, *GRI 205: Anti-Corruption* (n 32).

67 Michael Volkov, 'ISO 37001: The Good, The Bad and the Ugly (Part II of V)' (*VolkovLaw*, 16 October 2017) <https://blog.volkovlaw.com/2017/10/iso-37001-good-bad-ugly-part-ii-v/> accessed 1 June 2020.

68 Behnam and McLean (n 53) 50.

69 Martha C Wilson, 'A Critical Review of Environmental Sustainability Reporting in the Consumer Goods Industry: Greenwashing or Good Business?' (2015) 3 Journal of Management and Sustainability 1.

70 MaryAnn Reynolds and Kristi Yuthas, 'Moral Discourse and Corporate Social Responsibility Reporting' (2008) 78 Journal of Business Ethics 47, 50.

6.6 Voluntary adoption

The proliferation of anti-corruption IASs is a positive move that drives integrity concerns to the center of business thinking. Their expansion raises awareness among various stakeholders making it possible to question the legitimacy of corporations that do not live up to the expectations of transparency and sound business practices.[71] As a result, businesses can no longer ignore their impact on society. More and more of them seek to demonstrate their willingness and commitment to preventing, detecting, and addressing bribery and corruption. To do that firms engage in various kinds of anti-corruption certification and/or reporting. These company-wide projects enhance the overall understanding of the anti-corruption agenda, what are risks a company is facing and how the overall strategy should be aligned with the compliance program.

However, some authors argue that the genuine interest of corporations towards IASs is mainly driven by the public perception of the negative effects of corruption and bribery. Adoption of voluntary standards improves brand image and reputation. Companies claim to act responsibly, but due to the lack of legal obligation, it is nothing more than PR and 'window-dressing.'[72] Scherer, Palazzo, and Seidl call it 'a strategic manipulation strategy' when a company attempts to create a positive public image not substantiated by the appropriate organizational changes.[73] As long as the IASs remain non-binding soft law, not only adoption but also implementation and compliance with their requirements are voluntary. This perception may lead to adverse selection when 'symbolic adopters' drive out the companies that implement standards substantively due to the existing information asymmetry.[74]

In the same vein, adoption of soft law guidelines does not provide a guarantee, nor it does act as a bar to corporate liability for bribery. Even in the case of a certification standard like ISO 37001, although the certification would provide some evidence of a company's anti-corruption efforts, DOJ and SEC have made it clear that it would not substitute a proper investigation.[75] As Chen puts it 'Prosecutors will not outsource their responsibilities.'[76]

71 Scherer and Palazzo (n 8) 922–936.

72 Bobby S Banerjee, 'Corporate Social Responsibility: The Good, the Bad and the Ugly' (2008) 34 Critical Sociology 51; Robert N Mefford, 'The Economic Value of a Sustainable Supply Chain' (2011) Business and Society Review 109.

73 Andreas G Scherer, Guido Palazzo, and David Seidl, 'Managing Legitimacy in Complex and Heterogeneous Environments: Sustainable Development in a Globalized World' (2013) 50 Journal of Management Studies 259, 263.

74 Oliver F Williams, 'The UN Global Compact: The Challenge and the Promise' (2004) 14 Business Ethics Quarterly 755.

75 Thomas R Fox, *Defects in ISO 37001 Certification* (FCPA Compliance Report 7 February 2018) <http://fcpacompliancereport.com/2018/02/defects-iso-37001-certification/> accessed 1 June 2020.

76 Hui Chen, 'Toward Evidence-Based Programs: Thoughts on ISO 37001 and Certifications' (Hui Chen Ethics, 21 October 2017) <https://huichenethics.com/2017/10/21/toward

6.7 Assurance and enforcement mechanisms

The existence of manipulative strategies points to another structural deficiency of anti-corruption IASs, i.e., the lack of proper steering. All of the anti-corruption IASs except for certification standards do not provide for assurance and/ or sanctions mechanisms. Even in case a company is subject to EU Directive 2014/95/EU on non-financial reporting and uses GRI standards as reporting framework to meet a legally binding requirement, still, as the Directive clearly states 'statutory auditors and audit firms should only check that the non-financial statement or the separate report has been provided.'[77] Other than that, no external check is required.

On a positive side, no external assurance means no associated costs. Hiring an independent audit firm to go through a review is an expensive exercise, and some organizations (especially SMEs) might not have sufficient resources to afford this. Budget constraints should not be an obstacle to making a public commitment to the principles of business integrity. Adoption of a reporting framework like GRI doesn't provide for organizational changes or performance assessment, therefore, it is also affordable cost-wise. However, the IASs with low costs of adoption are also likely to be chosen by organizations wishing to appear supportive of anti-corruption issues but not willing to make actual organizational changes.[78]

External assurance process is crucial to the aspect of credibility. Research on compliance programs shows that those IASs that lack assurance mechanisms are easily decoupled from actual organizational practice.[79] The degree of accountability for compliance with IASs has an impact on the extent of the standard integration into business processes. Missing control over implementation results leads to symbolic adoption and decoupling.

Decoupling is one of the core problems associated with IASs.[80] According to the neo-institutional theory, decoupling occurs when expectations of external stakeholders appear to conflict with managerial interests.[81] Organizational structures required by external stakeholders are adopted in form but not in function. Research suggests that IASs with ambiguous expectations, low cost of adoption, high cost of compliance, and lack of assurance and enforcement mechanisms are likely to be decoupled.[82] On the contrary, clearly defined

-evidence-based-programs-thoughts-on-iso-37001-and-certifications/> accessed 1 June 2020.

77 Non-Financial Reporting Directive (n 12) rec. 16.

78 Behnam and McLean (n 53) 51.

79 Gary R Weaver, Linda K Treviño, and Philip Cochran, 'Integrated and Decoupled Corporate Social Performance: Management Commitments, External Pressures, and Corporate Ethics' (1999) 42 Academy of Management Journal 539.

80 Behnam and McLean (n 53) 48; Gilbert, Rasche, and Waddock (n 10) 34.

81 William R Scott, *Institutions and Organizations* (4th edn, Sage Publications 2014).

82 Lauren B Edelman, 'Legal Ambiguity and Symbolic structures: Organizational Mediation of Civil Rights Law' (1992) 97 American Journal of Sociology 153; Weaver, Treviño, and Cochran (n 79) 539–552; Alexandra Kalev, Frank Dobbin, and Erin Kelly, 'Best Practices or

standards with high cost of adoption, requiring evidence of compliance as well as providing for sanctions for non-compliance are likely to be integrated into the business processes.

According to Behnam and McLean, this is the case for certification standards.[83] Indeed, certification is often considered as a promising mechanism to ensure accountability because of the inherent independent assurance. However, the quality of this assurance regularly raises concerns.

On January 25, 2017, Eni Corporation announced its ISO 37001 certification. The press release stated that 'certification confirms the quality of the system of rules and controls aimed at preventing corruption, developed by Eni since 2009 in line with the principle of "zero tolerance" expressed in its Code of Ethics.'[84]

Two weeks later the company's current and most recent CEOs were charged with international corruption by Italian prosecutors following an investigation into the company's 2011 purchase of a Nigerian exploration license.[85] Unaoil, a Monaco-based oil consultancy prosecuted by the Serious Fraud Office (UK) in 2018, had a TRACE certification.[86] What are the shortcomings of the certification process that lead to such cases?

First, there are no common standards on qualifications required to perform an anti-corruption compliance audit. For example, ISO 37001 certification body *can* have an accreditation from a national accreditation body, but it's not compulsory. The national accreditation body evaluates certifying bodies seeking accreditation and decides whether they follow the auditing criteria set out in the standard ISO/IEC TS 17021:2015 'Conformity assessment – Requirements for bodies providing audit and certification of management systems' and its supplement 'Competence requirements for auditing and certification of anti-bribery management systems' added to the standard because of the anti-corruption specifics.[87] Some of the ISO advocates claim that it is a rigorous process,[88] but that is true only for the certifying bodies which haven't been accredited before.

Best Guesses? Assessing the Efficacy of Corporate America's Affirmative Action and Diversity Policies' (2006) 71 American Sociological Review 589; Behnam and McLean (n 53) 50.

83 Behnam and McLean (n 53) 54–65.

84 'Eni becomes the first Italian company to obtain the ISO 37001:2016 "Antibribery Management Systems" certificate of conformity for its Anti-Corruption Compliance Program' (Eni.com 25 January 2017) <https://www.eni.com/en_IT/media/2017/01/eni-becomes-the-first-italian-company-to-obtain-the-iso-370012016-antibribery-management-systems-certificate-of-conformity-for-its-anti-corruption-compliance-program> accessed 1 June 2020.

85 James Politi, 'Eni Chief Claudio Descalzi Charged with International Corruption' *Financial Times* (Rome, 8 February 2017) <https://www.ft.com/content/87983836-ee13-11e6-930f-061b01e23655> accessed 1 June 2020.

86 Alexandra Wrage, 'UNAOIL vs the Compliance Community' (TRACE 31 March 2016).

87 ISO, 'FAQ on ISO 37001: 2016' (n 26).

88 Kristy Grant-Hart, 'Accreditation Hits the Mainstream: ISO 37001' (Compliance and Ethics Blog, 8 August 2018) <http://complianceandethics.org/accreditation-hits-the-mainstream-iso-37001/> accessed 1 June 2020.

In case a certifying body has already received the accreditation for ISO/IEC TS 17021:2015 (to issue ISO 9001 certification, for example), the accreditation procedure is considerably simplified—one-day documentation review and one-time observation of audit procedures at auditee's premises is enough.[89] That explains how Eni could manage to get the certification so fast—with the standard published in October 2016, the official announcement came out already in January 2017.

Second, the broadness of the standards requires compliance managers to rely on professional judgment when implementing anti-corruption measures and controls. That means that a certification auditor needs to be at least equally qualified to assess the adequacy and proportionality of the implemented measures and controls and whether they are in compliance with the standard's requirements. Taking into account the loopholes in the accreditation process, it doesn't seem to be the case. In this instance, a certification audit appears to turn into a 'seal of approval' exercise for managerial decisions, which can't be regarded as a meaningful external assurance.

7 Conclusion: moving forward with anti-corruption standards effectiveness

This chapter discusses the proliferation of international anti-corruption initiatives, standards, and guidelines in recent decades. The IASs emerged as a new form of global governance 'above and beyond the state'[90] due to the decline in regulatory power of national government bodies. In today's globalized world MNCs are able to escape 'home' jurisdictions by shifting operations to developing countries where the rule of law may be less apparent. This has led to a highly heterogeneous and imbalanced global legal environment. In this regard, the purpose of the IASs, at the same time representing their major benefit, is to fill in the gaps in global governance and, at least partially, help to align the imbalanced rulemaking.[91]

The variety of anti-corruption initiatives is compelling. The existing IASs provide various mechanisms for how to facilitate corporate accountability, ranging from making a public commitment to going through an independent certification. This chapter attempts to classify anti-corruption IASs along two dimensions. First, the application of corporate responsibility initiatives classification[92] to anti-corruption standards allowed us to cluster them along four categories. Then, using several examples in each category, the IASs were analyzed along a set of

89 Emanuele Riva, 'Informativa in merito all'accreditamento per lo schema di certificazione ISO 37001 Prevenzione della corruzione' (Circolare Tecnica N° 28/2017, Accredia 20 November 2017) 7–8.

90 Scherer and Palazzo (n 8) 904.

91 John G Ruggie, 'Trade, Sustainability and Global Governance' (2002) 27 Columbia Journal of Environmental Law 297.

92 Gilbert, Rasche, and Waddock (n 10) 26.

criteria to arrive at an overview of the differences and similarities of existing anti-corruption IASs. The analysis suggests that the developers of the standards do not explore in a sufficient manner the existing complementarities between IASs remaining too focused on their own projects. Some of the standards compete with each other, others complement each other, and again others overlap. This situation creates uncertainty and confusion for those who develop the standards and for the end-users. Therefore, the convergence between the standards should be encouraged.

Elaborating further on the shortcomings associated with IASs, the chapter explored how swift expansion of anti-corruption standards brings not only opportunities for enhanced corporate accountability, but also a comparable number of problems. Extending this perspective, the two-fold analysis of standards' inherent features shows that opportunities often turn into problems, as will be true the other way round. The broadness of IASs makes most of them applicable to organizations of any size, type, sector, or geographic location. At the same time, generic requirements create ambiguity and can lead to the adoption of a standard in form but not in function. Flexibility makes them scalable to apply to individual risk-specific programs, subsidiaries, business units, or entire organizations, with a varying extent of application. However, it also means less completeness and comparability. The proliferation of IASs in their variety creates awareness among stakeholders and drives anti-corruption agenda to the mainstream of business thinking, but as long as they remain soft law not only adoption but also implementation and compliance with their requirements are voluntary. The costs of actual organizational change necessary to incorporate IASs into daily operations can be high enough for companies to be tempted by low-hanging fruits of window-dressing and focusing on a 'paper program.' With the lack of audit regulation and existing loopholes in auditors' accreditation process even certification standards, although often considered as the most promising,[93] are prone to decoupling. Therefore, the effectiveness and efficiency of anti-corruption accountability standards remain limited, since they lack accountability *per se*.

This chapter has several implications for future research on anti-corruption IASs. First, to advance the understanding of their effectiveness, future investigations should consider an empirical study exploring which types of standards are more likely to be decoupled. The negative aspects of standards' inherent features surfaced here should also be tested to identify which of them contribute the most to decoupling intentions and how they interact with each other. Second, we still have a limited understanding which factors facilitate or hamper the diffusion of IASs in terms of geography and time. One of the research priorities could be to understand the role of national governments in shaping the global anti-corruption landscape by supporting existing standards (e.g., in Malaysia the launch of an internal version of ISO 37001 by the Ministry of Science, Technology and

93 Behnam and McLean (n 53) 48; Gilbert, Rasche, and Waddock (n 10) 34.

Innovation in cooperation with the Malaysian Anti-Corruption Commission has led to a burgeoning number of certified organizations[94]) and translating voluntary rules into enforceable regulations (e.g., EU Directive 2014/95/EU on non-financial reporting with anti-corruption component). Longitudinal studies are likely to be the best way to address this research avenue.

94 Simon (n 27).

10 In the ocean of anti-corruption compliance standards and guidelines

Time for codification?

Eduard Ivanov

The active implementation of anti-corruption compliance in the business sector began in 2008 firstly under the influence of the increasing application of the US Foreign Corrupt Practices Act (FCPA) 1977 after the global financial crises in 2007–2008 and secondly after the adoption the UK Bribery Act in 2010. In the last few years, anti-corruption compliance has been becoming a growing field in the general framework of compliance. More and more organizations in various parts of the World decide to implement anti-corruption compliance programmes. The ethical norms and values are significant for designing an anti-corruption compliance programme. However, organizations should also decide which laws, regulations, standards, and guidelines to consider.

The United Nations Convention against Corruption of 2003 contains general provisions regarding cooperation with the private sector, promoting integrity and transparency among private entities.[1] It does not define the structure of, and formal requirements to, an anti-corruption compliance programme.

In contrast to the international standards on combating money laundering, the financing of terrorism, and proliferation 2012, developed by the Financial Action Task Force (FATF)—the main international policy maker in anti-money laundering/countering the financing of terrorism, none of the standards or guidelines on anti-corruption compliance published by international organizations became globally recognized, nor provided countries with a detailed framework of anti-corruption compliance in organizations.

At the national level, legal incentives for organizations to implement anti-corruption compliance, e.g., opportunities to avoid corporate liability or reduce fines in some jurisdictions should be not underestimated. However, as a rule, domestic laws neither establish obligations for organizations to implement anti-corruption compliance programmes, nor define detailed requirements to such programmes. Not many jurisdictions have published domestic guidelines on anti-corruption (anti-bribery) compliance. Besides France, the United Kingdom, the United

1 United Nations Convention against Corruption (opened for signature 9 December 2003, entered into force 14 December 2005) 2349 UNTS 41.

States, whose guidelines are very well known, countries which have adopted ISO 37001, Russia,[2] and Ukraine,[3] should be mentioned here.

In this regard, numerous international standards and guidelines have been becoming important sources for designing, implementing, and benchmarking anti-corruption compliance programmes in organizations. How can organizations navigate in the ocean of standards and guidelines? The aims of the chapter are to propose an answer to the above question, identify existing problems in regulation of anti-corruption compliance, and suggest possible solutions.

The author used the functional and analytical methods of comparative legal research as the most appropriate method for this study.[4] The sources for the research included comprehensive international conventions, anti-corruption compliance standards and guidelines, reports and other documents of international intergovernmental and non-governmental organizations, selected national laws and regulations, academic publications, and publications in professional blogs.

1 Distinctive features of anti-corruption compliance regulation

In 2017–2018, the author conducted a comparative study on Anti-Money Laundering/Countering the Financing of Terrorism (AML/CFT) and anti-corruption compliance regulation. The AML/CFT compliance regulation was selected as an opposite approach to anti-corruption compliance regulation because it is a classic model of legal regulation based on international law and domestic laws and regulations, which establish binding legal obligations for financial institutions and designated non-financial businesses and professions. Regulatory and supervisory functions of governmental authorities or central banks are also key components of the AML/CFT compliance regulatory framework.

The approach of international organizations and national governments to anti-corruption compliance differs significantly. The study identified several distinctive features of anti-corruption compliance regulation:

- None of the existing international standards and guidelines on anti-corruption compliance became globally recognised;

2 Методические рекомендации по разработке и принятию организациями мер по предупреждению и противодействию коррупции (утв. Министерством труда и социальной защиты РФ 8 ноября 2013 г.).

3 Lina Nemchenko and Mariana Marchuk, 'Typical Anti-Corruption Program for Legal Entity is Approved' *Global Compliance News* (20 April 2017) <https://globalcompliancenews.com/ukraine-anti-corruption-program-20170420/> accessed 1 June 2020.

4 Mathias Reimann and Reinhard Zimmermann (eds), *The Oxford Handbook of Comparative Law* (OUP 2006); Mark Van Hoecke, 'Methodology of Comparative Legal Research. Law and Method' (2015) 4 Boomjuridischtijdschriften <www.bjutijdschriften.nl/tijdschrift/lawandmethod/2015/12/RENM-D-14-00001> accessed 1 June 2020.

- In contrast to the strict AML/CFT legal regulation, most national anti-corruption laws create incentives rather than binding legal obligations for organizations to implement anti-corruption compliance programmes;
- The significant role of international soft law in contrast to the 'hard law' of AML/CFT regulation;
- The serious influence of domestic laws that have transnational application on anti-corruption compliance programmes of foreign organizations, including those which do not have legal obligations under these laws;
- The replacement of public supervision by private certification of anti-corruption (anti-bribery) compliance management systems and compliance officers by a number of private certification services providers in various countries.

The International standards on combating money laundering, the financing of terrorism, and proliferation 2012 (FATF Standards) define a detailed framework for AML/CFT compliance in financial institutions and designated non-financial businesses and professions. The FATF standards are incorporated into national laws and, in some jurisdictions, in industry-specific regulations and guidelines. National laws define the types of financial institutions and non-financial businesses and professions that have a binding legal obligation to have AML/CFT compliance system in place, and the structure and detailed requirements for AML/CFT compliance programmes.

The role of the FATF standards as comprehensive international standards was recognized in the UN Security Council Resolution 1617 adopted under Chapter VII of the UN Charter,[5] and then in the UN Global Counter-Terrorism Strategy adopted in the form of a General Assembly Resolution.[6] There are 35 states and two regional organizations that are members of the FATF, and two states with observer status. The nine FATF-style regional bodies (FSRBs) comprise 185 members (APG – 41 members, CFATF – 27 members, MONEYVAL – 34 members, EAG – 9 members, ESAAMLG – 18 members, GAFILAT – 16 members, GIABA – 15 members, MENAFATF – 19 members, GABAC – 6 members). In general, the FATF's framework includes 204 states and territories representing all continents and legal systems. Ten states are members of the FATF and one of the FSRBs. Three states (China, India, and the Russian Federation) are members of the FATF and of two FSRBs.[7]

The FATF established an effective mechanism of standards implementation. The prerequisite for FATF or FSRB membership is a willingness to cooperate with the FATF, FSRBs, and other member states on the bases of FATF standards.

5 UNSC Res 1617 (2005) SCOR Resolutions and Decisions 63.

6 UNGA Res 60/288 (2007) UN Doc A/60/49.

7 FATF, 'Members and Observers' <https://www.fatf-gafi.org/about/membersandobservers/#d.en.3147> accessed 1 June 2020.

The acts establishing FSRBs include provisions on recognition and implementation of FATF standards.[8]

There are effective mechanisms utilizing mutual evaluation in the FATF and FSRBs frameworks.[9] Based on the evaluation reports, the FATF Plenary identifies high-risk and non-cooperative jurisdictions. As a rule, listed jurisdictions cooperate with the FATF to improve their AML/CFT systems and present follow-up reports to the FATF Plenary. In case of non-cooperation, the FATF issues a public statement and calls on its members and other states to apply counter-measures to protect the international financial system from money laundering and financing of terrorism. The FATF Plenary takes place three times a year and updates lists of high-risk and non-cooperative jurisdictions accordingly. The most recent public statement confirms the effectiveness of the FATF global efforts. The Democratic People's Republic of Korea (DPRK) is the only jurisdiction which does not cooperate with the FATF. In the statement, the FATF calls on its members and other jurisdictions to apply counter-measures against DPRK, including closing 'existing branches, subsidiaries and representative offices of DPRK banks within their territories and terminat[ing] correspondent relationships with DPRK banks, where required by relevant UNSC resolutions.' The second jurisdiction mentioned in the statement, the Islamic Republic of Iran, adopted an Action Plan and took other relevant steps to address its strategic AML/CFT deficiencies. In this regard, the FATF decided to continue the suspension of counter-measures.[10]

Due to the efforts of the FATF and FSRBs, the FATF standards became, in the author's view, international customary law.

Currently, there are more than 30 international standards and guidelines on anti-corruption compliance published by various stakeholders in different periods of time. The most well-known standard on anti-corruption (anti-bribery) compliance is ISO 37001—Anti-bribery management systems. The standard has influence on the implementation of the anti-bribery management system in organizations and even a particular influence on governmental anti-corruption policies in several countries. In April 2017, Peru and Singapore officially adopted ISO 37001. In 2018, the standard was officially recognized by governmental authorities in Indonesia and Malaysia. In China, the Market Supervision Commission of the Shenzhen Municipality published in June 2017 the Anti-bribery Management System Shenzhen Standard based on ISO 37001. It became

8 APG, *Terms of Reference* (2012); EAG, *Agreement on the Eurasian Group on Combating Money Laundering and Financing of Terrorism* (2011); MENAFATF, *The Memorandum of Understanding Between the Governments of the Member States of the Middle East and North Africa Financial Action Task Force Against Money Laundering and Terrorist Financing* (signed on 30 November 2004, amended 26 November 2013).

9 FATF, *Methodology for Assessing Technical Compliance with the FATF Recommendations and the Effectiveness of AML/CFT Systems* (2013).

10 FATF, 'Public Statement—June 2019' (21 June 2019) <http://www.fatf-gafi.org/publications/high-risk-and-other-monitored-jurisdictions/documents/public-statement-june-2019.html> accessed 1 June 2020.

the first anti-bribery standard adopted by a Chinese local regulator to support the implementation of anti-bribery compliance programs in organizations. However, it is too early to judge the potential role of ISO 37001 as a global, widely recognized standard at the current stage of implementation.

In the absence of formal legal requirements for anti-corruption compliance in many jurisdictions, organizations design and implement anti-corruption compliance programs based on various international standards and guidelines, foreign anti-corruption laws and guidelines, and compliance programs of multinational corporations.

The main reasons for organizations to implement anti-corruption compliance programs can be classified into four groups: the personal positions of shareholders, board members and/or CEOs regarding corruption, legal obligations and incentives, market requirements, and participation in Collective Action initiatives.

The personal positions of shareholders, board members, and/or CEOs is a key factor for the implementation of anti-corruption compliance. Even in the absence of any formal legal requirements, they may decide to implement a compliance program, and promote business based on ethical principles and values, including integrity and zero tolerance of corruption in an organization.

Legal incentives include provisions of legal acts that give organizations the opportunity to use an effective compliance programme as a defense to avoid corporate criminal liability (UK) or to mitigate punishment (Brazil, US). Court decisions can also create legal incentives for organizations. In May 2017, the German Supreme Court declared in its decision that an effective compliance management system required remedial action to be taken into account by calculating fines.[11]

An interesting example of promoting anti-corruption compliance is the requirement of the European Parliament and Council Directive, 2014/95/EU of 22 October 2014, amending Directive 2013/34/EU as regards disclosure of non-financial and diversity information by certain large undertakings and groups ([2014] OJ L330/1), to include information necessary for an understanding of organizations' positions and activities relating to, as a minimum, environmental, social, and employee matters, respect for human rights, anti-corruption, and bribery. The necessary information includes, among other things, descriptions of anti-corruption policies, due diligence, and risk management. The first annual management reports containing information about anti-corruption measures were published in 2018.

A formal legal requirement to have anti-corruption compliance programmes in place is a rare exception in domestic legislations, e.g., in the Russian Federation. Article 13.3 of Russia's Federal Law on Combating Corruption 2008 established the obligation for all organizations in the Russian Federation to take measures to prevent corruption. The General Prosecutor's office, which is responsible for supervising the implementation of anti-corruption legislation, is entitled to order

11 StR 265/16 (2017) Bundesgerichtshof Urteil vom 9 Mai 2017.

or request a court to order organizations to implement measures in accordance with Article 13.3. However, despite the general legal obligation there is no special liability of organizations under Russian law for not having an anti-corruption compliance programme.

Market requirements to implement an anti-corruption compliance programme are interesting indirect results of proactive application of anti-corruption laws and of growing risk of corporate liability. To mitigate the risks, organizations request their business associates to demonstrate effective compliance. Market requirements include, among others:

- requirements of counterparties to have a compliance programme in place;
- requirements of counterparties to have a certified compliance programme;
- requirements of counterparties to apply an anti-corruption clause to contracts.[12]

The World Bank Institute defines an anti-corruption Collective Action as:

> a collaborative and sustained process of cooperation amongst stakeholders. It increases the impact and credibility of individual action, brings vulnerable individual players into an alliance of like-minded organizations and levels the playing field between competitors.[13]

According to the B20 Collective Action Hub, there are more than 100 Collective Action initiatives in all parts of the World.[14] Many of them receive support from international organizations and global corporations. Collective Action initiatives play an important role in promoting anti-corruption and compliance. They provide support to organizations, especially to SMEs in implementation anti-corruption compliance programs.[15]

Comparative analyses of AML/CFT and anti-corruption compliance regulation bring us to the two questions: why regulation of AML/CFT and anti-corruption compliance, which are in general aimed at prevention of two quite often connected types of crime, is so different, and whether the soft law approach is more suitable for anti-corruption compliance regulation. The very simplified explanation is that these two types of compliance have different natures. The purpose of AML/CFT compliance is to identify and report suspicious financial transactions of customers to an authorized governmental authority. It is more or

12 Eduard Ivanov, 'AML/CFT and Anti-Corruption Compliance Regulation: Two Parallel Roads' (IACA Research Paper Series 2/2018, 2018) 9.

13 World Bank Institute, *Fighting Corruption Through Collective Action: A Guide for Business* (2008).

14 Basel Institute on Governance, 'B20 Collective Action Hub' <https://www.baselgovernance.org/b20-collective-action-hub> accessed 1 June 2020.

15 Gemma Aiolfi, 'The Value and Importance of Collective Action' in IBA, *Anti-Corruption Law and Practice Report 2017: Innovation in Enforcement and Compliance* (May 2017) 29.

less a technical exercise which can be standardized. The aim of anti-corruption compliance is to influence behavior of people associated with an organization to prevent their involvement in corruption relationships. It is much more difficult to develop standard solutions that can influence human behavior in different countries, cultures, social groups, and industries. However, a number of policies in both types of compliance, e.g., policies on due diligence and risk management, are very similar.

The hard law approach can be criticized for its strict and sometimes formalistic regulation, that does not always allow one to tailor compliance programs considering the specifics of an organization.

There are several arguments in support of the soft law approach. Many compliance professionals underline that one size does not fit all. According to the US Department of Justice and the US Securities and Exchange Commission, one-size-fits-all compliance programs are generally ill-conceived and ineffective.[16] Another serious argument is that the so-called tick-box exercise is not effective enough to prevent corrupt behavior in an organization. The compliance program should not only meet formal requirements on the paper but also consider the cultural context of countries where an organization is doing or going to do business.

The soft law approach gives organizations more freedom for maneuver in designing and implementing anti-corruption compliance programs. They have an opportunity to consider risk profile, all the specific risk factors identified in the framework of risk assessment, specifics of industry, and available resources. At the same time, more freedom means also more responsibility. Organizations should design and implement effective anti-corruption compliance programs based on numerous general international guidelines, and considering applicable foreign anti-corruption laws. Large multinational enterprises solve this problem by hiring external lawyers and consultants. The reality of many SMEs is that one person is responsible for designing and implementing an anti-corruption compliance program. For compliance officers of SMEs, clear guidelines describing framework and requirements to the content of an anti-corruption compliance program are of significant importance.

In the author's opinion, another issue with the soft law approach is legal uncertainty. In the absence of clear legal rules and formal requirements, prosecutors and judges can also enjoy a particular level of freedom in evaluating effectiveness of anti-corruption compliance programs. In countries with corrupt judicial systems such legal uncertainty could even encourage other corruption offences, such as the extortion of a bribe by a judge in return for a positive assessment of a compliance program.

16 US Department of Justice and US Securities and Exchange Commission, *FCPA: A Resource Guide to the US Foreign Corrupt Practices Act 2012* (2012) 58.

It is hard to overestimate the role of the FCPA and the UK Bribery Act in the global anti-corruption system due to the transnational application of these laws, and numerous enforcement actions.

Corporations invest significant amounts to implement effective anti-corruption compliance management systems and prevent violations of anti-corruption laws, first of all violations of the FCPA and the UK Bribery Act. However, despite all efforts, we still regularly read reports about new investigations against large multinational corporations that paid a bribe to foreign public officials. The amount of fines for violations of the FCPA and of the UK Bribery Act paid by foreign companies is impressive. Corporations pay hundreds of millions or sometimes billions of US dollars for corporate misconduct.

There is no doubt that corruption must pay. The only question arises—who should receive these fines? Who are the victims struggling from corrupt corporate practices? Nowadays, corporations pay fines to the budgets of the most developed countries in the World. For citizens of less developed countries these payments look like an additional price that corporations shall pay for obtaining business in their countries through corrupt deals. Beneficiaries are the countries that are able to enforce their anti-corruption laws globally.

In the author's opinion, the victims of corrupt corporate practices are citizens of countries where corrupt practices of global corporations destroy public governance and kill trust between governments, the business sector, and citizens. In this regard, it would be logical that corporations pay fines directly to the citizens of countries where they bribed local officials. It is important to underline that money should be transferred not to the governments that are sometimes corrupt and can misuse the received funds but directly to citizens.

The developed countries that apply anti-corruption laws against corporations can receive compensation of investigations and prosecution costs. The remaining part of fines could be transferred directly to citizens of countries where corruption offences were committed. This new approach to punishment for corporate corruption offences could create an additional opportunity for developed countries to support needy people in the less developed countries.

The opportunity to receive compensation for corrupt corporate practices will create additional incentives for citizens to support global anti-corruption efforts and to use the official financial system.

In some countries not all the citizens have access to the banking system. However, the author believes that modern technologies including new payment methods and use of electronic currencies will solve this problem.

Not all countries are happy with the transnational application of the UK and US laws. Noteworthy in this regard is the new Chinese International Criminal Judicial Assistance Law. According to this law, domestic organizations and individuals must not provide evidence materials and assistance to foreign nations.[17] According to Carlson, Article 4 may prevent China-based subsidiaries

17 International Criminal Judicial Assistance Law of the PRC 2018, art 4.

of multinationals from providing evidence to UK and US criminal enforcement authorities, and may apply even to parent companies outside of China.[18]

Despite some criticism, there is no doubt that proactive application of the FCPA and the UK Bribery Act has had a serious positive influence on the implementation of anti-corruption compliance. Even organizations that are not obliged subjects under these laws take them into consideration. In countries that do not have legal rules and guidelines on anti-corruption compliance, organizations often use guidelines published in the UK or US to design anti-corruption compliance programs. This approach has at least two weak points. Firstly, a compliance program designed according to foreign guidelines does not always consider local risks and specifics. Secondly, local compliance officers and lawyers often do not have UK or US legal education and sufficient knowledge, and use guidelines without consideration of legal frameworks of respective countries.

A distinctive feature of AML/CFT regulation is a strong role for regulatory and supervisory authorities that have the power to evaluate the quality of compliance programs of financial institutions and designated non-financial businesses and professions. In anti-corruption compliance, the approach is completely different. Public authorities will evaluate an anti-corruption compliance program only in cases when an organization is involved in an anti-corruption investigation.

In certification of anti-corruption (anti-bribery) management systems, compliance programs and officers were the market reaction on the absence of public supervision. Certification by external service providers allows organizations to evaluate the quality of own compliance programs, and to have confirmation of quality of the compliance programs of current or future business partners. We can speak about the 'privatization' of particular regulatory and supervisory functions by companies, providing certification services.

Guidance issued by various international institutions recommends external reviews of the effectiveness of anti-corruption programs.[19] According to the TI, where appropriate, the enterprise should undergo voluntary independent assurance on the design, implementation, and/or effectiveness of the program. Where such independent assurance is conducted, the enterprise should consider publicly disclosing that an external review has taken place, together with the related assurance opinion.[20] After the ISO 37001 standard was published, many organizations, including market leaders, started seeking certification services.[21]

18 Eric Carlson, 'Practice Alert: China asserts "Judicial Sovereignty" with new blocking Statute' (*The FCPA Blog*, 10 December 2018) <http://www.fcpablog.com/blog/2018/12/10/practice-alert-china-asserts-judicial-sovereignty-with-new-b.html> accessed 1 June 2020.

19 Barbara Neiger, *Successful Compliance* (Austrian Standards plus GmbH 2015) 33

20 Transparency International, *Business Principles for Countering Bribery* (2013) 12.

21 Kristy Grant-Hart and Diana Trevley, 'Microsoft and Wal-Mart Seek ISO 37001 Anti-Bribery Certification' (*The FCPA Blog*, 11 May 2017) <http://www.fcpablog.com/blog/2017/5/11/microsoft-and-wal-mart-seek-iso-37001-anti-bribery-certifica.html> accessed 1 June 2020.

In the author's opinion, there are several pros and cons of certification. Certification can at least confirm that an anti-corruption compliance program of a current or future business partner meets particular requirements defined in one of the international compliance standards. It is an organization's responsibility to decide whether it trusts the certificate presented by its counterparty. This decision may consider the standards used for certification, and the business reputation of the certificate issuer.

For organizations from countries with a high level of corruption the international certification by solid service providers might be the only way to build trust with business partners abroad.

At the same time, certification means additional costs. Organizations pay initially to external service providers for designing compliance programmes and then to other service providers for certification services. In some cases, organizations go through the certification procedure only due to the requirements of a business partner in the framework of due diligence.

The legal significance of certification is an open question. Courts and prosecutors may take certificates into account in criminal, administrative, or civil procedures. MacMurray provided interesting examples of the use of ISO 37001 by the Brazilian and Danish prosecutors in settlement agreements.[22] However, neither courts nor prosecutors are obliged to consider certification. Legal criteria for evaluation of certificates are net defined. Evaluating certificates as evidence of effectiveness of compliance programs or compliance management systems, courts have to answer at least the following questions:

- whether certification according to one or another standard or guide should be taken into consideration;
- whether experts of the certificate's issuer have sufficient professional experience and reputation;
- whether a certificate issued by a foreign service provider should be taken into consideration.

In the author's opinion, the legal significance of certification needs clarification in national anti-corruption, criminal, administrative, and civil procedure laws.

2 Main categories of anti-corruption compliance standards and guidelines

As follows from the previous chapter, international standards and guidelines are useful sources for the design, implementation, and evaluation of anti-corruption compliance programs. In the absence of one comprehensive and widely

22 Worth MacMurray, 'Three Predictions for the Future of ISO 37001' (*The FCPA Blog*, 13 February 2019) <https://fcpablog.com/2019/02/13/three-predictions-for-the-future-of-iso-37001/> accessed 1 June 2020.

recognized international standard or guide, organizations should navigate the ocean of international standards and guidelines, and decide which of them to use. The selection of a relevant standard or guidance is also important when organizations take decisions regarding certifications of anti-corruption (anti-bribery) compliance management systems or programmes. Certification according to one or another standard or guidance may be considered by prosecutors or courts.

Domestic guidelines published in France, the UK, and the US should be also considered for the purposes of this study.

There are several possible classifications of anti-corruption compliance standards and guidelines based on different criteria.

International and domestic standards and guidelines differ in geographical application. Comprehensive international standards and guidelines are addressed to organizations in any country. There are a few regional guidelines. Domestic standards and guidelines are addressed to organizations which are subjects of particular domestic legislation. Domestic standards and guidelines may be developed and published by governmental agencies and/or business associations. In the author's view, anti-corruption Collective Action initiatives, in particular those supported by international organizations and/or multinationals, could also develop compliance standards and guidelines to support the implementation of anti-corruption compliance in countries or regions of their activities.

Standards and guidelines adopted by various stakeholders. In the context of this study, the author identified standards and guidelines adopted by international intergovernmental organizations, bodies, and public-private initiatives, non-governmental organizations, chambers of commerce, business associations, and private companies, e.g., law firms and consultants. There are 17 standards and guidelines developed by international intergovernmental organizations and bodies, four standards and guidelines developed by NGOs, eight guidelines developed by international business associations, and four guidelines developed by a private company.

General and topic-specific standards and guidelines defer in the scope of regulation. General standards and guidelines cover all main components of the anti-corruption compliance management system or programme. Specific standards and guidelines refer to one or several elements of anti-corruption compliance programmes. There are 12 general and 21 specific international standards and guidelines analyzed in this study.

General and sector-specific standards and guidelines. As a rule, international standards and guidelines are addressed to all types of organizations. The only exception is the Wolfsberg Group's Guidance for financial institutions.

Specific guidelines for small and medium-sized enterprises (SMEs). SMEs are vulnerable to corrupt practices such as extortion of bribe. Most of them have very limited resources for the implementation of compliance programmes and need support. All the more surprising is that only three guidelines take into account the specificities of SMEs. The UNODC's Guide analyzes after each chapter

Table 10.1 Includes international standards and guidelines.

Standards and guidelines developed by international intergovernmental organizations, bodies, and public-private initiatives		
Organization	*Standard/guidance*	*General/Special*
UNODC	An Anti-Corruption Ethics and Compliance Programme for Business: A Practical Guide 2013	General
UN Global Compact	Reporting Guidance on the 10th Principle Against Corruption (joint Guidance with TI) 2009	Special
	Resisting Extortion and Solicitation in International Transactions, A Company Tool for Employee Training (joint publication with ICC, TI, WEF) 2011	Special
	A Guide for Anti-Corruption Risk Assessment 2013	Special
OECD	Recommendation of the Council for Further Combating Bribery of Foreign Public Officials in International Business Transactions 2009	Special
	Principles for Integrity in Public Procurement 2009	Special
	Good Practice Guidance on Internal Controls, Ethics and Compliance 2010	General
	Anti-Corruption Ethics and Compliance Handbook for Business (joint Guidance with UNODC and World Bank) 2013	General
	Anti-Bribery Policy and Compliance Guidance for African Companies 2016	General, Regional
OSCE	Handbook on Combating Corruption 2016	General
World Bank Group	Integrity Compliance Guidelines 2010	General
FATF	International Standards on Combating Money Laundering, the Financing of Terrorism and Proliferation (the FATF Recommendations) 2012	General
	A Reference Guide and Information Note on the Use of the FATF Recommendations to support the fight against Corruption 2012	Special
	Guidance: Politically Exposed Persons 2013	Special
	Guidance on Transparency and Beneficial Ownership 2014	Special
G20	High-Level Principles on Beneficial Ownership Transparency 2014	Special
APEC	APEC Anti-Corruption Code of Conduct for Business 2007	Special

(*Continued*)

Table 10.1 Continued

Standards and guidelines developed by international intergovernmental organizations, bodies, and public-private initiatives		
Organization	*Standard/guidance*	*General/Special*
Standards and guidelines developed by international non-governmental organizations		
Organization	Standard/guidance	General/Special
ISO	Standard 37001 Anti-Bribery Management Systems – Requirements with Guidance for Use 2016	General
Transparency International	Business Principles for Countering Bribery 2013	General
World Economic Forum	Global Principles for Countering Corruption 2013	General
	Good Practice Guidelines on Conducting Third Party Due Diligence 2016	Special
Standards and guidelines developed by international business associations		
Organization	Standard/guidance	General/Special
ICC	Guidelines on Whistleblowing 2008	Special
	Guidelines on Agents, Intermediaries and Other Third Parties 2010	Special
	Rules on Combating Corruption 2011	General
	Anti-Corruption Clause 2012	Special
	Guidelines on Gifts and Hospitality 2014	Special
	Anti-Corruption Third Party Due Diligence: a Guide for Small and Medium Size Entities 2015	Special
	Guidelines on Conflicts of Interest in Enterprises 2018	Special
Wolfsberg Group	Anti-Bribery and Corruption (ABC) Compliance Programme Guidance 2017	General

Table 10.2 Presents guidelines published by international consultants.

Guidelines developed by international consultants		
Organization	*Guidance*	*General/Special*
NAVEX Global	Definitive Guide to Policy and Procedure Management 2017	Special
	Definitive Guide to Third Party Risk Management 2017	Special
	Definitive Guide to Ethics and Compliance Training 2017	Special
	Definitive Guide to Compliance Programme Assessment 2017	Special

Table 10.3 Includes European Union guidelines and selected domestic guidelines.

European Union guidelines and domestic guidelines from selected jurisdictions	
European Union	Guidelines on non-financial reporting (methodology for reporting non-financial information)
Country	*Guidance*
France	Anti-Corruption Agency's Guidelines to Help Private and Public Sector Entities Prevent and Detect Corruption, Influence Peddling, Extortion by Public Officials, Unlawful Taking of Interest, Misappropriation of Public Funds and Favoritism 2017
United Kingdom	Guidance about Procedures which Relevant Commercial Organisations Can Put into Place to Prevent Persons Associated with Them from Bribing (Section 9 of the Bribery Act 2010) published by the UK Ministry of Justice 2011
United States	A Resource Guide to the US Foreign Corrupt Practices Act published by the Criminal Division of the US Department of Justice and the Enforcement Division of the US Securities and Exchange Commission 2012
	Evaluation of Corporate Compliance Programs published by the Criminal Division of the US Department of Justice 2017

challenges and opportunities for SMEs.[23] The OECD Guidance for African companies identified the specific challenges confronted by SMEs in implementing an anti-bribery policy, related compliance measures and insights on ways to overcome some of those obstacles.[24] The ICC published a special Guide for SMEs on anti-corruption third party due diligence.[25]

Standards and guidelines on anti-corruption or anti-bribery compliance. Bribery is just one of the corruption offences. Most of the standards and guidelines were developed to prevent all kind of corruption offences. However, there are four standards and guidelines that use the term 'anti-bribery compliance' instead of 'anti-corruption compliance.'

The proposed classification includes the FATF standards and several guidelines adopted to support preventing and combating money laundering. Developing standards and guidelines on anti-corruption is not a key area of responsibility for the FATF. At the same time, the FATF Mandate 2012–2020 and the new open-ended Mandate adopted on April 12, 2019 define as one of the FATF tasks 'preparing guidance as needed to facilitate implementation of relevant international

23 UNODC, *An Anti-Corruption Ethics and Compliance Programme for Business: A Practical Guide* (2013).

24 OECD, *Anti-Bribery Policy and Compliance Guidance for African Companies* (2016).

25 ICC, *Anti-Corruption Third Party Due Diligence: A Guide for Small and Medium Size Entities* (2015).

obligations in a manner compatible with the FATF standards (e.g., continuing work on money laundering, terrorism financing, including new and emerging trends, and other misuse of the financial system relating to corruption).'[26] Based on these provisions, the FATF published several guides relevant for anti-corruption. In the author's opinion, general FATF standards can be also helpful for designing anti-corruption compliance programs.

3 Structure and content of anti-corruption compliance standards and guidelines

International standards and guidelines differ significantly in structure, scope, and level of detail. There are several comprehensive standards and guidelines that provide organizations with rather detailed recommendations on designing and implementing anti-corruption/anti-bribery compliance programs. The ISO Standard 37001, the OECD Guidance, the UNODC Guide, the World Bank Group's Guidelines, and the Wolfsberg Group's Guidance for financial institutions should be mentioned in this regard. Many others contain only general principles and brief descriptions of key components of an anti-corruption compliance program.

In general, international standards and guidelines contain recommendations on the following components of anti-corruption compliance:

- Developing an anti-corruption compliance program, including risk assessment (risk mapping), defining applicable laws, principles and values, assessment of available resources, and communication on anti-corruption compliance program;
- Code of Conduct;
- Anti-corruption compliance management system;
- Anti-corruption clause;
- Third party due diligence;
- Third party risk management;
- Mergers and acquisitions;
- Staff recruitment, promotion, and performance evaluation;
- Conflict of interest;
- Gifts and hospitality;
- Charitable donations and sponsorship;
- Political contributions;
- Reporting misconduct and hot lines;
- Internal investigations and addressing violations;
- Cooperation with authorities;
- Training and communication;

26 FATF, *Mandate 2012–2020* [3(f]; FATF, *Mandate 2019* [3(f)].

- Monitoring, review, and evaluation of an anti-corruption compliance program.

There are several components of anti-corruption compliance that are most developed in international and domestic standards and guidelines: risk assessment as a background for designing an anti-corruption compliance program, third party due diligence and risk management, gifts and hospitality, charitable donations and sponsorship, political contributions, and reporting misconduct.

To bring other components to the same level of details, additional efforts of international organizations, and professional anti-corruption community are required. Surprisingly, international standards and guidelines only mention the importance of the Code of Conduct but do not provide organizations with recommendations on the structure and content of the Code. For a long time, the same situation was with conflict of interest management. The UNODC Guide was a rare exception.[27] The ICC Guidelines on Conflicts of Interest in Enterprises were published in 2018 and filled this gap.[28] The anti-corruption compliance requirements for mergers and acquisitions are presented only in the Wolfsberg Group's Guidance for financial institutions[29] and in a Resource Guide to the US Foreign Corrupt Practices Act.[30] However, general recommendations regarding due diligence and risk management are also applicable to mergers and acquisitions.

International standards and guidelines sometimes use different terminology. There are various terms, e.g., defining subjects that implement anti-corruption compliance. The ISO Standard 37001 is addressed to 'organization.' The OECD Guidance and the UNODC Guide use the term 'companies.' The Anti-Corruption Ethics and Compliance Handbook for Business published by OECD/UNODC/World Bank uses the term 'enterprise.'

Usually, standards and guidelines use the term 'risk assessment.' However, some guidelines, e.g., the French Anti-Corruption Agency's Guidelines to Help Private and Public Sector Entities Prevent and Detect Corruption, Influence Peddling, Extortion by Public Officials, Unlawful Taking of Interest, Misappropriation of Public Funds and Favoritism, uses the term 'risk mapping' instead.

Some international standards and guidelines demonstrate a different understanding of the correlation between third party due diligence and risk management. According to the ISO Standard 37001, 'where the organization's bribery risk assessment has assessed a more than low bribery risk in relation to: b) planned or on-going relationships with specific categories of business associates, the organization shall assess the nature and extent of the bribery risk in relation to

27 UNODC (n 23) 49–53.

28 ICC, *Guidelines on Conflicts of Interest in Enterprises* (2018).

29 Wolfsberg Group, *Anti-Bribery and Corruption (ABC) Compliance Programme Guidance* (2017) 9–10.

30 US Department of Justice and US Securities and Exchange Commission (n 16) 62.

specific transactions, projects, activities, business associates and personnel falling within those categories. This assessment shall include any due diligence necessary to obtain sufficient information to assess the bribery risk.'[31] According to the WEF Guidelines, third party risk assessment and risk mitigation are parts of the due diligence process.[32] The OECD Guidance use the term 'risk-based due diligence.'[33]

There is no doubt that due diligence and risk management are closely connected. At the same time, controversial provisions in various standards and guidelines can mislead employees responsible for the relevant functions. In the author's view, conducting risk assessment is hardly possible without at least simplified or standard due diligence. Organizations should collect reliable data first to assess the risk. Based on the risk assessment, organizations can decide whether the enhanced due diligence is required to take a decision on entering into business relationships with a potential partner, and, if necessary, develop appropriate risk mitigation measures.

The definitions proposed by NAVEX Global may be considered to identify the scope of due diligence and risk management. According to NAVEX Global, third-party risk management is the process of assessing and controlling reputational, financial, and legal risks to the organization posed by parties outside the organization. Third party due diligence is the investigative process by which a third party is reviewed to determine any potential concerns involving legal, financial or reputational risks. Due diligence is a disciplined activity that includes reviewing, monitoring, and managing communication over the entire vendor engagement life cycle.[34]

In addition to anti-corruption compliance standards and guidelines, the FATF Standards and guidelines can be considered for risk assessment, and for designing compliance policies on third party due diligence and risk management. They contain useful recommendations on identification of beneficial owners, politically exposed persons and sources of their incomes, high risk jurisdictions, and suspicious transactions.

A hierarchical system of international standards and guidelines does not exist. Organizations may select any general international standard of guidance for certification of compliance programs if service providers offer such an opportunity. We cannot argue that the UNODC Guide is more important than OECD Guidance or ISO Standard 37001.

31 ISO Standard 37001, 15.

32 WEF, *Good Practice Guidelines on Conducting Third Party Due Diligence* (2013) 7.

33 OECD, *Good Practice Guidance on Internal Controls, Ethics and Compliance* (2010) 3.

34 NAVEX Global, *Definitive Guide to Third Party Risk Management* (2017) 2.

4 Benchmarking reports

The idea of benchmarking was developed and pioneered by Xerox Corporation in the 1970s. There are two most comprehensive definitions of the benchmarking. According to Kelessidis, benchmarking is the process of improving performance by continuously identifying, understanding, and adapting outstanding practices and processes found inside and outside an organization.[35] According to Stapenhurst, benchmarking is a method of measuring and improving our organizational performance by comparing ourselves with the best.[36]

Organizations can benchmark anti-corruption compliance programs against international or domestic standards and guidelines, against compliance programs of their peers or against best practices in the same industry or sector. They can benchmark the whole compliance program or just one or several components.

In the context of this study, benchmarking reports should be mentioned as useful tools for designing, implementing, and evaluating anti-corruption compliance programs.

Internationally recognized consultants and law firms published several interesting benchmarking reports on compliance in general or anti-corruption compliance benchmarks. Kroll and NAVEX Global have been conducting benchmarking studies and publishing reports on a regular basis.

The author would suggest consideration of two general studies:

- Anti-Bribery & Corruption Benchmarking Report – 2017;[37]
- Compliance Essentials.[38]

Many other studies are focused on several components of anti-corruption compliance. The key topics of the benchmarking studies are:

- place of compliance in the corporate structure;[39]
- leadership, tone at the top;[40]
- costs of risks and compliance;[41]
- third party due diligence;[42]
- risk management;[43]

35 Vassilis Kelessidis, *Benchmarking: Report Produced for the EC Funded Project 'Innoregio: Dissemination of Innovation Management and Knowledge Techniques'* (Thessaloniki Technology Park 2000) 2

36 Tim Stapenhurst, *The Benchmarking Book: A How-to-Guide to Best Practice for Managers and Practitioners* (Elsevier Ltd 2009) 6.

37 Kroll and Ethisphere Institute, *Anti-Bribery & Corruption Benchmarking Report* (2017).

38 Konstanz Institute on Corporate Governance, *Compliance Essentials* (Taylor Wessing).

39 EY, *Compliance-Studie Aktuelle Trends, Herausforderungen und Benchmarks* (2014).

40 PwC, *State of Compliance Study. Laying a Strategic Foundation for Strong Compliance Risk Management* (2016); Kroll and Ethisphere Institute (n 37).

41 Thomson Reuters, *Cost of Compliance Report 2018* (2018).

42 Kroll and Ethisphere Institute (n 37).

43 PwC, *Risk in Review: Managing Risk from the Front Line* (April 2017).

- oversight and responsibility;[44]
- training and communication;[45]
- hotlines and whistleblowing.[46]

Benchmarking reports do not establish compliance standards. However, they summarize the current best practices, and can cover existing gaps in anti-corruption compliance standards and guidelines. The outcomes of benchmarking studies can be implemented into new standards and guidelines.

5 Conclusion

In the absence of formal legal requirements in many jurisdictions, organizations may use various sources when drafting anti-corruption compliance programs and implementing anti-corruption compliance management systems. Usually, they consider ethical principles and values, international soft law (international standards and guidelines), applicable domestic laws, foreign laws that have transnational application, benchmarking reports and best practices, and compliance programs of the main business partners.

International intergovernmental and non-governmental organizations, business associations, and internationally recognized consultants and law firms have put in a lot of effort to provide organizations with necessary guidelines and to support the implementation of anti-corruption compliance management systems. As a result, more than 30 standards and guidelines on anti-corruption compliance in general or on particular components of an anti-corruption compliance program were published.

The international standards and guidelines are important sources for designing and implementing anti-corruption compliance programs and management systems in organizations. However, it is very challenging for organizations to navigate the current ocean of standards and guidelines.

In the author's opinion, it is time to open discussion on the systematization and codification of existing international standards and guidelines. Codification can simplify the use of standards and guidelines and support implementation of anti-corruption compliance in various jurisdictions.

The international codification may:

- define standardized terms and definitions;
- define the recommended structure of the Code of Conduct and anti-corruption compliance program. The structure may be amended in each particular case considering domestic laws, regulations, and specifics of an organization;
- eliminate certain gaps and contradictions in existing standards and guidelines;

44 PwC, *State of Compliance Study* (n 40).
45 NAVEX Global, *Ethics & Compliance Training Benchmark Report* (2018).
46 NAVEX Global, *Hotline Benchmark Report* (2015). NAVEX Global, *EMEA & APAC Whistleblowing Hotline & Incident Management Benchmark Report* (2017).

- provide detailed recommendations for SMEs taking into account their realities and resources;
- integrate pioneering provisions of recently published domestic guidelines and benchmarking reports;
- integrate applicable recommendations from FATF standards and guidelines developed to prevent and combat money laundering and financing of terrorism.

The codified standard or guideline may be used for:

- drafting domestic laws and regulations on anti-corruption compliance;
- designing and implementing anti-corruption compliance programmes, especially by SMEs;
- support the implementation of anti-corruption compliance in framework of Collective Action initiatives;
- benchmarking of anti-corruption compliance programmes;
- certification of anti-corruption (anti-bribery) compliance programmes (management systems).

The codification process could be led by the most influential international intergovernmental organizations, UNODC and OECD, in the anti-corruption field. The participation of business associations, NGOs and other stakeholders is an important precondition for broad recognition and application of codified standard or guideline.

11 State capture through corruption

How can human rights help?

Jimena Reyes

In Latin America, the early 2000s marked a democratic renewal with the end of internal conflicts and dictatorships, with the exception of Colombia and Cuba. However, today, almost 20 years later, the basis of democratic regimes—an independent judiciary, free and transparent elections, respect for the rule of law, and the state-controlled monopoly on violence—is being profoundly undermined in most Latin American countries. This chapter examines one cause of this undermining: the takeover of the public sphere by private interests through corruption. This threat is not new; it is even inherent to the existence of democracy.

It is useful to gain a better understanding of how this corruption occurs today in Latin American democracies. Indeed, among the various acts which may be described as corrupt, acts intended to capture state institutions are particularly damaging to democracy and the fulfillment of the state's obligation to respect and guarantee human rights. The considerable levels of impunity surrounding cases of corruption in the region reinforce their negative impact.

This chapter seeks to answer the question of how to characterize this capture through corruption. How can we move from empirical description to operational characterization? And finally, could human rights help fight state capture through corruption?

This chapter argues that there is a need to develop the concept of state capture through corruption. It hypothesizes that the prism of inter-American human rights can contribute to a more fully realized description of state capture through corruption and reveal its detrimental impact on the functioning of the state and its society. It also hypothesizes that occurrences of state capture through corruption could trigger Latin American states' responsibility to guarantee the free and full exercise of human rights. In these cases, inter-American case law could contribute to the development of regional standards for states' anti-corruption obligations.

The first section of this chapter summarizes the state of play between the United Nations (UN), the inter-American systems of human rights protection, and the fight against corruption. In particular, it shows that the anti-corruption consensus was built in isolation from the world and concepts of human rights. Likewise, the UN and inter-American systems of human rights protection have shown considerable timidity in dealing with human rights violations resulting from corruption.

In the second section, the chapter develops the concept of state capture through corruption. State capture through corruption is a relatively new and underdeveloped concept, which needs to be defined and distinguished from related notions such as regulatory capture, grand corruption, and kleptocracy. The concept is further developed by examining characteristics common to the following three case studies: (1) Mexico and organized crime in Coahuila and Texas; (2) Nicaragua and the awarding of megaprojects to a Chinese company; and (3) embezzlement in Guatemala's customs and duty service.

These three examples are emblematic of state capture through corruption in Latin America. Indeed, they illustrate the different groups involved in this kind of corruption—organized crime (Mexico example), a foreign company (Nicaragua example), and top-level state representatives (Guatemala example). These case studies also illustrate the main methods of corruption (bribes and embezzlement) and give examples of the impact these corrupt acts may have on human rights violations.

In the third and final section, we show how inter-American human rights case law could help better describe state capture through corruption and address its human rights impact by engaging the state's responsibility under international human rights law. Indeed, there are many academic articles on the question of the negative impact of corruption on human rights, but very few deal with issues of hard law and how corrupt acts can engage the responsibility of the state.

We will argue that the duty to prevent human rights violations resulting from the obligation to guarantee to all persons the free and full exercise of the rights and freedoms contained in the American Convention on Human Rights (ACHR) could constitute a basis for engaging the state's responsibility for acts of state capture through corruption.

1 The fight against corruption and the international system for protecting human rights: a slow awakening

While a broad consensus exists today within international governance bodies of the need to fight corruption, this does not translate into powerful, effective international instruments for monitoring cases of corruption, and even less for sanctioning states that fail to vigorously fight corruption. Until 2015, international and regional systems for safeguarding human rights played a purely rhetorical role when it came to countering the negative impact of corruption on human rights.

1.1 Weak consensus and fragmented international law in the fight against corruption

As a number of academics have shown, the need to fight corruption in the 20th century was not always self-evident.[1] It is, therefore, worth noting that at the

1 Susan Rose-Ackerman, *Corruption and Government: Causes, Consequences, and Reform* (CUP 2016); Robin Theobald, 'So What Really is the Problem about Corruption' (1999) 20 Third World Quarterly 491; James Gathii, 'Defining the Relationship between Human Rights and Corruption' (2009) 31 University of Pennsylvania Journal of International Law 125.

moment when the two principal treaties on protecting human rights were being negotiated and ratified—the International Covenant on Civil and Political Rights (ICCPR) and the International Covenant on Economic, Social and Cultural Rights (ICESCR)—the international community perceived the phenomenon of corruption as inevitable and even, in the view of some, useful. Thus, in 1968 Samuel Huntington in *Political Order in Changing Societies* wrote:

> In terms of economic growth, the only thing worse than a society with a rigid, overcentralized, dishonest bureaucracy is one with a rigid, overcentralized, honest bureaucracy. A society which is relatively uncorrupt – a traditional society for instance where traditional norms are still powerful – may find a certain amount of corruption a welcome lubricant easing the path to modernization.

It is only from the 1990s that one can talk of the birth of an anti-corruption consensus. Rose-Ackerman[2] attributed the emergence of this consensus to two events: the end of the Cold War, which reduced the incentives for more powerful countries to tolerate corruption in their allies, and the transition from a centrally planned economy to market economies, which opened up new opportunities for both licit and illicit profits. Other factors included the accelerated globalization and the 1977 US Foreign Corrupt Practices Act (FCPA), which criminalized overseas bribery and pressured governments to reduce unfair dealing and firms to re-examine their overseas practices.[3] The founding[4] of Transparency International (TI) and the publication of its corruption perception index, which caused alarm and anger among poorly rated countries is also considered a relevant factor. Finally, the intellectual underpinnings of development policy began to recognize the key role of public institutions. Development economists started to look to the field of political science and sociology and incorporated work on the functioning of institutions into their conceptual frameworks. In doing so, development economists described corruption as a particularly obvious pathology.[5] Thus, this consensus arose also from the evolving agenda promoted by the Bretton Woods institutions, which from 1992 onwards placed good governance at the center of development policies. Corruption was considered an indicator of poor governance and thus an obstacle to the proper functioning of the economy.

2 Rose-Ackerman (n 1) 6.

3 Gathii also recalls the importance of the non-aligned will in the 1970s to curb multinational corporation bribery within the UN, in a context of discussions on a 'New International Economic Order' that was then rejected in particular by the US, but led to the FCPA. James Gathii (n 1) 138–41.

4 Transparency International was founded in 1993 and the first perception index was launched in 1995: see Transparency International, 'Overview' <https://www.transparency.org/research/cpi/overview> accessed 1 June 2020.

5 Rose-Ackerman (n 1).

The beginnings of this consensus in the 1990s led to the negotiation and subsequent ratification of various international anti-corruption texts,[6] including two ratified by most Latin American countries: the Inter-American Convention Against Corruption[7] (IACAC), which came into force on March 6, 1997 and was ratified by 33 States, and the United Nations Convention against Corruption[8] (UNCAC), which came into force in 2005 and has been ratified by almost every country in the world.

The negotiations for these two conventions clearly prioritized a broad consensus on the strength of the obligations of states.[9] In summary, the conventions focus mostly on the obligation or possibility for a ratifying state to include a certain number of offenses as acts of corruption in its criminal code. They set out how cooperation between states operates (particularly through extradition and mutual legal assistance), and they provide options for preventative action and mandatory rules on asset recovery. The mechanisms for verifying that the obligations contained in the conventions are respected are weak and the sanctions for lack of respect non-existent.[10]

In addition to international conventions, the past 15 years have seen the emergence of numerous voluntary initiatives, including those issued by international financial institutions, company initiatives—for example, relating to extractive businesses ('publish what you pay')—and also individual sanction mechanisms introduced by countries like the United States. All of this has led to an anti-corruption global governance that is still embryonic and highly fragmented.

6 European Union, 'Convention Drawn Up on the Basis of Article K.3 of the Treaty on European Union, on the Protection of the European Communities' (1995) Financial Interests 49; Convention on Combating Bribery of Foreign Public Officials in International Business Transactions (adopted 17 December 1997, entered into force 15 February 1999) 37 ILM 1 (OECD Convention); Council of Europe Criminal Law Convention on Corruption, ETS No.173, 27 January 1999; Council of Europe Civil Law Convention on Corruption, ETS No.174, 4 November 1999; Additional Protocol to the Criminal Law Convention on Corruption, ETS No. 191, 15 May 2003; Southern African Development Community, Protocol against Corruption, opened for signature 14 August 2001; African Union Convention on Preventing and Combating Corruption (adopted 11 July 2003) (2004) 43 ILM 5.

7 Inter-American Convention against Corruption (entered into force 6 March 1997) 35 ILM 724.

8 United Nations Convention against Corruption (opened for signature 9 December 2003, entered into force 14 December 2005) 2349 UNTS 41.

9 Martine Boersma, *Corruption: A Violation of Human Rights and a Crime under International Law?* (Intersentia 2012) 64; Peter Schroth, 'The United Nations Convention Against Doing Anything Serious About Corruption' (2005) 12 Journal of Legal Studies in Business 1. Schroth considers that the provisions of the UN Convention on asset recovery are close enough to what they should be but the remainder of the articles does not provide international standards, many of the mandatory clauses will have little impact either; consensus was achieved to make them mandatory in the UN convention because they only reiterate obligations already existing in other international agreements.

10 Roberto de Michele, 'The Follow-Up Mechanism of the Inter-American Convention against Corruption: A Preliminary Assessment: Is the Glass Half Empty' (2004) 10 Southwestern Journal of Law & Trade in the Americas 295.

1.2 The slow awakening of the United Nations and the Inter-American human rights' protection systems

In 2003, at a time when discussions on the United Nations Convention Against Corruption were reaching their final stages, the United Nations Human Rights Commission, superseded by the Human Rights Council, began considering corruption and its impact on the full enjoyment of human rights. It commissioned a three-year mandate for a Special Rapporteur on corruption and human rights[11] and created a new Advisory Committee of the Human Rights Council.[12] Its 2015[13] final report on the question of the negative impact of corruption on the enjoyment of human rights, unlike previous reports, explicitly recognized that acts of corruption may constitute violations of human rights, thus making the state accountable under the 'respect, protect, fulfil' framework.[14]

Between 1994 and 2012, treaty bodies have referred to the negative impact of corruption on the enjoyment of human rights 131 times, and stressed in their recommendations the importance of combating this scourge.[15] No reference has been made to human rights violations as a result of corruption, but the vocabulary used by these bodies rarely refers to violations and instead describes the negative impacts of corruption and their concerns regarding them.

Out of the 182 States reviewed between 2007 and 2017 by the Human Rights Committee, one of the committees which has most often mentioned corruption in its observations, 39 Concluding Observations mention corruption (21%). Of those 39, 32 fall under Article 14 (rights relating to the judiciary).[16]

Compared to the UN system, the inter-American system of human rights protection has made very few references to the links between acts of corruption and human rights violations. Prior to 2017, the only mention of this link was found in two Inter-American Commission of Human Rights (IACHR) reports.[17] As we will see in section 3, the Inter-American Court of Human rights

11 OHCHR, *Report of Ms. Christy Mbonu, Special Rapporteur on Corruption and Its Impact on the Full Enjoyment of Human Rights* (Human Rights Council, 11th Session, UN Doc. A/HRC/11/CRP.1, 2–19 June 2009).

12 See, e.g., Human Rights Commission, Res. E/CN.4/Sub.2/2005/18; Human Rights Council Res 23/9, Rep. of the Human Rights Council, 23rd Sess., A/HRC/RES/23/9 (7 June 2013).

13 UN General Assembly, *Final Report of the Human Rights Council Advisory Committee on the Issue of the Negative Impact of Corruption on the Enjoyment of Human Rights* (UN Doc. A/HRC/28/73, 5 January 2015).

14 UN General Assembly, *Final Report of the Human Rights Council Advisory Committee on the Issue of the Negative Impact of Corruption on the Enjoyment of Human Rights* (UN Doc. A/HRC/28/73, 5 January 2015) [7], [9].

15 Boersma (n 9) ch 3.

16 This section relies heavily on Làzarie Eeckeloo, *The Human Rights Committee and Its Approach to Corruption* (Centre for Civil and Political Rights 2018).

17 OAS, *Annual Report of the Inter-American Commission on Human Rights 2005* (OEA/Ser.L/V/II.124, 27 February 2006); OAS, *Tercer Informe sobre la Situación de los Derechos Humanos en Paraguay 2001* (OEA/Ser./L/VII.110, 9 March 2001), devoting an entire

(IACrtHR) has mentioned corruption at least eight times in its rulings but has never acknowledged a violation of human rights or an obligation caused by facts of corruption alone.

Since 2017, an awareness has emerged within inter-American and universal[18] human rights systems. The IACHR issued two resolutions, one[19] in support of the Commission Against Impunity in Guatemala (CICIG) and a second in 2018[20] prior to the meeting of the General Assembly of the Organization of American States (OAS), where the central theme was the fight against corruption. That resolution underlines:

> Dismayed because corruption prevails, *the actors involved establish structures that capture state entities*, through different criminal schemes …
>
> Aware … That *under the inter-American legal framework, States have the duty to adopt legislative, administrative and other measures to guarantee the exercise of human rights against the violations and restrictions caused by the phenomenon of corruption.*

We have clearly reached a turning point, where the UN and OAS human rights institutions and civil society are discussing the issue of how human rights can contribute to the fight against corruption. It is in this context that we seek to develop the notion of state capture through corruption and then seek to reflect on how inter-American case law might chart the impact of corruption on human rights.

2 State capture through corruption: developing the concept

The objective of this section is to contribute to the definition of the social sciences concept of state capture through corruption by examining recent examples from Latin America. As this concept is relatively new and not very developed, it will first need to be distinguished from related concepts.

chapter to the question of corruption, particularly underlining the link with impunity and the impact of corruption on the fulfillment of social, economic and cultural rights.

18 OCHR, 'Workshop on Preventing and Fighting against Corruption' <https://www.ohchr.org/EN/Issues/CorruptionAndHR/Pages/WorkshopPreventingFightingAgainstCorruption.aspx> accessed 1 June 2020.

19 OAS, *Resolucíon 1/17 Derechos Humanos y Lucha contra la Impunidad y la Corrupcíon* (12 September 2017).

20 OAS, *Resolution 1/18 Corruption and Human Rights* (16 March 2018). See also CIDH, *Institucionalidad Democrática, Estado de Derecho y Derechos Humanos En Venezuela* (17 February 2018).

2.1 Existing concepts and definitions of grand corruption, kleptocracy, and state capture through corruption

International anti-corruption conventions do not give a definition of corruption. What these conventions do contain is a list of offenses occasionally included under the explicit umbrella of the concept of corruption. The offenses differ between conventions but always include bribery and embezzlement. The precise definition of corruption (even beyond the legal sphere) is subject to much debate.[21] We do not engage in this debate. We acknowledge the fluidity inherent in the overarching concept of corruption at the international level and use the term corruption in accordance with the basic social sciences definition where corruption is the abuse of public or entrusted[22] power for private gain.[23] In academic literature, this definition is often presented together with numerous typologies, which lend greater precision. One of the most common is the distinction between grand corruption and petty corruption.

The standard example of petty corruption is the police officer who demands a bribe in return for not imposing a fine. The standard example of grand corruption is the embezzlement of important amounts of public funds by a high-ranking public official or politician. Most definitions of these two notions base the distinction between grand and petty corruption on the amounts of private gain (i.e., scale) and/or on the public official corrupted (i.e., high level/low level). For example, Rose-Ackerman[24] defines grand corruption as high-level payments to government officials in the procurement process or as embezzling of state funds, and petty corruption as small payments to public officials that citizens hand over in the process of everyday public affairs.[25] Transparency International distinguishes between these two notions in terms both of their scale and impact.[26] The organization finds that grand corruption occurs when

> a public official or other person deprives a particular social group or substantial part of the population or a State of a fundamental right; or causes the State or any of its people a loss greater than 100 times the annual minimum

21 Rose-Ackerman (n 1).

22 There is a debate, which we will not get into, as to whether it should be 'entrusted power,' thus including possible corruption in private relations, or 'public power.' This chapter deals here only with cases of corruption involving public agents, thus we hereafter refer to 'public power.'

23 First formulated in 1931 as 'Corruption is the Misuse of Public Power for Private Gain.' See Joseph J Senturia, *Encyclopedia of Social Sciences*, vol VI (1967).

24 Rose-Ackerman (n 1).

25 See also Johann Lambsdorff, *The Institutional Economics of Corruption and Reform: Theory, Evidence and Policy* (CUP 2007).

26 Transparency International, 'What Is Grand Corruption and How Can We Stop It?' <https://www.transparency.org/news/feature/what_is_grand_corruption_and_how_can_we_stop_it> accessed 1 June 2020.

subsistence income of its people; as a result of bribery, embezzlement or other corruption offence.

We argue that this definition of grand corruption is less useful for human rights entities, despite its mention of fundamental rights. State capture is an easier concept to leverage for vindicating rights.

The World Bank developed the concept of state capture at the beginning of the 21st century to evaluate the governance of Eastern European countries transitioning from communism. After 2005, it was only used sporadically by the World Bank.

The World Bank defined state capture as firms shaping the formation of the basic rules of the game (i.e., laws, rules, decrees, and regulations) through illicit and non-transparent private payments to public officials and politicians[27] to obtain unjustified revenue from the state.[28] The World Bank contrasts this with administrative corruption, which it defines as private payments to public officials to distort the prescribed implementation of official rules and policies.[29] This classification, by distinguishing between state capture and administrative corruption, places the emphasis on the objective of corruption. In the case of state capture, the content of the rules of the game must be influenced, while for administrative corruption the application of those rules is distorted.

World Bank officials have made clear that although they focus solely on businesses, other actors can also be behind state capture.[30] They consider that executive, legislative, and judicial power are equally likely to be captured and that the concept of state capture may be included in the wider one of grand corruption.[31]

Lastly, the World Bank explains that the definition of state capture is derived from the concept of regulatory capture, already well established in economics literature: state regulatory agencies are said to be captured when they regulate businesses in accordance with the private interests of those regulated as opposed to the public interest for which they were established.[32] The economist George

27 Joel S Hellman, Geraint Jones, and Daniel Kaufmann, 'Seize the State, Seize the Day: State Capture, Corruption and Influence in Transition' (The World Bank 2000) 6.

28 James Anderson and others, 'Anticorruption in Transition: A Contribution to the Policy Debate' (The World Bank 2000) xvi.

29 Hellman, Jones, and Kaufmann (n 27); James Anderson and others (n 28). In this first document, the World Bank equates administrative corruption with petty corruption but it later explained that at the root of this form of corruption is public officials' discretion to grant selective exemptions, to prioritize the delivery of public services, or to discriminate in the application of rules and regulations. As scale is not the distinguishing criterion, administrative corruption seems to us wider than petty corruption.

30 Hellman, Jones, and Kauffman (n 27) n 3.

31 Ibid 7.

32 Anderson and others (n 28) 3.

Stigler is acknowledged as having developed the concept of regulatory capture in economics.[33]

State capture, as defined by the World Bank, is a broader concept than regulatory capture in that it encompasses the formation of law, rules, and decrees by a wider range of state institutions than simply regulatory agencies, i.e., the executive, the legislature, and the judiciary. At the same time, it has a narrower definition in that it focuses exclusively on the illicit and non-transparent provision of private benefits to public officials to influence the formation of laws, regulations, decrees, and other government policies to their own advantage.[34]

When mentioning 'state capture' or 'state capture through corruption,' we are referring to the same concept as that defined by the World Bank as state capture. It is important to make this clear as, in addition to the neighboring concept of regulatory capture, Transparency International and civil society often use the concept of state capture as encompassing both state capture through corruption and through other means. Transparency International thus explains in its glossary:

> As such, state capture can broadly be understood as the disproportionate and unregulated influence of interest groups or decision-making processes, where special interest groups manage to bend state laws, policies and regulations through practices such as illicit contributions paid by private interests to political parties and for election campaigns, parliamentary vote-buying, buying of presidential decrees or court judgments, as well as through illegitimate lobbying and revolving door appointments. State capture can also arise from the more subtle close alignment of interests between specific business and political elites through family ties, friendship and the intertwined ownership of economic assets.[35]

State capture through corruption must also be distinguished from the notion of kleptocracy. Kleptocracy comes from the Greek *klepto* meaning to steal and *cratie* meaning authority. It is used to refer to a political system founded entirely on the corruption of a leader or group of leaders. The first mention of the term in its current accepted form seems to originate in Stanislav Andreski's 1966 work *Parasitism and Subversion: The Case of Latin America*, in which he called it a 'self-explanatory neologism.' Subsequently, in his 1968 book *The African Predicament*, he described a system where 'the ruling classes of the recently independent ex-colonies had little if any loyalty to the countries for which they

33 Daniel P Carpenter and David A Moss, *Preventing Regulatory Capture: Special Interest Influence and How to Limit It* (CUP 2014).

34 Anderson and others (n 28) 18.

35 Transparency International, *State Capture: An Overview* (12 March 2014) 8.

worked, instead prioritizing ties to their tribes or families.'[36] More recently, Rose-Ackerman[37] categorized highly corrupt states under four types based on economic analysis and political economics, stressing the differences in opportunities and bargaining power. The nature of corruption depends not only on the organization of government but also on the organization and power of private actors. For Rose-Ackerman, the critical issue is how much bargaining power the government and the private sector have in dealing with one another. The four categories are: (1) kleptocracy; (2) bilateral monopolies; (3) mafia-dominated states; and (4) competitive bribery. In short, when speaking of kleptocracy, she refers solely to dictatorships and distinguishes between the strong kleptocrat, who runs a brutal but efficient state limited only by his or her own ability to make credible commitments, and the weak kleptocrat, who runs an intrusive and inefficient state organized to extract bribes from the population and the business community.[38]

Three elements differentiate the concept of state capture through corruption from the notion of kleptocracy. Firstly, while kleptocracy is used to describe dictatorial regimes, state capture through corruption refers to democratic albeit dysfunctional regimes. Secondly, the notion can also be used when only a structure of the state is captured, which is not the case with a kleptocracy. Thirdly, the notion of kleptocracy focuses more on the leader or leaders who accumulate wealth by plundering the state, while state capture concentrates particularly on third parties who succeed in capturing part of the state. The line between the two notions may however be blurred, and one may imagine a state where many structures are captured by the same kleptocratic elites, thereby becoming a kleptocracy.

A typology that differentiates between the concepts of state capture through corruption and administrative or petty corruption should have a greater presence in social sciences and in debates about corruption and human rights. It seems more useful for human rights analysis than, for example, the typology based on petty and grand corruption. Firstly, because for state capture through corruption, the seriousness of the situation comes not from the importance of the amount of money involved in the corruption or how high in the hierarchy the person corrupted is, but from a precise impact: the capture of a state structure. This also points to one of the possible links between corruption and human rights: the impact corruption has on the functioning of the state and, in some cases, on the obligation of the state to guarantee the full and free enjoyment of human rights that belong to citizens. Secondly, the measurement of capture and its description gives a more detailed view of the organization and responsibilities not

36 As explained in Oliver Bullough, 'The Dark Side of Globalization' (2018) 29 Journal of Democracy 25.

37 Rose-Ackerman (n 1) ch 8.

38 Ibid 282. When describing kleptocracies, Rose-Ackerman gives the examples of the following dictatorships: Alfredo Stroessner in Paraguay 1954–1989, Mobutu Sese Seko in Zaire 1965–1997, Jean-Claude Duvalier in Haiti 1957–1986, Hosni Mubarak in Egypt 1981 and Zine El Abidine Ben Ali in Tunisia 1987–2011.

only for the facts of corruption but also for the capture of the state or one of its structures. Finally, the concept of state capture through corruption is also useful to distinguish between systematic (organized) corruption (which may lead to state capture) and widespread (uncoordinated) corruption. Both have a negative impact on the functioning of the state but this distinction may help refine public policies and accountability strategies against those phenomena.

We will examine three examples of state capture through corruption in Latin America to develop the current definition.

2.2 Case studies

2.2.1 Case 1: Corruption and forced disappearances in Coahuila, Mexico

Coahuila is one of the five northern Mexican states bordering the United States and, as such, is an important and contested zone for criminal organizations involved in trafficking activities.

In 2009, the Zetas, a recent cartel of their own, entered the scene in order to lay claim to the territory of Coahuila.[39] The Zetas included a group of army deserters who had been trained in counter-insurgency tactics for use against the Zapatista uprising. They adopted a strategy to eliminate their perceived enemy and display their violence. This method became the hallmark of the Zetas' actions and transformed them into the most violent group in the country.[40] Anyone could be considered their enemy, including those who did not collaborate with the Zetas' activities and any innocent person whose disappearance could contribute to reinforcing their control.[41] The Zetas' strategy was also to take control of institutions by corrupting municipalities, their police, the government of Coahuila, the security forces, and the judiciary.[42]

39 Aguayo Quezada Sergio, *En El Desamparo: Los Zetas, El Estado, La Sociedad y Las víctimas De San Fernando, Tamaulipas (2010), y Allende, Coahuila (2011)* (El Colegio de México, Centro de Estudios Internacionales 2016) 11–14 <http://eneldesamparo.colmex.mx/> accessed 1 June 2020. Arturo Rodriguez, 'La batalla de Torreón' *El Diario de Coahuila* (24 February 2008) <http://www.eldiariodecoahuila.com.mx/locales/2008/2/24/batalla-torreon-88075.html> accessed I June 2020.

40 Jan Martínez Ahrens, 'Silencio, aquí se mata' *El País* (8 June 2016) <https://elpais.com/internacional/2014/07/05/actualidad/1404594964_269006.html> accessed 1 June 2020.

41 International Federation for Human Rights, Centro Diocesano para los derechos humanos Fray Juan de Larios, Familias unidas para nuestros desaparecidos, *Mexico, Coahuila: Ongoing Crimes against Humanity* (2017).

42 Eduardo Guerrero Gutiérrez, 'El dominio del miedo' *Nexos* (1 July 2014) <https://www.nexos.com.mx/?p=21671> accessed 1 June 2020. See also Guillermo Vázquez Del Mercado, *Organization Attributes Sheet: Los Zetas* (Ridgway Research 2012) 3. Regarding the Zetas' objective of obtaining territorial control, also see the report, Open Society Justice Initiative, *Atrocidades Innegables. Confrontando crímenes de lesa humanidad en México* (2016) 97–98.

In trials in San Antonio, Austin, and Del Rio in Texas, testimonies against members of the Zetas have demonstrated that the whole chain of public forces from the state of Coahuila supported this criminal group in exchange for money.[43] High-level government, security, and judicial officials profited from millions of dollars in return for helping or allowing the Zetas to commit their crimes without being prosecuted. Low-level security forces worked for the Zetas, and some formed part of their hierarchy, receiving monthly salaries from the cartel.[44]

Between 2009 and 2016, 1,886 persons disappeared in Coahuila.[45] Most of the disappearances that occurred between 2009 and 2011 had the same *modus operandi*: they began with arbitrary detentions by state forces, without any judicial order or warrant, and led to persons being handed to the Zetas and never seen again.[46]

2.2.2 *Case 2: Nicaragua, the concession awarded to Wang Jing[47] for several megaprojects*

In 2013, Chinese entrepreneur Wang Jing obtained a rare multiple concession agreement with the Nicaraguan government through his company HK Nicaragua Development Investment (HKND). This concession agreement allowed for the development and operation of different megaprojects including canals, railways, an oil pipeline, deep-water ports, free trade zones, airports, and a hydroelectric plant, with unrestricted rights for at least 116 years over priceless land, territories, and natural resources, including majestic Lake Nicaragua (Cocibolca), Central America's primary freshwater reserve. The absence of competitive tendering, the inexperience of the investor who was awarded the concession agreement, in conjunction with the leonine character of the contracts that were signed with the Nicaraguan State and the existence and indirect involvement of a web of at least 15 shell companies (registered in Nicaragua, the Cayman Islands, the Netherlands, Hong Kong, and Beijing) all point to the possibility of a corrupt scheme centered on the canal concession agreement. At the time of the approval, the project was estimated to cost $50 billion.[48]

43 Anna Smulders and others, *'Control ... Over the Entire State of Coahuila', an Analysis of Testimonies in Trials against Zeta Members in San Antonio, Austin and Del Rio, Texas* (Human Rights Clinic, University of Texas School of Law 2017).

44 Ibid.

45 Federación Internacional por los Derechos Humanos, *México: Asesinatos, desapariciones y torturas en Coahuila de Zaragoza constituyen crímenes de lesa humanidad* (2017).

46 International Federation for Human Rights, Centro Diocesano para los derechos humanos Fray Juan de Larios, Familias unidas para nuestros desaparecidos (n 41) 40–60.

47 According to the documents available, Wang Jing is the sole or main shareholder (and other minority shareholders appear to comply only with the commercial regulations of the country of registration) in the 15 companies relating to the canal concession. Henceforth we will refer to 'the investor,' meaning any company affiliated to Wang Jing or Wang Jing himself.

48 ERM, *Canal de Nicaragua Estudio de Impacto Ambiental y Social* (2015).

The National Assembly of Nicaragua voted to create a special legal framework under Law 840 to allow HKND Group to execute different agreements between the various companies and the Nicaraguan government.[49] The legal framework excludes the application of the constitutional and legal guarantees that protect the interests of the Nicaraguan State and its citizens, including with respect to property rights, water concessions and free, prior and informed consent. Since 2013, the State has penalized several leaders opposed to the construction of the inter-oceanic canal or to the whole concession agreement. Violent repression, criminal charges, arrest warrants, and public vilification have been used to delegitimize communities' mobilizations against the canal.[50] The state also intensified the police and military presence in the affected areas with checkpoints, searches, and other measures reinforcing the continual presence of armed government agents. A migration policy was also put in place permitting the expulsion of foreign nationals with any links to the area affected by the concession, whether they were researchers, journalists, or human rights campaigners.[51]

Since April 2018, following an important demonstration unrelated to the canal project, this same repressive policy has been extended to the entire territory and state violence has dramatically intensified. In three months, 300 demonstrators were shot dead by soldiers or militias while more than 500 people were arbitrarily detained.[52] Many mark April 2018 as the date when the State of Nicaragua became a dictatorship.[53]

2.2.3 Case 3: Corruption and the diverting of funds in the Línea case in Guatemala

This case relates to a corruption network in a multimillion-dollar customs fraud scheme. It led to the 2015 indictment of Guatemala's former Vice-president Roxana Baldetti, former President Otto Pérez Molina, and more than 20 other persons for the crimes of passive bribery, conspiracy, and customs fraud. Public outrage forced the resignation and indictment of the President and Vice-President of Guatemala after months of demonstrations.[54]

49 *Ley* N° 840—*Ley especial para el desarrollo de infraestructura y transporte nicaragüense atingente a El Canal, zonas de libre comercio e infraestructuras asociadas* 2013 (Nicaragua).

50 Mõnica López Baltonado, Vilma Nuñez, Jimena Reyes, *Nicaragua: Government Must Revoke the Interoceanic Canal Concession* (2016).

51 Arlen Cerda, 'Ortega ha expulsado de Nicaragua a 25 extranjeros' *Confidencial* (29 June 2016) <http://confidencial.com.ni/ortega-ha-expulsado-de-nicaragua-a-25-extranjeros/> accessed 1 June 2020.

52 OAS, *Nicaragua: Gross Human Rights Violations in the Context of Social Protests* OEA/Ser.L/V/II (21 June 2018).

53 Rafael Solis, 'Texto íntegro de la carta de renuncia de Rafael Solís' *Nicaragua Investiga* (11 January 2019) <https://www.nicaraguainvestiga.com/nicaragua-investiga-reproduce-de-manera-integra-la-carta-de-renuncia-de-rafael-solis/> accessed 1 June 2020.

54 Azam Ahmed and Elisabeth Malkin, 'Otto Pérez Molina of Guatemala Is Jailed Hours after Resigning Presidency' *The New York Times* (3 September 2015) <https://www.nytimes.

In the corruption network, companies called a special phone number and corrupted customs staff would reduce the amount of the tariffs to be paid in exchange for bribes.[55] Importers with goods being processed through the fairly long bureaucratic process of customs taxes would be able to use this scheme. The importers had to call a telephone number, 'The Linea,' to use this service. The leaders of the network would share the money. Middle and lower management took 39% of the profits, and the high commands, composed of former President Otto Pérez Molina, former Vice President Roxana Baldetti, the private secretary of the Vice Presidency, Juan Carlos Monzón, and the head of the external structure, Estuardo González, took 61% of the profits.[56] The network earned approximately $300,000 every week.

In the indictment of Otto Pérez Molina, the judge stressed that in the Superintendency of Tax Administration (SAT), an internal and an external structure was formed, composed of approximately 50 people whose objective was to benefit monetarily through this customs scheme by undervaluing merchandise and facilitating the entry of containers. The judge added that the purpose of this structure was to control the SAT and its dependencies, which included technicians, heads of customs, human resources, and the Superintendent of Customs, so that members of the corrupt network could obtain a percentage of money.[57]

2.3 *How these examples contribute to the notion of state capture through corruption*

The three cases reinforce Hellman's definition of state capture through corruption. They also help articulate additional criteria for identifying certain practices as state capture through corruption.

2.3.1 The state capture

Who is behind the capture of the state structure? Hellman specifies that actors other than companies may be behind the capture of state structures. In the three examples, these actors are the Zetas' cartel, the HKND Group, and the

com/2015/09/04/world/americas/otto-perez-molina-guatemalan-president-resigns-amid-scandal.html> accessed 1 June 2020; CICIG, 'A prisión preventiva ex presidente Otto Pérez Molina' (8 September 2015) <https://www.cicig.org/casos/a-prision-preventiva-ex-presidente-otto-perez-molina/> accessed 1 June 2020.

55 CICIG, 'Caso la línea: A juicio expresidente y exvicepresidenta' (27 October 2017) <https://www.cicig.org/casos/caso-la-linea-a-juicio-expresidente-y-exvicepresidenta/> accessed 1 June 2020.

56 CICIG, 'A prisión preventiva ex presidente Otto Pérez molina' (n 54).

57 Oswaldo J Hernández, 'Otto Pérez Molina o la resignación del expresidente' *Plaza Pública* (8 September 2015) <http://www.plazapublica.com.gt/content/otto-perez-molina-o-la-resignacion-del-expresidente> accessed 1 June 2020.

Guatemalan President, Vice-president, and customs staff. The actors consist of organized crime, companies, and kleptocratic elites.

How was state capture through corruption executed? In answer to this question, one needs to distinguish between the corruption facts, the capture, and the link between the two. Hellman's original definition refers to only one category of corruption, namely illicit and non-transparent payments to public officials and politicians.

The three Latin American examples offer a broader range of acts of corruption. There are the monthly or one-off payments to the police and governor respectively in the Mexican example, and the embezzlement of public funds in the Guatemalan example. In contrast, in the Nicaraguan example, as often happens in corruption cases, there are elements that point to the possible existence of acts of corruption but no proof, and thus, no information on the nature of the possible corruption.

This chapter suggests that the definition of state capture through corruption should include the embezzlement of public funds and any other offence mentioned in international anti-corruption conventions, in addition to illicit and non-transparent payments to public officials and politicians (as contained in Hellman's original definition).

Besides the acts constituting criminal offences, we believe that the existence of a covert, coordinated network is at the heart of the notion of capture. This also distinguishes it from generalized, uncoordinated corruption, which can weaken a state or a public structure (like a prison where most guards are corrupted for their own interest, for example) but is different from capture. However, the original definition does not mention the existence of a network. Instead, it refers to illicit and non-transparent private payments (i.e., to the corruption offences) and capture is only characterized by the effect or aim of corruption.

The existence of a covert, coordinated network is an important part of the process of state capture through corruption, and an element that should be added to the prevailing definition. This covert network can, but does not have to be, an element of the corruption offence, i.e., the network may concern only the process of capture.

The Guatemalan case involved a secret network of at least 20 people, each of whom played a part in the embezzlement and the capture. In the Coahuila example, the cartel members judged in Texas have given information on how the coordination between state representatives and the Zetas cartel would function, describing, in particular, the distribution of bribes and the contribution or inaction of the police when the crimes were committed.[58]

While we have very little information on how the Nicaraguan case transpired, we do know that the executive power made the main decision to grant the concession and Ortega's son led the negotiation with the HKND Group. A legislative assembly dominated by Orteguists also voted for Law 840, and the Supreme Court rejected all the actions challenging both the law and the

58 CICIG, 'Caso la línea: A juicio expresidente y exvicepresidenta' (n 55).

concession. In 2016, it seemed that the HKND Group had captured various state structures, probably through corruption in favor of the Orteguist, in order to obtain favorable conditions for revenue and control over key territories. In early 2019,[59] it seemed that the Ortega Murillo network(s) had become a dictatorial regime.[60] In 2016, the Nicaraguan case was at the frontier between state capture through corruption and kleptocracy with an operating network functioning well beyond the HKND concession. It is now in a clear kleptocracy.

2.3.2 The purpose of corruption

The original definition considers that state capture through corruption focuses on the ability to decisively influence how the rules of the game are formulated to obtain unjustified revenue from the state. However, state capture through corruption goes beyond this. For example, in cases of state capture by organized crime like the case of Coahuila, the ultimate objective is not to extract revenue from the state but from a criminal activity. Corruption buys the complicity of the state in the crimes committed and the control over a territory, which, in principle, the state should exert. Here, capture seeks to ensure that the state acts in the interests of a third-party captor in order for the captor(s) to obtain money illegally.

More generally, the aim of state capture through corruption is to permanently deflect the state or a structure of the state from its objective of acting in the general interest. Though most acts of corruption are intended to deflect state action from the public interest, one of the elements that distinguishes state capture through corruption is the lasting impact on the general interest that state capture will have. This element is a clear feature in the examples of Coahuila, Guatemala, and Nicaragua.

The exact definition of 'general interest' is subject to much debate. However, a state making individuals disappear, diverting customs duties on a massive scale, or awarding a leonine contract that harms state interests undeniably acts contrary to the general interest.

2.3.3 Suggesting a new definition of state capture through corruption

The three Latin American examples demonstrate gaps in Hellman's original definition of state capture through corruption. We propose four elements to define the phenomena:

59 European Parliament resolution of 14 March 2019 on the situation in Nicaragua (2019/2615(RSP)).

60 See, for example, the letter of resignation of Rafael Solis, Judge from the Supreme Court of Nicaragua: Solis, 'Texto íntegro de la carta de renuncia de Rafael Solís' (n 53).

1. owing to acts of corruption (bribery, embezzlement, or any offence defined in the international conventions against corruption or any act of abuse of public or entrusted power for private gain);
2. committed through a covert coordination at least among state representatives who benefit from the acts of corruption;
3. captor(s) decisively influence the formulation of the state's rules of the game to ensure unjustified revenue from the state or make the state complicit in criminal activities in order for the captor(s) to obtain money illegally; and
4. these three elements result in a state structure or the whole state diverting durably from the general interest.

These elements can be used to identify the possible existence of state capture. However, more precise instruments of measurement of this capture or the degree of this capture are needed. Indeed, just as the notion of state capture through corruption has not been studied extensively yet, the question of methodology and criteria for measuring the degree of capture of a structure of a state or the state itself is even more underdeveloped. The World Bank itself recognized the limitations of the business survey method it had used in the early 2000s.[61] Some scholars have presented methods for identifying and measuring state capture through corruption concentering in a specific category of captor.[62] For example, Fazekas and Tóth developed an analytical framework for gauging state capture based on microlevel contractual networks in public procurement. They analyzed the likelihood of corruption occurring in a given tender by screening a wide range of microlevel 'red flags' such as a short deadline for submitting bids, only one candidate in a competition, eligibility criteria, change to the biding conditions, etc.[63] The development of methods for assessing or measuring the capture of a state structure through corruption focusing on sectors or captors through a 'red flags' approach would be extremely useful to the fight against corruption. A more comprehensive assessment such as the one put forward by Sarah Chayes, who has analyzed sophisticated corruption networks that cross sectoral and national boundaries in their drive to maximize returns for their members, also constitutes an interesting path forward.[64] As demonstrated in the next section, inter-American case law on this issue could also be useful to describe the processes of state

61 Hellman, Jones, and Kaufmann (n 27) n 3.

62 Luis Jorge Garay Salamanca (ed), *La Captura y Reconfiguración Cooptada Del Estado En Colombia* (Avina: Corporación Transparencia por Colombia 2008); Mihály Fazekas and István János Tóth, 'From Corruption to State Capture: A New Analytical Framework with Empirical Applications from Hungary' (2016) 69 Political Research Quarterly 320.

63 Fazekas and Tóth (n 62). We develop a new conceptual and analytical framework for gauging state capture based on microlevel contractual networks in public procurement.

64 Sarah Chayes, *When Corruption is the Operating System, the Case of Honduras* (Carnegie Endowment for International Peace, 2017). She does not speak of state capture but of corrupted networks.

capture through corruption and their impact on persons and on the human rights obligations of the state.

3 The role of inter-American litigation in the fight against state capture through corruption

Acts of corruption can violate human rights. Looking at key universal and Inter-American human rights conventions, scholars such as Bacio Terracino[65] and Nash Rojas[66] have shown ways in which corruption can violate substantive human rights covered by those treaties. The main legal issue at stake in the analysis of the link between acts of corruption and a violation of human rights is causality. As those scholars have shown, it is possible to identify examples where the causal link is immediate enough for the acts of corruption to violate human rights. For example, when a person is detained for the sole purpose of extracting from him a bribe, the right to liberty and security of that person is violated through corruption. These scholars focus mostly on cases of petty corruption—that is, small scale corruption.

This section addresses the question of whether there is a path to establishing a legal link between corrupt acts and human rights violations in cases of systematic corruption.

3.1 The corruption loophole

It is increasingly common in Latin America for powerful actors—such as organized crime groups, kleptocratic elites, or corporations—to organize covert networks to illegally enrich themselves, either at the expense of the state or through complicity of the state in the commission of crimes.[67] From 2009 to 2012 in Coahuila, Mexico, for example, the Zetas cartel was able to gain control of the regional public forces, as well as members of the executive and judiciary, through bribery, thereby influencing them to collaborate with or at least tolerate the crimes committed by this illegal group. The crimes included hundreds of forced disappearances committed by the police jointly with the Zetas cartel.

In terms of establishing a factual causal link, the acts of corruption described above are a condition *sine qua non* of the state forces' participation in the forced disappearances. Currently, however, human rights courts focus on the forced disappearances without considering the corruption that contributed to their occurrence. This impunity creates a form of loophole for corrupt acts that lead

65 Julio Bacio Terracino, 'Hard Law Connections between Corruption and Human Rights' (International Council on Human Rights Policy Working Paper 2007) 57.

66 Claudio Nash Rojas, Pedro Aguiló Bascuñán, and María Luisa Bascur Campos, *Corrupción Y Derechos Humanos: Una Mirada Desde La Jurisprudencia De La Corte Interamericana De Derechos Humanos* (Centro de Derechos Humanos 2014) 129.

67 See Jimena Reyes, 'State Capture through Corruption: How Can Human Rights Help?' (Harvard Law School Working Paper No. HRP 19-002, 2019) 9–19.

to human right violations even if they do not directly violate human rights. The existence of this loophole calls for the Inter-American Court of Human Rights to adapt its case law, as we argue below.

3.2 Inter-American case law on corruption

The Court has referred to corruption in at least eight different cases.[68] In three of these cases, the Court has taken into account acts of corruption in the contextual section of the judgments, a section that does not constitute a part of the Court's legal analysis *stricto sensu*.[69] In two cases, the Court referred to corruption in the section on proven facts, as part of a larger set of facts constituting the violation of a right.[70] The Court has also ordered a state to investigate facts of corruption in at least two cases.[71]

The Court has never explicitly held that acts of corruption alone constituted a violation of an obligation or a right derived from the American Convention on Human Rights (ACHR). In 2018, however, the Court recognized a scheme of corruption as a proven fact and recalled that states must adopt measures to prevent, punish and eradicate corruption effectively and efficiently.[72] On this occasion, the acts of corruption were detailed at length in the section describing the proven facts, the subject of the Court's legal discussion. The negative impact of organized corruption on the enjoyment of human rights was explicitly recognized, even if it was not qualified as a breach of a human rights obligation. The Court stated:

> The Court recalls that States must adopt measures to prevent, punish and eradicate corruption effectively and efficiently … The Court highlights that the international adoptions took place within a framework of corruption, in which a set of actors and public and private institutions operated under the

68 For a full description see Corte Interamericana de Derechos Humanos, Cuadernillo de la Jurisprudencia de la Corte Interamericana de Derechos Humanos No. 23: Corrupción y Derechos Humanos (2019) .

69 *Comunidad Indígena Sawhoyamaxa v Paraguay*, Fondo, Reparaciones y Costas, Sentencia, IACtHR Series C No 146 (29 March 2006); *Montero Aranguren y otros (Retén de Catia) v Venezuela*, Excepción Preliminar, Fondo, Reparaciones y Costas, Sentencia, IACtHR Series C No 150 (5 July 2006); *Tibi v Ecuador, Preliminary Objections*, Merits, Reparations and Costs, Judgment, IACtHR Series C No. 114 (7 September 2004).

70 *Pueblo Indígena Kichwa de Sarayaku v Ecuador*, Fondo y Reparaciones, Sentencia, IACtHR Series C No 245 (27 June 2012); *'Instituto de Reeducación del Menor' v Paraguay*, Excepciones Preliminares, Fondo, Reparaciones y Costas, Sentencia, IACtHR Series C No. 112 (2 September 2004).

71 *A Respeito do Brasil Asunto do Complexo Penitenciário de Curado*, Medidas Provisórias, Resolução da Corte IACtHR (7 October, 2015), F*orneron e Hija v. Argentina*, Fondo, Reparaciones y Costas, Sentencia, IACtHR Series C No. 242 (27 April 2012).

72 *Ramírez Escobar y otros v. Guatemala*, Fondo, Reparaciones y Costas, Sentencia, IACtHR Series C No. 351 (9 March 2018).

> mantle of the protection of the best interest of the child, but with the real purpose of obtaining their own enrichment. In this sense, the machinery that was mounted and tolerated around illegal adoptions, which affected particularly poor sectors, had a strong negative impact on the enjoyment of human rights of children and their biological parents.

This *obiter dictum* may indicate the Court's willingness to put greater emphasis on the role of corruption and, in particular, of systematic corruption, in human rights violations. It could also signal a first step towards recognizing corruption as an operative factor in the breach of the obligation to guarantee human rights as set out in Article 1 of the ACHR. Such an argument could be made through the duty to prevent human rights violations or even, more pointedly, through the recognition of a special obligation to prevent acts of corruption that cause human right violations.

3.3 *The duty to prevent human rights violations in contexts of corruption*

The ACHR, like other human rights treaties, simultaneously establishes individual rights and state obligations. Thus, Article 1 of the ACHR, which sits in the opening chapter entitled 'General Obligations,' mandates that state parties respect the rights and freedoms recognized within the convention and guarantee the full and free exercise of these rights and freedoms by all those subject to their jurisdiction.

Since its first decision, the Court has identified several specific obligations or duties derived from the general obligation to guarantee the full and free exercise of these rights and freedoms recognized within the convention.[73] Among those specific obligations is the obligation to prevent human rights violations:

> As a consequence of the obligation of guarantee, the States must prevent, investigate and punish any violation of the rights recognized by the Convention … [This] duty to prevent includes all those means of a legal, political, administrative and cultural nature that promote the protection of human rights and ensure that any violations are considered and treated as illegal acts.[74]

The state bears responsibility for preventing human rights violations by nonstate actors as well as by state actors. This can take two forms. On the one hand, there is the doctrine of complicity of the state, establishing the direct responsibility of the state for actions that tolerate, accept, or support those human rights violations

73 *Velásquez-Rodríguez v. Honduras*, Merits, Reparations, and Costs, Judgment, IACtHR Series C No. 04 (29 July 1988).

74 Ibid [166].

committed by private actors. On the other, there is indirect state responsibility for breaching the obligation to guarantee the enjoyment of human rights, and in particular, of the specific duty to prevent human rights violations.

Of course, the state does not have unlimited responsibility for all the acts of private actors. Rather, the Court has limited indirect responsibility for cases of foreseeable and avoidable risk. Three elements must be met: (1) the state must have 'awareness of a situation of real and imminent danger;' (2) the danger must threaten 'a specific individual or group of individuals;' and (3) there must be 'reasonable possibilities of preventing or avoiding that danger.'[75] Using the foreseeable and avoidable risk criteria described above, the Court has also established the responsibility of the state for a breach of its duty to prevent and protect human rights in cases where the state has itself contributed to creating the risk of human rights violations.[76]

As mentioned, the main legal issue at stake in the analysis of the link between acts of corruption and a violation of human rights is causality. As Bacio and Nash have shown, it is possible to identify examples where the causal link is immediate enough for the acts of corruption to violate human rights.

However, when the human rights violation is caused by actions triggered by corruption rather than directly due to corruption, the Court could move from an analysis of the human rights violation to one of the breach of the obligation to prevent human rights violations by the state. This approach will allow the Court to overcome the above-described loophole and enable it to look at the whole picture. The criterion of the doctrine of foreseeable and avoidable risk, used in the following case, enables the Court to analyze the causal link between the facts of corruption and a human rights violation. In the case of Coahuila, in addition to stating the direct responsibility of the state for the forced disappearances, the Court would seek to ascertain the existence of corruption of the authorities by the Zetas as evidence of a foreseeable and avoidable risk of the occurrence of enforced disappearances.

3.4 Proposal for a duty to prevent corruption

In *Ramirez Escobar*, the Court stated in *obiter dictum* that the state must adopt measures to prevent, punish, and eradicate corruption effectively and efficiently. It is the first time that an international court acknowledged the existence of this obligation. This case may also mark the Court's first step toward bridging the legal obligations of the Inter-American Convention Against Corruption and the ACHR.

75 *Gonzalez y otras ('Campo Algodonero') v. México*, Merits, Reparations, and Costs, Judgment, IACtHR Series C No. 205 (16 November 2006).

76 Víctor Abramovich, 'Responsabilidad Estatal por Violencia de Género: Comentarios Sobre el Caso 'Campo Algodonero' en la Corte Interamericana de Derechos Humanos' *Anuario de Derechos Humanos Numero 6* (Centro de Derechos Humanos 2010) 167, 176.

Moving forward, the Court could also develop a new duty to be monitored by the Inter-American System of Human Rights: the duty to prevent corruption that leads to human rights violations.[77] Besides the preamble and section on preventive measures against corruption of the Inter-American Convention Against Corruption, the sources of such a duty could be found in the UN Convention against Corruption, the Inter-American Democratic charter (in particular, Article 4), and the UN treaty bodies' observations on the issue of corruption.

If a duty to prevent corruption that causes or contributes to human rights violations were recognized, the Court would be able to focus on the content of the obligation to prevent corruption. It would be able to articulate what a state must or must not do to fulfill its obligation to prevent corruption and whether it has complied with this obligation. As the Court cannot require that states prevent all corruption entirely, this obligation would necessarily be a requirement of means, not of result. In the case of Coahuila, for example, in addition to stating the responsibility of the state for the enforced disappearances, the Court would evaluate whether the state did enough to prevent this network of corruption in light of the systematic corruption of public forces that led to the disappearances.

In the case of the obligation to prevent human rights violations in context of corruption, the Court would ascertain the existence of corruption as evidence of the creation of a risk of a violation of human rights. However, in this case, there would be a more implicit obligation to prevent corruption as part of the prevention of a risk of a human rights violation.

There are several reasons why either of the two moves by the Court would be a positive step. First, it would allow the Court to describe and acknowledge the existence of systematic corruption, and perhaps help states hold actors accountable. The standard of proof in Inter-American human rights law is more flexible than in national criminal law. Moreover, the Court has frequently admitted as evidence the existence of acts that could also constitute a criminal offence, such as enforced disappearances, even in the absence of a domestic legal judgment qualifying those acts. For example, with regard to crimes against humanity committed during Latin American dictatorships, the Court's case law condemning states for those crimes included descriptions of the acts, which clearly contributed not only to breaching the wall of impunity at a national level but also to advancing the search for the truth about what happened to the victims of these crimes.

Second, the analysis of the foreseeable and avoidable risk would give visibility to the link between corruption, on the one hand, and a specific victim or group of victims harmed by human rights violations, on the other. Thus, establishing a hard legal link between facts of corruption and the violation of substantive rights would demonstrate that corruption is not victimless. In summary, when corruption

77 *Glenister v. President of the Republic of S. Afr.* 2011 (3) SA 347 (CC) [177] (South Africa) has made a similar link: 'The state's obligation to "respect, protect, promote and fulfil" the rights in the Bill of Rights thus inevitably, in the modern state, creates a duty to create efficient anti-corruption mechanisms.'

directly violates a human right, the possessor of that right would also be a victim of corruption. Similarly, if the duty to prevent human rights violations is breached because of the existence of a foreseeable and avoidable risk of a violation due or partly due to corruption, the victims of that human rights violation are also victims of corruption. In both cases, the Court could identify those victims. Indeed, the Court recognizes the victims of human rights violations by name.

Most national legal systems have not translated into legal terms the existence of victims of corruption. This is due both to the difficulty of analyzing causation in corruption cases and to the historic treatment of corruption offenses in both civil and common law criminal systems, which conceive of corruption as an offence against public order, where victims have no standing.

Finally, such a doctrine would contribute to the creation of public policy standards in the fight against corruption. The Court could contribute to standard-setting both when establishing the responsibility of the state for its breach of the duty to prevent human rights violations and when deciding on the guarantees of non-repetition. To ensure both of these, the Court could develop and detail the actions that a state must take to prevent networks of corruption that cause human rights violations and to ensure that its structures comply with its obligations. This would resemble the work that the Court has done in the area of gender violence crimes, for example.

4 Conclusion

Despite the existence of several international anti-corruption conventions, there are no mechanisms through which state responsibility can be engaged when states do not fight against corruption or do not fulfill their obligation to prevent corruption. The inter-American mechanism for the protection of human rights could contribute to achieving greater accountability in those cases. The Court could acknowledge the responsibility of the state that has breached its duty to prevent human rights violations by contributing to or tolerating opaque networks of corruption that create an avoidable and foreseeable risk of human rights violations, highlighting thereby that corruption is not victimless. This could also contribute to standard-setting on what the state should do to prevent the creation of such risk. This would be particularly useful when a state structure is captured through systematic corruption and does not fulfill its duty to prevent human rights violations.

To date, the phenomenon of state capture through corruption has not been described and analyzed enough in the academic literature. Prevailing accepted definitions of state capture through corruption do not adequately describe this type of corruption in the way that it takes place on the ground, as demonstrated by the three Latin American case studies described in this chapter. Therefore, a revised definition should be considered.

This chapter proposes the following new definition:

1. owing to acts of corruption (bribery, embezzlement, or any offence defined in the international conventions against corruption or any act of abuse of public or entrusted power for private gain);

2. committed through a covert coordination at least among state representatives who benefit from the acts of corruption;
3. captor(s) decisively influence the formulation of the state's rules of the game to ensure them unjustified revenue from the state or make the state complicit in criminal activities in order for the captor(s) to obtain money illegally; and
4. these three elements result in a state structure or the whole state diverting durably or through a durable impact from the general interest.

It would also be useful to further develop methods that make it possible to evaluate the level of capture through corruption of state structures or powers to better understand and fight this phenomenon. The Inter-American Human Rights System could contribute to this description in particular by analyzing the existence of a breach of the duty to prevent human rights violations.

It is urgent to intensify the fight against corruption and in particular to give visibility to and refine the fight against state capture through corruption. Indeed, there are very concerning trends in democratic governance in Latin America closely linked to state capture though corruption. On the one hand, the current feeling that there is widespread corruption in most structures and in the highest spheres of the state certainly influences the rise in populism in Latin America. This perception gives the impression that there is no other solution to the scourge of corruption than to make a clean sweep of all elites and replace them with leaders like President Bolsonaro who promise simple solutions to complicated problems. On the other hand, we may be entering an era of new dictatorial regimes but this time resulting not from military coup but from elected governments who enrich themselves through systematic corruption, then illegally stay in power, as is the case in Nicaragua and Venezuela.

12 Impact of corruption on the implementation of international law

An international criminal law perspective

Vishal Sharma

Corruption is a common phenomenon all over the world. According to the world corruption index 2017, New Zealand is the least corrupt state in the world. It does not mean that any state in the world is corruption free. There are examples of corruption occurring in New Zealand.[1] Why is it then that corruption is so prevalent worldwide? When analysing this question, one must see the meaning and nature of corruption. Corruption in common parlance can be defined *inter alia* as a deviant moral behaviour, especially of a public administrator, to provide undue benefits to some people in the lieu of undue gains for himself in any form.[2] Kautillya, an ancient scholar, professor, and legendary statesman of India in the 3rd century BC, discussed the phenomenon of corruption among public officials elegantly in the following words:

> Just as it is impossible not to taste the honey or the poison that finds itself at the tip of the tongue, so it is impossible for a government servant not to

1 Business Anti-Corruption Portal, *New Zealand Corruption Report* (February 2016). There is a low risk of corruption in New Zealand's public procurement sector, but some fraud risks exist. The diversion of public funds is uncommon, and businesses report that officials do not show favoritism to well-connected firms and individuals when deciding upon policies and contracts (GCR 2015–2016). Companies report no irregular payments in connection with the awarding of public contracts (GCR 2015–2016), but a few companies report other forms of corruption: out of the 33% of companies that have experienced economic crime in the past two years, 19% out of the New Zealand companies report to have experienced procurement fraud (PwC 2014). While globally fraud commonly occurs during the invitation of quotes and the bids process, New Zealand respondents report fraud-related concerns during vendor selection, the payment process, and vendor contracting or maintenance (PwC 2014).

2 Rollin M Perkins and Ronald N Boyce, *Criminal Law and Procedure* (3rd edn, Foundation Press 1982) 855. The definition of 'corruption' is as follows: 1. Depravity, perversion, or taint; an impairment of integrity, virtue, or moral principle; esp., the impairment of a public official's duties by bribery. 'The word "corruption" indicates impurity or debasement and when found in the criminal law it means depravity or gross impropriety.' 'The act of doing something with an intent to give some advantage inconsistent with official duty and the rights of others; a fiduciary's or official's use of a station or office to procure some benefit either personally or for someone else, contrary to the rights of others.'

> eat up, at least, a bit of the King's revenue. Just as fish moving under water cannot possibly be found out either as drinking or not drinking water, so government servants employed in the government work cannot be found out (while) taking money (for themselves).[3]

This quotation shows that small-scale corruption is inevitable. However, what if the officials swallow all the honey rather than just tasting it? Transparency International has termed extreme corruption of this nature by state officials as grand corruption.[4] In a democratic system, state revenue is not personal revenue of heads of state and government. It is the property of the state and *per extensionem* of its citizens. Hence, in democracies, the crime of grand corruption is not limited only to bureaucrats, but even political heads can be held liable of grand corruption if they usurp state revenue.

Corruption is present in all the spheres of life to a variable degree and has an impact on both national and international institutions. Corruption can undermine the working of vital international institutions, i.e., the International Criminal Court. The Rome Statute has four crimes under its primary jurisdiction: genocide, crimes against humanity, war crimes, and crimes of aggression; however, under secondary jurisdiction, in Article 70, the International Criminal Court can deal with the offense of 'corruptly influencing a witness.' War crimes in common parlance are understood as an excessive use of violence, as a part of plan or policy, by an army or a combatant group, against non-combatant soldiers or civilians, during the course of its primary attack against another army or combatant group. However, crimes against humanity are understood as a widespread or systematic attack, with the knowledge of the attack, during war or otherwise, when it is (primarily) targeted against any civilian population. On the other hand, with genocide there is an attempt to destroy in part or whole a national, ethnical,

3 R Shamasastry (tr) *Kautilya's Arthashastra* (Chaukhamba 2014).

4 Transparency International, 'What is Grand Corruption and How Can We Stop It' (19 August 2016) <https://www.transparency.org/news/feature/what_is_grand_corruption_and_how_can_we_stop_it> accessed 1 June 2020. The following points are relevant to note: (i) Grand Corruption occurs when: apublic official or other person deprives a particular social group or substantial part of the population of a State of a fundamental right; or causes the State or any of its people a loss greater than 100 times the annual minimum subsistence income of its people; as a result of bribery, embezzlement or other corruption offence; (ii) Transparency International has developed this legal definition of grand corruption to encourage advocates, scholars, lawmakers, and others to seek ways to enhance accountability of high-level public officials and others whose corruption harms their citizens egregiously and too often with impunity. The definition gives legal relevance to the harms and voice to the victims. Grand corruption is a human rights crime and deserves adjudication and punishment accordingly. The terms defined below may have existing definitions in legislation or elsewhere. The definitions here are only illustrative; (iii) 'Annual minimum subsistence income' shall be defined as 60% of the most recently officially published median household income or an equivalent measure of a state's official designation of the income level entitling the receipt of social benefits based on economic need; (iv) 'Public official' shall be understood as defined by Article 2(a) of the United Nations Convention against Corruption.

racial, or religious group. Whereas, 'crime of aggression' for the purpose of the Rome Statute means:

> the planning, preparation, initiation or execution, by a person in a position effectively to exercise control over or to direct the political or military action of a State, of an act of aggression which, by its character, gravity and scale, constitutes a manifest violation of the Charter of the United Nations.

The International Criminal Court, like any other criminal court, works on principles of fair trial where witness testimony has a great importance. If a witness is influenced by bribery, then perpetrators of war crimes, crimes against humanity, genocide, and crimes of aggression can easily escape the scales of justice. This chapter has tried to highlight the importance of Article 70 of the Rome Statute, when it deals with the offence of corruptly influencing witness. Moreover, how this 'secondary jurisdiction' of the International Criminal Court can have a direct impact on the International Criminal Court's exercise of its 'primary jurisdiction.' The first part of this chapter has dealt with the offence of grand corruption and its impact on the national systems. The second part deals with the Rome Statute offence of 'corruptly influencing witness' read with other rules of procedure, and its significance. To understand the gravity of grand corruption, it is important to analyze its impact on the lives of ordinary people.

1 Impact of grand corruption on fundamental rights and development

In 2002, grand corruption on the part of the leaders of Malawi led to an exacerbation of the Malawian famine. Associate Professor Olivier Rubin from University of Copenhagen explained the situation in Malawi in the following words:[5]

> Government corruption seems to have played a very direct role in perpetuating the Malawian food crisis into a famine. Politically connected persons allegedly sold some 168,000 tons of corn from the Strategic Grain Reserve for huge profits during the food crisis (Boston Globe). According to Devereux, the Catholic Commission for Justice and Peace released a list of names that contained a number of prominent people who benefited from purchasing maize cheaply from the reserve and selling it after the price hike. Although many prominent persons have subsequently been prosecuted, their actions withdrew food from the market, drove prices up further and created an artificial shortfall in the short term.[6]

5 Olivier Rubin, 'Malawi 2002 Famine—Destitution, Democracy and Donors' (2008) 17 Nordic Journal of African Studies 47, 59–60.

6 Ibid.

The reaction of the international community can also be given responsibility to some extent in aggravating the problem, as international support was withdrawn due to allegations of corruption and mismanagement against the Malawian government.[7] The International Monetary Fund (IMF) aggravated the problem as well by withholding balance of payment support and being extended only when reports of large-scale deaths appeared. Nevertheless, this does not reduce the culpability of the elected democratic government of Malawi. The famine was aggravated due to rampant corruption in the government.

Grand corruption is fatal not only in times of disaster; it can throttle the economic prosperity of the country even in normal circumstances. Grand corruption is not a localised crime; it shocks the collective consciousness of the international community, hence it may be termed as a crime against humanity. It depletes the faith of the people in governing bodies. Not only are the rights of ordinary citizens affected but also the rights of foreign investors are violated. Numerous times foreign investors of high repute also have to face incidents of huge corruption. For example, telecom company Millicom had to face corruption in Senegal.[8] On the other hand, sometimes multinational companies have also used corruption. For example, the World Duty Free company (WDF) paid bribes to enter into a business agreement in Kenya. Later on, they had to lose that agreement, and even international arbitration did not protect the WDF's rights which they obtained by using corruption.[9] Such situations have a negative impact on the inflow of foreign direct investment and economic growth as well. Today, grand corruption is the biggest obstacle in the growth of many developing and under-developed countries.

7 Roshni Menon, *Famine in Malawi: Causes and Consequences* (Human Development Report Office, Occasional Paper, 2007/2008). Donor-government relations were also terse at this time, as a result of donor claims of economic mismanagement and governance failures. In fact, the IMF withheld balance of payment support, DFID, the EU and USAID suspended development assistance, and Denmark terminated its development projects and withdrew from Malawi entirely. Much of these suspensions were based on the belief that corruption and fraud were rampant in government, though these could not have occurred at a worse time for Malawi. In fact, it was only after reports of starvation-related deaths had been published by the media that the donors reversed their hard-line stance and offered food aid without condition.

8 Lawrence Delevingne, 'The Joy of Doing Business in Africa: How Senegalese Politicians Tried to Shake Down Millicom for $200 Million' *Business Insider* (Senegal, 4 February 2010) <https://www.businessinsider.com/business-in-africa-how-corrupt-senegalese-politicians-tried-to-shake-down-millicom-for-200-million-2010-2?IR=T> accessed 1 June 2020: 'In a meeting in the summer of 2008 with Millicom CEO Mark Beuls, the son of Senegalese President Abdoulaye Wade was clear: fork over $200 million—or kiss your license to operate a cellular business in Senegal good-bye.'

9 World Duty Free Company Limited (Claimant) and The Republic of Kenya (Respondent) ICSID Case No. ARB/00/7.

2 Malabo protocol: an insufficient response to grand corruption

To solve issues of grand corruption, the African Union (AU) has come up with an adequate response. In 2014, the African Union proposed the Malabo protocol to amend the existing protocol of the African Court of Justice and Human Rights. The AU has proposed to add corruption as a separate crime under the jurisdiction of the African Court of Justice and Human Rights.[10] In Article 28A of the Malabo protocol, it has kept corruption as an international crime along with war crimes, crimes against humanity, and genocide.[11] This Protocol will come into force when at least 15 African states ratify it. So far only 11 African states have signed this protocol, none of which has ratified it. Nonetheless, it shows the vision of diplomats and political leaders of the African Union. There is a good amount of scepticism also regarding this 'vision' of African leaders. The African Court of Justice and Human Rights will have only 16 judges to hear cases related to 14 different crimes, whereas the International Criminal Court has 18 judges to hear only four crimes. Amnesty International raised concerns on the capacity of the court.[12] By adding corruption in the proposed amended jurisdiction of the court, the AU has moved towards fulfilling its obligations in the African Convention to combat corruption.[13] More specifically, the Malabo protocol has targeted only grand corruption, where it states that corruption of such a nature is detrimental for the stability of the state.[14] However, the immunity granted to the head of states and governments puts a serious question mark on the legitimacy of the African Court.[15] With these weak provisions, this court cannot practically address the crime of grand corruption. Nonetheless, the Malabo protocol should be given credit for purporting the idea that the crime of corruption should be dealt with on par with heinous international crimes such as genocide and crimes against humanity.

10 Protocol on Amendments to the Protocol on the Statute of the African Court of Justice and Human Rights.

11 Ibid art 28 cl 1, 8.

12 Amnesty International, *Malabo Protocol: Legal And Institutional Implications of The Merged And Expanded African Court Snapshots* (2017).

13 African Union Convention on Preventing and Combating Corruption (adopted 11 July 2003) (2004) 43 ILM 5.

14 Gerhard Werle and Moritz Vormbaum (eds) *The African Criminal Court – A Commentary on the Malabo Protocol* (T.M.C. Asser Press 2017): Article 28I of the Malabo Protocol, annex: regulates the crime of corruption. It replicates what the African Convention on Preventing and Combating Corruption lists as 'acts and practices' deemed to constitute corruption. But the Annex to the Malabo Protocol differs from the Convention in that it criminalizes corruption only if it is 'of a serious nature affecting the stability of a state, region, or the Union.' This suggests that the corruption targeted here is 'grand corruption.'

15 Ibid 89: 'The immunity granted to heads of state or government raises valid concerns about the legitimacy of the African Court of Justice and Human and Peoples' Rights in the eyes of the public.'

Contrastingly, this vision is not found in the members of the United Nations Diplomatic Conference of Plenipotentiaries on the Establishment of an International Criminal Court. In the International Criminal Court Rome Statute, corruption is not considered as an international crime. The crime of corruption is not even discussed in the Kampala Review Conference of 2010.[16] From examples of Malawi and Senegal, it is evident that the crime of grand corruption is a serious problem. It does not mean that corruption or grand corruption is a crime specific to the continent of Africa. There are severely corrupt states like Columbia and Venezuela in South America.[17] In Europe, Romania has high levels of corruption according to Transparency International.[18] In Asia, Afghanistan, Pakistan, and Bangladesh are very corrupt states.[19] In India, the then Prime Minister Rajiv Gandhi in 1985 said only 15% of released funds reach the intended beneficiaries.[20] However, at the same time the Indian judicial system is the most independent and probably the most powerful judicial system in the world.[21] Due to the efficiency of the Indian courts, five chief ministers of Indian provinces have been sent to jail in corruption cases.[22] At present, the head of the Indian National Congress party, the principal opposition political party of India, Mr Rahul Gandhi, is also out on bail in a corruption related case.[23] However, not every state of the developing world has a judicial system as strong as India's. When corruption is affecting people's livelihoods across the world, it should then be given a place in the Rome Statute as an international crime.

16 Review Conference of the Rome Statute of The International Criminal Court (Kampala, 31 May–11 June 2010).

17 Transparency International, 'Corruption Perceptions Index 2017' <https://www.transparency.org/news/feature/corruption_perceptions_index_2017> accessed 1 June 2020.

18 Ibid.

19 Ibid.

20 PTI, 'Only 15 Paise Reaches the Needy: SC Quotes Rajiv Gandhi in Its Aadhaar Verdict' *Hindustantimes* (New Delhi, 11 June 2017) <https://www.hindustantimes.com/india-news/only-15-paise-reaches-the-needy-sc-quotes-rajiv-gandhi-in-its-aadhaar-verdict/story-I8dniDGXF6ksulggTDgb9L.html> accessed 1 June 2020.

21 PTI, 'Indian Judiciary Strongest, Most Robust in the World: CJI Dipak Mishra' *The Times of India* (New Delhi, 1 October 2018) <https://timesofindia.indiatimes.com/india/indian-judiciary-strongest-most-robust-in-the-world-cji-dipak-misra/articleshow/66030379.cms> accessed 1 June 2020.

22 IANS, 'Corrupt Chief Ministers are Now in Jail: PM Modi's Dig at Lalu Prasad Yadav' *Business Standard* (New Delhi, 29 January 2018) <https://www.business-standard.com/article/politics/corrupt-chief-ministers-are-now-in-jail-pm-modi-s-dig-at-lalu-prasad-yadav-118012900108_1.html> accessed 1 June 2020. Five erstwhile Chief Ministers of India who had to go jail for corruption- Mr Lalu Prasad Yadav, Mr Madhu Koda, Mr Sukhram, Ms J Jayalalita, and Mr O P Chautala.

23 E T Bureau, 'National Herald Case: Sonia and Rahul Gandhi Granted Bail' *The Economics Times* (New Delhi, 20 December 2015) <https://economictimes.indiatimes.com/news/politics-and-nation/national-herald-case-sonia-and-rahul-gandhi-granted-bail/articleshow/50245031.cms> accessed 1 June 2020.

3 The Rome Statute: a lacklustre approach to the problem of corruption

It seems that the international community is not serious about the crime of corruption, which is reflected in the jurisdiction of the International Criminal Court. The Rome Statute is not only lacking in taking note of grand corruption as an international crime, but it also has weak provisions to deal with corruption when used to influence the witnesses and officers related to prosecution of ongoing cases of international crimes. Article 70 of the Rome Statute in clauses (c) and (d) of sub Article 1 deals with the offence of using corrupt practices to wrongly influence the proceeding of the court.[24] It is pertinent to analyse the efficacy of the provisions related to the offence of corruptly influencing witnesses and officers in the terms of proposed procedure and punishment.

4 Problematic rules of the International Criminal Court to deal with the offense of corruption

Sub Article 2 of Article 70, provides:

> the principles and procedures governing the Court's exercise of jurisdiction over offences under this article shall be those provided for in the Rules of Procedure and Evidence' of International Criminal Court. The conditions for providing international cooperation to the Court with respect to its proceedings under this article shall be governed by the domestic laws of the requested State. [25]

The first part of this provision brings rule 162 of s 1 of Chapter 9 of International Criminal Court rules into the picture, which decides whether the court will exercise its jurisdiction on the offense of using corrupt influence or not? Rule 162 has full potential to make Article 70 of the Statute ineffective. It provides *inter alia* many problematic provisions.

Before making a decision on whether or not to exercise jurisdiction, the court may consult the state party concerned. A consultation with a state, where a sitting or even outgoing official could be an offender under Article 70, might prove to be counterproductive. For example, in the case of Libya, even a new government,

24 Rome Statute of the International Criminal Court, 17 July 1998, 2187 UNTS 90, art 70(1) (Rome Statute). Article 70 relevantly provides: ... (c) Corruptly influencing a witness, obstructing or interfering with the attendance or testimony of a witness, retaliating against a witness for giving testimony or destroying, tampering with or interfering with the collection of evidence; (d) Impeding, intimidating or corruptly influencing an official of the Court for the purpose of forcing or persuading the official not to perform, or to perform improperly, his or her duties.

25 *Rules of Procedure and Evidence of International Criminal Court* (2nd edn, International Criminal Court Publication 2013).

which came after the fall of Muammar Gaddafi, was not willing to hand over Saif-Al-Islam, the son of Muammar Gaddafi to the International Criminal Court, due to domestic political considerations.[26] If states can refuse to hand over the offenders of crimes against humanity to the International Criminal Court, then refusing to hand over an individual accused of corruptly influencing witnesses could also pose a problem for the International Criminal Court.

Other than the consultation with the state, the court will consider the availability and effectiveness of prosecution in a state party. This is an unreasonable provision, as the prosecution of international crimes is taking place at the International Criminal Court. This fact is in itself evidence that according to the principle of complementarity, the state party was unwilling or unable to investigate or prosecute the crime in its domestic jurisdiction.[27] In such a scenario, if the prosecution of offences against justice related to the international crime happens in the domestic courts of the state party, then it will be detrimental for the prosecution of the main crime itself at the International Criminal Court.

Another important question is whether the principle of complementarity can be presumed to be satisfied in the cases referred by the states themselves and the UN Security Council (UNSC). To satisfy the principles of complementarity, generally in situations taken *proprio motu*, the court must expressly pronounce on the 'unwillingness or inability' of the domestic courts to 'investigate or prosecute.' However, in situations referred by the states themselves, there is an implied acceptance by the states that they are 'unwilling or unable' to 'investigate or prosecute' the crimes under the primary jurisdiction of the International Criminal Court. Otherwise, any state that is willing and able to instigate or prosecute these crimes would not refer its own situation to the International Criminal Court. Similarly, a situation referred by UNSC shows that the international community feels that the state concerned is not only 'unwilling or unable' to 'investigate or prosecute' these international crimes, but also state officials themselves are perpetrators of the crimes. This approach can be criticised on the grounds that even if the 'unwillingness or inability' of the state is implied, but that is to 'investigating or prosecuting' primary international crimes and not the secondary crimes like 'corruptly influencing the witness.' Nevertheless this 'secondary offense' of 'corruptly influencing witness' has a direct impact on the outcome of the prosecution of 'primary crimes;' hence, in the interest of justice and for protecting victim's faith in the International Criminal Court, primary satisfaction of principle of complementarity should be used for the 'secondary offences' as well.

Further, rule 162 provides that the court will consider the seriousness of the offense. This provision might be relevant to the offense of disturbing the

26 Fadil Aliriza, 'Is Libya Too Scared to Put Saif Gaddafi on Trial?' *The Independent* (Libya, 16 August 2013) <https://www.independent.co.uk/news/world/africa/is-libya-too-scared-to-put-saif-gaddafi-on-trial-8771495.html> accessed 1 June 2020.

27 The Rome Statute, s 17 (on issues of admissibility).

court proceedings, and the offense related to use of corrupt practices is *ipso facto* serious. The weak handling of the offenses of bribing witnesses or court officers has the potential to divert attention away from the Court's key work.

Clause 3 of rule 162 provides further that the court may waive its jurisdiction of the offense under Article 70, if concerned state party requests for the same. However, according to clause 4, if the International Criminal Court decides not to exercise its jurisdiction, then it 'may' ask the state party to exercise its jurisdiction on the offense. Use of discretionary vocabulary shows that there might be cases when neither the International Criminal Court nor the concerned state party will exercise its jurisdiction on the offense of corruptly influencing justice at the International Criminal Court. Such a lacklustre provision signals a clear instigation to perpetrators for using corrupt methods to influence the results of an ongoing prosecution.[28]

5 International Criminal Court's experience to deal with the offense of corruptly influencing witnesses (situation in Kenya)

It is relevant to analyze the court's approach to actual situations where crimes against the administration of justice, especially offenses related to use of corruption were involved. In the situation of Kenya, in January 2008, post-election violence resulted in widespread and systematic attacks against the non-Kikuyu population by the Mungiki criminal organisation.[29] Many people were killed, several women were raped, and thousands of innocent civilians were forcibly displaced.[30] It was alleged that Mr Uhuru Kenyatta, the President of Kenya, was involved in planning these attacks.[31] As a result of these attacks, a political compromise was reached in which Mr Kenyatta became Deputy Prime Minister of Kenya. He was accused

28 Rule 162 concerns the exercise of jurisdiction. It provides as follows: 1. Before deciding whether to exercise jurisdiction, the Court may consult with States Parties that may have jurisdiction over the offense; 2. In making a decision whether or not to exercise jurisdiction, the Court may consider, in particular: (a) The availability and effectiveness of prosecution in a State Party; (b) The seriousness of an offense; (c) The possible joinder of charges under article 70 with charges under articles 5 to 8; (d) The need to expedite proceedings; (e) Links with an ongoing investigation or a trial before the Court; and (f) Evidentiary considerations; 3. The Court shall give favorable consideration to a request from the host State for a waiver of the power of the Court to exercise jurisdiction in cases where the host State considers such a waiver to be of particular importance; 4. If the Court decides not to exercise its jurisdiction, it may request a State Party to exercise jurisdiction pursuant to article 70, paragraph 4.

29 Xan Rice, 'Death Toll Nears 800 as Post-Election Violence Spirals Out of Control in Kenya' *The Guardian* (Nairobi, 28 January 2008) <https://www.theguardian.com/world/2008/jan/28/kenya.international> accessed 1 June 2020.

30 See 'Victims' Response to the "Prosecution's Notice of Withdrawal of the Charges against Uhuru Muigai Kenyatta"' (ICC-01/09-02/11, 9 December 2014) [2]–[3].

31 ICC, 'Case Information Sheet—The Prosecutor v. Uhuru Muigai Kenyatta' (ICC-01/09-02/11, 13 March 2015) <https://www.icc-cpi.int/CaseInformationSheets/kenyattaEng.pdf> accessed 1 June 2020, 3.

of crimes against humanity at five counts: i.e., murder (art 7(1) (a)); deportation or forcible transfer of population (art 7(1)(d)); rape (art 7(1)(g)); persecution (art 7(1)(h)); and other inhumane acts (art 7(1)(k)).[32]

However, the International Criminal Court had to close the case against Mr Kenyatta because witnesses changed their statements due to alleged bribes, and there was no support from the government of Kenya. The International Criminal Court prosecutor Ms Fatou Bensouda, while declaring her decision to request the court to close prosecution against Mr Kenyatta, provided *inter alia* the following reasons for her action:

> I have explained to the people of Kenya the severe challenges my Office has faced in our investigation of Mr Kenyatta. These include the fact that:
>
> - Several people who may have provided important evidence regarding Mr Kenyatta's actions, have died, while others were too terrified to testify for the Prosecution;
> - Key witnesses who provided evidence in this case later withdrew or changed their accounts, in particular, witnesses who subsequently alleged that they had lied to my Office about having been personally present at crucial meetings; and
> - The Kenyan Government's non-compliance compromised the Prosecution's ability to thoroughly investigate the charges, as recently confirmed by the Trial Chamber.[33]

Mr Uhur Kenyatta became Deputy Prime Minister in 2008 after these violent events. In 2013, he became President of Kenya. As a result, there was no support given to the International Criminal Court from the government of Kenya. In 2014, when the International Criminal Court prosecutor decided to close the prosecution against Mr Kenyatta, she expressly blamed the government of Kenya for not providing help to her office. Initially, the government of Kenya filed official representations against the revised request of the office of prosecutor for additional evidence. When the revised request of the prosecutor was approved, the government of Kenya did not provide any information regarding vital points of investigation. As most of the evidence was in Kenya, it was almost impossible for the prosecutor to pursue the investigation without the help of the government of Kenya.[34]

32 Ibid.

33 See 'Statement of the Prosecutor of the International Criminal Court, Fatou Bensouda, on the Withdrawal of Charges against Mr Uhuru Muigai Kenyatta' (ICC-01/09-02/11, 5 December 2014).

34 Ibid: 'However, I wish to say a few words about the failure of the Government of Kenya to cooperate fully and effectively with my investigations in this case. From the time that the Prosecution submitted its revised 8 April 2014 Request to the Government of Kenya, the material the Government sent us simply did not respond to a significant portion of our

This situation has defeated the purpose for which the International Criminal Court was created. Political leaders have committed crimes against humanity with impunity. Not only has Mr Uhur Kenyatta committed these crimes, but also his associates like Mr Francis Kirimi Muthaura have managed to dodge prosecution from the International Criminal Court.[35] According to reports, Mr Muthaura, an ex-civil servant of Kenya, was also involved in the planning of post-election violence in Kenya in 2007–2008.[36] In May 2018, Mr Kenyatta has appointed Mr Muthaura as Chairman of Kenya Revenue Authority.[37] Given that the International Criminal Court is dependent on the support of states which are run by the accused themselves, faith in international justice in specific and international law is bound to erode. Poor victims of this post-election violence of Kenya responded to the closure of prosecution against Mr Kenyatta and Mr Muthaura in the following pitiful words:

> Nearly seven years ago, tens of thousands of civilians in Naivasha and Nakuru were targeted, for no reason other than their tribe. Men were beheaded. Others suffered the pain and humiliation of forcible circumcision and castration. Human heads were paraded on sticks to instil terror. Women were serially raped. Children and their mothers were locked in buildings and burnt alive. Houses, and small business premises (such as welding and carpentry shops; tea houses; hairdressing salons), were pillaged and destroyed in their thousands. Pigs and dogs fed on the remains of the dead: the murdered were denied dignity even after death. The surviving victims received no justice from the Kenyan criminal justice system. If the Prosecution now also walks

---

Revised Request for Records. In short, most of the material sought in my Revised Request was not provided. This is despite the fact that International Criminal Court Judges clearly confirmed that my Revised Request was valid, and dismissed all of the Government's objections to it. In this situation, the most relevant documentary evidence regarding the post-election violence could only be found in Kenya. Yet, despite assurances of its willingness to cooperate with the Court, the Government of Kenya failed to follow through on those assurances. Ultimately, the hurdles we have encountered in attempting to secure the cooperation required for this investigation have in large part, collectively and cumulatively, delayed and frustrated the course of justice for the victims in this case. To conclude, today is a dark day for international criminal justice. Be that as it may, it is my firm belief that today's decision is not the last word on justice and accountability for the crimes that were inflicted on the people of Kenya in 2007 and 2008; crimes that are still crying out for justice.'

35 ICC, *Prosecutor v. Francis Kirimi Muthaura and Uhuru Muigai Kenyatta* Decision on the withdrawal of charges against Mr Muthaura (ICC-01/09-02/11, 18 March 2013).

36 Ibid.

37 Emmanuel Wanjala, 'Uhuru Appoints Muthaura as KRA Chairman, Karangi Pushed Out of KAA' *The Star* (Nairobi, 15 November 2018) <https://www.the-star.co.ke/news/2018/05/25/uhuru-appoints-muthaura-as-kra-chairman-karangi-pushed-out-of-kaa_c1763901> accessed 1 June 2020.

away from them, it will betray thousands who have already had their lives torn asunder.[38]

The victims in their response have specifically mentioned that the state of Kenya has not fulfilled its duties under Part 9 of the Rules and Procedures to the Rome Statute. Neither were the assets of Mr Kenyatta frozen nor did it investigate all post-election violence cases. The government of Kenya even went to the extent of providing false information to the International Criminal Court, and an international crimes division was set up in the High Court of the country. The government of Kenya misinterpreted Kenyan laws and said the President cannot be held responsible for the failure of the government to stop post-election violence in the country. Particularly, the provision of Part 9 of the Rules and Procedures were grossly abused, to protect those who defused the court's judicial process under the Rome Statute. These deliberate attempts of the Kenyan government have led to the closure of the prosecution against Mr Kenyatta.[39] The key witnesses of the prosecution against Mr Kenyatta and other accused of being bribed. The International Criminal Court Prosecutor, Fatou Bensouda, accepted that witness no. 4, whose evidence was critical for a potential conviction, was bribed by the representatives of Mr Kenyatta.[40] These were offences against the administration of justice under Article 70 of the Rome Statute. Hence, the International Criminal Court registered the cases against Mr Paul Gicheru and Mr Philip Kipkoech Bett in 2015. It was alleged that these two had committed offences against the administration of justice, by corruptly influencing the witnesses of the prosecution in Ruto and Sang, and Mr Uhur Kenyatta in the situation in Kenya.[41] The warrant for the arrest of these two individuals was issued against on March 10, 2015 and unsealed on September 10, 2015. The two accused were arrested and presented in the High Court of Kenya, but they were not transferred to the International Criminal Court. So

38 See 'Victims' Response to the "Prosecution's Notice of Withdrawal of the Charges against Uhuru Muigai Kenyatta"' (ICC-01/09-02/11, 9 December 2014) [2]–[3].

39 Ibid 11, n 11: '1. The Government failed to freeze any of Mr Kenyatta's assets, in violation of Part 9 of the Statute; 2. The Government failed to bring its purported legal objections to the Pre-trial Chamber's asset-freezing order to the Court's attention, in violation of Part 9 of the Statute; 3. The Government failed to provide the 'key documents' referred to in the annex to the Prosecution's filing of 31 January 2014, in violation of Part 9 of the Statute; 4. The Government failed to provide the material sought in the original records request, in violation of Part 9 of the Statute'.

40 Emeka-Mayaka Gekara 'Key Witness was Bribed: Bensouda' *Daily Nation* (The Hague, 27 February 2013): 'This is the witness who said he was present at meetings in State House and the Nairobi Club where Mr Kenyatta and former head of Public Service Francis Muthaura allegedly planned violence. "Witness Four revealed in an interview in May 2012 that he had been offered and accepted money from individuals holding themselves out as representatives of the accused to withdraw his testimony and provided e-mails and records that confirmed the bribery scheme," said the prosecutor.'

41 Ibid.

far, they are not been convicted by the Kenyan court. It is easy to imagine that this is a sham investigation and that the prosecution is compromised, as they allegedly offered bribes to witnesses in order to protect the President and Deputy President of Kenya from the International Criminal Court. While Mr Kenyatta is in power, he will likely never hand over these individuals to the International Criminal Court, as sending them to International Criminal Court custody would prove detrimental for Mr Kenyatta himself. Rather, Mr Uhur Kenyatta started a vehement campaign against the International Criminal Court. He alleged that since the International Criminal Court is a foreign court it was unduly targeting the Kenyan people. Mr Kenyatta himself appeared in the International Criminal Court in October 2014,[42] but before that the key witnesses were already bribed.[43] Mr Kenyatta used his personal appearance at the International Criminal Court to earn political capital back home.[44] After coming back from The Hague, he campaigned in Kenya and stated that no Kenyan would ever be handed over to the International Criminal Court in the future.[45] Consequently, it means that the investigation and prosecution against Mr Gicheru and Mr Bett would be pursued only in Kenya. In such a scenario, it should not be any surprise if Mr Gicheru and Mr Bett are acquitted by the Kenyan court or are given only meagre punishments.

Another important case concerning an offence against the administration of justice is the case of Walter Osapiri Barasa.[46] The Warrant of Arrest for Mr Barasa accused him of offering bribes to three witnesses: P-0336, P-0536, and P-0256. He offered these witnesses one million to one and a half million Kenyan Shillings. He committed all these offences near Kampala, i.e., in Kenyan Territory.[47] Until now, Mr Barasa has not been arrested, so the trial has yet to begin at the International Criminal Court.

It is clearly visible that the three accused persons, Mr Barasa, Mr Gicheru, and Mr Bett, committed the offenses of bribing key witnesses to weaken the cases against powerful political personalities in their country. The accused were successful in their objective as the criminal cases against Mr Ruto and Mr Kenyatta were closed by the International Criminal Court. Even now, the political system of Kenya is denouncing the International Criminal Court for implicating the

42 'Kenyatta Appears at International Criminal Court in Hague for Landmark Hearing' *BBC News* (Nairobi, 8 October 2014) <https://www.bbc.com/news/world-africa-29530638> accessed 1 June 2020.

43 Mike Pflanz, 'With Landmark Kenyatta Case in Disarray, International Criminal Court Prosecutor has One Last Shot' *The Christian Science Monitor* (11 March 2014).

44 'Uhuru Kenyatta Denounces International Criminal Court as Kenya Charges Dropped' *BBC News* (5 December 2014) <https://www.bbc.com/news/world-africa-30344320> accessed 1 June 2020.

45 Geoffrey Lugano, 'Counter-Shaming the International Criminal Court's Intervention as Neocolonial: Lessons from Kenya' (2017) 11 The International Journal of Transitional Justice 9.

46 *The Prosecutor v. Walter Osapiri Barasa* (ICC-01/09-01/13, 2013).

47 *The Prosecutor v. Walter Osapiri Barasa* Warrant of arrest for Walter Osapiri (ICC-01/09-01/13, 2 August 2013).

Kenyans. After the closure of cases against Mr Kenyatta and Ruto, in 2015, Mr Barasa offered to the International Criminal Court that he would attend the hearing in The Hague if his arrest warrant were changed to a summons.[48] However, his request was rejected by the Court in September 2015.[49] He appealed the decision but it was not refused.[50] The International Criminal Court has tried its best to minimise the chances of misuse of Part 9 of the Rules of Procedure and Evidence. For example, the International Criminal Court did not consult the state of Kenya under Part 9 before starting proceedings under Article 70. This action of the International Criminal Court was justified for two reasons. Firstly, the main case was a *proprio motu* case taken up by the International Criminal Court prosecutor against the sitting head of state, so consulting him for the related cases was illogical. Secondly, when the International Criminal Court has taken up a case under the principle of complementarity, it is evidence in itself that the national judicial system of the state is unwilling or unable to investigate or prosecute the main offense and other offences related to the administration of justice in relation to the main case. However, the International Criminal Court is still waiting to get into custody the three accused, as Kenya is not cooperating. Kenya is misusing the International Criminal Court rule 167, read with Article 70 (2), which provides that the states will provide international cooperation to the International Criminal Court according to their own domestic laws and procedures. This is a fatal drawback in the Rome Statute and its rules. Since Mr Kenyatta is himself the President of Kenya, the Kenyan government is using this provision to shield those offenders who saved Mr Kenyatta and others by bribing the witnesses. This contrasts with the situation of the Central African Republic, where a war crimes case was brought against Congo politician Mr Jean Peare Bemba Gombo, and the International Criminal Court was able to acquire international cooperation, because Mr Bemba is not in power presently. In June 2018, Mr Bemba was acquitted in the main case, but he was convicted for the offence of using corrupt methods to influence the witnesses at the court.[51]

48 Walter Menya, 'International Criminal Court wanted man Walter Barasa Wants to Clear Name' *Daily Nation* (Nairobi, 4 March 2018) <https://www.nation.co.ke/news/International Criminal Court-wanted-man-Walter-Barasa-ready-to-surrender/1056-4327624-fr l0bf/index.html> accessed 1 June 2020.

49 *The Prosecutor v. Walter Osapiri Barasa* Decision on the 'Defence challenge to the warrant for the arrest of Walter Osapiri Barasa' (ICC-01/09-01/13-35, 2013).

50 *The Prosecutor v. Walter Osapiri Barasa* Decision on the 'Defence request for leave to appeal decision International Criminal Court-01/09- 01/13-35' (ICC-01/09-01/13, 2013); (ICC-01/09-01/13-35, 2013).

51 International Bar Association International Criminal Court and ICL Programme, *Offences against the Administration of Justice and Fair Trial Considerations Before the International Criminal Court* (Coalition for the International Criminal Court, August 2017). To date, the Court has issued one judgment on Article 70 charges, in October 2016. In the *Bemba et al* case, Trial Chamber VII found Jean-Pierre Bemba Gombo, two members of his defence team and two associates guilty of corruptly influencing 14 defence witnesses, and presenting false evidence to the Court in the *Bemba* main case.

International cooperation with the International Criminal Court depends very much on who is in power in the concerned country. If domestic political leaders wanted the conviction of an offender, they would provide full support to the International Criminal Court, and if leaders want to protect the offender then they will not extend any help to the International Criminal Court's investigation authorities. To eliminate this element of political discretion in extending international cooperation, the relevance of domestic laws must be eliminated. The state parties to the Rome Statute have to frame uniform rules for states to provide international support. State parties can begin to provide a mandate to the International Criminal Court by way of using the rules of international cooperation mentioned in chapter IV of United Nations Convention against Corruption.[52] Experience shows the relevance for domestic laws for providing international cooperation to the International Criminal Court has proven an obstacle more than a help.[53]

These lacunae are due to the fact that in the Rome conferences there was no unanimity among the member states regarding rules applicable in the matter of international cooperation. Moreover, many states were of the view that the offences against the administration of justice should not be taken as seriously as other international crimes mentioned in Article 5 of the statute.[54] This thinking is visible even in the quantum of punishment for these offences. Minimum punishment which can be awarded by the International Criminal Court for this offence according to sub-article (3) of Article 70 is only fine. This mentality is visible even in the proceedings of the court. The International Criminal Court considers offences against the administration of justice as offences of 'lesser gravity.'[55] Collectively, these provisions have a potential to defuse the power of the International Criminal Court even to prosecute in the matters of main crimes. If the international community is concerned about crimes against humanity, then

52 United Nations Convention against Corruption (opened for signature 9 December 2003, entered into force 14 December 2005) 2349 UNTS 41.

53 Otto Triffterer and Kai Ambos (eds), *The Rome Statute of the International Criminal Court: A Commentary* (3rd edn, Hart 2016) 1757: 'where the Court seeks international cooperation from a State Party with respect to an article 70 offence that the Court is investigating or prosecuting, 'the conditions for providing international cooperation … shall be governed by the domestic laws of the requested State. This formulation provides greater scope for a State to deny cooperation than provided in the provisions of Part 9' (emphasis added).

54 *United Nations Diplomatic Conference of Plenipotentiaries on the Establishment of an International Criminal Court*, vol 1 (Rome, 15–17 June 1998, A/CONF.183/13).

55 Carsten Stahn (ed), *The Law and Practice of the International Criminal Court* (OUP 2015):

> 'in *Bemba* et al. where four individuals were accused of offences against the administration of justice under Article 70 of the Rome Statute. When deciding their applications for interim release, Single Judge Tarfusser held that the lesser gravity of these offences is not 'per se suitable to diminish the risk of flight'. The Appeals Chamber found this conclusion 'problematic'; it emphasized that the offences under Article 70 cannot be considered as grave as the core crimes under Article 5, and thus the gravity of such offences should not be given undue weight in assessing the risk of flight.'

it should be equally concerned about plugging such lacunae, which can indirectly extend impunity for perpetrators of the crimes against humanity.

6 Conclusion

Grand corruption can deprive innocent people of the basic amenities of life. It can impoverish them, which can lead to malnutrition of children or even to deaths by starvation, as seen in the case of Malawi. Hence, grand corruption in itself should be taken as an international crime on par with the other international crimes such as genocide, war crimes, crimes of aggression, and crimes against humanity. At the same time, the provisions of the Rome Statute dealing with the offense of using corrupt methods are very weak. These provisions have defeated the whole aim of the International Criminal Court. To remove these drawbacks, the provisions of the International Criminal Court Rome statute should be amended. However, there will always be a clash between the International Criminal Court jurisdiction and principle of state sovereignty; hence, to begin with these rules might be applied when a case is concerned with an ousted head of state, and not with an incumbent head of state. The International Criminal Court should have its own team of investigators, and the UNSC should ensure that the states should cooperate with the International Criminal Court investigation, especially when an investigation is against an erstwhile ruler. Although these suggestions might appear far from reality they are from a victim-centric approach. The international community might take more time to digest the idea of *in situ* with international criminal investigations, but it is necessity for ensuring justice to the victims of crimes against humanity and other international crimes. To deal with the problem of corruption and grand corruption, this chapter suggests the following amendments in the International Criminal Court Rome Statute:

1. Huge corruption in governance by heads of states or the grand corruption should be added as a new international crime in the Rome Statute. To implement this suggestion, Article 5 of the Rome Statute will require an amendment.
2. There should be no relevance for the domestic laws and procedures of a state if the principle of complementarity is applied to a situation. For this para 2 of Article 70 and sub rule 2 of rule 167 should be amended. Until new universal rules and procedures of international cooperation are framed, the International Criminal Court should be mandated to use rules regarding international cooperation as mentioned in chapter IV of the UN Convention against Corruption.
3. The quantum of punishment for the offence of corruptly influencing witnesses should be increased. There should be a provision of compulsory punishment of five years for using corrupt methods to influence witnesses or the officers of the court. For this, para 3 of Article 70 should be amended.

4. The UNSC has power to refer or defer any case to the International Criminal Court.[56] However, it has no power to get arrest warrants of the International Criminal Court implemented, even when they are not against the sitting state officials. The Rome Statute should be amended to empower the UN Security Council to get the arrest warrants of the International Criminal Court honoured by the states at least when sovereignty issues are not involved, i.e., when arrest warrants are not against sitting heads of the state or government. To implement this suggestion, para 7 of Article 87 should be amended to empower the International Criminal Court to refer a matter to the UNSC if a state is not cooperating to implement the arrest warrants; even against the people who are not in ruling positions. At the same time, state parties to the Rome Statute should work on ensuring the presence of a sitting head of states in the court. Appearance of Mr Uhur Kenyatta at the International Criminal Court has shown if summons rather than arrest warrants against a sitting head of the state are issued, then leaders might attend the hearings at the International Criminal Court.

Implementing these suggestions might reduce the incidents of grand corruption and the use of corruption to protect the perpetrators of international crimes at the International Criminal Court.

56 The Rome Statute, art 13(b) (Referral by UNSC); art 16 (Deferral by UNSC).

Part III

The new frontiers of compliance

13 Whistleblower protection

The next frontier in the transnationalization of anti-corruption law

Leah Ambler and Claire Leger[1]

The international legal architecture to combat corruption has now been in place for almost two decades. The 44 parties to the OECD Convention, along with a number of other countries, have enacted laws to criminalize foreign bribery and hold companies liable for corruption offences. Enforcement of these laws is gathering momentum, although half of the 44 member countries of the OECD Working Group on Bribery (WGB) have yet to conclude a foreign bribery enforcement action.[2] Many recent corruption scandals with cross-border impacts point to the need to strengthen the enforcement of anti-corruption laws. To do this, the first step—and challenge—is detecting the offence.[3]

Whistleblowers[4] are ideally positioned to reveal inside information that would otherwise go undetected, leading to effective prevention, detection, investigation, and prosecution of wrongdoing. However, of the 263 foreign bribery cases sanctioned between 1999 and June 1, 2017, only 2% were detected by reporting persons. In contrast to the universal adoption of anti-bribery and corporate liability legislation among the 44 Parties to the OECD Convention, only 21 have enacted some form of public and private sector whistleblower protection legislation. At both an international and a national level, there is a relative legal vacuum when it comes to norms for protected reporting of corruption offences and those that exist are inadequate for ensuring that whistleblowers reporting corruption are protected from retaliation or entitled to adequate remedies. Comprehensive and consistent international standards for protected reporting are required in order to increase corruption reporting and thereby strengthen enforcement of

1 This chapter presents the views of the authors and does not necessarily represent the views of the member countries of the OECD, OECD Working Group on Bribery.

2 OECD, *Data on Enforcement of the Anti-Bribery Convention* (2017).

3 OECD, *The Detection of Foreign Bribery* (2017).

4 There is no internationally accepted definition of 'whistleblower.' While the terms 'whistleblower' and 'reporting person' are used interchangeably in this chapter, the authors prefer the term 'reporting person,' consistent with the terminology of the *UN Convention against Corruption Resource Guide on Good Practices in the Protection of Reporting Persons* (UN, 2015) and *Committing to Effective Whistleblower Protection* (OECD, 2016), which adopt a neutral terminology to avoid negative connotations often associated with 'whistleblowers.'

anti-corruption laws. In this respect, whistleblower protection is the next frontier in the transnationalization of anti-corruption law.

This chapter is divided into three parts. First, the authors identify reasons for underreporting of corruption offences by whistleblowers and argue that legal uncertainty is one of the key dissuasive factors. The current international legal framework for protection of persons who report acts of corruption is outlined in part two, including the continuing evolution of international standards and their crucial role in shaping national whistleblower protection frameworks. Part three compares and contrasts national whistleblower protection frameworks and emphasizes the disparities within and between national laws relating to information disclosure and protected reporting, outlining the key elements that such legal protection should include. The authors argue that the current uncertain and contradictory legal landscape for reporting demonstrates a need for stronger, overarching legal standards to promote more comprehensive, effective whistleblower protection. The chapter concludes with a case for the transnationalization of legal protection for reporting acts of corruption, starting with harmonised, overarching international standards.

1 Underreporting of corruption offences by whistleblowers

Whistleblowers can reveal information that would otherwise go undetected through measures such as internal audits or investigations. Underreporting of corruption offences undermines efforts to detect and prevent this crime and results in weakened enforcement. The 2017 Special Eurobarometer Survey of over 28,000 individuals from 28 EU member countries found that 81% of respondents did not report corruption that they experienced or witnessed to anyone.[5] Respondents considered the reasons for such underreporting to be difficulty proving the allegations (45%); lack of consequences for perpetrators (32%); lack of protection for those who report corruption (22%); and not knowing where to report (22%). A further 18% of respondents considered that corruption goes underreported because of fear of criminal consequences for reporting or not wanting to betray others.[6] The inadequacy of protected reporting legislation and its implementation underpins all of these perspectives on underreporting. Part one examines the main causes behind underreporting of corruption, namely cultural barriers, a real threat of retaliation, and lack of legal protection. It concludes that the greatest disincentive to speaking up is an inadequate and inconsistent international and national legal framework for protected reporting.

5 *Special Eurobarometer 470 Report: Corruption* (October 2017) 93.
6 Ibid 98.

1.1 Poor organizational culture as a barrier to reporting corruption

Criminalization of corruption coupled with a real threat of enforcement has led to a seismic shift in the private sector towards almost universal adoption of anti-bribery ethics and compliance programs by major multinationals. Furthermore, with ethics and compliance programs increasingly recognized either in mitigation of criminal sanctions for corruption offenses or in the context of pre-trial resolution (or settlement) procedures, companies have responded through major organizational and, as a consequence, cultural change. However, companies have not achieved the same cultural shift with respect to internal reporting of corruption. This is due, in part, to a lack of general legal obligation or incentive to put such protected reporting frameworks in place: only nine G20 and OECD WGB countries' protected reporting legislation currently requires companies to implement protected reporting frameworks.[7] In practice, corporate whistleblower protection frameworks fall short: 86% of companies surveyed for the 2015 OECD Survey on Business Integrity and Corporate Governance had a mechanism to report suspected instances of serious corporate misconduct, but over one-third of these either did not have a written policy of protecting whistleblowers from reprisals or did not know if such a policy existed.[8] Reporting channels without a clearly stated and demonstrated commitment to protect those who report from retaliation will inevitably lead to underreporting and a lack of confidence in the system. Culture is a key factor. The 2018 US Global Business Ethics Survey reports that in companies with weak ethical cultures, employees are three times more likely to observe ethical misconduct but 41% less likely to report such conduct; they are also 27% more likely to suffer retaliation after reporting misconduct.[9]

The authors contend that an inadequate and under-enforced legal framework for protected reporting is one of the main reasons that culture remains a barrier to speaking up about corruption. For example, many studies show that employees prefer to report first, if at all, inside their organization. The US Securities and Exchange Commission (SEC) 2018 Annual Report to Congress on its Whistleblower Program indicates that of the whistleblower award recipients who were current or former employees, 83% raised their concerns internally, or understood that supervisors or relevant compliance personnel were aware of the violations, before reporting to the Commission.[10] A new Australian survey of 17,778 individuals across 46 organisations in Australia and New Zealand showed that in both public and private sectors, on average over 85% of respondents reported internally only.[11] In contrast, most protected reporting provisions in international

7 France, India, Italy, Latvia, Lithuania, Netherlands, Norway, Slovak Republic, US.

8 OECD, *Committing to Effective Whistleblower Protection* (n 4).

9 European Commission, *Global Business Ethics Survey: The State of Ethics and Compliance in the Workplace* (Ethics and Compliance Initiative March 2018) 10.

10 US SEC, *Annual Report to Congress: Whistleblower Program* (2018) 17.

11 Integrity@Werq, *Whistleblower: New Rules, New Policies, New Vision* (November 2018) (survey of 17,778 individuals across 46 organisations in Australia and New Zealand).

anti-corruption instruments limit protection to those reporting corruption externally to competent authorities (see Table 13.1), whereas four countries currently limit protection to external reporting to the competent authorities only.[12] Current international legal standards on protected reporting are therefore ill-adapted to the cultural reality of reporting within organizations.

1.2 The reality of retaliation against whistleblowers reporting corruption

The forms of retaliation that can be inflicted on those reporting corruption are limited only to the bounds of human imagination. The Australian survey cited above showed that 81.6% of respondents who reported cases of unethical behaviour in their workplaces faced repercussions for speaking up.[13] The 2018 Global Business Ethics Survey results support these findings, noting that 83% of respondents who reported 'accepting gifts/giving kickbacks or bribing public officials' suffered retaliation, making corruption the category of misconduct with the single highest rate of retaliation.[14] This could be indicative of underreporting specifically when it comes to corruption offenses. To note, the 2018 and 2019 US SEC Annual Report to Congress show that US Foreign Corrupt Practices Act offences were seventh out of the 11 categories of wrongdoing reported to the SEC between 2015 and 2019.[15] In comparison, fraud is consistently the most common type of corporate misconduct reported via internal company mechanisms[16] and 40% of all detected fraud cases are uncovered by whistleblowers.[17] Employees may be more likely to report wrongdoing perpetrated by other employees that it is directly in the company's interest to address, for example fraud or theft of corporate assets, rather than corruption which has potentially much more serious implications for the company and its leadership and therefore carries a higher risk of retaliation.

Reporting corruption can also have much more dire consequences than the standard forms of workplace retaliation contemplated in many protected reporting frameworks and particularly those based on labor law principles. In many jurisdictions, reporting persons (and journalists who report the information they disclose) expose themselves to the risk of defamation or libel suits which are

12 Brazil, Chile, Greece, Peru.

13 Integrity@Werq (n 11).

14 Ethics and Compliance Initiative, *Global Business Ethics Survey: The State of Ethics and Compliance in the Workplace* (March 2018) 10.

15 US SEC, *2018 Annual Report* (n 10) 32. US SEC, *Annual Report to Congress: Whistleblower Program* (2019): The SEC received nearly the same number of FCPA tips (on average around 200 in total) 23. The SEC received nearly the same number of FCPA tips (on average around 200 in total).

16 OECD, *Committing to Effective Whistleblower Protection* (n 4).

17 Association of Certified Fraud Examiners, *Report to the Nations 2018 Global Study on Occupational Fraud and Abuse* (2018) 4: analysis of 2,690 cases of occupational fraud that were investigated between January 2016 and October 2017.

Table 13.1 Comparison of provisions on protection of reporting persons in multilateral anti-corruption instruments.

Treaty	*Are Parties required to protect?*	*Protection against what?*	*Protection for whom?*	*Protection conditional on what?*	*Protection for reporting what?*	*Protection for reporting to whom?*
IACAC (1997) Article III(8)	Parties agree to consider the applicability of … systems for protecting	Unspecified	Public servants and private citizens	In good faith	Acts of corruption	Unspecified
CoE Civil Law Convention (1999) Article 9	Each Party shall provide in its internal law	Any unjustified sanction	Employees	Have reasonable grounds to suspect … and report in good faith	Corruption	Responsible persons or authorities
CoE Criminal Law Convention (1999) Article 22(a)	Each Party shall adopt such measures as may be necessary	Unspecified	Unspecified	Unspecified	Criminal offenses established in accordance with Articles 2 to 14	Investigating or prosecuting authorities

(*Continued*)

Table 13.1 (Continued)

Treaty	*Are Parties required to protect?*	*Protection against what?*	*Protection for whom?*	*Protection conditional on what?*	*Protection for reporting what?*	*Protection for reporting to whom?*
African Union Convention on Preventing and Combating Corruption (2003) Article 5(6), (7)	Parties undertake to adopt measures	Reprisals	Citizens	Parties are required to adopt legislative measures to punish those who make false and malicious reports against innocent persons	Corruption	Unspecified
UNCAC (2005) Article 33	Each Party shall consider incorporating into its domestic legal system appropriate measures	Any unjustified treatment	Any person	In good faith and on reasonable grounds	Any facts concerning offences established in accordance with this Convention	Competent authorities
OECD 2009 Recommendation IX(i), (iii)	Member countries should ensure that appropriate measures are in place	Discriminatory or disciplinary action	Public and private sector employees	In good faith and on reasonable grounds	Suspected acts of bribery of foreign public officials in international business transactions	Competent authorities

lengthy and costly, regardless of the outcome. Worse still, whistleblowers may be subject to criminal prosecution, often involving sanctions up to and including incarceration, for violation of criminal provisions prohibiting the disclosure of information (e.g., bank, professional, commercial or national secrecy, and corporate espionage).[18] In some cases, those who report corruption are actually putting their lives and the lives of others at risk. This was chillingly highlighted in the recent murders of European journalists working on corruption stories,[19] as well as the recent alleged murder of former Grupo Aval auditor Jorge Enrique Pizano in connection with his revelations about alleged bribery by Brazilian construction giant Odebrecht for the Ruta del Sol II roadway concession in Colombia.[20] Legal frameworks that do not envisage protection for physical security and immunity from any kind of liability for making the protected disclosure fall dramatically short of addressing the stark reality of the kinds of retaliation facing whistleblowers reporting corruption offences.

18 See, e.g., Matthew Allen, "Whistleblower" Rudolf Elmer Given Suspended Sentence' (*Swissinfo.ch*, 23 August 2016) <https://www.swissinfo.ch/eng/breaking-news_whistleblower-rudolf-elmer-given-suspended-sentence/42392846> accessed 1 June 2020; Stephanie Nebehay, 'Swiss Top Court Knocks Down Bid to Extend Banking Secrecy' *Reuters* (10 October 2018) <https://www.reuters.com/article/us-swiss-banking-secrecy/swiss-top-court-knocks-down-bid-to-extend-banking-secrecy-idUSKCN1MK0TK> accessed 1 June 2020; Sudip Kar-Gupta, 'HSBC Whistleblower Falciani Sentenced to Five Years in Prison' *Reuters* (27 November 2015) <https://www.reuters.com/article/us-hsbc-tax-falciani/hsbc-whistleblower-falciani-sentenced-to-five-years-in-prison-idUSKBN0TG1I520151127> accessed 1 June 2020; Jesús Aguado, 'Spain Rejects Latest Swiss Bid to Extradite HSBC Whistleblower' *Reuters* (18 September 2018) <https://www.reuters.com/article/us-hsbc-tax-spain/spain-rejects-latest-swiss-bid-to-extradite-hsbc-whistleblower-idUSKCN1LY1EG> accessed 1 June 2020; Simon Bowers, 'LuxLeaks Whistleblower Avoids Jail after Guilty Verdict' *The Guardian* (29 June 2016) <https://www.theguardian.com/world/2016/jun/29/luxleaks-pwc-antoine-deltour-avoids-jail-but-is-convicted-of-theft> accessed 1 June 2020; 'LuxLeaks Whistleblower Antoine Deltour Has Conviction Quashed' *BBC News* (11 January 2018) <https://www.bbc.com/news/world-europe-42652161> accessed 1 June 2020.

19 Amy Wilson-Chapman, 'Malta Investigative Journalist Killed in Bomb Blast' *International Consortium of Investigative Journalists*, 16 October 2017 <https://www.icij.org/blog/2017/10/investigative-malta-journalist-killed-bomb-blast/> accessed 1 June 2020; 'Death of Investigative Journalist Sparks Mass Protests in Slovakia' *The Guardian* (8 March 2018) <https://www.theguardian.com/world/2018/mar/09/death-of-investigative-journalist-sparks-mass-protests-in-slovakia> accessed 1 June 2020; Chris Baynes, 'Bulgarian Journalist Investigating Alleged Corruption Found Raped and Murdered in Park' *Independent* (8 October 2018) <https://www.independent.co.uk/news/world/europe/bulgaria-journalist-murder-viktoria-marinova-ruse-rape-corruption-investigation-eu-funds-tvn-a8573686.html> accessed 1 June 2020.

20 Helen Murphy, Julia Symmes Cobb, 'Colombia to Probe Deaths of Odebrecht Whistleblower, Son' *Reuters* (14 November 2018) <https://www.reuters.com/article/us-odebrecht-colombia/colombia-to-probe-deaths-of-odebrecht-whistleblower-son-idUSKCN1NJ2Y2?feedType=RSS&feedName=worldNews> accessed 1 June 2020.

1.3 Legal uncertainty over protections for disclosure and remedies for retaliation

For those brave enough to speak up about corruption, the questions of how, when, what, and where to report are complex and heavily dependent on the subject matter of the report, the person's employment situation and his or her country of residence. Legal uncertainty over protected reporting frameworks is one of the major contributing factors to underreporting of corruption. The European Commission conducted an open public consultation in 2017 to collect views on the issue of whistleblower protection at the national and EU level.[21] A total of 5,707 replies were received, of which 69% of individuals and 65% of organisations indicated that the private workers are reluctant to report wrongdoing because of insufficient protection of whistleblowers. The 2017 OECD Survey on Investigative Journalists found that whistleblower protections were considered the second most valuable support for journalists investigating corruption (63%), behind strong editorial board backing (77%). However, journalists acknowledged the significant risks to sources as a result of non-existent or vastly inadequate whistleblower protection frameworks in many countries.[22] It is, therefore, urgent to address the current legal vacuum in the area of protection of reporting persons, both at national and international level. This chapter makes a case for transnationalising legal protection for reporting acts of corruption, in order to ensure the development of more consistent national whistleblower protection frameworks and increase enforcement of anti-corruption laws. Part two describes and analyzes the current international legal architecture for whistleblower protection.

2 A dissonant international legal framework for whistleblower protection

The current international legal framework for protection of persons who report acts of corruption plays a crucial role in shaping national whistleblower protection laws. However, the various instruments and standards are divergent, creating disharmony among national laws seeking to transpose them and general confusion for law and policy makers, reporting persons, and entities seeking to implement protected reporting frameworks, alike. In addition to these international legal standards, several soft law instruments such as anti-bribery guidance[23]

21 European Commission, 'Public Consultation on Whistleblower Protection' (2017) <https://ec.europa.eu/newsroom/just/item-detail.cfm?item_id=54254> accessed 1 June 2020.

22 OECD, *The Detection of Foreign Bribery* (OECD Publishing Paris 2017) 60.

23 For example, OECD, *OECD Recommendation on Public Integrity* (2016); G20/OECD, *Principles for Corporate Governance* (2015); OECD, *Good Practice Guidance on Internal Controls, Ethics and Compliance* (2010); OECD, *OECD Guidelines for Multinational Enterprises* (OECD Publishing Paris 2011); Asia-Pacific Economic Co-operation, *Anti-Corruption Code of Conduct for Business* (2007); Transparency International, 'Business Principles for Countering Bribery' (2013) <https://www.transparency.org/whatwedo/publication/business_principles_for_countering_bribery> accessed 1 June 2020; World Bank, *Integrity*

acknowledge protected reporting frameworks as a component of an effective organizational anti-corruption ethics and compliance program. The International Organization for Standardization (ISO) also recently announced the preparation of a new ISO standard on whistleblowing management systems.[24] This guidance seeks to complement the protected reporting standards in the anti-corruption treaties and instruments described below; however, it has not been included in the analysis undertaken for the purposes of this chapter.

2.1 International anti-corruption instruments

All multilateral anti-corruption instruments recognize whistleblower protection as an essential element of an effective framework to combat corruption. However, as illustrated in Table 13.1, the standards vary widely between instruments. First and foremost, not all instruments require countries to implement protected reporting frameworks. For example, the UN Convention against Corruption (UNCAC) and Inter-American Convention against Corruption (IACAC) provisions on protection of reporting persons are optional measures for state parties, whereas parties to the Council of Europe (CoE) Civil Law Convention on Corruption are required to provide for protection in their internal law. In addition, protection of reporting persons is not expressly included in the OECD Convention but it is one of the so-called 'soft law' recommendations in the 2009 OECD Recommendation on Further combating Foreign Bribery (2009 Recommendation). Even when these anti-corruption instruments require countries to protect reporting persons, they do not always call for legislative measures to ensure protection. Definitions also diverge when it comes to reporting persons, protected disclosures, conditions for protection, and reporting channels. A common requirement is that the report is made in good faith and on reasonable grounds. The African Union Convention goes so far as to require parties to adopt legislative measures to punish those who make false and malicious reports against innocent persons, which is discussed below (in part 3.7), can have a chilling effect on reporting. All of the instruments are deficient in that they do not define the scope and the form of the protection or remedies that should be available to reporting persons.

The monitoring mechanisms of the UNCAC, IACAC, CoE, and OECD conventions regularly review and make recommendations on countries' frameworks to facilitate reporting of corruption and protect reporting persons. As a result of monitoring by the OECD Working Group on Bribery (WGB), countries have taken concrete action to legislate for or reform whistleblower protection laws: as of 2017, 18 had introduced or strengthened whistleblower protection laws

Compliance Guidelines (2010); World Economic Forum, *Partnering Against Corruption Initiative Global Principles for Countering Bribery* (2016); International Chamber of Commerce, *ICC Rules on Combating Corruption* (2011).

24 ISO, *ISO/NP 37002: Whistleblowing Management Systems—Guidelines* (2018).

in response to peer evaluation reports and recommendations.[25] The recently announced review of the OECD 2009 Recommendation[26] has strong potential to harmonize OECD standards for protected reporting legislation with those of other fora, and most importantly, with the higher standards that exist in certain members' whistleblower protection laws. To support implementation of the IACAC, in 2013, representatives of the 33 member countries of the Mechanism for Follow-Up on the Implementation of the IACAC approved by consensus a Model Law to Facilitate and Encourage the Reporting of Acts of Corruption and to Protect Whistleblowers and Witnesses.[27] However, given the scarcity of comprehensive public and private sector whistleblower protection legislation in the region, it appears that the Model Law has yet to be implemented by many members of the Organization of American States (OAS).[28] More recently, the Lima Commitment on Democratic Governance against Corruption adopted at the Eighth Summit of the Americas in April 2018 called on OAS members to protect whistleblowers, witnesses, and informants of acts of corruption from intimidation and retaliatory actions.[29] The implementation of the Lima Commitment will be evaluated at the next Summit in 2021.

While protection of those reporting corruption is recognized as a universal priority across international anti-corruption instruments, the standards are divergent and lack detail. Opportunities to update, review, and revise these standards should be used to promote greater consistency and clarity, in turn ensuring that the countries adhering to them have the means to transpose effective and comprehensive whistleblower protection laws.

2.2 G20 action on whistleblower protection

The importance of whistleblower protection legislation was recognised for the first time by G20 Leaders at the 2010 Seoul Summit where they identified it as one of the priority areas in the 2011–2012 G20 Anti-Corruption Action Plan. In 2011, the G20 adopted its Compendium of Best Practices and Guiding Principles for Whistleblower Protection Legislation, as a reference for enacting

25 OECD, *Fighting the Crime of Foreign Bribery: The Anti-Bribery Convention and the OECD Working Group on Bribery* (2017).

26 OECD, 'Strengthening the Anti-Bribery Convention: Review of the 2009 Anti-Bribery Recommendation' (2019) <http://www.oecd.org/corruption/2019-review-oecd-anti-bribery-recommendation.htm> accessed 1 June 2020.

27 OAS, *Model Law to Facilitate and Encourage the Reporting of Acts of Corruption and to Protect Whistleblowers and Witnesses* (2013).

28 See, e.g., Latin America Advisor, 'Are Latin America's New Whistleblower Laws Working?' (*The Dialogue*, 8 May 2017) <https://www.thedialogue.org/analysis/are-latin-americas-new-whistleblower-laws-working/> accessed 1 June 2020.

29 'Lima Commitment 'Democratic Governance against Corruption' (VIII Summit of the Americas, Lima, B.22, 14 April 2018).

and reviewing whistleblower protection rules in G20 countries by the end of 2012.[30] Since then, the importance of whistleblower protection has featured in each of the subsequent G20 Anti-Corruption Action Plans, and lead to the endorsement of the G20 High-Level Principles for the Effective Protection of Whistleblowers, developed under Japan's G20 Presidency. From calling on G20 countries to enact legislation by end-2012, the G20 subsequently:

- indicated that members without protections would 'take specific actions, suitable to the jurisdiction, to ensure that those reporting on corruption, including journalists, can exercise their function without fear of any harassment or threat or of private or government legal action for reporting in good faith' (2013–2014);
- identified public sector whistleblower protection as an issue which merits 'particular attention' (2015–2016) and reaffirmed the importance of providing effective and easily accessible reporting mechanisms and whistleblower protection in the private sector in the 2015 G20 High Level Principles on Private Sector Transparency and Integrity;[31]
- committed to 'reviewing our progress in implementing legislative and institutional protections for whistleblowers' (2017–2018);
- undertook to 'assess and identify best practices, implementation gaps and possible further protection measures as appropriate' (2019–2020); and, most recently,
- developed the High-Level Principles for the Effective Protection of Whistleblowers,[32] built upon existing standards and good practices from the United Nations,[33] and several other international / regional bodies and reaffirming the importance of acting collectively to ensure the effective protection of whistleblowers.

The G20 took a leading role in setting international standards in the field of protected reporting. The High-Level Principles provide reference for countries intending to establish, modify, or strengthen protection framework, legislation, and policies. They intend to complement existing anti-corruption commitments and offer flexibility to enable countries to effectively apply them in accordance with their respective legal traditions.

30 G20, *Anti-Corruption Action Plan: Protection of Whistleblowers—Compendium of Best Practices and Guiding Principles for Legislation* (2011).

31 G20, *High Level Principles on Private Sector Transparency and Integrity* (2015).

32 G20, *High-Level Principles for Effective Protection of Whistleblowers* (2019).

33 Article 33 of the UNCAC states that 'Each State Party shall consider incorporating into its domestic legal system appropriate measures to provide protection against any unjustified treatment for any person who reports in good faith and on reasonable grounds to the competent authorities any facts concerning offences established in accordance with this Convention.'

2.3 Europe: leading the legal revolution

Aside from the whistleblower protection provisions in multilateral anti-corruption treaties and instruments mentioned above, the 2014 CoE Recommendation of the Committee of Ministers to member states on the protection of whistleblowers[34] is currently one of the only specific whistleblower protection standards at an international level. It envisages protection of both public and private sector whistleblowers who report or disclose information within an organization; to relevant external regulatory or supervisory bodies or law enforcement agencies; or to the public, on a threat or harm to the public interest in the context of their work-based relationship. Despite this standard, whistleblower protection continues to be fragmented across EU member states, with only ten EU countries (France, Hungary, Ireland, Italy, Lithuania, Malta, Netherlands, Slovakia, Sweden, and the UK) currently considered as providing comprehensive legal protection.[35] Furthermore, a 2017 study carried out for the Commission estimated the loss of potential benefits to the EU as a whole due to a lack of whistleblower protection, in public procurement alone, to be in the range of EUR 5.8 to EUR 9.6 billion annually.[36]

Building on the 2014 Recommendation, and propelled by the public outcry at several high profile cases of whistleblower retaliation, such as LuxLeaks,[37] the European Parliament called on the European Commission, in its resolution of October 24, 2017, to present: 'a horizontal legislative proposal establishing a comprehensive common regulatory framework which will guarantee a high level of protection across the board, in both the public and private sectors as well as in national and European institutions, including relevant national and European bodies, offices and agencies, for whistle-blowers in the EU.'[38] The Proposal for a Directive of the European Parliament and of the Council on the Protection of Persons Reporting on Breaches of Union Law (COM/2018/218 final) was issued in April 2018 (draft EU Directive).[39] A revised draft was adopted by the

34 Council of Europe, Recommendation on the protection of whistleblowers, 2014/7 of 30 April 2014.

35 European Commission Directorate General for Justice and Consumers, *Fact Sheet on Whistleblower Protection* (April 2018).

36 European Commission Directorate General for Internal Market, Industry, Entrepreneurship and SMEs, *Estimating the Economic Benefits of Whistleblower Protection in Public Procurement—Final Report* (9 June 2017).

37 For a summary of the case, see: 'The Case of LuxLeaks' (*Global Freedom of Expression, Columbia University*, June 2016) <https://globalfreedomofexpression.columbia.edu/cases/the-case-of-luxleaks/> accessed 1 June 2020.

38 European Parliament, Resolution on legitimate measures to protect whistle-blowers acting in the public interest when disclosing the confidential information of companies and public bodies, 2016/2224(INI) of 24 October 2017.

39 European Council, Proposal for a Directive on the protection of persons reporting on breaches of Union law, COM/2018/218 of 23 April 2018.

European Parliament's Legal Affairs Committee on November 20, 2018.[40] On October 7, 2019 the European Council approved the Whistleblower Protection Directive, which was first adopted by the European Parliament in April 2019 (EU Directive). The legislation still needs to be formally signed and published in the *Official Journal*.[41]

The Directive sets out common, mandatory minimum standards for EU member states to transpose into domestic legislation by the end of 2021. These include protection for a broad range of reporting persons and facilitators (e.g., journalists) working in the private or public sector who report internally or externally, as well as for public disclosures under certain conditions (art 15). The threshold for protection is defined as 'reasonable grounds to believe that the information on breaches reported was true at the time of reporting and that such information fell within the scope of this Directive' (arts 6). Protection is provided for reporting on breaches of specific EU acts (arts 1 and 2), although reporting on corruption is not mentioned and protection is excluded in areas where the Commission has no legislative power such as human rights, health services, or education.[42] Retaliation is defined broadly (art 5) 'any direct or indirect act or omission which occurs in a work-related context, is prompted by internal or external reporting or by public disclosure, and which causes or may cause unjustified detriment to the reporting person;' and the burden of proof rests with the person who retaliated, indeed 'it shall be presumed that the detriment was made in retaliation for the report or the public disclosure … it shall be for the person who has taken the detrimental measure to prove that that measure was based on duly justified ground' (art 21(5)). Protections include exemption from liability of any kind in respect of a report or public disclosure (art 21) and the right to seek dismissal of proceedings for defamation, breach of copyright, breach of secrecy, breach

40 European Parliament, 'EU-Wide Protection and Support for Whistle-Blowers' (20 November 2018) <https://www.europarl.europa.eu/news/en/press-room/20181120IPR19504/eu-wide-protection-and-support-for-whistle-blowers> accessed 1 June 2020; Committee on Legal Affairs, 'Voting List on the Draft Report on Protection of persons reporting on breaches of Union law 2018/106(COD)' (19 November 2018) <https://www.europarl.europa.eu/cmsdata/157100/juri-committee-voting-list-protection-persons-breaches-EU-law.pdf> accessed 1 June 2020.

41 European Council, 'Better Protection of Whistle-Blowers: New EU-Wide Rules to Kick in in 2021' (7 October 2019) <https://www.consilium.europa.eu/en/press/press-releases/2019/10/07/better-protection-of-whistle-blowers-new-eu-wide-rules-to-kick-in-in-2021/#> accessed 1 June 2020.

42 According to Directive, breaches of EU law include breaches affecting the financial interests of the Union (art 325 TFEU), breaches relating to the internal market (art 26(2) TFEU), and a list of breaches falling within the scope of the Union acts annexed to the Directive, and concern the following areas: (i) public procurement; (ii) financial services, prevention of money laundering and terrorist financing; (iii) product safety and compliance; (iv) transport safety; (v) protection of the environment; (vi) radiation protection and nuclear safety; (vii) food and feed safety, animal health and welfare; (viii) public health; (ix) consumer protection; (x) protection of privacy and personal data, and security of network and information systems.

of data protection rules, disclosure of trade secrets, or for compensation claims based on private, public, or on collective labor law (art 21(7)), or compensation for damage suffered (art 21(8)). The EU Directive also envisages the provision of support measures for the reporting person from an independent third party, including 'an information centre or a single and clearly identified independent administrative authority' (art 20(3)). It provides for interim relief pending the resolution of legal proceedings (art 21 (6)), legal aid, and further measures of legal aid, financial assistance, and psychological support for reporting persons in the framework of legal proceedings (art 20(2)). The text also foresees effective, proportionate, and dissuasive penalties for hindering or attempting to hinder reporting, retaliation or vexatious proceedings against reporting persons, breaching confidentiality of the reporting person. It nevertheless asks states to ensure that penalties are applicable to reporting persons making reports demonstrated to be knowingly reported or publicly disclosed false information. Compensating damage should be available to those who suffer detriment as a result (art 23). The EU Directive provides that EU member states shall designate the authorities competent to receive, give feedback, and follow up on reports, and shall provide them with adequate resources. Member states shall ensure that the competent authorities establish independent and autonomous external reporting channels, for receiving and handling information on breaches (art 11).

However, and as explored below (part 3.7), there are potential conflicts with other EU laws (in particular, those relating to trade secrets and data protection) that risk undermining the EU Whistleblower Protection Directive if care is not taken in their transposition by EU members. The EU Directive 2016/943 on the protection of undisclosed know-how and business information (EU Trade Secrets Directive)[43] had a deadline of June 2018 for transposition in all EU Member States. The Directive aims to ensure that there is a sufficient and consistent level of civil redress in the internal market in the event of unlawful acquisition, use, or disclosure of trade secrets. Exceptions to liability for violating trade secrecy include cases where the alleged acquisition, use, or disclosure of the trade secret is carried out in exercise of the right to freedom of expression and information of the media; as well as for the purpose of protecting the general public interest or a legitimate interest recognized by EU or national law. The EU Trade Secrets Directive, therefore, introduces a public interest test for whistleblowers that was not previously a criterion for protection under some national frameworks and puts the focus back on the motive, rather than the messenger.[44] The EU General

43 Council Directive 2016/943 of 8 June 2016 on the protection of undisclosed know-how and business information against their unlawful acquisition, use and disclosure [2016] OJ L 157/1.

44 See, for example, Transparency International Ireland, 'Irish whistleblowers could face criminal prosecution for reporting white-collar-crimes and cover-ups' (4 July 2018) <https://www.transparency.ie/news_events/irish-whistleblowers-could-face-criminal-prosecution-reporting-white-collar-crimes-and> accessed 1 June 2020 (following transposition of the EU Trade Secrecy Directive in Ireland).

Data Protection Regulation (GDPR) and Data Protection Directive (2016/680) bind all EU member countries from May 25, 2018. As organizational reporting mechanisms rely on the processing of personal data (both of the reporting person and the subject of the report), they are subject to this strengthened data protection framework. This means that, depending on how the GDPR is transposed in each EU country, organizations that have implemented, or intend to implement internal reporting mechanisms may need to obtain prior approval from national data protection authorities. Furthermore, companies could be liable to pay administrative fines amounting to the greater of EUR 20 million or 4% of total worldwide annual turnover should data protection authorities consider that their internal reporting mechanisms and subsequent internal investigation procedures violate GDPR provisions on data processing, data subjects' rights (i.e., the subject of the whistleblower report), or transfer of personal data to third countries or international organizations.[45] The requirement for prior approval of reporting mechanisms coupled with the risk of significant financial penalties could be a major deterrent for companies considering whether to implement protected internal reporting channels. However, under some national whistleblower reporting legislation and the draft EU Directive, companies may be legally required to implement such protected reporting mechanisms. Much will depend on how the respective instruments are transposed into domestic law; however, concerns have already been raised about potential conflicts arising from the interaction of these various legal regimes.[46]

Potential conflicts with other EU laws aside, the EU Directive as adopted is nothing short of a legal revolution in the international architecture for whistleblower protection. The Directive set a new benchmark for other international organizations to follow, in the update and revision of their protected reporting standards. If its text can ensure sufficient complementarity with other EU laws on information disclosure, the EU Directive will pave the way for greater harmonization of national whistleblower protection laws in Europe and beyond.

45 Council Regulation 2016/679 of 27 April 2016 on the protection of natural persons with regard to the processing of personal data and on the free movement of such data, and repealing Directive 95/46/EC (General Data Protection Regulation) [2016] OJ L 119, art 83(5).

46 Vera Cherepanova, 'GDPR Implications for the Whistleblowing Process' (*The FCPR Blog*, 3 May 2018) <https://fcpablog.com/2018/5/3/vera-cherepanova-gdpr-implications-for-the-whistleblowing-pr/> accessed 1 June 2020; Claire Guyot, 'Caution Needed in Transposing Whistleblowing and Trade Secrets Directives' (24 April 2018) <https://www.euractiv.com/section/justice-home-affairs/news/caution-needed-in-transposing-whistleblowing-and-trade-secrets-directives/> accessed 1 June 2020.

3 Disparities in national whistleblower protection laws

There are vast discrepancies between the various legal standards for protected reporting across G20 and OECD WGB member countries.[47] Sixteen of the 48 countries (33%) making up the combined membership have no form of whistleblower protection legislation applicable to either public or private sector employees. Six of the 32 countries (19%) that do have some form of whistleblower protection legislation limit legal protection to reporting persons in the public sector.[48] There has nevertheless been a marked uptake in whistleblower protection legislation over the last decade. Figure 13.1 provides a timeline of the enactment of specific whistleblower protection provisions in G20 and OECD WGB member countries. Some countries appear twice in the table as they have enacted different laws on whistleblower protection, for example, covering the public and private sectors. However, despite a flurry of legislative activity in this field, many national whistleblower protection laws reflect the disharmony of the international instruments they are transposing, and are usually reactive and scandal-driven instead of

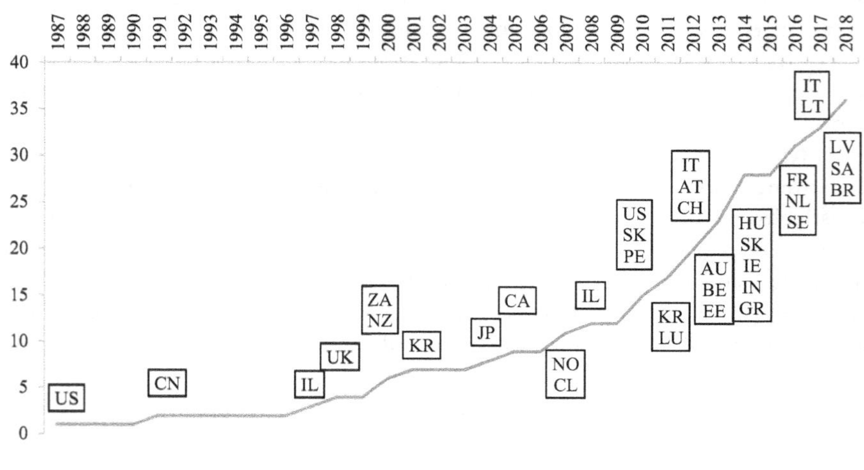

Figure 13.1 Timeline of enactment of specific whistleblower protection laws in G20 and OECD WGB member countries. Source: Information compiled by the authors, December 2018. Country abbreviations based on ISO 2-letter country codes.

47 All references to countries' protected reporting frameworks in this chapter are based on the information which was compiled in December 2018 by the authors following research into reports of countries' implementation of international anti-corruption treaties, as well as independent research and analysis.

48 Austria, Belgium, Canada, Chile, Estonia, Switzerland.

forward-looking. *Ad hoc* protection through fragmented provisions continues to be the norm, which risks providing less comprehensive protection than a specific protected reporting law that clarifies and streamlines the processes for disclosing wrongdoing and provides remedies for victims of retaliation.[49] As a result and as explored in this section, current protected reporting laws in many countries create uncertainty for potential whistleblowers as to the nature and scope of protection they are entitled to, and the conditions for accessing that protection. This section considers the main disparities in national whistleblower protection frameworks. It explores the differing requirements to qualify as a reporting person, prescribed subject matter of protected disclosures, avenues, and procedures for protected reporting, scope of protection, and remedies for retaliation, and the role, if any, for competent authorities to receive reports, advise reporting persons, and remediate. The authors argue that the current disparity in national laws demonstrates a need for stronger, harmonised international legal standards to promote more comprehensive and effective whistleblower protection.

3.1 *A panoply of legal forms and definitions*

At the national level, the source of protection for whistleblowers may originate either from comprehensive and dedicated laws on whistleblower protection, or from specific provisions in different laws such as public service laws, labour codes, criminal codes, and sector-specific laws, such as anti-corruption laws, competition laws, and financial or banking laws. Seventeen of the 48 member countries (35%) have enacted dedicated legislation that covers both public and private sector employees and does not limit protection to a certain area of wrongdoing but promotes and facilitates the reporting of illegal, unethical, or dangerous activities, in general.[50] In countries that have separate whistleblowing legislation for public and private sectors, the definition of protected disclosures in the private sector law tends to be narrower than that in the public sector law.[51] Eight countries limit protection to reports of corruption or corruption-related offences, largely to implement their international obligations under the various anti-corruption treaties.[52] As described above (part 1.2), there may be a heightened risk of retaliation and, therefore, a greater fear involved in reporting corruption, specifically. This is one of the reasons why limiting protection to reporting of corruption could result in underreporting and undermine the protective framework. Furthermore, reporting persons may not have sufficient information or knowledge to be able to categorize the wrongdoing they have witnessed into a specific type of offense.

49 OECD, *Committing to Effective Whistleblower Protection* (n 4) 118.

50 China, France, Hungary, Ireland, Israel, Japan, Korea, Latvia, Lithuania, Netherlands, New Zealand, Norway, Slovak Republic, South Africa, Sweden, United Kingdom, United States.

51 For example, Australia and US. See also Kim Loyens and Wim Vandekerckhove, *The Dutch Whistleblowers Authority in an International Perspective: A Comparative Study* (USBO 2018) 30.

52 Australia, Greece, India, Italy, Luxembourg, Peru, Saudi Arabia, Slovenia.

Finally, limiting protection to disclosures of corruption can be problematic in countries that have not fully criminalized all forms of corruption (for example, bribery of foreign public officials or private sector bribery), as reporting of these offenses would not qualify for protection.[53]

3.2 *Focus on motive rather than information*

If whistleblower protection is to be considered a key element in the arsenal of anti-corruption enforcement, then the focus needs to shift from the messenger to the message. The majority of multilateral anti-corruption treaties predicate protection for corruption reporting on 'good faith.' Thirteen countries (27%) require that reporting persons report in 'good faith,' or not for their own benefit,[54] whereas four countries apply a less onerous but nevertheless challenging public interest test,[55] to benefit from protection. Ireland, New Zealand, and Sweden have provided that a person is entitled to protection if, when they report, they have a 'reasonable belief' that the disclosure is true or accurate. Ireland's Protected Disclosures Act (2014) even contains a presumption in favor of the disclosure being protected (s 5(8)). Compounding the confusion over motive is the provision, in many whistleblower protection laws, for sanctions for malicious or false reporting. Nine countries specifically provide for criminal or disciplinary sanctions for malicious or false reporting.[56] Only six countries[57] envisage some form of immunity from liability (e.g., defamation, disclosure offenses) for making the protected disclosure and of these, only Ireland, Lithuania, and New Zealand provide for near complete immunity (see also part 3.7 for a discussion of the conflict between whistleblower protection and secrecy and defamation laws).

3.3 *Reporting channels and criteria*

Whistleblower protection legislation should facilitate protected reporting by clearly defining the correct protected reporting frameworks. The current and proposed EU whistleblower protection provisions are the only standards at an international level that do not limit protected reporting to external disclosures to competent authorities. This is at odds with the abovementioned empirical evidence that whistleblowers tend to report internally within their organizations, if at all (part 1.1). Given the importance of the issues being reported, particularly in corruption cases, protected reporting frameworks should provide reporting persons the option to either report internally, externally to regulatory authorities,

53 For example, India and Saudi Arabia.

54 Australia, Austria, Canada, France, Greece, Hungary, India, Israel, Latvia, Luxembourg, Slovenia, South Africa.

55 Korea, Lithuania, Netherlands, UK.

56 Belgium, Canada, Chile, China, India, Italy, Latvia, Peru, South Africa.

57 Australia, Greece, Ireland, Latvia, Lithuania, New Zealand.

or to the public (for example, through disclosures to the media or civil society), depending on the specific circumstances. Only 14 countries allow for either internal, external, or public disclosures, and of these, 11 make protection conditional on a so-called 'tiered approach' to reporting, requiring the exhaustion of internal channels before resorting to external whistleblowing, subject to certain exceptions.[58] However, only five of the countries with a strict tiered approach to protected reporting require organizations to implement protected reporting channels, further complicating the situation.[59] Brazil, Chile, Greece, and Peru currently only provide protection for external reporting exclusively to the competent regulatory or law enforcement authorities.

The recent burst of legislative activity in the area of corporate liability for corruption offenses—largely in response to recommendations from the OECD WGB—has resulted in countries legislating to require companies to implement protected reporting frameworks, or to incentivize them to do so through the possibility of mitigated liability or sanctions. Ironically, Argentina, Colombia, and Mexico's new corporate liability provisions now have some form of requirement or recognition of private sector protected reporting frameworks but these countries continue to have a complete absence of overarching whistleblower protection legislation. In this context, while there is a positive uptake of protected reporting mechanisms in private entities, potential reporting persons cannot be guaranteed effective protection against retaliation and remedies for reprisals without an overarching legislative framework. Countries therefore need to ensure that protected reporting legislation evolves at the same rate as corresponding anti-corruption and corporate liability laws, to avoid the possibility of reporting persons falling through the gaps in legal protection. This requires, as a first step, greater harmony between anti-corruption and whistleblower protection standards at the international level.

3.4 Inadequate protections and remedies

As noted above (part 1.2), there are a myriad of ways in which employers and others can retaliate against reporting persons. To counter this, whistleblower protection laws should provide for the broadest range of protections against retaliation possible, and ensure that there are adequate remedies for those who are victims of reprisals.

The possibility for confidential and/or anonymous reporting is considered one of the most basic forms of protection. The UNCAC requires parties to

58 Australia (public sector only), Canada (public sector only), France (tiered approach), Ireland (tiered approach), Korea, Latvia (tiered approach), Lithuania (tiered approach), Netherlands (tiered approach), New Zealand (tiered approach), Norway (tiered approach), South Africa (tiered approach), Sweden (tiered approach), UK (tiered approach), and US (public sector only; tiered-approach).

59 France, Latvia, Lithuania, Norway, US.

facilitate anonymous reporting by the public to anti-corruption bodies, where possible, whereas the IACAC and African Union Conventions refer to protection of the identity of the reporting person. From a practical perspective, it is difficult to provide comprehensive protection to a person whose identity is unknown and equally difficult to obtain additional information from that person in order to understand and remediate the wrongdoing. Nineteen countries provide for confidential reporting, whereas three ensure anonymity.[60] Ensuring confidentiality may require harmonization with other laws, including those regarding data protection and freedom of information. Italy and New Zealand have legislated to ensure that whistleblower reports are exempt from freedom of information legislation.[61]

Another form of protection is the dissuasive effect of criminal or disciplinary sanctions for violation of confidentiality or reprisals. Sixteen countries currently provide for sanctions against those who retaliate under their whistleblower protection legislation.[62] In France and Korea, disclosure of a whistleblower's identity, or facts that may infer it, is punishable by imprisonment or a fine (Loi Sapin II, art 9; PPIWA art 30 (1)). Further protection can be ensured by providing for a legal presumption in favor of the reporting person, or, in other words, reversing the burden of proof such that the employer must demonstrate that the retaliatory actions were not connected with the protected disclosure. Eleven countries reverse the burden of proof for retaliation in their whistleblower protection legislation.[63]

Remedies for reprisals should cover all direct and indirect consequences of the discriminatory or retaliatory action. Most jurisdictions provide for traditional employment law remedies, such as compensation for unfair dismissal or reinstatement,[64] although the latter is not always appropriate in the context of workplace reprisals. Other remedies include causes of action to claim compensation (available to differing extents in 19 countries),[65] including for pain and suffering and for past or future losses arising from the retaliation. Financial support should also cover legal, medical, or relocation expenses, as well as other reasonable and foreseeable costs linked to the proceedings; without this support,

60 Confidentiality: Australia, Belgium, Canada, Chile, China, Estonia, France, Ireland, Italy, Korea, Lithuania, Netherlands, New Zealand, Norway, Peru, Slovak Republic, Slovenia, South Africa, US. Anonymity: Australia, Austria, Brazil.

61 The NZ PDA provides that a request under the Official Information Act may be refused if it might identify a person who has made a protected disclosure (see s 19(2)).

62 Australia, Belgium, Canada, China, France, Hungary, Ireland, Israel, Italy, Korea, Latvia, Lithuania, Norway, Peru, South Africa, US.

63 Belgium, France, Ireland, Italy, Korea, Lithuania, Luxembourg, New Zealand, Norway, Sweden, US.

64 See, UK PIDA ss 5, 47(B); Korean ACA, arts 31–33; Japanese WA, arts 3–5; US WPA s 2(b)(2)(C), 5; South African PDA ss 2(1)(a–b), 3, 4; Australian PDA s 25; Canadian PSPDA, art 19.

65 Australia, Canada, France, Ireland, Israel, Japan, Korea, Latvia, Lithuania, Luxembourg, Netherlands, New Zealand, Norway, Peru, Slovenia, South Africa, Sweden, UK, US.

reporting persons often do not have the means to access the remedies available to them. Reporting persons should be also able to seek interim relief in the form of a provisional measure to stop threats or continuing acts of retaliation, or prevent irreversible damage, while proceedings are ongoing. The international legal framework for protected reporting of corruption is silent on the forms of protection and remedies that should be made available to reporting persons. This deficiency should be urgently rectified if potential whistleblowers are to have confidence in the legal framework for reporting.

3.5 The distorting effect of financial incentives

Five countries have, to date, introduced financial incentives for reporting and others are considering introducing rewards in the context of reforms or draft whistleblower protection legislation.[66] The most established frameworks for financial incentives are those in the US and Korea.

Following the enactment of the Dodd-Frank Act in 2010, section 21F,5 entitled 'Securities Whistleblower Incentives and Protection' was inserted into the US Exchange Act and directs the US SEC to 'make monetary awards to eligible individuals who voluntarily provide original information that leads to successful Commission enforcement actions resulting in monetary sanctions over $1 million and successful related actions.' Awards must be made in an amount equal to 10 to 30% of the monetary sanctions collected. To ensure that whistleblower payments would not diminish the amount of recovery for victims of securities law violations, Congress established a separate fund, called the Investor Protection Fund (Fund), from which eligible whistleblowers are paid. To date, over 59 individuals have been awarded over $326 million for having provided information and cooperation which assisted the Commission in bringing successful enforcement actions. Twelve of these individuals were foreign whistleblowers.[67]

Korea's Anti-Corruption and Civil Rights Commission (ACRC) is mandated under the Anti-Corruption Act and the Act on the Protection of Public Interest Whistleblowers (2011) to provide financial rewards to public and private sector whistleblowers who report internally within their organization or directly to the ACRC in cases of internal reporting which has led to direct recovery or increase of revenue of central or local governments, awards can range from 4 to 20% of the assets recovered up to KRW 2 billion; or up to KRW 20 million in cases of whistleblowing which contributed to upholding the public interest or prevented losses to, or led to pecuniary advantages for, central or local governments.

66 Brazil, Korea, Lithuania, Slovak Republic, United States. Australian Parliamentary Joint Committee on Corporations and Financial Services, Whistleblower Protections (Senate Printing Unit, Parliament House, Canberra, 2017): Recommendations 11.1 and 11.2, p. xvii, recommends that, following the imposition of a penalty against a wrongdoer by a Court, a whistleblower protection body or prescribed law enforcement agencies may give a 'reward' to any relevant whistleblower.

67 US SEC, *2018 Annual Report* (n 10) 1.

In addition, the Act permits whistleblowers to request compensation for their expenses, such as medical or psychological treatment, removal costs due to job transfer, and legal fees. To date, the ACRC has paid rewards totalling KRW 11.8 billion ($10.6 million) in 412 corruption cases, in relation to which the Korean government was able to recover KRW 137 billion ($122.9 million) for public organizations.[68]

While financial rewards can contribute to covering costs and compensating damages suffered as a result of retaliation, they can have a distorting effect on reporting and potentially expose reporting persons (particularly those located abroad) to additional risks when not accompanied by other forms of protection. A recent study has shown that the existence of financial rewards 'hijacks the moral imperative' of whistleblowers by introducing a cost-benefit analysis into the decision as to when (e.g., allowing the fraud or misconduct to create the maximum damage and thereby potentially increase the sanction and accompanying reward), or even whether to report.[69] Rewards are often conditional on reporting to designated authorities, which can also be problematic for employees who may be primarily inclined to report within their organization (see discussion above, part 1.1).

3.6 *Absence of oversight authorities or monitoring and evaluation mechanisms*

Twenty countries have designated a specific authority to receive whistleblower reports and/or advise and ensure statutory protections are offered to whistleblowers.[70] The majority (12) have nominated the Ombudsman,[71] or public sector equivalent,[72] to oversee whistleblower protection legislation, although others have entrusted this role to anti-corruption authorities,[73] prosecutorial authorities or financial regulators,[74] or NGOs.[75] Several countries also require these agencies to provide annual reports detailing information such as the number of protected disclosures, action taken in response to those disclosures, and other information as may be requested (without prejudice to maintaining the confidentiality of the reporting person). While these agencies carry out an array of roles with respect to

68 Anti-corruption and Civil Rights Commission, *Annual Report* (2017).

69 Leslie Berger, Stephen Perreault, and James Wainberg 'Hijacking the Moral Imperative: How Financial Incentives can Discourage Whistleblower Reporting' (2017) 36(3) Auditing: A Journal of Theory & Practice 1.

70 Australia, Belgium, Canada, France, Greece, Hungary, India, Ireland, Israel, Italy, Korea, Latvia, Lithuania, Luxembourg, Netherlands, New Zealand, Peru, Slovak Republic, Slovenia, US.

71 Australia, Belgium, France, Hungary, Israel, Italy, New Zealand, Slovak Republic.

72 Canada, India, Israel, Peru, US.

73 Italy, Korea, Slovenia.

74 Australia, Greece, Lithuania, US.

75 Ireland, Luxembourg.

receiving and treating protected disclosures, in most countries, reporting persons have to turn to court(s) to seek remedies for retaliation. The Netherlands is the only country to have established a dedicated, independent, government-funded agency to implement its whistleblower protection legislation and perform the combined tasks of advice, psychosocial care, investigation of alleged wrongdoing and retaliation, and prevention.[76] There are obvious resource implications for empowering existing agencies—or creating independent authorities—to oversee and enforce whistleblower protection. However, with such a scattered approach across jurisdictions between designated authorities and reporting frameworks (see above part 3.3, in relation to tiered approaches to reporting), there is an increasing lack of clarity and certainty for whistleblowers as to how, where, and when to report, as well as the consequences for doing so.

Monitoring and evaluation mechanisms for protected reporting frameworks are essential to their effectiveness and to enable such systems to adjust to new challenges that arise following enactment (e.g., the need for encrypted reporting; appropriate 'carve-outs' to take into account subsequent information disclosure legislation). The whistleblower protection laws in Australia, Ireland, Japan, and New Zealand all originally provided for a statutory review of the operation of the legislation within a prescribed timeframe.[77] These provisions for ongoing monitoring and evaluation, if entrenched more broadly in the international legal framework for whistleblower protection (see, for example, the EU Directive), would provide an important opportunity to ensure greater harmony of standards across jurisdictions and identify emerging trends to be addressed in future reforms.

3.7 An uncertain and contradictory legal landscape for disclosure

Countries with comprehensive, standalone whistleblower protection legislation can risk undermining its effectiveness if they do not address potential conflicts with other laws governing issues such as prohibition of disclosure of information (i.e., secrecy laws), data protection, and defamation. By reporting wrongdoing, in addition to exposure to workplace retaliation, and in the absence of appropriate legislative 'carve-outs,' whistleblowers in many jurisdictions also risk criminal prosecution or civil claims in relation to their disclosures. Even laws intended to promote greater transparency and accountability, such as freedom of information legislation, could be used to uncover the identities of reporting persons and their facilitators.[78]

76 See also Loyens and Vandekerckhove (n 51).

77 Public Interest Disclosure Act (2013) s 82A (Australia); Protected Disclosures Act (2014) (Ireland) s 2; Whistleblower Protection Act (2004) (Japan), supplementary provisions, art 2; Protected Disclosures Act (2000) (NZ) s 24 (repealed).

78 See, for example, Vlad Lavrov and Eva Kubaniova, 'Freedom of Information Law: Reporter's Best Friend or Killer?' (2018) <https://www.occrp.org/en/amurderedjournalistslastinvestigation/freedom-of-information-law-reporters-best-friend-or-killer> accessed 1 June

As emphasized above (part 2.1), even at a multilateral level, there are incongruous standards with respect to obligations, on the one hand, to legislate for violation of trade secrecy, and on the other, potentially to protect whistleblowers. Transposition of the EU Trade Secrets Directive in France and Ireland, for example, has resulted in different thresholds and definitions being introduced for reporting persons disclosing commercial information, as opposed to other categories of information. The EU GDPR also creates a dichotomy for companies that, in some jurisdictions, are required to implement protected reporting frameworks, while risking hefty sanctions should that framework violate strict EU data protection rules. Time limits for data conservation could also be problematic for companies or indeed law enforcement or regulatory authorities that may need to refer to, or investigate, information disclosed by reporting persons in the context of internal protected reporting procedures but that has had to be destroyed for data protection purposes. Recent cases in Luxembourg and Switzerland have highlighted the potential criminal consequences for reporting persons in the financial sector.[79] Some of these cases embody the dichotomy of the whistleblower: s/he is offered financial bounties from foreign tax agencies for information leading to the recovery of evaded taxes, but risks gaol time in the country where the alleged misconduct took place for disclosing the same information. Certain employees or professions must navigate a labyrinth of legal reporting obligations violation of which could expose them to criminal liability (for example, with respect to anti-money laundering and counterterrorism financing), whilst also ensuring they are not liable for the same disclosure under professional or national secrecy laws or inadvertently expose themselves to liability for libel or defamation.[80]

The conflict between whistleblower protection and other laws is escalated in cases involving multiple jurisdictions and in the context of the increasingly global workplace. Piecemeal national whistleblower protection laws are not adapted to the globalized workforce and the negative consequences of the current disparity in national laws on reporting demonstrate a need for stronger, overarching legal standards to promote more comprehensive and effective whistleblower protection. Law enforcers lack resources to detect wrongdoings. Employees of multinational organizations are uniquely placed to report on corrupt practices and act as a valuable intelligence source for investigators and law enforcement bodies, particularly where the alleged misconduct extends beyond

2020. As discussed, Italy and New Zealand have both exempted their protected disclosures from the scope of their Freedom of Information legislation.

79 See, for example, the cases of Swiss Leaks (Hervé Falciani) and LuxLeaks (Antoine Deltour, Raphael Halet and Edouard Perrin): see n 18.

80 See, for example, James Exelby, 'The Cover Up at Dutch Multinational SBM' (*Vridj Nederland*, 13 February 2015) <https://www.vn.nl/the-cover-up-at-dutch-multinational-sbm/> accessed 1 June 2020.

their jurisdiction.[81] Recent cases exposed by whistleblowers include industrial scale tax avoidance, abuse of environmental protections, illegal mass surveillance, election tampering, grand corruption, and even the sexual abuse of children by peacekeepers. However, cross-border reporting requires harmonized legal protections. Whistleblowers may unwittingly expose themselves to criminal or civil actions in foreign jurisdictions in relation to their disclosures and face legal uncertainty between different scopes and definitions, conflicts of laws, and procedures. As a case in point, only four countries currently provide immunity from civil, criminal, or disciplinary proceedings arising from the protected disclosure,[82] whereas nine expressly provide for sanctions for malicious or false reporting.[83] The growing disparities between national whistleblower protection legal frameworks and the consequent uneven protection across countries have a seriously dissuasive effect on reporting and translate into missed opportunities to detect, prevent, and punish corruption. This disharmony within and between national legislative frameworks provides all the more justification for harmonization of standards at an international level.

4 Conclusion: towards transnationalization of whistleblower protection law

This chapter has sought to illustrate that, against a backdrop of near universal standards for criminalising corruption, the legal architecture for protected reporting, at both an international and national level, is ineffective at best and contradictory at worst. This situation dramatically undermines efforts to detect, prevent, and punish corruption and other forms of misconduct. In general, reporting persons are afforded insufficient protection, the protection granted is sometimes limited to specific sectors or circumstances, to restricted categories of persons, for reporting limited types of violations, or only against specific forms of workplace retaliation and often undermined by contradictions or conflicts with other laws governing, *inter alia*, information disclosure. The authors argue that one of the first steps towards a solution is the transnationalization of whistleblower protection law. The anti-corruption experience has demonstrated that uniform and universal legislation is not the panacea to the problem; however, it creates the necessary foundation for subsequent enforcement and cultural change. The current momentum for new EU-level protected reporting legislation is mirrored in other fora such as, for example, the G20 in the context of its Anti-Corruption Working Group's continued emphasis on whistleblower protection or the OECD in the context of the review of its 2009 Recommendation on further combating

81 Ashley Savage, 'Challenges and Opportunities of Cross-jurisdictional Whistleblowing' (OECD 2018) <http://www.oecd.org/corruption/integrity-forum/academic-papers/Savage.pdf> accessed 1 June 2020.

82 Ireland, Latvia, Lithuania, New Zealand.

83 Belgium, Canada, Chile, China, India, Italy, Latvia, Peru, South Africa.

foreign bribery.[84] Above all, there should be coordination to ensure common minimum standards and avoid inconsistent or contradictory obligations. Once in place, the transposition and implementation of these standards should be closely monitored, with a focus on their effectiveness in providing protection to those who are brave enough to speak the truth about corruption.

84 OECD, 'Strengthening the Anti-Bribery Convention: Review of the 2009 Anti-Bribery Recommendation' (2019) <http://www.oecd.org/corruption/2019-review-oecd-anti-bribery-recommendation.htm> accessed 1 June 2020.

14 The contract as anti-corruption platform for the global corporate sector

Jeffrey R. Boles[1]

In the current age of economic globalization and open-border commerce, the fight against corruption is developing into a worldwide movement flowing through the public and private sectors. Companies wishing to avoid prosecution for corruption-related offenses confront a growing and complex nexus of anti-corruption laws affecting their local and global operations, with non-compliance penalties posing significant criminal and civil liability coupled with reputational harm and potential exclusion from public contracts. Increased enforcement of anti-corruption law governing international commerce, including the Foreign Corrupt Practices Act (FCPA), Bribery Act 2010 (Bribery Act), and Criminal Code Act 1995 (Cth) in the United States, United Kingdom, and Australia, respectively, has dramatically changed the global anti-corruption compliance landscape.[2] Companies that operate internationally, or contract with third party agents that do so, face increased scrutiny under these laws and the accompanying need to implement compliance measures to avoid prosecution.[3]

The rise of anti-corruption legislation and enforcement has, in turn, shifted corporate culture towards a zero tolerance approach to bribery and other forms of corruption. Corresponding changes to corporate governance materialize in the formulation and implementation of internal anti-corruption policies and practices, typically centralized through a compliance program designed to ensure adherence with external anti-corruption regulations as they develop. Such programs properly structured can detect and address corrupt activity involving companies or their employees, with policies and practices incorporating anti-corruption principles that harmonize with existing legal and ethical obligations alongside business operations. The programs' features may include employee trainings, detailed codes of conduct, and anonymous and confidential reporting systems.

1 An earlier version of this chapter was first published as an article in the University of Pennsylvania Journal of Business Law.

2 Ben Allen, 'Contracting Out of Corruption' (*LinkedIn*, 2 March 2015) <https://www.linkedin.com/pulse/contracting-out-corruption-can-done-ben-allen?trk=portfolio_article-card_title> accessed 1 June 2020.

3 Ibid.

Heightened corruption risks surround third party agents, such as business development consultants, sales representatives, subcontractors, distributors, lawyers, accountants, and other intermediaries, as they pose immense liability concerns for companies conducting international business indirectly through these third parties.[4] The FCPA and Bribery Act, for example, impose liability upon organizations for the actions of their employees, distributors, and other agents when acting on their principals' behalf.[5] Moreover, a majority of recently reported FCPA cases involve bribery schemes that rely upon third-party intermediaries, highlighting the prevalence of this corrupt practice.[6]

Even with the most robust anti-corruption compliance program in place, a company cannot necessarily dictate how its third party agents carry out their internal operations, and no company can guarantee that its agents will bring zero corruption risk. This exposure leaves companies vulnerable to corrupt acts, with the third party agents constituting 'a chink in [organizations'] armour against bribery and corruption prosecution.'[7] Companies as a result 'are alive to the risk of being tainted by the corrupt action of a counterparty,'[8] rendering third-party risk management a necessity for companies with any direct or indirect international operations.

To address third party risk more effectively, the tools of contract law offer the private sector a form of protection from potential corrupt and unethical conduct arising from their consultants or other agents. Companies can include anti-corruption compliance provisions within their contracts with third party intermediaries, and the provisions can fundamentally proscribe by contract any corrupt activity related to the contract while it remains in force. If properly drafted and enforced, the provisions may shield a company from corrupt acts perpetrated by its third party intermediaries and in connection with any corresponding criminal, civil, or administrative proceedings.[9] Functioning as a warranty, the provisions may also serve as evidence that a company has not engaged in corrupt activity related to the contract prior to execution and during its lifetime. As the contract sets the bar for the principal–agent relationship, it offers a critical yet underutilized mechanism to help shield companies from criminal liability arising from this third party risk.

4 See F Joseph Warin and others, 'The British are Coming!: Britain Changes Its Law on Foreign Bribery and Joins the International Fight Against Corruption' (2010) 46 Texas International Law Journal 1 38.

5 15 US Code 2018 s 78dd-2(a)(3); Bribery Act 2010 (UK) ss 7(1), 8(1). See also Warin and others (n 3) 40–41 (comparing FCPA and Bribery Act provisions).

6 Arthur and Toni Rembe Rock Center for Corporate Governance, 'Third Party Intermediaries' (*FCPA Clearinghouse*, 7 January 2019) <http://fcpa.stanford.edu/chart-intermediary.html> accessed 1 June 2020.

7 Allen (n 2).

8 Katherine Meloni and Gabrielle Ereira, *Anti-Corruption Provisions in Loan Documentation* (Slaughter and May 2016).

9 Juan Francisco Gonzalez Guarderas, 'What Should You Know when Entering into a Contract with an Anti-Corruption Clause?' (*PBP*, 14 October 2016) <https://www.pbplaw.com/en/a-que-me-obligo-cuando-firmo-contrato-clausula-anticorrupcion/> accessed 1 June 2020.

While a party cannot contract out of criminal liability, anti-corruption contractual provisions may effectively shift liability risk such that it remains with the agent engaged in wrongdoing, provided such provisions are structured appropriately and integrated within a larger compliance program. Parties may draft anti-corruption contractual provisions to create mutual trust and cooperation, provide assurance of integrity, and protect the business relationship from the taint of corruption during the pre-contractual period through the lifespan of the contract. No set formula or government-endorsed standards exist internationally in relation to recommended content of anti-corruption provisions, leaving companies with a plethora of protection options from which to choose. Provisions could address suitable record-keeping measures, adequate internal controls and procedures, ongoing monitoring, and objective audit, suspension, termination, and indemnification rights in connection with the agreement, among other possibilities.

This chapter scrutinizes the synthesis between contract and anti-corruption law in the context of third party intermediary risk, explores the conceptual landscape and spectrum of anti-corruption contractual provisions available to business arrangements, and offers suggested models for drafting and enforcement as a risk-reduction strategy to minimize exposure in light of existing international anti-corruption legislation. Part 1 of the chapter provides overviews of the nature of corruption in the corporate sector, international anti-corruption enforcement through domestic legislation and international instruments, and the role of the corporate compliance program to address anti-corruption obligations. Part 2 examines the origins and legal background of anti-corruption contractual provisions as a corporate due diligence tool in commercial agreements, critiques existing model clauses proffered by international organizations, and surveys the range of possible anti-corruption rights and obligations available to contracting parties. Part 3 concludes with recommendations for harmonizing balanced and commercially workable contractual provisions with anti-corruption compliance program operations through structured risk management, analyzes the potential legal shortcomings with such provisions, and suggests ways in which subsequent legislative efforts can capitalize upon the beneficial effects of provision usage from a public policy perspective.

1 Business corruption and corresponding legal regulation

1.1 Corruption pervades the private sector

Corruption, the misuse of entrusted authority for private gain, permeates the private sector globally.[10] Corrupt acts, such as bribery, fraud, abuse of power, embezzlement, extortion, and money laundering, entice perpetrators to gain a

10 Transparency International, 'What Is Corruption?' <https://www.transparency.org/what-is-corruption> accessed 1 June 2020; Transparency International, 'Engaging the Private Sector in the Fight against Corruption' <https://www.transparency.org/whatwedo/activity/engaging_the_private_sector_in_the_fight_against_corruption> accessed 1 June 2020.

business advantage or garner illicit profit *sub rosa*, and research findings indicate such activity remains widespread across industries.[11] The International Monetary Fund estimates that businesses and individuals annually pay $1.5 trillion in bribes, amounting to roughly 2% of global GDP.[12] World Bank surveys from more than 135,000 firms across 139 countries show roughly 20% of such firms reported experiencing at least one bribery request.[13]

While no industry is immune, the energy, mining, construction, military defense, oil, telecommunications, medical and pharmaceutical, transportation, and property development sectors are particularly prone to corruption.[14] Across industries, ever-present opportunities to engage in corruption could surface at seemingly any point in the lifecycle of a transaction. Corruption may insert itself, for instance, in an infrastructure or construction project's identification, financing, planning, design, tendering, execution, operation, and/or maintenance phases.[15]

Deemed 'the single greatest obstacle to economic and social development around the world,' corruption ushers in economic, social, political, and environmental harms to societies it touches.[16] While companies may perceive that by engaging in corrupt acts, they may reap competitive advantages, empirical studies illustrate the damage corruption brings to the commercial realm. For example, empirical findings demonstrate that corruption creates operational inefficiencies in the business sector, requiring more employees to complete the same amount of work, ultimately making companies less productive.[17] Firms operating in corrupt regions show, *inter alia*, more inefficient management practices, smaller product

11 See Kathleen A Lacey and Barbara Crutchfield George, 'Crackdown on Money Laundering: A Comparative Analysis of the Feasibility and Effectiveness of Domestic and Multilateral Policy Reforms' (2003) 23 Northwestern Journal of International Law and Business 263, 303 (summarizing types of foreign corrupt activities); Transparency International, 'Our Priorities' <https://www.transparency.org/en/our-priorities> accessed 1 June 2020 (identifying industries prone to corruption).

12 International Monetary Fund, *Corruption: Costs and Mitigating Strategies* (IMF Staff Discussion Note SDN/16/05 2016) 5.

13 The World Bank, 'Enterprise Surveys: Corruption' <http://www.enterprisesurveys.org/data/exploretopics/corruption> accessed 1 June 2020.

14 OECD, 'Foreign Bribery Fact Sheet' (2014) <https://www.oecd.org/daf/anti-bribery/Foreign_Bribery_Factsheet_ENGLISH.pdf> accessed 1 June 2020, 1.

15 GIACC, 'How Corruption Occurs' <http://www.giaccentre.org/how_corruption_occurs.php> accessed 1 June 2020.

16 UNODC, '"It's a Crime": Corruption' (12 February 2015) <http://www.unodc.org/unodc/en/frontpage/2015/February/its-a-crime_-corruption.html> accessed 1 June 2020. See generally Susan Rose-Ackerman and Bonnie J Palifka, *Corruption and Government: Causes, Consequences, and Reform* (2nd edn, CUP 2016) 27–36 (summarizing empirical findings addressing the effects of corruption); Philip M. Nichols, 'The Business Case for Complying with Bribery Laws' (2012) 49 American Business Law Journal 325, 338–340 (analyzing harmful economic effects of corruption in the business sector).

17 Ernesto Dal Bóa and Martín A Rossi, 'Corruption and Inefficiency: Theory and Evidence from Electric Utilities' (2007) 91 Journal of Public Economics 939, 958–960.

markets, lower export prospects, and lower levels of innovation and R&D investment.[18] Indeed, a large academic consensus identifies the corrosive impact of corruption on economic growth.[19]

1.2 International anti-corruption enforcement through domestic legislation and international instruments

Most countries outlaw bribery and other forms of corruption through domestic legislation, and many use criminal sanctions and civil penalties with supplemental regulatory action to enforce and deter.[20] Typically an anti-corruption law extends its reach to transactions occurring within the respective jurisdiction, but a number of countries have enacted expansive criminal legislation with extraterritorial scope that forbids bribes to foreign officials in international transactions.[21] The FCPA and Bribery Act are perhaps the most prominent examples of such an approach.

The United States enacted the FCPA in 1977 to outlaw payments to foreign government officials that are made to assist in securing or retaining business.[22] The first criminal statute to outlaw international corruption, it prohibits individuals and companies from corruptly offering, promising, or providing anything of value to foreign officials in order to secure or retain an improper advantage.[23] It requires as well companies whose securities are listed in the United States to maintain books and records that accurately and fairly reflect the companies' transactions and maintain an adequate system of internal accounting controls.[24] Due to its broad jurisdictional interpretation, the law extends its reach extraterritorially

18 Daphne Athanasouli and Antoine Goujard, 'Corruption and Management Practices: Firm Level Evidence' (2015) 43 Journal of Comparative Economics 1014, 1032.

19 See, e.g., Transparency International, 'The Impact of Corruption on Growth and Inequality' (15 March 2014) <https://www.alreporter.com/media/2014/06/Impact_of_corruption_on_growth_and_inequality_2014.pdf> accessed 1 June 2020 (examining how corruption 'adversely affect long-term economic growth through its impact on investment, taxation, public expenditures and human development'); Giorleny D Altamirano, 'The Impact of the Inter-American Convention Against Corruption' (2007) 38 University of Miami Inter-American Law Review 487, 492–497 (discussing research findings regarding the negative impact of corruption on the economy).

20 See Jeffrey R Boles, 'Criminalizing the Problem of Unexplained Wealth: Illicit Enrichment Offenses and Human Rights Violations' (2015) 17 NYU Journal of Legislation and Public Policy 835, 842 (providing overview of international anti-corruption efforts).

21 See, e.g., 15 US Code 2018 ss 78dd-1ff; Antonio Argandoña, 'The 1996 ICC Report on Extortion and Bribery in International Business Transactions' (1997) 6 Business Ethics 134, 136 (discussing countries enacting anti-corruption legislation).

22 See Gideon Mark, 'Private FCPA Enforcement' (2012) 49 American Business Law Journal 419, 422 (providing a brief history of the FCPA).

23 15 US Code 2018 ss 78m, 78dd-1-78dd-3, 78ff. Rahul Kohli, 'Foreign Corrupt Practices Act' (2018) 55 American Criminal Law Review 1269, 1301: ('No other country enacted a similar piece of anti-bribery legislation until 1997 when the international community began to take substantial steps to criminalize corruption in transnational commercial dealings.')

24 15 US Code ss 78m(b)(2)(A)–(B).

to business transactions conducted entirely outside of the US.[25] Moreover, general corporate liability principles apply to the FCPA, rendering a company liable for FCPA violations through the actions of its officers, directors, employees, or agents acting within the scope of their employment and intended to benefit the company.[26]

The United Kingdom enacted the Bribery Act in 2010[27] to modernize and strengthen its anti-bribery laws, creating what 'has been widely received as one of the most far-reaching anti-bribery laws of any country or international organization.'[28] The Bribery Act criminalizes active bribery (offering, promising or giving a bribe), passive bribery (requesting, accepting or agreeing to receive a bribe), commercial bribery (private-to-private bribery), and bribery of a foreign official to obtain or retain business or advantage in conducting business.[29] It also creates a new type of corporate liability in the failure of a commercial organization to prevent bribery by persons associated with it.[30] This latter provision, the first of its kind globally, effectively imposes strict liability for organizations that fail to prevent bribery by their employees or agents,[31] and its broad extraterritorial reach covers any entity that conducts 'part of a business' in the UK[32] The Act tempers its 'failure to prevent' offense with a full defense available to any organization that has implemented adequate procedures to prevent bribery by persons associated with it.[33]

A growing, cross-border anti-corruption regime recently surfaced to coordinate national enforcement system efforts and encourage the development of

25 See Peter W Schroth, 'The United States and the International Bribery Conventions' (2002) 50 American Journal of Comparative Law 593, 602–604: ('In its current form, the FCPA purports to reach foreigners who have virtually any sort of contact with the United States in furtherance of a violation of the act and US nationals who do anything in furtherance of such a violation anywhere in the world.')

26 See US Department of Justice and US Securities and Exchange Commission, *FCPA Resource Guide to the US Foreign Corrupt Practices Act* (2012) 27 (discussing corporate liability principles for bribery violations).

27 Bribery Act 2010.

28 Kohli (n 23) 1307.

29 Bribery Act 2010 ss 1, 2, and 6.

30 Ibid s 7.

31 See Warin and others (n 4) 38.

32 Jon Jordan, 'Recent Developments in the Foreign Corrupt Practices Act & the New UK Bribery Act: A Global Trend towards Greater Accountability in the Prevention of Foreign Bribery' (2010) 7 NYU Journal of Law and Business. 845, 866: ('[A]ny international corporation that does any kind of business in the [UK] can be held criminally liable for failure to prevent bribery even when the corporation is not based in the [UK], the offensive bribe did not take place in the [UK], or the recipient of the bribe is not from the [UK].')

33 Bribery Act 2010 s 7; Ministry of Justice, *The Bribery Act 2010: Guidance* (2011) 8 ('The defence is also included in order to encourage commercial organisations to put procedures in place to prevent bribery by persons associated with them.'). The FCPA does not contain a similar defense. Jon Jordan, 'The Adequate Procedures Defense Under the UK Bribery Act: A British Idea for the Foreign Corrupt Practices Act' (2011) 17 Stanford Journal of Law Business and Finance 25, 33.

domestic criminal legislation.[34] The anti-bribery measures of international organizations largely facilitated the growth of this infrastructure, as the organizations' multilateral agreements require signatory nations to maintain criminal laws that penalize corruption and to implement other anti-corruption mechanisms.[35] The 1997 OECD Convention on Combatting Bribery of Foreign Public Officials in International Business Transactions,[36] the 1999 Council of Europe Criminal Law Convention on Corruption,[37] and the 2003 United Nations Convention against Corruption,[38] for instance, require signatory countries to criminalize bribery involving foreign public officials, and the agreements significantly facilitated the development of transnational bribery laws.[39] These collective efforts propelled the global anti-corruption movement, with most nations now retaining substantive laws that prohibit various corrupt activities.[40]

1.3 Attacking corruption in the private sector through the corporate compliance function

A self-policing private sector is necessary to fight corruption effectively, and governments can incentivize organizations to self-police and cooperate through reward-and-penalty approaches.[41] To manage the massive issue of identifying and

34 See Thomas R Snider and Won Kidane, 'Combating Corruption through International Law in Africa: A Comparative Analysis' (2007) 40 Cornell International Law Journal 691, 698–711 (detailing international anti-corruption initiatives).

35 See Peter J Henning, 'Public Corruption: A Comparative Analysis of International Corruption Conventions and United States Law' (2001) 18 Arizona Journal of International and Comparative Law 793, 814.

36 OECD, *Convention on Combatting Bribery of Foreign Public Officials in International Business Transactions and Other Related Documents* (2011) 7.

37 Council of Europe Criminal Law Convention on Corruption, ETS No.173, 27 January 1999.

38 United Nations Convention against Corruption (opened for signature 9 December 2003, entered into force 14 December 2005) 2349 UNTS 41, annex, art 16.

39 See Jeffrey R Boles, 'The Two Faces of Bribery: International Corruption Pathways Meet Conflicting Legislative Regimes' (2014) 35 Michigan Journal of International Law 673, 680. TRACE International, *Global Enforcement Report 2011* (2011): ('[t]he goal of such laws and conventions is to create a fair and transparent international business market rather than one skewed by under-the-table deals that enrich government officials at the expense of their fellow citizens.')

40 See Benjamin B Wagner and Leslie Gielow Jacobs, 'Retooling Law Enforcement to Investigate and Prosecute Entrenched Corruption: Key Criminal Procedure Reforms for Indonesia and Other Countries' (2008) 30 University of Pennsylvania Journal of International Law 183, 194: ('[M]ost developing countries now have a range of substantive provisions prohibiting bribery and other acts of public corruption.')

41 Julie R O'Sullivan, 'Some Thoughts on Proposed Revisions to the Organizational Guidelines' (2004) 1 Ohio State Journal of Criminal Law 487, 494 (examining how a corporation's liability exposure can significantly be reduced resulting from awarded credits for compliance programs, self-reporting, cooperation during the investigative stage, and accepting responsibility).

investigating corporate wrongdoing, particularly involving crimes like international bribery that may be virtually impossible to detect without corporate admission, governments can employ the threat of corporate criminal liability with the prospect of leniency as a dual mechanism to induce companies to monitor their own agents, identify wrongdoing, and make disclosures to the relevant government agency.[42] In doing so, governments shift the investigatory burden to companies, easing the practical difficulties governments face with the expensive and time-consuming nature of investigatory work, the complexity of corporate accounting and bookkeeping, and limited budgets.[43]

The US Sentencing Guidelines demonstrate this carrot-and-stick approach by offering to reward organizations that voluntarily disclose violations, cooperate with law enforcement, and 'promote an organizational culture that encourages ethical conduct and a commitment to compliance with the law' with a reduction in offense level.[44] The UK follows a similar approach,[45] and a number of international instruments also advocate for companies to adopt and implement compliance programs and codes of conduct.[46] With this growing dynamic, multinational companies have legal and financial incentives to exercise diligence in detecting and preventing wrongdoing and to sustain an ethical corporate culture with an effective compliance program.[47]

42 Rachel Brewster and Samuel W Buell, 'The Market for Global Anticorruption Enforcement' (2017) 80 Law and Contemporary Problems 193, 211.

43 Robert S Bennett and others, 'From Regulation to Prosecution to Cooperation: Trends in Corporate White Collar Crime Enforcement and the Evolving Role of the White Collar Criminal Defense Attorney' (2013) 68 Business Law 411, 417; William R McLucas and others, 'The Decline of the Attorney-Client Privilege in the Corporate Setting' (2006) 96 Journal of Criminal Law and Criminology 621, 639: (examining how 'private lawyers are effectively "deputized" in many internal investigations, and the government obtains the facts of their inquiry through waiver of attorney-client privilege.')

44 US Sentencing Guidelines Manual s 8B2.1(a)(2) (US Sentencing Commission 2004); Justice Manual s 9-28.300 (November 2018) (discussing factors to be considered when deciding whether to bring charges against a corporate target, including, *inter alia*, 'the corporation's willingness to cooperate, including as to potential wrongdoing by its agents').

45 Ministry of Justice, *The Bribery Act 2010: Guidance* (n 32) 8: ('The commercial organisation's willingness to co-operate with an investigation under the Bribery Act and to make a full disclosure will also be taken into account in any decision as to whether it is appropriate to commence criminal proceedings.'); Kevin J Smith, 'The Foreign Corrupt Practices Act: Set Aside the Moral and Ethical Debates, How Does One Operate within this Law?' (2017) 45 Hofstra Law Review 1119, 1134–1135 (comparing US and UK approaches).

46 See, e.g., OECD, Recommendation of the Council for Further Combating Bribery of Foreign Public Officials in Internal Business Transactions (26 November 2009) III, X (recommending that its signatory countries adopt business sector requirements regarding the implementation of accounting, external audit, internal control, ethics, and compliance requirements and practices in order to detect and prevent bribery of foreign public officials).

47 Maurice E Stucke, 'In Search of Effective Ethics & Compliance Programs' (2014) 39 Journal of Corporation Law 769, 775. But see, *United States v. Potter* 463 F.3d 9, 25–26 (1st Cir. 2006) (noting that a corporation cannot 'avoid liability by adopting abstract rules' that prohibit its agents from engaging in illegal conduct, as '[e]ven a specific directive to an agent or

Compliance programs constitute a fundamental component of a company's enterprise risk management and internal controls framework that assesses the operative risks and realities inherent in the company's operations.[48] Properly structured compliance programs can effectively detect and address instances of corruption involving companies or their agents, with such anti-corruption practices serving to protect corporate reputations and stakeholder interests.[49] While no compliance program could detect every instance of criminal activity involving a company, critical factors inherent in any program, from the lens of the Department of Justice (DOJ), center upon 'whether the program is adequately designed for maximum effectiveness in preventing and detecting wrongdoing by employees and whether corporate management is enforcing the program or is tacitly encouraging or pressuring employees to engage in misconduct to achieve business objectives.'[50]

There is no set formula for structuring a compliance program, but prosecutors, when assessing such programs, typically examine whether a program is well designed, effective in application, and applied earnestly and in good faith, as they differentiate between mere 'paper programs' and suitably designed and implemented programs that are reviewed and revised as appropriate.[51] Companies with effective programs maintain sufficient compliance staff to document, analyze, utilize, and audit results from the programs and provide adequate training to employees and other agents regarding the program's operations and company's commitment to the program.[52] Such programs tailor their functions to align with the fundamentals of company product lines or services and attendant market supply chain and work force, the degree of regulation and government interaction, and the extent to which the company operates in countries with a high risk of corruption.[53]

Through its operations, an effective compliance program bridges legal, risk management and ethics policy and practice by thwarting corruption and other illicit activity in a risk-based approach tailored to the company's industry, size,

employee or honest efforts to police such rules do not automatically free the company for the wrongful acts of agents'); Justice Manual s 9-28.800 (November 2015) ('[T]he existence of a compliance program is not sufficient, in and of itself, to justify not charging a corporation for criminal misconduct undertaken by its officers, directors, employees, or agents.').

48 Ibid.

49 United Nations Global Compact, 'Eliminate Corruption to Build Sustainable, Inclusive and Transparent Societies' <https://www.unglobalcompact.org/what-is-gc/our-work/governance/anti-corruption> accessed 1 June 2020 (discussing how mobilizing business can provide a united voice against corruption, as '[c]ollective action is essential for bringing an end to a systemic issue that is too complex for any company to tackle alone.').

50 Justice Manual s 9-28.800.B (November 2015).

51 Ibid.

52 Ibid; Ministry of Justice, *The Bribery Act 2010: Guidance* (n 33) 20–31 (detailing its six guiding principles for effective compliance programs).

53 US Department of Justice and US Securities and Exchange Commission, *FCPA Resource Guide* (n 26) 40.

and location and focused upon identified corruption risks and schemes.[54] Such a compliance program can deter corruption from multiple angles by overseeing proper accounting and auditing practices that ensure all firm expenditures have been authorized and accounted for, taking appropriate disciplinary action against any employee or agent who has violated company anti-corruption policies, and providing an anonymous reporting system where any employee or agent can report apparent anti-corruption policy violations without fear of retribution.[55]

2 Contract law as anti-corruption mechanism to fight third party risk

2.1 The advent of anti-corruption contractual provisions as corporate due diligence tools

Business development consultants, sales representatives, subcontractors, distributors, lawyers, accountants, and other intermediaries pose corruption risks that constitute massive liability concerns for companies conducting overseas business indirectly through such third parties.[56] The FCPA and Bribery Act impose liability upon organizations for the actions of their employees, distributors, and other third party agents when acting on their principals' behalf.[57] Recent FCPA enforcement actions show how third party intermediaries frequently engage in international business transactions and attempt to conceal bribery payments to foreign officials.[58] Roughly 90% of all recently reported FCPA cases involve bribery schemes that rely upon third party intermediaries, rendering third party risk management a critical concern for companies with overseas operations.[59]

In apparent recognition of the fulsome liability danger, the primary internationally recognized business instruments on anti-bribery, including those from the World Bank, OECD, International Chamber of Commerce (ICC), and Transparency International, offer guidance on internal controls and compliance practices pertaining to third party risk in order to assist companies in addressing

54 Professors David Hess and Thomas Dunfee have argued that, to impact corrupt practices, a company's anti-corruption principles 'must (1) emphasize transparency; (2) provide guidance concerning specific practices associated with paying bribes; (3) be relevant to organizational environments; (4) identify itself with and be supported by an independent entity such as a non-governmental organization or an academic center, and, perhaps most importantly; (5) be capable of monitoring and assessment by external, independent entities, such as social and financial auditors.' David Hess and Thomas W Dunfee, 'Fighting Corruption: A Principled Approach: The C Principles (Combating Corruption)' (2000) 33 Cornell International Law Journal 593, 618.

55 Ibid 621.

56 See Warin and others (n 4) 38.

57 15 US Code 1998 s 78dd-2(a)(3) ; Bribery Act 2010 ss 7(1), 8(1). See also Warin and others (n 3) 40–41 (comparing the FCPA and Bribery Act provisions).

58 KPMG, *Third-Party Risk Management* (2014) 2–3.

59 Arthur and Toni Rembe Rock Center for Corporate Governance (n 6).

this precarious area.[60] The instruments advocate for the adoption of corporate policies that support third party compliance with anti-corruption rules.[61] Recurring advice in such instruments surrounds the need to conduct 'properly documented risk-based due diligence pertaining to the hiring, as well as the appropriate and regular oversight of business partners,'[62] to notify business partners of a company's commitment to abiding by the terms of applicable anti-bribery laws and of the company's compliance program addressing anti-bribery practices, and to seek a reciprocal commitment from business partners.[63]

To mitigate the risk that third party payments will constitute bribery violations, many companies now implement extensive compliance policies and practices that govern third party intermediary conduct as part of their due diligence processes.[64] One due diligence process, in particular, the inclusion of anti-corruption compliance provisions in agreements with third party intermediaries, has been recognized as one the most effective ways to mitigate liability risks posed by third parties.[65] If structured and enforced properly, the provisions may effectively protect a company from corrupt acts perpetrated by its third party intermediaries and in connection with any resulting criminal, administrative, or civil proceedings.[66]

These provisions essentially prohibit by contract third party intermediaries and their agents from engaging in any corrupt activity related to the contract while it remains in force. Moreover, the provisions may provide evidence that a company has not paid bribes or otherwise engaged in corrupt activity related to the contract prior to the contract's execution and during its lifetime.[67]

60 OECD and others, *Anti-Corruption Ethics and Compliance Handbook for Business* (2013) 38–46 (detailing provisions of business guidance instruments on anti-bribery).

61 Ibid.

62 OECD, *Good Practice Guidance on Internal Controls, Ethics and Compliance* (18 February 2010, adopted 26 November 2008) Annex II, [6.i]. *See also* World Bank Group, *Integrity Compliance Guidelines* (September 2010) 5.1: ('Conduct properly documented, risk-based due diligence (including to identify any beneficial owners or other beneficiaries not on record) before entering into a relationship with a business partner, and on an ongoing basis')

63 OECD, *Good Practice Guidance* (n 62) s A.6.ii–iii.

64 Warin and others (n 4) 40 (discussing diligence regarding FCPA risks of third-party business partners); Priya Cherian Huskins, 'FCPA Prosecutions: Liability Trend to Watch', (2008) 60 Stanford Law Review 1447, 1456.

65 See Kohli (n 23) 1322: ('Addressing FCPA compliance in the formative contract is widely recognized as the best way to mitigate risks posed by 'red flag' transactions.'); Daniel J Grimm, 'Traversing the Minefield: Joint Ventures and the Foreign Corrupt Practices Act' (2014) 9 Virginia Law and Business Review 91, 146: ('FCPA risks can be further reduced by including various contractual provisions within joint-venture agreements and contracts with third parties.'); Meloni and Ereira (n 8) 1 (discussing usage of anti-corruption provision in English law loan documentation); Neil McInnes, 'Addressing the Bribery Act in Your Contracts: A Tiered Approach' *Thomson Reuters Construction Blog* (13 June 2012) <http://constructionblog.practicallaw.com/addressing-the-bribery-act-in-your-contracts-a-tiered-approach/> accessed 1 June 2020 (analyzing effective use of anti-corruption clauses in supply chain and subcontractor contracts).

66 Guarderas (n 9).

67 Ibid.

Government agencies through earlier enforcement activity served as initial catalysts to raise private sector awareness on the use of anti-corruption contractual provisions with third party agents. They have required defendants in enforcement actions to insert anti-corruption provisions in their third party contracts as part of their larger due diligence compliance efforts. For instance, defendant Metcalf and Eddy agreed as part of its consent agreement with the DOJ in 1999 to implement an anti-corruption compliance program where contracts with its agents and other representatives include a clause stating that the parties will not offer bribes and that the counterparty agent will not employ a sub-agent without the prior written consent of Metcalf and Eddy.[68] The DOJ also endorsed the use of anti-corruption compliance provisions in third party contracts through issued opinions[69] and deferred prosecution agreements,[70] and the SEC has noted in prior complaints whether defendants contractually bound their third party consultants to comply with the FCPA.[71]

The UK Ministry of Justice likewise advocates for firms to follow this approach.[72] It strongly advocates for companies to employ anti-corruption provisions with counterparties in their supply chain.

The principal way in which commercial organisations may decide to approach bribery risks which arise as a result of a supply chain is by employing the types of anti-bribery procedures referred to elsewhere in this guidance (e.g., risk-based

68 Consent and Undertaking of Metcalf and Eddy Inc: *United States v. Metcalf & Eddy, Inc.* No. 99-cv-12566 (D. Mass. 1999) [4.i]. This case constitutes the first instance where the DOJ provided a detailed list of features that a defendant corporation should include in a remedial compliance and ethics program; Philip Urofsky and others, 'How Should We Measure the Effectiveness of the Foreign Corrupt Practices Act? Don't Break What Isn't Broken-The Fallacies of Reform' (2012) 73 Ohio State Law Journal 1145, 1153–54.

69 See US Department of Justice, 'FCPA Opinion Procedure Release No 2008–02' (13 June 2008) <https://www.justice.gov/sites/default/files/criminal-fraud/legacy/2010/04/11/0802.pdf> accessed 1 June 2020, 3. ('All agents and other third parties … will as soon as commercially reasonable be required to sign new contracts … with Halliburton that incorporate appropriate FCPA and anti-corruption representations and warranties, anti-corruption provisions, and audit rights, as provided for under Halliburton's Code of Business Conduct and related policies and procedures.')

70 See Deferred Prosecution Agreement, C-7, *United States v. Panalpina World Transport (Holding) Ltd.*, No. 4:10-cr-00769 (S.D. Tex. Nov. 4, 2010) ('Panalpina will include standard provisions in agreements, contracts, and renewals thereof with all agents and business partners that are reasonably calculated to prevent violations of the anticorruption laws').

71 See Complaint at [17], *Securities and Exchange Commission v. Avon Products, Inc.*, No. 14-CV-9956 (S.D.N.Y. Dec. 17, 2014) ('Avon Products China did not contractually bind Consulting Company 1 to comply with the FCPA').

72 See Ministry of Justice, *The Bribery Act 2010: Guidance* (n 33) 39 (endorsing the use of suitable contractual terms on bribery prevention measures in agreements between parties). Notably, the US Sentencing Commission in its Sentencing Guidelines for Organizations does not explicitly address the use of anti-corruption contractual provisions, but comments that large organizations should encourage smaller organizations that seek to contract with them to implement effective compliance and ethics programs. US Sentencing Guidelines Manual, s 8B2.1(b), cmt. 2(C)(ii) (US Sentencing Commission 2004).

due diligence and the use of anti-bribery terms and conditions) in the relationship with their contractual counterparty, and by requesting that counterparty to adopt a similar approach with the next party in the chain.[73]

Scholars and practitioners have also endorsed the application of anti-corruption contractual provisions to corporate business partners and stressed their utility in helping to control difficulties companies face in complying with anti-corruption laws.[74] David Hess and Thomas Dunfee have highlighted how agents, particularly those that facilitate sales and marketing, are often conduits by which firms make payments, and such firms may not be aware of their sales and marketing agents making improper payments to government officials using commissions and fees.[75] Their anti-corruption C2 Principles require firms to obtain from all of their suppliers affirmation that the suppliers have not and will not make improper payments in any contract to which the firm is a party.[76]

Others note how anti-corruption contractual provisions containing appropriate remedies for breach[77] may prevent a company from having to choose between continuing an agreement that raises corruption risks or subsequently breaching the agreement due to previously unknown corruption liability.[78] The provisions may allow the company to exit the contractual relationship cleanly.[79]

Warin and colleagues emphasize the benefits of combining anti-corruption contractual provisions with appropriate due diligence on a third party, as such a combination may significantly decrease the likelihood that prosecutors would allege that a company 'consciously disregarded or remained deliberately ignorant of the possibility of a corrupt payment, even if the third party does make such a payment.'[80] Beyond reducing the risk of prosecution, companies that include properly enforced anti-corruption contractual provisions in their third party contracts may pursue a private cause of action against their agents for breach of contract if the agents materially violate the provisions.[81]

73 Ministry of Justice, *The Bribery Act 2010: Guidance* (n 33) 16.

74 See Ike Adams and Robert Keeling, 'Vicarious Liability Risks Facing the Financial Industry under the FCPA' (2017) 9 George Mason Journal of International Commercial Law 1, 32 (advocating for 'appropriate contractual representations with third-party intermediaries relating to compliance with the FCPA and relevant foreign anti-corruption laws'); Christopher F Corr and Judd Lawler, 'Damned If You Do, Damned If You Don't? The OECD Convention and the Globalization of Anti-Bribery Measures' (1999) 32 Vanderbilt Journal of Transnational Law 1249, 1343.

75 Hess and Dunfee (n 54) 622.

76 Ibid 621. Designed for voluntary adoption by firms, the C2 Principles 'require firms to implement procedures to prevent the payment of bribes and to publicly disclose their progress and efforts towards these ends': ibid 594.

77 See text at n 122 (examining termination rights).

78 Kohli (n 23) 1322.

79 Grimm (n 65) 146–147.

80 Warin and others (n 4) 41.

81 Brian C Harms, 'Holding Public Officials Accountable in the International Realm: A New Multi-Layered Strategy to Combat Corruption' (2000) 33 Cornell International Law Journal 159, 205 n 290.

2.2 *Formalizing anti-corruption contractual provisions with model clauses*

While the benefits of anti-corruption contractual provisions have been recognized for roughly two decades, there has been no apparent consensus or uniform approach regarding when to require such provisions in a contract or what types of anti-corruption commitments within which to include.[82] For instance, many international anti-bribery business instruments stress the importance of including anti-corruption commitments in contracts with business partners but differ in the specific types of commitments and breach remedies they recommend.[83]

To illustrate, the OECD Good Practice Guidance on Internal Controls, Ethics and Compliance advises companies to consider informing their business partners of their anti-corruption commitments and ethics and compliance program and to seek 'a reciprocal commitment from business partners.'[84] The World Economic Forum's PACI Principles for Countering Bribery (the PACI Principles) advises that an enterprise's 'agent, adviser or other intermediary should contractually agree in writing to comply with the enterprise's [compliance program]' and that '[p]rovision should be included in all contracts with agents, advisers and other intermediaries relating to access to records, cooperation in investigations and similar matters pertaining to the contract.'[85] Regarding breach of an anti-corruption provision, the PACI Principles advise that an enterprise 'should monitor the conduct of its agents, advisers and other intermediaries and should have a contractual right of termination in case of conduct inconsistent with the [enterprise's compliance program].'[86]

Providing companies with more concrete direction, the International Chamber of Commerce (ICC) in 2012 published a model anti-corruption clause (ICC Clause) as guidance 'designed to be applied by enterprises of any size, whether large, medium or small.'[87] The ICC Clause aims 'to provide parties with a contractual provision that will reassure them about the integrity of their counterparts during the pre-contractual period as well as during the term of the contract and even thereafter,' and offers two contractual alternatives that parties

82 See McInnes (n 65) (noting that the Ministry of Justice guidance does not provide detail on anti-bribery terms and conditions).

83 See text at n 56 (discussing recommendations of international anti-bribery instruments).

84 OECD, *Good Practice Guidance* (n 62) s A.6.ii.

85 See World Economic Forum, *Anti-Corruption Handbook: Implementing the PACI Principles for Countering Bribery* (2007) 31.

86 Ibid. The World Bank Group Integrity Compliance Guidelines Similarly Recommend the Inclusion of a Contractual Termination Right in the Event of a Business Counterparty's Corrupt Misconduct. World Bank, *Integrity Compliance Guidelines* (n 62) s 6.2 (advising that business partner contracts should include 'express contractual obligations, remedies and/or penalties in relation to [m]isconduct (including in the case of business partners, a plan to exit from the arrangement, such as a contractual right of termination, in the event that the business partner engages in [m]isconduct)).'

87 ICC, *ICC Anti-Corruption Clause* (2012) 1.

can insert into a contract, with the first constituting a more substantive anti-corruption undertaking by the parties.[88]

This first alternative incorporates Part I of the ICC Rules on Combating Corruption (ICC Rules),[89] where each party agrees that it, its officers, directors, or employees

> have not offered, promised, given, authorized, solicited or accepted any undue … advantage … in any way connected with the [c]ontract and that it has taken reasonable measures to prevent … third parties, subject to its control or determining influence, from doing so.[90]

The parties also agree that, 'at all times in connection with and throughout the course of the [c]ontract and thereafter,' they will not engage in bribery, extortion or solicitation, trading in influence or money laundering, and that they will take 'reasonable measures' to ensure that the third parties they engage will likewise refrain from such activity.[91] Finally, the first alternative provides a right to suspend or terminate the contract if a party provides evidence that its counterparty has materially breached the above anti-corruption provisions, and the counterparty fails to take the necessary remedial action.[92] Upon notice of apparent breach, the notified counterparty may invoke a defense by proving that, at the time the evidence of breach had arisen, it had implemented 'adequate anti-corruption preventive measures … capable of detecting corruption and of promoting a culture of integrity in its organization.'[93]

The second alternative offers a weaker undertaking for the contracting parties. It mandates that each party simply commits to putting into place a corporate anti-corruption compliance program at the time the parties enter into the contract or soon thereafter, and advises that the compliance program should be 'adapted to

88 Ibid 2.

89 Ibid. The ICC presents two options for inclusion, either by reference or by incorporation of the full text of Part I, as in some jurisdictions incorporation by reference may be inadequate to create legal effects. See Lauri Railas, 'The Origins and Advantages of the International Chamber of Commerce Anti-Corruption Clause' (Ethic Intelligence November, 2013) (analyzing the ICC Clause).

90 ICC (n 87) 4.

91 Ibid. In connection with taking 'reasonable measures' with third party agents, the ICC Clause mandates that the contracting parties 'should instruct them neither to engage nor to tolerate that they engage in any act of corruption; not use them as a conduit for any corrupt practice; hire them only to the extent appropriate for the regular conduct of the [p]arty's business; and not pay them more than an appropriate remuneration for their legitimate services': ibid 5.

92 Ibid. For a discussion on how a breach of a non-corruption obligation can be remedied, see Railas (n 89) (arguing that the breaches that are not attributable to the directing mind of an organization may be remedied by a reorganization of work, increased surveillance, or firing the individuals who committed the offense).

93 Ibid.

[each party's] particular circumstances and capable of detecting corruption and of promoting a culture of integrity in its organization.'[94] The parties must maintain such program throughout the contract's lifetime,[95] and if one party proffers evidence that the counterparty's compliance program contains material deficiencies that undermine its efficiency, it can require the counterparty to take remedial action upon notice. If the counterparty fails to remediate, the notifying party has the right to suspend or terminate the contract.[96]

The Global Infrastructure Anti-Corruption Centre (GIACC) also issued guidance on anti-corruption model clauses that can be included in organizations' contracts with business associates, and the GIACC model terms expand the range of anti-corruption commitments beyond those proffered by the ICC Clause.[97] Like the ICC, the GIACC offers two contractual alternatives, with the first constituting a simple commitment for the contracting business associate 'not to participate in any corrupt conduct.'[98] The second alternative offers more comprehensive anti-corruption commitments for an organization's choosing, including provisions concerning corruption prevention, training, auditing, investigating, and termination rights.[99]

The GIACC's more comprehensive provisions mandate that, *inter alia*, the business associate agree that it, its personnel, subsidiaries, and related companies will not participate in any corrupt practices relating to the contract and that it will take reasonable steps to ensure that its agents and associates do not participate in any corrupt practices.[100] The business associate must also confirm that it,

94 Ibid. Lauri Railas explains that the ICC included the second alternative in the final days of preparation to address concerns over a contracting party's improper motives. See Railas (n 89) (explaining that '[t]here was a fear that random actions of insignificant employees would jeopardise the existence of a long-term contractual relationship in a situation where a contracting partner wants to get rid of a binding contract that has become disadvantageous due to commercial developments.').

95 ICC (n 87) 5.

96 Ibid at 6.

97 GIACC, 'Contract Terms' <http://www.giaccentre.org/contract_terms.php> accessed 1 June 2020, pts 1–5. The GIACC is an independent non-profit organization whose mission is to provide resources to assist in understanding, identifying, and preventing corruption in the infrastructure, construction, and engineering sectors. GIACC, 'About GIACC' <http://www.giaccentre.org/index.php> accessed 1 June 2020.

98 GIACC, 'Contract Terms' (n 96) pt 4. The GIACC defines a 'business associate' to mean 'any party with which the organisation contracts, including but not limited to clients, customers, joint venture partners, consortium partners, contractors, consultants, sub-contractors, suppliers, vendors, advisors, agents, distributors, representatives and intermediaries (but excluding the organisation's personnel).' GIACC, 'Business Associate Corruption Risk Assessment' <http://www.giaccentre.org/RiskAssessment-BusinessAssociate.php> accessed 1 June 2020.

99 GIACC, *Sample Anti-Corruption Contract Commitments* (19 February 2016) 1–12.

100 GIACC, 'Contract Terms' (n 97) pt 5. The GIACC defines corrupt conduct to include bribery, extortion, fraud, cartels, abuse of power, embezzlement, and money laundering. GIACC, *Sample Anti-Corruption Contract Commitments* (n 99) 1.

its owners, directors, and managers 'have not been investigated, convicted or debarred for corruption.'[101] Moreover, the business associate must agree to provide anti-corruption training to its personnel, and allow the contracting counterparty to (i) audit the business associate in relation to the underlying transaction,[102] (ii) undertake an investigation in the event of suspected or actual corruption involving the business associate,[103] and (iii) terminate the contract immediately in the event that the business associate breaches any of the anti-corruption provisions.[104] Finally, the business associate must agree to indemnify the counterparty for any liability or loss suffered due to any breach by the business associate of the anti-corruption provisions.[105]

2.3 *Parties may harness broad powers through an expanded range of anti-corruption commitments*

Anti-corruption contractual provisions offer basic protection that can address compliance obligations under the FCPA, UK Bribery Act, and other applicable laws when a company enters into an agreement with a business associate. Contracting parties may avail themselves of a wide range of anti-corruption undertakings and representations that can further strengthen anti-corruption commitments and that extend beyond those proffered by the ICC Clause and the GIACC model provisions. Such clauses fall into nine broad categories: (i) representations and warranties pertaining to compliance with relevant anti-corruption laws, (ii) rights to conduct audits of the third party's books and records, (iii) termination rights connected to any breach of the anti-corruption provisions, (iv) indemnification rights, (v) cooperation rights, (vi) restrictions on the use of sub-contractors, (vii) on-going training requirements, (viii) annual certification requirements, and (ix) re-qualification requirements.

101 Ibid pt 5(c). Under this provision, the business associate also agrees to notify its counterparty immediately in writing if at any time it becomes aware of any such investigation, conviction, or debarment. GIACC, *Sample Anti-Corruption Contract Commitments* (n 99) pt 2(b).

102 The purpose of the audit is for an organization to ensure as far as practicable that any payments it made to the business associate under the contract have not been used corruptly. Ibid pt 7.

103 The investigation provision requires the business associate to 'provide all reasonable assistance, information and documentation' to the counterparty during the course of the investigation: ibid 10.

104 GIACC, 'Contract Terms' (n 97) pt 5(g).

105 Ibid pt 5(h).

2.3.1 *Representations and warranties pertaining to anti-corruption compliance*

To follow a minimal requirement for an anti-corruption contractual commitment, a company can implement as an administrative procedure including in contracts between the company and any relevant business associate a simple provision that prohibits corruption.[106] The clause could require the parties to agree that they have not, and will not, participate in any corrupt practices in relation to the contract.[107] The ASCO Transport & Logistics client terms & conditions contract contains a clause that exemplifies this approach, where '[e]ach party warrants and represents that in negotiating and concluding the contract it has complied, and in performing its obligations under the contract it has complied and shall comply, with all applicable anti-bribery laws.'[108]

A company could more rigorously expand the scope of this clause, thereby expanding its protection, such that the business associate agrees to ensure that its personnel, partners, sub-contractors, suppliers, consultants, and other agents, as well as its subsidiaries and related companies, will not participate in any corrupt practices related to the contract. It could further supplement this protection by requiring the business associate to confirm that it, its owners, directors, and officers have not been investigated, convicted, or debarred for corruption.[109] In

106 Corrupt practices are typically defined to include bribery, extortion, fraud, abuse of power, cartels, embezzlement, money laundering, and any similar activities. See GIACC, *Sample Anti-Corruption Contract Commitments* (n 99) 1 (defining corrupt practices); International Financial Institutions Anti-Corruption Task Force, *Uniform Framework for Preventing and Combating Fraud and Corruption* (September 2006) 1 (defining fraudulent and corrupt practices).

107 Per the British Bankers' Association (BBA) guidance, '[t]he contracts should warrant that the associated person has not and will not breach relevant anti-corruption laws.' Meloni and Ereira (n 8) 6 (quoting the BBA guidance).

108 ASCO Transport & Logistics, *AT&L Client Terms & Conditions* (2 March 2017) pt 28.1; TUI Group, 'Information on the Anti-Corruption Clause' <https://www.tuigroup.com/en-en/meta/purchase_conditions/anti-corruption-clause> accessed 1 June 2020: (stating that '[t]he supplier agrees to comply with all German legislation to combat corruption in the execution of the contractually agreed services.'). For an alternative approach that includes bribery-specific compliance template language, see Michael Volkov, 'Contracts and Anti-Corruption Compliance' (*Volkov*, 17 July 2011) <https://blog.volkovlaw.com/2011/07/contracts-and-anti-corruption-compliance/> accessed 1 June 2020: (providing that the business associate in all undertakings 'will make no payments of … anything of value, nor will such be offered, promised, or paid, directly or indirectly, to any foreign officials, political parties, party officials, candidates for public or political party office, to influence the acts of such [persons] in their official capacity, to induce them to use their influence … to obtain or retain business or gain an improper advantage in connection with any business venture or contract in which the company is a participant.').

109 See McInnes (n 65) 3 (discussing anti-corruption contractual warranties).

connection with such provisions, some companies make reference to their business partner-specific ethical codes of conduct to set broader ethical expectations.[110]

Finally, a company could require the business associate to warrant further that the business associate has implemented an anti-corruption compliance program that sets out adequate procedures designed to comply with the applicable anti-corruption laws and that the business associate will maintain and comply with its program for the duration of the contract.[111] Veolia follows this approach in its agreements with its suppliers, where a '[s]upplier undertakes to put in place and implement all necessary and reasonable policies and measures to prevent corruption.'[112] Such a provision effectively compels the business associate to maintain an internal anti-corruption compliance program for the duration of the contract.

2.3.2 *Rights to conduct audits on a counterparty*

As corruption by its nature transpires in secrecy, typically leaving no evidence trail, a company faces practical difficulties in determining whether its business partner has infringed upon an anti-corruption provision in an agreement.[113] The conclusions of an audit of a business partner's financial books and records may produce evidence of infringement, rendering an audit one of the few means for companies to detect corruption and resulting infringement by a business partner.[114] A contractually provided audit right can, accordingly, provide a party with a mechanism to monitor compliance with its anti-corruption commitments. The purpose of the audit confirms to a party that, as far as practicable, no payments made by that party to its counterparty under the agreement have been used

110 See, e.g., Phillips 66, 'Standard Compliance Clauses' (20 January 2017) <https://www.phillips66.co.uk/EN/about/commercial-uk/Documents/compliance%20clauses%20%20trading%20170124.pd> accessed 1 June 2020, 1–2 (referencing standards of business ethics and business partner principles of conduct).

111 See ASCO Transport & Logistics (n 108) pt 28.2 ('The contractor warrants that it has [a compliance program] setting out adequate procedures to comply with applicable anti-bribery laws and that it will comply with such [compliance program] in respect of the contract').

112 Veolia, 'Anti Corruption Clause' <https://www.veolia.com/anz/anti-corruption-clause-0> accessed 1 June 2020, [1.3].

113 See, e.g., *JSG Trading Corp. v. United States Department of Agriculture* 176 F.3d 536, 545 (D.C. Cir. 1999): (stating that '[w]ithout a finding of secrecy and intent to induce, there appears to be nothing to distinguish an illegal bribe from a simple promotional gift.'); *United States v. Holzer* 816 F.2d 304, 309 (7th Cir. 1987) (observing that 'no public official … takes bribes openly'); *Sirkin v. Fourteenth Street Store* 124 A.D. 384, 391 (NY App. Div. 1908): (remarking that '[t]he vice [of bribery] lies in making the agreement without the knowledge of the master.')

114 Witness statements, particularly as a result of a whistleblowing mechanism, are another avenue to produce such evidence. See ICC (n 87) 10 (discussing evidence of non-compliance with anti-corruption commitments).

corruptly.[115] Parties can draft audit rights provisions to provide assurance that a counterparty maintains accurate financial books and records and well-functioning anti-corruption internal controls.[116]

Companies have also drafted audit rights provisions to include an express right to audit the existence, content, and implementation of a counterparty's compliance program.[117] From the range of anti-corruption provisions available, audit rights provisions are possibly the most contentious, due to the intrusive nature of the audit process. In the event of objections, a party can narrow the scope of audit rights to apply only to those financial records that pertain to the performance of the relevant contract, or structure the audit provisions such that a third party would conduct any audit, to overcome the possibility of such objections.[118]

The DOJ has signaled the importance of audit rights in its issued FCPA guidance to individuals and companies,[119] and through its Opinion Procedure Releases,[120] where the inclusion of audit rights in contracts with business partners comprised a feature of the opinion requestors' compliance programs.[121] The Ministry of Justice likewise has acknowledged the significance of including such provisions in contracts with business partners to prevent bribery.[122]

115 See GIACC, *Sample Anti-Corruption Contract Commitments* (n 98) pts 4–8 (detailing the purpose of audit rights provisions).

116 See Grimm (n 65) 147 (explaining that audit rights provide insurance that books and records are accurate, and the counterparty has strong internal controls).

117 See ASCO T&L (n 108) pt 28.3 (saying 'on provision of no less than thirty (30) days' formal notice, the Company … shall have the right to audit, at its own cost, the existence, content and implementation of the Contractor's [compliance program], but such right shall not include access to documents that are legally privileged or were created for the purpose of an on-going internal investigation.'); Paul Marshall and Eve Brazier, 'The Oil & Gas 'Contracting Compass': Pointing the Compass Toward Anti-Bribery & Corruption' (*Brodies LLP*) <https://brodies.com/sites/default/files/brodies_llp_-_anti-bribery_corruption_white_paper.pdf> accessed 1 June 2020, 12 (analyzing audit rights provisions).

118 Law360, 'Contracting with Third-Party Reps: FCPA Risks' (1 August 2012) <https://www.law360.com/articles/361944/contracting-with-third-party-reps-fcpa-risks> accessed 1 June 2020, 2.

119 See US Department of Justice and US Securities and Exchange Commission, *FCPA Resource Guide* (n 26) 60: (saying that 'companies should undertake some form of ongoing monitoring of third-party relationships … this may include … exercising audit rights.')

120 The FCPA Opinion Procedure process allows private parties to obtain the DOJ's opinion as to whether certain specified, prospective—not hypothetical—conduct conforms with the DOJ's present enforcement policy regarding the anti-bribery provisions of the FCPA. Foreign Corrupt Practices Act Opinion Procedure 2014 28 C.F.R. s 80.1.

121 See US Department of Justice, 'FCPA Opinion Procedure Release No 2004–02' (12 July 2004) <https://www.justice.gov/sites/default/files/criminal-fraud/legacy/2010/04/11/0802.pdf> accessed 1 June 2020: (acknowledging the 'inclusion in all agreements … with all … Business Partners of provisions … allowing for internal and independent audits of the books and records of the … Business Partner to ensure compliance with the [anti-corruption contractual provisions]'). US Department of Justice, 'FCPA Opinion Procedure Release No 2008–02' (n 69) 3: (making a similar acknowledgement).

122 Ministry of Justice, *The Bribery Act 2010: Guidance* (n 33) 39: (acknowledging the inclusion of 'suitable contractual terms on bribery prevention measures in [an] agreement

2.3.3 Addressing infringement through termination, suspension, cooperation, and indemnification rights

If a party breaches its obligations under an anti-corruption clause, the breach may trigger termination of the contract. Options abound, as parties may include rights to suspend and terminate a contract unilaterally in the event of a material breach of an anti-corruption commitment within,[123] such as a party violating an applicable anti-corruption law.[124] A party can further include in the provision an agreement that in the event corrupt payments are made in connection with the contract, the contract is void, and deem any violation of an applicable anti-corruption law to constitute grounds for withholding any outstanding payments related to the illicit conduct.[125]

Parties can structure a termination right to provide the alleged breaching party an opportunity to remedy a suspected breach[126] if such remedy is possible under the circumstances.[127] In some instances, companies include an obligation to notify in connection with any instance of corruption, essentially requiring their suppliers as part of their engagement terms and conditions to notify within a reasonable time any breach of any anti-corruption clause.[128] When a party exercises its right of termination, it typically bears the burden of proof that its counterparty has infringed the relevant anti-corruption provision(s).[129]

---

between [parties], for example: ...giving [one party] the ability to audit [the counter-party's] activities and expenditure.')

123 See, e.g., Phillips 66 (n 110) 2: (stating that '[e]ither party may terminate the [a]greement forthwith upon written notice to the other at any time, if in its reasonable judgment, the other is in breach of any of the representations, warranties or undertakings in this anti-corruption section.'); Veolia (n 112) s 7: (saying that '[i]f Supplier breach any term of this [anti-corruption] clause ... Veolia may immediately terminate this [a]greement without notice and without incurring any liability.')

124 See Xenakis (n 118): (advising to '[i]nclude a provision stating that a violation of anti-corruption laws constitutes a material breach of contract.')

125 Ibid. But see Marshall and Brazier (n 117) 13: (explaining that '[t]he right to suspend payment is not an absolute right but is qualified by reasonableness.')

126 See ASCO Transport & Logistics (n 108) pt 28.5(a) (stating that 'if the C[ompany] has a reasonable belief that the C[ontractor] has breached [the anti-corruption commitments], the C[ompany] may give formal notice of its intention to suspend payments under the C[ontract] to the C[ontractor] ... and [i]f within seven (7) days of receipt ... the C[ontractor] neither responds with information reasonably satisfactory to the C[ompany] to refute such belief nor commences and continues with action reasonably satisfactory to the C[ompany] to remedy such suspected breach ... the C[ompany] may ... suspend with immediate effect any payments due ... without liability').

127 While certain infringements may be impossible to remedy (e.g., a party engaging in criminal activity), the ICC provides examples of possible remedial actions where the gravity of infringement is relatively minor: issuing warnings, reorganizing work, terminating employment for any personnel involved in misconduct, terminating contracts with any sub-contractors involved in misconduct. See ICC (n 87) 9.

128 Veolia (n 112) pt 5.

129 See ICC (n 87) 10 (analyzing the effects of termination). Amounts contractually due at the time of termination typically remain payable, if permitted by applicable law: see ibid.

Suspension rights allow a company to suspend performance of the relevant contract and any associated payments thereof, with or without notice, often for either a defined period, or for as long as the company considers necessary to investigate any alleged infringement by its business partner of any material anti-corruption provision. The company, in drafting a suspension rights clause, can include language noting that it will not incur liability or obligation to its counterparty for exercising a suspension right.[130] Moreover, a company can obligate its business partner by contract to initiate a document hold exercise where the business partner agrees to take all reasonable steps to prevent the loss or destruction of any documentary evidence related to the relevant alleged infringing conduct.[131]

In connection with suspension rights, the company can also require its business partner to provide all reasonable information, documentation, and assistance to the company during the course of the investigation.[132] Such a cooperation right can require a business provider to cooperate fully with any corruption-related investigation, including the review of any emails and bank account information pertinent to the underlying transaction.[133]

In the event that a party breaches an anti-corruption clause, an indemnification provision requires the breaching party to agree to indemnify its counterparty for damages, losses, or expenses incurred by that counterparty arising out of the breach.[134] The provision can cover the indemnified party's expenses from any corruption investigation or prosecution brought about by the breaching party's activities.[135] Certain indemnities, however, may be contrary to public policy and unenforceable, such as an indemnity to cover criminal fines and penalties.[136]

130 See Veolia (n 112) pt 6.1 (asserting a suspension right without notice).

131 Ibid pt 6.2.

132 GIACC, *Sample Anti-Corruption Contract Commitments* (n 99) pt 10.

133 See Volkov (n 108).

134 See Veolia (n 112) pt 7.2 (asserting an indemnification right to the maximum extent allowed by law); Joanna Kay, 'Anti-Corruption Provisions and Upstream Joint Ventures-Boilerplate or Bespoke?' (*Hunton Andrews Kurth LLP*, 20 April 2015) <http://www.mondaq.com/unitedstates/x/390538/Oil+Gas+Electricity/AntiCorruption+Provisions+and+Upstream+Joint+Ventures+Boilerplate+or+Bespoke> accessed 1 June 2020 (explaining that each party may undertake to indemnify the other for any losses suffered as a result of the admission of allegations of an anti-corruption violation, or the final adjudication that there has been a corruption violation applicable to that party).

135 See Xenakis (n 118) (describing termination provision structuring). For a sample anti-corruption indemnity clause, see Shevan Algama, 'BIMCO Anti-Corruption Clause' (2016) <https://www.shipownersclub.com/media/2016/04/BIMCO-Anti-Corruption-Clause.pdf> accessed 1 June 2020, 2 (remarking that '[i]f either party fails to comply with any applicable anti-corruption legislation it shall defend and indemnify the other party against any fine, penalty, liability, loss or damage and for any related costs (including, without limitation, court costs and legal fees) arising from such breach.').

136 *Lincoln Logan Mut. Ins. Co. v. Fornshell*, 722 N.E.2d 239, 242 (Ill. Ct. App. 1999) (holding that '[a]n agreement to indemnify against intentional misconduct would, as a general rule, be contrary to public policy and unenforceable … [C]riminals should not be permitted to

2.3.4 *Additional rights, restrictions, and requirements available by contract*

The remaining set of rights and restrictions available to contracting parties largely center upon ongoing compliance monitoring and review. In connection with a party's engagement of subcontractors, a company can require its business partner to agree that it will not engage any subcontractor, consultant, or other agent without the company's prior written consent.[137] Such a restriction may allow either contracting party to conduct appropriate anti-corruption due diligence on any proposed intermediary.[138] The company can ensure that any intermediaries are instructed not engage in any corrupt practice, hired only to the extent appropriate in connection with the underlying transaction, and paid only an appropriate remuneration for legitimate services provided.[139]

On-going training requirements require that a party undertake any pertinent anti-corruption training that its counterparty reasonably requires. The counterparty requiring such training is often responsible under the terms of the agreement for the costs of any such training.[140] The purpose of this provision aims to ensure that a business partner's relevant personnel receive anti-corruption training.[141] The business partner's top management and all persons performing services in connection with the underlying transaction would presumably receive such training too.[142]

Annual certification clauses typically require a counterparty to certify that it remains aware of its anti-corruption obligations, it has not engaged in conduct that violates any applicable anti-corruption laws, and it is not aware of any such conduct by its employees and agents.[143] Finally, re-qualification clauses require a counterparty to re-qualify as a legitimate business partner at regular intervals.[144] The re-qualification process allows a party to conduct updated due diligence on its business partner and review the relevant contract during its lifespan to assess any corruption concerns that may have arisen.[145]

---

profit from their own intentional misconduct.') (citations omitted). See also Marshall and Brazier (n 117) 6 (discussing how criminal fines are not insurable in England and Wales).

137 See Volkov (n 108) (discussing subcontractor compliance efforts).

138 See McInnes (n 65) (examining intermediary due diligence initiatives); Xenakis (n 118) (discussing intermediary due diligence initiatives as well).

139 ICC (n 87) 8 (providing a sample provision addressing intermediaries).

140 GIACC, *Sample Anti-Corruption Contract Commitments* (n 99) pt 3 (evaluating training obligations).

141 See GIACC, 'Contract Terms' (n 97) pt 5(d).

142 See Volkov (n 108) (analyzing training best practices).

143 See Xenakis (n 118) (providing an overview of annual certification requirements in contract).

144 See Volkov (n 108) (discussing re-qualification obligations for contracting parties).

145 See McInnes (n 65) (noting the use of anti-corruption clauses in supply chain and subcontractor contracts).

3 Recommendations for harnessing contractual law to fight corruption in the corporate sector

Anti-corruption provisions in contracts with third parties constitute a critical soft-law initiative that can facilitate constraining corruption in international business transactions.[146] From a corporate perspective, they provide a means for private sector entities to signal their commitment to abiding by pertinent anti-corruption law(s), to integrate anti-corruption commitments into their commercial dialogue with agents, to strengthen the monitoring and supervision of projects with such agents, and to address corruption risks at all stages of the pertinent contract's lifespan with predictability.[147] From the perspective of corporate directors and officers, who potentially face personal liability for attributable breaches of their company's business partners, the provisions reduce the risk of liability for these individuals. More broadly, the provisions promote greater corporate transparency and disclosure, 'help preserve trust between [contracting] parties and prevent corruption in both the negotiation and performance of contracts.'[148]

3.1 Harmonizing anti-corruption compliance program operations with contractual provisions through structured risk management

Any company seeking to avoid corrupt practices abroad should construct an effective anti-corruption compliance program through a structured risk management approach, whether that company is a multinational corporation or simply conducts business overseas.[149] An increasingly critical feature of the compliance program involves conducting due diligence on the selection and retention of any third party that aims to serve as agent. Programs should facilitate as part of their mission the use of anti-corruption provisions in contracts with third party agents, given companies can be held liable for the acts of its agents under the FCPA and UK Bribery Act.[150] Companies should design such programs with adequate resources and with the objective to assess and address firmly the nature and scope of corruption risks at all stages of engagement with any third party agents subject

146 See Susan Rose-Ackerman and Sinead Hunt, 'Transparency and Business Advantage: The Impact of International Anti-Corruption Policies on the United States National Interest' (2012) 67 NYU Annual Survey of American Law 433, 433 (discussing benefits and costs to the US from anti-corruption soft-law initiatives).

147 See Marie Chêne, 'Examples of Anti-Corruption Clauses in Cooperation Agreements' (U4 Anti-Corruption Resource Centre, 2010) <https://www.u4.no/publications/examples-of-anti-corruption-clauses-in-cooperation-agreements.pdf> accessed 1 June 2020 (demonstrating the role of anti-corruption clauses in cooperation agreements).

148 See Allen (n 2).

149 For an overview of corporate compliance programs tailored to address international white-collar crime, see Colin R Jennings, 'Avoiding Criminal Liability for Corrupt Practices Abroad Through Effective Corporate Compliance' (2011) WL 6740787 *1.

150 See text at n 20ff (detailing the FCPA and UK Bribery Act liability provisions); Jennings (n 149) *6 (analyzing due diligence inquiries pertinent to third party agents).

to company control or determining influence. The programs should be capable of detecting corruption and should, accordingly, allow for training of company directors, officers, and employees. Inclusion of anti-corruption contractual provisions serves as an effective corporate tool functioning as a component of a company's larger compliance program.

Companies face three disparate options in including anti-corruption provisions within contracts with third party agents: whether to include the provisions in all of their contracts, in contracts over a certain amount, or to include depending upon the results of a risk assessment exercise, where companies assess, *inter alia*, the underlying risk, the business relationship and commercial needs, and the nature of the negotiations. Very few companies follow the latter approach,[151] which allows companies to construct a specific model of risk assessment that best suits their purposes. The risk assessment model categorizes agents into risk bands by reference to specific objective criteria and applies different levels of due diligence and internal controls to such agents according to the criteria.[152]

A risk-based approach presents an optimal method, as it can offer simplicity and proportionality to companies by providing the ability to group anti-corruption clauses into risk bands to be deployed based upon appropriate risk categories as a result of the risk assessment conducted. A simple example of a tiered approach involves standard anti-corruption provisions for lower risk relationships (such as for supply chain partners who have existing, robust compliance programs in operation) and enhanced provisions for higher risk relationships (such as for joint ventures, consultants, and counterparties operating in countries classified with high corruption risk).[153] Such an approach may avoid unnecessarily burdensome obligations in connection with lower risk relationships.[154]

Some advocate for the blanket inclusion of anti-corruption provisions in all third party contracts,[155] but the use of robust provisions may add unnecessary cost and inconvenience to the business relationship. While no contract modality is free from corruption risks,[156] longer term contracts, contracts with large magnitude or complexity, and acquisition contracts present higher risk, along with contracts with higher risk business associates.[157] Companies entering into such high-risk contracts could benefit from including an expansive set of anti-corruption protections as discussed in part 2. For instance, inserting a warranty for an agent's

151 Eduard Ivanov and others, 'Legal Regulation of Combating Corruption: Report of the LSGL's Research Group' Law Schools Global League Research Paper No 2 (1 July 2014) <https://ssrn.com/abstract=2461487> accessed 1 June 2020, 14.

152 See GIACC, 'Business Associate Corruption Risk Assessment' (n 98) 1 (providing detailed guidance on business associate corruption risk assessment).

153 See McInnes (n 65) (outlining steps for risk assessment).

154 Ibid.

155 Jennings (n 149) *14: (advising companies to 'include anticorruption elements in contracts wherever possible').

156 Chêne (n 147) 1 (providing overview of corruption risk).

157 See Railas (n 89) (detailing business arrangements carrying high corruption risk).

compliance with anti-corruption law may entitle an innocent party in the event of corruption to a civil claim for breach of contract and to recover damages that would not otherwise arise under the relevant statutory provisions.[158]

Termination is notably the most effective mechanism for a company to disavow itself of its counterparty's corrupt activities.[159] While companies generally allow for the immediate termination of the relevant contract if a counterparty violates any pertinent anti-corruption law or any substantive anti-corruption contractual provision, companies seldom include penalty clauses within their anti-corruption provisions.[160] Penalties obligating a non-compliant party to reimburse its innocent counterparty for any fines and losses incurred as a result of the non-compliance, in addition to the innocent party's unilateral right to terminate the agreement, may be an efficient starting approach for negotiations in order to address a party's potential failure to comply. The provisions in sum should 'shield each party from the corrupt practices of the other, while preserving the continuity of their contractual relationship.'[161]

Any set of anti-corruption provisions should at minimum include an agreement that the parties have and will comply with the applicable anti-corruption laws, with clear definitions and descriptions of prohibited conduct, and an agreement that the parties will implement reasonable and necessary policies and practices to prevent corruption while the contract remains in force. The provisions should also allow for a party to conduct legitimate inquiries should red flags arise during the contract's duration.[162] More expansive provisions providing for training, audit, investigation, termination, and indemnification rights can solidify further the parties' anti-corruption commitments and protections if necessary given the risk levels present.[163]

3.2 *Enhancing anti-corruption initiatives globally through expansive use of anti-corruption provisions*

The use of anti-corruption provisions in contracts with foreign parties who would otherwise not be obligated to respect anti-corruption legislation serves to advance international anti-corruption objectives.[164] The provisions can compel foreign parties to respect anti-corruption legislation of other jurisdictions, to implement internal anti-corruption compliance policies and programs, and to subject their facilities and financial statements to audit.[165] Potential substantive sanctions for

158 Marshall and Brazier (n 117) 10–11.
159 See Xenakis (n 118) (noting the benefits of anti-corruption provisions).
160 Ivanov and others (n 151) 14.
161 See Allen (n 2).
162 See Xenakis (n 118) (noting the benefits granted by an anti-corruption provision).
163 See text at n 106ff (discussing the comprehensive set of anti-corruption provisions available to parties).
164 See text at n 11ff (discussing international anti-corruption initiatives).
165 See Guarderas (n 9) (bringing attention to the powers of anti-corruption clauses).

noncompliance would increase the likelihood that such parties carry out their obligations under these provisions. For these reasons, the provisions may assist in shifting norms toward corporate anti-corruption commitments on a global level and raising awareness of the need to avoid corruption. They signal to all involved that corrupt actions will not be tolerated.[166]

Regardless of its location, a company could take the position that anti-corruption contractual provisions are extraneous contract mechanisms that may cause the company to lose business to (corrupt) competitors.[167] Such a position ignores the significant liability risks under the FCPA, Bribery Act, and other laws companies may face in connection with the corrupt activities of their third party agents, as well as the economic harm corruption brings to the private sector.[168] Moreover, companies using the provisions have a mechanism to oppose corrupt payments and to monitor their agents' behavior without any external pressure from law enforcement. Individual profit-maximization and the avoidance of corruption can harmonize together through effective provision usage.[169]

From a public policy perspective, anti-corruption contractual provisions can reinforce a strong corporate stance against foreign bribery and other forms of corruption and signal the value of an honest business environment. The provisions allow corporations to participate in global anti-corruption efforts, help level the corporate playing field, and harmonize with international public order.[170] The 10th Principle of the UN Global Compact implores companies to 'work against corruption in all its forms, including extortion and bribery,' calling on companies to develop policies and practices to address corruption: 'We challenge companies to join peers, governments, UN agencies and civil society to realize a more transparent global economy.'[171] Anti-corruption provisions harmonize with this movement.

3.3 *Recognizing the limitations of anti-corruption contractual provisions for corporate actors*

While anti-corruption provisions offer benefits directly to companies and more broadly to the larger society in connection with combatting corruption, the

166 See Allen (n 2).

167 Cf Richard Levick, 'The Foreign Corrupt Practices Act at 40: No Shortage of Challenges' *Forbes* (16 May 2017) <https://www.forbes.com/sites/richardlevick/2017/05/16/the-foreign-corrupt-practices-act-at-40-no-shortage-of-challenges/#25f81c3a5f90> accessed 1 June 2020: ('Detractors [of the FCPA] say its benefits are exaggerated, that it puts American companies at a competitive disadvantage, and that its compliance costs are prohibitive for many companies.')

168 See text at n 19 (analyzing the effects of corruption upon economic growth).

169 See Rose-Ackerman and Hunt (n 146) 461–462 (examining how corruption can introduce inefficiencies that decrease competitiveness).

170 ICC (n 87) 1.

171 United Nations Global Compact (n 49).

provisions are not a compliance panacea for the company that engages third party agents. The provisions alone constitute insufficient protection for companies in connection with their liability under anti-bribery laws, as companies should integrate these provisions into a larger anti-corruption compliance program.[172] Government agencies in assessing a company's compliance with and liability under anti-corruption law may look to whether the company not only adopts but also enforces anti-corruption provisions where reasonable in its contracts with counterparties and links such enforcement to a larger compliance program.[173] Companies arguably court liability if they use anti-corruption provisions in their contracts as mere boilerplate without giving the attendant obligations under the provisions due attention.

Companies should not over-engineer anti-corruption provisions when drafting, such that the provisions are imbalanced, one-sided, and onerous, potentially reaching beyond the law and potentially too broad to be practicable and enforceable.[174] Given the various rules of contract interpretation, companies should ensure that the provisions receive respect and enforcement via the ordinary course of the parties' performance of their contractual obligations.[175] The validity of these provisions have largely been untested in courts, and whether a court will enforce such provisions, interpret strictly or allow as a defense against a corruption provision based upon a default of a noncompliant counterparty remains to be seen.[176] Whether such provisions will be deemed valid judicially should not weaken their intent when coupled with a company's robust anti-corruption compliance program.[177]

Regardless of the anti-corruption provisions' specific breadth, they should present a balanced approach that effectively regulates and manages corruption risk. The provisions should neither be particularly onerous to the parties, nor disproportionate to the level of risk present, nor 'create unexpected consequences by

172 See discussion about integration of anti-corruption provisions within corporate compliance program operations.

173 See Gordon Kaiser, 'Corruption in the Energy Sector: Criminal Fines, Civil Judgments, and Lost Arbitrations' (2013) 34 Energy Law Journal 193, 210; Volkov (n 108) ('A company's commitment to anti-corruption compliance can be quickly tested by examining its contracting practices and its use of anti-corruption provisions.'); Xenakis (n 118) ('The US Securities and Exchange Commission and US Department of Justice will expect companies to exercise such rights and will look unfavorably on companies that have included audit rights but not exercised them when there are red flags.')

174 See Marshall and Brazier (n 117) 9 (analyzing contract drafting principles).

175 Daniel Schimmel and others, 'Bridging the Cultural Gap in International Arbitrations Arising from FCPA Investigations' (2016) 39 Fordham International Law Journal 829, 838.

176 See Allen (n 2).

177 Ibid. See also ICC, (n 87) 2: ('An entity, whether an arbitral tribunal or other dispute resolution body, rendering a decision in accordance with the dispute resolution provisions of the contract, shall have the authority to determine the contractual consequences of any alleged non-compliance with the [anti-corruption] [c]lause[s].')

way of its exploitation for commercial purposes.'[178] The provisions should reflect the parties' genuine intent to combat corruption and not function to exploit corruption as an unfair or sham mechanism for terminating contractual arrangements.[179] For instance, the provisions should enable the parties to work together when confronting and resisting demands for illicit payments.[180]

3.4 Encouraging the usage of anti-corruption provisions through expanded domestic legislation and regulation

Over the last two decades, government enforcement agencies have been enforcing anti-corruption legislation with increased rigor,[181] creating what has been deemed a 'highly adversarial relationship between enforcement agencies and firms.'[182] Companies may implement numerous strategies to reduce their exposure to corrupt practices, including robust due diligence, rigorous compliance systems, and expansive contractual remedies, but these efforts may not ultimately protect when operating in an uncertain enforcement landscape.[183]

Given the degree of uncertainty surrounding the FCPA, in particular, recent calls to amend this law abound.[184] In connection with the corporate compliance function, Professor Steve Salbu argues for the establishment of 'standards for rigorous compliance programs that would provide qualifying companies with a defense against entity liability for the corrupt behavior of individuals.'[185] Under Salbu's proposal, business entities could enjoy robust, clearly defined defenses upon implementing qualifying good-faith compliance programs through well-articulated and formulated standards.[186] His qualified good-faith compliance program defense can be further enhanced by explicitly incorporating the use of anti-corruption provisions with third party agents as a required practice where appropriate.

Such a good-faith defense can offer a safe harbor in connection with third party agent liability for companies that (i) insert substantive anti-corruption provisions within their contracts with such agents, and (ii) incorporate enforcement of such provisions as appropriate within a larger internal compliance program

178 See Railas (n 89).

179 See Kay (n 134) (examining termination rights).

180 See Algama (n 135) 1 (discussing contractual provisions that facilitate cooperation in connection with illegal payment requests in the shipping industry).

181 Michael S Diamant and others, 'Sanctionable Practices at the World Bank: Interpretation and Enforcement' (2016) 18 University Pennsylvania Journal of Business Law 985, 992.

182 Steven R Salbu, 'Mitigating the Harshness of FCPA Enforcement through a Qualifying Good-Faith Compliance Defense' (2018) 55 American Business Law Journal 475, 475.

183 Grimm (n 65) 93.

184 See, e.g., Daniel J Grimm, 'The Foreign Corrupt Practices Act in Merger and Acquisition Transactions: Successor Liability and Its Consequences' (2010) 7 NYU Journal of Law and Business 247, 299–300, 331.

185 Salbu (n 182) 475.

186 Ibid 479.

designed to comply with relevant anti-corruption laws. Companies meeting the above conditions should enjoy a full defense from liability arising from corrupt acts of third party agents. The 'policies and procedures' defense to 'failure to prevent' offenses under s 7 of the Bribery Act could also benefit from legislative reform such that it explicitly endorses anti-corruption contractual provision usage as a compliance program component that shields entities from third party liability concerns.[187]

Revising anti-corruption legislation such as the FCPA and Bribery Act in this manner could benefit both private and public sectors. The revisions could provide businesses with direct incentives to develop strong anti-corruption compliance programs that use and enforce anti-corruption contractual provisions appropriately. The revisions could also decrease transaction costs related to uncertainty in the domestic and international marketplace,[188] help prevent future corruption violations, facilitate companies' self-policing in the fight against corruption, and boost ethics-centered corporate cultures along with the credibility of government enforcement agencies.[189]

4 Conclusion

Contract law offers a unique platform to assist a company in avoiding corruption actions. Properly structured anti-corruption contractual provisions with third parties can significantly reduce legal and performance risks and reputational concerns associated with third party corrupt action, provided the provisions receive due enforcement in conjunction with the operations of an internal compliance program. Companies can draft these provisions most effectively in a risk-sensitive manner, recognizing that using these provisions contributes toward an ultimate purpose of removing corruption from the companies' relevant industries.

187 See discussion on the Bribery Act 'policies and procedures' defense.

188 See Adam Prestidge, 'Avoiding FCPA Surprises: Safe Harbor From Successor Liability in Cross-Border Mergers and Acquisitions' (2013) 55 William and Mary Law Review 305, 333: ('A safe harbor rule … removes the need to compensate for uncertainty with expensive due diligence, decreasing the costs of these types of transactions because companies are able to pursue transactions with greater assurance that even if violations exist, they will not be penalized for those violations if otherwise compliant.')

189 See Salbu (n 182) 535 (noting the benefits of a compliance program defense to the credibility of the FCPA and the DOJ's and SEC's FCPA enforcement system and practices).

15 Linear and non-linear modeling techniques in transnational corruption risk assessment

Robert E. Clark

Any rationalized attempt to confront corruption on a global scale requires a model of the problem—a way to determine where attention is needed and to legitimate a responsive course of action. The model needn't be complicated; a fairly simple ranking algorithm can accomplish the basic function of organizing institutional efforts and resources. But while a simplified model can be useful in communicating the imperative and building large-scale political support, it can also embody and perpetuate distortions of the underlying phenomenon.

Over the past two decades, the tasks of publicizing corruption as a transnational issue and galvanizing its structured opposition have been accomplished largely through the use of country-level corruption indexes. The most prominent are the Corruption Perceptions Index (CPI) published since 1995 by Transparency International[1] and the 'Control of Corruption' metric included among the World Bank's Worldwide Governance Indicators (WGI) since 1999.[2] Both indexes are composed by aggregating and averaging (with or without weights) certain corruption-related scores from a variety of other sources, typically representing the assessments of experts in the relevant topics or regions. Both indexes have been subjected to substantial methodological criticism,[3] but have nevertheless largely retained their authoritative status in public discourse.

1 Transparency International, 'Corruption Perceptions Index' <https://www.transparency.org/research/cpi/overview> accessed 1 June 2020.

2 Daniel Kaufmann, Aart Kraay, and Pablo Zoido-Lobatón, 'Aggregating Governance Indicators' (1999) World Bank Development Research Group Policy Research Working Paper 2195; Daniel Kaufmann, Aart Kraay, and Massimo Mastruzzi, 'The Worldwide Governance Indicators: Methodology and Analytical Issues' (2010) Policy Research Working Paper 5430.

3 Staffan Andersson and Paul M Heywood, 'The Politics of Perception: Use and Abuse of Transparency International's Approach to Measuring Corruption' (2009) 57 Political Studies 746; Carmen R Apaza, 'Measuring Governance and Corruption through the Worldwide Governance Indicators: Critiques, Responses, and Ongoing Scholarly Discussion' (2009) 42 Political Science and Politics 139; Danielle E Warren and William S Laufer, 'Are Corruption Indices a Self-Fulfilling Prophecy? A Social Labeling Perspective of Corruption' (2009) 88 Journal of Business Ethics 841; MA Thomas, 'What Do the Worldwide Governance Indicators Measure?' (2010) 22 The European Journal of Development Research 31; Stuart Vincent Campbell, 'Perception Is Not Reality: The FCPA, Brazil, and the Mismeasurement

That authority carries both commercial and political weight. Multinational businesses that are required to implement anti-corruption controls commensurate with corruption risk commonly refer to the CPI to inform investment decisions and focus the deployment of private-sector safeguards.[4] State leaders, sensitive to their countries' rankings in such lists—and to the investment and foreign aid decisions those rankings may influence—can be spurred toward implementing anti-corruption measures to obtain better positioning.[5] Academic researchers have also used these composite indexes to assess corruption's relationship to other societal and economic factors of interest.[6]

In all of these areas, the function of ranking responds to a specific imperative: to know where things stand. Having identified corruption as an impediment to an ideal state of development, the apparatus organized around furthering that ideal needs to formulate a response. Addressing and limiting corruption will, it is anticipated, have a positive effect on the desired outcomes of growth, equity, and sustainability. Measuring corruption, however imperfectly, allows this premise to be acted upon and the results evaluated.

The question, then, is how the currently recognized yardsticks fall short in advancing that goal and what other kinds of approaches might yield valuable results. The problem has generated substantial attention of late, with a number of recent volumes dedicated to understanding and improving our use of corruption- and governance-related data and rankings.[7] The present chapter will focus on issues raised by one specific characteristic shared by most such rankings: their construction as linear models.

1 The structure of linear indexes

Put simply, a linear function is one in which the output changes in direct proportion to the input. The longer the cab ride, for example, the higher the fare. A single-variable linear function takes the form $y = mx + b$, with m and b representing

of Corruption Note' (2013) 22 Minnesota Journal of International Law 247; Alex Cobham, 'Corrupting Perceptions' *Foreign Policy* (22 July 2013) <https://foreignpolicy.com/2013/07/22/corrupting-perceptions/> accessed 1 June 2020.

4 Richard L Cassin, 'TI's Corruption Perceptions Index Plays Role in SEC Risk Warnings' *The FCPA Blog* (18 December 2017) <http://www.fcpablog.com/blog/2017/12/18/tis-corruption-perceptions-index-plays-role-in-sec-risk-warn.html> accessed 1 June 2020.

5 Christiane Arndt and Charles P Oman, *Uses and Abuses of Governance Indicators* (OECD Publishing 2006) 48.

6 Andersson and Heywood (n 3).

7 Alexander Cooley and Jack Snyder (eds), *Ranking the World: Grading States as a Tool of Global Governance* (CUP 2015); Sally Engle Merry, Kevin E Davis, and Benedict Kingsbury (eds), *The Quiet Power of Indicators: Measuring Governance, Corruption, and Rule of Law* (CUP 2015); Dan Hough, *Analysing Corruption* (Agenda Publishing 2017); Debora Valentina Malito, Gaby Umbach, and Nehal Bhuta, *The Palgrave Handbook of Indicators in Global Governance* (Springer 2017); Helmut K Anheier, Matthias Haber, and Mark A Kayser, *Governance Indicators: Approaches, Progress, Promise* (OUP 2018).

constant values, x representing the input, and y representing the output. If the value for m is positive, the output increases with any increase to the input; if it's negative, any increase to the input leads to a decrease in the output.

A linear equation can be more complex than a single-input function. My cab fare may depend on a combination of distance, time spent in traffic, and how long the driver has to wait for me. Each input variable will have its own constant multiplier (or *coefficient*), and there may again be a stand-alone constant included in the equation (e.g., the initial cost of getting into the cab). To avoid running out of letters, we can distinguish our several inputs (and their respective coefficients) with numeric subscripts:

$$y = m_1x_1 + m_2x_2 + m_3x_3 + b$$

Or, if we want to generalize to an unspecified number of inputs, we can represent the sum using the slightly more imposing notation:

$$y = \sum_{i=1}^{n} m_ix_i + b$$

The CPI and the WGI are both derived in an essentially linear fashion. The CPI's methodology involves four steps: 'selection of source data, rescaling source data, aggregating the rescaled data and then reporting a measure for uncertainty.'[8] The source data consist of quantitative assessments obtained from various international and non-governmental organizations—each covering a distinct range of countries—regarding the extent of certain corruption-related behaviors and the availability of certain dissuasive mechanisms.[9]

The aggregation of these scores (following their conversion to a common scale) is performed by calculating their average—specifically, their arithmetic mean. For a given country, each available source contributes to the outcome in proportion to the number of available sources (ranging in practice from three to ten out of 13, depending on the country) and the relative degree of its initial scaling. This is roughly equivalent to the above formula for a linear equation, with the coefficients and the constant for each country mirroring the effect of the scaling algorithm. Under either formulation, a change to any one input factor will result in a corresponding and proportionate change in the country's final score.

The WGI is more explicit in its assumptions regarding linearity:

> [W]e interpret the [source] data as being generated by an unobserved components or multiple-indicator model in which the observed data on

8 Transparency International, 'Corruption Perceptions Index 2017: Technical Methodology Note' (February 2018) <https://www.transparency.org/en/news/corruption-perceptions-index-2017> accessed 1 June 2020.

9 Ibid.

> governance can be expressed as a linear function of unobserved governance plus a random error term.[10]

Like the CPI, the WGI draws upon data from a range of primary sources (21 in all for the 'Control of Corruption' indicator) and calculates each country's score by averaging the available inputs. It differs from the CPI in deriving a separate weight to be applied to the data from each source—meaning, in effect, that its coefficients are not solely a reflection of the data's conversion to a common scale.

The procedure for determining these weights deserves closer attention. It hinges on two concepts: (1) the observed data for each country (generally consisting of expert opinion) is assumed to be an imperfect linear function of each country's underlying quality of governance; and (2) the degree of that imperfection is assumed to vary from one data source to another. These assumptions are characterized using the metaphor of signal extraction:

> [E]ach of the individual data sources provides an imperfect signal of some deeper underlying notion of governance that is difficult to observe directly. This means that, as users of the individual sources, we face a signal-extraction problem—how do we isolate an informative signal about the unobserved governance component common to each individual data source, and how do we optimally combine the many data sources to get the best possible signal of governance in a country based on all the available data?[11]

The WGI's answer to this problem is to identify which sources carry the hypothesized governance signal with the greatest clarity—with a minimal degree of 'noise'—and give those sources proportionally greater weight in the linear aggregation. The differences among these ascribed weights can be dramatic: the 2017 formula for the Control of Corruption indicator assigns data from the Political Risk Services International Country Risk Guide (PRS) a weight amounting to 20.9% of the total score, while data from the Asian Development Bank Country Policy and Institutional Assessments (ASD) is accorded a weight of just 0.2%.[12]

Accounting for these differences and how they arise is non-trivial. It would be conclusory to assume that the PRS simply reflects the quality of anti-corruption governance one hundred times more accurately than the ASD—nor does that appear to be what the WGI is suggesting. At the same time, the extent of this variability may warrant approaching the signal-extraction metaphor with some skepticism.

10 Kaufmann, Kraay, and Zoido-Lobatón (n 2).

11 Kaufmann, Kraay, and Mastruzzi (n 2).

12 Aart C Kraay, 'WGI_Weights.Xlsx' (2018) <http://info.worldbank.org/governance/wgi/#doc> accessed 1 June 2020.

We can articulate our skepticism more precisely. Signal extraction is a familiar econometric technique, but it is generally applied in the study of time-series data rather than in the analysis of a composed set of single-year data.[13] It is analogous to the identification of a specific electromagnetic wave within a spectrum, filtering and isolating its oscillations from other extraneous fluctuations within the field, often through the use of sophisticated techniques for weighting particular observations.[14] In the context of economics, one uses such techniques to help identify and analyze the cyclical factors that might otherwise obscure long-term trends—the so-called 'unobserved components' of the economic cycle.[15]

The WGI is presented as deploying this sort of model to generate its assessments: 'We combine the many individual data sources into six aggregate governance indicators, corresponding to the six dimensions of governance described above. We do this using a statistical tool known as an unobserved components model (UCM).'[16] But because there is no cyclical aspect to the data upon which the WGI draws, it is difficult to characterize precisely what kind of signal it means to extract.

A signal conveys information by propagating the alteration of a state through a given medium. For a common radio signal, the medium is an electromagnetic field and the alteration is to the amplitude (AM) or the frequency (FM) of a specific wavelength. In statistical analysis, the medium is the field of surveyed facts and the signal—to the extent one is found—represents the regular operation of a hypothesized phenomenon upon the field.

The use of the signal metaphor to discuss governance implies an expectation of such regularity. If the quality of governance can be discerned through its effects on measured data, then those data can presumably be changed by improving the quality of governance.

This is a reasonable expectation, and the presumption of effectiveness could be formulated as a testable hypothesis. But that would require assessing the relationship *over time* between one or more hypothesized 'governance factors' and the medium in which they are presumed to operate. More pointedly, that medium would need to be defined in societal terms, such that one would be investigating the relationship between, for example, governance and the economy, or governance and health, or governance and family stability. No such medium is specified in the WGI's methodology.

The rationale for using an unobserved components model therefore appears dubious. But what about the results? As a quantitative matter, the WGI's

13 D Stephen G Pollock, 'Statistical Signal Extraction and Filtering: A Partial Survey' in David A Belsley and Erricos John Kontoghiorghes (eds), *Handbook of Computational Econometrics* (John Wiley & Sons, Ltd 2009) 321.

14 Andrew Harvey and Siem Jan Koopman, 'Signal Extraction and the Formulation of Unobserved Components Models' (2000) 3 The Econometrics Journal 84.

15 Diego J Pedregal, 'Analysis of Economic Cycles Using Unobserved Components Models' (2001) 2 Review on Economic Cycles 1.

16 Kaufmann, Kraay, and Zoido-Lobatón (n 2).

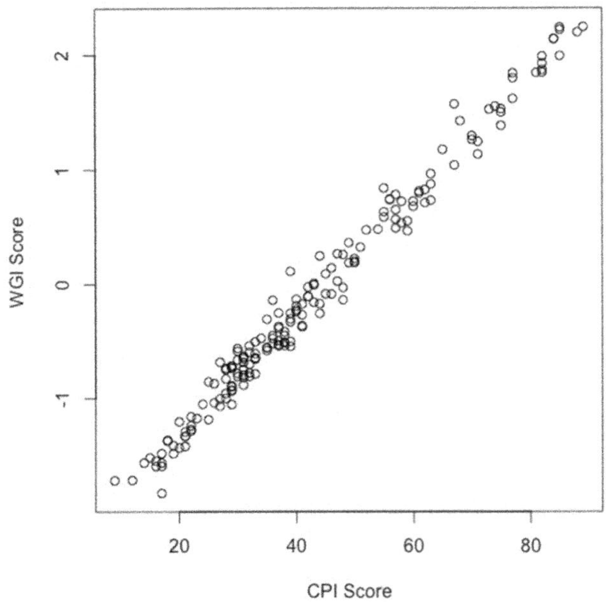

Figure 15.1 Comparison of CPI 2017 and WGI Control of Corruption 2017 Scores.

application of the model's formulas to derive data-source weights leads to a familiar outcome: for the 180 countries covered by both the CPI and the WGI in 2017, the correlation between the two indexes is better than 0.991—an almost perfect linear relationship.

This similarity gives rise to a certain form of mutual legitimation. The fact that the two separate calculations yield nearly identical results serves to bolster the credibility of both indexes, fostering the sense that whatever they are measuring—though it may be something other than corruption as such—is real.[17]

However, this apparently corroborative correlation becomes less surprising—and less illuminating—once we take into account the overlap between the data sets used in constructing the two indexes: of the CPI's 13 sources, 12 are included in the WGI's Control of Corruption calculation. The effect of this overlap is heightened by the WGI's weighting scheme, under which the 12 shared sources account for more than 85% of the final score set, making the index's remaining

17 Alexander Hamilton and Craig Hammer, 'Can We Measure the Power of the Grabbing Hand? A Comparative Analysis of Different Indicators of Corruption' (2018) The World Bank Group Policy Research Working Paper 8299 <https://elibrary.worldbank.org/doi/pdf/10.1596/1813-9450-8299> accessed 1 June 2020.

nine sources largely irrelevant. In effect, the two indexes are telling us the same thing based on the same information.

2 Measurement, modeling, and metaphor

So what is it that these indexes tell us? In one respect, they are simply saying that certain countries appear to be more corrupt than others, in a way that can be quantified and ordered. As discussed above, this has implications at the level of the global economy, affecting investment decisions, aid allocation, and governance reform initiatives. But there is a subliminal message as well, conveyed by the metaphoric frame in which the rankings are presented.

Specifically, the CPI is consistently promoted as a measure not of corruption itself, but of the *perception* of corruption—specifically the perception of experts regarding levels of actual corruption. The emphasis on 'perception' is notable: it does not attach in the same way to other policy-oriented indexes that are also based largely or exclusively on survey data—for example, the World Justice Project's Rule of Law Index,[18] the Press Freedom Index published by Reporters Without Borders,[19] or the World Bank's Doing Business rankings.[20] We may wonder whether the insistent specification that the CPI measures only perception has a function beyond pure description.

We get a hint of that function from the proffered rationale for relying on perceptions:

> Corruption generally comprises illegal activities, which are deliberately hidden and only come to light through scandals, investigations or prosecutions. There is no meaningful way to assess absolute levels of corruption in countries or territories on the basis of hard empirical data.[21]

Corruption is by nature *hidden*. This hidden character impedes direct assessment and mandates recourse to indirect forms of measurement.

A separate rationale underpins the WGI's reliance on the idea of governance as a *signal*. Like corruption, governance is understood as difficult to observe directly. But while it is not deliberately hidden in the same way as corruption, it is subject to similar observational constraints. For example: 'Just as alternative survey-based measures are imperfect proxies for the overall level of corruption in

18 World Justice Project, 'Methodology' <https://worldjusticeproject.org/our-work/research-and-data/wjp-rule-law-index-2019/methodology> accessed 1 June 2020.

19 Reporters Without Borders, 'Detailed Methodology' (19 April 2016) <https://rsf.org/en/detailed-methodology> accessed 1 June 2020.

20 World Bank Group, 'Methodology' <https://www.doingbusiness.org/en/methodology> accessed 1 June 2020.

21 Transparency International, 'Corruption Perceptions Index 2013' <https://www.transparency.org/cpi2013/in_detail#myAnchor2> accessed 1 June 2020.

a country, fact-based description of the legal regulatory framework are also only imperfect proxies for the overall business environment facing firms.'[22]

For the CPI, corruption is deliberately hidden and must be assessed by surveying perceptions; for the WGI, corruption and governance are too abstract to be measured directly and must be inferred through proxy data. Each of these gestures effectively frames its object as something distant that cannot be immediately apprehended, but that becomes accessible through a process of indirect discernment.

In both cases, the relation between the invisible and the visible is linear. This too is metaphorically significant. If governance can be improved and corruption controlled, we can expect those changes to have a linear effect on things that—unlike governance and corruption—we do experience directly. Critically, in positing the underlying phenomena as distant and opaque, we construct them as unitary sources of calculable influence. We also render them immediately comparable from one instance to the next, allowing us to grade, sort, and rank the status of each. We are able to conceptualize the matter under a single rubric, globally subject to a uniform metric, radiating predictably into practical civic life.

In short, by placing ourselves at a distance from corruption, we isolate it and identify it as a distinct problem to be engaged, with the conviction that our engagement will have a positive effect. This is a useful and powerful abstraction, largely responsible for maintaining global focus on the problem of corruption over the past decades. In practice, though, these models have little to say about what kind of engagement might be effective. The problem as such isn't the models' linearity, but their metaphoric construction of corruption as unobservable. We would do well to look at other approaches to assessing corruption that aren't tethered to the linearity metaphor.

3 Non-linear modeling alternatives

Mathematically, non-linearity is a catch all term encompassing any relationship whose description cannot be accounted for in terms of linear equations—that is to say, anything in which the output is not directly proportionate to the input. These include polynomial relationships, in which the input has a varying effect on the output (yielding more or less 'bang for your buck'), and exponential relationships, in which the input has a compounding effect on the output (leading something to 'spiral out of control').

Most real-world systems are, in fact, non-linear. They are also complex—composed of multiple linear and non-linear relationships whose effect on one another can be difficult to trace and even more difficult to predict. One way of handling these complexities is by finding useful approximations that can be expressed in linear terms, rendering them more amenable to calculation. Another is to bring massive computational power to bear upon the problem, making

22 Kaufmann, Kraay, and Mastruzzi (n 2).

it possible to offer plausible forecasts of systems—like the weather—whose fundamental mechanisms are reasonably well understood.

Other approaches may be better suited to the transnational study of corruption, given that the subject doesn't require—or even allow—a high degree of computational specificity. As an example of such innovation, a group of Belgian scholars has applied neural-network techniques from the data-mining world to produce high-dimensional 'self-organizing maps' based on country-level characteristics that might be expected to affect corruption levels.[23] Those maps then form the domain for application of another machine-learning technique—'support vector machines'—to classify and forecast changes to corruption levels in a manner that respects non-linear causality.[24]

Classification and forecasting are useful additions to our collection of metaphors. At the same time, there may be limits to how well they can inform our judgment about appropriate interventions. The old joke—'everyone talks about the weather, but nobody does anything about it'—is (mildly) funny precisely because nothing *can* be done about the weather. Forecasting is subliminally tied to a sense of fatalism, while classification suggests a certain rigidity of distinction. Neither of these brings us significantly closer to practical engagement.

There are other metaphors we can look to if we aim not to produce a more accurate calculation, but to express a more nuanced understanding of the phenomenon. We want our analysis to help us find ways to remedy what we recognize as a societal ill. We might accordingly ask what use can be made of the metaphor of *diagnosis*.

The process of diagnosis can be described as a form of decision tree. A patient presents with a given set of symptoms from which the physician can infer a range of possible causes. To narrow down that range, the physician asks questions about behavior and family history, performs physical examinations, and orders specific tests. At each stage, the results will increase or decrease the probability of certain conclusions, and the physician must exercise judgment in determining if and when to exclude those from further consideration.

Critically, the path the physician traces—from symptom through examination and on to diagnosis—need not be supported by a causal understanding of the disease. Such an understanding, while valuable, is the domain more of physiology than of medicine. In diagnosis (literally, the knowledge of distinctions), what matters is experience—codified, aggregated, and systematized. And as statistical techniques of linear signal extraction have been developed to gauge distant electromagnetic activity, so have statistical techniques of non-linear decision-tree

23 Johan Huysmans and others, 'Country Corruption Analysis with Self Organizing Maps and Support Vector Machines' in Hsinchun Chen and others (eds), *Intelligence and Security Informatics*, vol 3917 (Springer Berlin Heidelberg 2006) 103.

24 Ibid. ('Support vector machines have proven to be excellent classifiers in other application domains (e.g., credit scoring) and are able to capture nonlinear relationships between dependent and independent variables.')

classification been developed to assist in the process of diagnosis—particularly in the context of emergency medicine, where decisions must be made quickly based on limited information.[25]

With its combination of causal agnosticism and practical intention, the metaphor of diagnosis may help produce a valuable supplement to the linear models exemplified by the CPI and the WGI. Corruption, like an underlying disease, can remain essentially hidden, but through examination of its symptomatic manifestations we might nevertheless aim to devise an appropriate treatment, the details of which would not be constrained by a presumption of linear effectiveness.

There are, of course, limits to such an approach. Although a decision-tree algorithm can make use of a wider range of input data than a straightforward linear regression, the number of subject countries is likely too low to support genuinely robust statistical inference. But the metaphor of diagnosis needn't be tied to a particular form of calculation. As a polemical device, it can still carry significant weight.

In her 2006 paper 'Corruption: Diagnosis and Treatment,'[26] Alina Mungiu-Pippidi pins the failure of many anti-corruption initiatives on a misapprehension of the specific nature of corruption in the targeted countries:

> Donors gather in grand anticorruption meetings, but they all result in the same stereotypical strategies. Impressive efforts have been undertaken to formulate better theories of corruption, to develop comprehensive strategies to battle it, and to review anticorruption efforts around the world. Yet we still cannot properly diagnose corruption.[27]

There follows a rough definition of the task: 'A proper diagnosis means that we understand the causes of a malady in the context of a given organism.'

As her primary context, Professor Mungiu-Pippidi proposes a continuum between ***particularism*** and ***universalism***—that is, between societies in which rent seeking and favoritism are deemed the natural perquisites of a traditional rulership, and societies in which government is supposed to provide equal treatment for all. The continuum includes a transitional zone of 'competitive particularism' in which the old, tolerably corrupt order has fallen but the ideals of universalist governance have not yet been established.

The typology developed within this framework is unabashedly prescriptive; it aims not just to diagnose but also to cure. The analysis proceeds with increasing granularity to identify likely obstacles and opportunities. For example, a system

25 Terry M Therneau, Elizabeth J Atkinson, and Mayo Foundation, 'An Introduction to Recursive Partitioning Using the RPART Routines' (April 2019) <https://cran.r-project.org/web/packages/rpart/vignettes/longintro.pdf> accessed 1 June 2020 (using data on revival of cardiac arrest patients to illustrate the use of classification-tree algorithms).

26 Alina Mungiu-Pippidi, 'Corruption: Diagnosis and Treatment' (2006) 17 Journal of Democracy 86.

27 Ibid 91.

with some room for social advancement will be more resilient and less vulnerable to intervention than a system in which social roles are absolutely fixed; while a system producing identifiable and consistent losers will have a base through which remedial measures can be introduced. These clinical histories unfold in a decidedly non-linear manner: the upheavals that mark the transition from 'pure' to 'competitive' particularism may lead to more pervasive and virulent corruption, but they also produce the conditions under which an effective treatment can be administered.

Here, the metaphor of diagnosis is used to structure and animate a vigorous contextual survey. It is invoked precisely to underscore that different circumstances require different interventions—that a given input does not always yield the same output.

The essay is also unapologetic in its embrace of a certain metaphoric collateral. The treatment of illness—particularly the terminal kind—is often characterized in militaristic terms: as a fight, a struggle, a battle. In a parallel deployment not signaled in the paper's title, Professor Mungiu-Pippidi repeatedly turns to the language of warfare to describe the course of treatment, sometimes in ways that seem to bleed over into literalism. This goes hand-in-hand with the author's insistence on addressing corruption as a political matter: 'The argument I advance is that many anti-corruption initiatives fail because they are nonpolitical in nature, while most of the corruption in developing and post-communist countries is inherently political.'[28]

We began this chapter with the premise that modeling corruption has a political function: to focus collective attention on the problem, and to build support and legitimacy for any proposed intervention. We can conclude by briefly taking notice of a final non-linear frame of analysis, inextricably tied to the details of practical political life, established through the metaphor of governance as a *machine*.

The discipline of systems analysis aims to understand specific, delimited social and institutional dynamics within a defined network of interaction. It does this by identifying the network's constituent types in all their variety, establishing each one's aims, interests, and interactions, and charting a map that captures the full range and complexity of their interrelated effects upon one another. Requiring assessment of unevenly distributed allocations of power, the tracking of competing feedback loops of virtue and vice, and concrete representation of the most abstract motives and responses, the creation of such maps is extraordinarily challenging and time-intensive.

And yet progress can be made. Scholars have recently been able to produce detailed maps of the criminal justice systems in Uganda[29] and the Central African

28 Ibid 86.

29 Cheyanne Scharbatke-Church and Diana Chigas, *Facilitation in the Criminal Justice System: A Systems Analysis of Corruption in the Police and Courts in Northern Uganda* (Institute for Human Security, 2016).

Republic[30] and of kleptocratic networks in Azerbaijan, Kyrgyzstan, and Moldova.[31] The utility of these maps remains to be seen—their creators, while expressing and demonstrating a clear sense of imperative, do not clearly identify specific interventions the maps have made possible. However, we can see the potential in such an analysis in a comparable project carried out by the World Bank in the 1990s charting the process by which school grant funds from the central government in Uganda were diverted from their intended purpose, with a rate of 'leakage' approaching 80%.[32] Within a few years, a targeted public information campaign by the Ugandan government had successfully empowered the local populace to monitor the points at which loss was evident, resulting in a complete reversal of the situation and a leakage rate of less than 20%.[33]

Quick fixes like this are likely to be uncommon. When a machine isn't working properly, you take it apart and figure out what's broken. But corruption is more systemic, like the corrosion suffered by an automobile after too many winters on salted roads. Systems analysis recognizes corruption's pervasive character and the inextricability of the machine's interlocked parts. But it stands firm in the conviction that by coming to understand those parts and their mutual dependencies, we can get the machine to run more smoothly and comfortably.

30 Ladislas de Coster, Cheyanne Scharbatke-Church and Kiely Barnard-Webster, *Pity the Man Who Is Alone: Corruption in the Criminal Justice System in Bangui, Central African Republic* (CDA Collaborative Learning Projects 2017).

31 Sarah Chayes, 'The Structure of Corruption: A Systemic Analysis Using Eurasian Cases' *Carnegie Endowment for International Peace* (30 June 2016) <https://carnegieendowment.org/2016/06/30/structure-of-corruption-systemic-analysis-using-eurasian-cases-pub-63991> accessed 1 June 2020.

32 Ritva S Reinikka and Jakob Svensson, *Measuring and Understanding Corruption at the Micro Level* (2002).

33 Ritva Reinikka and Jakob Svensson, 'The Power of Information: Evidence from a Newspaper Campaign to Reduce Capture of Public Funds' (*Mimeo, IIES* 2004).

16 Transnationalization of anti-corruption trainings

Nuria González

During the last years, globally we have witnessed a proliferation of anti-corruption standards applicable to private organizations, which has been accompanied by a growing tendency to enforce them.[1]

This set of rules has emerged in different settings as part of the international legal framework created to counter corruption, which includes multilateral instruments, such as the United Nations Convention against Corruption (UNCAC), and the Organisation for Economic Cooperation and Development Convention on Combating Bribery of Foreign Public Officials in International Business Transactions (OECD Convention), and an array of regional treaties such as the Inter-American Convention Against Corruption, African Union's Convention on Preventing and Combating Corruption, the Council of Europe's Criminal Law Convention on Corruption and Civil Law Convention on Corruption, and the European Union's anti-corruption policy *ex* Article 29 of the Treaty on European Union.[2]

Systematically, this 'anti-corruption *acquis*' of hard and soft rules built across the world considers trainings as one of the key elements of anti-corruption compliance programs,[3] while setting specific requirements for their implementation.[4] Is it possible then to find a *transnational* common ground in the anti-corruption trainings realm?

1 Jonathan Webb, 'Anti-Bribery Enforcement Actions Increase across the Globe: Prosecutors Crack Down On Corruption' *Forbes* (2 March 2017) <www.forbes.com/sites/jwebb/2017/03/02/anti-bribery-enforcement-actions-increase-across-the-globe-prosecutors-crack-down-on-corruption/#25c552311819> accessed 1 June 2020.

2 UNODC, *An Anti-Corruption Ethics and Compliance Programme for Business: A Practical Guide* (2013) 2.

3 Thomas Fox, 'What are the Essential Elements of a Corporate Compliance Program?' *JDSupra* (22 May 2013) <https://www.jdsupra.com/legalnews/what-are-the-essential-elements-of-a-cor-08825/> accessed 1 June 2020; Richard Cassin, 'Ten Elements of an Effective Compliance Program' *The FCPA Blog* (2 October 2007) <www.fcpablog.com/blog/2018/8/13/back-to-basics-the-ten-elements-of-an-effective-compliance-p.html> accessed 1 June 2020.

4 OECD, UNODC, and The World Bank, *Anti-corruption Ethics/Compliance Handbook for Business* (2013) 13.

In order to answer this, in the first part of this chapter I will present how training is addressed *generally* in a group of anti-corruption hard and soft law rules. In the second section, I will refer to *specific* requirements grouped in major topics where it is possible to find similarities. In the third section, I will propose a conclusion to determine whether it is possible to find transnational standards in this field and what are the expected trends that will follow.

As a note, throughout this chapter, I will use hard law to refer to different types of rules that are somehow binding and soft law to encompass rules that despite not being mandatory, nonetheless, bestow some legal relevance.[5] I will also refer to anti-corruption *acquis* to include jointly the group of hard and soft law standards herein covered. The chapter is not aimed at encompassing the whole universe of existing rules and standards but a representative group of them. When mentioning compliance programs, or its equivalent *nomen iuris*, I will be alluding to anti-corruption programs. Also, I will use the term anti-corruption training, encompassing ethics, integrity and/or compliance trainings. This broad definition also covers all forms of training on this field, irrespective of their form (in-person, online, virtual, blended, etc.). Finally, where alphabetical order is not observed, the sequence of the standards is without prejudice to their legal status, hierarchy, or importance.

1 Anti-corruption trainings as a requirement derived from hard law and soft law

1.1 Domestic approaches

Relevant anti-corruption legal frames, and their guiding documents, coincide with the inclusion of training requirements.[6]

1.1.1 Argentina

Argentine Law 27.401, effective as of March 2018, makes legal entities liable for bribery and other crimes related to interactions with public officials. Whereas the adoption of a compliance program is only compulsory for companies which operate as government contractors, other entities may also opt to implement 'adequate' integrity programs in order to mitigate penalties for infringing this piece of legislation. Such is the importance allotted to trainings that they are considered amongst the three minimum *must-haves* for an integrity program to be adequate. In October 2018, the Argentine Anti-corruption Office published the *Guidelines on the design, implementation and maintenance of Integrity Programs governed by Law 27.401.* This instrument stresses the heightened relevance of

5 Bryan A Garner, *Black's Law Dictionary* (7th edn, West Group 999) 1397.

6 Keith Korenchuk and others, 'Anti-corruption Compliance: Meeting the Global Standard' *Bloomberg Law* (23 April 2014) <https://news.bloomberglaw.com/white-collar-and-criminal-law/anti-corruption-compliance-meeting-the-global-standard> accessed 1 June 2020.

compliance trainings and provides stakeholders with detailed orientation on this matter.[7]

1.1.2 Australia

Pursuant to the Australian Criminal Code, compliance programs can be a mitigating or exonerating factor on criminal liability of legal entities. Neither this body of law nor other secondary sources define the elements of a compliance program. As a result, further informal guidance on the matter is to be sought, for example, in the Australia Standard on Compliance Programs AS. 3806-2006, which specifically targets compliance trainings.[8]

1.1.3 Brazil

Brazilian Clean Act Company Act 12.846/2013 and its regulation by Decree 8420/2015 describe the delivery of periodic trainings as an element to validate the existence and application of integrity programs.[9] Further guidance on trainings is offered by the document entitled *Integrity Programs–Directives for Private Companies* issued in 2015 by the Ministry of Transparency, Supervision, and Control of Brazil.[10]

Beyond formal regulations, Pró-Ética Initiative, launched by the Brazilian Ministry of Transparency, encourages companies to voluntarily adopt integrity measures, including the conducting of trainings, by providing incentives of public recognition. For example, validated organizations are included in a specific registry and may use the brand 'Empresa Pró-Ética.'[11]

In a different setting, the Corporate Pact for Integrity and Against Corruption (*Pacto Empresarial pela Integridade e Contra a Corrupção*), launched in 2005 as a joint initiative of the NGO Ethos Instititue (UniEthos), the United Nations Office on Drug and Crime (UNODC), and the Brazilian Chapter of the UN Global Compact, states the commitment from signatory organizations to inform and spread its principles both internally and externally.[12] Member organizations may check up their integrity and corporate social responsibility practices through

7 Oficina Anticorrupción de Argentina, Lineamientos de Integridad para el mejor cumplimiento de lo establecido en los artículos 22 y 23 de la Ley 27.401 de Responsabilidad Penal de las Personas Jurídicas (octubre de 2018) s 3.4.

8 Robert R Wyld and Jasmine Forde, 'The Anti-Bribery and Anti-Corruption Review—Australia' *The Law Reviews* (6th edn, January 2018).

9 Decreto Nro 8420 de 14 de março de 2015, art 42.

10 Ministério da Transparência, Fiscalização e Controladoria-Geral da União, República Federativa do Brasil, *Programa de integridade–Diretrizes para Empresas Privadas* (setembro 2015) 20.

11 Ministério da Transparência, Fiscalização e Controladoria-Geral da União, República Federativa do Brasil, *Regulamento Empresa Pró-Ética* (janeiro de 2017).

12 Pacto Contra a Corrupção, Termo de Adesão, s 2.1.

the Ethos Indicators for sustainable and responsible business (*Indicadores Ethos para Negócios Sustentáveis e Responsáveis*), which is a questionnaire that also targets training efforts.[13]

1.1.4 Chile

Chilean Law No. 20.393 (2009) lays down corporate criminal liability applicable to money laundering, financing of terrorism, and bribery of domestic and foreign public officials.[14] In order to prevent these offenses, companies may adopt models consisting of specific obligations, prohibitions, and sanctions. These models should be mainstreamed to employees through channels such as communication and trainings.[15]

1.1.5 Colombia

Pursuant to Colombian Anti-corruption Law No. 1778 (2016), the Superintendency of Corporations will encourage the adoption of compliance programs. In this regard, this agency issued *Guidelines for Anti-bribery Prevention* aimed at orienting companies in the devise of compliance programs. These guidelines require companies to establish proper communication channels for compliance programs, including training exercises for employees and third parties.[16]

1.1.6 France

French Law No. 2016-1691 on transparency, fight against corruption, and modernization of economic life (Sapin II) provides that organization leaders and

13 Instituto Ethos de Empresas e Responsabilidade Social, *Indicadores Ethos para Negócios Sustentáveis e Responsáveis—Guia Temático: Integridade, Prevenção e Combate à Corrupção*, Dimensão Governança e Gastão (maio de 2019).

14 Chilean Law No. 20.393 (2009), art 4. See also, Osvaldo Artaza Varela, 'Sistemas de prevención de delitos o programas de cumplimiento. Breve descripción de las reglas técnicas de gestión del riesgo empresarial y su utilidad en sede jurídico penal' (2013) 8 Política criminal 1; Matteson Ellis, 'Anti-Corruption Laws in Chile: Three things companies should know' *FCPAméricas Blog* (December 2013) <www.fcpamericas.com/english/anti-corruption-compliance/anti-corruption-laws-chile-companies/> accessed 1 June 2020.

15 Fiscalía Nacional del Ministerio Público de Chile, Oficio FN Nro 440/2010 9; Hernán Fernández Aracenal, 'Comentarios al modelo de responsabilidad penal de las personas jurídicas establecido por la Ley Nro. 20.293 en relación a los delitos de cohecho' (Junio 2010) Revista Jurídica del Ministerio Público Nro. 42 90.

16 Superintendencia de Sociedades, República de Colombia, Circular Externa 100-000003 contentiva *de una guía con las instrucciones administrativas relacionadas con la promoción de los programas de integridad empresarial, así como de los mecanismos internos de auditoría, anticorrupción y prevención del soborno transnacional, en el contexto de la Ley 1778 de 2016* (26 julio de 2016) 19ff.

employees exposed to higher corruption risks should receive training.[17] Further clarification on the matter is provided by the French Anti-Corruption Agency's *Guidelines to help private and public sector entities prevent and detect corruption, influence peddling, extortion by public officials, unlawful taking of interest, misappropriation of public funds and favoritism*, issued on December 2017.[18] Furthermore, the *Mouvement des entreprises de France* (MEDEF), France's largest business association, released in September 2017 the *Practical Guide on Anti-corruption measures of the Sapin II Law*, which also targets training touchstones.[19]

1.1.7 Italy

Italian Legislative Decree 231/2001 entitled 'Administrative liabilities of legal entities deriving from offences' provides for the creation of an appropriate organization and management model to prevent certain crimes.[20] These models should be adopted efficiently for companies to benefit from penalty reductions.[21] Whereas this piece of legislation does not specifically mention trainings, in 2002 Confindustria, Italy's major industry association, issued guidelines on how to implement compliance programs, which were later approved by the Italian Ministry of Justice in 2008. This document expressly refers to the necessity of developing a suitable system of compliance trainings and communications.[22]

1.1.8 Japan

In Japan, domestic corruption is regulated in the Criminal Code, and foreign bribery is governed by the Unfair Competition Prevention Act. None of these

17 Loi no 2016–1691 du 9 décembre 2016 relative à la transparence, à la lutte contre la corruption et à la modernisation de la vie économique, art 42. Maria Lancri, 'Anti-corruption issues: New French Sapin II Law on transparency' (2017) Compliance & Ethics Professional 89ff.

18 *Recommandations de l'Agence française anticorruption destinées à aider les personnes morales de droit public et de droit privé à prévenir et à détecter les faits de corruption, de trafic d'influence, de concussion, de prise illégale d'intérêt, de détournement de fonds publics et de favoritisme* (Decembre 2017) 30ff.

19 MEDEF, *Guide pratique: dispositif anticorruption de la Loi Sapin II* (22 Septembre 2017) 49ff.

20 Decreto Legislativo 8 giugno 2001, n. 231, Disciplina della responsabilita' amministrativa delle persone giuridiche, delle societa' e delle associazioni anche prive di personalita' giuridica, a norma dell'articolo 11 della legge 29 settembre 2000, n. 300.

21 Di Marilisa De Nigris, Andrea Strippoli Lanternini, and Antonio Arrotino, 'The Legislative Decree no. 231/01 the Test of the International Law' *Il diritto penale della globalizzazione* (6 giugno 2016) <www.dirittopenaleglobalizzazione.it/the-legislative-decree-no-23101-the-test-of-the-international-law> accessed 1 June 2020.

22 Confindustria, *Linee Guida per la costruzione dei modelli di organizzazioni, gestioni e controllo ai sensi del Decreto Legislativo 8 Giugno 2001 N. 231* (marzo 2014), 39; Giulio Rivera, 'Il training dei dipendenti e la formazione sui reati presupposto' *Il Sole 24 Ore—Diritto 24* (Roma, Novembre 2013).

bodies expressly touches upon compliance programs. Nonetheless, they can be deemed as a valid instrument to prevent violations under the Unfair Competition Prevention Act.[23] In this sense, in 2015 the Japanese Ministry of Economy, Trade and Industry (METI), which is the agency that administers the later regulation, issued the *Guidelines for the Prevention of Bribery of Foreign Public Officials.* This document provides that 'appropriate educational activities should be conducted within the company to promote the improvement of employees' ethical awareness toward prevention of bribery and to enhance the effectiveness of the operation of internal control.'[24] As a supplement, the Japan Federation of Bar Associations rendered in 2016 the *Guidance on Prevention of Foreign Bribery*, which also encompasses training requirements as an indispensable element of anti-bribery compliance programs.[25]

1.1.9 Mexico

The Mexican General Law of Administrative Responsibilities, enacted in 2016, includes adequate systems of trainings amongst the key elements of an integrity policy.[26] With the aim of providing guidance on the implementation of integrity programs, in 2017 the Mexican Secretary of Public Function released the document entitled *Models of Corporate Integrity programs*, which makes specific reference to training requirements and good practice on this subject.[27] Furthermore, the Consejo Coordinador Empresarial of Mexico's (CCE) (Mexico employers' association) *Code of Integrity and Business Ethics*, as well as its *Integrity Manual*, also outline training requirements.[28]

1.1.10 Peru

Peruvian Law 30424, modified by Legislative Decrees 1052 and 3083, in force since January 2018, introduced corporate liability for criminal offenses related to corruption, money laundering, and finance of terrorism. This statute lays down the implementation of prevention models or compliance programs, which entail

23 Kana Manabe, Hideaki Umetsu, and Shiho Ono, 'The Anti-Bribery and Anti-Corruption Review—Japan' *The Law Reviews* (6th edn, January 2018).

24 Japan Ministry of Economy, Trade, and Industry, *Guidelines for the Prevention of Bribery of Foreign Public Officials* (July 2015) ch 2, s 5.

25 Japan Federation of Bar Associations, *Guidance on Prevention of Foreign Bribery* (January 2017) art 6.

26 Mexican General Law of Administrative Responsibilities (2016), art 25. See also PwC, *El Nuevo Sistema Nacional Anticorrupción en México Impactos Importantes en las Empresas* (septiembre 2016); Luis F Ortiz, 'Elementos esenciales de un programa de compliance' *El Economista México* (agosto de 2018).

27 Secretaría de la Función Pública de México, *Modelo de Programa de Integridad* (mayo de 2017) 8ff.

28 Consejo Coordinador Empresarial de México (CCE), *Código de integridad y ética empresarial* (octubre de 2017) principio 7; *Manual de Integridad* (octubre de 2017) 25ff.

adequate trainings. Further guidance on the implementation of compliance programs was provided by the project of Regulation published by Peruvian Ministry of Justice on February 2018 through Ministerial Resolution N°0061-2018-JUS. This project (*lege ferenda*) encompassed the delivery of periodic trainings aimed at enabling a culture of corporate integrity in companies.[29] Regulation was finally passed in January 2019 through Decree N° 002-2019-JUS, which sets forth that all legal entities, regardless of their size and capacity, must inform employees and third parties of their prevention models. [30]

1.1.11 Spain

Organic Law 5/2010, which introduced to the Spanish Criminal Code liability of legal entities for bribery and other crimes, sets forth the effective adoption of an organization and management model implementing supervision and effective control measures capable of preventing such offenses. To provide orientation on this, the National Prosecutor Office of Spain issued Circular 1/2016, which serves as an interpretation aid. This guidance embraces training requirements for both board members and associates.[31] Furthermore, UNE (the standardization body of Spain) also requires training as part of its certification 191601:2017 on criminal compliance.[32]

1.1.12 South Korea

South Korea's Improper Solicitation and Graft Act, effective as of September 2016, contains rules on corporate legal liability and leaves room for companies to undertake voluntary measures to prevent corruption under this legal frame. With the purpose of providing orientation on this matter, the Korean Anti-corruption and Civil Rights Commission issued *Guidelines for Companies*, which specifically enumerate integrity education as one of the basic elements for the implementation of anti-corruption programs.[33]

29 Ministerio de Justicia del Perú, Resolución Ministerial N° 0061-2018-JUS sobre el Proyecto Reglamento de la Ley N°30424 que regula la responsabilidad administrativa de las personas jurídicas por el delito de cohecho activo transnacional' (27 de febrero de 2018) art 40.

30 Decreto Supremo N° 002-2019-JUS art 4, s 10.

31 Fiscalía General del Estado, Circular 1/2016 sobre Responsablidad Penal de las Personas jurídicas conforme a la Reforma del Código Penal Efectuada por Ley Orgánica 1/2015. Similarly, legal scholars have included here the necessity of disseminating legal knowledge in companies. Enrique Bacigalupo, *Compliance y derecho penal* (Hammurabi, Buenos Aires, 2012) 134ff.

32 Abogacía Española, 'Publicada la norma UNE 19601 que establece los requisitos para sistemas de gestión de compliance penal' (18 mayo 2017) <www.abogacia.es/2017/05/18/publicada-la-norma-une-19601-que-establece-los-requisitos-para-sistemas-de-gestion-de-compliance-penal/> accessed 1 June 2020.

33 Korea Anti-corruption and Civil Rights Commission, *Anti-corruption Guidelines for Companies* (December 2016) 28ff.

1.1.13 United Kingdom

Under the Bribery Act of 2010, companies can resort to anti-bribery trainings as one of the measures to deter corruption. Educational activities are oriented to raise alertness and comprehension of organizational procedures and its commitment to their proper application.[34] Training good practices and recommendations are also found in the Transparency International UK Report, *Global Anti-bribery Guidelines for Companies.*[35]

1.1.14 United States

In the United States, when outlining the elements of an effective anti-corruption compliance program, the Federal Sentencing Guidelines, applicable to evaluate adherence to the Foreign Corrupt Practices Act (FCPA), amongst others, provide that the organization shall take 'reasonable steps to communicate periodically and in a practical manner its standards and procedures … by conducting effective trainings.'[36] Similarly, in relation to the FCPA, the United States Department of Justice (DOJ) and Securities Exchange Commission (SEC) also assess whether a company has taken measures to ensure training.[37]

1.2 International business standards and 'friends' from civil society

This section covers a non-exhaustive bundle of standards from international organizations and civil society developed as part of the international anti-corruption framework. Whereas these sources may not be purported *per se* to create new touchstones or to serve as binding legal rules, they may have a potential snowball effect and have influence in the development or deepening of anti-corruption standards. Hence, they are considered soft law for the purposes of this work.

In the OECD arena, the *Good Practice Guidance on Internal Controls, Ethics, and Compliance* (2010) states that entities should consider 'measures designed to ensure periodic communication and documented training for all levels of the company, on ethics and Compliance programs or measures regarding foreign bribery, as well as, where appropriate, for subsidiaries.'[38] Also, under the auspices of the OECD, the *Directives for Multinational Companies* (2008) call

34 UK Ministry of Justice, *Anti-Bribery Act Guidance About Procedures Which Relevant Commercial Organizations Can Put in Place to Prevent Persons Associated with Them From Bribing (Section 9 of the Bribery Act 2010)* (March 2011) 29ff.

35 Transparency International UK, *Anti-Bribery Guidance* (October 2017) ch 15.

36 United States Sentencing Commission, *Sentencing Guidelines* (2015) s 8B2.1.

37 United States Department of Justice and Securities Exchange Commission, *A Resource Guide to the U.S. Foreign Corrupt Practices Act* (November 2012) 59; US Department of Justice Criminal Division Fraud Section, *Evaluation of Corporate Compliance Programs* (2016) [6].

38 OECD, *Good Practice Guidance on Internal Controls, Ethics, and Compliance* (2010) [8].

corporations to counter corruption through measures which entail providing trainings to its employees.[39]

The World Bank Group *Integrity Compliance Guidelines* (2011) sets forth the delivery of periodical trainings to all employees and third parties,[40] as one of the elements to evaluate compliance and good standing from institutions that were sanctioned for infringing the Bank's anti-corruption and fraud policies.[41]

The United Nations Global Compact is an international initiative that promotes sustainable development, inviting companies to conduct business in accordance with principles which englobe the fight against corruption (Principle 10 derives from the United Nations Convention Against Corruption). In this context, the Global Compact calls on participant institutions to take concrete measures to combat corruption, including the conducting of trainings that enable the development of a culture of integrity organizations.[42]

Under the umbrella of the World Economic Forum, the 'Partnering Against Corruption Initiative' (PACI) was launched in 2004 as a cross-industry alliance of companies committed to fight corruption through collective actions. The PACI *Principles to Combat Corruption* also enumerate compliance trainings targeting employees and third parties.[43]

Under the auspices of the Asia-Pacific Economic Cooperation (APEC), the *Anti-corruption Code for Business* (2007) provides that organizations must maintain a zero-tolerance internal culture against corruption through training programs for leaders, associates, and agents, tailored to specific needs and circumstances.[44]

The International Chamber of Commerce (ICC) *Rules to Combat Corruption* (2011) also refer to periodic trainings as one of the elements of an efficient compliance program.[45]

In the civil society arena, Transparency International's *Business Principles for Countering Bribery* (2013) provide that companies must conduct appropriate training for employees and third parties as part of their programs to tackle corruption.[46]

39 OECD, *Directives for Multinational Companies* (2008) s VII.4 21.

40 The World Bank, *Integrity Compliance Guidelines* (2011) s 7.

41 World Bank, *Sanctions Procedures* (2012).

42 United Nations Global Compact, Transparency International and The Prince of Wales International Business Leaders Forum, *Los negocios contra la corrupción. Un marco para la acción. Implementación del 10mo principio del Pacto Global de las Naciones Unidas contra la corrupción* (2011) 11.

43 World Economic Forum, *Global Principles for Countering Corruption, Application & General Terms of Partnership* (May 2016) s 9 (PACI *Principles*).

44 APEC Anti-Corruption and Transparency Working Group, *Implementing the APEC Anti-Corruption Code of Conduct for Business* (June 2013) 18.

45 ICC, *Rules on Combating Corruption* (2011) 10.

46 Transparency International, *Business Principles for Countering Bribery* (2013) s 6.4.

Still in the civil society scene, the U4 think-tank also includes training as one of the elements of anti-corruption programming.[47]

Alliance for Integrity is a 'business driven multi-stakeholder initiative between private sector, civil society, political organizations and international institutions,' which was initiated by the German Government, with the aim of providing transparency and integrity in the economic sector by generating compliance capacity-building in companies. This initiative particularly targets compliance trainings through a train-the-trainers approach.[48]

Anti-corruption trainings are also present in the certifications field. ISO 37001:2016 on Anti-Bribery Management Systems published by the International Organization for Standardization considers the raising of awareness and formation as one of the measures companies can undertake when implementing Compliance programs that are to be certified under those standards.[49] Similarly, trainings are required by ISO 19600:2014 on Compliance Management Systems.[50] Also, when it comes to providing compliance credential to companies, TRACE International considers anti-bribery trainings as one of the steps organizations should complete as part of its due diligence process.[51]

Finally, when assessing 'the World's most ethical companies,' the Ethisphere Institute also evaluates ethics and compliance programs, including trainings.[52]

In sum, similar to the findings in the major anti-corruption legal frames analyzed, the array of international standards or soft law sources described systematically include trainings as a key element in the fight against corruption.

2 Transnational anti-corruption training requirements

As seen above, anti-corruption trainings are included consistently in a plethora of different sources. Yet, when it comes to their implementation, is it possible to extract some international commonality from this anti-corruption *acquis*? In other words, when private organizations implement educational activities, can we find that expectations align transnationally in the anti-corruption realm? Amongst the above-analyzed sources of our 'anti-corruption *acquis*,' it is possible

47 U4 Anti-Corruption Resource Centre, 'Anti-Corruption Basics' <www.u4.no/topics/anti-corruption-basics/basics#addressing-corruption> accessed 1 June 2020.

48 Alliance for Integrity, 'About Us' <www.allianceforintegrity.org/en/alliance-for-integrity/about-us/> accessed 1 June 2020.

49 ISO 37001:2016, Sistemas de gestión antisoborno Requisitos con orientación para su uso s 7.3.

50 ISO 19600:2014, Sistemas de gestión de Compliance s 7.2.

51 Trace International, 'Anti-Corruption Certification' <https://tpms.traceinternational.org/> accessed 1 June 2020.

52 Ethisphere Institute, 'World's Most Ethical Companies' <www.worldsmostethicalcompanies.com> accessed 1 June 2020.

to present, amongst others, the following patterns based on common areas of contact.[53]

2.1 *Risk assessment*

How are risk assessments and anti-corruption trainings connected? As a component of anti-corruption programs, the linkage between trainings and risk assessments is a regular topic in the anti-corruption *acquis*, particularly considering the limited resources in the area.[54] This can be inferred, for example, from the standards rendered by international organizations such as UNODC, the OECD and the World Bank.[55] Also, it is frequently at the national level in countries such as Argentina,[56] France,[57] Japan,[58] Mexico,[59] Peru,[60] and the UK.[61]

Risk assessments also play a part in justifying a focus on specific populations which are highly exposed to corruption or bribery challenges. For instance, they also sustain the customization of training programs regarding content, time factors, and its very own improvement.[62]

2.2 *Periodicity*

How often should anti-corruption trainings be conducted in an organization? Recurrence of trainings, based upon risk mapping, prevails across this anti-corruption *acquis*. This includes, *inter alia*, Argentina,[63] Brazil,[64] France,[65] Mexico,[66]

53 For other general training topics, see Nuria González, 'La formación en compliance en organizaciones privadas' in Raúl R Saccani and Gustavo L Morales Oliver (eds), *Tratado de Compliance*, vol 1 (Thomson Reuters 2018) 215.
54 OECD, UNODC and The World Bank (n 4) 14.
55 Ibid; UNODC (n 2) 59.
56 Oficina Anticorrupción de Argentina, *Lineamientos de Integridad* (n 7) s 3.4.
57 *Recommandations de l'Agence française anticorruption* (n 18) 31.
58 Japan Federation of Bar Associations, *Guidance* (n 25) art 6.
59 Consejo Coordinador Empresarial de México (CCE), *Código de integridad* Principio 7° (n 28).
60 Ministerio de Justicia del Perú, Resolución Ministerial N°0061-2018-JUS (n 29) art 40.
61 UK Ministry of Justice, *Anti-Bribery Act Guidance* (n 34) 30.
62 United Nations Global Compact, *A Guide for Anti-corruption Assessment* (2013) 14.
63 Oficina Anticorrupción de Argentina, *Lineamientos de Integridad* (n 7) s 3.4.
64 Brazilian Clean Act Company Act Nro 12.846/2013 and its regulation by Decree 8420/2015 art 42.
65 MEDEF, *Guide pratique* (n 19) 50.
66 Secretaría de la Función Pública de México, *Modelo de Programa de Integridad* (n 27) 8; Consejo Coordinador Empresarial de México (CCE), *Código de integridad* Principio 7 (n 28).

Peru,[67] the United States,[68] the UK,[69] the World Bank *Integrity Guidelines*,[70] the OECD business guiding instruments,[71] ICC *Rules on Combating Corruption*,[72] UN Global Compact *Guidelines for the implementation of the 10th principle*,[73] UNODC *Guidelines*,[74] and ISO 37001:2016.[75]

Some of the studied sources, such as Argentina,[76] Mexico,[77] Peru,[78] and the UNODC *Guidelines*,[79] recommend anti-corruption training to be delivered at least on an annual basis.[80] In Italy, for example, periodicity is deemed as one of the elements to consider when devising training systems. In Japan, for example, it is advised that anti-corruption training regularity is determined based on a risk assessment.[81] A similar criterion is found in Argentina where training frequency is encouraged based on employees' risk profiles.[82] Finally, Australia's Standard on Compliance Programs, AS 3806-2004.3.3, includes *on-going* trainings as one of the factors which support the development of a compliance culture in an organization.

2.3 Audience

Who should be trained? When answering this question, our anti-corruption *acquis* appears to be less uniform. Standards vary including some or even all of the following potential individuals: employees (all or some), top management, board or governing body members, key stakeholders such as agents and business partners.

As per employees, many of the existing standards require a certain level of training or awareness to be provided across the whole organization irrespective of

67 Ministerio de Justicia del Perú, Resolución Ministerial N°0061-2018-JUS (n 29) art 40.
68 United States Sentencing Commission (n 36) s 8B2.1. United States Department of Justice and Securities Exchange Commission (n 37) 59; US Department of Justice Criminal Division Fraud Section (n 37) [6].
69 UK Ministry of Justice, *Anti-Bribery Act Guidance* (n 34) 30.
70 The World Bank, *Integrity Compliance Guidelines* (n 40) s 7.
71 OECD, *Good Practice Guidance* (n 38) [8].
72 ICC, *Rules on Combating Corruption* (n 45) art 10.
73 United Nations Global Compact, Transparency International and The Prince of Wales International Business Leaders Forum (n 42) 11.
74 UNODC (n 2) 2.
75 ISO 37001:2016, Sistemas de gestión antisoborno—Requisitos con orientación para su uso s 7.
76 Oficina Anticorrupción de Argentina, *Lineamientos de Integridad* (n 7) s 3.4.
77 Consejo Coordinador Empresarial de México, *Manual de Integridad* (n 28) 26.
78 Ministerio de Justicia del Perú, Resolución Ministerial N°0061-2018-JUS (n 29) art 40.
79 UNODC (n 2) 2.
80 On the idea that trainings should not be a special and unique yearly event, see Debbie Troklus and Sheryl Vacca, *International Compliance 101—How to Build and maintain an effective compliance and ethics program* (Society of Corporate Compliance and Ethics 2013) 21.
81 Japan Federation of Bar Associations, *Guidance* (n 25) art 2.
82 Oficina Anticorrupción de Argentina, *Lineamientos de Integridad* (n 7) s 3.4.

workers' level or hierarchy. For example, this is the case of anti-corruption standards from Argentina,[83] Brazil,[84] the United States,[85] the UK,[86] France,[87] Peru,[88] Mexico,[89] the OECD *Guidance on Internal Controls, Ethics and Compliance*,[90] the World Bank's *Integrity Guidelines*,[91] the PACI *Principles*,[92] and ISO 37001:2016 on Anti-Bribery Management Systems.[93]

Regardless of whether certain training targets all of the organization, a commonality found throughout the anti-corruption *acquis* is the focus on those who are highly exposed to risks. As an illustration, this standard is found in, for example, Argentina,[94] Colombia,[95] France,[96] Japan,[97] the UK,[98] ISO 37001:2016 on Anti-Bribery Management System,[99] and the World Bank's *Integrity Guidelines*.[100] The criterion lies in accordance with the above-referred linkage between risks assessments and anti-corruption trainings.

As a trend, some of the sources target specific populations such as new employees who are in need of specific 'on-boardings.'[101] These examples of orientation are found in, for example, the UK,[102] Argentina,[103] Brazil,[104] and South Korea[105] (with specific reference to even newly promoted employees). The

83 Ibid s 3.4.
84 Ministério da Transparência do Brasil, *Programa de integridade–Diretrizes* (n 10) 20.
85 United States Department of Justice and Securities Exchange Commission (n 37) 59.
86 UK Ministry of Justice, *Anti-Bribery Act Guidance* (n 34) 30; Transparency International UK, *Anti-Bribery Guidance* (n 35) ch 15.5.
87 *Recommandations de l'Agence française* (n 18) 31. MEDEF *Guidelines* also make specific reference to targeting employees based on their fonctional and roles within the organization. MEDEF, *Guide pratique* (n 19) 51.
88 Ministerio de Justicia del Perú, Resolución Ministerial N°0061-2018-JUS (n 29) art 40.
89 At least with regard to the Code of Conduct. Secretaría de la Función Pública de México, *Modelo de Programa de Integridad* (n 27) 4.
90 OECD, *Good Practice Guidance* (n 38) [8].
91 The World Bank, *Integrity Compliance Guidelines* (n 40) s 7.
92 World Economic Forum, PACI *Principles* (n 43) s 4.
93 ISO 37001:2016, Sistemas de gestión antisoborno—Requisitos con orientación para su uso sec 7.3.
94 Oficina Anticorrupción de Argentina, *Lineamientos de Integridad* (n 7) s 3.4.
95 Superintendencia de Sociedades, República de Colombia, Circular Externa 100-000003 del 26 de julio de 2016 (n 16) 20.
96 *Recommandations de l'Agence française anticorruption* (n 18) 30.
97 Japan Ministry of Economy, Trade and Industry, *Guidelines* (n 24) ch 2, s 5; Japan Federation of Bar Associations, *Guidance* (n 25) arts 2, 9.
98 UK Ministry of Justice, *Anti-Bribery Act Guidance* (n 34) 30.
99 ISO 37001:2016, Sistemas de gestión antisoborno—Requisitos con orientación para su uso s 7.3.
100 The World Bank, *Integrity Compliance Guidelines* (n 40) s 7.
101 Similar findings were identified in NAVEX 2018 Ethics & Compliance Training Benchmark Report, 26.
102 UK Ministry of Justice, *Anti-Bribery Act Guidance* (n 34) 30.
103 Oficina Anticorrupción de Argentina, *Lineamientos de Integridad* (n 7) Sec 3.4.
104 Ministério da Transparência do Brasil, *Programa de integridade–Diretrizes* (n 10) 20.
105 Korea Anti-corruption & Civil Rights Commission, *Anti-corruption Guidelines* (n 33) 26.

UN Global Compact *Guide* also covers new hires as part of the risk assessment anti-corruption training scoring matrix.[106] Whereas this group is particularly targeted in the latter sources, they could also be considered indirectly targeted in others when defining relevant populations in training programs.

Pertaining to anti-corruption training for management and members of governing bodies, analyzed sources coincide with their inclusion. Along these lines, it is possible to enumerate standards set by, for example, *Transparency International Business Principles*,[107] the ICC *Rules for Combating Corruption*,[108] and PACI *Principles*.[109] Similar requirements are found domestically in Argentina,[110] France,[111] the UK,[112] and the USA.[113] Also, and related to governing authorities, sources from Argentina,[114] Italy,[115] and the United States[116] mention their oversight role and support to the training program as an expression of the tone-at-the-top principle and as an opportunity to understand how workers are trained on anti-corruption.[117] As seen, most of the sources focus on high management of the organization. Sources highlight the need for management support, oversight, and commitment. An interesting standard regarding *tone-in-the middle* is found in the UNODC *Guide*, which stresses the vital role played by middle managers when deploying trainings.[118]

Beyond the organization, the trend is to extend anti-corruption training to third parties or stakeholders such as contractors, agents, suppliers, and business partners, as appropriate or to the extent possible. Such standards are set forth in APEC's *Anti-Corruption Code of Conduct for Business*,[119] ICC *Rules on Combatting Corruption*,[120] Transparency International's *Business Principles*,[121] the PACI *Principles*,[122] and the UNODC *Guide*.[123] Similar principles are also

106 UN Global Compact, *A Guide for Anti-corruption Assessment* (n 62) 64.
107 Transparency International, *Business Principles* (n 46) s 6.4.1.
108 ICC, *Rules on Combating Corruption* (n 45) art 10.
109 World Economic Forum, PACI *Principles* (n 43) s 4.
110 Ley de Responsabilidad Penal de las Personas Jurídicas Nro. 27.401 art 23 c); Oficina Anticorrupción de Argentina, *Lineamientos de Integridad* (n 7) s 3.4.
111 *Recommandations de l'Agence française anticorruption* (n 18) 30.
112 For an example of a specific board training syllabus, see Transparency International UK, *Anti-Bribery Guidance* (n 35) ch 15.8.
113 United States Sentencing Commission (n 36) s 8B2.1.
114 Ley de Responsabilidad Penal de las Personas Juridicas Nro. 27.401 Art 23 c); Oficina Anticorrupcion de Argentina, *Lineamientos de Integridad* (n 7) s 3.4.
115 Confindustria, *Linee Guida* (n 22) 38.
116 United States Sentencing Commission (n 36) s 8B2.1.
117 David A Katz and Laura McIntosh, 'The Board's Role in FCPA Compliance' (Harvard Law School Forum on Corporate Governance and Financial Regulation, 23 September 2016).
118 UNODC (n 2) 40.
119 APEC Anti-Corruption and Transparency Working Group (n 44) 18.
120 ICC, *Rules on Combating Corruption* (n 45) art 10 (k).
121 Transparency International, *Business Principles* (n 46) s 6.4.
122 World Economic Forum, PACI *Principles* (n 43) s 4.
123 UNODC (n 2) 69.

found in domestic rules from the UK,[124] the US,[125] Argentina,[126] Colombia,[127] Mexico,[128] and South Korea.[129]

2.4 Training content and approach

How should anti-corruption trainings be? What should they cover? As a cross-border commonality identified in most of the studied sources, content should be risk-based (as presented above), practical, content specific, and tailored.

The myriad of analyzed sources addresses practicality with a similar spirit. As an illustration, in Argentina it is recommended that trainings encompass dialogue and discussion of dilemmas so as to generate decision-making skills in difficult situations.[130] Likewise, in Brazil it is desired that trainings include practical aspects, including discussion of dilemmas and case studies, so that participants *actually* know how to apply this knowledge.[131] In France, anti-corruption education is expected to be pedagogical, pragmatic, and adapted to the dynamic risk mapping of the organization.[132] It is also advised that trainings cover how to handle corruption when it happens.[133] Similarly, in Japan training should be oriented to provide understanding of applicable anti-bribery regulations, as well as internal policies and procedures (SOPs) with the inclusion of practical examples, bribery challenges, and how to say no to bribe requests beyond the mere knowledge of applicable rules.[134] In Mexico, it is recommended that trainings encompass how to deal with corruption in daily situations.[135] In Peru, trainings are expected to teach how to identify and face risks.[136] In South Korea, anti-corruption educational activities should be aimed at explaining to participants *how* to operate with integrity and probity every day.[137] A practical approach to trainings is also found in the United States,[138] where content is expected to include real life scenarios

124 UK Ministry of Justice, *Anti-Bribery Act Guidance* (n 34) 30.

125 United States Department of Justice and Securities Exchange Commission (n 37) 59; United States Sentencing Commission (n 36) s 8B2.1.

126 Oficina Anticorrupción de Argentina, *Lineamientos de Integridad* (n 7) s 3.4.

127 Superintendencia de Sociedades, República de Colombia, Circular Externa 100-000003 del 26 de julio de 2016 (n 16) 18.

128 Training to third parties with regard to Code of Conduct. Secretaría de la Función Pública de México, *Modelo de Programa de Integridad* (n 27) 8.

129 Korea Anti-corruption & Civil Rights Commission, *Anti-corruption Guidelines for Companies* (n 33) 14.

130 Oficina Anticorrupción de Argentina, *Lineamientos de Integridad* (n 7) s 26.

131 Ministério da Transparência do Brasil, *Programa de integridade–Diretrizes* (n 10) 20

132 MEDEF, *Guide pratique* (n 19) 51.

133 *Recommandations de l'Agence française anticorruption* (n 18) 31.

134 Japan Federation of Bar Associations, *Guidance* (n 25) art 6; Japanese Ministry of Economy, Trade and Industry, *Guidelines* (n 24) ch 2, s 5.

135 Consejo Coordinador Empresarial de México (CCE), *Manual de Integridad* (n 28) 26.

136 Ministerio de Justicia del Perú, Resolución Ministerial N°0061-2018-JUS (n 29) art 40.

137 Korea Anti-corruption & Civil Rights Commission, *Anti-corruption Guidelines* (n 33) 26.

138 United States Sentencing Commission (n 36) 8B2.1.

and case studies beyond the mere explanation of rules.[139] In the United Kingdom, the goal of training activities is to develop a firm comprehension of relevant rules and procedures in *praxis*.[140] Hence, it is suggested that trainings include thought-provoking case studies, dilemmatic situations, and hypotheses so as to learn how to navigate grey areas.[141] The UNODC *Guidelines* also highlight the importance of practical examples to show coherence between individual actions and organizational values.[142] With a similar approach, the UN Global Compact provides online trainings through interactive-video dilemma scenarios.[143] Additionally, ISO 37001:2016 on Anti-Bribery Management Systems states that, as a result of the training, participants should be able to *understand* bribery risk and their compliance obligations with the applicable anti-bribery policy.[144]

In addition to the risk assessment anchor and practical approach, some of the analyzed sources make specific reference to minimum topics or curricula to be covered from a normative or rule-based perspective. For example, the Argentine standards require synchronization with the organization's code of conduct and internal rules (policies and SOPs). The French standards also recommend that training cover specific matters such as top management's commitment, corruption problematics, its causes and forms, applicable legal rules and consequences for its infringement, anti-corruption compliance framework, etc. The Japanese standards define training subject matter targeting relevant laws and regulations, as well as internal policies and SOPs.[145] In Peru, training curricula expectations include an array of items ranging from internal policies aimed at preventing specific bribery crimes, risks for the organization and its personnel, situations in which these risks may arise, tools to identify and manage them, avenues of communication, reporting channels, collaboration forms to prevent risks and enhance the program, non-compliance legal consequences, and information on available educational resources.[146] In South Korea, activities of integrity education are expected to

139 United States Department of Justice and Securities Exchange Commission (n 37) 59.

140 UK Ministry of Justice, *Anti-Bribery Act Guidance* (n 34) 30.

141 Transparency International UK, *Anti-Bribery Guidance* (n 35) ch 15 2.

142 UNODC (n 2) 69.

143 This approach can be also found in specific training tools offered by international organizations. For example, the United Nations Global Compact provides online trainings through interactive-video dilemma scenarios. Similar responses can be found in RESIST, the company tool for training employees how to resist extortion and solicitation in international transactions through scenarios developed jointly by the United Nations Global Compact, the World Economic Forum, the ICC, and Transparency International in 2011. See, e.g., UN Global Compact, *The Fight Against Corruption: E-Learning Tool* (2010) <www.unglobalcompact.org/library/152> accessed 1 June 2020; UN Global Compact, RESIST—*A company tool for training employees* (March 2011).

144 ISO 37001:2016, Sistemas de gestión antisoborno—Requisitos con orientación para su uso s 7.3.

145 Japan Federation of Bar Associations, *Guidance* (n 25) art 6; Japanese Ministry of Economy, Trade and Industry, *Guidelines* (n 24) ch 2, s 5.

146 Ministerio de Justicia del Perú, Resolución Ministerial N°0061-2018-JUS (n 29) art 40.

touch upon main laws applicable to business.[147] A similar approach appears in ISO 37001:2016 on Anti-Bribery Management Systems, which require organizations to cover anti-bribery-policies, the duty to comply with it, risk and damage to both company and its personnel derived from non-adherence; how bribery can appear in relation to specific functions and how to handle it.[148]

Interestingly, some of the analyzed sources in scope make reference to anti-corruption programs enshrined in organizational values. Standards from Argentina,[149] and Brazil,[150] specifically include these amongst the topics to be covered by trainings (without excluding others). This could be interpreted as an alignment with the dichotomy that distinguishes between anti-corruption compliance programs that are rule-based and value-based.[151] However, from a holistic standpoint, this binary distinction appears to be superseded by a *tertium genus* or a mixed category, which combines both rule-based aspects with organization values embodied in an organizational culture that promotes simultaneously legal compliance and ethical conduct.[152][153]

Many of the consulted sources coincide in including training customization based on audiences and contexts (see above). For example, adaptation to local languages, circumstances,[154] and audiences is found in Argentina,[155] France,[156] Japan,[157] and the United States with specific case law related to this matter.[158]

147 Korea Anti-corruption & Civil Rights Commission, *Anti-corruption Guidelines* (n 33) 26.

148 ISO 37001:2016, Sistemas de gestión antisoborno—Requisitos con orientación para su uso s 7.3.

149 Oficina Anticorrupción de Argentina, *Lineamientos de Integridad* (n 7) s 3.4

150 Ministério da Transparência do Brasil, *Programa de integridade–Diretrizes* (n 10) 20.

151 Harlan Loeb, 'Principles-Based Regulation and Compliance: A Framework for Sustainable Integrity' *Huffpost The Blog* (May 5, 2015) <www.huffingtonpost.com/harlan-loeb/princ iplesbased-regulaton_b_7204110.html> accessed 1 June 2020.

152 Michael Volkok, 'The Important Distinction Between Ethics & Compliance' *Corporate Compliance Insights* (3 November 2014); Roy Snell, 'Teaching Values is Not Enough' *Compliance & Ethics Professional—A Publication of the SCCE* (16 June 2015).

153 For example, this is the criterion found in the US. United States Sentencing Commission (n 36) ch 8, s 8B2.1.4.

154 APEC Anti-Corruption and Transparency Working Group (n 44) 18.

155 Oficina Anticorrupción de Argentina, *Lineamientos de Integridad* (n 7) s 3.4.

156 *Recommandations de l'Agence française anticorruption* (n 18) 30. See also Christophe Collard and others, *Risque juridique et Conformité* (Wolters Kluwer 2011) Ch 3, 249.

157 Japanese Ministry of Economy, Trade and Industry, *Guidelines* (n 24) ch 2, s 5. The later document refers to local circumstances. The same criterion is also found in: Transparency International UK, *Anti-Bribery Guidance* (n 35) ch 15.

158 US Department of Justice and Securities Exchange Commission (n 37) 59; US Department of Justice Criminal Division Fraud Section (n 37) [5]. For specific enforcement on this matter, consult Ellis Matteson, 'SEC: Local Language Essential to "Effective" FCPA Compliance' *FCPAAmericas Blog* (11 July 2012); Carlos Ayres, 'Conducting Effective FCPA Training in Latin America' *FCPA Americas Blog* (29 November 2013).

Similar criteria can be inferred from the UNODC *Guidelines*[159] and the UN Global Compact risk assessment anti-corruption training scoring matrix.[160]

References to cultural aspects are specifically found in the aforementioned Argentine and UNODC standards.[161] Irrespective of the specific treatment conferred in the assessed sources, it could be worth asking whether training customization could be implied in the very global concept of effective training itself.

2.5 Training formats: in-person vs. e-learnings

How should trainings be conducted? Whereas some of the sources provide guidance on how training should be delivered with specific advice or preference, others solely present potential learning channels.

For example, in Argentina, it is preferable that organizations blend both methods to the greatest possible extent.[162] Italy also favors a mixed scheme based on risk: e-learnings should be accompanied by appropriate testing and monitoring, and be complemented with in-person formative activities.[163]

In France, highly exposed associates should receive in-person training, with e-learning only as a complement.[164] In the United Kingdom, although both methodologies are accepted,[165] the face-to-face format is considered essential and more effective than e-learnings.[166] In South Korea, aside from the traditional formats, the range of proposed options also include innovative participatory methodologies such as the 'Integrity Concert,' which resorts to culture and entertainment.[167] In the United States, a blended approach is mentioned with regard to large organizations.[168] Also, the UNODC standards call for a mix between more standardized web-based solutions with more personal avenues that encourage in-person exchanges, based on customization for specific audiences.[169] Finally, sources from Peru refer to both traditional methodologies and web-based/e-learning without any further orientation.[170]

159 UNODC (n 2) 69.

160 UN Global Compact, *A Guide for Anti-corruption Assessment* (n 62) 64.

161 For more general ideas about the linkage between training and cultural aspects, see Mary Gentile, 'Taking About Ethics Across Cultures' *Harvard Business Review* (23 December 2016); Mark Dorosz, 'Cultural Identities & Compliance Training: Reaching Your Employees' *Ethics & Compliance SCCE Blog* (16 February 2017).

162 Oficina Anticorrupción de Argentina, *Lineamientos de Integridad* (n 5) s 3.4.

163 Confindustria, *Linee Guida* (n 22) 39.

164 *Recommandations de l'Agence française anticorruption* (n 18) 30.

165 UK Ministry of Justice, *Anti-Bribery Act Guidance* (n 34) 30.

166 Transparency International UK, *Anti-Bribery Guidance* (n 35) ch 15.8.

167 Korea Anti-corruption & Civil Rights Commission, *Anti-corruption Guidelines* (n 33) 26.

168 United States Department of Justice and Securities Exchange Commission (n 37) 59.

169 UNODC (n 2) 69.

170 Ministerio de Justicia del Perú, Resolución Ministerial N°0061-2018-JUS, (n 29) art 40.

2.6 Testing in anti-corruption education

Should participants be tested? Some of the sources of our anti-corruption *acquis* answer affirmatively. In this sense, the Argentine standards call for an evaluation of attendees.[171] In Italy, the standards recommend appropriate intermediate and final assessments in e-learning activities.[172] In Mexico, private organizations are expected to implement testing to the greatest possible extent.[173] In the United States, there is an expectation for organizations to measure training effectiveness, and even more generally, to take reasonable measures so as to ensure the ethics and compliance program is actually followed. The latter can also be interpreted teleologically so as to support some ground for training assessment.[174] In the United Kingdom, it is also expected that participants be examined to show their understanding.[175] The desirability of testing trainings can also be traced in the UN Global Compact risk assessment anti-corruption training scoring matrix.[176]

2.7 Mandatory trainings and incentives

Can trainings be compulsory? Some of the assessed sources respond affirmatively, such as in, among others, Argentina,[177] Brazil,[178] and France.[179] Whereas other standards do not necessarily touch upon this topic expressly, again it could be worth asking whether obligatory trainings could be derived from the very effectiveness idea.

Can organizations provide incentives related to anti-corruption trainings? Most of the sources under review respond affirmatively, either in a generic (group 1) or specific fashion (group 2). The first group approach can be found in, for example, the United States,[180] the ICC Rules,[181] TI Principles,[182] PACI *Principles*,[183] and the World Bank Integrity Guidelines.[184] The methodology followed by the

171 Oficina Anticorrupción de Argentina, *Lineamientos de Integridad* (n 7) s 3.4.
172 Confindustria, *Linee Guida* (n 22) 39.
173 Consejo Coordinador Empresarial de México (CCE), *Código de integridad* (n 28) principio 7.
174 US Department of Justice Criminal Division Fraud Section (n 37) [5]; United States Department of Justice and Securities Exchange Commission (n 37) 59.
175 Transparency International UK, *Anti-Bribery Guidance* (n 35) ch 15.4.
176 UN Global Compact, *A Guide for Anti-corruption Assessment* (n 62) 64.
177 Oficina Anticorrupción de Argentina, *Lineamientos de Integridad* (n 7) s 3.4.
178 Ministério da Transparência do Brasil, *Programa de integridade—Diretrizes para Empresas Privadas* (n 10) 20.
179 Managers must ensure employees complete trainings. *Recommandations de l'Agence française anticorruption* (n 18) 30.
180 United States Sentencing Commission (n 36) s 8B2.1.
181 ICC, *Rules on Combating Corruption* (n 45) art 10 (k).
182 Transparency International, *Business Principles* (n 46) s 2.6.3.1.
183 World Economic Forum, PACI *Principles* (n 43) s 5.4.3.
184 The World Bank, *Integrity Compliance Guidelines* (n 40) s 8.

second group of sources can be traced in, for example, Argentina,[185] Brazil (with a possibility to link participation to career development),[186] France,[187] the United Kingdom,[188] and UNODC *Guidelines.*[189]

2.8 *Anti-corruption training records*

Should anti-corruption trainings be documented? When answering this question, most of the studied sources share unanimously the necessity to record trainings. The need to have documentation lies in an array of reasons ranging from gathering evidence as to prove undertaken efforts in this realm, to serving as a defense against rules violation or even while seeking external certifications. As an illustration, training records are present in the UNODC *Guidelines*,[190] ICC *Rules on Combatting Corruption*,[191] the OECD *Good Practices Guidance*,[192] as well as standards from Argentina,[193] Brazil,[194] Peru,[195] and the United Kingdom.[196]

2.9 *Monitoring and assessment*

Should anti-corruption trainings be monitored? Many of the studied sources of the *acquis* respond affirmatively, including, for example, Argentina (with the purpose of updating content and including lessons learned),[197] France (to enable oversight),[198] the UK,[199] APEC *Anti-Corruption Code for Business Conduct*,[200] and the World Economic Forum PACI *Principles.*[201]

3 Conclusion

Existing standards in both hard law and soft law in relation to training requirements enabled the creation of an anti-corruption *acquis.* Based on shared

185 Oficina Anticorrupción de Argentina, *Lineamientos de Integridad* (n 7) s 3.4
186 Ministério da Transparência do Brasil, *Programa de integridade—Diretrizes para Empresas Privadas* (n 10) 20.
187 *Recommandations de l'Agence française anticorruption* (n 18) 31.
188 Transparency International UK, *Anti-Bribery Guidance* (n 35) ch 15.
189 UNODC (n 2) 74.
190 Ibid 69.
191 ICC, *Rules on Combating Corruption* (n 45) art 10(k).
192 OECD, *Good Practice Guidance* (n 38) [8].
193 Oficina Anticorrupción de Argentina, *Lineamientos de Integridad* (n 5) Sec 3.4.
194 Ministério da Transparência do Brasil, *Programa de integridade—Diretrizes para Empresas Privadas* (n 10) 20.
195 Ministerio de Justicia del Perú, Resolución Ministerial N°0061-2018-JUS (n 29) art 40.
196 Transparency International UK, *Anti-Bribery Guidance* (n 35) ch 15.
197 Oficina Anticorrupción de Argentina, *Lineamientos de Integridad* (n 7) s 3.4.
198 *Recommandations de l'Agence française anticorruption* (n 18) 31.
199 Transparency International UK, *Anti-Bribery Guidance* (n 35) ch 15.
200 APEC Anti-Corruption and Transparency Working Group (n 44) 4 (h).
201 World Economic Forum, PACI *Principles* (n 43) s 5.4.3.

commonalities, it is possible to infer transnational common ground pertaining to this area. Consensus can be found mostly in topics such as linkage between trainings and risk-assessments, recurrence, targeted audiences, content, incentives schemes, and records.

As hard and soft law rules with international elements will continue to grow rapidly, commonalities in the transnational anti-corruption *acquis* will increase through different avenues, either deepening current similarities or reaching areas that are currently 'untouched' or in 'limbo.'

This burgeoning trend in transnational anti-corruption training requirements can be inferred from multiple reasons.

First, for the sake of efficiency and alignment, multinational private organizations tend to make uniform internal programs incorporating cross-border standards, while allowing tailoring as needed. As a result, even with certain customization, anti-corruption trainings requirements are probably one of the elements of compliance programs that are more fertile to allow standardization and uniformity across jurisdictions. In addition to this *in-house* influence in the *transnationalization* process of anti-corruption training requirements, this self-regulation can also have an expansive effect externally through interactions in industry associations and involvement in collective actions efforts, where experiences and practices shared may also lead to a certain 'alignment.' In sum, *transnationalization* could also be grounded in the pursuit of having more state-of-the-art, top-notch, or world-class compliance programs.

Second, advancement in the *transnationalization* path can be seen as new standards or updated ones influence existing sources in a sort of 'virtuous cycle.' This can be seen, for instance, in the use of comparative methods, benchmarking exercises, and the attention paid to foreign sources during the drafting of some of the documents analyzed. All this activity can trigger, consequently, a snowball effect making the playground more even or aligned in terms of anti-corruption trainings.[202]

Third, the path towards further guidance and standards is eased as anti-corruption programs evolve becoming more complex and exigent, more oriented

202 As an illustration, in Brazil the guiding document *Diretrizes para empresas* includes standards from the UK, the United States, UNODC, and OECD amongst the documents consulted for its drafting. Also, the guiding document *Modelo de Programa de Integridad* published by the Mexican Secretary of Public Function makes reference to standards from the United States, the UK, and organizations such as the OECD, UNODC, and ICC. The Argentine *Guidelines* issued by the Ant-corruption Office cite as consulted documents sources utilized for its preparation—standards from Brazil, Colombia, the United States, UNODC, OECD, United Nations Global Compact, Transparency International, and the ICC. In Japan, the METI *Guidelines* mention the OECD standards. Similarly, the *Guide* published by Japan Federation of Bar Associations refers to standards from the United States, the UK, and the OECD. In Mexico the *Integrity Manual* published by the Consejo Coordinador Empresarial includes references to the United Nation Global Compact.

to creating a *culture of integrity* over ticking-the-box schemes.[203] As a result of this, there is an opportunity to *welcome* guiding standards that, as explained, might eventually take shape to become more and more transnational.

Fourth, anti-corruption transnational standards continue to build as more and more scholarship and contributions from players, stakeholders, and the anti-corruption community itself take place in specialized events and publications which transcend borders and continuously nourish this *acquis*.[204]

The journey towards a stronger global anti-corruption *acquis* on trainings is only starting and will only be further invigorated.

203 Peter Verhezen, 'Giving Voice in a Culture of Silence. From a Culture of Compliance to a Culture of Integrity' (2010) 96 Journal of Business Ethics 187.

204 An example of this is the very conference where this chapter was presented. Also, when examining the agenda or programs or anti-corruption events, trainings are often times addressed in sharing good practices sessions. As an illustration see the Day 2 agenda of the 17th Annual Compliance & Ethics Institute (Las Vegas, October 2018); Day 3 agenda of the Compliance Week Annual Conference for Compliance and Risks Professionals (Washington DC, May 2018).

Part IV

Anti-corruption considerations in international dispute resolution

17 Methodologies for proving corruption in arbitration

Uses and limitations of red flags

Lucinda A. Low

As arbitration—both commercial and investor-state—increasingly confronts the issue of the effects on claims of alleged bribery, corruption, or related conduct, by a claimant, often acting through third parties, questions of proof assume central importance. Corruption, when it occurs, is typically concealed due to its illicit nature. Direct proof of an improper payment is often not available, for various reasons: failures of investigation and prosecution at the national level, limitations on the availability of evidence in other jurisdictions, and others. Resort to circumstantial evidence, even by criminal prosecutors, is common.

A successful corruption defense to a claim can result in the dismissal of the claim for lack of jurisdiction, a determination that the claim is inadmissible for public policy reasons, or other significant consequences for the claim. Few other issues, in fact, have the potential for such a dramatic effect on the claim.

For respondents advancing a corruption defense to a claim, which is the most frequent context at present in which such issues are presented, the benefits of a successful corruption defense can be great. And given the challenges of proof, the temptation to argue for reliance on 'red flags' as a basis for establishing corruption is therefore also great. And even without such a defense, arbitral tribunals determined to investigate signs of potential bribery or corruption will also likely confront the role of such 'red flags.'

The use of indirect proof and 'red flag' methodologies, given the widely recognized challenges of locating direct proof of corruption, has thus become a key issue in such cases. Along with questions of burden and standard of proof, the use of adverse inferences, and other techniques for fact-finding, the role of such 'red flags' in establishing corruption, are much debated. Terms such as 'connecting the dots,' the identification of '*faisceaux concordants et précis*,' which also involve methodologies of proof, particularly in circumstantial cases, are related even if differently framed.

This chapter discusses the uses and limitations of red flags and similar types of analyses. It begins by identifying the origin and evolution of red flag analysis in the prevention and control of corruption more generally. Part 2 then discusses some leading arbitration cases, both from the commercial sphere and the investor-state sphere, in which 'red flag' analysis has been at issue. Part 3 sets forth a critical analysis of 'red flag analysis' as a method of proof in international arbitration, and suggests the proper scope of red flag analysis and similar methodologies in proving corruption in this area.

The thesis of this chapter is that while red flags, properly understood, can be a useful tool in identifying areas of inquiry in relation to corruption allegations involving third parties, they also have their limitations. It is essential that such limitations be recognized by tribunals if decisions are to have the necessary evidentiary foundation. Red flags typically do not even constitute circumstantial evidence, but are mere risk indicators that may or may not lead to evidence, direct or circumstantial. Some red flags, moreover, especially those that are transaction-specific, are more probative than others; conversely, general red flags such as country risk have very limited probative value. And in any event any red flags that are specific to the third party or the transaction, rather than being of a general nature, need to be pursued to determine whether the red flag is, in fact, substantiated by evidence or not. Only after that follow-on exercise can more informed judgments be made about the relevant evidence, its probative value, and the most likely factual scenario when considered in its totality. Virtually every red flag scenario is susceptible to multiple explanations, and what appears to be questionable at first blush (for example, alleged excessive compensation of a third party) may in fact have a legitimate explanation. Some assessments of red flags are judgment-laden, and these judgments should be understood and critically examined. Thus, even transaction-specific red flags should not be taken at face value as 'evidence,' even circumstantial evidence. Nor would simply an aggregation of red flags to reach a conclusion represent a proper methodology. Regardless of what standard of proof a tribunal determines it should apply to allegations of corruption, red flags alone, even if numerous, would not in the author's view be a proper foundation for a conclusion of corruption, but would require further examination and substantiation. Parties and arbitral tribunals also need to be aware of letting 20/20 hindsight affect their analysis. Adverse inferences should be approached with caution.

When the corruption allegation involves contracts allegedly procured via corruption (as opposed to contracts for corruption) the additional legal requirement of causation, or linkage, needs to be considered, and should not be presumed even when the facts reveal third-party involvement in a contract for corruption relating to the contract.

1 Red flags—origins and evolution

The concept of red flags in the bribery and corruption context comes from the regulatory and enforcement arena. It is not limited to the area of bribery and corruption, but has been picked up in a number of other areas of international regulatory compliance, including anti-money laundering, export controls, and economic sanctions. This analysis will, however, focus on their use in relation to allegations of bribery and corruption.

Red flags in the bribery and corruption area are associated with the use of third parties' agents, representatives, consultants, finders, and others—as a conduit for improper payments.[1] While third party relationships are generally a lawful and even sometimes mandated structure for doing business,[2] they may also be used as a vehicle for making illicit payments. We first address how this risk has been addressed in the context of laws criminalizing bribery in international business transactions.

1.1 The US FCPA and the OECD Convention

The world's first law criminalizing the bribery of foreign public officials (also referred to herein as transnational bribery or TNB) was the US Foreign Corrupt Practices Act (FCPA).[3] The FCPA made it a crime for persons covered by the statute corruptly to give anything of value to a 'foreign official' and certain other covered recipients in order to secure action, inaction, influence, or an undue advantage in order to obtain, retain, or direct business to any person.[4]

The FCPA recognized the risk that third parties, such as agents or consultants, would be employed to make improper payments on a company's behalf. Instead of simply proscribing 'indirect' as well as direct payments, as many anti-bribery statutes do, it adopted a specific standard of liability for third-party payments, criminalizing payments or other transfers of value made to 'any person' with the requisite degree of awareness (discussed further below) that the payment or value would be passed on, in whole or in part, to a government official or other prohibited recipient.[5]

In the FCPA as originally enacted in 1977, this standard was framed as 'reason to know.'[6] However, this standard was roundly criticized as inappropriately

1 Of course, companies may make payments through their own employees or other personnel, which payments may be attributed to the company under principles of vicarious liability or *respondeat superior*. This chapter refers to payments by company personnel as direct payments, and payments through third parties as indirect payments.

2 Some jurisdictions, particularly in the Middle East, require use of a local agent as a precondition to doing business in the country. Others may restrict the use of third parties in certain sectors, particularly the defense sector, or require disclosure of the use of third parties, particularly marketing or commission agents.

3 15 US Code ss 78dd-1 (applying to 'issuers'), dd-2 (applying to 'domestic concerns'), dd-3 (applying to 'any person').

4 The FCPA's anti-bribery provisions apply solely to foreign governmental corruption, from the so-called 'supply' side—the offeror or giver of a bribe rather than the 'demand' side—the solicitor or recipient. Private sector bribery is left to other statutes, although the FCPA's accounting provisions apply to all transactions of covered persons, not just those involving foreign government officials.

5 Accordingly, the statute provides that it is not only unlawful to make an improper payment to a 'foreign official,' foreign political party, party official, or candidate for office, but also to 'any person, while knowing that all or a portion of such money or things of value will be offered, given or promised, directly or indirectly, to any foreign official, to any foreign political party or official thereof, or to any candidate for foreign political office.' 15 US Code ss 78dd-1(a)(3), 78dd-2(a)(3), 78dd-3(a)(3).

6 See FCPA Pub L No 95–213, 91 Stat 1494 (1977), s 103(a).

establishing a negligence standard as the basis for vicarious criminal liability, and in 1988, as part of a broader set of amendments to the FCPA,[7] the statute was changed and new definitions of 'knowledge' and 'knowing' were adopted.

Under this vicarious liability provision for indirect payments, the definition of 'knowledge' is broader than actual knowledge: a company is deemed to 'know' that a third party will use money provided by the company to make an improper payment or offer if it is aware of, but consciously disregards, a 'high probability' that such a payment or offer will be made.[8] The purpose of this standard is to prevent companies from adopting a 'head in the sand' approach to the activities of their agents and partners.[9] Both knowledge and recklessness with respect to a third party's conduct can, therefore, be the basis of criminal liability for the principal under the FCPA.

In 1997, the United States ratified the OECD Convention on Combating Bribery of Foreign Public Officials in International Business Transactions.[10] Although the FCPA was amended in various respects at the time, particularly to expand its jurisdictional reach, in connection with this ratification, the FCPA's third-party liability provision remained unchanged.

The convention itself, in Article 1(1), does not articulate a specific standard for third-party liability, but requires states parties to criminalize the bribery of foreign public officials, when carried out either 'directly or through intermediaries.'

1.2 Anti-bribery compliance programs and third parties

But criminalization is only part of the story. The FCPA has spawned a host of expectations regarding preventive compliance measures. Companies are expected today to adopt and maintain programs that are designed to prevent, detect, and remediate bribery and corruption in their business activities, not only by their employees but by third parties as well. These programs are to be designed on a risk-appropriate basis, following a risk assessment process that takes into account the nature of the company's business, including the extent of its touch points with government, where the company operates, and how the company operates, including its use of third parties in carrying out its business.[11]

7 See HR Conf Rep No. 576, 100th Cong 2d Sess 920 (1988).

8 15 US Code ss 78dd-1(f)(2)(B), 78dd-2(h)(3)(B), 78dd-3(f)(3)(B).

9 See HR Conf Rep No. 576, 100th Cong 2d Sess 920 (1988).

10 See International Antibribery and Fair Competition Act of 1998, s 2375, Pub L No 105–366, 112 Stat 3302 (1998). See Convention on Combating Bribery of Foreign Public Officials in International Business Transactions (adopted 17 December 1997, entered into force 15 February 1999) 37 ILM 1 (OECD Convention).

11 See US Department of Justice and US Securities and Exchange Commission, *FCPA: A Resource Guide to the US Foreign Corrupt Practices Act* (2012). On compliance programs generally, see at: 56–63; on the role of risk assessment to the development of an effective anti-bribery compliance program, see especially at: 58–59.

This movement towards compliance standards has been picked up by other countries, and internationally. Some jurisdictions, such as the UK, have adopted as a defense to strict corporate liability standards an 'adequate procedures' exception (essentially a compliance program defense).[12]

With respect to third parties, Good Practice Guidance issued by the OECD in 2009 states that:

> Member countries should ensure that, in accordance with Article 1 of the OECD Anti-Bribery Convention, and the principle of functional equivalence in Commentary 2 to the OECD Anti-Bribery Convention, a legal person cannot avoid responsibility by using intermediaries, including related legal persons, to offer, promise or give a bribe to a foreign public official on its behalf.[13]

The Guidance goes on to encourage companies to adopt and maintain programs of internal controls, ethics, and compliance to deal with bribery and corruption risks and sets out the elements of such programs. In relation to third parties, such programs are to include:

> measures designed to present and detect foreign bribery applicable ... to third parties such as agents and other intermediaries, consultants, representatives, distributors, contractors, and suppliers, consortia and joint venture partners (hereinafter 'business partners'), including, *inter alia*, the following essential elements:
>
> i) Properly documented risk-based due diligence pertaining to the hiring, as well as the appropriate and regular oversight, of business partners.[14]

This Guidance followed studies done by the OECD Working Group on Bribery (in which states parties to the OECD Convention are required to participate)

12 Section 7 of the Bribery Act 2010 (UK) creates strict corporate liability for a 'failure to prevent' bribery by an 'associated person'—a term defined in s 8 of the Act as a person who performs services on behalf of the company. The compliance defense set forth under s 9 of the Bribery Act relates to this 'failure to prevent' liability. Other sections of the Bribery Act also create corporate liability for organizations that commit bribery either directly or through a third party. See the discussion of associated persons in Ministry of Justice, *The Bribery Act 2010 Guidance* (March 2011) 1, 16–18.

13 'Recommendation of the Council for Further Combating Bribery of Foreign Public Officials in International Business Transactions,' approved November 26, 2009 ('2009 OECD Recommendation'). See 'Good Practice Guidance on Implementing Specific Articles of the Convention on Combating Bribery of Foreign Public Officials in International Business Transactions,' Annex I, [C].

14 See 2009 OECD Recommendation entitled 'Good Practice Guidance on Internal Controls, Ethics and Compliance' Annex II, sub-s A [6].

that demonstrated a high incidence of the use of intermediaries in cases involving improper payments.[15]

Compliance guidance issued by other authorities, including the International Chamber of Commerce (ICC), Transparency International, the World Economic Forum, and the International Standards Organization, also include a focus on managing third party risk, some as a part of overall guidance on anti-bribery and anti-corruption compliance programs, and others more targeted.[16] An example of the latter is the ICC, which in 2010 issued Guidelines on Agents, Intermediaries, and other Third Parties.[17]

1.3 Red flags

That brings us to red flags. The concept of 'red flags' emerged early in the history of the FCPA. It may surprise some readers to know that there exists no regulation or binding legal document definitively identifying red flags under the FCPA. The first red flags were identified in the late 70s by enforcement officials in speeches, as businesses focused on the compliance and liability implications of the 'reason to know' standard in the FCPA at the time. Commentators picked up and elaborated on the concept, and compliance standards for third parties began to emerge.

As the US Congress specified in adopting the FCPA's current third party liability standard:

> [T]he so-called 'head-in-the-sand' problem—variously described in the pertinent authorities as 'conscious disregard,' 'willful blindness' or 'deliberate ignorance'—should be covered so that management officials could not take refuge from the Act's prohibitions by their unwarranted obliviousness to any action (or inaction), language or other 'signaling device' that should reasonably alert them of the 'high probability' of an FCPA violation.[18]

From this approach to preventive compliance measures was a logical, but far-reaching, step.

15 See generally, e.g., OECD Working Group on Bribery in International Business Transactions, *Final Report—Typologies on the Role of Intermediaries in International Business Transactions* (2009)

16 See, e.g., World Economic Forum, 'Partnering Against Corruption Initiative' <https://www.weforum.org/communities/partnering-against-corruption-initiative> accessed 1 June 2020; Transparency International, 'Business Principles for Countering Bribery' (17 December 2013) <https://transparency.ch/publikationen/business-principles-for-countering-bribery/> accessed 1 June 2020; ISO, 'ISO 37001—Anti-Bribery Management Systems' <https://www.iso.org/iso-37001-anti-bribery-management.html> accessed 1 June 2020.

17 International Chamber of Commerce, *Guidelines on Agents, Intermediaries and other Third Parties* (2010).

18 HR Rep No 100–576, 920 (1988).

In the 2012 FCPA Resource Guide jointly issued by the Department of Justice and the SEC, the agencies identified the following common red flags in their discussion of third party liability:

- Excessive commissions to third party agents or consultants;
- Unreasonably large discounts to third party distributors;
- Third party 'consulting agreements' that includes only vaguely described services;
- The third party consultant is in a different line of business than that for which it has been engaged;
- The third party is related to or closely associated with the foreign official;
- The third party became part of the transaction at the request or insistence of the foreign official;
- The third party is merely a shell company incorporated in an offshore jurisdiction; and
- The third party requests payment to offshore bank accounts.[19]

Other red flags identified in the literature have included: where the country in question has traditionally had a bribery problem; the agent's commission is paid in cash; it is illegal under the local law for the agent to act as an agent; the agent has indicated that a particular amount of money is needed in order for him to 'get the business' or 'make the necessary arrangements;' the agent has requested that the company prepare false invoices or any other type of false documentation; or the agent has refused to promise in writing that he will abide by the FCPA (or similar substantive anti-bribery prohibitions).[20]

International standards have embraced the red flag concept as well. The ICC's Guidelines on Agents, Intermediaries and other Third Parties referenced earlier has a section on red flags, in the context of recommended due diligence for third parties, introduced as follows:

> In conducting anti-bribery due diligence, it is important that enterprises be sensitive to circumstances that suggest bribery risks. Circumstances that may indicate a Third party's propensity to make illegal payments to public or private sector officials or employees are commonly referred to as 'red flags'. Indeed, any fact that suggests commercial, financial, legal, or ethical irregularity can constitute a 'red flag'. 'Red flags' can arise at any stage of a Third-party relationship, including during an enterprise's selection of a Third party, during contract negotiations, in the course of operations, or at termination. 'Red flags' that do not present serious issues at one stage

19 US Department of Justice and US Securities and Exchange Commission, *FCPA: A Resource Guide* (n 11) 22–23.

20 See Lucinda A Low and John Davis, 'The FCPA in Investment Transactions: An Overview' (2005) Business Law Inc 106.001, 106.007–106.008.

> of a relationship may pose significant risks of liability when they appear at a different stage or in combination with a different overall set of facts. Thus, enterprises may wish to evaluate the significance of 'red flags' in the context of all of the facts, rather than in isolation. However, depending on the nature of their business and their enterprise policies, enterprises can define one or several of these red flags as general showstoppers.
>
> Although such 'red flags' may not themselves constitute violations of the anti-bribery laws, they are warning signs that need to be taken seriously and investigated. The presence of one or more 'red flags' does not necessarily mean that the transaction cannot go forward, but it does suggest the need for a more in-depth inquiry and the implementation of appropriate compliance safeguards. Any red flags must be addressed to the satisfaction of the enterprise prior to entering into the relationship.

The Guidance goes on to enumerate specific red flags:

> Red flags that warrant further review when selecting and working with a Third party are varied and numerous. The following are a few examples:
>
> - A reference check reveals the third party's flawed background or reputation, or the flawed background or reputation of an individual or enterprise represented by the third party;
> - The operation takes place in a country known for corrupt payments (e.g., the country received a low score on Transparency International's Corruption Perceptions Index);
> - The third party is suggested by a public official, particularly one with discretionary authority over the business at issue;
> - The third party objects to representations regarding compliance with anti-corruption laws or other applicable laws;
> - The third party has a close personal or family relationship, or business relationship, with a public official or relative of the official;
> - The third party does not reside or have a significant business presence in the country where the customer or project is located;
> - Due diligence reveals that the third party is a shell company or has some other non-transparent corporate structure (e.g., a trust without information about the economic beneficiary);
> - The only qualification the third party brings to the venture is influence over public officials, or the third party claims that he can help secure a contract because he knows the right people;
> - The need for the third party arises just before or after the contract is to be awarded;
> - The third party requires that his or her identity or, if the third-party is an enterprise, the identity of the enterprise's owners, principals, or employees, not be disclosed;

- The third party's commission or fee seems disproportionate in relation to the services to be rendered;
- The third party requires payment of a commission, or a significant portion thereof, before or immediately upon, the award of a contract;
- The third party requests an increase in an agreed commission in order for the third party to 'take care of' some people or cut some red tape; or
- The third party requests unusual contract terms or payment arrangements that raise local law issues, payments in cash, advance payment, payment in another country's currency, payment to an individual/entity that is not the contracting party; payment to a numbered bank account or a bank account not held by the contracting individual/entity, or payment to a country that is not the contracting individual/entity's country of registration or the country where the services are performed.[21]

Others have elucidated red flag lists as well. For example, the Woolf Report, issued in 2008 in relation to the defense sector and in particular to BAE in the wake of its prosecution for bribery and related issues in the US and UK, listed 16 red flags, many of which are similar to those listed above but with variations (e.g., 'an Adviser represents companies with a questionable reputation').[22] The OECD Report on Intermediaries cited above also contains a list of red flags.[23]

Transparency International and others have identified certain industries or sectors that, because of their characteristics, are more susceptible to corruption.[24] These include the extractive industries, such as mining, oil & gas, and related services; construction and engineering; telecommunications; certain highly regulated industries; and others. It should be emphasized, however, that virtually every sector has 'touch points' with government around taxation, permitting,

21 International Chamber of Commerce, *Guidelines on Agents, Intermediaries and other Third Parties* (n 17) s VI.

22 Woolf Committee, *Report on BAE System Plc's Ethical Policies and Processes* (6 May 2008) 28. See also Basel Institute on Governance, 'Corruption and Money Laundering: A Toolkit for Arbitrators' (2019) <https://arbcrime.org/a-toolkit-for-arbitrators> accessed 1 June 2020.

23 OECD Working Group on Bribery in International Business Transactions (n 15) [86].

24 Global Witness has focused significant attention on the extractive industries (oil, gas and mining), see, e.g., Global Witness, 'Oil, Gas and Mining' <https://www.globalwitness.org/en/campaigns/oil-gas-and-mining/#more> accessed 1 June 2020. The Publish What You Pay movement, focused on these sectors, and the Extractive Industries Transparency Initiative (EITI) are transparency initiatives growing out of the focus on the corruption risks presented by these industries. Transparency International has spotlighted issues in the defense and pharmaceutical sectors. See, e.g., Transparency International, *Corruption in the Pharmaceutical Sector: Diagnosing the Challenges* (2016); Transparency International UK, 'Defense & Security Corruption' <https://www.transparency.org.uk/our-work/defence-security-corruption/> accessed 1 June 2020. Construction and engineering and telecommunications are other sectors that have been the subject of analysis and found to have characteristics that give rise to corruption risks. See Transparency International, *Overview of Corruption in the Telecommunications Sector* (2014); PWC, *Economic Crime: A Threat to Business Globally* (2014).

and regulation to at least some extent. Any of these touch points can give rise to bribery and corruption risks, especially if they involve discretionary governmental action.

As the above lists demonstrate, red flags fall into two general categories:

(1) *General Red Flags*: relating to the geography (usually the country, although it can be a sub-national geography as well), the particular industry or sector, or even a particular regime within a country; and
(2) *Party- or Transaction-Specific Red Flags*: relating to the characteristics of the third party; or specific features of the business opportunity or proposed transaction.

We will return to these two categories, which differ both in their risk profile and in available risk mitigation options, in the discussion below.

1.4 Role of red flags in both compliance and enforcement liability analyses

As the ICC Guidance quoted above suggests, it is well established that red flags are not violations, but only risk indicators. As such, red flags play a central role in third party risk management. This is largely a preventive activity, although it can also be remedial.

1.4.1 The role of red flags in prevention

When entering into relationships with third parties, particularly those who will interact with government officials, companies are now expected as part of their preventive efforts to conduct due diligence on a proposed third party, and as part of that due diligence, to investigate any red flags that may be presented.[25] That investigation can result in a red flag being confirmed or negated, or continued uncertainty—in any event the analysis then moves to risk mitigation based on the information available.

For general red flags such as country or sectoral risks, mitigation options are limited given the immutability of these factors. Companies can, and sometimes do, decide that the risks of doing business in a particular country, area, or sector are too great to justify the benefits. No anti-bribery law or enforcement policy requires that decision—FCPA enforcement officials have always been clear that they do not require companies not to do business in countries ranked as highly corrupt—but they have said that companies should exercise greater caution when operating in those areas.

25 There is also an expectation that this diligence will be periodically refreshed, either as part of a periodic renewal exercise, or independently. See, e.g., OECD Working Group on Bribery in International Business Transactions (n 15) [98].

Similarly, industry risks are a function of the innate characteristics of specific industries and are not susceptible to change, at least in the short term.[26] And they may be related to country risk. Extractive industries, for example, are risky in part because they have no choice but to operate where the relevant resources are located. These may be fragile states, with a poorly developed rule of law. But they are also risky because the projects often depend on discretionary government licenses, permits, contracts or concessions that are high-value, long-term and may attract corrupt demands. Once established, these businesses' substantial fixed in-country investments also make them vulnerable to solicitation and extortion. And their interactions with government are extensive and often highly discretionary. These features are difficult or impossible to change.

For party- or transaction-specific red flags, on the other hand, there may be many options for risk mitigation. At the extreme, a company may choose not to do business with a particular third party, or even for that matter entire categories of third parties (such as agents).[27] But often the business decision is to try to find ways to mitigate risk to an acceptable level. Mitigation may take the form of contractual measures, non-contractual measures such as due diligence and heightened oversight, and others.[28] Some have by now become standard practice, while others will be highly party- and transaction-specific. Different companies may have different risk appetites as well.

In devising risk mitigation strategies, companies are often acutely aware of the problem of 20/20 hindsight (a phenomenon with important implications for disputes as well): Risk assessment and risk mitigation are based on the information that is available at the time of the transaction, which is often imperfect. But if a problem later emerges, the temptation to judge the adequacy of risk mitigation measures based on that later-acquired information about the conduct of an intermediary—even if legally unjustified—may be strong. And yet companies must make decisions on the basis of what is known at the time, and if they have not put their heads in the sand, those decisions should not give rise to enforcement liability.

26 Tools such as integrity pacts may, however, be used to mitigate risk in a particular project or procurement.

27 After being prosecuted in 2008 for FCPA violations, Alcatel made it publicly known that it would cease doing business with agents. 'Alcatel-Lucent Says "No Thanks" to Middlemen,' *Bus Week* (7 January 2009). More recently, Airbus has terminated many long-time consultants in the wake of its anti-bribery prosecutions and record settlement of almost $4 billion with authorities in the US, France, and the UK. See, e.g., Sudip Kar-Gupta and Tim Hepher, 'Airbus Faces Record $4 Billion Fine after Bribery Probe' *Reuters* (28 January 2020) <https://in.reuters.com/article/airbus-probe-idINKBN1ZR0IQ> accessed 1 June 2020.

28 This is not just an issue at the time of hiring. As part of prevention, companies are also expected to exercise continued oversight over third party activities from a compliance perspective, and respond to red flags that present themselves in the course of performance or even termination of a relationship.

1.4.2 Red flags in the enforcement context

Ignoring red flags can lead to either criminal or civil liability under the anti-bribery provisions of the FCPA, if their disregard reflects the necessary elements of belief and intent.[29]

Much ink has been spilled in the 40-year history of the FCPA regarding the third party liability provision. For many years, the vast majority of cases prosecuted by the US enforcement authorities have involved third parties. However, the 'floodgates' of prosecutions of companies for the acts of third parties in cases falling short of demonstrated knowledge and intent—i.e., involving recklessness—feared by some have never come to pass. Indeed, what is striking is how few cases have been prosecuted on the basis of 'head in the sand,' or reckless, behavior, as opposed to actual knowledge.

One of the few adjudicated cases involving the FCPA's 'willful blindness,' or recklessness, standard involved the case of Frederick Bourke, a businessman who was convicted of conspiring to violated the FCPA's anti-bribery provisions by agreeing to make payments to officials in Azerbaijan in connection with a scheme to promote the privatization of the State Oil Company of Azerbaijan (SOCAR).[30] On appeal, the US Court of Appeals for the Second Circuit found that Mr Bourke had been properly convicted on a conscious avoidance charge, although he was also found in the alternative to have had actual knowledge based on the facts that: he knew corruption was pervasive in Azerbaijan; he was aware of the reputation of his business partner, Viktor Kozeny (the so-called 'Pirate of Prague'), for misconduct; he had created two US companies in order to shield himself and other investors in the SOCAR privatization scheme from potential liability for payment made in violation of the FCPA; and he had expressed concerns to his lawyers and others (which were recorded) about whether his business partner and company were bribing officials.[31]

Most FCPA prosecutions, of course, whether of individuals or corporate entities, are resolved via one of the available forms of negotiated resolution, so the issue is not frequently examined by a court in detail. Nonetheless, the vast majority of cases involving third parties are cases where a factual finding has been made that there has been deliberate and intentional use of a third party as a vehicle for improper payments. This use takes a myriad of forms, sham consulting or other types of supply agreements (for goods or services), to distributor discounts

29 The FCPA's anti-bribery and accounting provisions are enforced civilly as well as criminally. The Department of Justice has civil as well as criminal enforcement authority over all persons subject to the FCPA, although it uses its civil authority relatively rarely, but the US Securities and Exchange Commission regularly enforces the FCPA against 'issuers' (SEC filing and reporting companies) and related persons.

30 *United States v. Kozeny* [2008] 582 F Supp 2d 535, 537–540 (SDNY).

31 *United States v. Kozeny* [2011] 667 F3d 122 (2d Cir).

that are given for improper purposes, to legitimate service agreements with customs brokers, finders, or others that have incorporated improper elements, and others.[32]

Criminal liability, of course, requires a high standard of proof—in the United States, the standard of 'beyond a reasonable doubt' applies.[33] There must be sufficient evidence—whether direct or circumstantial—to support the finding of corruption. A disregard for, or inadequate attention to, red flags in a third party relationship may result in an inference of knowledge or reckless disregard. They may also be used to establish direct or circumstantial evidence of other elements of the offense. As noted earlier, the offense of transnational bribery has numerous elements, each of which must be established to the requisite degree of proof. Although a chain of circumstantial evidence may be used to prove bribery, proof to the applicable standard in a criminal case through such evidence alone is difficult and quite rare.

But although this standard of proof may be a factor in explaining why there are so few criminal cases of third party liability that are not based on recklessness rather than positive knowledge, it likely does not provide a complete explanation. It may well be that proving a corrupt practice where the evidence does not support positive knowledge is fraught with difficulty, as well.

We now turn to the arbitration arena. Before turning to red flag analysis, we will touch briefly on the question of standard and burden of proof and definitional issues that must be confronted in connection with the corruption defense.

2 Use of red flags in civil disputes, particularly in arbitration

2.1 Preliminary issues

2.1.1 Standard and onus of proof

In arbitration cases, a civil standard of proof—generally preponderance of the evidence—rather than the criminal standard of beyond a reasonable doubt, discussed above, generally applies.

Having said that, the question of precisely what standard should be applied to allegations of corruption has resulted in the spilling of much ink by the parties to disputes submitted to arbitration. The party advancing the defense will typically argue that because of the difficulties in proving corruption, the standard of proof should not be higher than the normal one of preponderance of the evidence.

32 For examples, see Lucinda Low and others, *FCPA/Anti-Corruption Developments: 2019 Year in Review* (Steptoe & Johnson 2020), and prior years' publications as well.

33 Civil or administrative enforcement, for example by the US Securities and Exchange Commission, which shares enforcement authority with the US Department of Justice for so-called 'issuers' (companies which a class of securities registered with the SEC or required to file periodic reports with the SEC) and related persons, is based on a lower standard, the balance of probabilities.

The party resisting the defense will typically counter that the seriousness of the charge requires clear and convincing evidence. Tribunals have gone both ways, and some have eschewed articulating a precise standard or articulated a standard of 'reasonable certainty.' And some tribunals have bypassed the issue entirely, as we will see in the discussion of selected cases below.

The onus or burden of proof is also contentious. The party advancing a corruption defense often also argues for a shifting of the burden of proof once a *prima facie* case has been established, and / or for the use of adverse inferences. Burden shifting, although used in some contexts,[34] has not been widely embraced by arbitration tribunals in the context of corruption allegations. The use of adverse inferences, on the other hand, is an accepted technique in international arbitration, and is applied in this context. The latter, of course, takes us into methods of proof, a topic to which we will return later in this chapter, and which is often raised in the context of red flag analysis.

2.1.2 Definitional issues

Another threshold issue is what misconduct in particular is being alleged when a 'corruption' defense is raised. Corruption as a term has no single precise legal meaning. Treaties such as UNCAC specify a wide range of offenses as corruption-related offenses in their criminalization chapters and it will often be important to clarify precisely what is meant when the term is invoked in a given case. Most frequently in the author's experience what is really at issue is bribery, particularly bribery of a public official for a business advantage. But the elements of different types of corrupt practices differ, and having the relevant elements clearly in mind is a key exercise before issues of proof, including red flag analysis, can even come into play.[35] Applicable law will, of course, play an important role in this definitional exercise. Where international law governs, at least in part, tribunals are increasingly looking to the OECD Convention and other international anti-corruption instruments, as the examples discussed below will illustrate. However, the standard will not always come from international law. Arbitrators are, of course, bound to apply the applicable law, and a failure to do so may lead to the annulment or setting aside of the award. International public policy, and the public policy of the jurisdiction where the award is to be recognized and enforced, will also play a role.

34 See, e.g., The World Bank, *Bank Procedure: Sanctions Procedures and Settlements in Bank Financed Projects* (28 June 2016) (effective 1 July 2016).

35 One only has to consider the different between bribery and trading in influence in terms of the elements constituting the offense to recognize that, especially when contracts or rights allegedly resulting from corruption are it issue, the distinctions can be critical.

2.1.3 Typologies

The different typologies of corruption must be distinguished as well, as they may have different requirements of proof and potentially different consequences.

One typology is where a party is trying to enforce a contract which the respondent asserts is tainted by corruption. Here we must distinguish between contracts *for* corruption and contracts *resulting from, or procured by*, corruption.

2.1.3.1 CONTRACTS FOR CORRUPTION

A contract for corruption is a contract whose purpose is illicit (or in civil law terms, *cause illicite*)—the party that is engaged, often ostensibly to provide legitimate services (typically marketing-type activity), is actually being engaged to commit corrupt practices—typically bribery, although trading in influence or other forms of corruption may come into play as well. Often these contracts take the form of intermediary arrangements, including agreements with agents, representatives, brokers, consultants, or other third parties, but joint venture or partnership arrangements may also sometimes be contracts for corruption.

Most of the international instruments in the anti-corruption area do not focus on civil liability, or if they do, it is only briefly. One important exception is the Council of Europe Civil Law Convention on Corruption.[36] Under this convention, states parties are required to enact provisions in their internal laws specifying that contracts (or contract clauses) for corruption are automatically null and void.[37]

2.1.3.2 CONTRACTS RESULTING FROM CORRUPTION

A contract resulting from corruption, in contrast, is a contract whose purpose is lawful, for example, the supply of goods or services, or a concession, but which has arguably been procured through unlawful means. It may have been secured through the efforts of a third party (indirect corruption) or the direct efforts of the company in question, (direct corruption), or (most often) some combination of the two. These are most frequently commercial cases, although they increasingly involve respondents that are state enterprises, but sometimes are presented as investor-state cases, as where a relevant bilateral investment treaty (BIT) has an umbrella clause permitting contract claims of a foreign investor to be heard under the BIT's arbitration mechanism.

Under the CoE Civil Law Convention, contracts resulting from corruption are not automatically null and void, but are subject to being voided upon application to a court, and may give rise to a right to claim damages.[38]

36 Council of Europe Civil Law Convention on Corruption, ETS No.174, 4 November 1999.
37 Ibid art 8(1).
38 Ibid art 8(2).

In addition to establishing that corruption has taken place, an additional hurdle that must be met for such contracts to be subject to voidability is a requirement of linkage or causation—namely, that the corruption must be shown to have resulted in the issuance of the contract. This causal requirement is not present with contracts for corruption. It is recognized by the CoE Civil Law Convention, which makes the showing of a causal link between the act of corruption and the damage an essential element for eventual compensation. The linkage requirement has also been accepted by arbitral tribunals.[39]

Under the United Nations Convention Against Corruption (UNCAC), a global anti-corruption treaty,[40] the state party must 'take measures ... to address [the] consequences of corruption.' Corruption may be considered a 'relevant factor in legal proceedings to annul or rescind a contract, withdraw a concession or other similar instrument or take any other remedial action.'[41] Therefore, UNCAC similarly does not treat a contract procured by corruption as requiring states to provide for an automatic nullification of the contract, but considers the corruption to be a relevant factor in proceedings (including arbitration) to address its consequences. This approach opens the door for states to adopt a wide array of remedies under applicable law.

2.1.3.3 INVESTOR-STATE CLAIMS

In addition to being grounded in contract (for investment treaties that contain 'umbrella' clauses, as just discussed), investor-state claims submitted to arbitration may be based on rights granted by the investment treaty,[42] or both. The former are simply another form of contract procured by corruption, while the latter are akin to those contracts and will be referred to as investments allegedly procured by corruption.

Corruption has increasingly been invoked as a defense in investor-state cases, both based in contract and in treaty rights, in recent years. And when that occurs, red flag analysis has often come into play. The reason is simple: it is the exceptional

39 The CoE Civil Law Convention defines corruption as including an offer or authorization, or a failure to prevent, but since the conditions also include actual damage and linkage it is somewhat difficult to imagine how those conditions might be fulfilled by a mere offer. See CoE Civil Law Convention, arts 2, 4; discussion of *Niko* section at text to n 83 (attempt not sufficient to invalidate contract); *Gustav F W Hamester GmbH & Co KG v. Republic of Ghana*, ICSID Case ARB/07/24, Award of 18 June 2010; *Getma Int'l & ors v. Republic of Guinea*, ICSID Case ARB/11/29, Award of 16 August 2016; *Nat'l Iranian Oil Co v. Crescent Petroleum Co Int'l* [2016] EWHC (Comm) 510, [36].

40 United Nations Convention against Corruption (opened for signature 9 December 2003, entered into force 14 December 2005) 2349 UNTS 41, art 34.

41 Ibid.

42 Such as fair and equitable treatment, expropriation, full protection and security, national and most-favored-nation treatment, and others, depending on the particular treaty.

case where the foreign investor effectively admits to the commission of bribery,[43] where the host state has investigated or prosecuted the corruption allegations,[44] or where the party advancing the defense will have access to the information necessary to establish the claim. Rather, the usual posture is that the claimant denies engaging in any corrupt practices, leaving the tribunal to determine how to explore and assess the issue, including grappling with alleged red flags and their asserted implications.

Many investment treaties contain provisions that require that the investment be made 'in accordance with law' in order for the host state of the investment to consent to arbitration of disputes. As will be discussed below, in such cases, where the host state believes this legality clause has been violated, they may seek to have the case dismissed on jurisdictional grounds or the claims declared inadmissible due to the alleged corruption on the part of the investor in the making of the investment.[45] Most treaties do not specify what consequences arise from a failure of the investor to act in accordance with the legality clause, leaving the arbitral tribunal to grapple with the consequences.

Allegations of corrupt practices may be made with respect to post-investment conduct, i.e., activities occurring during the course of operations or even during the windup or termination of the investment. If the conduct involves foundational rights for the investment, e.g., renewal of a key license or permit, the issues raised will be more akin to investments allegedly procured by corruption and contracts for corruption, while if they involve other types of advantages (for example, better regulatory or tax treatment, or advantages in immigration or customs matters) the benefits secured may not be foundational but may still be significant to the business.

Other variations of these issues that corruption allegations may present involve conduct by a predecessor-in-interest to the rights at issue (for example where the claimant has succeeded to contract or other right by merger, acquisition or succession), or conduct involving other members of a corporate group, such as a subsidiary, raising issues of attribution.

Although most corruption issues arise in a defensive context, occasionally allegedly corrupt conduct by the host state is part of the claim-in-chief in investor-state cases. It may be alleged, for example, that state actors demanded improper payments as part of a fair and equitable treatment claim (allegations of

43 The oft-cited case of *World Duty Free Co v. Republic of Kenya*, ICSID Case ARB/00/7, Award of 4 October 2006, involved an admission of bribery of the Kenyan head of state (later argued to constitute a customary payment, i.e., *harambee*) by the shareholder of the claimant, a company that had received a concession to operate duty-free stores at Kenyan airports, in an affidavit submitted in evidence).

44 This was the case in *Niko Resources*, discussed at text to n 83.

45 In treaties that do not have explicit legality clauses, the respondent may argue that such a clause is implicit. They may also assert contributory fault or other defenses to the merits.

solicitation or even extortion).[46] In such cases, although tribunals may be asked to rely on circumstantial evidence or 'connect the dots,'[47] red flag analysis as such does not arise. Thus, this chapter will focus on corruption as a defensive issue, rather than an element of a claim-in-chief.

With these typologies and other foundational issues in mind, let us turn to a few examples of red flag analysis in different types of disputes.

2.2 Case examples

2.2.1 Contracts for corruption

The best-known case involving contracts for corruption is ICC Case No. 1110 of 1963, in which Judge Lagergren held that a contract that he had determined to have an illicit cause was null and void and he lacked jurisdiction to enforce it. Since then, numerous cases have grappled with contracts for corruption; two that are particularly interesting from a red flag analysis point of view are detailed below.

2.2.1.1 ICC CASE 13914 (2008)[48]

This case involved a consultancy and other agreements between the respondent, a US company, and the claimant, a businessman from an African state and former employee of a national oil company and government contractor. The respondent's defense was that the payment of the claimed commissions had been forfeited by the claimant's unlawful activities, vitiating his right to payment under the contract, and that payment would violate the FCPA. The contract was governed by US law.

The tribunal held that the contracts at issue were void and dismissed the claims.

In defining bribery, the tribunal looked to the OECD Convention and the US FCPA.[49] They cited a list of red flags highlighted by the US government as indicators of improper payments.[50]

In this case, they found a number of red flags, general and specific, in the evidentiary record of the case:

- The prevalence of corruption in the state in question;
- The size of the commission payments in comparison to the claimant's expected performance, leading to a 'strong suspicion' that his testimony about 'door opening' services really consisted of pass-through payments;

46 E.g., *EDF (Servs) Ltd. v. Romania*, ICSID Case ARB/05/13 (2009), Award of 8 October 2009; *Rumeli Telekom v. Kazakhstan*, ICSID Case ARB/05/16, Award of 29 July 2010 and Decision of the ad hoc Comm of 25 March 2010.

47 See, e.g., *Methanex v. United States*, UNCITRAL, Final Award of the Tribunal on Jurisdiction and Merits of 3 August 2005.

48 Reprinted in the ICC Bulletin (2013), vol 24, Special Supp 77.

49 Ibid 78.

50 Ibid.

- A lack of transparency in the claimant's expenses and accounting records, as produced to the tribunal;
- The claimant's lack of qualifications in the technical area in which the services were to be rendered;
- The fact that the hiring of the claimant was recommended by an official of the potential government customer; and other conduct of the government customer in connection with the contract, including efforts to keep the consultancy in force and to continue the payments thereunder, that indicated that officials of a state-owned enterprise had a 'substantial personal interests' in the claimant's commission payments.

Although the tribunal framed this as a red flag analysis, the extract of the award makes it clear that the tribunal relied on the evidence that was adduced during the proceedings as well as what was not adduced or produced.[51] This included evidence that the claimant had paid more than US $6 million to key officials of the state-owned enterprise without giving any credible explanation for the payments.[52] The tribunal found there was only 'one reasonable conclusion' from this evidence, namely, that the intermediary had made improper payments, and that there was clear and convincing evidence that the commission payments under the contract were used to pay bribes.

The consulting agreement was, therefore, declared null and void on the basis of public policy. Although the tribunal refused to enforce the contract, it did not term it a contract for corruption as such. Rather, the illicit purpose was inferred from the evidence, including the evidence of the intermediary's conduct after the conclusion of the contract.

2.2.1.2 ICC CASE NO. 12290 (2005)[53]

This case involved a series of agreements, that, in essence, gave a multinational company the right to purchase five million barrels of oil from an African state in return for money and assistance from the MNC with the latter's IMF Structural Adjustment Program. The claimant was a subsidiary of the MNC, based in an unspecified tax haven jurisdiction. The respondent state sought to have the claim, governed by French law, declared null and void on public policy grounds, arguing that the contract had an illicit cause.

The tribunal looked to the OECD Convention's definition of bribery of foreign public official for the elements of corruption.[54] It went on to note the

51 Ibid 79–80.

52 Bank account information of the claimant was part of the evidentiary record in this case, unusually.

53 Jean-Jacques Arnaldez, Yves Dérains, and Dominique Hascher (eds), *Collection of ICC Arbitral Awards, 2008–2011* (Wolters Kluwer 2013) 831.

54 Ibid 833.

need to look behind the contract terms, to the behavior of the parties, including conduct that preceded the execution of the contract, to discern the true intent underlying the contract.

While the burden of proof was placed on the party seeking to have the contract invalidated,[55] the Tribunal noted that it could use all means of proof authorized by law to determine the true meaning of the contract, and had no choice but to look at '*extracontractual indicators*' ('*les arbitres n'ont d'autre chois que de se réposer sur des indications extracontractuelles*'). Because of difficulties of proof, it believed it could resort to presumptions based on indicators ('*L'exigence en matière de preuve est des lors reduite et peut se limiter à une présomption réposant sur des indices*').[56]

The indicators identified by the tribunal in this case were:

- The inability of the claimant to bring forward any proof of actual services rendered with respect to the structural adjustment element of the contract;
- The short duration of negotiations on this point;
- The fact that remuneration was based on a percentage;
- The excessive level of remuneration; and
- The reputation for corruption of the country in question.[57]

On this basis, the tribunal declared the contract null and void. It declined to reach the question of the effect of the complicity of state agents in the corrupt practice, reasoning that the state itself was not corrupted. However, it rejected the state's demand for restitution.

2.2.2 *Contracts allegedly procured by corruption: Niko Resources (Bangladesh) Ltd. v. People's Republic of Bangladesh*[58]

Niko Resources (Bangladesh) Ltd. V. People's Republic of Bangladesh is a contract case that arose from agreements containing an ICSID arbitration clause. The claimant, Niko Resources (Bangladesh) Ltd. (Niko), the Barbados subsidiary of a Canadian company, brought claims against Bangladesh,[59] and two SOEs, Bapex and Petrobangla, arising out of the respondents' alleged breach of contracts for development of gas fields and the sale of gas. The gas was to be developed

55 Ibid 834.

56 Ibid.

57 Ibid 835.

58 *Niko Resources (Bangladesh) Ltd. v. People's Republic of Bangladesh*, ICSID Cases ARB/10/11 and ARB/10/18, Decision on Jurisdiction of 19 August 2013.

59 The tribunals concluded that they did not have jurisdiction over Bangladesh and thus dismissed Bangladesh from the case; ibid [256].

pursuant to the claimant's gas purchase and sales agreement (GPSA) through a joint venture with Bapex and Petrobangla.[60]

During the course of the GPSA negotiations, Niko provided a Toyota Land Cruiser (worth approximately C$191,000) to the Bangladeshi State Minister for Energy and Mineral Resources and sponsored his travel to a conference in Canada. These gifts became publicly known and ultimately led to the company's prosecution and conviction in Canada under its foreign anti-bribery law.[61] The Canadian authorities found that the gifts were made for the purpose of inducing the Minister to issue the GPSA to Niko.

The matter was investigated in Bangladesh but no charges were ultimately filed. There were also judicial proceedings instituted to cancel the joint venture agreement, but these did not result in a finding of impropriety in the formation of the agreement.[62]

The respondents sought to have Niko's claims dismissed for lack of jurisdiction on the grounds that the corruption led to violations of good faith and international public policy. The tribunals rejected this request for dismissal on each ground, finding that the lack of good faith did not justify the denial of jurisdiction but must instead be considered as part of the merits of the dispute. Concerning international public policy, the tribunals found that while bribery is a violation of international public policy,[63] this did not warrant the exclusion of a case where the bribery could not be causally linked to the procurement of the contracts at issue.[64] The tribunals relied on the findings of the Canadian prosecutions to conclude that acts of corruption were committed.[65] As to any other acts of corruption that the respondents suggested had occurred, the tribunals noted that any such acts needed to be proven and could not simply be based on inferences.[66] Citing the local proceedings and the findings (or lack of prosecution thereof), the tribunals concluded that there were no other acts of corruption.[67]

The tribunals discussed the difference between contracts that were allegedly for corruption and contracts allegedly procured by corruption, finding that the contracts at issue in the case fell into the latter category.[68] Such contracts, if proven, are voidable rather than void, but in this case, there was no proof that

60 There were two separate claims, one under the joint venture agreement and one under the GPSA. These were not formally consolidated, but it was agreed that they would be heard in parallel and decided together. See ibid [138].

61 Niko was also ordered to pay a fine of approximately C$9.5 million. Ibid para 389 (citing [2011] *R v. Niko Res Ltd*, 101 WCB (2d) 118 (Can Alta QB)).

62 *Niko Resources* (n 58) [394]–[405].

63 Ibid [433].

64 Ibid [454]–[455].

65 Ibid [423].

66 Ibid [424], citing *Gustav F W Hamester GmbH & Co KG v. Republic of Ghana*, ICSID Case ARB/07/24, Award of 19 June 2010 [134].

67 Ibid [429].

68 Ibid [438].

the influence sought via the gifts was obtained; rather, the case was analyzed as involving only attempt.[69]

Further, even if the instrument had been voidable, the respondents had not voided the contract.[70] Even in the arbitration proceedings, the respondents had not argued for voidability.[71] Rather, the respondents argued that the attempted bribery was sufficient to make the arbitration clauses in the contracts unenforceable. The tribunals rejected this position, stating that there was no link between the established acts of corruption and the procurement of the contracts at issue.[72] They rejected the respondents' argument that the arbitration clauses had been rendered unenforceable by the claimant's conduct, and also rejected additional arguments of unclean hands.[73] The tribunals found that there was valid consent to arbitrate and that if the claimant 'had unclean hands, the respondents disregarded this situation.'[74]

Although the case thus proceeded on the merits, the respondents subsequently raised a new corruption defense: that the GPSA and joint venture agreement were procured by corruption. This resulted in a decision by the tribunals of a need to examine the claim,[75] and a stay of the proceedings except for that defense and an interim measures request. The tribunals issued a decision on the corruption claim on February 25, 2019, concluding, in an analysis requiring almost 600 pages to complete, that the evidence did not establish that the agreements in question or the governmental acts leading up to them were procured by corruption.[76]

In terms of methodology, the *Niko* corruption decision was anything but a red flag analysis. The tribunals assessed both the third-party contracts whose purpose was at issue, and the government contracts allegedly procured by corruption.

69 The respondent had argued that corruption in either the making or performance of the investment should be sufficient for a denial of jurisdiction: see ibid [375]; and that attempts to bribe were still sufficiently linked to the investment: ibid [377]; the tribunals rejected these arguments without explicitly addressing the making versus performance issue. Other tribunals, however, have distinguished between conduct at the time of the investment and conduct during performance. See, e.g., *Fraport AG Frankfurt Airport Servs Worldwide v. Republic of the Philippines*, ICSID Case ARB/11/12, Award of 10 December 2014; *Yukos Universal Ltd (Isle of Man) v. Russian Fed'n*, PCA Case 2005-04/AA 227, Final Award of 18 July 2014.

70 *Niko Resources* (n 58) [438].

71 Ibid.

72 Ibid [455].

73 Ibid [484].

74 Ibid.

75 *Niko Resources (Bangladesh) Ltd v. People's Republic of Bangladesh* (n 58) Procedural Order No. 13 of 26 May 2016 [7]. ('The Tribunals have noted that other ICSID tribunals have taken the initiative of examining alleged acts of corruption without being restricted by the specific allegations of the Respondents and their burden of proof with respect to them. Mindful of their responsibility for upholding international public policy, the Tribunals will therefore examine the corruption charges that have been raised by the Respondents.')

76 *Niko Resources* (n 58) Decision on the Corruption Claim of 25 February 2019.

The respondents had argued that 'certain classic "red flags" of corruption can suffice to shift the burden of proof.'[77] While the claimant had accepted that red flags justified particular scrutiny of a transaction, it emphasized that red flags are not evidence of corruption. It went on to cite the *Kim v. Uzbekistan* decision on jurisdiction, in which the tribunal stated that:

> Respondent has not established that red flags can of themselves substantiate the most basic requirements of the crime of bribe giving [to government officials] as set forth in Article 211 [of the Uzbek Criminal Code].[78]

The tribunals declined to decide the issue of burden-shifting in the abstract, finding it not to be an issue of principle that could be decided in that fashion.[79] Rather, they concluded that:

> The Tribunals must therefore examine whether (i) the circumstances on which the Respondents rely as red flags are established and, if so, (ii) what evidentiary conclusions should be drawn from them, taken individually and collectively. In this process, the Tribunals will also have to consider circumstances which point in the opposite direction.[80]

The tribunals made it clear that they viewed red flags as 'warning signals and possible clues but not evidence.'[81] Moreover, their analysis negated the existence of certain asserted red flags.[82] They declined to make certain adverse inferences requested by the respondent, deciding the case on the evidence before them.[83]

2.2.3 Other investor-state cases

2.2.3.1 METAL-TECH V. UZBEKISTAN[84]

Metal-Tech Ltd. V. Republic of Uzbekistan represents one of the high-water marks to date of an arbitral tribunal's independent assessment of corruption issues. The claim was made under the Israel-Uzbekistan BIT, which contained a legality requirement, raising the issue as a jurisdictional one.[85]

77 Ibid [787], citing to the respondent's Memorial on Corruption, [165].
78 Ibid, citing *Vladislav Kim v. Republic of Uzbekistan,* ICSID Case ARB/10/3, Decision on Jurisdiction of 8 March 2017 [589].
79 Ibid [796].
80 Ibid [797].
81 Ibid [1477].
82 Ibid [1630], referencing the question whether the compensation agreed by Niko in certain third-party agreements was disproportionate to the services to be provided.
83 Ibid [963].
84 *Metal-Tech Ltd. v. Republic of Uzbekistan*, ICSID Case ARB/10/3, Award of 4 October 2013.
85 Ibid [131].

The case involved a joint venture to build and operate a molybdenum products plant in Uzbekistan. The claimant engaged several third parties in connection with the making of its investment and investment approvals. These included three consultancies, one with the brother of the then-Prime Minister, one with a senior government official responsible for human resources functions in the President's office, and one with an individual with no identified government positions or blood relationships.[86] Metal-Tech Ltd. paid these three 'consultants' large sums for their services.[87]

Although the parties disagreed on burden and standard of proof, the tribunal sidestepped those issues by determining that because the facts had given rise to suspicions of bribery, it must inquire into the facts using its *ex officio* powers under Article 43 of the ICSID Convention on the Settlement of Investment Disputes Between States and Nationals of Other States.[88] In the course of those inquiries, including its questioning of witnesses, additional facts emerged.

The tribunal used circumstantial evidence, classic red flags, and inferences from missing evidence to sustain the corruption defense. The evidence reviewed by the tribunal included:

- the disproportionately large size of the payments made to the consultants;
- the inability of the company to establish legitimate services for which the consultants received compensation;
- the consultants' lack of relevant qualifications; and
- the fact that two of the consultants were in a position to exercise influence over the investment at the time of its establishment.[89]

The decision was not, however, simply a matter of connecting the dots or aggregating risk factors; rather, the tribunal evaluated witness testimony and other evidence on the key elements. The tribunal also reviewed the chronology of events, including the fact that the last payment to certain of the consultants was made at the same time the Prime Minister left his position.[90]

The tribunal compared the payment of the two consultants who maintained government connections with a third whose legitimate activities were well documented and transparent.[91] The tribunal found that the actions of the third consultant did not show a violation of law even though a few facts surrounding the payments raised doubts.[92] Based on the finding of corruption in the first two

86 Ibid [209]–[212].
87 Ibid [197].
88 Ibid [239], [241].
89 Ibid [199]–[212]; [225]–[226].
90 Ibid [227]; [267]–[273].
91 Ibid [359]–[363].
92 Ibid [364].

contracts, the tribunal went on to find that it had no jurisdiction and dismissed the case.[93]

2.2.3.2 SPENTEX V. UZBEKISTAN[94]

A second relatively recent investor-state case against Uzbekistan, brought under the Netherlands–Uzbekistan BIT, also bears reviewing for its reported methodology in addressing allegations of corruption.

The claimant, a company based in New Delhi, India, had sought to establish a spinning mill in Uzbekistan. The project was subject to a government tender. To assist it and entering the market, the claimant hired a third party (A) under the auspices of a services agreement, and a second third party (B), as a consultant for the same purpose. Other third parties were engaged as well, including an Uzbek state-owned enterprise (C), and a third party based in an offshore haven (G) (the British Virgin Islands).

Shortly after hiring G, the claimant increased its tender offer for the mill from $75 to $81 million. It was ultimately successful with the tender.

The tribunal defined foreign public bribery in terms of Article 1(1) of the OECD Convention and Article 16(1) of the UNCAC, considering corruption to be '[a]ny promise, offering or giving to a (foreign) public official, directly or indirectly, of an undue financial or other advantage in order that the official act or refrain from acting in the exercise of his or her official duties, for the purpose of obtaining business advantages.'[95]

Although the tribunal declined to establish a specific applicable standard of proof, it found evidence on the record to establish corruption. While citing the statement of Judge Higgins in the *Oil Platforms* case that 'the graver the charge the more confidence must there be in the evidence relied on,'[96] its methodology was one of 'connecting the dots,' thereby assessing all individual indicia of corruption in detail and seeking to verify the plausibility of an emerging picture from their assemblage.[97]

The tribunal found no corruption with respect to A, notwithstanding some references to bribery in the documents. The tribunal found that A had performed legitimate services and payments received were not clearly disproportionate. In

93 ibid [389].

94 *Spentex v. Uzbekistan*, ICSID Case ARB/13/26, Award of 27 December 2016. This decision is not yet published, so this summary is based on published commentary. See Kathrin Betz, *Proving Bribery, Fraud and Money Laundering in International Arbitration: On Applicable Criminal Law and Evidence* (CUP 2017) 128ff.

95 Betz (n 94) 130–31, quoting *Spentex* (n 94) [842].

96 *Oil Platforms* (*Islamic Republic of Iran v. United States*), Judgment of 6 November 2003, 2003 ICJ 161, [33] (separate opinion by Higgins J); see Betz (n 94) 131.

97 Betz (n 94) 131–32, citing Spentex (n 94) [857]ff with further references to case law.

addition, timing factors played a role in that the conduct attributable to A took place in 2004, two years before the tender.[98]

With respect to third parties B and G, however, the tribunal identified a number of red flags for which no legitimate explanation could be identified. These included:

- the strikingly high commission to be received by G;
- concealment and attempted concealment of the consulting contracts from the tribunal;
- the consultants' lack of qualifications;
- a vague description of services and the lack of record demonstrating legitimate services in return for payments;
- the short time period between G's engagement and bid submission; and
- failure on the part of the claimant to produce relevant records and the implausibility of the explanation provided by the claimant for the same.[99]

There was no evidence of payments received by Uzbek officials, but the tribunal noted contradictions between the arguments of the respondent state and its own witnesses. Despite the respondent's lack of prosecution, the tribunal concluded that 'the most compelling explanation of the events surrounding the tender process in June 2006 and the making of the investment is clearly that it involved corrupt activities on the part of the [intermediaries] of … the [r]espondent.'[100]

This decision has been described by commentators as the first case in which bribery was successfully proven on the basis of an accumulation of red flags.[101] Although it is difficult to determine that methodology definitively from secondary sources, if that were to be the case, it would be highly troubling. And it does not appear that was in fact what occurred from the available information. Rather, it appears that the tribunal sought to marshal the available evidence, made inferences from the presence or lack of evidence on several of the indicators, and sought to assess, based on all the totality of the testimony and evidence received, the most plausible explanation for the third-party payments. It was on this basis that the tribunal concluded that bribery had taken place.[102] If so, its methodology in 'connecting the dots' would go beyond red flag analysis.

98 Betz (n 94) 132, citing *Spentex* (n 94) [865]ff.

99 Betz (n 94) 132–33.

100 Ibid 134, quoting *Spentex* (n 94) [934].

101 See Betz (n 94) 135.

102 The decision has also garnered attention for its novel approach to costs. Instead of awarding costs to the successful party (the respondent state), the tribunal 'ordered both parties to bear their own costs and fees, and to equally share the costs and fees of the proceedings:' see ibid. Additionally, the tribunal urged the respondent to donate to a United Nations anti-corruption project or suffer an adverse cost award: see ibid, citing *Spentex* (n 94) [981] ff. See also Luke Eric Peterson and Vladislav Djanic, 'In an Innovative Award, Arbitrators Pressure Uzbekistan—Under Threat of Adverse Cost Order—to Donate to UN Anti-

3 Further observations and recommended approach

What are the lessons that can be drawn from the foregoing cases in terms of methodology and the actual use of red flags?

The cases show a variety of approaches. Some, e.g., *ICC Case No. 13914*, appear to give lip service to red flag analysis as being central to the tribunal's conclusions; however, when they are more closely parsed, it appears that the decision finding a contract for corruption was very much evidence-based. The extract cites one general red flag, but does not appear to rely on it in the ultimate analysis. Others, such as *Niko*, explicitly reject a red flag analysis as a basis for findings and demonstrate a careful probing of asserted red flags to determine if they are in fact corroborated.

On the other hand, the ICC tribunal in *Case No. 12290* stated that it was applying presumptions based on indicators. This approach goes well beyond a red flag analysis, and even beyond a 'connect the dots' approach, in applying a legal presumption based on the presence of red flags. The cited flags include a general one (the country in question) as well as several transaction-specific red flags. But despites its assertion, it appears that the tribunal's analysis did not rely entirely on indicators. The extract noted that the claimant had been unable to bring forward any proof of actual services rendered in relation to the elements of the contract that were at issue—in effect an adverse inference from the lack of evidence.

The *Spentex* case, as reported, appears also to have relied on indicators, which were then aggregated to find corruption. But again it appears that some of what may have started as indicators—e.g., questions about whether the third parties at issue had performed legitimate services—were pursued for probative evidence, and decisions were ultimately made on the basis of the presence or lack of evidence considering the totality of the facts and circumstances. Timing issues also played an important role in the analysis.

Finally, *Metal-Tech*, like *Niko*, reflects an evidence-based approach, notable for the fact that it was the arbitral tribunal that drove the fact-finding inquiries on the corruption issue after developing concerns about possible corruption on the part of the claimant, rather than the issue having been raised as a defense by the respondent. As with some of the other cases, the lack of evidence on certain key issues played an important role in the tribunal's ultimate conclusions, as did timing considerations.

These decisions illustrate both the value of the red flag concept as an organizing tool and the slippery slope it presents for arbitrators. It is possible to use red flags for their intended purpose—i.e., as risk indicators only and not as evidence—as some of these decisions demonstrate. The tribunals that have eschewed the application of presumptions from indicators, or direct use of red flags, have not ignored the red flag concept, but are using the tool in a manner which is

Corruption Initiative; Also Propose Future Treaty-Drafting Changes that Would Penalize States for Corruption' [2017] Investment Arbitration Reporter 261.

consistent with its intended function—to identify relevant areas of potential risk for further inquiry. Conversely, the tribunals that have made direct use of red flags or indicators, and particularly to the extent they are applying indicators on a presumptive basis to find corruption, or are simply aggregating indicators, are not only distorting the function of red flags but also embarking on dangerous territory. While circumstantial evidence is often going to be used to assess corruption allegations, tribunals should guard against conflating indicators with such evidence. For that reason, it is important for tribunals to exercise caution in using terms such as 'red flag analysis' when it comes to an actual assessment of conduct and emphasize the distinction between risk indicators and evidence.

These decisions also illustrate other limitations of red flag analysis. Several of the decisions reviewed above have cited general red flags, particularly country risk, in connection with their findings on the corruption issue. It is difficult for the reader to discern from the available materials how much weight has been given to this red flag in their analyses, but in any event, for the reasons set forth earlier, reliance on general red flags for a finding of corruption is particularly problematic. At most, given that the function of a general red flag is to suggest the possibility of a heightened risk environment, arbitrators would want to look in response for indicators of measures taken by the claimant that would be responsive to such heightened risks. It is therefore not the country risk itself that is ultimately probative, but whether it was recognized as a heightened risk factor and what steps, if any, were taken commensurate with such risk in response. But temporal questions come into play here; as compliance standards become internationalized, it will be more reasonable for tribunals to inquire about the preventive measures taken. And what may be adequate preventive measures even a few years ago may not meet today's 'good practice' standards. The bar for an effective compliance program has been rising, but the progressive development of standards and the uneven adoption of standards around the world need to be taken into account.

The decisions reviewed in this chapter that have cited red flags in their analysis have focused principally on party- and transaction-specific red flags, and particularly the latter. This seems appropriate, as it is transaction-specific red flags that, if confirmed, would present the strongest risk indicators. Indeed, while party-specific risk indicators such as a third party's reputation or qualifications may be stronger than more general indicators, the most relevant risk indicators and those most apt to lead to probative evidence are likely to be those that are specific to the transaction at issue.

Yet even these, as the *Niko* corruption decision demonstrates, should not be taken at face value but should be tested for their value as indicators, as they may not be borne out after further inquiry.

One of the most difficult risk indicators in the author's experience, highlighted in several of the decisions reviewed above, is the proportionality between a third party's compensation and the services to be rendered. How should one determine whether in fact compensation is excessive? This is often not a question of determining an objective fact but is a judgment call. Certainly it cannot be the subjective judgment of the tribunal but must be based on objective criteria. In some cases there may be established industry standards or benchmarks. But in many there is not, and compensation is often highly contextual. What is appropriate in a small project may not be appropriate for a large project, for instance. And the more complex the project, the more difficult the analysis will be.

Although not presented in any of the cases reviewed above, in some cases (and perhaps increasingly going forward as good compliance practices are adopted by an increasing number of firms), evidence of due diligence at the time of the third party engagement may be available and could be an important area of inquiry on this issue. Companies with robust compliance programs not only do due diligence on the third party, but also endeavor to benchmark the compensation to be paid. Where available, such due diligence information would represent contemporaneous evidence of the steps taken and information available to and belief of the principal at the relevant time, not as assessed some years (perhaps even decades) later, when the issue has ripened into a dispute. The availability of such information would also alleviate the 20/20 hindsight risk alluded to earlier.

Faced with a lack of contemporaneous evidence regarding the proportionality of compensation, the above decisions show that tribunals have responded by seeking evidence of the legitimate services that a third party has provided. This is appropriate—after all, it represents the other side of the proportionality analysis to compensation—but again may run into evidentiary obstacles arising from lapse of time, the nature of a course of dealing, or the like. The issue is particularly difficult when the third party is engaged in activities that require government interface rather than a technical service. In this case, the value of legitimate services may be great, but the intermediary is operating at a risk juncture, perhaps under time pressures that are not conducive to leaving a detailed paper trail of his activities. The reality is that not every legitimate engagement fits into a fee for defined service model. Today, companies operating defensively may seek to create and retain such a paper trail against this possibility, but that practice is far from universal and, given that disputes often arise many years after the conduct at issue, arbitrators should expect that there could be continue to be gaps.

There will, of course, almost never be evidence that the intermediary has made payments to a government official, unless the conduct has been investigated by enforcement authorities and there is a public record of findings. Nor should it be expected that the tribunal will be able to access bank records of the third party at issue to determine the outflow of funds received from the principal, although that occasionally occurs, as we have seen. One may hope that enforcement will increase over time as barriers to cross-border investigations and enforcement, and enforcement capacity, increase, but experience to date has shown this is a slow and spotty process. Tribunals should approach with skepticism corruption allegations that have been known to a state for some time, but have not been investigated by that state on a timely basis; conversely, they should be alert to potential misuse by a state of its enforcement resources to target companies for litigation advantage.

Temporal considerations have been considered circumstantially in several cases, as we have seen, including the timing of a third party engagement in relation to a government procurement decision or other governmental actions. However, while timelines are a frequently used tool in corruption investigations, temporal evidence alone only shows correlation, and will rarely be probative as to either purpose or causation. It is only when it is linked with other evidence that it takes on significance. It must, therefore, be considered in the larger context and its limitations borne in mind.

Accordingly, the tribunal will have to evaluate the totality of the evidence emanating from further examination of those red flags that are confirmed to be valid and relevant—as noted above, these are most likely to be any transaction-specific red flags—together with the relevant circumstances, for their implications as to whether a contract has a licit or illicit purpose and, in the case of contracts allegedly procured by corruption, whether causation has been shown.

Here an important difference between contracts for corruption and contracts allegedly procured by corruption must be emphasized. For the criminal offense of bribery to have taken place, it is not necessary to prove that a payment was actually made: a promise of payment, offer of payment, authorization of payment, or act in furtherance of a corrupt scheme will generally be enough. Similarly, for a contract to have a *cause illicite*, it is not necessary that its illicit object have been fulfilled—a finding of an improper purpose should be a sufficient basis on which to conclude that the contract should not be enforced. But in the case of a contract allegedly procured by corruption, showing the payment—the actual pass through—may be of critical importance given the requirement of causation.

A hypothetical scenario will illustrate this point. Company A is seeking a contract from the Defense Ministry of Country X. Company A hires intermediary B with the purpose of improperly influencing the award of the contract by the Defense Ministry, and pays B with the intention that B pass the funds to the Defense Minister (D) for purposes of securing his influence over the contract award. But B, unbeknownst to A, pockets the money and did not pass it through. A is awarded the contract (let us call it Contract C) without any corrupt payment.

The arrangement between A and B in that scenario is undoubtedly corrupt. It is a contract for corruption—based on its purpose. And there was even performance on one side: A paid the money to B. It was B that did not perform its side of the bargain. A strong argument can be made that it is a tainted contract that should not be enforced.

But in order for Contract C to be tainted, there has to have been an actual pass-through of money, or at least some proof that D was improperly induced to award the contract to A. There thus needs to be sufficient proof of performance of the corrupt bargain by the intermediary to conclude that the contract was in fact procured through corruption.

Any 'connect the dots' exercise thus has to take into account what must ultimately be proven given the typology of the issue involved. One cannot conclude that that the Contract C award was *ipso facto* tainted on the basis of a determination that the A/B arrangement was corrupt. While the finding of a corrupt intermediary arrangement may increase the likelihood that a subsequent contract procured with the assistance of the intermediary was tainted, it is a leap without sufficient foundation to conclude that it was. The requirement to show causation thus takes the tribunal beyond red flag analysis.

The cases reviewed above do not involve any shifting of the burden of proof. They do reflect the use of adverse inferences by tribunals, albeit sparingly. This seems appropriate. Just as a red flag should not be conflated with evidence, so should a red flag not form the basis for an adverse inference to be made. Inferences relate to evidence, and it should only be once a red flag is pursued for probative evidence should a possible inference be considered. And the inference should be based not on the red flag or indicator, but on the presence or absence of evidence at the end of the day. There can be many reasons why a party will not have access to evidence—lack of custody or control, lapse of time, intervening mergers and acquisitions, or other corporate changes—to name only a few, and tribunals should not be too quick to respond to the demand for adverse inferences on a matter have such significant consequences unless they are satisfied that the necessary conditions have been met.[103]

Tribunals are being encouraged to address corruption issues in both contracts and investment treaty claims *sua sponte*, even if the parties have not raised the issue, and the review of cases in this chapter has corroborated that this is occurring.[104] The Toolkit for Arbitrators argues the point as follows:

> While arbitrators are not state judges, they do fulfil [sic] a certain public function because—in general terms—arbitral awards are enforceable like court decisions. Furthermore, arbitrators have a duty to issue an enforceable award. If arbitrators ignore issues of corruption, there is a risk that their award will be challenged in front of state courts in set-aside proceedings or at the enforcement stage on the ground that it is contrary to the national or transnational public policy. While in ICSID arbitration, the possibilities to challenge an award are limited to the review procedures provided for in the

103 The Toolkit for Arbitrators (n 22) states in tool 6, that: Arbitrators should consider applying adverse inferences if the following conditions are fulfilled:

i. the party that seeks the adverse inference must produce compelling indicators of corruption and must itself have produced all available evidence to corroborate the inference sought, or the tribunal itself has identified sufficient indicia of corruption;
ii. the party of whom evidence has been requested must have access to such evidence;
iii. the party of whom evidence has been requested failed to give any convincing reason for not producing such evidence; and
iv. the inference must be reasonable, consistent with the facts and logically related to the likely nature of the withheld evidence.

The use of the term 'compelling indicators' here, however, raises a question about whether inferences are in reality arising from red flags, or evidentiary matters.

104 Ibid Step 4.

> ICSID Convention, parties may equally seek revision or annulment of an award before an annulment committee. Therefore, whether in the context of commercial or investor-state arbitration, if a party alleges or arbitrators suspect that corruption was involved in the underlying dispute, arbitrators should consider investigating (also on a *sua sponte* basis) those issues. Arbitrators should do so even if the allegations or suspicions arise only at the final stages of the proceedings.[105]

But arbitrators will proceed at their peril if they do not consider the scope of their authority to investigate *sua sponte* under the applicable rules and law governing the proceeding. That authority may be clearer in the ICSID context than in other contexts, justifying the questions raised by the tribunal in the *Metal-Tech* case, but should not be taken for granted.

Finally there is the question of standard of proof. As the cases reviewed in this chapter demonstrate, there appears to be a tendency on the part of tribunals to sidestep the issue of standard of proof to a certain extent. But tribunals using red flag analysis may need to take extra caution in this regard. Perhaps it does not matter whether the standard is a preponderance of the evidence or clear and convincing evidence at the end of the day if the tribunal is reasonably satisfied regarding the evidence that has been adduced. But satisfaction to whatever standard should be evidence-based, and not red flag or indicator-based; otherwise it may be argued that the decision does not even meet what surely must be the minimum standard—preponderance of the *evidence*.

This does not mean that 'connect the dots' is necessarily an improper methodology. If connect the dots means assessing a chain of largely circumstantial evidence in its totality, it can be reconciled with an evidence-based standard and may be simply another name for assessing such evidence. On the other hand, if it means aggregating risk indicators, particularly on a presumptive basis, such methodology would raise serious questions about its validity.

In conclusion, allegations of corruption raise difficult issues of proof in arbitration. Although those issues of proof are largely factual matters, they raise important methodological concerns that ultimately tie into key legal issues in the proceedings. This chapter has attempted to demonstrate the proper use and limitations of the 'red flag' tool and similar approaches in addressing allegations of corruption, particularly when a tribunal is confronted with circumstantial evidence. Further, this chapter has sought to provide an analytical framework for different types of red flags, in the context of third-party relationships, with the goal of assisting arbitral tribunals in dealing with these issues.

105 Ibid.

18 The World Bank Group in international dispute resolution of fraud and corruption

Examining the practice and jurisprudence of the Sanctions Board and ICSID Arbitral Tribunals

Anna Lorem Ramos and Charlene Valdez Warner[1]

Former World Bank Group ('WBG' or the 'Bank') President James D Wolfensohn's prominent speech in 1996 about the 'cancer of corruption' put this issue front and center in the development world.[2] Since then, the WBG has made the fight against corruption a priority, viewing corruption as a hindrance to the Bank's twin goals of ending extreme poverty and boosting shared prosperity. The WBG's well-known initiatives in combatting corruption primarily revolve around technical assistance and capacity building in areas such as governance, transparency, rule of law, and asset recovery. Less explored, however, is its growing role in the international dispute resolution of fraud and corruption allegations.

Two institutions within the WBG, while having different mandates and spheres of competence, contribute to the Bank's fight against corruption. One is the WBG Sanctions Board (the 'Sanctions Board'), which has over a decade of experience in resolving fraud and corruption claims in WBG-financed projects. Through its publicly available, fully reasoned decisions, the Sanctions Board has progressively developed its own jurisprudence on fraud and corruption with the aim of protecting Bank funds and deterring potential misconduct. The other is the International Centre for Settlement of Investment Disputes ('ICSID' or the 'Centre'), the world's leading international investment arbitration institution established in 1966 to further the Bank's objective of promoting international

1 The opinions expressed in this chapter are those of the authors alone.

2 Note, this chapter uses the term 'World Bank Group' to refer to the International Bank for Reconstruction and Development (IBRD), the International Development Association (IDA), the International Finance Corporation (IFC), and the Multilateral Investment Guarantee Agency (MIGA). As stipulated in decisions of the Sanctions Board, the 'World Bank Group' includes Bank Guarantee Projects and Bank Carbon Finance Projects but does not include the International Centre for the Settlement of Investment Disputes (ICSID). In addition, this chapter uses the term 'World Bank' to refer to both IBRD and IDA.

investment. A number of ICSID arbitral tribunals have issued awards and decisions in investment arbitration cases, in which allegations of fraud and corruption figured in the disputes between investors and states.

This chapter examines how the WBG, through the Sanctions Board and ICSID, is pioneering efforts in the international dispute resolution of fraud and corruption allegations. This chapter first briefly discusses the scope of jurisdiction and competence of the Sanctions Board and ICSID. This chapter then explores the practice and jurisprudence of the Sanctions Board and ICSID arbitral tribunals with respect to three issues: burden of proof; standard of proof and evidence; and red flags. Finally, this chapter identifies lessons learned from the practice and jurisprudence of the Sanctions Board and ICSID arbitral tribunals that may be of value to international litigation and arbitration of fraud and corruption allegations.

1 Jurisdiction and competence

1.1 Sanctions system

The WBG sanctions system was created in furtherance of the Bank's fiduciary duty to ensure that the funds it provides are used only for their intended purposes.[3] Through this system, the WBG sanctions firms and individuals found to have engaged in certain types of misconduct ('Sanctionable Practices') in Bank-financed projects,[4] with the aim of protecting Bank funds and deterring those who might otherwise misuse them.[5]

Sanctions proceedings are administrative in nature,[6] and cover five types of Sanctionable Practices: fraud, corruption, collusion, coercion, and obstruction.[7] The definitions of these Sanctionable Practices can be found in the different versions of the Anti-Corruption Guidelines, Procurement Guidelines, and Consultant Guidelines applicable to a given case.[8] While the definitions of these

3 IBRD Articles of Agreement, art III, s 5(b); IDA Articles of Agreement, art V, s 1(g).

4 'World Bank Procedure: Sanctions Proceedings and Settlements in Bank Financed Projects Issued by the World Bank' (28 June 2016) s III.A, sub-para 1.01(a) (Sanctions Procedures). See also 'WBG Policy: Sanctions for Fraud and Corruption' (13 June 2015) s III.A.1 (Sanctions Policy). The term 'Bank-Financed Projects' encompasses an investment project or a program for results operation, for which IBRD or IDA (as the case may be), whether acting for its own account or in the capacity as administrator of trust funds funded by donors, has provided financing in the form of a loan, credit or grant and governed by the Bank's Procurement Guidelines, Consultant Guidelines, or Anti-Corruption Guidelines: Sanctions Procedures, s II(e). See 'WBG Sanctions Regime Information Note' (November 2011) 14 (Sanctions Regime).

5 Sanctions Policy, s III.A, sub-paras 1–3; Sanctions Regime, 14.

6 Sanctions Procedures, s I.1; Sanctions Board Decision No. 89 (2016) [12]; Sanctions Board Decision No. 93 (2017) [36]; Sanctions Board Decision No. 97 (2017) [30]; Sanctions Board Decision No. 98 (2017) [31]; Sanctions Board Decision No. 108 (2018) [27].

7 Sanctions Procedures, s II(r).

8 Ibid.

Sanctionable Practices have been revised over the years, the essence of the definitions practically remains the same. Based on the latest versions of the Procurement Guidelines and Consultant Guidelines,[9] fraud and corruption are defined in the following terms:

- fraud is 'any an act or omission, including (a) misrepresentation, that knowingly or recklessly misleads, or attempts to mislead, a party to obtain a financial or other benefit or to avoid an obligation';[10]
- corruption is the 'offering, giving, receiving, or soliciting, directly or indirectly, of anything of value to influence improperly the actions of another party.'[11]

The range of sanctions that can be imposed are the following: (i) reprimand (in the form of a 'Letter of Reprimand'); (ii) conditional non-debarment (the sanctioned party is required to comply with certain remedial, preventative or other conditions to avoid debarment); (iii) debarment (either indefinitely or for a fixed period of time); (iv) debarment with conditional release (the sanctioned party is released from debarment upon compliance with certain conditions); and (v) restitution[12] (the sanctioned party is required to make restitution, financial or otherwise, to the borrowing country or to any other party, but is not to be construed as a fine).[13]

The WBG sanctions regime is a quasi-judicial, two-tier system. The Integrity Vice Presidency ('INT') investigates allegations of sanctionable practices, and refers the case to the appropriate Evaluation and Suspension Officer ('EO')—the first tier of review[14]—in cases where INT finds evidence of misconduct.[15] If the EO determines that INT's accusations are supported by sufficient evidence, then the EO issues a Notice of Sanctions Proceedings, recommends a sanction, and may temporarily suspend the respondent firm or individual from eligibility for new WBG-financed contracts pending the final outcome of the sanctions

9 To date, no case brought before the Sanctions Board has ever involved the Anti-Corruption Guidelines.

10 'The World Bank's Guidelines, Procurement of Goods, Works, and Non-Consulting Services under IBRD Loans and IDA Credits & Grants by World Bank Borrowers' (January 2011, revised July 2014), s 1.16(a)(ii) (July 2014 Procurement Guidelines); 'The World Bank's Guidelines: Selection and Employment of Consultants under IBRD Loans and IDA Credits & Grants by World Bank Borrowers' (January 2011, revised July 2014), s 1.23(a)(ii) (July 2014 Consultant Guidelines).

11 July 2014 Procurement Guidelines, s 1.16(a)(i); July 2014 Consultant Guidelines, s 1.23(a)(i).

12 Note that restitution is not equivalent to a fine.

13 Sanctions Policy's III.C, sub-para 1; Sanctions Procedures, s III.A.1, sub-para 9.01.

14 Sanctions Procedures, s III.A.1, sub-para 3.01.

15 The WBG has four EOs with separate responsibilities for cases pertaining to the Bank, MIGA, IFC, and Bank guarantee projects.

proceedings.[16] If the respondent does not contest INT's allegations or the EO's recommended sanction, then the EO's recommended sanction is imposed.[17] Otherwise, the respondent may refer the case to the Sanctions Board,[18] which serves as the second and final tier of review.[19]

The Sanctions Board reviews all contested sanctions cases *de novo*, which means that it does not engage in a reconsideration of the decisions of the first tier. The Sanctions Board conducts oral hearings, which is not available at the first tier, as requested by the parties or convened by the Sanctions Board Chair in his discretion.[20] The Sanctions Board is composed of seven members, all external to the WBG. It began publishing its fully reasoned decisions in January 2011.[21]

1.2 ICSID tribunals

Article 25 of the ICSID Convention governs the Centre's jurisdiction and provides as follows:

> The jurisdiction of the Centre shall extend to any legal dispute arising directly out of an investment, between a Contracting State (or any constituent subdivision or agency of a Contracting State designated to the Centre by that State) and a national of another Contracting State, which the parties to the dispute consent in writing to submit to the Centre. When the parties have given their consent, no party may withdraw its consent unilaterally.[22]

Therefore, for ICSID to have jurisdiction, three requirements must be satisfied under Article 25. First, the dispute must be a 'legal' dispute arising 'directly out of an investment,' (subject matter jurisdiction). Second, the parties to the dispute must be a contracting state (or a designated constituent subdivision or agency of a contracting state) and a national of another contracting state (personal jurisdiction). Lastly, the parties must have consented to submit their dispute to ICSID jurisdiction in writing, either in their contract or treaty before the dispute arose or after the dispute has arisen (consent).

16 Sanctions Procedures, s III.A.1, sub-paras 4.01–4.02.

17 Ibid s III.A.1, sub-para 4.04.

18 Ibid s III.A.1, sub-para 5.01.

19 Sanctions Policy, s III.B, sub-para 1; Sanctions Procedures, s III.A.1, sub-para 8.03.

20 Sanctions Procedures, s III.A.1, sub-para 6.

21 Ibid s III.A.1, sub-para 10.01(b). The holdings in unpublished decisions between 2007 and 2012 were presented in the first edition of the Sanctions Board's Law Digest published in December 2011.

22 Convention on the Settlement of Investment Disputes Between States and Nationals of Other States, (opened for signature 18 March 1965, entered into force 14 October 1966) 575 UNTS 159 (ICSID Convention).

Article 25(1) of the ICSID Convention limits ICSID's jurisdiction to 'any legal dispute arising directly out of an investment.'[23] This limitation gives rise to differing interpretations with regard to the nature of investments that fall within ICSID's subject matter jurisdiction. Some investment treaties provide that an investment must be 'in accordance with' or 'in conformity with' the laws and regulations of the host state.[24] In some cases, even where the treaty does not expressly so state, tribunals have held that an investment must have been made in accordance with the host state's law in order to come within the jurisdiction of the tribunal and the Centre.[25] This is the case under the Energy Charter Treaty ('ECT'), which unlike a number of Bilateral Investment Treaties ('BIT' or 'BITs'), does not contain a provision requiring that an investment conform with a particular law. However, the tribunal in *Plama v. Bulgaria* held that the lack of this provision under the ECT does not mean that 'the protections provided for by the ECT cover all kinds of investments, including those contrary to domestic or international law.'[26] According to the tribunal, 'the ECT should be interpreted in a manner consistent with the aim of encouraging respect for the rule of law,' as this furthers the fundamental aim of the ECT to strengthen the rule of law on energy issues.[27]

Some tribunals also discuss whether good faith in making the investment is relevant to Article 25 of the ICSID Convention. A split in decisions currently exists. Certain tribunals have found that an investment made illegally is determinative of whether the investment comes within ICSID's jurisdiction. One example is the *Phoenix Action v. Czech Republic* tribunal, which found that an investment must be made in good faith in order to come within the purview of Article 25.[28] Other tribunals have found that illegality of an investment is determinative of

23 Ibid art 25(1).

24 For example, Article 1(1) of the Ukraine-Lithuania BIT requires that investments be made in compliance with the laws. This requirement is common amongst modern BITs. See *Tokios Tokeles v. Ukraine*, ICSID Case No ARB/02/18, Decision on Jurisdiction of 29 April 2004 [84].

25 In *Inceysa*, the tribunal decided that the consent given by Spain and El Salvador in entering the BIT excludes investments not made in accordance with the laws of the host State. See *Inceysa Valiisoletana, S.L. v. Republic of El Salvador*, ICSID Case No. ARB/03/26, Award of 2 August 2006 [195]. In *Blusun*, the tribunal concluded that even though the Energy Charter Treaty does not lay down an explicit requirement of legality, 'it does not cover investments which are actually unlawful under the law of the host state at the time they were made....' See *Blusun SA, Jean-Pierre Lecorcier and Michael Stein v. Italian Republic*, ICSID Case No. ARB/14/3, Award of 27 December 2016 [264].

26 *Plama Consortium Ltd. v. Republic of Bulgaria*, ICSID Case No. ARB/03/24, Award of 27 August 2008 [138].

27 Ubid [139].

28 *Phoenix Action Ltd. v. The Czech Republic*, ICSID Case No. ARB/06/5, Award of 15 April 2009 [106]. According to the tribunal, at [100]: '[t]he purpose of the international mechanism of protection of investment through ICSID arbitration cannot be to protect investments made in violation of the laws of the host State or investments not made in good faith, obtained for example through misrepresentations, concealments or corruption.'.

outcome, and not of jurisdiction. For instance, the *Fakes v. Turkey* tribunal expressly disagreed with the approach followed in *Phoenix Action*, holding that:

> the principles of good faith and legality cannot be incorporated into the definition of Article 25(1) of the ICSID Convention without doing violence to the language of the ICSID Convention: an investment might be "legal" or "illegal," made in "good faith" or not, it nonetheless remains an investment.[29]

Similarly, the *Quiborax v. Bolivia* tribunal held that, while 'recourse to treaty arbitration and substantive treaty protections may in certain circumstances breach the prohibition of abuse of rights,' a notion which emanates from the principle of good faith, this does not mean that legality or good faith forms part of the *definition* of investment.[30] Note, however, that the *Fraport v. Philippines* tribunal drew a fine line in noting that illegality of investments must be considered in deciding whether legal remedies are available to such investment, where the illegality goes to the essence of the investment.[31] The *Fraport* tribunal found it important that the particular investment was lawful under the laws and regulations of the host state 'at the time [such investment was] made.'[32]

2 Practice and jurisprudence of the Sanctions Board and ICSID arbitral tribunals

2.1 Standard of proof; evidence

The Sanctions Procedures provide for the use of a 'more likely than not' standard in the resolution of sanctions cases.[33] The choice of this standard stems from the administrative nature of sanctions proceedings and the limited investigative tools available to INT.[34] 'More likely than not' means that, upon consideration of all the relevant evidence, a preponderance of the evidence – the standard commonly

29 *Saba Fakes v. Republic of Turkey*, ICSID Case No. ARB/07/20, Award of 14 July 2010 [112]. According to the *Fakes* tribunal, at [114]–[115], Article 25(1) of the ICSID Convention does not relate to the legality of investments but BITs are at liberty to condition their application and protection to a legality requirement. This is precisely the case in the Netherlands-Turkey BIT, which contains such requirement under Article 2(2): '[t]he present Agreement shall apply to investments … which are established in accordance with the laws and regulations in force [in the Host State].'

30 *Quiborax SA, Non Metallic Minerals S.A. and Allan Fosk Kaplún v. Plurinational State of Bolivia*, ICSID Case No. ARB/06/2, Decision on Jurisdiction of 27 September 2012 [226].

31 *Fraport AG Frankfurt Airport Services Worldwide v. Republic of the Philippines [II]*, ICSID Case No. ARB/11/12, Award of 10 December 2014 [332].

32 Ibid [331].

33 Sanctions Procedures, s III.A, sub-paras 8.01, 8.02(b)(i).

34 Anne-Marie Leroy, *Advisory Opinion on Certain Issues Arising in Connection with Recent Sanctions Cases* (No 2010/1 2010) [43].

used in civil cases[35]—supports a finding that the respondent engaged in a sanctionable practice.[36]

Formal rules of evidence do not apply in sanctions proceedings.[37] The Sanctions Board exercises discretion to determine the relevance, materiality, weight and sufficiency of all the evidence presented,[38] including hearsay[39] and circumstantial evidence.[40]

Two interesting cases illustrate how the Sanctions Board applies the 'more likely than not' standard and exercises its discretion in considering the evidence presented by the parties. In *Sanctions Board Decision No. 92* (2016), INT made three allegations of fraud and five allegations of corruption. With respect to the corruption allegations, INT relied on emails written and testimony provided by the respondent firm's regional manager, who detailed various bribes she allegedly made on behalf of her employer.[41] On their own, these emails and testimony may be considered as strong evidence of misconduct. However, the respondents challenged the credibility of this witness, prompting the Sanctions Board to make a preliminary determination on the weight of her testimonial and documentary evidence.[42] The Sanctions Board took into account relevant factors that bore on her credibility, including inconsistencies between her testimony before INT and her emails; her admission to owning a company supposedly formed in case the respondent firm becomes bankrupt; and a situation of conflict between this witness and the respondent firm, which allegedly reneged on its obligation to pay her salary and benefits, and had suspected her of financial impropriety.[43] Based on these factors, the Sanctions Board decided to accord limited weight to this witness' testimonial and documentary evidence.[44] As a consequence of this

35 John Coogan and others, 'Combatting fraud and corruption in international development' (2015) 22 Journal of Financial Crime 230.

36 Sanctions Policy, s III.B, sub-para 3; Sanctions Procedures, s III.A.1, sub-para 8.02(b)(i).

37 Sanctions Procedures, s III.A, sub-para 7.01.

38 Ibid.

39 For cases where the Sanctions Board considered hearsay evidence, see *Sanctions Board Decision No. 64* (2014) [33]; *Sanctions Board Decision No. 92* (2017) [57]; *Sanctions Board Decision No. 97* (2017) [31].

40 For cases where the Sanctions Board considered circumstantial evidence, generally, see *Sanctions Board Decision No. 47* (2012) [25]; *Sanctions Board Decision No. 87* (2015) [110]. For instances where the Sanctions Board considered circumstantial evidence as basis for inferring knowledge or recklessness on the part of the respondent in making the misrepresentation in alleged fraud cases, see, e.g., *Sanctions Board Decision No. 77* (2015) [33]; *Sanctions Board Decision No. 79* (2015) [23], [26]; *Sanctions Board Decision No. 81* (2015) [39]; *Sanctions Board Decision No. 82* (2015) [31]; *Sanctions Board Decision No. 86* (2015) [34]; *Sanctions Board Decision No. 88* (2015) [31]; *Sanctions Board Decision No. 90* (2016) [28]; *Sanctions Board Decision No. 97* (2017) [46]; *Sanctions Board Decision No. 98* (2017) [38], [42]; *Sanctions Board Decision No. 100* (2017) [34].

41 *Sanctions Board Decision No. 92* (2017) [51].

42 Ibid.

43 *Sanctions Board Decision No. 92* (2017) [53].

44 Ibid [54]

determination, the Sanctions Board found insufficient evidence of misconduct in three out of the five corruption allegations, where this witness's statements were not corroborated by other evidence. The Sanctions Board, therefore, concluded that it was not more likely than not that the respondents engaged in these three alleged counts of corruption.[45]

In *Sanctions Board Decision No. 96* (2017), INT alleged a total of three counts of corrupt practices against a firm and its managing director and regional director. The first two corruption allegations involved the purported provision of recreational 'study tours' to public officials to influence and reward their actions.[46] The third corruption allegation involved the supposed payment of bribes, which were disguised as 'study tours' and a 'ghost' contract in the respondent firm's records, to public officials to influence the award and execution of certain contracts.[47] With respect to the first corruption allegation, the Sanctions Board found that the respondent managing director and respondent regional director provided public officials with a trip, but found insufficient evidence of corrupt intent for lack of proof that the directors approved the trip knowing it to be recreational in nature.[48] With regard to the second corruption allegation, the Sanctions Board found the record insufficient to show that it was more likely than not that the respondent managing director provided a public official any trip.[49] With respect to the third corruption allegation, the Sanctions Board found insufficient evidence to hold the respondent regional director culpable or responsible for the alleged misconduct given, *inter alia*, the absence of evidence showing that he instructed or ordered the payment of bribes.[50] The Sanctions Board observed that '[w]hile the record includes some evidence indicating that misconduct may have taken place,' it found that 'the record, on balance, is insufficient to show that it is more likely than not' that the respondents engaged in the alleged corrupt practices.[51]

Both of these Sanctions Board decisions demonstrate how the use of the 'more likely than not' standard is able to balance, on the one hand, the reality that the limited investigative tools available to INT contribute to the existing difficulty of obtaining direct evidence in corruption cases; and on the other hand, the need to uphold due process in proceedings of an administrative nature. However, it is this very lack of direct evidence, as well as the parties' own hesitation to formally allege corruption, that appears to steer arbitral tribunals the other way by displaying a degree of reticence in dealing with corruption allegations.[52] This reluctance

45 Ibid [93], [96]–[97], [99]–[100].
46 *Sanctions Board Decision No. 96* (2017) [17]–[18].
47 Ibid [19].
48 Ibid [56], [58]–[59].
49 Ibid [63].
50 *Sanctions Board Decision No. 96* (2017) [67]–[69].
51 Ibid [73].
52 Aloysius Llamzon and Anthony Sinclair, 'Investor Wrongdoing in Investment Arbitration: Standards Governing Issues of Corruption, Fraud, Misrepresentation and Other Investor Misconduct' [2014] 18 ICCA Congress Series 451, 468.

is reflected in how some ICSID arbitral tribunals have imposed high standards of proof in resolving corruption allegations.

The tribunals in *Siag v. Egypt*, *EDF v. Romania*, and *Karkey v. Pakistan*[53] viewed fraud and corruption accusations as grave allegations that warrant the imposition of a high standard of proof. In *Siag*, the tribunal required parties to adduce 'clear and convincing evidence,' explaining the need to examine fraud allegations against a standard that is less than beyond reasonable doubt, but greater than the balance of probabilities.[54] In *EDF* and *Karkey*, the tribunals emphasized that the 'seriousness of the accusation of corruption,' which in both cases involved high-level government officials, demand that allegations must be proven by 'clear and convincing evidence.'[55]

The tribunals in *Fraport* and *Metal-Tech v. Uzbekistan* underscored the difficulty of proving corruption allegations, but nonetheless applied different standards of proof.[56] In *Fraport*, the tribunal recognized that corruption allegations are difficult to prove by direct evidence. The tribunal found that while circumstantial evidence may be considered, such evidence must still be clear and convincing 'so as to reasonably make-believe that the facts, as alleged, have occurred.'[57] In *Metal-Tech*, the tribunal held that 'it will determine on the basis of the evidence before it whether corruption has been established with reasonable certainty,' noting that 'corruption is by essence difficult to establish and that it is thus generally admitted that it can be shown through circumstantial evidence.'[58]

2.2 *Burden of proof*

Under the Sanctions Procedures, INT bears the initial burden of proof to present evidence sufficient to establish that it is more likely than not that a respondent engaged in a sanctionable practice. Once INT satisfactorily carries this burden, the burden of proof shifts to the respondent to demonstrate that it is more likely than not that the respondent's conduct did not amount to a sanctionable practice.[59] Two recent Sanctions Board decisions illustrate how burden-shifting on the specific issue of corrupt intent has resulted in opposing outcomes.

In *Sanctions Board Decision No. 103* (2017), INT alleged that the respondent, which was the local agent of a joint venture that won a Bank-financed contract,

53 *Waguih Elie George Siag & Clorinda Vecchi v. Arab Republic of Egypt*, ICSID Case No. ARB/05/15, Award of 1 June 2009; *EDF (Services) Limited v. Romania*, ICSID Case No. ARB/05/13, Award of 8 October 2009; *Karkey Karadeniz Elektrik Uretim A.S. v. Islamic Republic of Pakistan*, ICSID Case No. ARB/13/1, Award of 22 August 2017.

54 *Siag v. Egypt* (n 53) [325]–[326].

55 *EDF v. Romania* (n 53) [221]; *Karkey v Pakistan* (n 53) [491]–[492].

56 *See Fraport v. Philippines [II]* (n 31) [479]; and *Metal-Tech Ltd. v. Republic of Uzbekistan*, ICSID Case No. ARB/10/3, Award of 4 October 2013 [236]–[243].

57 *Fraport v. Philippines [II]* (n 31) [479].

58 *Metal-Tech Ltd. v. Republic of Uzbekistan* (n 56) [243].

59 Sanctions Procedures, s III.A.1, sub-para 8.02(b)(ii).

engaged in a corrupt practice by receiving or soliciting from one of the joint venture partners an improper payment to be passed along to public officials.[60] In support of its allegation, INT relied on an email from the joint venture partner's senior vice president to other members of the company's management, discussing the need to pay an amount to 'our agent' to 'ensure that … the [contract] goes to [the World Bank] for approval.'[61] Attached to the same email was a memorandum, in which a manager of this joint venture partner stated the need to pay public officials involved in the evaluation of the contact.[62] The record also included a bank statement from the respondent reflecting a payment from the joint venture partner that the respondent acknowledged it received from the joint venture partners six days after the date of the email.[63] The Sanctions Board found that INT had met its burden to show that the respondent's receipt of the improper payment was with corrupt intent given, *inter alia*, the language in the email; and the timing of both the email and the payment in relation to certain decisions handed down by the bid evaluation committee.[64] According to the Sanctions Board, the respondent then had the burden to show that its conduct did not amount to a corrupt practice. The respondent argued that the payment it received from the joint venture partner was for 'legitimate services' that the respondent had rendered in relation to a different project.[65] However, the Sanctions Board found that the respondent was unable to substantiate its claim with sufficient evidence. As the respondent failed to meet its evidentiary burden, the Sanctions Board held that it was more likely than not that the respondent engaged in a corrupt practice.[66]

In *Sanctions Board Decision No. 110* (2017), INT alleged that the respondent firm and the respondent managing director engaged in a corrupt practice by making an improper payment to a public official in order to influence the public official's acts during the implementation of a tracer study contract.[67] The Sanctions Board found that, consistent with the respondents' concession, the respondent manager made a payment to the public official on behalf of the respondent firm.[68] In determining that this payment was made with corrupt intent, the Sanctions Board considered evidence showing, *inter alia*, that the public official was in a position of authority with respect to the project; and that the respondent managing director knew that the public official had influence over the respondent firm's interests in relation to the contract. The Sanctions Board found that INT met its burden of proof, and stated that the burden shifted to the respondents

60 *Sanctions Board Decision No. 103* (2017) [6], [12].
61 Ibid [23].
62 Ibid.
63 *Sanctions Board Decision No. 103* (2017) [23].
64 Ibid [27], [28].
65 Ibid [29].
66 Ibid [29]–[30].
67 *Sanctions Board Decision No. 110* (2017) [6].
68 Ibid [22].

to demonstrate that it is not more likely than not that they acted with corrupt intent.[69] In their defense, the respondents argued, *inter alia*, that the payment was made to the public official for onward payment to field enumerators.[70] The Sanctions Board found the respondents to have satisfactorily carried their burden of proof, considering, *inter alia*, a sworn affidavit of a hired field enumerator, who stated that he collected stipends due him and the other field enumerators from the public official without issuing a receipt or signing a document. Despite noting its 'misgivings with regard to the payment,' the Sanctions Board found that it is more likely than not that the respondents did not act with corrupt intent.[71]

In international investment arbitration, tribunals adopt the 'nearly universal practice'[72] of placing the burden of proof on the party asserting a fact.[73] However, at least two ICSID arbitral tribunals have recognized the possibility of employing a burden-shifting approach in the resolution of corruption allegations.

In *Metal-Tech*, the tribunal raised the question of whether the burden should be shifted to the investor to establish that there was no corruption in cases where corruption allegations have been raised as a defense.[74] The tribunal noted that the Israel–Uzbekistan BIT did not provide rules for shifting the burden of proof or establishing presumptions.[75] The tribunal, therefore, concluded that it 'has relative freedom in determining the standard necessary to sustain a determination of corruption.'[76] Noting a similar set of circumstances in the case of *World Duty Free v. Kenya*,[77] the *Metal-Tech* tribunal did not resort to presumptions or rules of burden of proof. Instead, the tribunal determined, based on the evidence—which was adduced by the investor and sought by the tribunal itself—'whether corruption has been established with reasonable certainty.'[78] Without finding that Uzbekistan had established the existence of corruption *prima facie*, the tribunal noted that the facts did establish 'suspicions of corruption' that required explanations.[79] The tribunal further drew inferences from the investor's

69 Ibid [25].
70 *Sanctions Board Decision No. 110* (2017) [14].
71 Ibid [27].
72 *Marion Unglaube v. Republic of Costa Rica*, ICSID Case No. ARB/08/1, Award of 16 May 2012 [33]. See also *Metal-Tech v. Uzbekistan* (n 56) [237] ('The principle that each party has the burden of proving the facts on which it relies is widely recognised and applied by international courts and tribunals. The International Court of Justice as well as arbitral tribunals constituted under the ICSID Convention and under the NAFTA have characterized this rule as a general principle of law.')
73 See, e.g., *Unglaube v. Costa Rica* (n 72) [34]; *Metal-Tech v. Uzbekistan* (n 56) [237]; *Karkey v. Pakistan* (n 53) [497].
74 *Metal-Tech v. Uzbekistan* (n 56) [238].
75 Ibid.
76 Ibid.
77 *World Duty Free Company Ltd. v. Republic of Kenya*, ICSID Case No. ARB/00/7, Award of 4 October 2006.
78 *Metal-Tech v. Uzbekistan* (n 56) [243].
79 Because 'facts emerged in the course of the arbitration … [which] raised suspicions of corruption, the Tribunal [therefore] required explanations': ibid [239].

failure to produce certain evidence, taking into consideration Article 9(5) of the International Bar Association ('IBA') Rules on the Taking of Evidence in International Arbitration.[80] Because the investor was unable to rebut the suspicions of illicit conduct, the tribunal concluded that 'corruption is established to an extent sufficient to violate Uzbekistan law in connection with the establishment of the Claimant's investment in Uzbekistan.'[81] Therefore, the tribunal held that claimant's investment has not been 'implemented in accordance with the laws and regulations of the Contracting Party in whose territory the investment is made,' which was a requirement under Article 1(1) of the Israel-Uzbekistan BIT.[82]

In *Karkey*, the tribunal acknowledged the principle that the party asserting a fact must prove it. Nevertheless, the tribunal found that 'it can shift the burden of proof with respect to corruption and fraud' to the claimant investor should there be 'unequivocal (or unambiguous) prima facie evidence' of corruption and fraud to the tribunal's satisfaction.[83] However, in this case, the tribunal was not satisfied that the evidence before it warranted burden-shifting.[84] In particular, evidence consisted of questions raised by Pakistan 'based on alleged acts or omissions by Pakistani government officials which are not proven.'[85] The tribunal observed that even if these alleged acts or omissions are established, the government officials 'may have other explanations than corruption.'[86] These alleged acts or omissions include the 'haste of the Prime Minister and of the Minister to Water and Power' that, according to the tribunal, 'may just as well reflect their manner of exercising power.'[87] Another allegation involved 'advantages obtained by Karkey through contract modification' that, the tribunal noted, may be explained by Pakistan's inability 'to comply with some of its contractual obligations, such as the issuing of a guarantee, and the consequent need to offer a reciprocal benefit to Karkey.'[88] Because Pakistan failed to demonstrate that Karkey possessed evidence explaining the real motivation of Pakistani officials, the tribunal held that it 'would not be entitled to draw adverse inferences against Karkey, such as to shift the burden of proof.'[89]

80 Ibid [245]. Article 9(5) of the 2010 IBA Rules on the Taking of Evidence in International Arbitration provides that '[i]f a Party fails without satisfactory explanation to produce any Document... ordered to be produced by the Arbitral Tribunal, the Arbitral Tribunal may infer such document would be adverse to the interests of that Party.'

81 Ibid [239], [372]. See also Michael A Losco, 'Charting a New Course: Metal-Tech v Uzbekistan and the Treatment of Corruption in Investment Arbitration' (2014) 64 Duke Law Journal 37, 43–44.

82 *Metal-Tech v. Uzbekistan* (n 56) [372].

83 *Karkey v. Pakistan* (n 53) [497].

84 Ibid [521].

85 Ibid.

86 Ibid.

87 Ibid.

88 Ibid.

89 Ibid. The tribunal was unable to find 'red flags' that suggest corruption so as to shift the burden of proof to the claimant-investor in this case, and 'still less, any positive proof of corruption'. See discussion on 'red flags': text at n 90.

2.3 Red flags of fraud and corruption

In more than a decade of resolving fraud and corruption cases, the Sanctions Board has considered various types of circumstantial evidence and recurring fact patterns that can be distilled into useful red flags of fraud and corruption. Some examples of these red flags include the following:

i. Amount of commissions paid to an agent;[90]
ii. Indicia of falsity in bid documents;[91]
iii. Conclusion of agency agreements that do not articulate specific bid-related deliverables;[92]
iv. Provision of trips to public officials;[93]
v. Public officials' request to hire individuals;[94]
vi. Conclusion of 'ghost' contracts for services that were not performed or were performed at inflated prices.[95]

It must be emphasized that, based on the practice of the Sanctions Board, the mere identification of red flags does not supplant the need to ascertain whether the evidence on the record meets the 'more likely than not' standard. Thus, there have been cases where the Sanctions Board did not find sufficient evidence of corrupt practices despite the existence of certain red flags. For example, in *Sanctions Board Decision No. 96* (2017), INT relied on correspondence to support its allegation that the respondent approved and authorized illegitimate payments that were purportedly disguised by a 'study tour' and a 'ghost' contract.[96] The Sanctions Board found that:

> [W]hile red flags may be inferred from certain language in the emails, the evidence is insufficient to show on balance that the Respondent Regional Director approved the study tour and the contract with the Third Party Company knowing them to be a disguise for corrupt payments.[97]

90 See, e.g., *Sanctions Board Decision No. 72* (2014) [43]; *Sanctions Board Decision No. 88* (2017) [28]; *Sanctions Board Decision No. 97* (2017) [43]; *Sanctions Board Decision No. 106* (2018) [12].

91 See, e.g., *Sanctions Board Decision No. 52* (2012) [27]; *Sanctions Board Decision No. 79* (2015) [28]; *Sanctions Board Decision No. 112* (2018) [31].

92 *Sanctions Board Decision No. 97* (2017) [57].

93 See, e.g., *Sanctions Board Decision No. 78* (2015) [21]; *Sanctions Board Decision No. 85* (2016) [25], [30]–[32]; *Sanctions Board Decision No. 96* (2017) [58]; *Sanctions Board Decision No. 108* (2018) [56].

94 *Sanctions Board Decision No. 66* (2014) [24]; *Sanctions Board Decision No. 78* (2015) [20]; *Sanctions Board Decision No. 111* (2018) [13].

95 *Sanctions Board Decision No. 96* (2017) [11]; *Sanctions Board Decision No. 108* (2018) [31], [39].

96 *Sanctions Board Decision No. 96* (2017) [67].

97 Ibid [67].

Another example is *Sanctions Board Decision No. 110* (2017), where INT alleged that the respondents made an illegal payment by depositing a sum to the personal account of the public official. In finding that the respondents did not act with corrupt intent, the Sanctions Board held as follows:

> The Sanctions Board notes its misgivings with regard to the payment in question. It is particularly concerning that the deposit was made to the Deputy Director's personal bank account, that the Respondents failed to keep receipts and other primary records of the payments to the individual field enumerators, and that the Respondents were unable to provide a full explanation for this unsatisfactory practice. The Sanctions Board nevertheless finds that, on balance, the totality of the record supports a finding that it is more likely than not that the Respondent Managing Director did not act with corrupt intent.[98]

Some ICSID arbitral tribunals have acknowledged the value of red flags in dealing with corruption allegations, but have differed in the use and recognition of their import. For instance, the tribunal in *Metal-Tech* found the existence of certain internationally accepted red flags in that case:[99] the amount of payments made to the consultants;[100] the absence of services supposedly rendered by the consultants or lack of proof thereof;[101] the consultants' lack of qualifications to perform the required services;[102] the conclusion of a sham contract;[103] the lack of transparency in the payment arrangements to the consultants;[104] and the consultants' connections with relevant public officials.[105] The tribunal viewed some of these red flags as 'suspicions' of corruption that prompted it to seek further evidence from the parties[106] and served as the threshold for shifting the burden of proof to the investor.[107]

In *Karkey*, Pakistan alleged the existence of certain red flags, which indicate that the subject investment was procured through corruption that the claimant-investor supposedly needed to rebut.[108] The tribunal was not satisfied that these red flags created a *prima facie* case of corruption that would 'shift Pakistan's burden of proving its allegations of corruption' to the claimant-investor.[109] In

98 *Sanctions Board Decision No. 110* (2018) [27].
99 *Metal-Tech v. Uzbekistan* (n 56) [293].
100 Ibid [199]–[203].
101 Ibid [204]–[207].
102 *Metal-Tech v. Uzbekistan* (n 56) [208]–[212].
103 Ibid [213]–[218].
104 Ibid [219]–[224].
105 Ibid [225]–[227].
106 Ibid [239].
107 Ibid [372], [390].
108 *Karkey v. Pakistan* (n 53) [518].
109 Ibid [497], [521].

particular, the tribunal noted that the red flags listed by Pakistan consisted 'solely of questions' that were not of 'sufficient weight and credibility.'[110]

In *Kim v. Uzbekistan*, the tribunal found that red flags may be treated as circumstantial evidence that 'can play an important supporting role in the assessment of guilt'[111] and may serve to 'heighten scrutiny' of the allegations made.[112] Ultimately, the tribunal found that the host state 'has not established that red flags can of themselves substantiate the most basic required elements of the crime of bribe giving' under the applicable law in Uzbekistan.[113]

3 Lessons learned

Examining the practice and jurisprudence of the Sanctions Board and ICSID arbitral tribunals with respect to standard of proof and evidence, burden of proof, and red flags offers more than just an understanding of procedural issues encountered by these institutions. What this exercise leads us to contemplate is how the Sanctions Board and ICSID arbitral tribunals are able to maintain the importance of fairness and due process while wading through the evidentiary difficulties of proving fraud and corruption and contending with their limited means of seeking out evidence given these institutions' lack of subpoena powers.

First, the jurisprudence of the Sanctions Board demonstrates that its imposition of a 'more likely than not' standard and non-adherence to formal rules of evidence, including the consideration of circumstantial evidence, do not mean that mere assertions of fraud and corruption are enough to pass muster. The Sanctions Board cases discussed above illustrate how even the existence of what may first appear as strong evidence of misconduct may in fact be insufficient to meet the 'more likely than not' standard. This is because the Sanctions Board looks at the record as a whole and exercises discretion in determining the weight and relevance of all the evidence presented. With respect to international investment arbitration, some scholars have criticized the imposition of a higher standard of proof noting that while tribunals admit to the difficulty of proving corruption allegations, they nevertheless impose a high standard of proof that makes the misconduct even more difficult to prove.[114] However, although this approach may appear to create a contradiction, decisions like *Fraport* do offer some workable flexibility. Cognizant that the difficulty in proof lies in finding ***direct*** evidence of corruption,[115] the *Fraport* tribunal suggests that weight may be given

110 Ibid [521].

111 *Vladislav Kim and others v. Republic of Uzbekistan*, ICSID Case No. ARB/13/6, Decision on Jurisdiction of 8 March 2017 [548]–[589].

112 Ibid [589].

113 Ibid.

114 Constantine Partasides, 'Proving Corruption in International Arbitration: A Balanced Standard for the Real World,' (2010) 25 ICSID Review—Foreign Investment Law Journal 47 [43]–[44].

115 See *Fraport v. Philippines [II]* (n 31) [479].

to *circumstantial* evidence, so long as it is clear and convincing. Indeed, ICSID arbitral tribunals seem to focus less on which standard of proof to apply—whether clear and convincing evidence or otherwise—and more on the weight of the circumstantial evidence offered by the party making the allegation.[116]

Second, the jurisprudence of the Sanctions Board shows how shifting the burden of proof is used as a helpful tool in evaluating the evidence in its totality. In contrast to the Sanctions Board, however, international investment tribunals still treat this approach with controversy. It is important to note that in ICSID matters, either party may raise fraud or corruption as an allegation: the respondent-State as a defense to the legality of the investment on the matter of jurisdiction or on the merits; and the claimant-investor as a claim, for example, for violation of the fair and equitable treatment standard, as in the case of *EDF*.[117] Unlike the Sanctions Board, since ICSID arbitral tribunals do not have fixed rules on the standard of evidence, coming up with evidentiary threshold sufficient to shift the burden of proof becomes the crucial issue regardless of whether it is the host state or the investor that raises the allegation of fraud or corruption.

Finally, the jurisprudence of the Sanctions Board and ICSID arbitral tribunals demonstrate the roles that red flags may serve in resolving fraud and corruption allegations: first, red flags may serve as a cue to seek or require further evidence, or to heighten scrutiny; second, once found to be sufficient, red flags may be an evidentiary threshold to shift the burden of proof; and third, red flags may be weighed as circumstantial evidence. Regardless of how a tribunal wishes to treat red flags, mere identification thereof is not to be taken as proof in itself; substantiation that meets the requisite standard of evidence is still required.

Through the Sanctions Board and ICSID arbitral tribunals, the WBG has made great strides in contributing to the fight against corruption through dispute resolution. Considering that various efforts to establish an international or transnational system for adjudicating fraud and corruption cases have failed,[118] the practice and jurisprudence of the Sanctions Board and ICSID tribunals offer valuable lessons to future international litigation or arbitration of cases involving fraud and corruption allegations.

116 In *Kim*, the tribunal held that 'regardless of whether the standard of proof is 'reasonable certainty' or 'clear and convincing evidence,'... allegations of bribery and corruption have not been established by the evidence presented in this proceeding.' *Kim v. Uzbekistan* (n 111) [545].

117 See *EDF v. Romania* (n 53).

118 L Yves Fortier, 'Arbitrators, Corruption, and the Poetic Experience: 'When Power Corrupts, Poetry Cleanses' (2015) 31 Arbitration International 367, 371.

19 References to international anti-corruption conventions in international investment arbitration and international investment agreements

Yueming Yan[1]

Over years, corrupt acts have penetrated the boundaries of states in the context of globalization; the concept of 'transnational corruption' was then brought to the table and has thus become one of the main subjects in the global anti-corruption movement. This implies that anti-corruption efforts further require cross-border cooperation instead of completely being restricted to domestic initiatives.

In fact, the ongoing recognition of the devastating effects of corruption on global economic development has contributed to the creation of numerous anti-corruption instruments at the domestic, regional, and international levels, including major binding covenants and a variety of instructive guidelines oriented towards both the public and private sectors.[2] As a consequence of the transnationalization of anti-corruption laws, regulation against corruption is no longer a purely local issue and international anti-corruption norms have been showing rapid development in the past decades.

Remarkably, the United States (US) enacted the Foreign Corruption Practices Act (FCPA) in 1977, one of the most important domestic statutes addressing *bribery of foreign officials*, stimulating a large production of subsequent international anti-corruption treaties and, in some cases, directly imposing a substantive impact on the substance of a great number of international anti-corruption

1 The author wishes to thank her supervisor Prof. Andrea K Bjorklund for her valuable and precious comments on the early version of this chapter.

2 Stefan Mbiyavanga, *Improving Domestic Governance through International Investment Law: Should Bilateral Investment Treaties Learn from International Anti-Corruption Conventions?* (OECD Global Anti-Corruption & Integrity Forum 2017).

norms,[3] such as the United Nations Convention against Corruption (UNCAC),[4] and the OECD Convention on Combating Bribery of Foreign Public Officials in International Business Transactions (OECD Convention).[5] A large number of other multilateral anti-corruption treaties have also been concluded by states, with a number of them having binding effects on a regional basis, including the Inter-American Convention Against Corruption (IACAC),[6] the Council of Europe Criminal Law Convention on Corruption (CLCC),[7] the Council of Europe Civil Law Convention on Corruption (CivLCC),[8] and the African Union Convention on Preventing and Combating Corruption (AUCPCC).[9]

In addition, there are numerous documents in relation to corruption prevention and deterrence that are developed by international non-governmental organizations and/or economic cooperation organizations or communities, including the Asia-Pacific Economic Cooperation (APEC) Principles on the Prevention of Bribery and Enforcement of Anti-Bribery Laws, G20 High Level Principles on Organizing against Corruption, G20 Guiding Principles on Enforcement of the Foreign Bribery Offence, G20 High Level Principles on the Liability of Legal Persons for Corruption, and the Southern African Development Community (SADC) Protocol against Corruption, etc. Although these instruments have limited 'binding effects' on the states or regions concerned, they may help a big group of objectives as useful guidance and principles.

Admittedly, these anti-corruption norms were not initially designed to be used in international investment law, but to serve more general purposes, such as demonstrating the negative effects of acts of corruption, illustrating the universal or regional consensus on the measures and cooperation against corruption and promoting the in-depth and intensive cooperative measures and domestic measures against corruption. But this fact does not signify that there is no linkage between these two domains at all. We cannot deny that the negative effects of corruption

3 Kevin E Davis, 'Does the Globalization of Anti-Corruption Law Help Developing Countries' in Susan Rose-Ackerman and Paul D Carrington (eds), *Anti-Corruption Policy: Can International Actors Play a Constructive Role?* (Carolina Academic Press 2013) 169, 170; Jan Wouters, Cedric Ryngaert, and Ann Sofie Cloots, 'The International Legal Framework against Corruption: Achievements and Challenges' (2013) 14 Melbourne Journal of International Law 205; Aloysius Llamzon, *Corruption in International Investment Arbitration* (OUP 2014) 49, 51; Cecily Rose, *International Anti-Corruption Norms: Their Creation and Influence on Domestic Legal Systems* (OUP 2015) 64.

4 United Nations Convention against Corruption (opened for signature 9 December 2003, entered into force 14 December 2005) 2349 UNTS 41.

5 Convention on Combating Bribery of Foreign Public Officials in International Business Transactions (adopted 17 December 1997, entered into force 15 February 1999) 37 ILM 1.

6 Inter-American Convention against Corruption (entered into force 6 March 1997) (1996) 35 ILM 724.

7 Council of Europe Criminal Law Convention on Corruption, ETS No.173, 27 January 1999.

8 Council of Europe Civil Law Convention on Corruption, ETS No.174, 4 November 1999.

9 African Union Convention on Preventing and Combating Corruption (adopted 11 July 2003) (2004) 43 ILM 5.

seriously jeopardize the attractiveness of domestic laws, thereby discouraging foreign investment[10] and have indeed profoundly affected international and transnational investment and trade transactions. International investment law with a diversity of forms has genuinely evolved into an integral part of the global anti-corruption campaign.

It would not be quite as surprising when we hear the news about transnational corrupt acts in international investment activities. This type of corruption probably accounts for a large portion of the aggregate of corrupt acts. Bearing this in mind, collaborative measures against corruption in the domain of international investment law are reasonably necessary and imperative.

In fact, the above-mentioned anti-corruption treaties have been significant and indispensable sources of authority for policy-makers to draft their investment agreements in a new era of international investment agreements (IIAs) when we can observe an extensive reform of IIAs such as increasing sustainable development concerns and growing weight of society values. Other connections between international anti-corruption norms and international investment law are observed in national legislation and policies and international investment arbitration.[11] These major international and regional anti-corruption treaties require state parties to adopt legislative or other necessary measures to combat corruption, such as criminalizing corruption as offenses and imposing criminal and/or civil and/or administrative sanctions on entities and individuals involved. To implement these international obligations, states have accordingly issued or modified laws and regulations, including rules against corruption conducted in international business transactions. International arbitral tribunals have so far dealt with a few investment disputes where investor or host state parties raised submissions surrounding corruption. Some of the tribunals have referred to international anti-corruption conventions in making decisions on corruption issues, for instance in the case of *World Duty Free v. Kenya*.

In light of the above development, this chapter presents a study of international anti-corruption efforts in international investment law. In particular, how states and international investment arbitral tribunals rely on international anti-corruption conventions to address issues in relation to (anti-)corruption. The next two sections will respectively discuss the application of international or regional anti-corruption conventions in international investment arbitration and the existing anti-corruption provisions in over 3,000 IIAs where these anti-corruption norms have been incorporated. This chapter will then close with a brief conclusion.

10 Kofi A Annan, 'Forward—United Nations Convention against Corruption' in UNODC, *United Nations Convention against Corruption* (2004) <https://www.unodc.org/documents/treaties/UNCAC/Publications/Convention/08-50026_E.pdf> accessed 1 June 2020.

11 Kathryn Gordon, 'International Investment Agreements: A survey of Environmental, Labour and Anti-Corruption Issues' in OECD (ed), *International Investment Law: Understanding Concepts and Tracking Innovations* (2008) 135, 139.

1 Anti-corruption conventions in international investment arbitration

IIAs are important and one of the basic legal authorities that arbitrators should rely on when dealing with international investment disputes between foreign investors and host states. In cases where the parties raise corruption allegations, arbitrators will then need to address all such issues in accordance with the anti-corruption provisions incorporated in the applicable IIAs. This is to say, if states made any reference to international anti-corruption conventions, such norms should be the appropriate standards for application when arbitrators confronting with corruption submissions.

1.1 Overview

As a matter of fact, international investment arbitral tribunals have begun to address corruption issues raised by parties with an increasing frequency since 2000. Around 30 cases of investor-state disputes have so far involved corruption issues, showcasing varying degrees of prominence addressed by tribunals convened under the Convention on the Settlement of Investment Disputes between States and Nationals of Other States (ICSID Convention) or the United Nations Commission on International Trade Law (UNCITRAL).[12] In most of these cases, corruption allegations were raised by host states as an objection to the jurisdiction *rationae temporis* or *rationae personae* of the tribunals, or as a defense justifying the complete dismissal of investors' claims on the merits.[13] However, since corrupt activities are commonly conducted covertly, the alleged corruption facts are difficult to prove. As revealed by the current investment arbitration case law, the proportion of failed corruption allegations is particularly large. This, however, does not signify that corruption issues can never prosper; instead, arbitral tribunals have indeed supported several corruption allegations in distinct cases, including *World Duty Free v. Kenya*, *Metal-Tech v. Uzbekistan*, and *Spantex v. Uzbekistan.*

12 Cecily Rose, 'Questioning the Role of International Arbitration in the Fight Against Corruption' (2014) 31 Journal of International Arbitration 183, 183; Llamzon (n 3) 305–320. Dr Aloysius Llamzon identified 28 international investment cases addressed by ICSID arbitral tribunals or UNCITRAL tribunals with varying degrees of discussion about corruption issues in his book; after the publication of this book, other investment tribunals have heard several new investment disputes involving corruption issues, such as *Spentex v. Uzbekistan* (2016) and *Vladislav Kim and others v. Uzbekistan* (2017).

13 Llamzon (n 3) 198–200; Andreas Kulick and Carsten Wendler, 'A Corruption Way to Handle Corruption? Thoughts on the Recent ICSID Case Law on Corruption' (2010) 37 Legal Issues of Economic Integration 61, 62; Stephan Wilske & Willa Obel, 'The "Corruption Objection" to Jurisdiction in Investment Arbitration' in Krista Nadakavukaren Schefer (ed), *Poverty and the International Economic Legal System* (CUP 2013) 177, 185.

1.2 Anti-corruption conventions in international investment arbitration

It has to be highlighted that among all these corruption-involved arbitration cases, the arbitrators did not rely on any anti-corruption provisions to adjudicate corruption-related submissions.[14] This is because the state parties did not incorporate any such anti-corruption clauses (not to mention any reference to international anti-corruption conventions) into their bilateral investment treaties (BITs) or investment chapters in other forms of economic treaties applicable to the cases concerned.

Still, the international investment arbitral tribunals have occasionally resorted to the international and regional anti-corruption conventions to deal with allegations of corruption raised by the parties. For instance, in *World Duty Free v. Kenya* (2006), the tribunal firstly noted that 'bribery or influence peddling, as well as both active and passive corruption, are sanctioned by criminal law in most, if not all, countries'[15] and then presented a number of international and regional anti-corruption conventions and their ratifications in chronological order, aiming at 'render[ing] more effective this general condemnation.'[16] This includes those instruments developed by the Organization of American States, the Organization for Economic Cooperation and Development, the Council of Europe, the African Union, and the United Nations.[17] In particular, the tribunal attached great importance to the AUCPCC and the UNCAC and concisely illustrated the anti-corruption commitment and international obligations therein.[18] This is because Kenya is one of the contracting states to these two treaties and such emphasis assists the interpretation of anti-corruption standards, mainly from the criminal law aspect, confirmed by the parties involved in this case.

In another case, namely *Metal-Tech v. Uzbekistan* (2013), the arbitrators also briefly discussed the current effective international anti-corruption conventions and affirmed their 'administrative and civil law aspects relating to the fight against corruption.'[19] The tribunal then made a mention of the award of the *World Duty Free v. Kenya* case to confirm the existence of international public policy against corruption.[20] Whereas in *Vladislav Kim and others v. Uzbekistan* (2017), the tribunal focused on the scope of corruption aspect after reviewing the international

14 Yueming Yan, 'A Comprehensive Chapter on Anti-Corruption in the China-EU CAI: A Progressive or an Unnecessary Step?' in Yuwen Li, Tong Qi, and Cheng Bian (eds), *China, the EU and International Investment Law: Reforming Investor-State Dispute Settlement* (Routledge 2020) 227, 231.

15 *World Duty Free Company v Republic of Kenya*, ICSID Case No Arb/00/7, Award of 4 October 2006 [142].

16 Ibid [143].

17 Ibid [143]–[145].

18 Ibid [143]–[145].

19 *Metal-Tech Ltd v. Republic of Uzbekistan*, ICSID Case No ARB/10/3, Award of 4 October 2013 [290]–[291].

20 Ibid [290]–[292].

instruments on corruption. It observed that there actually exists 'a lower level of consensus as to corruption within the private sector'[21] and concluded that the present international public policy against corruption mainly focuses on 'situations that aim at the corruption of governmental officials.'[22]

In spite of the absence of anti-corruption provisions in the IIAs concerned, international and regional anti-corruption conventions play an important role in the decision-making process in the investor-state arbitration. By examining these anti-corruption norms, the tribunals were able to identify the current status of the 'anti-corruption policy issue' worldwide. So far, the international and regional anti-corruption conventions were approached by arbitral tribunals to confirm the presence of the consensus on combating and condemning corruption achieved among states, no matter from the criminal, civil or administrative aspects. This observance is essential for the tribunal in the case of *World Duty Free v. Kenya* to draw the conclusion that 'bribery is contrary to the international public policy of most, if not all, States or, to use another formula, to transnational public policy,'[23] which was afterwards constantly supported by tribunals in *Metal-Tech v. Uzbekistan* and in *Vladislav Kim and others v. Uzbekistan.*

1.3 Providing tools for arbitrators to address corruption allegations

Other than the above recognition, there are indeed some to-be-clarified problems in the corruption context, such as the precise definition and scope of corruption, the appropriate standard of proof and admissible evidence, and the legal consequence of corruption in international investment activities. These contentious issues are hard to solve in cases where arbitrators are not able to refer to international anti-corruption standards due to its silence in the applicable IIA. This scenario may yet occur even when arbitrators have introduced international anti-corruption conventions and make decisions in accordance with these conventions.

For instance, the 'clear and convincing evidence' and 'reasonably certainty' standards of proof have been applied respectively by the tribunal in *EDF (Services) v. Romania* (2009),[24] and the tribunal in *Metal-Tech v. Uzbekistan* (2013).[25] The arbitrators in the former case considered it as a much higher standard of proof of corruption considered the 'seriousness of the accusation of corruption in the present case,'[26] whereas the tribunal in the latter one considered standard of proof as a '*lex causae*' issue when it provided that:

21 *Vladislav Kim and others v. Republic of Uzbekistan*, ICSID Case No ARB/13/6, Decision on Jurisdiction of 8 March 2017 [596].
22 Ibid [594].
23 *World Duty Free v. Kenya* (n 15) [157].
24 *EDF (Services) Ltd. v. Romania*, ICSID Case No ARB/05/13, Award of 8 October 2009 [221].
25 *Metal-Tech v. Uzbekistan* (n 19) [243].
26 *EDF (Services) v. Romania* (n 24) [221].

> Rules establishing presumptions or shifting the burden of proof under certain circumstances, or drawing inferences from a lack of proof are generally deemed to be part of the lex causae. In the present case, the lex causae is essentially the BIT, which provides no rules for shifting the burden of proof or establishing presumptions. Therefore, the Tribunal has relative freedom in determining the standard necessary to sustain a determination of corruption.[27]

The tribunals have also applied distinct proving standards in some other cases: in *Vladislav Kim v. Uzbekistan*, the tribunal noted that since the alleged corrupt act was in violation of a particular domestic law, 'the standard of proof to be employed is that provided for in that law;'[28] in *African Holding v. Democratic Republic Congo*, irrefutable evidence was required by the tribunal to prove the serious defense of bribe allegations;[29] in *TSA Spectrum v. Argentina*, the tribunal required the most rigorous level of proof as to an accusation of bribery but did not specify the precise one;[30] in *Wena Hotels v. Egypt*, the tribunal examined the evidence presented in connection with corruption allegations but did not point out a specific applicable standard of proof.[31]

As stated in the case of *Vladislav Kim and others v. Uzbekistan* (2017), 'the task of specifying the content of an international public policy against corruption may be undertaken by reference to international instruments addressing corruption.'[32] The fact that international anti-corruption obligations and standards have seldom been incorporated into IIAs thus possibly contributes to the above uncertainties, leading to a lack of substantive guidance for arbitrators to address corruption allegations,[33] as well as a shortage of affirmative decisions on this matter.[34] On the other hand, standardization of anti-corruption issues (both substantive and procedural) in detail in IIAs by states will provide arbitrators necessary tools to address corruption allegations, which will contribute to avoiding the above dilemma, explicating competence of arbitrators, mitigating critics of legitimacy and consistency of arbitration awards and engaging in international anti-corruption movement in a more effective way.

27 *Metal-Tech v. Uzbekistan* (n 19) [238].

28 *Vladislav Kim and others v. Uzbekistan* (n 21) [545].

29 *African Holding Company of America, Inc and Société Africaine de Construction au Congo SARL v. La République démocratique du Congo*, ICSID Case No ARB/05/21, Sentence sur les déclinatoires de compétence et la recevabilité of 29 July 2008 [52].

30 *TSA Spectrum de Argentina SA v. Argentine Republic*, ICSID Case No ARB/05/5, Award of 19 December 2008 [172].

31 *Wena Hotels Ltd v. Arab Republic of Egypt*, ICSID Case No ARB/98/4, Award of 8 December 2000, 41 ILM 896 (2002) 917–18.

32 *Vladislav Kim and others v. Uzbekistan* (n 21) [594].

33 Llamzon (n 3) 62.

34 Mbiyavanga (n 2) 5.

2 Anti-corruption conventions in international investment agreements

Incorporating international anti-corruption standards into IIAs not only enables international investment arbitral tribunals to participate in this global anti-corruption campaign but also indicates intensified efforts by states to combat corruption in international investment activities.

2.1 Overview

It is fair to say that a growing recognition has been achieved that addressing transnational anti-corruption issues requires not only effective international and regional conventions aiming at combating corruption, but also considerations against corruption in the legal frameworks that facilitate international trade and investment. In practice, among the existing over 3,000 IIAs, there are indeed some provisions addressing anti-corruption issues in both the preamble and the main text, engaging in substantive and/or procedural issues with a broad variety.[35]

As a most recent revolution, we do witness some changes in coverage of this issue over the past decade as well as a concurrence of both the variation and harmonization in the treatment of issues. Although countries have adopted distinct approaches to anti-corruption concerns in their IIAs and a great diversity has been observed in these anti-corruption provisions in terms of the forms, the wording language and the content, the treatments that states employ to anti-corruption in IIAs do not present a comprehensive or embedded framework.

First and foremost, many states chose to incorporate anti-corruption statements in the preamble of BITs or free trade agreements (FTAs), which forms an integral part of an IIA and in most times serves as guidance when drafting and validating the main text of the treaty. States manage to express their commitment to combating corruption either in explicit or implicit ways. For instance, in the European Union (EU)–Singapore Investment Protection Agreement (2018), the preamble provides:

> DETERMINE to strengthen their economic, trade, and investment relations in accordance with the objective of sustainable development, in its economic, social and environmental dimensions, and to promote investment in a manner mindful of high levels of environmental and labor protection and

35 See UNCTAD (United Nations Conference on Trade and Development), 'Mapping of IIA Content' <https://investmentpolicy.unctad.org/international-investment-agreements/iia-mapping#iiaInnerMenu> accessed 1 June 2020.

> relevant internationally-recognized standards and agreements to which they are parties.[36]

This is a case where the parties of the investment agreement implicitly state their determination to combating corruption through words like 'objective of sustainable development' and 'relevant internationally-recognized standards and agreements.' While in the preamble of the Canada-Burkina Faso BIT (2015), the two states confirm their engagement of anti-corruption in a much more explicit manner where they recognize 'the undertakings in the *United Nations Convention against Corruption*.'[37]

Another way of engaging in anti-corruption relied upon by states in the IIA-making practice is inserting anti-corruption obligations within clauses addressing other issues, like corporate social responsibility.[38] For instance, in the Colombia–Costa Rica FTA (2013), Article 12.9 (Corporate Social Responsibility) stipulates that:

> Each Party shall encourage companies that operate in its territory or that are subject to its jurisdiction to voluntarily incorporate within its internal policies, internationally recognized standards of corporate social responsibility that have been approved by the Parties. These principles address issues such as labor rights, environment, human rights, community relations and the fight against corruption.[39]

Even though the state parties are not imposing a direct obligation of anti-corruption upon investors, this clause truly reveals their collaborative intention with regard to eliminating corrupt acts in enterprises within their respective jurisdictions. In spite of the feature of 'soft law' of the corporate social responsibility clause, the word 'shall' indeed represents states' affirmation of their anti-corruption responsibilities and duties under the universal anti-corruption campaign.

More importantly, a separate clause or even chapter addressing corruption issues has recently been approached by states, signifying the increasing importance attached to the fight against corruption in international investment law. Such a type of separate clause might be abstract where no specific measures are proposed, such as in the Japan-Oman BIT (2015) where Article 8 (Measures against Corruption) provides that '[e]ach Contracting Party shall ensure that

36 Preamble, EU–Singapore Investment Protection Agreement (2018), signed on 15 October 2018.

37 Preamble, Burkina Faso–Canada (2015), signed on 20 April 2015, entered into force on 11 October 2017.

38 Andrea Bjorklund, Yarik Kryvoi, and Jean-Michel Marcoux, 'Investment Promotion and Protection in the Canada-UK Trade Relationship' (2018) SSRN Working Paper <https://papers.ssrn.com/abstract=3312617> accessed 1 June 2020, 24–26.

39 Costa Rica–Colombia FTA (2013), signed on 22 May 2013, entered into force on 1 August 2016, art 12.9 (Corporate Social Responsibility).

measures and efforts are undertaken to prevent and combat corruption regarding matters covered by this Agreement in accordance with its laws and regulations.'[40]

On the other hand, states may also incorporate a range of concrete obligations, such as establishing the definition, scope, and liability of corruption in domestic legislation and promoting bilateral, multilateral cooperation measures in relation to corruption prevention. An appropriate example here should be the Comprehensive and Progressive Agreement for Trans-Pacific Partnership (CPTPP) (2018) where a comprehensive and lengthy chapter (Chapter 26 Transparency and Anti-Corruption) is provided, including Article 26.6 (Scope), Article 26.7 (Measures to Combat Corruption), Article 26.8 (Promoting Integrity among Public Officials), Article 26.9 (Application and Enforcement of Anti-Corruption Laws), Article 26.10 (Participation of Private Sector and Society), Article 26.11 (Relation to Other Agreements), and Article 26.12 (Dispute Settlement).[41]

2.2 Anti-corruption conventions in IIAs

Another type of anti-corruption provision observed in the present IIAs is establishing international/regional anti-corruption conventions as references and standards that state parties should rely on when confronting any potential corruption-related issues in this investment promotion and protection collaboration (see the attached Annex). The reference to international anti-corruption conventions plays an important role in regulating rules towards international investment transactions. They affirm the anti-corruption standards that states should comply with when establishing international investment cooperation and when dealing with any disputes arising from the involved investment treaty.

This type of anti-corruption provisions can, in practice, be divided into different groups in accordance with distinct criteria. First of all, such reference to international anti-corruption standards can be either direct or indirect. Among most of this type of anti-corruption provisions, the parties generally gave very specific standards that states shall refer to. For instance, in the Guatemala-Trinidad and Tobago BIT (2013), Article 17 states that '[i]n accordance with their respective laws and regulations, each Contracting Party shall endeavor to … uphold anticorruption practices in accordance with the United Nations

40 Japan–Oman BIT (2015), signed on 19 June 2015, entered into force on 21 July 2017, art 8 (Measures against Corruption).

41 The Comprehensive and Progressive Agreement for Trans-Pacific Partnership (CPTPP) (2018), signed on 8 March 2018, entered into force on 30 December 2018, ch 26 (Transparency and Anti-Corruption).

Convention Against Corruption, done at New York, October 31, 2003.'[42] However, in other cases, international anti-corruption standards were not precisely or clearly pointed out, such as in the US–Singapore FTA (2003), Article 21.5 says that '[t]he Parties further commit to undertake best efforts to associate themselves with appropriate international anti-corruption instruments and to encourage and support appropriate anti-corruption initiatives and activities in relevant international fora.'[43]

Among those specific international anti-corruption conventions, their binding effects may be at an international level or a regional one. In the US–Peru Trade Promotion Agreement (2006), Article 19.8.2 (Cooperation in International Fora) provides that '[t]he Parties reaffirm their existing rights and obligations under the 1997 Inter-American Convention Against Corruption and shall work toward the implementation of measures to prevent and combat corruption consistent with the 2003 United Nations Convention Against Corruption.'[44] While the instruments of the Council of Europe are also frequently referred to in some of the EU's IIAs, for instance, the EU–Moldova Association Agreement (2014) where the contracting parties:

> are committed to implementing effectively the relevant international standards, and in particular those enshrined in the United Nations Convention against Transnational Organized Crime of the 2000 and its three Protocols, the United Nations Convention against Corruption of 2003, and relevant Council of Europe instruments on preventing and combating corruption.[45]

The standards may highly depend on whether the conventions are effective among both contracting parties, but in some cases, other conventions or instruments may also be cited even though they are not contracting parties to this specific anti-corruption convention. A pertinent example should be the EU–Armenia Comprehensive and Enhanced Partnership Agreement (2017) where Article 16 provides that '[t]he Parties shall cooperate in preventing and fighting corruption in line with the UN Convention Against Corruption of

42 Guatemala–Trinidad and Tobago BIT (2013), signed on 13 August 2013, entered into force 23 June 2016, art 17 (General Provisions).

43 US–Singapore FTA (2003), signed on 6 May 2003, entered into force 1 January 2004, art 21.5 (Anti-Corruption).

44 Peru–US Trade Promotion Agreement (2016), signed on 12 April 2006, entered into force on 1 February 2009, art 19.8 (Cooperation in International Fora).

45 EU–Moldova Association Agreement (2014), signed on 27 June 2014, entered into force on 1 July 2016, art 16 (Preventing and combating organized crime, corruption and other illegal activities).

2003, the recommendations of the Group of States against corruption and the OECD.'[46]

Instruments having limited binding effect may also be referred by states, such as in the CPTPP (2018) where parties 'affirm their adherence to the APEC Conduct Principles for Public Officials, encourage observance of the APEC Code of Conduct for Business: Business Integrity and Transparency Principles for the Private Sector.'[47] While in the United States–Mexico–Canada Agreement (2018), in addition to the OECD Convention, IACAC and UNCAC, a number of anti-corruption documents developed by the APEC or the G20 anti-corruption fora are recommended to be supported by states, such as the G20 Guiding Principles on Enforcement of the Foreign Bribery Offence (2013), G20 Guiding Principles to Combat Solicitation, G20 High Level Principles on the Liability of Legal Persons for Corruption, APEC Conduct Principles for Public Officials, and the APEC Principles on the Prevention of Bribery and Enforcement of Anti-Bribery Laws.[48]

It is worthy to note that, as seen in the Annex, the reference to the international and regional anti-corruption conventions does not normally present in treaties addressing bilateral investment transactions (except the Guatemala–Trinidad and Tobago BIT). Rather, parties prefer to incorporate such standards in clauses or chapters discussing general issues in FTAs (not the investment chapter) or other forms of trade agreements, like EU's association agreements while these provisions are, at the same time, applicable to investment activities. The information in this Annex table also allows us to believe that such practice was formally initiated by the US since we can observe several implicit statements of referring anti-corruption treaties in the US FTAs signed in the early years. The EU then followed this practice in some of its association agreements and framework agreements in the past ten years.

Overall, the number of anti-corruption provisions where international and/or regional anti-corruption conventions are inserted as references is quite limited. In other words, incorporating anti-corruption conventions as standards is not a common practice engaged by states when formulating their new bilateral or multilateral investment agreements. In spite of that, we do witness a growing awareness of the importance of reaffirming the standards incorporated in international anti-corruption conventions as well as an increasing number of such types of anti-corruption provisions in the IIA-making practice.

46 Armenia–EU Comprehensive and Enhanced Partnership Agreement (2017), signed on 24 November 2017, art 16 (Fighting against organized crime and corruption).

47 CPTPP ch 26 (Transparency and Anti-Corruption).

48 United States–Mexico–Canada Agreement (2018), signed on 30 November 2018, ch 27 (Anti-Corruption).

2.3 Fulfilling international anti-corruption commitment

Considering the small number of anti-corruption provisions in the present IIAs, the statements are somehow acceptable that IIAs are not frequently utilized by states as a tool to achieve their objectives of anti-corruption and that international and national policies against corruption remain the main avenues states take on this challenge.[49] However, a critical ground explicating this phenomenon should be the fact that global anti-corruption movement has effectively taken place in the last 20 years. This is why corruption deterrence and elimination, particularly transnational corruption, was not one of states' major concerns until the late 20th century when the first international anti-corruption convention—the IACAC—became effective in 1997. Afterwards, an international framework of anti-corruption laws has sprouted and almost all states have more or less involved in this worldwide campaign.

For instance, the OECD Convention was adopted by the negotiating conference on November 21, 1997 and entered into force on February 15, 1999.[50] It now has 44 signatories consisting of all OECD countries and eight non-OECD countries and has been recognized as the first and so far the only international anti-corruption instrument that is focused on the supply side of an act of bribery.[51] In the preamble, the convention in the very first sentence points out that 'bribery is a widespread phenomenon in international business transactions, including trade and investment,' and immediately in the second paragraph recognizes that 'all countries share a responsibility to combat bribery in international business transactions.'[52]

More importantly, the UNCAC, the first universal anti-corruption treaty with 186 state parties, was adopted by the United Nations on October 31, 2003 and became effective on December 14, 2005.[53] The high number of ratifications reflects the collective intent and strong determinations of the international

49 Gordon (n 11) 139.

50 Besides, the OECD also adopted various related recommendations and guidelines, most notably the 2009 Recommendation of the Council for Further Combating Bribery of Foreign Public Officials in International Business Transactions, the 2009 Recommendation of the Council on Tax Measures for Further Combating Bribery of Foreign Public Officials in International Business Transactions, the 2006 Recommendation of the Council on Bribery and Officially Supported Export Credits, and the 2016 Recommendation of the Council for Development Co-operation Actors on Managing the Risk of Corruption. Although these instruments are non-binding, their accompanying the binding OECD Convention will further the implementation and enforcement of the OECD Convention in a more effective way. See OECD, 'OECD Convention on Combating Bribery of Foreign Public Officials in International Business Transactions' <http://www.oecd.org/daf/anti-bribery/oecdantibriberyconvention.htm> accessed 1 June 2020.

51 Ibid.

52 OECD Convention, preamble.

53 See UNODC, 'United Nations Convention against Corruption' <https://www.unodc.org/unodc/en/corruption/uncac.html> accessed 1 June 2020.

community on corruption elimination and deterrence. Furthermore, the comprehensive and in-depth provisions regarding preventive measures, criminalization and law enforcement, international cooperation, asset recovery, and technical assistance and information exchange evidence the treaty's innovation and significance to the global anti-corruption campaign.

The emergence of international anti-corruption conventions and increasing ratifications by states indicate incremental awareness of the importance of collectively combating corruption, along with other implications. Since then, the need to include terms with respect to anti-corruption in investment treaties has gradually come to countries' notice. It is fair to say that provisions addressing anti-corruption issues started to be included in IIAs right after the emergence of an international consensus on combating corruption was evidenced by the conclusions of international anti-corruption conventions. These instruments not only require member states to take effective measures to combat corruption within states but also to cooperate in international and regional fora.

Inserting anti-corruption provisions in IIAs, although not explicitly required by these principal international anti-corruption treaties, enables states, in a novel way, to achieve the aims of eliminating corruption, and thus forms an important part of implementing obligations under these international anti-corruption conventions. By doing so, international investment law acts as a complementary contributor to curbing corruption worldwide, and all states are therefore advised to incorporate anti-corruption clauses into their new IIAs.

The fact that states have reiterated their adherence to international anti-corruption conventions in their newly signed IIAs should be deemed as their direct response to the international obligations created in these instruments. More precisely, the UNCAC is the most commonly referred-to instrument, partly because it has the largest number of contracting parties and partly because of its emphasis on prohibiting both sides of corruption, namely giving and accepting (or soliciting) a bribe, which is aligned with the inherent bilateral feature of a corrupt act conducted between an investor and a public official in the international investment activities context. Some states have additionally included standards in the OECD Convention or other regional anti-corruption treaties, such as the IACAC, as supplemental resources to carry out their commitments. The selection of international anti-corruption standards highly depends on the geographical area to which the states belong and on their association with the treaties concerned.

Furthermore, incorporating relevant international and/or regional anti-corruption standards into IIAs is also an approach to promote harmonization of the domestic legal systems of the states concerned.[54] Virtually every state has outlawed corruption and has established the standards that should be employed to evidence such acts,[55] whereas there are indeed considerable divergences among

54 Yan (n 14) 231.
55 Llamzon (n 3) 70.

these resources.[56] The enforcement of the award rendered will then be challenged when the tribunal applied the standards largely different from those employed in domestic courts or tribunals, thereby jeopardizing the integrity of national legal system and international investment arbitration regime.[57] However, the standards in the international anti-corruption conventions may be different. For instance, the scope and definition of an act of corruption in different anti-corruption conventions may vary greatly. The OECD Convention does not embrace the demand side of a corrupt act and only covers certain types of corruption of foreign public officials. The silence in this treaty on the legal consequences of solicitation or acceptance of a bribe[58] might lead to an asymmetric result for the two parties to a corrupt act, i.e., the giver and the accepter (or the solicitor). The two parties in an international investment activity are investors and public officials of host states. This asymmetry in liability may evolve into an incentive of encouraging transnational corruption rather than having the effect of deterring and combating corruption,[59] thereby conflicting with the object and purpose of the OECD Convention. Nevertheless, the UNCAC comprehensively addresses both supply side and demand side, both solicitation and acceptance, of corruption and enumerates a wider range of corrupt acts of both foreign and national officials as well as private sectors. Precisely, the UNCAC sheds light on the necessity of criminalizing the soliciting and accepting of a bribe by a public official, in addition to the supply side of a corrupt act, requiring that all state parties establish both givers and accepters (in other words, bribers and bribees) as offenses and impose sanctions through domestic legislation.[60] It seems that balancing liabilities for both parties could essentially promote good governance and transparency and effectively achieve the desired outcomes. International investment arbitration may also benefit from this approach when tribunals are called on to adjudicate anti-corruption allegations raised by investors or host states. This might constitute another reason to explain why the UNCAC is much more preferred, than the OECD Convention, by investment arbitrators and in the IIA formulating process.

Another significant inconsistency relates to issues of facilitation payments. When the clarification in the Commentaries on the OECD Convention on

56 Lorenzo Cotula, *Foreign Investment, Law and Sustainable Development: A Handbook on Agriculture and Extractive Industries* (2nd edn, Institute for Environment and Development 2016) 120.

57 Yan (n 14) 231.

58 In fact, in the preamble of the OECD Convention, all parties have recognized 'the role of governments in the prevention of solicitation of bribes from individuals and enterprises in international business transactions', but no corresponding provisions were offered in the main text.

59 Llamzon (n 3) 242, 256, 277–279; Jason Webb Yackee, 'Investment Treaties and Investor Corruption: An Emerging Defense for Host States Essay' (2012) 3 Virginia Journal of International Law 723, 744.

60 UNCAC, art 15.

Combating Bribery of Foreign Public Officials in International Business Transactions (Commentaries on the OECD Convention) stated that facilitation payments do not constitute bribery offenses as described under Article 1 of the OECD Convention,[61] the UNCAC has explicitly outlawed such conduct. The UNCAC has stated, in a clear manner, that small facilitation payments are not excluded from the scope of corruption defined under the UNCAC, which covers bribes undertaken for both the purpose of obtaining or retaining business and attaining 'other advantage in relation to the conduct of international business.'[62] Provided that facilitation payments do not impede fair and free business activities, the reason for the disparity in treating 'grease' payments between these two conventions arguably lies in their respective focuses. While the OECD Convention mainly addresses corruption 'as a distortion of free competition,' the UNCAC emphasizes 'a much more comprehensive penalization of bribery.'[63] More precisely, the UNCAC is not basically concerned with ensuring 'fair and free trade,' but suggests the problems and threats brought by corruption to the stability and security of societies need to be addressed.[64]

In other words, an IIA that simply refers to these international anti-corruption conventions may also generate innumerable challenges to tribunals with regard to applicable standards or other associated issues and, accordingly, jeopardize the effectiveness of their efforts to eliminate corruption. Consequently, to pursue the objective of effective corruption deterrence in the international investment law domain, an operative measure would be introducing relevant international anti-corruption standards into IIAs along with necessary clarifications and adequate explanations when the standards listed are inconsistent; accordingly, challenges due to the vagueness of the legal rules and standards will be avoided. Alternatively, rules with enhanced precision about how should states and arbitrators address corrupt acts while no reference to international anti-corruption standards could also ensure the rule of justice domestically and internationally and the effectiveness of corruption prevention at the same time.

3 Conclusions

This chapter intends to present a study between international anti-corruption conventions and international investment law, in particular, how arbitrators utilize international anti-corruption conventions to adjudicate corruption

61 Commentaries on the Convention on Combating Bribery of Foreign Public Officials in International Business Transactions, adopted on 21 November 1997, [9].

62 UNCAC, art 16(1).

63 Michael Kubiciel, 'Core Criminal Law Provisions in the United Nations Convention against Corruption' (2009) 9 International Criminal Law Review 139, 154.

64 Ibid.

submissions and how states formulate their anti-corruption provisions by incorporating universal or regional legal anti-corruption norms in their recently signed IIAs.

The current major international or regional anti-corruption conventions are not initially concluded under the purpose of serving the international investment law system; however, eliminating and deterring corruption in international investment activities indeed falls within the aims of these norms. On the other hand, a variety of practice has been observed that international anti-corruption conventions are referred to in the bilateral and multilateral investment treaty drafting and in the investor-state arbitration.

It is true that the applicable IIAs in corruption-involved cases contain none of anti-corruption provisions, accordingly nothing about international or regional anti-corruption conventions. But these norms were yet relied upon in several cases (such as *World Duty Free v. Kenya*, *Metal-Tech v. Uzbekistan*, and *Vladislav Kim and other v. Uzbekistan*) by arbitrators to address some basic issues of corruption like confirming the presence of international public policy against corruption. However, a large number of other issues in relation to this concept, such as the applicative standard of proving corruption acts, remain controversial and need to be solved consistently and urgently. These uncertainties might to some extent be avoided by introducing anti-corruption provisions to IIAs, thereby standardizing anti-corruption issues.

At the same time, we do witness an increase in anti-corruption provisions in the recent IIA-making practice. In addition to approaching anti-corruption in the preamble, within other clauses and through a comprehensive chapter, referring to international and regional anti-corruption conventions has become one of the categories of provisions addressing anti-corruption. Although this is not a prevailing practice engaged by states, it implies their intensified efforts to combat corruption in international investment activities and indicates states' growing recognition of the importance of reaffirming the standards incorporated in the international anti-corruption conventions. However, incorporating these norms into IIAs is far from satisfactory due to some intrinsic inconsistencies in relation, for instance, to the scope of corruption. The divergence on the facilitation payment in the UNCAC and the OECD Convention should be one such significant difference.

All in all, it is suggested to introduce relevant international anti-corruption standards into IIAs with necessary clarifications, or alternatively, to insert rules with enhanced precision about how should states and arbitrators treat corruption in cases where no reference to international anti-corruption conventions is made. This will then benefit to achieving multi-fold purposes, including fulfilling international anti-corruption commitment in the international investment law domain, offering practical tools for arbitrators to address corruption allegations, and eventually combating and preventing corruption in a more effective way.

International Anti-Corruption Conventions in IIAs

No.	*Parties*	*Agreement Title*	*Status*	*Date of Signature*	*Date of Entry into Force*	*Clause(s)*	*Referred International/Regional Anti-Corruption Norms*
1	United States Singapore	Free Trade Agreement	In force	06-May-03	01-Jan-04	Chapter 21 (General and Final) Art.21.5 Anti-Corruption	'appropriate international anti-corruption instruments'
2	United States Morocco	Free Trade Agreement	In force	15-Jun-04	01-Jan-06	Chapter 18 (Transparency) Art.18.5 Anti-Corruption	'regional and multilateral initiatives to eliminate bribery and corruption'
3	United States Oman	Free Trade Agreement	In force	19-Jan-06	01-Jan-09	Chapter 18 (Transparency) Art.18.5 Anti-Corruption	'regional and multilateral initiatives to eliminate bribery and corruption'
4	United States Peru	Trade Promotion Agreement	In force	12-Apr-06	01-Feb-09	Chapter 19 (Transparency) Section B Anti-Corruption	UNCAC IACAC
5	United States Korea	Free Trade Agreement	In force	30-Jun-07	15-Mar-12	Chapter 21 (Transparency) Art.21.6 Anti-Corruption	'regional and multilateral initiatives to eliminate bribery and corruption'
6	European Union Cameroon	Economic Partnership Agreement	Signed (not in force)	15-Jan-09	/	TITLE VIII (General and Final Provisions) Art.105 Collaboration in tackling illegal financial activities	UNCAC UNCTOC and its protocols
7	European Union Korea	Framework Agreement	Signed (not in force)	10-May-10	/	TITLE VII (Cooperation in the area of justice, freedom and security) Art.35 Combating organised crime and corruption	UNCAC UNCTOC and its supplementing protocols
8	European Union Iraq	Partnership and Cooperation Agreement	Signed (not in force)	11-May-12	/	TITLE IV (Justice, Freedom and Security) Art.106 Combating organised crime and corruption	UNCAC UNCTOC and its supplementing protocols
9	European Union Viet Nam	Framework Agreement on Comprehensive Partnership and Cooperation	Signed (not in force)	27-Jun-12	/	TITLE V (Cooperation in the area of justice) Art.23 Combating organized crime	UNCAC UNCTOC and its supplementing protocols

(*Contined*)

(Contined)

International Anti-Corruption Conventions in IIAs

No.	Parties	Agreement Title	Status	Date of Signature	Date of Entry into Force	Clause(s)	Referred International/Regional Anti-Corruption Norms
10	European Union CACM (Central American Common Market)	Association Agreement	Signed (not in force)	29-Jun-12	/	TITLE II (Justice, Freedom and Security) Art.37 Organised Crime and Citizen Security	UNCAC UNCTOC and its supplementing protocols
11	Guatemala Trinidad and Tobago	Bilateral Investment Treaty	In force	13-Aug-13	23-Jun-16	Art.17 General Provisions	UNCAC
12	European Union Georgia	Association Agreement	In force	26-Jun-14	01-Jul-16	TITLE III (Justice, Freedom and Security) Art.37 Fight against organized crime and corruption	UNCAC UNCTOC and its three protocols
13	European Union Ukraine	Association Agreement	In force	27-Jun-14	01-Jan-16	TITLE III (Justice, Freedom and Security) Art.22 Fight against crime and corruption	UNCAC UNCTOC and its three protocols
14	European Union Moldova	Association Agreement	In force	27-Jun-14	01-Jul-16	TITLE III (Justice, Freedom and Security) Art.16 Preventing and combating organised crime, corruption and other illegal activities	UNCAC 'relevant Council of Europe instruments on preventing and combating corruption'
15	European Union Kazakhstan	Enhanced Partnership and Cooperation Agreement	Signed (not in force)	21-Dec-15	/	TITLE V (Cooperation in the area of freedom, security and justice) Art.242 Fight against organized and transnational crime and corruption	UNCAC UNCTOC and its three protocols 'Council of Europe relevant instruments on preventing and combating corruption'
16	European Union Armenia	Comprehensive and Enhanced Partnership Agreement	Signed (not in force)	24-Nov-17	/	TITLE III (Justice, Freedom and Security) Art.16 Fight against organized crime and corruption	UNCAC 'recommendations of the Group of States against Corruption (GRECO) and the OECD'

(Contined)

(*Contined*)

International Anti-Corruption Conventions in IIAs

No.	*Parties*	*Agreement Title*	*Status*	*Date of Signature*	*Date of Entry into Force*	*Clause(s)*	*Referred International/Regional Anti-Corruption Norms*
17	Australia Brunei Canada Chile Japan Malaysia Mexico New Zealand Peru Singapore Vietnam	Comprehensive and Progressive Agreement for Trans-Pacific Partnership (CPTPP)	In force	08-Mar-18	30-Dec-18	Chapter 26 (Transparency and Anti-Corruption) Section C Anti-Corruption	UNCAC UNCTOC OECD Anti-Bribery Convention with its Annex IACAC APEC Conduct Principles for Public Officials APEC Code of Conduct for Business: Business Integrity and Transparency
18	United States Mexico Canada	United States-Mexico-Canada Agreement (USMCA)	In force	30-Nov-18	2-Jul-20	Chapter 27 Anti-Corruption	OECD Anti-Bribery Convention with its Annex IACAC UNCAC UNCTOC G20 High Level Principles on Organizing against Corruption G20 High Level Principles on Corruption and Growth G20 Guiding Principles on Enforcement of the Foreign Bribery Offence (2013) G20 Guiding Principles to Combat Solicitation G20 High Level Principles on the Liability of Legal Persons for Corruption APEC Conduct Principles for Public Officials APEC Principles on the Prevention of Bribery and Enforcement of Anti-Bribery Law APEC Code of Conduct for Business: Business Integrity and Transparency Principles for the Private Sector APEC General Elements of Effective Voluntary Corporate Compliance Programs G20 High Level Principles on Private Sector Transparency and Integrity

UNCAC United Nations Convention Against Corruption; IACAC Inter-American Convention Against Corruption; OECD Anti-Bribery Convention OECD Convention on Combating Bribery of Public Officials in International Business Transactions; UNCTOC United Nations Convention against Transnational Organized Crime

Part V

Challenges in the transnational enforcement of anti-corruption laws

20 The global diffusion of DPAs

The not so functional remaking of the rules against business corruption

Simon St-Georges and Denis Saint-Martin

This chapter focuses on the international proliferation of new alternative justice mechanisms developed to fight business corruption since the early 2000s. We examine how political science and sociology could explain the proliferation of deferred prosecution agreements (DPAs), non-prosecution agreements (NPAs), and of similar instruments in various jurisdictions, including the United Kingdom, France, and Canada. Originally developed for individual first-time offenders with rehabilitation potential, DPAs now allow states to suspend and eventually rescind criminal proceedings against businesses, without formal recognition of criminal liability. This solution allows the entity to preserve its public contracts, and arguably to minimize the impacts on its reputation, leading proponents of DPAs to argue that it can save business entities while allowing proper consequences. Businesses signing DPAs will suffer financial penalties, and they should, in principle, adopt internal reforms in addition to committing to proper behaviour for the duration of the DPA.

Are these new justice instruments uncontentious, agreed upon, and spreading because of their inherent merits? Or are they proliferating despite their more controversial features and policy implications? Further to a critical review of the specialized literature on DPAs, we show that the latter hypothesis is more convincing.

In the first section of this chapter, we describe and analyze DPAs in a context where key anti-corruption laws became increasingly extraterritorial in their nature, notably with the rise of the 1977 American *Foreign Corrupt Practices Act* (FCPA). In the second section, we critically review how the diffusion of DPAs in the major western economies hardly fits 'functionalist' or explanations of rational learning: where a good public policy would travel to other countries because of its capacity to obtain its desired goals, because of its outcomes and merits. In the third section, we introduce the reader to different approaches in political science and sociology that provide alternative explanations for the rise of DPAs.

1 DPAs in a nutshell: focusing on the non-recognition of liability

Originating from America, DPAs essentially allow companies to put an end to criminal judicial procedures, without formal recognition of guilt, based on payments of fines and in exchange of commitments for better governance.[1] This absence of a formal recognition of guilt is, of course, the main difference between the DPA and the plea agreement. More precisely, DPAs are administrative arrangements between, on the one hand, a justice department and, on the other hand, a business accused of a crime.[2] The terms of these agreements may provide that corporate controllers will ensure the satisfactory implementation of good governance reforms, such as a code of ethics and anti-corruption compliance measures. DPAs sometimes contain factual admissions on the part of the business surrounding the events of the criminal accusation. In principle, if the business commits another related offence during the term of a DPA, the prosecutors may revive the criminal file and take advantage of the factual admissions that will have been agreed upon during the negotiation of the DPA. In reality, however, at least in the United States and the UK, the lawsuits are abandoned, even in cases where repeated breaches are found.[3]

Although some DPAs include factual admissions of 'wrongdoing,' their main effect is therefore to avoid a finding of guilt and the consequences that ensue for businesses. In some cases, the loss of public contracts that this recognition of guilt would entail would be so important that it would lead the business entity to bankruptcy. The DPA is therefore different from the guilty plea on this crucial point. The other characteristics of the DPAs mentioned above are not exclusive to these instruments: one could very well monitor the rehabilitation of the particular business culture, charge penalties, or compensate victims without introducing DPAs in the criminal system.[4] The main debate surrounding DPAs is therefore to determine whether it is appropriate to allow a business entity to escape recognition of criminal culpability through the payment of sums of money

1 Note that American DPAs have some technical variations. When an agreement is reached before a company is indicted, it is referred to as a non-pursuit agreement (NPA). NPAs are not allowed in the UK or in Canada. There are many nuances between the DPAs of different countries. The notion of negotiation to avoid a recognition of guilt, however, remains intact and that is what we focus on in this chapter.

2 We refer to businesses, business entities, and 'corporate' as generic terms—to include corporations, holdings, and other forms of entities—and to simplify the text, although corporations almost exclusively sign DPAs given their legal personality.

3 Brandon L Garrett, *Too Big to Jail: How Prosecutors Compromise with Corporations* (Harvard University Press 2014); Greg Farrell, 'Senate Democrats Seek Answers from DOJ on Latest HSBC Agreement' *Bloomberg* (2 July 2018) <https://www.bloomberg.com/news/articles/2018-07-02/senate-democrats-seek-answers-from-doj-on-latest-hsbc-agreement> accessed 1 June 2020.

4 Brandon L Garrett, 'Structural Reform Prosecution' (2007) 93 Virginia Law Review 853; Garrett (n 3).

and good governance commitments. That is why they are controversial among legal experts as to their efficiency and fairness.

For instance, law Professor Peter Reilly writes that DPAs turn the criminal justice system into a 'mockery' because they allow for abuse of discretion while involving inequities between litigants.[5] Among other critical analyses, law Professors Brandon Garrett and Rena Steinzor respectively demonstrate that DPAs are controversial across the partisan lines, since they run counter to ideals of law, order, and social cohesion.[6] Nevertheless, despite criticism from many law professors, DPAs have spread to the United Kingdom, Brazil, Canada, France, Singapore, Japan, and other jurisdictions in various forms.[7]

DPAs therefore evolved in various jurisdictions. We are a long way from the first corporate DPA in the United States, which occurred in 1992. It was only in 2002, after the Enron scandal and the bankruptcy of their accounting firm Arthur Andersen, that the instrument really gained momentum.[8] The Bush administration and Deputy Attorney General Larry Thompson then revised the administrative guidelines for corporate indictments.[9] The 'Thompson Memo' allowed for DPAs to avoid or suspend the charge of large companies.[10] As the subsequent 'Filip Memo' explicitly points out, DPAs and NPAs should now be considered in some criminal corporate cases if they can protect innocent third parties.[11] Between the Thompson and Filip Memos, and around 2006–2007, the use of DPAs in the US was consolidated, as we describe below. We also focus our review on

5 Peter Reilly, 'Justice Deferred Is Justice Denied: We Must End Our Failed Experiment in Deferring Corporate Criminal Prosecutions' (2015) Brigham Young University Law Review 307; Peter Reilly, 'Corporate Deferred Prosecution as Discretionary Injustice' (2017) Utah Law Review 46; Peter Reilly, 'Sweetheart Deals, Deferred Prosecution, and Making a Mockery of the Criminal Justice System: US Corporate DPAs Rejected on Many Fronts' (2018) 50 Arizona State Law Journal 1113.

6 Garrett (n 3); Rena Steinzor, *Why Not Jail?: Industrial Catastrophes, Corporate Malfeasance, and Government Inaction* (CUP 2015).

7 Michel A Perez and Alizée Dill, 'The Rise of the American Deferred Prosecution Agreement ('DPA') and Its European Avatars' (2016) 2 Revue Trimestrielle de Droit Financier 43; Michaël Fernandez-Bertier, Mona Giacometti, and Nathalie Van der Eecken, 'La Transaction Pénale et La Reconnaissance Préalable de Culpabilité Comme Modes Alternatifs de Règlement Des Conflits Pénaux: L'heure Des Comptes a Sonné' in Marie-Aude Beernaert, Henri-D Bosly, and Christian De Valkeneer (eds), *La loi pot-pourri II: un an après* (Larcier 2017) 171.

8 Court E Golumbic and Albert D Lichy, 'The "Too Big to Jail" Effect and the Impact on the Justice Department's Corporate Charging Policy' (2014) 65 Hastings Law Journal 1293.

9 Mark J Stein and Joshua A Levine, 'The Filip Memorandum: Does It Go Far Enough?' *Law. Com* (11 September 2008) <https://www.law.com/newyorklawjournal/almID/1202424426861/> accessed 1 June 2020.

10 Larry D Thompson, 'Principles of Federal Prosecution of Business Organizations' (20 January 2003).

11 Mark Filip, 'Principles of Federal Prosecution of Business Organizations' (28 August 2008) 18.

corruption of foreign public officials and provide more details about the definition, origins, and prevalence of DPAs below.

1.1 The growth of DPAs in the United States

The use of DPAs has become so prevalent in the US that about 80% of all cases of corporate bribery would now be resolved through this intermediary.[12] Given the absence of an official national corporate offender registry, some researchers and law firms have compiled their own data.[13] According to the law practice Gibson Dunn, from January 1, 2000 to June 10, 2019, the US Department of Justice (DOJ) and the Securities and Exchange Commission (SEC) concluded 523 DPAs or NPAs, for a total of approximately US $70.8 billion recouped in fines.[14] DPAs have greatly increased in the US since the beginning of the 2000s, especially under the Obama administration, from 2008 to 2016. Under the Trump Administration, corporate penalties from DPAs and prosecutions alike are so far in decline, but court declinations are on the rise, which suggests that corporate crime is quite simply less monitored.[15]

1.2 The international proliferation of DPAs and other instruments

After DPAs became the norm in the US, they proliferated around the Western World, and even now in Asia. Brazil emulated the United States as early as 2013, allowing similar tools to the DPA and NPA. The United Kingdom authorized DPAs in 2014 while Australia began its consultations on the subject the same year, but to date they still haven't been approved.[16] In 2016, France adopted a criminal transaction regime for legal persons in the 'Sapin II Law,' which also enabled companies accused of corruption to negotiate a fine without going to trial or pleading guilty.[17] Singapore and Canada adopted their own DPA regimes

12 Mike Koehler, 'Measuring the Impact of Non-Prosecution and Deferred Prosecution Agreements on Foreign Corrupt Practices Act Enforcement' (2015) 49 UC Davis Law Review 69.

13 Brandon L Garrett and Jon Ashley, 'Corporate Prosecution Registry, Duke University and University of Virginia School of Law' <http://lib.law.virginia.edu/Garrett/corporate-prosecution-registry/index.html> accessed 1 June 2020; Stephanie Brooker, Richard Grime, and Patrick Stokes, 'Negotiating Closure of Government Investigations: NPAs, DPAs, and Beyond' (Gibson Dunn LLP, Washington DC, 11 June 2019) <https://www.gibsondunn.com/wp-content/uploads/2019/06/WebcastSlides-Negotiating-Closure-of-Government-Investigations-NPAs-DPAs-and-Beyond-11-JUN-19.pdf> accessed 1 June 2020.

14 Brooker and others (n 13).

15 Brandon L Garrett, 'Declining Corporate Prosecutions' (2020) 57 American Criminal Law Review 109.

16 Perez and Dill (n 7); Fernandez-Bertier and others (n 7).

17 Ingrid Feuerstein, 'Corruption : la transaction pénale revient à l'Assemblée' *Les Echos* (24 May 2016) <https://business.lesechos.fr/directions-juridiques/droit-des-affaires/contentieux/021956937826-corruption-la-transaction-penale-revient-a-l-assemblee-210719.php#Xtor=AD-6000> accessed 1 June 2020.

in 2018. Other countries recognizing corporate criminal culpability (e.g., the Czech Republic, Belgium, and Switzerland) have similar measures to DPAs.[18] In other countries where corporate criminal liability is not recognized, administrative and civil instruments similar to DPAs also exist, notably for corruption and fraud in Germany, Italy, Norway, the Netherlands, and Denmark.[19]

2 The functionalist and rational learning explanations for the proliferation of DPAs

How, then, can we explain the international proliferation of DPAs? Functionalism and rational learning offer a first hypothesis. In political science, functionalism arises when a given policy innovation is thought to be effective in responding to the policy goals, which are themselves set on the shared knowledge among the decision makers.[20] Functionalist arguments therefore imply that outcome X (an institution, policy, or an organization) exists because it serves the function Y.[21] The explanation of new institutional forms, such as DPAs, would therefore be found in their functional consequences based on the expectations of its creators.[22]

The functional hypotheses are not without their merit to account for some social innovations, or to explain, if only in part, the causality of new institutional forms. However, their plausibility rests upon demanding assumptions. As argued by Paul Pierson, for functionalist arguments to succeed, the actors who participated in the innovation must act instrumentally (prioritizing effectiveness over other goals, such as optics or legitimacy), they must give weight to the long term functional outcomes, and they must also control a fair share of the unanticipated consequences of their design.[23] Therefore, functionalist hypotheses risk being invoked as 'an easy rationale for evading the thorny issues of institutional emergence and change.'[24] It is best to treat functionalism as a starting point for rigorous analysis, while understanding that it will often hide other causal explanations.

Among these are rational learning mechanisms based on lesson-drawing, such as when a policy with unintended consequences is adapted by purposive and rational actors. 'Improvements' in the understanding of a problem or of its

18 Corruption Watch UK, *Out of Court, Out of Mind—Do Deferred Prosecution Agreements and Corporate Settlements Deter Overseas Corruption?* (2016).

19 Ibid.

20 Beth A Simmons, Frank Dobbin, and Geoffrey Garrett, *The Global Diffusion of Markets and Democracy* (CUP 2008) 25; Ernst B Haas, 'Why Collaborate? Issue-Linkage and International Regimes' (1980) 32 World Politics 367, 368.

21 Paul Pierson, 'The Limits of Design: Explaining Institutional Origins and Change' (2000) 13 Governance 476.

22 Ibid 475.

23 Ibid 478–79, 483.

24 Ibid 477.

solutions will, therefore, lead to an ameliorative revision of public policies.[25] In terms of policy diffusion, governments would draw relatively well thought out conclusions 'based on the data generated by policy experiments elsewhere, thus narrowing the range of interpretations regarding the causal relationship between the policy and its hypothesized outcome.'[26] However, the explanatory power of rational learning is prone to similar shortcomings compared to functionalism: it tends to underestimate the complexity of the real political world, including the multiplicity and ambiguity of actors' motivations.[27]

For instance, in her study on the independence of central banks as a new international standard, Professor Kathleen McNamara argued that discourses focused on the functional and rational motives for adaptive public policies also contained mimicry reflexes, cultural influence of economic elites, and capitalistic structural concerns.[28] To test the limits of the functionalist hypotheses or the application of rational learning mechanisms in the case of DPAs, we therefore critically review four of their main and purported advantages, while contrasting these with three of their main and purported disadvantages. Our limited review cannot establish that DPAs are 'dysfunctional' policy tools, but we minimally demonstrate that they are controversial instruments, that functionalism alone cannot explain their diffusion.

2.1 *Summary and critical review of the arguments in favour of DPAs*

We proceed to a summary and critical analysis of the discourses justifying DPAs, although a more thorough review remains to be completed. If many articles by law firms or legal periodicals presenting DPAs are optimistic, more rigorous academic publications are critical, or they at least temper their enthusiasm towards DPAs. Also noteworthy is the lack of empirical research from public policy or political science articles, with most work on DPAs coming from law or business administration. One notable exception is the cooperative work of King and Lord, which also includes perspectives from criminology.[29] Several researchers also question the link between the recognition of criminal liability and the 'corporate death sentence.' Furthermore, there is contradictory evidence

25 Hugh Heclo, 'Modern Social Politics in Britain and Sweden: From Relief to Income Maintenance. Yale University Press, 1974' (1976) 6 Politics & Society 119; Colin J Bennett and Michael Howlett, 'The Lessons of Learning: Reconciling Theories of Policy Learning and Policy Change' (1992) 25 Policy Sciences 275.

26 Simmons and others (n 20) 27.

27 Pierson (n 21) 488.

28 Kathleen McNamara, 'Rational Fictions: Central Bank Independence and the Social Logic of Delegation' (2002) 25 West European Politics 47.

29 Colin King and Nicholas Lord, *Negotiated Justice and Corporate Crime: The Legitimacy of Civil Recovery Orders and Deferred Prosecution Agreements* (Springer International Publishing 2018).

on how DPAs may favor self-disclosure. It is therefore necessary to recognize that the 'competitiveness' argument is the main, and most logical one in favor of these new instruments.

2.1.1 The prevention of systemic risk and the protection of third parties against the corporate death penalty

According to the proponents of DPAs, these instruments would better protect innocent parties such as employees, shareholders, and suppliers of a business. These parties would be negatively and unfairly affected in the event of formal recognition of guilt on the business entity, yet they have done nothing wrong and they should not be penalized if they are innocent bystanders. In cases where the survival of an important company could even be questioned, following an indictment or a recognition of guilt, the DPA would also protect the population from the systemic risk that a major bankruptcy would have on the economy.[30]

These arguments have been repeatedly mentioned in the United States as DPAs increased in popularity. For instance, when HSBC Bank signed a DPA, Deputy Attorney General Eric Holder explained that his goal was to avoid causing systemic effects to the economy and to prevent the loss of thousands of jobs.[31] It was even necessary to worry about the possible fall of HSBC, and to avoid another 'corporate death sentence' as in the case of Arthur Andersen. Mr Holder testified before the Senate Judiciary Committee that he was concerned that the size of some of these institutions is becoming so important that it is now difficult to prosecute them, thus referring to a 'too big to jail' dilemma, and the moral hazard problem it implies.[32]

However, this logic presents several factual and historical problems.[33] After all, the problematic corporate culture that led to Arthur Andersen's indictment may have been enough to undermine its reputation. The criminal charge may only have contributed to the inevitable. Civil lawsuits against the company alone would have destroyed what was left of the company's credibility.[34] In the same

30 Golumbic and Lichy (n 8); Polly Sprenger, *Deferred Prosecution Agreements: The Law and Practice of Negotiated Corporate Criminal Penalties* (Sweet & Maxwell 2014); Elizabeth K Ainslie, 'Indicting Corporations Revisited: Lessons of the Arthur Andersen Prosecution' (2006) 43 The American Criminal Law Review 107; Scott A Resnik and Keir N Dougall, 'The Rise of Deferred Prosecution Agreements' (2006) New York Law Journal 3.

31 James O'Toole, 'HSBC: Too Big to Jail?' *CNN Business* (12 December 2012) <http://money.cnn.com/2012/12/12/news/companies/hsbc-money-laundering/index.html> accessed 1 June 2020.

32 Patrick Radden Keefe, 'Why Corrupt Bankers Avoid Jail' *The New Yorker* (24 July 2017) <https://www.newyorker.com/magazine/2017/07/31/why-corrupt-bankers-avoid-jail> accessed 1 June 2020.

33 Gabriel Markoff, 'Arthur Andersen and the Myth of the Corporate Death Penalty: Corporate Criminal Convictions in the Twenty-First Century' (2013) 15 University of Pennsylvania Journal of Business Law 797; Garrett (n 3); Steinzor (n 6).

34 Markoff (n 33).

fashion, from 2001 to 2010, Markoff found that, when companies are not able to benefit from a DPA, 90% of them plead guilty instead of going to trial. According to his research, no publicly traded company went bankrupt as a result of these guilty pleas. The impact on their economic viability is also variable, but often limited. For example, the guilty plea of BP following the spill in the Bay of Mexico, included a fine of US $4.5 billion, but the stock price would not have been affected at the end of 2012 and its profits rose to $27.6 billion.[35]

2.1.2 The levelling the playing field argument

The 'international competition' rationale for DPAs is based on 'fairness' for national companies with respect to competitors benefiting from these instruments, or even to the competitors who are not bound by either strong anti-corruption laws, or enforcement thereof. National companies with stronger laws and enforcement are, therefore, at risk of losing contracts abroad to dishonest competitors.[36] Foreign companies that are subject to US laws have quickly put pressure on their national government to obtain the same DPA regimes, and thus compete on 'equal terms' with their US counterparts.[37] This 'competitive' argument seems internally logical, but its implications are controversial: there should be a limit to how far countries can relax the content of their criminal law or its enforcement based on international competition. Levelling the playing field could also mean levelling it down or racing to the bottom in the worst scenario.

2.1.3 Effectiveness, efficiency, and increased flexibility due to DPAs?

Several researchers recognize that 'one of the great attractions of DPA systems is its effectiveness.'[38] DPAs are legitimized by their proponents for being new, easier-to-use instruments that would lead to more prosecutorial interventions, with a corresponding increase in financial penalties. Administrations could therefore save on investigation and trial costs, but the comparison should also be examined with respect to negotiated guilty pleas. These also allow for resource efficiency, and they should be signed after prosecutors gave enough time and resources to ensure that their case is strong enough to lead to charges.

The notion of greater 'flexibility' of DPAs for the application of criminal law is contested by former Chief Public Prosecutor David Uhlmann. According to him, plea agreements could lead to the same corporate reforms, financial penalties, and factual admissions as DPAs. The real benefits of DPAs to the administration are

35 Ibid 833.

36 Antoine Garapon and Pierre Servan-Schreiber, *Deals de justice: le marché américain de l'obéissance mondialisée* (Presses Universitaires de France 2013).

37 Brandon L Garrett, 'Globalized Corporate Prosecutions' (2011) 97 Virginia Law Review 1775; Garrett (n 3).

38 Garapon and Servan-Schreiber (n 36) 126.

that the costs are lower, which leads Uhlmann to conclude that 'the motivation of the Department of Justice to pursue DPAs ... has been much less thoughtful than the concern for collateral consequences or desire cooperation or structural reform.'[39] The argument that DPAs allow for more 'flexibility' would have been developed as a form of legitimation well after DPAs were established as a money-saving and moneymaking practice in the United States. Uhlmann therefore highlights the weak foundation of DPAs in policy and their inconsistent use by the Justice Department.[40]

2.1.4 *The alleged effect of DPAs on the self-disclosure of crimes*

According to proponents of DPAs, these instruments would promote greater self-disclosure of criminal activities. This would help to increase the effectiveness of anti-corruption laws since DPAs would lead to enforcement in cases that would have otherwise remained secret. Unfortunately, this hope is not supported by empirical evidence either, despite several attempts to demonstrate that logic.[41] There are cases where 'self-disclosing' companies have been rewarded, but there are also several cases where they may have been more harshly penalized than if they had not collaborated with the authorities. It is also very difficult, if not impossible, to compare the reality where a corporate entity divulges an offence to try to obtain a DPA and the alternative reality where it does not disclose at all, given that the absence of disclosure is obviously not documented, except *a posteriori*, when it is discovered. Moreover, there may be better ways to enhance the disclosure of crimes, such as the protection of whistleblowers.

2.2 Critical review of the main arguments against DPAs

The following section shows how certain researchers believe that DPAs reduce the deterrent effect of criminal law, threaten the independence of prosecutors and undermine the rule of law. As a result, and because DPAs involve an inequality in the application of the criminal law between corporate and individual citizens, people's faith in their public institutions and in the administration of justice may suffer.

39 David M Uhlmann, 'Deferred Prosecution and Non-Prosecution Agreements and the Erosion of Corporate Criminal Liability Symposium: Too Big to Jail: Overcoming the Roadblocks to Regulatory Enforcement' (2012) 72 Maryland Law Review 1324.

40 Ibid 1315.

41 Matthew Stephenson, 'Do Companies Benefit from Self-Disclosing FCPA Violations?' *The Global Anticorruption Blog* (27 March 2014) <https://globalanticorruptionblog.com/2014/03/27/do-companies-benefit-from-self-disclosing-fcpa-violations/> accessed 1 June 2020; Stephen J Choi and Kevin E Davis, 'Foreign Affairs and Enforcement of the Foreign Corrupt Practices Act' (2014) 11 Journal of Empirical Legal Studies 409.

2.2.1 *DPAs undermine the rule of law and may hinder the independence of prosecutors*

From both sides of the political spectrum, DPAs are criticized for undermining the rule of law. On the one hand, several experts who support shareholder and corporate rights believe that DPAs provide too much discretion to prosecutors. For example, one American researcher states that DPAs erode the most basic protections of criminal law, turning the prosecutor into a judge and jury, undermining the principles of separation of powers, and thereafter sending justice monitors into corporate boardrooms.[42] Since the leniency or severity of DPAs can vary greatly from case to case, these authors are also concerned about the effect on the consistency of the law if the judicial review is minimal.

On the other hand, critics such as law Professor Rena Steinzor see DPAs as a tax on crime (and corruption) for the companies that are 'too big to jail.'[43] The investigative journalist Jessie Eisinger brings the logic even further.[44] After hundreds of interviews with American prosecutors, judges, and other legal actors, he illustrates how DPAs may threaten their independence and expertise. He is not particularly afraid of extortion by the Justice Department. Quite the contrary, he argues that it is much more common for prosecutors to terminate prosecutions or to refrain from pursuing them when they in fact have faith in their merits. In some cases, they opt for a DPA or a NPA to avoid the risk of losing in court, and they are often pressured into considerations of judicial economy. Rather than undertaking a long and costly process, they reap the lesser, but immediate, benefits that DPAs offer. Politicized prosecutors will also be more favorable toward the faster obtainment of penalties as a tangible demonstration that a scandal has been addressed by the authorities, independently of the 'qualitative' shortcomings of the consequence.[45] The problem that DPAs present for the independence of prosecutors is also linked with other dynamics threatening the public trust in their democratic and judicial institutions, to which we now turn.[46]

42 Richard A Epstein, 'The Deferred Prosecution Racket' *Wall Street Journal* (28 November 2006) <https://www.wsj.com/articles/SB116468395737834160> accessed 1 June 2020; Richard A Epstein, 'Deferred Prosecution Agreements on Trial: Lessons from the Law of Unconstitutional Conditions' in Anthony S Barkow and Rachel E Barkow (eds), *Prosecutors in the Board Room: Using Criminal Law to Regulate Corporate Conduct* (NYU Press 2011) 38.

43 Garrett (n 3); Steinzor (n 6).

44 Jesse Eisinger, *The Chickenshit Club: Why the Justice Department Fails to Prosecute Executives* (Simon & Schuster 2018).

45 Mike Koehler, 'The Facade of FCPA Enforcement' (2010) 41 Georgetown Journal of International Law 907.

46 Reilly, 'Justice Deferred Is Justice Denied' (n 5).

2.2.2 DPAs, their lack of consistency for criminal law enforcement, and their threat to the level of public trust

Some authors criticize the inequity or the lack of social coherence that DPAs engender. The low conviction rate of corporate crime is often compared to the very large prison population in the United States.[47] Even the highly respected Judge Jed S Rakoff of the Southern District of New York, and former prosecutor of economic crimes, implies that DPAs protect the rich, while the poor do not have access to the same privileges under the law.[48]

This issue of legal coherence also goes beyond the contrasts between the marginalized individuals and large multinational corporations. Professor Garrett has identified highly problematic trends in how DPAs were awarded to different kinds of companies. DPAs and NPAs are indeed more often awarded to public rather than private entities, and smaller companies are less likely to obtain them as well. In addition, domestic firms are more likely to obtain these conciliatory instruments than foreign firms.[49]

2.2.3 DPAs as a threat to the deterrent effect of criminal law

The risk that DPAs erode the deterrent effect of corporate criminal law is one of the main arguments invoked by critics.[50] If the pecuniary solution for corporate accountability becomes the main thing there is, the fight against corruption could be turned into a tax on corruption. The lure of profit and the economic logic can already motivate certain companies to break the law in order to obtain important contracts. Although the dynamics are very difficult to quantify, a study concludes that companies earn US $11 for every dollar spent on bribes.[51] The reliance on anticorruption fines may harm the normative environment of companies and may detrimentally alter the cost/benefit incentives for corporate crime. Moreover, the fines that are collected with DPAs may seem important in absolute terms, but they are often secondary in relative terms, as they often represent only a small part of the expected revenues.[52]

47 Garrett (n 3); Steinzor (n 6).

48 Jed S Rakoff, 'Justice Deferred Is Justice Denied' *The New York Review of Books* (19 February 2015) <http://www.nybooks.com/articles/2015/02/19/justice-deferred-justice-denied/> accessed 1 June 2020.

49 Garrett (n 3).

50 Garrett (n 3); Steinzor (n 6); Eisinger (n 44).

51 Yan Leung Cheung, Raghavendra Rau, and Aris Stouraitis, 'How Much Do Firms Pay as Bribes and What Benefits Do They Get? Evidence from Corruption Cases Worldwide' (2012) NBER Working Paper No 17981 <http://www.nber.org/papers/w17981> accessed 1 June 2020.

52 Dominic Rushe, 'HSBC "Sorry" for Aiding Mexican Drugs Lords, Rogue States and Terrorists' *The Guardian* (17 July 2012) <http://www.theguardian.com/business/2012/jul/17/hsbc-executive-resigns-senate> accessed 1 June 2020.

The available empirical evidence also shows that the financial penalty is less of a deterrent than the restrictions on business opportunities or the imprisonment of offending officers. In this regard, the Humboldt-Viadrina Anti-Corruption Governance School in Berlin conducted an anonymous survey of 1,000 anti-corruption experts from the public sector, the business sector and civil society.[53] Their investigation revealed that the two best ways to deter companies from engaging in corruption are precisely the criminalization of corporate executives and the restriction of commercial opportunities, such as the suspension or exclusion of public contracts (debarment).

It is therefore dangerous to rely too heavily on fines to deter bribery if they are not accompanied by more severe sanctions such as individual prosecutions and the restriction of commercial opportunities. However, expert work on the issue shows that individual prosecutions occur in just a minority of cases where DPAs are granted.[54] Between 2001 and 2012, when public companies obtained DPAs or NPAs, Professor Garrett calculated that individual prosecutions arose in only 35% of cases.[55] Moreover, in 2016, the DOJ recorded the lowest corporate crime prosecution rate in 20 years, with a 40% drop, according to the Transactional Records Access Clearinghouse.[56] At the same time, several companies have benefited from a DPA for FCPA charges while subsequently reoffending, such as Halliburton, Biomet, Orthofix, or Marubeni.[57]

3 Alternative approaches of political science and sociology

We reviewed arguments against DPAs that question the validity and primacy of functionalist or rational explanations to explain their international diffusion. How then do we best explain the diffusion of DPAs? Political science offers us alternative hypotheses to answer that question. On the one hand, some states—and the US, in particular—may have a power of coercion in international relations that explains how anti-corruption laws and enforcement trends are exported around the world. On the other hand, a particular model of business power in political economy could help us understand how major businesses can influence both the development and the diffusion of DPAs. Short of testing our hypothesis,

53 Jennifer Schöberlein, Sven Biermann, and Sebastian Wegner, 'Motivating Business to Counter Corruption: A Global Survey on Anti-Corruption Incentives and Sanctions' (Humboldt-Viafrina School of Governance 2012).

54 Garrett (n 3); Koehler, 'Measuring the Impact of Non-Prosecution and Deferred Prosecution Agreements on Foreign Corrupt Practices Act Enforcement' (n 12).

55 Garrett (n 3) 83.

56 Transactional Records Access Clearinghouse (TRAC), 'White Collar Crime Prosecutions through July 2016' <http://tracfed.syr.edu/results/9x7057c8a7ee9c.html> accessed 1 June 2020.

57 Mike Koehler, 'Corporate FCPA Repeat Offenders' *FCPA Professor* (3 August 2017) <http://fcpaprofessor.com/corporate-fcpa-repeat-offenders/> accessed 1 June 2020.

our aim in this chapter is to provide an overview of the variables and to present observations which can serve research agendas.

3.1 *'Coercion,' the state, and extraterritorial enforcement of the FCPA*

In this section, we examine how international relations, with the power of the United States as the main driving force for policy change, can explain the spread of both anti-corruption laws and its enforcement mechanisms, such as DPAs. We can see patterns of 'internationalization' of American anti-corruption law that 'coerce' other states into adopting similar measures, including DPAs. Coercion arises when governments, international organizations, or non-governmental actors use their stronger power asymmetries to impose their preferences for policy change on weaker governments. Coercion can be subtle or overt and take the form of threats, physical force, and even manipulation of economic costs and benefits.[58] After an overview of the historical context, we examine below how coercion played an important role in the dominance of the FCPA and in the proliferation of DPAs.

In 1977, the FCPA was adopted in a very particular domestic context following the Watergate scandals.[59] For several years, European countries did not share this American concern, until corruption scandals became a major election issue in Germany, France, and the United Kingdom.[60] In 1996, the World Bank (finally) classified corruption as an economic issue, not just a political one.[61] Helped by new studies, the decision makers in international organizations changed their view of bribery as a counterproductive economic factor, rather than a harmless or business-enabling phenomenon.[62] In this context, the OECD countries signed, in 1997, the International Convention on Combating Bribery of Foreign Public Officials (OECD Convention). This rare binding convention at the level of the OECD compelled all member countries to adopt their own domestic anti-corruption legislation. In 1999, the OECD Convention was ratified, and the United States could increase its level of enforcement of the FCPA now that competing jurisdictions were collaborating. Previously, US companies would have been at a disadvantage compared to their main competitors if the US had rigorously applied the FCPA against them despite the inaction of other states. This problem of collective action was thus targeted by a new multilateral institution.

58 Simmons and others (n 20) 10.

59 Mark Pieth and Radha Ivory (eds), *Corporate Criminal Liability: Emergence, Convergence, and Risk* (Springer Netherlands 2011); Rachel Brewster and Samuel W Buell, 'The Market for Global Anticorruption Enforcement' (2017) 80 Law and Contemporary Problems 193.

60 Pieth and Ivory (n 59).

61 *Voice for the World's Poor: Selected Speeches of the World Bank President James D. Wolfensohn, 1995-2005* (World Bank 2005).

62 Brewster and Buell (n 59).

Table 20.1 Evolution of FCPA proceedings and associated amounts, years 1977–2015.

Period (inclusive)	*Number of Years*	*Total Number of indictments*	*Average of indictments / year*	*Total amount recovered (US $ - approximate)*	*Average amount recovered (US $ / year – approximate)*
1977 to 2000	23	52	2	129 million	5.6 million
2001 to 2015	15	379	25	8 billion	533 million

Source: Stanford Law School 2018

As shown in Table 20.1, between the time of the enactment of the FCPA in 1977 and the year 2000, the federal government undertook only 52 enforcement actions for a total recovery of US $129 million.[63] During a shorter period of time, between 2001 and 2015, seven times more enforcement actions were initiated with total revenues up to 60 times greater (approximately US $8 billion).

While investigations and prosecutions under the FCPA multiplied, the extra-territoriality and the complexity of cases also increased. Through the FCPA, the US can sue foreign-registered companies if they have a US subsidiary, or such a tenuous attachment as trading shares in the United States.[64] In addition, the territory where there is an exchange of bribes does not matter to the application of the FCPA. This is why the FCPA is often described as being 'extraterritorial,' which could also be analyzed under the lens of 'coercion.'

In response to the DOJ's criminal actions against foreign businesses with trade in the US, home jurisdictions may have wanted to react and take the criminal process in their own hands. Authors Garapon and Servan-Schreiber notably saw a link between the introduction of DPAs in France and the fact that several French groups, such as Total SA, had been the subject of lawsuits and sanctions under the American FCPA.[65] As described below, a similar reaction was noted for the BAE Systems plc case, when the UK government introduced DPAs to respond to the criminal accusations against its national champion, a British multinational in the defence business.[66]

63 'Foreign Corrupt Practices Act Clearinghouse (FCPAC)' *Stanford Law School* (15 May 2018) <https://law.stanford.edu/foreign-corrupt-practices-act-clearinghouse-fcpac/> accessed 1 June 2020; Brewster and Buell (n 59).

64 Garrett (n 3).

65 Department of Justice of the United States, 'French Oil and Gas Company, Total, S.A., Charged in the United States and France in Connection with an International Bribery Scheme' (29 May 2013) <https://www.justice.gov/opa/pr/french-oil-and-gas-company-total-sa-charged-united-states-and-france-connection-international> accessed 1 June 2020.

66 Garrett (n 3); Lawrence A Cunningham, 'Deferred Prosecutions and Corporate Governance: An Integrated Approach to Investigation and Reform' (2014) 66 Florida Law Review 1.

3.2 Business power and political economy analysis

The business power model, notably developed by Professor Pepper Culpepper in '*Quiet Politics*,' would be another alternative for understanding the proliferation of DPAs, especially where the interests of large corporations are involved.[67] This model sharpens the debate between those who believe that the interests of business lobbies always triumph and others who place businesses on an equal footing with various social actors in a pluralistic vision of politics. Culpepper demonstrates that the interests of corporate lobbies will generally prevail in situations of low salience and when governance rules are informal.[68] Conversely, companies would not be more powerful than other political actors when the public issues that concern them are publicized and when formal governance rules apply to the debate. In other words, companies will not necessarily lose their political fight in high-profile situations, but both their lobbying tools and their important position in the economy will generally be insufficient to convert their preferences into public policies.

3.2.1 Business power and DPAs: the Canadian example

The process leading to the Canadian adoption of DPAs is an interesting case to explore for a business power hypothesis. On June 6, 2018, the Canadian House of Commons indeed adopted its own version of DPAs. They were subtly included in the Budget Implementation Act,[69] which compiled more than 500 pages of different dispositions. All the members of the Standing Committee on Finance, mandated to adopt DPAs, expressed their discomfort and even their opposition to the omnibus legislation process for such a significant change to the Criminal Code. Some would have liked to hear more independent experts seeing the controversy implied by the DPAs. But time was running out for SNC-Lavalin, one of Canada's national champion companies, accused of corruption.

According to Culpepper, salience will have a greater impact than formality in determining corporate power.[70] Even though the Canadian process was 'formal' as opposed to informally adopted by the executive and Attorney Generals in the US, the process was rushed, opaque and possibly, *quiet* as well. The public consultation on the adoption of DPAs was already oriented towards the desired result. The consultation was led by a more industry-oriented Department of Public Works—rather than Justice Canada—and it was mostly attended by business lobbies and other corporate interests. The fact that the briefs filed were

67 Pepper D Culpepper, *Quiet Politics and Business Power Corporate Control in Europe and Japan* (CUP 2011); Pepper D Culpepper and Raphael Reinke, 'Structural Power and Bank Bailouts in the United Kingdom and the United States' (2014) 42 Politics & Society 427.

68 Culpepper (n 67) 181.

69 2018, C-12. An Act to implement certain provisions of the budget tabled in Parliament on February 27, 2018 and other measures C-74.

70 Culpepper (n 67) 186.

not public, or that they could not be reviewed in the parliamentary process, also contributed to the interpretation of a 'silent' and technical process.

The timeline also suggests the preference for protecting the business interest of SNC-Lavalin. Accused of corruption and criminal fraud in February 2015, SNC-Lavalin was about to start its criminal trial scheduled for September 2018, while DPAs were adopted in March 2018 in the hope of providing enough time for negotiations in this specific case. While the US had been increasing its use of DPAs since 2005, it is only after SNC was formally charged by the RCMP that the Canadian government seriously considered their adoption. If their functional or rational merits were as conclusive as their proponents suggested, then why would the Canadian government have waited for more than a decade to replicate the US experiment, and then rush the legislative process the way it did? There was no reason for such an eagerness other than the commencement of SNC's trial. The Trudeau Cabinet was well aware of the controversy over DPAs as it was raised by all of the members of the Standing Committee on Finance who studied their adoption, including by a Liberal MP. The government could have responded to the requests of all members of this committee and taken more time to study the allowance of DPAs in a separate bill, and with broader participation of interest groups. However, such a process would have prevented SNC from negotiating a DPA before the commencement of its trial, and it may have raised the salience of a controversial issue. After all, DPAs may be an uneasy fit in the particular culture of Canadian corporate criminal law.[71] In any event, they played an important role in a political scandal that erupted in Canada after their implementation. Prime minister Justin Trudeau and members of his team were found by the ethics commissioner to have exerted undue influence on the Minister of Justice and Attorney General, Judy Wilson Raybould, in order to help SNC-Lavalin in its quest towards a DPA.[72]

3.2.2 Business power and DPAs: the United Kingdom example

In the 2000s, the United Kingdom risked its own version of an 'Arthur Andersen' case in connection with the FCPA and its extraterritoriality. As indicated above, the case of the British arms manufacturer BAE Systems plc (BAE) influenced the United Kingdom to modify its anti-corruption laws, and to open the door to DPAs. The case goes back to the 1980s when BAE sold US $80 billion worth of fighter planes to Saudi Arabia. Evidence of bribes was collected around 2004, but the English Serious Fraud Office (SFO) did not lay charges. Several statements by officials, including a statement by Prime Minister Tony Blair, demonstrate a

71 Jennifer Quaid, 'Negotiated Justice and Economic Crime: Lessons from the Canadian Experience' (2017) SSRN No 3039707 <https://papers.ssrn.com/abstract=3039707> accessed 1 June 2020.

72 Mario Dion, *Trudeau II Report* (Office of the Conflict of Interest and Ethics Commissioner 2019).

special concern to refrain from indicting BAE, a national champion of the UK with leading strategic and military interests. The UK may have hoped that the US prosecutors would do the same, but they didn't. BAE's Chief Executive Officer and officers received subpoenas to compel them to appear in front of a grand jury, while they were passing through Houston, where BAE has a subsidiary.[73] Diplomatic and legal negotiations continued between the two countries until 2010. In the end, only the American subsidiary of BAE signed a plea agreement (with penalties of US $400 million). The parent company avoided charges that would have cut off access to several markets, but the recognition of guilt on the part of its subsidiary was still problematic. In the face of this partially averted catastrophe, the United Kingdom began, as early as 2012, the revision of its anti-corruption laws to increase their extraterritoriality and to allow the signature of DPAs for corporate crimes.[74] The UK can now also respond to the corruption scandals of its own national champions through DPAs. Just as it can monitor, like the US does, the behaviour of foreign companies that have a connection to UK markets.

For Professor Garrett, cases such as the one of BAE demonstrate a 'soft form of pressure(s)' by the United States as the 'leading exporter of corporate criminal law,' a particular form of dissemination of new anti-corruption instruments that echoes our previous section on the influence of the state and its coercive aspects.[75] But the BAE case also illustrates that business interests, and especially those of national champions, may highly influence the motivations of international actors involved. As with the concepts of isomorphism that we now turn to, we are working with ideal types that describe complex realities, and are not meant to be understood as watertight compartments.

4 Institutional isomorphism

In this section, we explore two sociological theories of 'isomorphism' that explain why institutions can present increasingly similar features over time. Based on the typology by DiMaggio and Powell, we review *normative isomorphism*, which is associated with professionalization, and *mimetic isomorphism*, which examines replication as a standard response to uncertainty.[76] Both types are strategies to legitimize the adoption of a policy, notwithstanding its policy merits or its rational appeal. Again, this typology 'is an analytic one: the types are not always empirically distinct.'[77]

73 Garrett (n 3) 225.

74 Ibid 248.

75 Ibid 246.

76 Paul J DiMaggio and Walter W Powell, 'The Iron Cage Revisited: Institutional Isomorphism and Collective Rationality in Organizational Fields' (1983) 48 American Sociological Review 147.

77 Ibid 150.

4.1 Normative isomorphism and the role of epistemic communities in the proliferation of DPAs

Normative isomorphic essentially means that professionalization plays a central role in policy diffusion, while epistemic communities refer to the networks of knowledge-based communities with policy-relevant knowledge within their domain of expertise.[78] There may be certain features in the education, training, and certification of professions that will influence the development of policies in a certain way.[79] Researchers document how normative isomorphism and epistemic communities play an important role in the development of new anti-corruption norms.[80] In the case of DPAs, this notably happens when American, Canadian, Australian, and UK lawyers internalize similar values or norms through their own—yet compatible—education, certification process, and on-going training. Normative isomorphism can also arise through the pressures of international organizations, such as the International Bar Association, or through inter-hiring when lawyers practice more and more internationally. In other words, because of their socialization, people with similar backgrounds will approach problems with similar ways of thinking.

Therefore, the important role of anti-corruption training and of epistemic communities at the level of international organizations and NGOs, such as Transparency International and the OECD, are directly relevant for an analysis of the DPA proliferation. The OECD, for instance, has released on March 20, 2019, a report on non-trial resolutions of foreign bribery cases. Despite acknowledging some institutional and procedural challenges, the report positively reviews the adoption of DPAs as a pragmatic and efficient way to resolve cases, while also promoting enforcement and self-reporting.[81] Earlier on, Transparency International Canada also played an important role in promoting DPAs in that country, especially through a special report published in July 2017, urging the government to consider the adoption of DPAs.[82] As the Canadian case exemplifies, an international organization's branches can directly or indirectly collaborate with business or other professional associations. For instance, in 2016, Transparency International Canada preceded its report on DPAs by collaborating with the

78 Peter M Haas, 'Epistemic Communities' in Bertrand Badie, Dirk Berg-Schlosser, and Leonardo Morlino (eds), *International Encyclopedia of Political Science* (SAGE 2011). See also Emanuel Adler and Peter M Haas, 'Conclusion: Epistemic Communities, World Order, and the Creation of a Reflective Research Program' (1992) 46 International Organization 367.

79 DiMaggio and Powell (n 76) 152–54.

80 See notably Jennifer L Mccoy, 'The Emergence of a Global Anti-Corruption Norm' (2001) 38 International Politics 65; Ellen Gutterman, 'The Legitimacy of Transnational NGOs: Lessons from the Experience of Transparency International in Germany and France' (2014) 40 Review of International Studies 391.

81 OECD, *Resolving Foreign Bribery Cases with Non-Trial Resolutions: Settlements and Non-Trial Agreements by Parties to the Anti-Bribery Convention* (2019).

82 Transparency International Canada, *Another Arrow in the Quiver?: Consideration of a Deferred Prosecution Agreement Scheme in Canada* (2017).

Institute for research in public policy, which brought together law and business administration professors alongside business representatives such as SNC-Lavalin and members of the Business Council of Canada.[83]

Furthermore, according to professors Brewster and Buell, the rise of FCPA-like practices, such as DPAs, are also influenced by defense lawyers' organizations, or by other law professional or bar associations.[84] Worldwide, the IBA Anti-Corruption Committee recognizes and studies the role of DPAs and other settlement tools for increasing the enforcement of anti-corruption rules.[85] In the US, Jessie Eisinger documented particularly well the phenomenon of revolving doors between the DOJ and major law firms or consultants who pushed for DPAs.[86] The rise of DPAs, and the legal monitoring obligations they imply, represents important business opportunities for major defense law firms. Eisinger fears that prosecutors may self-censor and offer DPAs when there are hopes for a future passage towards the large firms that defend business signatories of DPAs. Law professor Rena Steinzor is also concerned by the cultural proximity that DPAs imply. In effect, DPAs force prosecutors to consult economists, or worse, to think like them when deciding whether to prosecute or not. Prosecutors must 'predict whether a criminal conviction will drive a giant firm out of business.'[87] When they do so, 'they morph into policymakers determining the future rather than police ensuring consequences for the past.'[88]

4.2 *Mimetic isomorphism and the role of uncertainty for the spread of DPAs*

Finally, mimetic isomorphism arises when an organization imitates another because of the belief that the structure, or the policy preferences, of the latter organization are beneficial. Mimicking is more frequent when a weaker organization has no clearly defined policy goals, or means to achieve them. In the face of uncertainty, following the leader or walking in the footsteps of other countries can be 'safer' and it is seen as 'legitimate.'[89] Mimetic isomorphism can also be linked to 'reference group theory' in social psychology, which suggests that individuals emulate the behaviour of peers because they believe that the policies

83 Institute for Research on Public Policy, *Finding the Right Balance: Policies to Combat White-Collar Crime in Canada and Maintain the Integrity of Public Procurement—IRPP Round Table Report* (2016) 22.

84 Brewster and Buell (n 59).

85 Abiola Makinwa and Tina Søreide (eds), *Structured Settlements for Corruption Offences Towards Global Standards?* (International Bar Association Anti-Corruption Committee: Structured Criminal Settlements Subcommittee 2018).

86 Eisinger (n 44).

87 Steinzor (n 6) 275.

88 Ibid.

89 DiMaggio and Powell (n 76) 151–152.

of peers will 'work' for them as well.[90] Socio-cultural linkages may contribute to 'psychological proximity' among nations, as when the United Kingdom looks to North America for policy solutions.[91] Again, mimetic isomorphism is linked with other kinds of isomorphism, as when a policy is copied either because of 'expert theorization,' which is closer to normative isomorphism, or because of 'follow the leader' dynamics, which are closer to coercive isomorphism.[92] And mimicry comes at a price: the borrowed policies may be materially and culturally inappropriate to the local needs, or flawed by design.

At this stage, it is difficult to find clear evidence of mimicry for DPAs, but their fast proliferation in 'like-minded' countries could suggest such a phenomenon. In an article on the 'transgovernmental policy networks in the Anglo-sphere', Tim Legrand mentions that DPAs were discussed in 2012 at an Ottawa conference between the attorney generals of the US, England and Wales, Canada, Australia and New Zealand.[93] We need more research to establish if and how mimicking may have played a role in the policy diffusion of DPAs, especially since other compelling explanations could apply to at least some of these countries.

5 Conclusion

There is, therefore, a need for further research on DPAs and their proliferation in various forms, especially through OECD countries. In the meantime, this chapter weakened the hypothesis that DPAs are on the rise because they are well thought-out, functioning, or 'rational' policy instruments. Short of demonstrating that the arguments in favor of DPAs are based on 'rational fictions,' we showed that many are untested, historically misleading, or that they lead to controversial implications and important tradeoffs in values. As in the case of Canada, their adoption can be rushed to achieve short-term goals of protectionism towards national champions that are subject to a criminal procedure. They are also championed as a new mechanism to deal with corporate crime by the US, through extra-territorial criminal law and soft power. Foreign authorities must, therefore, adapt, given that international anti-corruption enforcement implies collective action challenges. Furthermore, the policy rationale for DPAs is promoted by epistemic communities composed of businesses and corporate defense lawyers, often with a stake in their implementation. The business power of national champions may well interact with some other policy diffusion and isomorphism mechanisms.

We wanted to introduce the reader to important models in political science and sociology that provide better alternative hypotheses, which would need to be

90 Simmons and others (n 20) 37.
91 Richard Rose, *Lesson-Drawing in Public Policy: A Guide to Learning across Time and Space* (Chatham House 1993).
92 Simmons and others (n 20) 38.
93 Tim Legrand, 'Transgovernmental Policy Networks in the Anglosphere' (2015) 93 Public Administration 973.

further tested through rigorous process-tracing and through comparative empirical analyses. It may be that DPAs do not end up being as counterproductive as some of their critics suggest, but our main thesis here is that their diffusion cannot only be explained by rational and functional arguments. We do not suggest that they are automatically a failed policy experiment, and further reviews would need to compare how states have learned from each other in implementing their DPA regimes, how authorities awarded them, and what is the resulting impact on the behavior of both political and corporate actors. The jury is still out, and history is in the making.

21 The impact of blocking statutes on the enforcement of anti-corruption laws

Stéphane Bonifassi and Caroline Goussé

While reasons differ, proponents and critics of blocking statutes enacted to prevent foreign authorities—critics mainly in the US—from accessing information or documents located abroad outside the mechanisms provided for in treaties and multilateral agreements, appear to at least agree on one thing: blocking statutes are causing more harm than not. Where countries have a strong interest in enforcing anti-corruption regulations outside their domestic settings, blocking statutes are preventing effective transnational efforts in combating corruption. And while these statutes were originally thought of as protection against threats to nations' sovereign interests, considering the French blocking statute—to take but one example—has been famously described as a 'paper tiger,'[1] one must admit that this protection is often inexistent.

On one hand, efficient transnational anti-corruption enforcement, which is admittedly the purpose of the OECD Convention on Combating Bribery of Foreign Public Officials in International Business Transactions (OECD Convention) and other globalized efforts against corruption, requires that enforcing authorities can readily access information located abroad. After all, blocking statutes are, by definition, a tool that prevents these authorities from having full and easy access to evidence of bribery, and they arguably allow potential defendants to escape prosecution on charges of corruption.

On the other hand, the track record in transnational cases of violations of the Foreign Corrupt Practices Act of 1977 (FCPA) of both the United States Department of Justice (DOJ) and the Security and Exchange Commission (SEC) arguably shows that there is no real hindrance to effective transnational anti-corruption enforcement, either because blocking statutes are designed to allow for efficient enforcement, or because these statutes are not that much relied upon.

In any case, in the interest of globalized efforts against international corruption, this interplay between blocking statutes and proper transnational enforcement should be assessed.

1 Constantin Achillas, Jeffrey S Russell, Cécile Terret ,and Nikki A Ott, 'The French Blocking Statute: Effective Protection against Cross-Border Discovery' (June 2014) Bryan Cave Bulletin 3, referencing US courts decisions.

Should blocking statutes be permitted to apply in the context of transnational anti-corruption? Blocking statutes, such as those in Switzerland and France, and similar provisions in China, which are those on which the chapter focuses, generally follow the premise that discovery mechanisms, at least as they apply in civil proceedings in common law countries, are fundamentally wrong and can be the source of espionage, theft of confidential information, and infringement of privacy. Defenders of blocking statutes therefore submit that these tools protect sovereign states from aggressive extraterritorial enforcement, especially from the US.

However, what have blocking statutes achieved so far? The 2014 OECD report has criticized France for having made no changes to its blocking statute to ensure that it does not hinder investigations or prosecutions of corruption cases by foreign governments.[2] And, in fact, France's recent law no. 2016-1691 of 9 December 2016 on corruption expressly refers to—and in a way, reinforces—the French blocking statute. But again, considering the number of cases against French companies brought in the US, it is far from obvious that these blocking statutes have achieved their purpose of reducing extraterritorial enforcement.

These are the questions this chapter explores.

1 An overview of blocking statutes in France, Switzerland, and China

1.1 France

The French law no. 68-678 of 26 July 1968 first applicable to maritime matters but whose scope was extended in 1980 is exceedingly broad in what it forbids. First, pursuant to Article 1, it provides that no natural or legal person of French nationality, or residing habitually in France, or having its headquarters on French territory may share, through any means, information of an economic, commercial, industrial, financial, or technical nature to foreign public authorities where it would threaten the sovereignty, security, or essential economic interests of France. Second, pursuant to Article 1bis, no person—irrespective of their nationality—may request, seek, or share information of an economic, commercial, industrial, financial, or technical nature 'intended for the establishment of evidence in connection with pending or prospective foreign judicial or administrative proceedings.' Both provisions apply except when international treaties or agreements provide otherwise, and violations carry a prison term of up to six months and/or a fine of up to €18,000 for natural persons, and up to five times this amount for legal entities.

While Article 1bis prohibits the transfer of information when done for a specific purpose, Article 1 straightforwardly forbids any transfer of certain information, to whichever ends. It is true that Article 1 applies not to just anyone. But it does apply

2 OECD, *France: Follow-Up to the Phase 3 Report & Recommendations* (December 2014) 5.

very largely not only to French nationals, residents, and companies headquartered in France, but also to any director, representative, or agent of a company having only an office in France. Finally, the criterion that sharing some information would pose a threat to the sovereignty, security, or essential economic interests is quite easily met. First, because the notions of sovereignty and national interests are very vague. Second, even if notions of sovereignty and national interests were not ambiguous, they do cover an exceedingly wide range of possible information. Third, and most importantly, because Article 1 only requires that the information be of *a nature* to pose a threat to sovereign and national interests, *not* that it actually does.

The scope of Article 1bis is especially broad as well. First, it applies to any person that shares or obtains, or tries to share or obtain, protected information. It also applies irrespective of the offender's nationality. Further, and while the intended purpose for the information is to be used abroad as evidence in a trial, it is not required that the information effectively be used. The mere communication of protected information will be in violation of Article 1bis. In addition, the criterion of pending or actual judicial or administrative proceedings is all-encompassing, and a threat to national interests need not be established.

Finally, both articles are written to prevent the communication of information that is of an economic, commercial, industrial, financial, or technical nature, i.e., almost if not everything. At the very least, it covers information that would be most important for purposes of anti-corruption enforcement: money transfers, commercial strategies, or internal policies of companies, and so forth.

While no changes have yet been made to the French blocking statute itself since 1994, Act n°2016-1691 of 9 December 2016 (Sapin 2) and a decree no. 2016-66 of 29 January 2016 have attempted to address the interplay between the requirements laid out in the blocking statute and imperatives of transnational anticorruption enforcement.

According to Sapin 2, the abovementioned 2016 decree, and a decree no. 2019-206 of 20 March 2019, a newly-created 'Service de l'information stratégique et de la sécurité économique' (Service for strategic information and economic security) and its Commissioner, within the Ministry of the Economy, are responsible for ensuring that the blocking statute is properly applied, and for providing compliance standards to companies notably on financial relations with foreign countries and matters regarding the fight against corporate fraud and corruption. The Service for strategic information and economic security has already reportedly been contacted by several companies concerned by the risks of proceedings abroad, and, more generally, by their compliance obligations. As such, it is meant to provide a contact point for companies in France caught between obligations under the blocking statutes, and information or document production requests by foreign authorities. The question remains, of course, whether companies will, in fact, be willing to inform the Service for strategic information and economic security of document production requests from abroad, when doing so would risk getting the unwanted attention of French authorities. Indeed, according to Article 40 of the French code of criminal procedure:

every constituted authority, every public officer or civil servant who, in the performance of his duties, has gained knowledge of the existence of a felony or of a misdemeanour is obliged to notify forthwith the district prosecutor of the offence and to transmit to this prosecutor any relevant information, official reports or documents.

It should be noted that in any case, Article 2 of the French blocking statute already required all persons listed under Article 1 and Article 1bis to alert the competent Minister when asked to respond to information production requests. But Sapin 2, and the 2016 and 2019 decrees, mark the increased—one might say long-due—willingness of French authorities to strengthen both the existing norms against bribery, and their enforcement. In this regard, companies may be facing a choice between complying with the blocking statute, alerting the Service for strategic information and economic security and thereby risking proceedings in France—which would incidentally allow French authorities to upstage foreign, i.e., American, authorities in anti-corruption enforcement or, at least, allow French authorities to be part of a global settlement such as a joint deferred prosecution agreement—and disregarding the French blocking statute to comply with requests of subpoenas from foreign regulators.

Along with this newly-created service is the new 'Agence française anticorruption' (French Anti-corruption Agency), formerly the 'Service central de prévention de la corruption' (Central Service on Preventing Corruption), in charge of ensuring compliance with the blocking statute where companies are under the monitorship of foreign authorities. Interestingly so, according to a June 2018 deferred prosecution agreement (DPA) between the French company Société Générale, and the DOJ and the US Attorney's Office for the Eastern District of New York, while Société Générale consented to 'any and all disclosures' of 'any information, testimony, documents, records, or other tangible evidence' as deemed appropriate by both the DOJ and the US Attorney's Office for the Eastern District of New York, it is also provided that any evidence of a violation of, among other provisions, the anti-bribery provisions of the FCPA should be disclosed 'in a manner that is consistent with its obligations to report to the PNF [National Financial Prosecutor] and the Agence Française Anticorruption (AFA).'[3] Likewise, DPAs signed by French companies Total and Technip, respectively in 2013 and 2010, provided that disclosures should be made in compliance with the French blocking statute under the supervision of the then-Service central de prévention de la corruption.[4] In this regard, the question as to whether the blocking statute is having an unfortunate

3 See United States Department of Justice, 'Press Release' (June 2018) <https://www.justice.gov/opa/press-release/file/1068521/download> accessed 1 June 2020, [6]; Claire Tetard, 'The Société Générale's Deferred Prosecution Agreement: The First Coordinated Settlement between French and American Authorities' *Ethnic Intelligence* (June 2018).

4 Thomas Rouhette and Ela Barda, 'The French Blocking Statute and Cross-Border Discovery' (2017) 84 Defense Counsel Journal 1.

impact on anti-corruption enforcement is all the more relevant: the French blocking statute, among other statutes of the type, might be preventing the proper monitorship of companies in France by foreign authorities. It might not, however, be preventing domestic anti-corruption enforcement as French authorities are now in a favourable position to do so, providing of course that they are willing to.

It should be noted that further amendments to law no. 68-678 could happen in the foreseeable future, following a June 26, 2019 report to the French Prime Minister titled '[r]estoring the sovereignty of France and Europe and protecting our companies from extraterritorial laws and measures' by MP Raphael Gauvain. In terms highly critical of both the United States and the inefficiency of the French blocking statute, the report argued that:

> the United States of America has led the world into an era of judicial protectionism: while the rule of law has always served as an instrument of regulation, it has now become a weapon of destruction in the United States' economic warfare against the rest of the world, including against its traditional and loyal allies in Europe.

And offered several amendments to the current French legislation, including that the Service for strategic information and economic security be the reporting authority under Article 2, that a penalty for non-compliance with the information obligation be imposed under a newly created article, and that sanctions pursuant to Article 3 be increased.

1.2 Switzerland

Although Switzerland does not have a similarly worded blocking statute, it has enacted several provisions which arguably have the same impact on transnational anti-corruption enforcement. Articles of the Swiss penal code and laws on banking secrecy, legal privilege, and personal data protection also provide limits to the transnational free-flow of evidence.

Article 271 of the Swiss penal code makes it a criminal offence to perform an act which would infringe on Switzerland's sovereignty. Specifically, Article 271 provides that:

> any person who carries out activities on behalf of a foreign State on Swiss territory without lawful authority, where such activities are the responsibility of a public authority or public official; any person who carries out such activities for a foreign party or organization; any person who encourages such activities, is liable to a custodial sentence not exceeding three years or to a monetary penalty, or in serious cases to a custodial sentence of not less than one year.

Similar to the French blocking statute, Article 271 has quite a broad scope of application. It forbids not acts that are precisely defined but any act which legally falls under the authority of a Swiss public official. It is not required that the act be performed at the request of a foreign authority, but only that it is performed either on behalf of a foreign state, or for the benefit of a foreign party or organization. Finally, Article 271 provides that the act be performed on Swiss territory and without authorization from Swiss authorities.

In many respects, Article 271 works like the French blocking statute. Collecting and gathering evidence in Switzerland is generally a judicial function. As such, Article 271 prevents any person—no mention is made in the statute as to the person's nationality—from collecting and gathering evidence in Switzerland when it is ordered by a foreign authority and for use in proceedings abroad, e.g., evidence collected in response to a subpoena or a court order. This applies whether said evidence is in the hands of the requested party, or a third party such as business partners and formers employees, and as much during pre-trial discovery, when made compulsory, as once proceedings have started. A violation of Article 271 is a criminal offense which carries a maximum three-year term of imprisonment or a fine of an unspecified maximum amount.

Article 271 is not *per se* a blocking statute, however: it is not a blanket interdiction of all evidence collecting and sharing for litigation purposes abroad. It does not prevent a person from voluntarily producing certain information or filing documents as evidence to substantiate a claim or a defense in foreign proceedings. And while information may not be collected or reviewed on Swiss soil by or on behalf of a foreign authority, any Swiss-based party may voluntarily do so. Most importantly, and while this seems to be very rarely the case, a foreign authority or party may still be authorized to perform acts—such as collecting evidence pursuant to a foreign court order—otherwise falling within the competence of Swiss public authorities.

Other provisions of the Swiss penal code restricting how evidence circulates abroad, notably Article 273, make it illegal for any person to make available, or to obtain in order to make available 'a manufacturing or trade secret to an external official agency, a foreign organization, a private enterprise, or the agents of any of these.' Article 273 is still not, however, a boundless limitation on sharing information or documents abroad which contain trade or manufacturing secrets. First, it only prohibits the intentional communication of such secrets, not negligent conduct. Second, a Swiss party, i.e., a party either residing or having its headquarters in Switzerland, may waive the protection afforded by Article 273.

1.3 China

On October 26, 2018, the People's Republic of China enacted a blocking statute on international criminal assistance, the International Criminal Judicial Assistance Law (ICJAL), whereby approval from Chinese authorities is necessary before providing evidence, or more generally assistance, in foreign criminal proceedings. This new statute immediately applied to, *inter alia*, the investigation, prosecution, trial, and enforcement of criminal cases, service of documents, collection of evidence, witness depositions, and asset forfeiture in criminal matters.

Internal investigations unrelated to ongoing criminal proceedings would thus not fall within this scope, but as some authors have pointed out, 'authorities could potentially make their own determination on whether a foreign country's proceeding is "criminal," and there is no clear guidance on how [Chinese] authorities might do so.'[5] The statute is mute on what factors Chinese authorities would favor in granting requests, but provides for six specific circumstances under which approval may be denied, and a seventh worded as broadly as 'other situations where refusal is allowed.'[6] Furthermore, the sharing of information and document production 'must not harm the People's Republic of China's sovereignty, security, or societal public interest; and must not violate the basic principles of the laws of the People's Republic of China.'[7] Interestingly, the statute does not (yet) address penalties for violations of its dispositions; some authors have already pointed out one instance where a US court has rejected a defense at least partly based on the ICJAL against subpoenas from the US Attorney's Office, considering among other criteria that sanctions were 'pure speculation.'[8]

Another piece of domestic legislation limiting the free-flow of information and document production abroad is China's secrecy laws, which notably prohibit the unauthorized transfer of state, trade, and bank secrets. The impact of these laws on how China-based companies have been responding to document production requests by foreign regulators is reportedly consequential, because a violation of these laws is heavily sanctioned pursuant to the Chinese penal code, and because the definition of what constitutes a state, or a trade secret is both broad and vague.

Regarding state secrets specifically, pursuant to Article 111 of the Chinese penal code:

> whoever steals, secretly gathers, purchases, or illegally provides state secrets or intelligence for an organization, institution, or personnel outside the country is to be sentenced from not less than five years to not more than 10 years of fixed-term imprisonment; when circumstances are particularly serious, he is to be sentenced to not less than 10 years of fixed-term imprisonment, or life sentence; and when circumstances are relatively minor, he is to be sentenced to not more than five years of fixed-term imprisonment, criminal detention, control, or deprivation of political rights.

5 Ryan Rohlfsen, David Zhang, and Karen Oddo, 'China's Blocking Statute Creates New Challenges for Multinational Companies' *FCPA Professor* (6 March 2019) <http://fcpaprofessor.com/chinas-blocking-statute-creates-new-challenges-multinational-companies/> accessed 1 June 2020.

6 ICJAL art 14.

7 Ibid art 4.

8 Eric Carlson and Helen Hwang, 'Practice Alert: What's the Impact of China's Year-Old Blocking Statute?' *The FCPA Blog* (2 December 2019) <https://fcpablog.com/2019/12/02/practice-alert-whats-the-impact-of-chinas-year-old-blocking-statute/> accessed 1 June 2020.

These penalties incurred for violating Chinese state secret laws are particularly heavy, even more so when one considers what falls under the definition of a state secret. According to Article 2 of the Law of the People's Republic of China on Guarding State Secrets, 'state secrets are matters which relate to the national security and interests' as defined by law. Pursuant to Article 9, these include classified matters in key policing decisions on state affairs, in national economic and social development, in science and technology, as well as other classified matters 'as determined by the state secrecy administrative department.' It would appear Chinese authorities take a broad view of what constitutes a classified matter under Article 9, and that many documents belonging either to state-backed companies, or to companies involved in sensitive industries would fall under the state-secret label. It was pointed out, for example, that internal policies and procedures of state-owned companies may, as such, be considered state secrets.

1.4 Three blocking statutes as a protection of sovereign interests

It goes without saying: blocking statutes or related provisions aim at protecting nations' sovereign interests and are, at least on paper, not meant to impede effective enforcement of anti-corruption regulations abroad. The French and Swiss statutes mentioned above are to apply except where international treaties or agreements provide otherwise, and considering the large number of legal instruments allowing for an effective flow of evidence abroad, one could make the argument that blocking statutes are merely a protection against demands that overlook principles of comity, or that show 'a disrespect for internationally recognized principles restricting the extraterritorial reach of a nation's laws, or an offense to public policy unworthy of recognition.'[9]

Sovereign interests that are sought to be protected lie partly with the 'power of a nation to prescribe laws regulating activities within its territory,' whether it be substantive or procedural laws.

With regard to transnational anti-corruption enforcement, however, blocking statutes can hardly be considered as a protection against the extraterritorial reach of substantive norms. There is arguably not much of a difference between national substantive legal rules regarding corruption, at least to the extent that corruption is generally made a criminal offense. Further, under the OECD Convention, signatory countries must also enact 'laws in conformity with its provisions designed to criminalize bribery of foreign officials.'[10] The OECD Convention, whose purpose is to 'further advance international understanding and co-operation in combating bribery of public officials,' very early declares that 'achieving equivalence among the measures to be taken by the Parties is an essential object and purpose of the Convention, which requires that the

9 Ken S Nakata, 'The SEC and Foreign Blocking Statutes: Need for a Balanced Approach' (1987) University of Pennsylvania Journal of International Business 549, 553.

10 Ibid 895.

Convention be ratified without derogations affecting this equivalence.' And while the convention leaves a certain freedom of interpretation of its rules to its parties, this freedom is limited, however, by the fact that such norms as are contained in the OECD Convention must not be defeated by too different interpretations, country to country.[11]

Procedural rules regarding the collecting and sharing of information or documents which might constitute evidence in anti-corruption proceedings are, on the other hand, very much opposed when it comes to common law and civil law countries. While not discussing the merits of each, it is a rather established fact that the United States and countries such as France regard each other's rules of evidence as either limitative to a party's right and an impediment to effective (here, anti-corruption) enforcement, or nothing less than a fishing expedition. It has even been argued by a French scholar that US rules of evidence, in this case rules of discovery in civil proceedings, were a denial of a party's right to a fair trial. Of course, this polar opposition between civil and common law countries, or at least between the French and American systems, exists arguably more in civil than in criminal matters. To cite but just two small examples in support of this argument is the fact that conditions for granting search warrants in criminal investigations are much stricter and more strictly enforced in the US than in France. Similarly, French courts admit evidence in criminal proceedings that would be excluded from American courts, such as evidence unlawfully obtained. In this respect, the protection of sovereign interests that is understood as a protection against an invasive means of acquiring evidence is less appealing when it comes to anti-corruption enforcement. But if one looks at the aggressive or committed enforcement of anti-corruption provisions in the US, to this date—at least—much more so than in France, and the means by which American enforcement authorities can coerce companies to cooperate, the differences between French and American procedure rules remain sharp. To this extent, blocking statutes are effectively meant to preserve a nation's sovereign interests.

Sovereign interests also evidently lie in the protection of a nation's economic affairs, and blocking statutes, especially as they apply to transnational anti-corruption enforcement, may in this respect be held by some as a necessary protection. The extraterritorial reach of the FCPA has now been debated and criticized for several years. The staggering amounts in fines imposed on European companies by both the DOJ and the SEC have been denounced as 'a significant levy on European economies to the benefit of the US public finances' and a way for the US to 'impose sanctions on the foreign companies that may harm their interests.'[12] Some argue that the $772 million fine imposed on Alstom in 2014,

11 To this end, the OECD Convention imposes many standards on each of its parties under the theory of functional equivalence.

12 Rouhette and Barda (n 5) 1, citing the Rapport Lellouche commissioned by the French parliament to review the impact of the extraterritorial reach of the US statutes on French and European economies.

the same year General Electrics acquired Alstom's power and grid division, is the perfect example of this. In any case, it is hardly debatable that the fines imposed on foreign companies by both the DOJ and the SEC in anti-corruption cases are excessively punitive, especially when compared to fines to which US companies were sentenced for similar violations.[13] In this sense, if we posit that blocking statutes effectively hinder, to some degree, transnational anti-corruption enforcement, it is because some consider these statutes as necessary to preserve some national sovereign interests. This is undoubtedly the rationale behind the French, Swiss, and Chinese statutes studied above, as much as behind the European Union blocking statute in support of the Iran nuclear deal following the US withdrawal from the Joint Comprehensive Plan of Action and the announcement that the US would reimpose sanctions on non-US persons involved in specific transactions with Iran.

2 Blocking statutes against effective transnational anticorruption enforcement

While not necessarily questioning their legitimacy, because blocking statutes are specifically designed to hinder the transfer abroad of information and documents that could serve as evidence, they could possibly be an impediment to effective transnational anti-corruption enforcement. One could indeed argue that blocking statutes are overly broad in their application, redundant with other statutes such as data protection regulations, that they in fact provide undue protection to persons committing acts of bribery, or that they contribute to a 'piling on' of regulatory enforcement and of obligations for both regulators and recipients of document production requests.

While Switzerland has admittedly a more restricted approach to rules preventing the free transfer of information to foreign entities, a most common critique of the French and Chinese statutes is indeed that they are exceedingly broad.

As indicated above, while China's ICJAL is limited to criminal proceedings abroad, the statute is unclear as to what actually are understood as criminal proceedings, and leeway is given to Chinese authorities to give these terms a broad interpretation. Conditions for approval or refusal of information communication requests seem to border on the arbitrary, and such communication is, in any case, forbidden wherever it would harm China's sovereignty, security, or societal public interests, however comprehensive such terms may be. Similarly, China's state secret law relies on an extremely comprehensive understanding of what constitutes a state secret. This incredibly large understanding of what is a state secret effectively ensures that not only companies that are state-backed, or companies in obviously sensitive sectors, but almost, if not all, companies based or having an

13 Richard L Cassin, '2017 FCPA Enforcement Index' *The FCPA Blog* (2 January 2018) <https://fcpablog.com/2018/01/02/2017-fcpa-enforcement-index/> accessed 1 June 2020.

office in China must abide by the blocking statute or fear prosecution by Chinese authorities.

Regarding the French blocking statute specifically, and as was mentioned above, Article 1 and Article 1bis of the French blocking statute forbid the transfer of information, in whichever form, of an economic, commercial, industrial, financial, or technical nature. This, in fact, covers most if not all information. Both articles also apply to an almost all-encompassing category of persons. Article 1 targets French nationals, French residents, as well as any director, representative, and agent of a company having either its headquarters or just an office in France. Article 1bis simply makes no mention of a specific group of people, and thus applies to all persons on French territory and to all French nationals abroad. Article 1bis also applies not only to persons who communicate privileged information, like Article 1, but to those who seek to obtain such information as well.

Furthermore, while Article 1 provides that relevant information should not be transferred when its communication would be of a nature to threaten national interests, Article 1bis is applicable irrespective of such threat and only requires that the communication of information be for the purpose of proceedings abroad, or in view of such proceedings. Questions as to the merits of an Article 1bis, which makes no mention of the protection of a sovereignty or national interests, are especially valid in the context of transnational anti-corruption enforcement: forbidding almost all transfer of information that is to be used in foreign enquiries or proceedings runs counter to a globalized effort against bribery. France, a signatory party to the OECD Convention, should supposedly be advocating for such globalized efforts. Of course, one could argue, as it has been done more than once by some French scholars and legislators, that Article 1bis purports to protect national interests or sovereignty, even if not mentioned, in hampering transnational anti-corruption enforcement that runs counter to those interests. But first, Article 1 already provides such protection. Second, Article 1bis applies not only to French nationals in France and abroad, but also to anyone on its territory. As such, the assertion that it only aims to prevent violation to French interests or sovereignty is either unconvincing or illustrates an understanding of notions of sovereignty and national interests that is as harmful in its extraterritorial reach as would be an alleged aggressive transnational enforcement of the FCPA.

In addition to some being excessively broad in scope, the French, Swiss, and Chinese statutes all provide extra limitations to the transfer of information in the name of a protection already guaranteed by data privacy laws. Responding to requests for information or document production first requires that a substantive amount of personal data be reviewed, and their processing and transfer abroad is heavily regulated in most jurisdictions that include Europe and China. In this regard, requiring that companies—for example—comply with blocking statutes when subject to court orders or subpoenas from foreign authorities is adding a layer of obligations that is arguably unnecessary and a hindrance to effective transnational anti-corruption enforcement. It is also placing companies between a rock and a hard place when they are willing to cooperate with foreign enforcement authorities but cannot do so because of such overly broad blocking statutes.

There is an undeniable overlap between blocking statutes and data privacy laws, considering that information often falls within the wide range of both regulations, which also have a large jurisdictional scope, that strict enforcement and penalties are made to ensure compliance with each of these laws (at least on paper), and that data protection much like blocking statutes are both at play in transnational corruption enforcement matters.[14] Personal data covers a wide range of information, including information that would be protected by blocking statutes, for instance credit information, or computer IP addresses. Further to this point, it should be noted that according to China's national standard on personal information protection issued on January 2, 2018,[15] personal data is not to be understood as information relating to identifying personal factors only, but also to sensitive data understood on a risk-based approach for persons or property,[16] and which could, as such, cover an even broader range of information also protected according to blocking statutes.

And much like blocking statutes, data privacy laws have a large jurisdictional scope of application. Swiss data privacy laws, for example, apply where the data subject is a Swiss resident, where the data controller or processor is Swiss-based, or if the damage resulting from data breach is sustained in Switzerland. The European Union's recent General Data Protection Regulation (GDPR) is applicable, pursuant to its Article 3, to data controllers or processors that are based in the Union, but also to foreign-based controllers or processors 'where the processing activities are related to: (a) the offerings of goods or services, irrespective of whether a payment of the data subject is required, to such data subjects in the Union; or (b) the monitoring of their behaviour as far as their behaviour takes place in the Union,' as well as where the data controller or processor is based in foreign territory subject to member-state law.

Compliance with data privacy laws is no less optional than to blocking statutes. As an example, penalties for violations of provisions of the GDPR regarding data transfer to third countries are particularly substantial: whichever is higher between a fine of €20 million or 4% of the firm's annual global turnover.

Transnational anti-corruption enforcement, most notably through the globalization of FCPA enforcement over the last decade or so, is necessarily impacted by both data privacy laws and blocking statutes, and there is hardly an argument that the double impact of these regulations is legitimate. As briefly laid out above, these statutes actually overlap in many ways, and they impose twice as many obligations on recipients of requests for information or document

14 See Katherine Morga, 'Data Privacy and the Foreign Corrupt Practices Act: A Study of Enforcement and Its Effect on Corporate Compliance in the Age of Global Regulation' (2012) 20 Commlaw Conspectus 415.

15 National Standards on Information Security Technology—Personal Information Security Specification, GB/T 35273-2017, 2018.

16 Yan Luo and Phil Bradley-Schmieg, 'China Issues New Personal Information Protection Standard' *Covington* (5 January 2018) <https://www.insideprivacy.com/international/china/china-issues-new-personal-information-protection-standard/> accessed 1 June 2020.

production that creates a risk of 'piling on,' as was described by then-Attorney General Rod Rosenstein in his remarks to the New York City Bar White Collar Crime Institute of May 9, 2018.[17] Mr Rosenstein was partly referring to joint or parallel investigations by US or foreign agencies and how their interplay may affect effective enforcement. But Mr Rosenstein was also referring to situations where 'a company may be accountable to multiple regulatory bodies' and how these created 'a risk of repeated punishments that may exceed what is necessary to rectify the harm and deter future violations.' It may be argued that compliance with data protection laws and blocking statutes, furthermore when they clash with obligations to cooperate, creates this 'piling on' that is regrettable first because it hinders effective enforcement. For instance, compliance with blocking statutes and data privacy laws imposes a reporting to different administrative bodies to secure the transfer of the same information. Second, because these statutes create a legal framework that is overly stringent if only in terms of penalties, which would exceed their punitive and deterrent objectives.

While the negative impact of blocking statutes is such, on paper, that one might wonder if the sovereign interests they aim to protect are not eventually outweighed, the reality of this impact is in fact much more questionable. American authorities appear to have had little deference to foreign blocking statutes, especially the French blocking statute, and considering how effective the transnational FCPA enforcement by the DOJ and the SEC has been, in terms both of the number of enforcement cases and amount of financial penalties, it is difficult to assert that blocking statutes would have had an effect, in the past, on transnational anti-corruption enforcement. There also have been very few convictions for violations of blocking statutes, at least in France and Switzerland. And while hard to assess, it does not appear that blocking statutes have effectively allowed companies or private individuals to evade proceedings on FCPA violations.

On a par with how the DOJ and the SEC have construed the extraterritorial reach of the FCPA in their mission to combat the bribery of foreign officials, American authorities seem to have afforded statutes hampering such extraterritorial reach with very little deference. This has been amply written about, specifically regarding the French blocking statutes and mostly regarding landmark American court decisions in civil matters holding the French statute as optional.

The fact that violations of the French and Swiss blocking statutes are, respectively, inexistent but for one peculiar example and relatively uncommon has contributed to this lack of deference from US courts and, supposedly, regulators. The French blocking statute, which, for memory, was enacted in 1968 and extended in 1980, has been the basis for a criminal conviction in French courts only once in 2007. The Criminal chamber of the *Cour de cassation* upheld the conviction of a French attorney pursuant to Article 1bis. Not only is there no

17 Rod Rosenstein, 'Remarks to the New York City Bar White Collar Crime Institute' (New York, 9 May 2018) <https://www.justice.gov/opa/speech/deputy-attorney-general-rod-rosenstein-delivers-remarks-new-york-city-bar-white-collar> accessed 1 June 2020.

criminal conviction based on Article 1, but we are not aware of any civil court decisions interpreting this article either. The enforcement by French courts of the blocking statute is quasi inexistent. It is no surprise, therefore, that American authorities should give it the responding amount of deference.

Admittedly, China appears to be much more serious in its enforcement of its blocking provisions.[18] While we have found no information as to the exact number of criminal convictions by Chinese courts for violations of the state, trade, or bank secrets laws, the difficulties for China-based companies when faced with document production requests from foreign authorities have been much reported. Nonetheless, at least in civil matters, American courts seem to have taken the same approach as with the French blocking statute, i.e., Chinese blocking statutes are optional and Chinese interests in protecting information and documents must be reviewed according to a balanced approach. Consequently, some US courts have alternatively accepted or rejected arguments as to the existence of harsh penalties for violating state secrecy laws. Worth mentioning as well is the impact of the Chinese state secrecy laws on the SEC general fraud investigations. Section 106 of the Sarbanes-Oxley Act of 30 July 2002 (SOX),[19] and the SOX's subsequent amendment in 2010 by the Dodd-Frank Act which was, in turn, arguably dismantled in 2018, have given tools to the SEC to force accounting firms to provide audit work papers, including from offices abroad. In two separate cases involving, respectively the Big-Four accounting firms, and the firm Deloitte, the SEC had issued subpoenas to produce audit documents regarding Chinese companies. In each case, the firms had refused to comply on grounds that they would infringe the Chinese state secrecy laws by doing so, an argument which had been rejected by the SEC and prompted enforcement actions before the courts. In the case involving the Big-Four, the court ruled out the defense based on compliance with the Chinese state secrecy laws. Desirous to avoid a severe sanction, the four affiliates reached a settlement with the SEC, according to which each of the companies agreed to pay USD $500,000. They also had to agree to comply with all future document production requests. However, in the case involving Deloitte, the SEC eventually moved to dismiss without prejudice its subpoena enforcement action after an agreement was reached with Chinese authorities to produce requested documents. Considering these two cases only, it does not appear that antifraud enforcement suffers much from the Chinese state secrecy laws: either the SEC forces through litigation the production of documents or manages to agree with the Chinese authorities through mutual assistance treaties. Companies caught in between the foreign regulators and Chinese laws are, on the other hand, bearing the brunt of this conflict of laws. And this would be

18 The ICJAL being in existence for just one year, as of the date of this chapter, we have little knowledge of China's actual enforcement of its provisions. We only considered, therefore, enforcement of China's state secret laws.

19 Public Law 116 STAT. 745, 30 July 2002. See at <https://www.gpo.gov/fdsys/pkg/PLAW-107publ204/pdf/PLAW-107publ204.pdf> accessed 1 June 2020.

particularly topical in case of increased tensions between the US and China which would render cooperation between authorities more difficult. In terms of FCPA enforcement, a definite understanding of the impact of China's blocking statutes on enforcement is not easy to reach,[20] but as one author pointed out: 'China has certainly been fertile ground for FPCA enforcement action – 31 percent of all corporate FCPA cases from 2011 to the present have involved improper conduct in part or in full in China.'[21]

3 Conclusion

Blocking statutes are much criticized, and with reason. They are hardly efficient; the French blocking statute is undoubtedly the least effective of all the statutes studied in this chapter. It is placing companies in a situation in which compliance with either the blocking statute or the production request may have adverse consequences. Blocking statutes, when read outside the context of a subpoena or a formal request by a foreign authority, prevent not only companies but also attorneys from requesting or sharing information abroad that would be paramount to the interests of their clients. It is noteworthy that the only criminal conviction ever rendered in France for a violation of the blocking statute is that of an attorney. The French and Chinese blocking statutes are also excessively large, and they range from difficult to impossible to enforce and/or comply with, for this reason also.

As to blocking statutes being nonetheless legitimate in that they aim to protect sovereign interests, and aside from the fact that this protection is virtually inexistent since blocking statutes are hardly applied, this legitimacy does not easily interplay with that of an effective transnational anti-corruption enforcement. If the United States has been much criticized for its aggressive enforcement of the FPCA, and while not necessarily dismissing all critics on this front, one must admit that US regulators would have had much less groundwork to do so if countries like France had effectively enforced their own anti-bribery provisions. Sapin 2 and other recent legal amendments to further combat bribery in France—if effectively enforced—will, in this regard, provide for an interesting chance to see how relevant the blocking statute is to preserve French sovereign interests.

20 Farrah Berse and others, 'Paul Weiss Discusses FCPA Enforcement and Anti-Corruption Developments' *The CLS Blue Sky Blog* (February 2017) <http://clsbluesky.law.columbia.edu/2017/02/08/paul-weiss-discusses-fcpa-enforcement-and-anti-corruption-developments/> accessed 1 June 2020.

21 Eric Carlson, 'National Security: Are Chinese Companies Targeted for FCPA Enforcement?' *The FCPA Blog* (November 2018) <http://www.fcpablog.com/blog/2018/11/8/national-security-are-chinese-companies-targeted-for-fcpa-en.html> accessed 1 June 2020.

22 The search for synergies

The utopian ideal of cooperation between international anti-corruption mechanisms

Camila Florencia Tort[1]

The 2030 Agenda for Sustainable Development, which came into force in January 2016, calls on states to build effective, accountable, and inclusive institutions at all levels and includes a specific target on substantially reducing corruption and bribery in all their forms.[2] Moreover, the Sustainable Development Goal Target 16.A urges states to strengthen relevant national institutions for building capacity at all levels to prevent violence, and combat terrorism and crime.[3] With this in mind, it is not only reasonable, but desirable to increase synergies between international/regional organizations and global anti-corruption mechanisms.

Over the last several years, a number of mechanisms within international institutions and organizations have been created to fight corruption at all levels. Nonetheless, the mandates and states members of these institutions oftentimes overlap, adding a new level of complexity to the call for increased cooperation to find effective and sustainable solutions.

Organizations and/or mechanisms may overlap under two 'dimensions.' On the one hand, the 'membership' dimension, and on the other hand, the 'mandate' dimension. The former simply refers to states that are part of an organization, which occurs when all member states of one of organization are also member states of another one, which is bigger in terms of number of member states. Both organizations are independent and autonomous, but they share membership of countries. Another variation of membership overlapping is when some, but not all, of the member states of one organization are also member states of another organization. The latter dimension usually occurs after one organization decides to increase the areas and topics covered by its work, or two organizations address the same issues or share the same organizational goals, but differ in the applicable normative framework.[4]

1 The views and/or opinions in the article are that of the author and do not necessarily represent the views and/or opinions of the Organization of American States.

2 'Transforming Our World: The 2030 Agenda for Sustainable Development', adopted by UN General Assembly Resolution, UN Doc. A/RES/70/1, 21 October 2015, target 16.5.

3 Ibid target 16.a.

4 Brigitte Weiffen, 'Institutional Overlap and Responses to Political Crises in South America' in Marcial A G Suarez, Rafael Duarte Villa, and Brigitte Weiffen (eds), *Power Dynamics and*

The proliferation of organizations and institutions has led to a considerable debate over the effects and effectiveness of overlapping mechanisms. Some scholars have argued that the proliferation of similar organizations may create tensions and competition instead of collaboration and unity between them.[5] Instead, others argue that the existence of multiple organizations and mechanisms may even lead to further cooperation, an integration of efforts, and homogenize standards.[6]

No state is immune from corruption and its transnational reach. In this context, the existence of more than one anti-corruption mechanism can be both desirable and reasonable in the fight against corruption.[7] Enhancing cooperation between international anti-corruption mechanisms can prove to be enormously beneficial for states to decrease the costs these international commitments impose on them and to ensure an effective and coordinated response against corruption. Nonetheless, one cannot ignore the structural differences between each mechanism that can hinder the potential for cooperation.

This chapter examines the main characteristics and describes the two dimensions—membership and mandate—of the principal anti-corruption mechanisms: the United Nations Convention against Corruption's Implementation Review Mechanism (UNCAC Review Mechanism), the Mechanism for Follow-Up on the Implementation of the Inter-American Convention against Corruption (MESICIC), the Group of States against Corruption of the Council of Europe (GRECO), and the monitoring body to the Organization for Economic Co-operation and Development's Anti-Bribery Convention.

Regional Security in Latin America (Palgrave Macmillan 2017) 173. See also Brigitte Weiffen, Leslie Wehner, and Detlef Nolte, 'Overlapping Regional Security Institutions in South America: The Case of OAS and UNASUR' (2013) 16 International Area Studies Review 370.

5 Laura Gómez-Mera, 'International Regime Complexity and Regional Governance: Evidence from the Americas' (2015) 21 Global Governance 19. See also Andrés Malamud and Gian Luca Gardini, 'Has Regionalism Peaked? The Latin American Quagmire and Its Lessons' (2012) 47 The International Spectator: Italian Journal of International Affairs 47 116; Andrés Malamud, 'Overlapping Regionalism, No Integration: Conceptual Issues and the Latin American Experiences' (2013) EUI RSCAS Working Paper 2013/20 <https://cadmus.eui.eu/bitstream/handle/1814/26336/RSCAS_2013_20.pdf?sequence=1&isAllowed=y> accessed 1 June 2020.

6 José Antonio Sanahuja, 'La construcción de una región: Suramérica y el regionalismo posliberal' in Manuel Cienfuegos and José Antonio Sanahuja (eds), *Una región en construcción: UNASUR y la integración en América del Sur* (Barcelona Center for International Affairs 2010) 87. See also Pia Riggirozzi and Diana Tussie, 'The Rise of Post-hegemonic Regionalism in Latin America' in Pia Riggirozzi and Diana Tussie (eds), *The Rise of Post-hegemonic Regionalism: The Case of Latin America* (Springer 2012) 1; Detlef Nolte, 'Latin America's New Regional Architecture: A Cooperative or Segmented Regional Governance Complex?' (2014) EUI RSCAS Working Paper 2014/89 <https://cadmus.eui.eu/bitstream/handle/1814/32595/RSCAS_2014_89.pdf?sequence=1&isAllowed=y> accessed 1 June 2020.

7 International organizations are actively interplaying and are dependent on each other to reach their goals. Malte Brosing, 'Overlap and Interplay between International Organizations: Theories and Approaches' (2011) 18 South African Journal of International Affairs 147.

1 The first dimension: differences in membership

Even though the differences in membership may seem obvious and irrelevant at first glance, the implications of said differences are quite relevant to better understanding the potential for cooperation. The fact that not all states are part of the same anti-corruption mechanism means, first, that not all states are bound by the same provisions and obligations. This also gives rise to a jurisdictional incompatibility, since each anti-corruption mechanism can only follow-up on the implementation of the provisions of its own specific anti-corruption convention or set of principles, as in the case of the GRECO.

The Inter-American Convention against Corruption (IACAC), adopted in 1996, was the first international legal instrument of its kind.[8] To date, all 34 active OAS member states have ratified the IACAC.[9] The IACAC follows a comprehensive approach to the problem of corruption and contains measures for the prevention, detection, and investigation of acts of corruption, for the punishment of those who commit them, and for the recovery of the proceeds of such acts.

Soon after its entry into force, the states parties to the IACAC began discussions to create a follow-up mechanism on the implementation of the IACAC obligations on a state. As a result, the Report of Buenos Aires on the Mechanism for Follow-Up on Implementation of the Inter-American Convention against Corruption (Report of Buenos Aires) was adopted in June, 2001.[10] Currently, 33 of the 34 states parties of the IACAC are member states of the MESICIC.[11]

Similarly, the GRECO was created in 1999,[12] thanks to the strong political will among the member states of the Council of Europe, which were determined to give birth to a mechanism with the objective to fight against corruption.[13]

8 Inter-American Convention against Corruption (entered into force 6 March 1997) (1996) 35 ILM 724.

9 See more information regarding the signatories and ratifications to the IACAC at: OAS, 'Inter-American Convention against Corruption (B-58)' <www.oas.org/en/sla/dil/inter_american_treaties_B-58_against_Corruption_signatories.asp> accessed 1 June 2020.

10 See OAS General Assembly, 'Mechanism for Follow-Up of Implementation of the Inter-American Convention Against Corruption' (Resolution adopted at the third plenary session, 5 June 2001), OAS Doc. AG/RES. 1784 (XXXI-O/01), including the Buenos Aires Report.

11 For general information on the MESICIC see: OAS, 'What is the MESICIC?'<www.oas.org/en/sla/dlc/mesicic/default.asp> accessed 1 June 2020. Additionally, it is important to note that the MESICIC is a voluntary mechanism within the IACAC. As a matter of fact, not all IACAC Member States are Member States of the MESICIC.

12 See 'Resolution (98) 7—Authorizing the Partial and Enlarged Agreement Establishing the "Group" of States against Corruption—GRECO', adopted by the Council of Europe Committee of Ministers, 5 May 1998. Resolution (98) 7 was followed by 'Resolution (99) 5—Establishing the Group of States against Corruption (GRECO)', adopted by the Council of Europe Committee of Ministers, 1 May 1999.

13 For more information regarding GRECO's historical background, see: Council of Europe, 'GRECO – Historical Background' <www.coe.int/en/web/greco/about-us/background> accessed 1 June 2020.

Since its inception, the GRECO has grown to include 49 member states, and although the GRECO is a group created within the Council of Europe, its membership extends to Asia and includes the United States of America.[14]

Following the example of the OAS and the Council of Europe, after the United Nations Convention against Corruption (UNCAC)[15] entered into force in December 2005, states negotiated the creation of an Implementation Review Mechanism (UNCAC Review Mechanism) in accordance with Article 63(7), which was finally established in 2009 during the Conference of the states parties in Doha.[16] As of June 2018, the UNCAC has been ratified by 186 member states, which at the same time are part of the UNCAC Review Mechanism.[17]

Lastly, the Organization for Economic Co-operation and Development (OECD), in 1997, passed the Convention on Combating Bribery of Foreign Public Officials in International Business Transactions (OECD Convention).[18] To date, 44 states have ratified the OECD Convention, 36 of which are also member states of the OECD.[19] In addition, 18 Recommendations[20] have been adopted for the successful implementation of the obligations provided in said Convention.

The OECD Convention itself establishes an open-ended, peer-driven monitoring mechanism to ensure the thorough implementation of the international obligations that countries have taken on under the convention. This monitoring is carried out by the OECD Working Group on Bribery. The establishment of this monitoring body was possible due to the provisions in Article 12 of the convention, which provides that this Working Group is to carry out a program of systematic follow-up to monitor and promote the full implementation of the convention.

Secondly, the differences in membership may also indicate that some states do not want to undertake the obligations of a convention they are not part of. For instance, all of the IACAC provisions are mandatory; on the contrary, the

14 For a detailed list of the member States, see: Council of Europe, 'Members and Observers' <www.coe.int/en/web/greco/structure/member-and-observers> accessed 1 June 2020.

15 United Nations Convention against Corruption (opened for signature 9 December 2003, entered into force 14 December 2005) 2349 UNTS 41 (UNCAC).

16 Resolution 3/1 established the Implementation Review Mechanism and contains its terms of reference. Resolution 3/1 was later modified by Resolution 4/1 which included the participation, in certain steps of the evaluation, NGOs.

17 For more information regarding signatures and ratifications of the UNCAC, see: UNODC, 'Signature and Ratification Status' <www.unodc.org/unodc/en/corruption/ratification-status.html> accessed 1 June 2020.

18 Convention on Combating Bribery of Foreign Public Officials in International Business Transactions (adopted 17 December 1997, entered into force 15 February 1999) 37 ILM 1.

19 See OECD, 'Country Reports on the Implementation of the OECD Anti-Bribery Convention' <www.oecd.org/daf/anti-bribery/countryreportsontheimplementationoftheoecdanti-briberyconvention.htm> accessed 1 June 2020.

20 Recommendation of the Council for Further Combating Bribery of Foreign Public Officials in International Business Transactions, adopted by the Council, 26 November 2009.

UNCAC has three levels of obligations: first, the mandatory provisions;[21] second, obligations that states should consider adopting;[22] and third, optional provisions.[23]

Thirdly, states might disagree on the specific processes the other anti-corruption mechanisms use to evaluate the level of implementation of the provisions under review. Or, they may want to keep their country report confidential, a possibility which may differ among the different mechanisms. For instance, within the framework of the MESICIC, the online distribution of all documentation—reports and annexes—is mandatory.

The above are some of the implications that result from having different states being members of different conventions and anti-corruption mechanisms, which follow-up on the implementation of the convention which created it. Despite having the same aim and sharing some of their obligations and standards, in this context, the little differences matter when determining the level of possible substantive synergies.

2 The second dimension: differences in mandates

As previously noted, while all international anti-corruption mechanisms review and assess the implementation of their corresponding international anti-corruption legal instruments, there are numerous substantive differences in the way these mechanisms operate and in the legal instruments these mechanisms oversee. These differences include:

1. Differences in the topics currently under review;
2. Differences in the timing of the rounds/phases of analysis;
3. Differences in the process of analysis;
4. Differences in the levels of transparency-confidentiality of the information;
5. Differences in the civil society participation throughout the review process;
6. Differences in the preparation of global/hemispheric reports and other activities within the mechanism.

This section addresses these differences by comparing the UNCAC Review Mechanism, the MESICIC, the GRECO, and the OECD Convention monitoring body.

21 See, e.g., UNCAC, art 12(4).
22 Ibid art 8(6).
23 Ibid art 57(5).

Table 22.1 Membership by the states of the Americas of the anti-corruption mechanisms.

States Membership to the Anti-Corruption Mechanisms							
STATE	*OAS*		*UN*		*OECD*		*GRECO*
	IACAC ratification	*MESICIC*	*UNCAC signature*	*UNCAC ratification*	*OECD Anti-Bribery*	*OECD Member*	*Member State*
Antigua and Barbuda	YES	YES	YES	YES	NO	NO	NO
Argentina	YES	YES	YES	YES	YES	NO	NO
Barbados	YES	NO	YES	NO	NO	NO	NO
Belize	YES	YES	YES	YES	NO	NO	NO
Bolivia	YES	YES	YES	YES	NO	NO	NO
Brazil	YES	YES	YES	YES	YES	NO	NO
Canada	YES	YES	YES	YES	YES	YES	NO
Chile	YES	YES	YES	YES	YES	YES	NO
Colombia	YES	YES	YES	YES	YES	NO	NO
Costa Rica	YES	YES	YES	YES	YES	NO	NO
Dominica	YES	YES	YES	YES	NO	NO	NO
Dominican Rep.	YES	YES	YES	YES	NO	NO	NO
Ecuador	YES	YES	YES	YES	NO	NO	NO
El Salvador	YES	YES	YES	YES	NO	NO	NO
Grenada	YES	YES	YES	YES	NO	NO	NO
Guatemala	YES	YES	YES	YES	NO	NO	NO
Guyana	YES	YES	YES	YES	NO	NO	NO
Haiti	YES	YES	YES	YES	NO	NO	NO

Honduras	YES	YES	YES	YES	NO	NO	NO
Jamaica	YES	YES	YES	YES	NO	NO	NO
Mexico	YES	YES	YES	YES	YES	YES	NO
Nicaragua	YES	YES	YES	YES	NO	NO	NO
Panama	YES	YES	YES	YES	NO	NO	NO
Paraguay	YES	YES	YES	YES	NO	NO	NO
Peru	YES	YES	YES	YES	YES	NO	NO
St. Kitts and Nevis	YES	YES	NO	NO	NO	NO	NO
St. Lucia	YES	YES	YES	YES	NO	NO	NO
St. Vincent and the Grenadines	YES	YES	NO	NO	NO	NO	NO
Suriname	YES	YES	NO	NO	NO	NO	NO
The Bahamas	YES	YES	YES	YES	NO	NO	NO
Trinidad and Tobago	YES	YES	YES	YES	NO	NO	NO
Uruguay	YES	YES	YES	YES	NO	NO	NO
USA	YES	YES	YES	YES	YES	YES	YES
Venezuela	YES	YES	YES	YES	NO	NO	NO

2.1 Differences in the topics that are currently under review in each mechanism

Given the length and complexity of the provisions of the anti-corruption conventions and the number of member states to be analyzed, all four anti-corruption mechanisms decided that the reviews should be conducted by rounds. Each round analyzes some of the provisions and, depending on the mechanisms, follows up on the recommendations made in previous rounds. For instance, currently, the MESICIC is on its fifth round of analysis.[24]

Like the MESICIC, the GRECO is currently undergoing its fifth evaluation round; however, the topics under analysis are not the same. The evaluation in GRECO's fifth round is focused on central government (including top executive functions) and law enforcement.[25,26] Regarding the UNCAC Review

24 Topics of the fifth round of analysis: instructions to government personnel to ensure proper understanding of their responsibilities and the ethical rules governing their activities; the relationship between compensation and probity in public service; systems od government hiring; systems of procurement of goods and services; and criminalization of acts of corruption and the protection of those who report it (the last three are topics of the second round which are being followed up). Topics of the fourth round of analysis: oversight bodies, with a view to implementing modern mechanisms for preventing, detecting, punishing, and eradicating corrupt acts (art 3(9)). The fourth round followed up the recommendations made in the first round of analysis. Topics of the third round of analysis: denial or prevention of favorable tax treatment for expenditures made in violation of the anticorruption laws (art 3(7)); prevention of bribery of domestic and foreign government officials (art 3(10)); transnational bribery (art 8); illicit enrichment (art 9); notification of criminalization of transnational bribery and illicit enrichment (art 10); extradition (art 13). The third round followed up the recommendations made in the first and second rounds of analysis. Topics of the second round of analysis: systems of government hiring and procurement of goods and services (art 3(5)); systems for protecting public servants and private citizens who, in good faith, report acts of corruption (art 3(8)); acts of corruption (art 6). The second round followed up the recommendations made in the first round of analysis. Topics of the first round of analysis: measures and mechanisms regarding standards of conduct for the correct, honorable, and proper fulfillment of public functions (art 3(1)–(2)); systems for registering income, assets and liabilities (art 3(4)); participation by civil society (art 3(11)); assistance and cooperation (art 14); central authorities (art 18). For more information, see: OAS, 'Anticorruption Portal of the Americas' <www.oas.org/en/sla/dlc/mesicic/documentos.html> accessed 1 June 2020. Pursuant to para 7(b)(i) of the Report of Buenos Aires, the MESICIC Committee of Experts in the Plenary Meeting that precedes the start of the respective round, determines which are the provisions to be analyzed and the schedule to be follow, based on the proposal presented by the Technical Secretariat.

25 It is worth mentioning that GRECO decided to begin its fifth evaluation round, before the fourth round had finished. The latter was launched in 2012, but the compliance report was still pending as at October 2018.

26 Topics of the fourth round of analysis: prevention of corruption in respect of members of parliament, judges and prosecutor. Topics of the third round of analysis: incriminations provided for in the Criminal Law Convention on Corruption (ETS 173), its Additional Protocol (ETS 191) and Guiding Principle 2 (GPC 2); and transparency of Party Funding with reference to the Recommendation of the Committee of Ministers to member states on common rules against corruption in the funding of political parties and electoral campaigns

Mechanism, it is carrying out its phase two of analysis which covers Chapter II of the convention regarding preventive measures and Chapter V regarding asset recovery.[27,28] The OECD Convention monitoring body is currently in its fourth phase of evaluation, focusing on enforcement and cross-cutting issues tailored to specific country needs, and outstanding recommendations from phase 3, and has the characteristic of being tailored according to the specific situation of each member state.[29,30]

As evidenced in the schedule of all four mechanisms, the topics under review in each mechanism vary. Therefore, there is no need to go into depth regarding the topics being evaluated in each mechanism to demonstrate the differences in the issues being analyzed, which would also include the actors, laws, and regulations being investigated and reviewed in each case. Given the diversity of the topics being analyzed, it is hard to imagine broad areas of joint substantive work. Even if synergies are a mutual goal between all four mechanisms, at least nowadays, it is not viable. *Per se,* the use of a joint questionnaire might be an area

(Rec (2003) 4). Topics of the second round of analysis: identification, seizure, and confiscation of corruption proceeds; public administration and corruption (auditing systems; conflicts of interest); prevention of legal persons being used as shields for corruption; tax and financial legislation to counter corruption; links between corruption, organized crime and money laundering. Topics of the first round of analysis: independence, specialization, and means available to national bodies engaged in the prevention and fight against corruption; extent and scope of immunities.For more detailed information regarding GRECO's Evaluation Rounds, see: Council of Europe, 'Evaluations' <www.coe.int/en/web/greco/evaluations#{%2222359946%22:[0]}> accessed 1 June 2020.

27 Because of its complexity, this phase took from 2010 to 2015 to be accomplished and there are still a couple of states that have not been evaluated (UNCAC Review Mechanism received 179 self-assessment check-list. There are 186 member states). The launching of a new phase of analysis is possible as 'the Conference [of the Parties] may decide to launch a new review cycle before the completion of all reviews of the previous cycle'. See UNODC, *Mechanism for the Review of Implementation of the United Nations Convention against Corruption—Basic Documents* (2011).

28 Topics of the Phase-One: Chapters III and IV regarding criminalization and law enforcement, and international cooperation, respectively. For more information regarding the phase of analysis and the country profiles, see: UNODC, 'Country Profiles' <www.unodc.org/unodc/en/treaties/CAC/country-profile/index.html> accessed 1 June 2020.

29 For detailed information regarding the Fourth Phase of analysis, see: OECD, 'Phase 4 country monitoring of the OECD Anti-Bribery Convention' <www.oecd.org/daf/anti-bribery/oecd-anti-bribery-convention-phase-4.htm> accessed 1 June 2020.

30 Topics of the third phase of analysis: Focus on enforcement and cross-cutting issues. This phase also evaluate the progress made by parties to the convention on weaknesses identified in Phase 2, and issues raised by changes in the domestic legislation or institutional framework of the parties. Topics of the second round of analysis: review of legislative and institutional framework.Topics of the first round of analysis: evaluates whether the legal texts through which participants implement the OECD Convention meet the standard set by the convention.For detailed information regarding OECD Convention monitoring body's Evaluation Phases, see: OECD, 'Country monitoring of the OECD Anti-Bribery Convention' <www.oecd.org/daf/anti-bribery/countrymonitoringoftheoecdanti-briberyconvention.htm> accessed 1 June 2020.

for anti-corruption mechanisms to join efforts, however, since the questions that need to be asked are different for the preparation of an evaluation report of the anti-corruption mechanisms, it makes no sense for these mechanisms to work on preparing a unique and, thus, extensive questionnaire. Moreover, the focus of each questionnaire is on different topics and, by extension, the government agencies and departments that are required to provide the requested information will vary. For the above-mentioned reasons, it follows that resources and efforts will not be duplicated if each mechanism prepares its own shorter questionnaire.

Moreover, the difference in the topics currently under review in each anti-corruption mechanism would also impact the possibility of coordinating joint on-site visits. This would not be viable or practical for mechanisms that require an on-site visit as a mandatory[31] step of the process of analysis (MESICIC,[32] GRECO,[33] OECD Convention monitoring body[34]) since, first of all, they do not have jurisdiction over the same states. Additionally, there is no added value in coordinating for the same dates for an on-site visit, especially given that the mechanisms are currently reviewing different topics. This would only occur if the same topics were being analyzed, reviewing the same legislations and legal frameworks, as well as government agencies, thus requiring the same public officials to provide information in one on-site visit, rather repeating them in three separate ones. However, as set out above, this is not the case. The anti-corruption mechanisms are not analyzing the same topics, nor reviewing the same governmental agencies and legislations, nor evaluating the same states.

Furthermore, and I will elaborate this point later, not all mechanisms are allowed to have meetings with all the actors within the civil society as part of the agenda of an on-site visit. This is another aspect to keep in mind. Even for those anti-corruption mechanisms that do allow the participation of civil society, this participation varies from one case to another.[35]

Finally, we have to consider the fact that there is a mismatch in relation of the states that are currently under review in each mechanism, the states that have already been analyzed in the specific round of analysis that each mechanism is conducting, and the states that have not yet been analyzed. In this regard, Table 22.2, Table 22.3, and Table 22.4 illustrate which states of the

31 It is important to clarify that even though the on-site visit might be a mandatory step of the process of analysis, within the MESICIC, the on-site visit can only be materialized insofar as the state under review has given its consent.

32 MESICIC, 'Methodology for Conducting On-Site Visits', approved in its entirety by the Committee of Experts of the MESICIC within the framework of its Eighteenth Meeting, OEA/Ser.L SG/MESICIC/doc.276/11, 25 March 2011, para 2.

33 Council of Europe, *Fifth Evaluation Round* (17 March 2017).

34 OECD, *OECD Anti-Bribery Convention: Phase 4 Monitoring Guide* (revised April 2020) [B(4)].

35 See section 2.5.

Table 22.2 UNCAC Review Mechanism's member states that are still to be reviewed in the current Round of Analysis.

UNCAC Review Mechanisms		
Member States under review	*Subgroup of Analysis*	
1st year of Evaluations		
Mexico	Guatemala	Sao Tome and Principe
Honduras	Trinidad and Tobago	Cook Island
Grenada	Chile	Nauru
Bolivia	Dominican Rep.	Slovenia
Panama	Jamaica	United Arab Emirates
2nd year of Evaluations		
Peru	Cuba	Fiji
Dominica	Guyana	Romania
Uruguay	Antigua and Barbuda	Bosnia and Herzegovina
Antigua and Barbuda	Belize	Belarus
Haiti	Colombia	Solomon Islands
Trinidad and Tobago	Peru	Nicaragua
St. Lucia	Venezuela	Grenada
3rd year of Evaluations		
Argentina	TBD	
Cuba		
Bahamas		
Dominican Rep.		
Nicaragua		
Guyana		
4th year of Evaluations		
Jamaica	TBD	
Chile		
Brazil		
Guatemala		
Colombia		
Venezuela		
Costa Rica		
5th year of Evaluations		
Ecuador	TBD	
El Salvador		
Paraguay		
Belize		

Table 22.3 MESICIC's member states that are still to be reviewed in the current Round of Analysis.

MESICIC				
		Fifth Round of Analysis		
	State under review	*Subgroup of Analysis*		*Beginning of analysis*
7th Group	USA	Costa Rica	St. Vincent and the Grenadines	May-18
	Antigua and Barbuda	Jamaica	Peru	May-18
	Haiti	Argentina	Panama	May-18
	St. Kitts and Nevis	Ecuador	The Bahamas	May-18
8th Group	Guatemala	Chile	Honduras	Nov-18
	Trinidad y Tobago	St. Kitts and Nevis	Belize	Nov-18
	St. Vincent and the Grenadines	Canada	Antigua y Barbuda	Nov-18
9th Group	Nicaragua	St. Vincent and the Grenadines	Chile	May-19
	Venezuela	Peru	Uruguay	May-19
	Dominica	St. Kitts and Nevis	Mexico	May-19
	St. Lucia	Antigua and Barbuda	Belize	May-19

Table 22.4 OECD Anti-Bribery Convention monitoring body's member states that are still to be reviewed in the current Round of Analysis.

OECD Anti-Bribery Convention monitoring body			
Member States under review	*Subgroup of Analysis*		*Working Group on Bribery Meeting*
Mexico (4th Phase)	Slovenia	Brazil	Oct-18
Costa Rica (2nd Phase)	Colombia	Latvia	TBD
Chile (4th Phase)	Greece	Spain	Dec-18
Peru (1st Phase)	TBD	TBD	Mar-19
Argentina (1st Phase-bis)	Slovak Republic	Spain	Jun-19
Colombia (3rd Phase)	Luxemburg	Costa Rica	Oct-19
USA (4th Phase)	Argentina	UK	Dec-19
Canada (4th Phase)	Austria	UK	Jan-21
Brazil (4th Phase)	Colombia	Russia	Dec-22
Argentina (4th Phase)	Slovak Republic	Mexico	Dec-23
Colombia (4th Phase)	Costa Rica	New Zealand	Mar-24

Americas[36] have not been analyzed yet by each anti-corruption mechanism. It should be noted that there is no table illustrating the States of the Americas that have not been reviewed by the GRECO in their fifth round of analysis, since the only state subject to that review is the United States, which has yet to be evaluated.[37]

2.2 *Differences in the timing of the rounds/phase of analysis*

The difference of states that have yet to be reviewed in each anti-corruption mechanism highlights that it is not possible to carry out or coordinate a review of a country that participates in these various mechanisms. Given that the length of the rounds of analysis diverge from one mechanism to another, and that each anti-corruption mechanism launches its round on different dates, this discrepancy will continue and hamper possible areas of mutual coordination. Figure 22.1 illustrates this aforementioned difficulty. It should be noted that the GREGO does not appear in Figure 22.1, as there is no scheduled year for completion of its current fifth round of analysis, which was launched in 2017.

Furthermore, there is a gap in relation to the months needed to complete the process of evaluation of one state by each mechanism. As a matter of formal procedure, the UNCAC Review Mechanism expects to allocate six months for the evaluation of each state.[38] However, the review process sometimes takes longer than stipulated. For instance, the Executive Summary of Argentina's Report was released in June 2014 during the Fifth Session of the Implementation Review Group,[39] despite the fact that the joint meeting took place in April 2011[40] meaning

36 The states of the Americas are taken as base for the comparison since it is the region with wider overlapping in terms of membership, and, therefore, the region were synergies between anti-corruption mechanisms could be enhanced.

37 Council of Europe, 'GRECO Table on Evaluation and Compliance Report of the 5th Round of Analysis' <www.coe.int/en/web/greco/evaluations/round-5-new> accessed 1 June 2020.

38 'Model Schedule for Country Reviews based on the Terms of Reference of the Review Mechanism and the Guidelines for Governmental Experts and the Secretariat' <www.unodc.org/documents/treaties/UNCAC/Review-Mechanism/IRG_model_country_review_schedule.pdf> accessed 1 June 2020.

39 'Argentina—Review of Implementation of the United Nations Convention against Corruption' Implementation Review Group, CAC/COSP/IRG/I/1/1/Add.17, 10 December 2013.

40 See UNCAC's Argentina Country Profile at <www.unodc.org/unodc/treaties/CAC/country-profile/CountryProfile.html?code=ARG> accessed 1 June 2020.

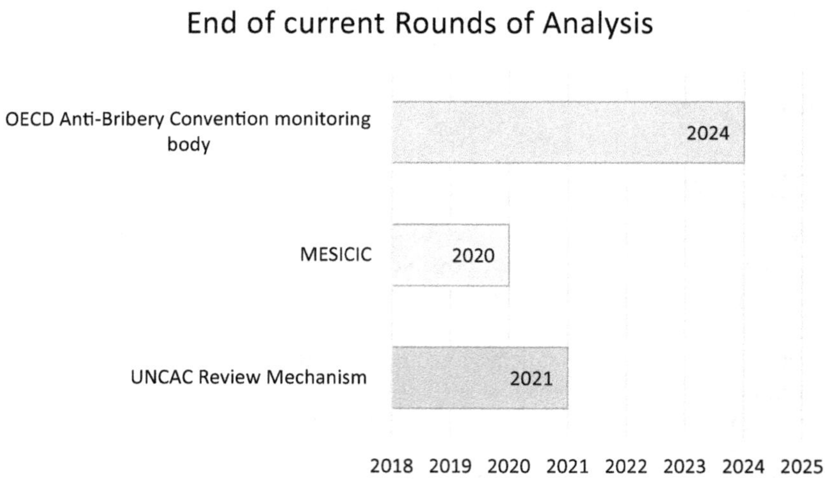

Figure 22.1 Finalization of current Rounds of Analysis.

that the review process had started at least a couple of months before.[41] On its part, the MESICIC follows a strict schedule which designates eight months for the review process to be carried out for each state under review.[42] On the other hand, the OECD Convention monitoring body review process for one state is a nine-month period.[43] Therefore, it is not only the date of the launching and completion of the rounds that needs to be taken into consideration when thinking about synergies, but also the period of time each anti-corruption mechanism allocates for the review process of each state.

41 For the joint meeting to take place, at least, the state under review would have answered the questionnaire and the subgroup of analysis would have reviewed the provided information. For detailed information regarding the steps of the countries' review, see the terms of reference of the Mechanism for the Review of Implementation of the United Nations Convention against Corruption in: UNODC, *Mechanism for the Review of Implementation of the United Nations Convention against Corruption* (n 26) [27]–[32].

42 For detailed information regarding the MESICIC Fifth Round Schedule, see: 'Calendario para la quinta ronda de análisis' (25 August 2016) <www.oas.org/juridico/PDFs/mesicic5_calendario.pdf> accessed 1 June 2020.

43 OECD, *Convention on Combating Bribery of Foreign Public Officials in International Business Transactions, Working Group on Bribery in International Business Transactions Monitoring Schedule December 2016–June 2024* <http://www.oecd.org/corruption/anti-bribery/Phase-4-Evaluation-Calendar-2016-2024.pdf> accessed 1 June 2020.

2.3 Differences in the process of analysis

Even though the processes of review for each mechanism have similar steps, there are certain differences that are worth noting. In this regard, the first issue to note is the way the order of analysis is determined. The order in which states are to be analyzed under the MESICIC follows a procedure that allows states to voluntarily offer to be analyzed at the start of a round, and then by order in which the other states ratified the IACAC.[44] On the contrary, the order of analysis in other anti-corruption mechanisms is random.[45,46]

The second issue to look at is the determination of the composition of subgroups of analysis. In this regard, the anti-corruption mechanisms determine the states by lottery; however, some of them follow additional rules. For instance, within the MESICIC, there are two rules that must be followed: (1) At least one of the reviewing states is to have the same legal tradition as the state under review; (2) states cannot analyze each other. Within the UNCAC Review Mechanisms, there is only one rule: that at least one of the states must be from the same geographical region as the state under review.[47] In relation to the OECD Convention monitoring body, one of the two states that are part of the group of analysis must have a legal system/tradition similar to that of the state under review, and, if possible, one of the two states that are part of the group of analysis of state 'A' must have been one of the two states that were part of the group of analysis of state 'A' during the previous phase of analysis.[48]

The third topic worth mentioning is that the MESICIC, the OECD Convention monitoring body, and the UNCAC Review Mechanism complete their country evaluation once the report of said country is adopted in the Plenary Meeting of each mechanism.[49] However, both the GRECO and the OECD Convention monitoring body incorporate, as part of the state's review process, a compliance report that follows up on the implementation of the recommendations formulated to the country in an original report of analysis. Specifically, as part of the GRECO evaluation, the state under review has 18 months to comply

44 MESICIC, 'Rules of Procedures and Other Provisions', adopted by the Committee in its First Meeting, OAS Headquarters, OEA/Ser.L SG/MESICIC/doc.9/04 rev.5, 14–18 January 2002, art 19.

45 Within the UNCAC Review Mechanism, the order is determined by the drawing of lots. See UNODC (n 27) [14].

46 It is important to note that within the GRECO, the Rules of Procedure neither specify the way in which the order of evaluation is determined nor how the experts reviewing the State under analysis are chosen. See Council of Europe, 'Rules of Procedure', adopted by GRECO, First Plenary Meeting, Strasbourg, 4-6 October 1999. The last amendment was made in Strasbourg, 23 June 2017.

47 See UNODC (n 27) [18]–[19].

48 OECD, *Phase 4 Monitoring Guide* (n 34) [19].

49 For the MESICIC, see MESICIC, 'Rules of Procedure and other Provisions' (n 44) art 25. For the OECD Convention monitoring body, see OECD, *Phase 4 Monitoring Guide* (n 34) [31]–[49]. For the UNCAC Review Mechanism, see UNODC, *Mechanism for the Review of Implementation of the United Nations Convention against Corruption* (n 27) s IV.B.2.

with the recommendations formulated in the adopted report and inform the status of implementation for each of them.[50] If the GRECO members determine that the state did not fulfill the recommendations, the GRECO can request the state under review to receive a high-level mission with the goal of reinforcing the importance of complying with the relevant recommendations. This mission is followed by a Compliance Report and might be followed by a Public Statement.[51]

Last, but not least, another difference is the manner in which on-site visits are carried out. The MESICIC, the OECD Convention monitoring body, and the GRECO adopted as a mandatory step of their process of analysis (as long as the states of review provides its consent) an on-site visit to the state under review. The purpose is to specify, clarify and/or complement the information provided by the state under review in its response to a questionnaire.[52]

2.4 *Differences in the levels of transparency-confidentiality of the information obtained by the mechanism*

The Regulations and Rules of Procedure of the MESICIC provide that all information related to the process of analysis will be published and disseminated on the internet through the mechanism's website.[53] Therefore, the MESICIC's Technical Secretariat does not need to have the consent of the states prior to uploading the information in the Anti-Corruption Portal of the Americas. In this sense, not only are the full national reports available online, but also, the responses to the questionnaire (both from the state and from civil society), the documents annexed to the report, the schedule for each round of analysis, the progress reports of each country in the implementation of the recommendations, the hemispheric reports of each round, and all the regulations and methodologies by which the mechanism is governed; the information gathered during the on-site visits; and even the documents and presentations of the MESICIC's Committee of Experts and the ones in relation to the Conferences of states parties. There is no private information that can only be accessed by representatives of the states or members of the mechanism. All information is uploaded to the website and is public.[54]

Almost at the complete opposite of the transparency spectrum one can find the UNCAC Review Mechanism. Despite the fact that the UNCAC has 186 member states, in the website of the UNCAC Review Mechanism, there are only 81 Country Reports of the First Cycle published and four of the Second

50 See Council of Europe, 'Rules of Procedure' (n 46), rr 30–31.
51 Ibid rr 32–33.
52 For the MESICIC, see MESICIC, 'Methodology for Conducting On-Site Visits' (n 32). For the OECD Convention monitoring body, see OECD, *Phase 4 Monitoring Guide* (n 34) [16]-[18]. For the GRECO, see Council of Europe, 'Rules of Procedure' (n 46) r 24(2).
53 MESICIC, 'Rules of Procedure and Other Provisions' (n 44) arts 9(i), 18(a), 19, 32, 34.
54 See OAS, 'Anticorruption Portal of the Americas' (n 24).

Cycle.[55] Furthermore, in relation to the questionnaire, the UNCAC Review Mechanism adopted the use of a Comprehensive Self-Assessment Checklist[56] which is a computer-based application to respond to the questionnaire.[57] Besides the particularity of using an Omnibus Survey Software, the other characteristic is that it is of restricted access. Thus, only the states which expressly give their authorization for the Self-Assessment Checklist to be uploaded for public view are available online. To date, there are only 15 Self-Assessment Checklist of the First Cycle published and two of the Second Cycle.[58] Thus, the information and documents available for the public online is very limited, only providing the Self-Assessment Checklist, Executive Summary, and Country Report of the states that have agreed to disclose them, the regulations and methodologies by which the mechanism is governed, and some general information about the mechanism itself and the date of past meetings.[59]

Somewhere in between the transparency spectrum, one can situate the GRECO and the OECD Convention monitoring body. Once in GRECO's website,[60] one can find main and basic information on the GRECO (such as the members of the GRECO Bureau, what the GRECO is, etc.), but also, GRECO's detailed calendar for 2018. Secondly, one can go to the evaluation section[61] and find the Countries Reports, as well as each country's Compliance Report and Second Compliance Report. Additionally, GRECO uploads all the relevant information regarding each Evaluation Round (e.g., of the information in relation to the fifth Round of Analysis: the themes to be analyzed, the table on evaluation and compliance, the questionnaire, the guidelines and schedule of the on-site visits, the guidelines for the evaluators, and a list of reference texts). Moreover, the decisions taken during the Plenary Meetings and the meetings reports are available to the public online. However, what is left confidential is the information gathered in relation to an evaluation or compliance procedure, including responses to the questionnaire.

Concerning the OECD Convention monitoring body level of transparency, all Country Reports are published in the OECD Convention monitoring body's website.[62] One can access both the original Country Report and the Follow-Up Reports of each country. By the same token, one can go through the relevant

55 For detailed information, see: UNODC, 'Country Profiles' (n 28).

56 Adopted for the second cycle and approved by the Implementation Review Group in June 2016.

57 For detailed information, see: UNODC, 'Comprehensive Self-Assessment Checklist on the Implementation of the United Nations Convention against Corruption' <www.unodc.org/unodc/en/treaties/CAC/self-assessment.html> accessed 1 June 2020.

58 For detailed information, see: UNODC, 'Country Profiles' (n 28).

59 For detailed information, see: UNODC, 'Implementation Review Group' <www.unodc.org/unodc/en/corruption/IRG/implementation-review-group.html> accessed 1 June 2020.

60 'GRECO' <www.coe.int/en/web/greco/home> accessed 1 June 2020.

61 Council of Europe, 'Evaluations' (n 26).

62 OECD, 'Country Reports on the Implementation of the OECD Anti-Bribery Convention' (n 19).

information and documents of each Phase of Analysis, for instance, the guidelines, principles to be followed, the schedule for the Phase of Analysis, the questionnaires, and the on-site visit information, among others.

The discrepancy in the levels of transparency and openness among anti-corruption mechanisms makes it difficult for any possible collaboration and hampers substantive synergies. Setting aside the good will of wanting to coordinate their work, there is an underlying constraint: confidentiality. Thus, either the exchange of information will require the prior express consent of the state in question, or it has to be limited to the information regarding the secretariats' work.

2.5 *Differences in the participation of civil society throughout the review process*

Another relevant issue to take into consideration before proposing areas of synergies is the extent of civil society participation through the review process. Regarding this issue, it is possible to plot each anti-corruption mechanism, more or less, between two points on a continuous line, from 'non-participation of civil society in the review process' to 'participation of civil society in every step of the process.'

Similar to the issue of transparency, the MESICIC is the mechanism that provides civil society with broader areas of participation within the activities of this mechanism. For example, if invited by the Conference of state parties to the MESICIC, civil society organizations can participate in said conference as observers.[63]

Secondly, within the framework of the meetings of the Committee of Experts, the civil society organizations registered before the OAS in the country under analysis can participate in the process of analysis by responding to the same questionnaire and in the same timeframe that the country under review is required to respond, for a round in question. In this line, the civil society organizations which answered the questionnaire and received an invitation from the Committee of Experts, may attend the meeting and verbally present those documents that they have sent to assist in the preparation of the analysis reports by country.[64] Also within the framework of the Committee of Experts meetings, civil society organizations can propose the debate of topics of general interests,[65] so long as the proposal is sent within the established timeframe to the MESICIC Technical Secretariat.

63 MESICIC, 'Rules of Procedure of the Conference of the States Parties to the Mechanism for Follow-Up on Implementation of the Inter-American Convention Against Corruption', First Meeting of the Conference of States Parties within the MESICIC framework, SG/MESICIC/doc.58/04 rev.7, 2 April 2004, art 18.

64 Ibid art 36.

65 Ibid art 34(c).

Thirdly, regarding the preparation of country reports, civil society organizations registered before the OAS may submit proposals for identifying future provisions of the convention to be analyzed, proposals on the methodology that they consider could be adopted, and proposals for the questionnaire of a new round of analysis.[66]

Lastly, in relation to the on-site visits, civil society organizations of the state under analysis may be invited to participate in the meetings to be held during the visit, whether or not they have responded to the analysis questionnaire and whether or not they are registered before the OAS.[67] Having described the different areas in which civil society can participate in the MESICIC process, it is important to highlight that if a civil society organization responded to the questionnaire of its state under review, as noted above, the information provided is taken into consideration by the subgroup of analysis and may be included in the final version of the country report. In addition, the information provided by civil society organizations during the meetings held during the on-site visit is also incorporated, if deemed relevant by the subgroup of analysis, in the country reports and considered when making recommendations to the state. Last but not least, it is important to note that 'civil society' for the MESICIC understand is broad, as it includes organizations from the private sector, professionals in the topic under review, scholars, and researchers.

When analyzing the extent of participation by civil society in the UNCAC Review Mechanism process of analysis, one can see that this participation is not mandatory and only slightly promoted. In order to further promote constructive dialogue with non-governmental organizations, the UNCAC Review Mechanism carries out a briefing on the outcomes of the review process, including identifying any technical assistance needs, but that is all.[68]

The GRECO, on its part, may permit civil society to participate during the meetings of the on-site visits and in the GRECO's Annual Conferences. Furthermore, some organizations from civil society are invited to exchange views with the GRECO and to contribute in the preparation of the countries-specifics evaluations. Nonetheless, civil society is neither allowed to participate in the adoption of the evaluation reports nor in the preparation of the compliance reports.

In relation to the OECD Convention monitoring body, in accordance with its Phase 4 Monitoring Guide,[69] organizations from civil society participate in the on-site visits but have no active role during the preparation of the reports.

Taking into account the manner in which these mechanisms address participation by civil society in their process of analysis, it further proves to be an

66 Ibid art 34.

67 MESICIC, 'Methodology for Conducting On-Site Visits' (n 32) art 13(e).

68 'Non-Governmental Organizations and the Mechanism for the Review of Implementation of the United Nations Convention against Corruption', adopted by resolution of The Conference of the States Parties to the United Nations Convention against Corruption, res 4/6, October 2011.

69 OECD, *Phase 4 Monitoring Guide* (n 34) [22].

obstacle to the idea that complete synergies could be possible between four said mechanisms. For instance, participation by civil society in the whole MESICIC process of review is an integral pillar of the mechanism. The MESICIC country reports even quote and refer to the perspective of civil society on the topics being evaluated, even if it contradicts the view of the state under review regarding its obligation to the IACAC. Having mechanisms so distant in the continuous line that 'measures' the participation of civil society in these mechanisms makes it almost impossible to merge them on a certain point of the line. This is especially true when considering the differences in the membership of all four mechanisms, and, in the case of the UNCAC, all the states that would have to agree on promoting the active role of civil society and the private sector in their respective country reviews.

2.6 Differences in the preparation of global/hemispheric reports and other activities within the mechanism

Besides following up on each country implementation of the obligations established by each anti-corruption convention that governs each of the four anti-corruption mechanisms, these mechanisms carry out other activities. For instance, in accordance with Article 30 of the Rules of Procedure and other Provisions Rules,[70] the MESICIC elaborates a hemispheric report at the end of each round of the analysis. The purpose of the report is to reflect general conclusions reached from recommendations of a collective nature, in the sense that they have been formulated to more than one state, and identifying common difficulties found in these states, which hinder the effective implementation of the IACAC. Additionally, the hemispheric report aims to summarize the progress achieved by the state, and the region as a whole. To sum up, the goal of said report is to reflect the overall situation of the region in relation to the IACAC articles and issues that were under review in the round. At the same time, the MESICIC works to promote the exchange of best practices amongst its member states,[71] and acts as a forum for the exchange of knowledge in matters relating to the prevention and fighting of corruption. For this latter end, the MESICIC invites specialists to present their work, analysis, and training programs, in the framework of the MESICIC Committee of Experts meeting.

Similarly, the UNCAC Review Mechanism prepares a thematic implementation report at the end of each cycle on the level of implementation of a determined issue in each region of the world, taking into account the achievements, good practices, and identified common difficulties, for the countries of a particular

70 MESICIC, 'Rules of Procedure and Other Provisions' (n 44).

71 For more information regarding MESICIC's best practices and their methodology, see: OAS, <www.oas.org/en/sla/dlc/mesicic/buenas-practicas.html> accessed 1 June 2020.

region.[72] However, and very importantly, in contrast to the MESICIC hemispheric report, the thematic report prepared by the UNCAC Review Mechanism is confidential and only states may read it, upon request. It is not made public and, therefore, is not available online on the webpage of the UNCAC.[73] In addition to said report, the UNCAC Review Mechanism, as an additional activity within the mechanism, provide opportunities to exchange views, ideas, and good practices, thus contributing to strengthening cooperation among states parties in preventing and fighting corruption.[74]

Regarding the GRECO activities, beyond the country reports, the GRECO annually releases a report which reflects trends among its member states and, additionally,[75] the GRECO publishes thematic reports on topics of collective interest.[76]

Concerning the other activities carried out by the OECD Convention monitoring body, as a 'global report' of the second phase of analysis, it compiled all the formulated recommendations in one report.[77] This was also carried out after the third phase of analysis with the recommendations formulated for that phase.[78] Furthermore, within the framework of the meetings of the Working Group on bribery (which meets four times a year in Paris), there is an opportunity for the dialogue of issues that is of common interest among the representatives of the states parties to the OECD Convention. For example, in the agenda of the March 2018 OECD Working Group on Bribery meeting, under the item 'other issues,' the topic of sports and corruption was discussed.[79]

For the foregoing reasons, substantive synergies in this area would also prove to be problematic. Despite the fact that the preparation of a general report with trends, difficulties, developments, and common recommendations seems to be an activity shared by all four anti-corruption mechanisms, the membership of each mechanism is not composed of the same states. Thus, the conclusions of each report are based on the situation of different states and regions. Even if the

72 Terms of reference of the Mechanism for the Review of Implementation of the United Nations Convention against Corruption in: UNODC, *Mechanism for the Review of Implementation of the United Nations Convention against Corruption* (n 27) [35]–[37].

73 Ibid [39].

74 Ibid [7]. For instance, within the UN Open-ended Intergovernmental Working Group on Prevention, member states can exchange information and experiences in relation to preventing corruption in their countries. For detailed information of the Open-ended Intergovernmental Working Group on Prevention, see: UNODC, 'Open-ended Intergovernmental Working Group on Prevention' <www.unodc.org/unodc/en/corruption/WG-Prevention/working-group-on-prevention.html> accessed 1 June 2020.

75 GRECO's publications are available at: Council of Europe, 'Publications' <www.coe.int/en/web/greco/publications> accessed 1 June 2020.

76 For GRECO's specific reports, see: Council of Europe, 'Specific Reports' <www.coe.int/en/web/greco/specific-reports> accessed 1 June 2020.

77 OECD, *Compilation of Recommendations Made in the Phase 2 Reports* (October 2010).

78 OECD, *Compilation of Recommendations Made in the Phase 3 Reports* (December 2014).

79 OECD Working Group on Bribery Agenda, Plenary Meeting 13–15 March 2018.

issue membership is set aside, the substantive information reflected in the reports is different since none of the anti-corruption mechanisms covered in this chapter are reviewing the same topics and provisions, nor are they being carried out in the same timeframe.

Moreover, by looking at the other activities carried out within the mechanism, even though good practices and topics of collective interest appear as a common denominator, the reason for their presentation varies. Regarding this point, the sharing of the product or outcome of the other activities carried out by each mechanism can be strengthened. In addition, even though the topics of the reports vary and the countries on which the conclusions are based differ, the information and findings are all relevant and should be distributed not only between the technical secretariats of each anti-corruption mechanism, but also among the member states of each mechanism. The findings of best practices should also be shared, which is an area in which the mechanisms can work together and help facilitate access by the participating states of their respective mechanisms.

3 Conclusion

Setting aside the fact that there are no conclusive studies to determine if overlap has *per se* a positive or negative impact,[80] international anti-corruption mechanisms may be dysfunctional in many ways but overlap does not rank high among their problems. This does not mean that certain level of synergies and joint cooperation cannot be arranged nor that that is not being done. Indeed, the interplay between these mechanisms is needed in order to provide solutions to corruption. For instance, annual meetings between the Technical Secretariats and joint events are already under way, as is the participation in each other's meetings and the use of each other's reports for the preparation of one country report and the identification of trends, so that they may be coherent.

The existence of a certain level of overlap between the anti-corruption mechanisms mandates allows them to act together and reinforce their main goals.[81] Moreover, a little competition among them can have positive effects as well, such as promoting innovation, promoting effectiveness, and diversifying risks. In addition, while at a first glance it may seem that compliance with the recommendations made by each anti-corruption mechanism might be overwhelming for a state, the fact that a single state is receiving similar recommendations from different anti-corruption mechanisms puts more pressure on said state to comply with

80 Weiffen (n 4) 192. See also Mario Prost and Paul Kingsley Clark, 'Unity, Diversity and the Fragmentation of International Law: How Much Does the Multiplication of International Organizations Really Matter?' (2006) 5 Chinese Journal of International Law 341.

81 Malte Brosing, 'Overlap and Interplay between International Organizations: Theories and Approaches' (2011) 18 South African Journal of International Affairs 147, 147. See also Prost and Clark (n 80).

them. In this sense, the existence of multiple anti-corruption mechanisms helps raise international standards and benchmarks for improving the implementation of certain anti-corruption measures.[82]

More synergies are not necessarily the answer to address possible weaknesses, nor is the need to decrease the economic cost a sufficient reason to increase synergies. Especially considering that there is a fundamental difference in the obligations that each mechanism follows up. The reasons set out in the previous sections demonstrate that increasing the steps already taken towards substantive synergies represents a near impossible task, if not a utopian ideal. The many operational and normative discrepancies between each anti-corruption mechanism may prove to be a barrier for substantive cooperation.

Within the context of the analyzed anti-corruption mechanisms, the most efficient way to maximize resources and positive impact is to enhance the existing information exchanges and dialogues between them. Moreover, in addition to enhanced dialogue, the anti-corruption mechanisms can work together to reach an agreement on the distribution of states to be analyzed each year, in order to prevent the overlap of dates, on-site visits, or in responding to similar questions in different questionnaires. The distribution of the states to be reviewed may also allow states to show their progress and developments from the report of one mechanism to the report of another. Furthermore, the anti-corruption mechanism can coordinate and agree upon their agendas and schedules and, more importantly, the topics and issues that each mechanism will be evaluating during the length of their round / cycle phase of analysis. By coordinating the topics and issues, the public officials will not be losing their time and resources in answering the same questions from different questionnaires, and nor will the same agencies and laws be under scrutiny at the same time. This will allow the anti-corruption community to monitor more constantly and in a more efficient way, the legal framework and practices of each state. In addition, the anti-corruption mechanisms can work together in the dissemination and publicity of their reports and findings.

In a world where corruption is increasing and widespread, the lack of enforcement power by anti-corruption mechanisms poses a great threat to citizens which are the ones that are ultimately impacted by the dire effects of corruption. However, the lack of enforceability should not be a barrier in the fight against corruption. Instead, anti-corruption mechanisms should find other ways to make their voices heard and create social pressure for the implementation of their recommendations. In this context, cooperation among these mechanisms is not only desirable, but necessary.

82 Karen Alter and Sophie Meunier, 'The Politics of International Regime Complexity' (2009) 7 Perspectives on Politics 13. See also Gómez-Mera (n 5) 23; Hannah Murphy-Gregory and Aynsley Kellow, 'Forum Shopping and Global Governance' in Wilhelm Hofmeister and Jan Melissen (eds), ***Rethinking International Institutions: Diplomacy and Impact on Emerging World Order*** (Konrad Adenauer Stiftung/Clingendael 2016) 41.

23 In search of a tailored approach to anti-corruption sanctions in the international development context

Financial remedies by the multilateral development banks

Alexandra Manea and Jamieson Smith[1]

While the concept of international development can be described in several ways, all definitions include the notion of addressing some of the toughest challenges of global society: poverty and inequality. Annually, ample financial contributions are made by development institutions toward improving the well-being of the poorest and most vulnerable people from around the world. Among the international development organizations, the multilateral development banks (MDBs) have specific features which have influenced the evolution of their responses to corruption. Once corruption was explicitly recognized by interdisciplinary research as a major hindrance to socio-economic development in the mid-1990s, MDBs acknowledged that corruption was an issue they needed to address through various entry points. Thus, MDBs began to assist countries that requested help to curb corruption by enabling them to build capable, accountable, and transparent institutions, and with assistance on tackling tax reform, illicit financial flows, procurement reform, legislation, and recovery of stolen assets, among others. But the MDBs also turned inward and established administrative mechanisms aimed at curbing fraud and corruption under MDB-financed projects.

These anti-corruption mechanisms sanction private entities that engage in specific forms of corruption while competing for or implementing MDB-financed contracts. Over time, these early mechanisms evolved into formal administrative sanctions systems with the explicit purpose of protecting MDBs' funds from corrupt actors. The World Bank Group (WBG) and the Asian Development Bank (ADB) were the first two MDBs to establish anti-corruption sanctions systems in the late 1990s, followed by the Inter-American Development Bank (IDB), the European Bank for Reconstruction and Development (EBRD), and the African

1 The observations, interpretations, and conclusions expressed herein are those of the authors and do not necessarily reflect the views of the World Bank Group or its Board of Directors. The authors would like to thank Frank Fariello, Leonardo Sempertegui, Collin Swan, Haiyue Xue, and Caroline Nagel Wachtell for their invaluable help in the preparation of this chapter.

Development Bank (AfDB) in the next decade.[2] Since then, the MDBs have invested significantly in the evolution of their sanctions systems, including the diversification of the applicable sanctions, in an effort to achieve proportionate justice and enhance protection of the institutions' funds.[3] With more than 3,000 sanctions cases adjudicated across the MDBs to date, a key challenge remains how to design sanctions that provide flexibility and uphold proportionality while contributing to the MDBs' development mandate.

This chapter looks at the MDBs' sanctioning policies and practices to date and analyzes the importance of connecting and adapting the evolution of the sanctions regimes to the broader international development context. It seeks to examine the panoply of available sanctions and to reflect on the use, or perhaps underuse, of financial sanctions, such as restitution and other financial remedies. Identifying a lack of consensus among MDBs and divergent approaches to imposing financial sanctions, the chapter discusses the MDBs' options going forward—maintain the status quo, with its shortcomings; undertake harmonization efforts; or undertake an innovation effort similar to the series of reforms that have over the past two decades, shaped the MDBs' remarkable sanctions systems. In this context, the research looks across leading common and civil law jurisdictions for principles and concepts from various disciplines that could be merged and kneaded into an alternative basis to be used to operationalize the high-potential instrument of financial sanctions.

Financial sanctions are notable in that they reach beyond ineligibility (which is the typical result of MDB sanctions) and may ensure greater deterrence by providing a measurable consequence of misconduct and by minimizing the profitability of wrongdoing.[4] Importantly, in contrast with other available sanctions, financial remedies are forward-looking measures that many view as capable of providing a meaningful reaction to harmful misconduct by redirecting resources to attenuate, directly or indirectly, the harm done in furtherance of developmental objectives.

2 For the purpose of this chapter, the term multilateral development banks (MDBs) refers to the ADB, AfDB, EBRD, IDB, and WBG. The WBG is composed of five institutions: International Bank for Reconstruction and Development (IBRD) and International Development Association (IDA), International Financial Corporation (IFC), Multilateral Investment Guarantees Agency (MIGA), and International Centre for Settlement of Investment Disputes (ICSID). Together, IBRD and IDA make up the 'World Bank.'

3 Inter-American Development Bank, 'IDB Sanctions System' <https://www.iadb.org/en/about-us/about-us-0> accessed 1 June 2020; African Development Bank, 'Sanctions System' <https://www.afdb.org/en/topics-and-sectors/topics/sanctions-system> accessed 1 June 2020; Asian Development Bank, 'Anticorruption and Integrity' <https://www.adb.org/site/integrity/main> accessed 1 June 2020; European Bank of Reconstruction and Development, 'Integrity and Compliance' <https://www.ebrd.com/integrity-and-compliance.html> accessed 1 June 2020; World Bank Group, *Sanctions System: Annual Report FY18* (2018).

4 Richard Thornburgh, Ronald L Gainer, and Cuyler H Walker, *Report Concerning the Debarment Processes of the World Bank* (2002) 63; Eugenia A Pyntikova, 'Exclusion and Rehabilitation: How Multilateral Development Banks Address Corrupt Behavior' (2018) 9 Jindal Global Law Review 43, 51.

Underscoring the MDBs' positive role as facilitators of loss recovery, an efficient use of financial remedies could close the loop on an effective protection of the institutions' funds which should be used as intended, to improve standards of living across the developing world.

1 MDB-specific characteristics influencing the evolution of the MDBs' sanctions systems

Three MDB-specific characteristics influenced the origination, subjects, and nature of the MDBs' sanctions systems. The MDBs were chartered to promote economic growth and thus have an apolitical character, with a specific mandate to not be influenced in their decisions by the political character of the governments that request funding.[5] Until the early 1990s, corruption was mainly perceived as a moral and political problem without any relation to economic development. This understanding of corruption traditionally precluded the MDBs from tackling the issue in any of its forms. By the mid-1990s, however, research in economics and sociology recognized a direct and negative correlation between corruption and economic growth.[6] In 1996, the then-President of the WBG, the largest MDB, gave a ground-breaking speech officially rejecting the old belief that corruption was a political problem and recognizing that corruption inhibits socio-economic growth.[7] This moment placed the issue squarely on the development agenda for the first time for a multilateral institution. It also marked the starting point of the WBG's response to corruption[8] 50 years into its history, including the adoption of measures intended to tackle corruption in WBG-financed projects, which subsequently evolved into a robust sanctions system, which the other MDBs have similarly instituted.[9]

5 International Bank of Reconstruction and Development, *Articles of Agreement* (1944) art IV, s 10: 'the Bank and its officers shall not interfere in the political affairs of any members; nor shall they be influenced in their decisions by the political character of the member or members concerned.'

6 Andrei Shleifer and Robert W Vishny, 'Corruption' (1993) 108 The Quarterly Journal of Economics 599, 600; Paolo Mauro, 'Corruption and Growth' (1995) 110 The Quarterly Journal of Economics 681; Ibrahim F I Shihata, 'Corruption—A General Review with an Emphasis on the Role of the World Bank' (1997) 15 Penn State International Law Review 454.

7 James Wolfensohn delivered what is now known as the 'Cancer of Corruption' speech during the WBG-International Monetary Fund Annual Meetings: see James Wolfensohn, 'People and Development: Annual Meetings Address' WBG-International Monetary Fund Annual Meetings (Washington DC, 1 October 1996).

8 The WBG anchored the legal basis for its sanctions regime in its 'fiduciary duty' to protect the use of the institutions' financing, set out in its Articles of Agreement which require the institution to make arrangements to ensure that financing provided by the Bank is used for its intended purposes and with due attention to economy and efficiency. See World Bank International Development Association, *Articles of Agreement* (1960) art III, s 5(b), art V, s 6.

9 The World Bank, *Helping Countries Combat Corruption: Progress at the World Bank since 1997* (2000).

Secondly, the MDBs' clients are mostly sovereign governments, which has two-fold implications ultimately leading to the MDBs' sanctions system limiting the parameters of who can be sanctioned to mainly private sector entities.[10] Some MDBs deem public entities, such as state-owned enterprises, or public officials susceptible to sanctions when they act in their individual capacity.[11] Thirdly, MDBs are international organizations dedicated to promoting socio-economic development. As such, these organizations have neither the power nor the mandate of sovereign jurisdictions to investigate and impose criminal sanctions when dealing with misconduct like fraud and corruption. Mindful of these limitations and in contrast to national criminal systems, the MDBs' sanctions systems are characterized as 'administrative,' having the primary purpose of protecting the institutions' funds.[12] This administrative nature implies that the system can be assessed and updated by the stakeholder institutions in a shorter period of time than national systems, which brings significant benefits. The administrative nature is also reflected in a series of elements that compose the system, including the range of applicable sanctions.[13]

With the narrowly stipulated goal of protecting the institutions' funds, the MDBs adopted a general utilitarian, as opposed to punitive, approach in developing the sanctions toolbox. In the first phase of evolution, advanced by the WBG in a context with no similar precedent, the only available sanction was the exclusion, or debarment, of a sanctioned entity from the pool of eligible entities for Bank-financed contracts. This approach sought to simply render the contractor incapable of obtaining the institution's funds for a period of time. As the volume of sanctions cases and the associated impact increased, the institution acknowledged the need to better connect its sanctions regime to its overarching international development goals and expanded, as well as gradually calibrated, the range of applicable sanctions to a set reflecting all the elements of a utilitarian approach: deterrence, rehabilitation, and restitution.

At different points in time, the other MDBs followed the WBG's model and developed similar sanctions systems as a formal tool against corruption and other harmful practices.[14] In 2006, the MDBs embarked in a harmonization

10 Anne-Marie Leroy, *Advisory Opinion on Certain Issues Arising in Connection with Recent Sanctions Cases* (No 2010/1 2010) 32.

11 Another rationale lies in the doubtful deterrence effect exacted by an MDB-specific sanction over a public official. Instead, some MDBs make referrals of findings of misconduct by public officials to the national authorities, in an assumption that the prospect of national law enforcement would have a stronger deterrent effect. Frank Fariello and Giovanni Bo, 'Development-Oriented Alternatives to Debarment as an Anticorruption Accountability Tool' (2015) 6 World Bank Legal Review 415, 429.

12 For a discussion regarding the 'administrative nature' of the WBG's sanctions system, see Laurence Boisson de Chazournes and Edouard Fromageau, 'Balancing the Scales: The World Bank Sanctions Process and Access to Remedies' (2012) 23 EJIL 972, 972–975.

13 Pyntikova (n 4).

14 The Asian Development Bank implemented its first Anticorruption Policy in 1998; the Inter-American Development Bank approved its first sanctions framework in 2001; the European

effort starting with the adoption of a 'Uniform Framework for Preventing and Combating Fraud and Corruption,' which standardized the definitions of corruption and three other sanctionable practices,[15] and continuing with a 2010 landmark 'Cross-Debarment Agreement,' agreeing to mutually recognize and enforce the debarments of the other MDBs when they are longer than one year.[16] The MDBs further harmonized their systems by agreeing on 'General Principles and Guidelines for Sanctions' and on 'Harmonized Principles on Treatment of Corporate Groups,' thus setting common sanctioning standards to ensure consistent treatment of entities in the determination of sanctions.[17] While differences among the MDBs' sanctions systems do exist, mainly with respect to procedural steps constituting each process, the overall approach remains common: a mainly adversarial system with both parties presenting evidence to at least one independent decision-maker who decides if the suspected misconduct occurred and if so, determines an appropriate sanction.

2 The MDBs' range of sanctions

All the MDBs have a shared range of applicable sanctions in accordance with the 'General Principles and Guidelines for Sanctions.'[18] The Guidelines highlight from the outset the administrative nature of the sanctions process and stipulate a non-exhaustive range of applicable sanctions:

- *Debarment*, involving a definite or indefinite period in which the sanctioned party is ineligible for the award of MDB-financed contracts.
- *Debarment with conditional release*, which involves a period of debarment after which the sanctioned party may become re-eligible for MDB-financing only if it complies with a set of defined conditions.

Bank for Reconstruction and Development began investigating external contractors' misconduct in 2005; the African Development Bank established its integrity and anti-corruption system in 2006.

15 The agreement harmonized the definitions of 'corrupt practice,' 'fraudulent practice,' 'coercive practice,' and 'collusive practice.' International Financial Institutions Anti-Corruption Task Force, *Uniform Framework for Preventing and Combating Fraud and Corruption* (2006).

16 Ibid. Steve S Zimmerman and Frank Fariello, 'Coordinating the Fight against Fraud and Corruption: Agreement on Cross-Debarment among Multilateral Development Banks' (2011) International Financial Institutions and Global Legal Governance 189, 189–204.

17 Inter-American Development Bank, 'Harmonization Efforts with Other International Financial Institutions' <https://www.iadb.org/en/transparency/harmonization-efforts-other-international-financial-institutions> accessed 1 June 2020.

18 African Development Bank Group, 'General Principles and Guidelines for Sanctions' <www.afdb.org/fileadmin/uploads/afdb/Documents/Generic-Documents/General_Principles_and_Guidelines_for_Sanctions_2015.pdf> accessed 1 June 2020.

- *Conditional non-debarment*, allowing the party to remain eligible for MDB-financed contracts, subject to defined conditions it must fulfil within a determined period.
- *Letter of reprimand*, consisting of a letter of reprimand addressed to the sanctioned party.
- *Restitution and other financial remedies*, requiring the sanctioned party to make a restitution payment or provide other financial remedies to an identified party, or to take other actions to remedy the harm it perpetrated.

The Guidelines recommend a default sanction of 'three years debarment (with or without conditional release),' adjustable depending on applicable mitigating and/or aggravating factors. Sanctions may be imposed singly or in combination, and some of them—letter of reprimand and restitution—may be applied as a condition that the sanctioned party needs to fulfill in order to avoid or be released from debarment. The Guidelines also recognize that MDBs may choose to add other types of sanctions. While some of the MDBs developed their own more detailed sanctioning guidelines,[19] the MDBs' approach to sanctions remains generally harmonized, with two exceptions embodied by 'private debarments' applied by the ADB and 'fines' applied by the AfDB, which are discussed in more detail below.[20]

3 The MDBs' sanctions evolution and practice

The WBG, ADB, and IDB have each sanctioned hundreds of entities, and the AfDB and EBRD have each imposed dozens of sanctions to date. The proportions of specific types of sanctions also vary across the MDBs' practice, with debarment in its various forms being by far the most commonly applied sanction. The early stages of the sanctions systems—particularly at the WBG and the ADB which started sanctioning in the 1990s—favored flat debarment (sometimes indefinite) considering that this was the only available sanction for misconduct. Under flat debarment, however, MDBs were left without any discretion as to whether sanctioned entities may become re-eligible for MDBs-financed activities upon the expiration of their debarment period and without any avenue to assess whether these entities have been rehabilitated or will simply re-engage in misconduct once they are allowed back into the pool of contractors.[21] These considerations

19 The World Bank, 'The World Bank Sanctioning Guidelines' <https://www.worldbank.org/content/dam/documents/sanctions/other-documents/osd/World%20Bank%20Group%20Sanctioning%20Guidelines%20January%202011.pdf> accessed 1 June 2020.

20 African Development Bank Group, 'AfDB Levies $17 Million in Financial Penalties in Corruption Case' <www.afdb.org/en/news-and-events/afdb-levies-us-17-million-in-financial-penalties-in-corruption-case-12923/> accessed 1 June 2020.

21 Frank Fariello and Anne Marie Leroy, *The World Bank Group Sanctions Process and Its Recent Reforms* (WBG 2012).

have led the MDBs to explore further instruments that would help mitigate such residual fiduciary risks and ensure a better protection of the institutions' funds.[22]

The MDBs initially considered addressing this risk by establishing a 'reinstatement' procedure upon expiration of the debarment period, whereby sanctioned parties would apply for re-eligibility and the relevant MDB would determine whether the party demonstrated 'present responsibility' by considering all relevant factors before it regained eligibility. This potential approach was seen as providing the MDBs with the highest possible degree of assurance that a reinstated party would not engage in misconduct again. However, the first two MDBs to implement sanctions systems acted divergently on this idea. The ADB went ahead and added 'debarment with conditional reinstatement' to its range of sanctions, making reinstatement possible upon a determination that the sanctioned party appears to be compliant.[23] The ADB may define conditionalities for reinstatement, such as improvements to the sanctioned party's ethics and business controls, but parties who petition for reinstatement may be evaluated against a holistic look at their businesses beyond their compliance with the defined imposed conditions.[24]

The WBG, however, opted not to establish such a procedure, citing as problematic the highly discretionary nature of the reinstatement decision and the potential absence of defined conditions for reinstatement, as well as considering that an exclusive focus on the present responsibility of a party might alter the general deterrent effect of its sanctions.[25] In pursuit of a greater emphasis on rehabilitation, the WBG instead adopted a new sanction of 'debarment with conditional release,' whereby before a sanctioned party is released from a minimum period of debarment, the party is required to meet a defined set of conditions intended to incentivize remedial actions and mitigate the chances of recidivism.[26] In practice, the conditions focus mainly on requiring the sanctioned party to undertake remedial measures addressing the misconduct and to implement or improve an integrity compliance program tailored to its risks and profile.[27] Over time, the IDB, AfDB, and EBRD have also included debarment with conditional release

22 Ibid 14. The authors describe the WBG's experience with considering addressing this risk by establishing a procedure upon expiration of the debarment period whereby sanctioned parties would apply for 'reinstatement' of their eligibility for World Bank-financed contracts. Such procedure would aim at demonstrating the party's 'present responsibility' prior to becoming re-eligible.

23 Asian Development Bank, *Anticorruption and Integrity Strategy* (2nd edn, 2010) 17–18; Asian Development Bank, *Office of Anticorruption and Integrity Annual Report 2017* (2017) 19.

24 Asian Development Bank, *Anticorruption and Integrity Strategy* (n 23) 17–18; Asian Development Bank, *Office of Anticorruption and Integrity Annual Report 2017* (n 23) 19.

25 Fariello and Leroy (n 21) 15. The authors also highlight that this approach might have endangered the World Bank's reputational risk if it decided to reinstate a party that subsequently engages again in misconduct, since 'reinstatement' could be seen as the institution's 'seal of approval.'

26 The World Bank, *The World Bank Sanctioning Guidelines* (n 19).

27 World Bank Group, *Sanctions System: Annual Report FY18* (n 3) 27.

in their sanctions arsenals, and have further diversified the potential conditions. For example, in a few cases, the AfDB has required that sanctioned parties make a financial contribution to the institution to be used in anti-corruption initiatives as a condition to regain eligibility.[28] Additionally, the ADB has solicited some sanctioned parties to sponsor integrity compliance seminars for other companies in an effort to 'promote integrity in the industry and/or region in which they operate.'[29] IDB and EBRD appear to have limited their conditionalities to integrity compliance improvements, restitution, and other remedial measures.

Conditional sanctions were deemed suitable in the development context to the point that stakeholders have suggested to shift the default sanction from debarment with conditional release to conditional non-debarment. However, the MDBs appear to have agreed that in cases of serious misconduct, the assumption is that a sanctioned party needs some time to change its culture to one of integrity; therefore debarment remains a vital sanction.[30] Moreover, the MDBs considered it important to get the balance of incentives right (by penalizing wrongdoing but rewarding self-cleaning and corrective actions) and to strike this balance, the MDBs try to incentivize the establishment of better compliance systems and increased recognition of remedial actions as a mitigating factor.[31]

Nevertheless, when evaluating the rate of sanctioned parties' compliance with conditions, the available data shows less than ideal overall rates of successful engagement with the system. This is particularly concerning given that absent the fulfillment of conditions attached to a debarment, an otherwise temporarily debarred party (with conditional release) becomes *de facto* permanently debarred. For example, at the WBG, which has the most experience with conditional sanctions, about one-third of the 328 parties debarred with conditional release by mid-2018 have failed so far to engage with the institution's Integrity Compliance Officer, which determines whether imposed conditions have been met.[32] The reasons for this lack of engagement may vary: some entities may be uninterested

28 African Development Bank, 'Integrity in Development Projects: AfDB and SNC-Lavalin Settle Corruption Allegations' (2015) <www.afdb.org/en/news-and-events/integrity-in-development-projects-afdb-and-snc-lavalin-settle-corruption-allegations-14760/> accessed 1 June 2020; African Development Bank, 'Integrity in Development: AfDB and Hitachi Ltd Conclude Settlement Agreement' (2015) <www.afdb.org/en/news-and-events/integrity-in-development-afdb-and-hitachi-ltd-conclude-settlement-agreement-15118/> accessed 1 June 2020.

29 Asian Development Bank, *Office of Anticorruption and Integrity Annual Report 2017* (n 23) 19.

30 World Bank Group, 'Review of the World Bank Group Sanctions System, Global Multi-Stakeholder Consultations, Phase I: July–October 2013, Feedback Summary' (2013) <https://consultations.worldbank.org/consultation/sanctions-reviews> accessed 1 June 2020.

31 Ibid 8.

32 The Integrity Compliance Officer (ICO) reaches out to debarred entities and assists them with meeting the conditions of their release from debarment. It monitors the entities' efforts and determines whether they have met the conditions and therefore are able to be released from debarment. World Bank Group, *Sanctions System: Annual Report FY18* (n 3) 15.

in receiving MDB-financed contracts in the future and therefore might not be disturbed by their ineligibility, while other entities may face difficulties in complying with conditionalities because of a lack of familiarity with integrity compliance standards.[33] Or possibly, the type of imposed conditionalities—requiring mostly the adoption of an integrity compliance program—need to be further diversified. Integrity compliance programs are believed to bring important benefits to companies in terms of preventing future corruption, but robust evidence for this belief is largely absent. Nevertheless, conditionalities seek to promote such programs based on a reasonable inference that, at the minimum, such programs do increase awareness that misconduct will have consequences and that 'clean business' is good business when handling MDB financing.

While the impact of mainstreaming the adoption of integrity compliance programs as a condition to avoid or to be released from debarment remains to be empirically studied, from among the conditions identified so far in the MDBs' practice, financial conditionalities (i.e., restitution, fines) also stand out as resulting in tangible beneficial results for development effectiveness. According to all MDBs' sanctioning guidelines, a financial measure can be imposed as an independent sanction or as a condition to the more complex sanctions of debarment with conditional release or conditional non-debarment. The latter option might be more effective as debarment remains the only enforcement mechanism of other types of sanctions, given that MDBs are non-sovereign organizations lacking the specific enforcement powers of national authorities. In practice, however, notwithstanding their obvious benefits, the use of financial sanctions by MDBs has proved to be challenging.

4 Use of restitution and financial remedies

As the MDBs' sanctions systems have matured and the impact of sanctions has increased, particularly with the advent of the 2010 Cross-Debarment Agreement, the MDBs have moved toward a framework allowing for more tailored sanctions to the point of today's range of applicable sanctions pliable to the circumstances of each case. A survey of the MDBs' practices to date shows that the prevalence of each type of sanction varies among the institutions. The IDB and ADB apply the sanction of fixed-term (or 'flat') debarment most commonly, while the WBG and the AfDB use debarment with conditional release for most cases. The EBRD has imposed mostly conditional non-debarment so far.[34] Letters of reprimand and restitution appear to be the least utilized from among the range of common available sanctions. While the underuse of reprimands can be easily seen as having a symbolic value in the face of serious misconducts of the type investigated, the

33 Fariello and Bo (n 11) 424–25.

34 European Bank of Reconstruction and Development, 'Integrity and Anti-Corruption Report 2017' <www.ebrd.com/integrity-and-compliance.html> accessed 1 June 2020, 22.

reasons underlying the underuse of restitution or 'other financial remedies' are much more complex.

As briefly noted earlier, 'restitution' and 'financial remedies' are explicitly recognized as possible sanctions under the MDBs' harmonized sanctioning guidelines.[35] These terms are, however, rather ambiguous and the existing public guidelines do not offer much clarification. A review of the concepts of restitution and financial remedies across common and civil law jurisdictions indicates three different understandings of the concepts:

- *Compensation or damages (or civil penalty).* This view focuses on the party harmed by the misconduct and requires the wrongdoer to undertake payments or actions to repair the harm. This non-punitive understanding of the concepts, specific to national tort and contracts law, generally tends to limit restitution/financial remedies to the cost of restoring the status quo prior to the misconduct.[36]
- *Disgorgement of illicit profits.* Focused rather on the wrongdoer who is considered to have engaged in misconduct to obtain a profit and has thus been unjustly enriched, disgorgement is not designed to punish but as a tool for preventing unjust enrichment.[37] Justice considerations mandate that the wrongdoer give up the illicitly obtained profits, which means that disgorgement is limited to the amount earned through the illicit activities.[38]
- *Fines.* The imposition of fines focuses on the harm caused by the wrongdoer to the public good and is unrelated to either the harmed party or the wrongdoer. As such, the limits for fines are determined by the system employing them depending on the type of offense they address and often take the form of mere punishment.[39]

While support for the first two forms of 'restitution' and 'financial remedies' can be easily distinguished in the MDBs' sanctions theoretical frameworks, only the IDB mentions explicitly 'fines' in its sanctions procedures, however, limiting them as 'reimbursement of the costs associated with the investigations' and

35 The World Bank, 'General Principles and Guidelines for Sanctions' <http://lnadbg4.adb.org/oai001p.nsf/0/CE3A1AB934F345F048257ACC002D8448/$FILE/Harmonized%20Sanctioning%20Guidelines.pdf> accessed 1 June 2020, [3(f)].

36 Restatement of Torts (Second) (US 1979) s 901; Restatement of Contracts (Second) (US 1981) s 344; David Pearce and Roger Halson, 'Damages for Breach of Contract' (2008) 28 OJLS 73.

37 For example, in US law, disgorgement is an equitable remedy authorized by the Securities Exchange Act of 1934 that is used to deprive wrongdoers of their ill-gotten gains and deter violations of federal securities law.

38 Ewoud Hondius and Andre Janssen, *Disgorgement of Profits: Gain-Based Remedies Throughout the World* (Springer 2015).

39 The US Sentencing Commission provides guidelines both on how to calculate fines for organizations operating mainly for criminal purpose and for all other organizations. United States Sentencing Commission, *Primer: Fines under the Organizational Guidelines* (2017).

sanctions proceedings.[40] As discussed in more detail below, the AfDB's procedures have come to be interpreted as also providing a basis for the use of fines under an 'other sanctions' provision.

According to available data, financial sanctions have been rarely used in the MDBs' practices to date. Although this type of sanction became an option more than ten years ago, the WBG has applied restitution and other financial remedies in only 12 of its 580 cases,[41] the AfDB has applied fines in seven of its 15 cases,[42] and the IDB has requested restitution in two of its 437 cases.[43] The ADB, which has applied 1,629 sanctions,[44] and the EBRD, which has applied 28 sanctions,[45] have not imposed any financial sanctions to date. This arguable underuse of financial sanctions raises two main questions. The first question relates to the degree to which the MDBs intended to mainstream such sanctions into their systems in the first place. The second, depending on the first, seeks to clarify whether financial sanctions are indeed 'underused,' and if yes, what could be the underlying reasons for such underuse.

One indicator in gauging the MDBs' openness to employing financial remedies could be the level of effort invested in the evolution of their sanctions systems, including the upgrading of the applicable sanctions. The MDBs' sanctions processes have been through a series of iterations and reforms aimed at providing the system with a variety of instruments to tackle corruption and other misconducts in their development projects. The MDBs devoted significant resources toward the improvement of their sanctions systems, with the overall objective of maximizing their effectiveness and efficiency, including by enhancing their independence and transparency, and with the more specific objective of achieving proportionate justice, by expanding the range of sanctions beyond debarment to include other four sanctions in an effort to provide tools that uphold flexible and proportional sanctions. If the range of sanctions has been diversified and upgraded to achieve proportionate justice, then it can be reasonably expected to see at least some more than marginal percentages of cases resulting in restitution and other financial remedies, even in the case of the MDBs that explicitly indicate

40 Inter-American Development Bank, 'Sanctions Procedures' (2015) <http://idbdocs.iadb.org/wsdocs/getdocument.aspx?docnum=39676437> accessed 1 June 2020, [8.2.5].

41 As of October 31, 2018. The figure represents the total number of sanctions cases since restitution and other financial remedies were adopted as potential sanctions in 2006. The total number of sanctions cases since the system was established (in 1998) is 912.

42 African Development Bank Group, *Sanctions Office Annual Report 2017* (2017) 19.

43 Inter-American Development Bank, *Office of Institutional Integrity and Sanction System Annual Report 2016* (2016) 36.

44 The figure represents the total number of sanctions cases since the system's inception, thus not necessarily since restitution and other financial remedies became an applicable sanction. Asian Development Bank, 'Anticorruption and Integrity: Sanctions' <www.adb.org/site/integrity/sanctions> 1 June 2020.

45 European Bank of Reconstruction and Development (n 3).

that restitution and other financial remedies, may 'be used in exceptional circumstances,' such as the WBG.[46]

Financial sanctions are notable in that they reach beyond ineligibility and can potentially ensure greater deterrence by providing a measurable consequence of misconduct and by minimizing the profitability of wrongdoing.[47] Importantly, in contrast with some other available sanctions, financial remedies are forward-looking measures capable of providing a meaningful reaction to harmful misconduct by redirecting resources in furtherance of developmental objectives. Underscoring the MDBs' positive role as potential facilitators of loss recovery, an efficient use of financial remedies may close the loop on an effective protection of the institutions' funds.

Notwithstanding their positive potential, in practice, financial remedies have been rarely used, likely mainly due to the challenging nature of two key issues: calculating the quantum of the sanction and identifying the appropriate beneficiary of the amount.[48] The challenge of identifying an appropriate beneficiary has been addressed in different ways by the three MDBs with experience in imposing financial sanctions—in most cases, the WBG has redirected the funds to the governments that implemented the project affected by the misconduct; the AfDB has collected the fines into a trust fund, the African Integrity Fund, with the intent of disbursing the funds for regional integrity initiatives; and the IDB, in one case, redirected the funds to the community affected by the misconduct.[49] An analysis of the broader issue of identifying the appropriate beneficiary of the payment and the mechanics of the transaction is beyond the scope of this chapter, but it merits further study in the context of the MDBs' divergent responses to the issue and the thought-provoking questions it poses.

The MDBs have responded to the greater challenge of calculating the quantum of financial sanctions by employing different views of the financial remedies concept. The WBG and IDB's practice could be best described as applying financial sanctions in the form of 'compensation or damages' and 'disgorgement of illicit profits.' This view of financial remedies, however, comes with a series of associated problems that may often prove insurmountable in practice. When viewing financial sanctions as a form of compensation or damages (or civil penalty), the

46 The World Bank, 'The World Bank Sanctioning Guidelines' (n 19) [II(F)].

47 Thornburgh and others (n 4) 63; Pyntikova, (n 4).

48 Fariello and Bo (n 11) 426; Inter-American Development Bank, *Office of Institutional Integrity and Sanction System Annual Report 2017* (2017) 63.

49 As of mid-2018, AfDB collected USD 55 million in fines. African Development Bank Group, *Establishment of the African Integrity Fund* (Integrity and Anti-Corruption Department 2016). In 2017, for example, upon a settlement with the World Bank Group in relation to findings of corrupt practices in the Democratic Republic of Congo, the Seves Group agreed to pay a financial remedy of Euro 6.8 million to the DRC government. See The World Bank, 'World Bank Settles with Seves Group, Debars Sediver SAS' (5 December 2017) <www.worldbank.org/en/news/press-release/2017/12/05/world-bank-group-settles-with-seves-group-debars-sediver-sas> accessed 1 June 2020.

payable quantum equals the costs of the harm done. However, the extent of the harm is often extremely difficult if not impossible to determine, especially if indirect harm such as unfulfilled potential (typical to acts of corruption) is to be taken into consideration. When looking at financial sanctions as a form of disgorgement, the amount to be paid equals the value of the wrongdoer's illicit gain. Determining such an amount requires distinguishing between licit and illicit profits and identifying a causal link between the illicit activity and the profit to be disgorged. But, in practice, proving such a causal link and calculating the illicit profits can involve complexities that may be beyond the scope of the sanctions systems' decision makers, especially where an uncooperative party may refuse to provide documentation regarding profits made. In the absence of clear assessment criteria, the MDBs' sanctions systems' decision makers have rarely issued financial sanctions. Most likely this explains why virtually all cases involving financial remedies have been resolved through settlements.[50] The settlement mechanism provides a platform for determining a quantum acceptable to both parties, rather than an MDB decision maker attempting to measure the harm done by a sanctionable practice or the illicit profit made by the sanctioned party. Given the absence of clear and more granular public guidance on how to overcome such calculation challenges and the relatively uncommon resolution of cases through settlements, the MDBs have made little use of a potentially effective sanction, with the exception of the AfDB.

The AfDB has appeared to embrace the use of fines. Under this view of financial remedies, the amount is not calibrated to either the harm caused or the wrongdoer's illicit profit. The AfDB's use of fines relies on a provision of its Sanctions Procedures which stipulates that 'other sanctions' may be applied, including 'but not limited to' reimbursements of the costs associated with the investigations and proceedings.[51] As of mid-2018, the AfDB has collected approximately US $55 million in fines pursuant to settlements in seven cases, but the guidelines for setting each fine have not been published.[52] The idea of imposing fines has been discussed by other MDBs as well in the past, emphasizing that fines could be an effective way to sanction contractors without the anticompetitive effects of debarments affecting various markets and without the unpredictable economic

50 Out of the World Bank's 12 sanctions involving financial remedies, only one case was resolved through sanctions proceedings. See The World Bank Group Sanctions Board, 'Decision No. 53' (involving overbilling, where the contractor admitted to overbilling by a certain amount). AfDB's seven cases involving financial sanctions were all settled through negotiated agreements. For more information about case resolution through settlements, see The World Bank Group, *Sanctions System: Annual Report FY18* (n 3) 22.

51 African Development Bank, 'Sanctions Procedures of the African Development Bank Group' (2014) <www.afdb.org/fileadmin/uploads/afdb/Documents/Generic-Documents/AfDB_Sanctions_Procedures_-_November_2014.pdf> accessed 1 June 2020, [11.2(g)].

52 African Development Bank Group, 'AfDB establishes Africa Integrity Fund' (2016) <www.afdb.org/en/news-and-events/afdb-establishes-africa-integrity-fund-16359/> accessed 1 June 2020.

impact of debarments on excluded parties.[53] But a set of concerns ultimately discouraged the other MDBs from applying fines. Among other things, concerns included the perception that corrupt contractors might view fines as an attractive way to 'buy their way out' of debarments. MDBs also noted that fines might lead to inequities for smaller companies and individuals who do not have the abundant financial resources of large companies. On the other hand, for companies with rich coffers, fines might not have as much deterrent effect as debarments, although, to increase deterrence, fines could be attached to a debarment period (to be calculated mindful of the proportionality principle). Concerns elated as well to a lack of legal basis for MDBs—as non-sovereigns—to levy fines, but this could be avoided by using fines as a component of a more complex sanction including debarment.[54]

More fundamental—and top among the reasons for lack of consensus among MDBs—are the concerns related to the punitive connotation of fines, which possibly contradicts the MDBs' consistent assertion that their sanctions systems are not meant to be punitive but protective and of an administrative nature.[55] As was noted in the report of former US Attorney General Richard Thornburgh, which has guided the evolution of the WBG's sanctions regime, in any sanctions system, the nature of the available sanctions depends upon the overall goal of the system, and the particular purposes sought to be achieved by the imposition of sanctions in individual cases passing through the system.[56] In an utilitarian system, such as that employed by the MDBs, the broader goal can be characterized, arguably, as segregating out actors that engage in harmful practices so as to leave a pool of honest firms to undertake MDB-financed project. The system is not intended to achieve its goal through punitive measures but rather through administrative measures such as incapacitation, rehabilitation, and deterrence.

Recognizing the MDBs' relative disuse of restitution and other financial remedies and the evident lack of consensus among MDBs regarding the use of fines, the MDBs can be viewed as having three options: (1) continue the currently divergent practices with all the associated challenges, (2) reflect whether to support the harmonization of guidelines on the use of restitution and fines across the MDBs, or (3) explore further options in the area of financial remedies via innovation. The first two options are relatively unattractive due to multiple

53 For a discussion about the downsides of debarment, see Tina Søreide, Linda Gröning, and Rasmus Wandall, 'An Efficient Anticorruption Sanctions Regime? The Case of the World Bank' (2016) 16 Chicago Journal of International Law; Pyntikova (n 4) 53–54. Arguably, the threat of fines might still negatively affect the competition in some markets. In markets where few companies wish to enter, the risk of sanctions—including fines—reduces the number of interested companies and therefore makes those markets more vulnerable to anti-competitive conduct.

54 Fariello and Bo (n 11) 427.

55 Fariello and Leroy (n 21) 15; Boisson de Chazournes and Fromageau (n 12) 972–75; Pyntikova (n 4) 47, 51.

56 Thornburgh and others (n 4) 59.

reasons, partly discussed above. The third option opens the door to innovation, perhaps by designing entirely new instruments, or more prudently, by rethinking the basis for applying financial sanctions which would lead to their enhanced use.

5 Alternative basis for financial remedies

In consideration of the foregoing, experience suggests that there may be an opportunity to rethink or expand the MDBs' sanctions 'toolkit' with a view towards complementing the MDBs' broader developmental goals. While remaining mindful of the sanctions systems' administrative nature and protective role, including by deterring future wrongdoing, this section discusses a potential alternative basis for rendering the instrument of financial sanctions more functional.

Following the MDBs' practice of creating administrative law by importing and adjusting concepts and elements from various legal systems and disciplines, one idea could be the formulation of an MDB-specific contractual clause that captures elements from two similar yet distinct concepts: 'liquidated damages' from common law and a '*clause penale*,' or penalty clause, from civil law jurisdictions.[57] Rooted in contract law, both clauses respond to the parties' difficulties in anticipating, calculating or proving losses likely to flow from a subsequent breach of contractual obligations.[58] Parties seek to eliminate dealing with these often insurmountable difficulties by agreeing ahead of time on the amount to be paid to the non-breaching party in case of breach. Such clauses are fundamentally justified by the non-feasibility or inconvenience of otherwise obtaining an adequate remedy and are not intended to provide a basis for the parties to pay their way out of contractual obligations.

Notwithstanding their common elements, liquidated damages and penalty clauses differ in scope, although recent research has suggested that the former would benefit from adopting a scope more similar to the latter's.[59] A liquidated damages clause is designed in an attempt to provide for just compensation in case of contractual breach. To the extent that it is not merely compensatory and might have punitive intent or effect, the clause becomes unenforceable.[60] In other

57 One dilemma in the comparison between common and civil law is the confusion of terminology regarding these clauses. This confusion arises because in some countries, whether under civil code or doctrine or case law, both concepts are recognized and the terms are used interchangeably. In the UNICITRAL uniform rules relating to liquidated damages and penalty clauses, this problem has been solved by simply referring to both as 'contract clauses for an agreed sum due upon failure of performance.' J Frank McKenna, 'Liquidated Damages and Penalty Clauses: A Civil Law versus Common Law Comparison' (Lexology 2008).

58 Charles Calleros, 'Punitive Damages, Liquidated Damages, and Clauses Penales in Contract Actions: A Comparative Analysis of the American Common Law and the French Code Civil' (2006) 32 Brooklyn Journal of International Law 67.

59 Solene Rowan, *Remedies for Breach of Contract* (OUP 2012) 175.

60 The US approach is illustrated by the Uniform Commercial Code s 2-718 and the Restatement of Contracts (Second) s 356: the key feature for upholding the validity of a liquidated

words, liquidated damages are not allowed as a punishment and, in common law practice, have been deemed enforceable 'as long as 'the amount stipulated for is not so extravagant, or disproportionate to the amount of property loss, as to show that compensation was not the object aimed at or as to imply fraud, mistake, circumvention, or oppression.'[61] However, where actual damages are proved, the fact that they may be less, or more, than the amount specified in the liquidated damages clause is insufficient by itself to render the clause unenforceable.[62] Moreover, liquidated damages may be collected even if actual damages are not proved.[63]

The approach is quite different in civil law jurisdictions, inspired by the Napoleonic code, where a penalty clause is inserted in a contract with the intention of encouraging the fulfillment, or deterring non-fulfillment, of obligations, rather than merely ensuring compensation in case of a contractual breach.[64] Unlike the case of liquidated damages, a penalty clause may establish the amount independently of the estimated damages and remain enforceable even if the amount appears to be disproportionate to the actual damage when this can be proved. However, no proof of any real damage is needed to enforce a penalty clause. In practice, civil law judges will reduce penalty amounts, based on factors similar to

---

damages clause is whether the amount of damages specified is 'reasonable.' The purpose of liquidated damages under both is to compensate the injured party, but not to penalize the breaching party. Thus, only a 'reasonable' amount of liquidated damages will be enforceable. Under the Restatement, the two factors to consider when making a judgment of reasonableness are (1) anticipated or actual loss caused by the breach, and (2) the difficulty of the proof of loss. The first factor examines whether the compensation provided by the liquidated damages is reasonable as compared to the loss which occurred as a result of the breach. The second factor looks at whether the loss would be difficult to prove given the elements that must be met to claim compensatory damages in general (i.e., under Restatement s 351 damages must be foreseeable and certain). Similarly, under the UCC, whether liquidated damages provisions may be upheld depends on (1) the anticipated or actual harm caused by the breach, (2) the difficulties of proof of loss, and (3) the inconvenience or non-feasibility of otherwise obtaining an adequate remedy.

61 *DF Mfg. Corp. v. United States* 86 F.3d 1130, 1134 (Federal Circuit 1996), quoting *Wise v. United States* 249 US 361, 365 (1919).

62 *Sun Printing & Publishing Ass'n v. Moore* 183 US 642 (1902).

63 Despite the longevity of the view that punitive damages are not available in common law for breach of contractual obligations, there is growing academic research supporting a reconsideration. See Rowan (n 59) 175.

64 Before April 2018, Article 1226 of the French Civil Code stipulated the following: 'La clause pénale est celle par laquelle une personne, pour assurer l'exécution d'une convention, s'engage à quelque chose en cas d'inexécution.' ('The penalty clause is the one by which a person, to ensure the execution of an agreement, commits to something in case of non-execution.') Upon the enactment of Law 2018-287 of April 20, 2018, the penalty clause is regulated in Article 1231-5 of the Civil Code. The Italian legislative provisions pertaining to penalty clauses are based on the French Civil Code. Harriet N. Schelhaas, 'The Penalty Clause in European Contract Law' (Trans-Lex 2004); Francesco Paolo Patti, 'The New English Law on Penalty Clauses: An Italian Perspective' (2017) 25 European Review of Private Law 227.

those considered in common law for determining whether a liquidated damages clause is penalizing, if part of the main contract obligation has been performed and the penalty thus appears to be 'manifestly excessive.'[65]

Variations can be found, for example, in Chinese and Indian law. The latter provides for an interesting mix of elements from common and civil law by not making a distinction between liquidated damages and penalties, and thus allowing for contractual damages in case of breach even if the intention is to deter non-fulfillment of obligations, and regardless of evidence of actual loss.[66] According to a similar type of clause in Chinese law, parties may prescribe that if one party breaches a contract, it will pay a certain sum to the other party in light of the degree of the breach or prescribe a method for calculation of damages for the loss resulting from the party's breach.[67]

6 An anti-corruption 'remedial clause' in the MDBs sanctions context

A 'remedial clause' built on selected principles specific to the concepts of liquidated damages and penalty clauses, to be included in MDBs-financed contracts, might help overcome the sanctions systems' current challenges with imposing financial sanctions, thus leading to a more effective protection of MDB funds. The envisaged 'remedial clause' would require the contractor to pay a specific percentage of the contract's value in the event that the MDB finds that the contractor engaged in a sanctionable practice.

A particularly attractive advantage of such a 'remedial clause'—and what may make this approach superior to the current status quo and other prior proposals—is its practicality. The use of the 'remedial clause' would eliminate the burden of quantifying the damages caused by the wrongdoing or the illicit profits of the wrongdoer. In the same vein as liquidated damages and penalty clause provisions, this 'remedial clause' would be justified by the often-insurmountable difficulties of proving actual loss resulting from corruption and the inconvenience or non-feasibility of otherwise obtaining an adequate remedy. Inspired by the common law approach, the 'remedial clause' would seek to compensate for the loss presumed to result from a corrupt act, although, designed along the principles found in civil law, the clause would allow for the imposition of financial remedies even if proportionality cannot be established between the stipulated amount to

65 For a brief overview of court decisions across European jurisdictions, see McKenna (n 57).

66 Section 74 of the Indian Contract Act: 'When a contract has been broken, if a sum is named in the contract as the amount to be paid in case of such breach, or if the contract contains any other stipulation by way of penalty, the party complaining of the breach is entitled, whether or not actual damage or loss is proved to have been caused thereby, to receive from the party who has broken the contract reasonable compensation not exceeding the amount so named or, as the case may be, the penalty stipulated for.' Indian Contract Act, s 74.

67 Contract Law of the People's Republic of China, art 114(1) (1999).

be paid as remedy (quantified as a percentage of the contract value) and the actual damage.

Other ideas to help boost the use of the entire range of MDBs' sanctions, especially of restitution, include a proposal to request 'community service' as a form of in-kind restitution. A company found to have engaged in corrupt acts would be required to serve the community affected by its misconduct by repairing the harm caused or by providing goods, works, or services to benefit the community.[68] The idea is particularly meritorious in that it holds the sanctioned party accountable in a way that directly addresses the harm done to development effectiveness, thus contributing directly to the MDBs' goals. Notwithstanding its many other merits, the value of the service to be provided to the community remains a difficult issue. In most cases where the actual harm cannot be quantified, the cost of the community service would be a notional value calibrated to the seriousness of the wrongdoing according to what is considered needed to act as effective deterrence against future wrongdoing. But such an approach renders the sanction riskily akin to applying a fine and, as discussed above, applying fines does not currently appear to be considered a feasible option across MDBs.

Using a 'remedial clause,' however, would address the persistent issue of determining the value of the remedy to be paid, along with most challenges associated with applying financial sanctions discussed above. In contrast with applying fines, using a 'remedial clause' as a basis for financial sanctions shift the focus away from punitive connotations of financial sanctions other than amounts involving strictly the direct actual loss or the exact illicit gain. The underlying intention of the 'remedial clause' would subscribe to a more comprehensive protection of MDBs' funds by not only excluding corrupt actors from MDB financing but also ensuring that they contribute to tackling, in one way or another, the harm done by their misconduct. In furtherance of this, debarment would still have a central role in directly protecting the MDBs' funds from contractors that have engaged in misconduct, as paying remedies pursuant to a 'remedial clause' would generally be coupled with debarment. Wealthier contractors would therefore not find this to be an attractive alternative to debarment. Less wealthy contractors could perhaps make the payments in installments over a period in which they could transition to conditional non-debarment, in order to avoid creating inequities, although, to some extent, such difficulties are attenuated by the remedy consisting of a percentage of the contract's value.

An equally desirable effect would be an arguable increase in deterrence. A 'remedial clause' would communicate more effectively the risks of engaging in sanctionable practices and would make the consequences of being sanctioned tangible to any MDB contractor. Deterrence and punishment are often thought of together, but the latter sanctions the culpability of the wrongdoer usually in proportion to the seriousness of his misconduct, while the former attempts to influence the future

68 Fariello and Bo (n 11).

behavior of the wrongdoer and others.[69] The effect of the financial sanctions, as supported by a 'remedial clause,' would be deterrence, not punishment. Deterrence is particularly important for the effectiveness of sanctions as an anti-corruption tool in the international development context. The MDBs' sanctions systems likely do not reach close to all contractors that engage in fraud and corruption on MDB-financed projects. In this context, the overall effectiveness of an MDB sanctions system depends on the demonstration effects of the imposed sanctions and on the level of general deterrence it generates against wrongdoing. For purposes of deterrence, debarment is considered, generally, to be a potent sanction in view of the potential loss of future MDB-financed business, as well as because of the collateral reputational costs debarment may involve.[70]

In terms of sanctions policy and a more specific framework, the MDBs would need to tackle several challenges, among which a primary one would be whether paying the remedy enshrined in the 'remedial clause' would serve as a separate independent sanction from restitution as currently used, or serve as a backup and be triggered based on a principle of subsidiarity (thus used only when restitution cannot be calculated as disgorgement or compensation). Other primary concerns include whether such a 'remedial clause' should be inserted in all MDB-financed contracts and attached to all sanctionable practices and all types of respondents, or reserved for a certain category of contracts, selected sanctionable practices, and a particular class of respondents. For example, MDBs could limit the use of such clause to contracts implemented in areas of the world or industries categorized as 'high-risk' based on internal indicators. In terms of the value set in the 'remedial clause,' MDBs could set a fixed percentage of the contract's value in all cases, or set different percentages depending, for example, on the sanctionable practice and the applicable aggravating or mitigating factors. Essentially, each MDB could tailor its method of putting this idea into practice, depending on varying objective and subjective limitations.

In terms of procedural advantages, such a 'remedial clause' would remove the burden of calculating financial sanctions from the MDBs' sanctions systems' decision-makers. The quantum of a financial sanction is difficult to measure, except in the limited cases of fraudulent overbilling, which explains why most of the MDBs' cases involving financial sanctions to date have been settled through negotiated agreements. But based on a 'remedial clause,' the quantum of financial sanctions would be already calculated before a sanctions case even began. To ensure enforcement, MDBs could consider requiring contractors to cause 'remedial bonds' to be issued in the relevant MDB's favor. Such a 'remedial bond' would be designed along the principles of performance bonds required

69 Rowan (n 59) 172.

70 For a discussion about the deterrence value of potential reputations costs, arguing that financial sanctions are a more effective threat to control misconduct, see Scott Baker and Albert H Choi, 'Reputation and Litigation: Why Costly Legal Sanctions Can Work Better than Reputational Sanctions' (2018) 47 The Journal of Legal Studies 45.

to guarantee the performance of contracts. In case a sanctionable misconduct occurs, the MDB would then be guaranteed payment of the remedy by the guarantor. Arguably, in the current context of a globally uneven playing field, a strict enforcement aspiring at reducing overall levels of corruption through deterrence might result in clients moving away toward lenders and donors with less related constraints. However, the MDBs can address this challenge by increasing harmonization of standards and enforcement with other financiers and donors, in the same vein as they managed to coordinate their systems and prompt others, such as the Asian Infrastructure Investment Bank, to establish similar ones.[71]

7 Conclusion

Each year, the MDBs commit hundreds of billions of dollars in loans, grants, equity investments, and guarantees to their partner countries and private businesses in pursuit of a world without extreme poverty and deep inequality.[72] The MDBs have built remarkable sanctions systems in an effort to protect the efficient and effective use of these funds. Notwithstanding such efforts, the MDBs need to enhance their positive role as facilitators of loss recovery. Restricting access of a corrupt contractor to further financing through debarment removes the risk of further waste of resources by this contractor, but it leaves the harm done by the misconduct, often severe, unaddressed. Although the MDBs have acknowledged the importance of financial remedies by integrating them into their sanctions toolbox, difficulties relating to determining an appropriate quantum have led to their relative disuse. Including an anti-corruption 'remedial clause' in the MDBs-financed contracts may help overcome the sanctions systems' current challenges with imposing financial sanctions, thus leading to a more comprehensive protection of MDB funds. While the envisaged idea might not provide for a perfect mechanism or solution, it tackles in an efficient and predictable (for all stakeholders) manner issues that have been so far challenging for all MDBs.[73] Considering the high stakes of addressing the harm done to development effectiveness, it might be worth discussing how to further refine the idea and exploring whether this could be feasible, and, if yes, how to best tailor it, in the MDBs' specific context.

71 The Asian Infrastructure Investment Bank (AIIB) has recently established an Integrity System aimed at investigating and sanctioning misconduct, including corruption, in the projects it finances. Pascale Hélène Dubois and others, 'The World Bank's Sanctions System: Using Debarment to Combat Fraud and Corruption in International Development' (2018) AIIB Yearbook of International Law 129, 133–35.

72 'Dollars' refer to US dollars. For example, in fiscal year 2018, the World Bank Group committed 66.9 billion dollars. The World Bank, *Annual Report 2018* (2018).

73 For some of the MDBs, such as the WBG, a 'remedial clause' partially inspired by and adapted from a civil law jurisdiction concept also responds to external suggestions that the WBG should make sure that its system is not 'Americanized,' as it must be understood by different legal traditions and systems around the globe. World Bank Group, 'Review of the World Bank Group Sanctions System' (n 30).

Index

Page numbers in *italics* denote figures; page numbers in **bold** denote tables

For Product Safety Concerns and Information please contact our EU representative GPSR@taylorandfrancis.com
Taylor & Francis Verlag GmbH, Kaufingerstraße 24, 80331 München, Germany

www.ingramcontent.com/pod-product-compliance
Lightning Source LLC
LaVergne TN
LVHW021003300926
849160LV00007B/231
9781032005447